FORESIGHT
and
EXTREME
CREATIVITY

FUTURELAB
2016

Also by
Langdon Morris

Agile Innovation
with Moses Ma and Po Chi Wu

Soulful Branding
with Jerome Conlon and Moses Ma

The Innovation Formula

The Chief Innovation Officer

The Innovation Master Plan

Permanent Innovation

The War for America

4th Generation R&D
with William L. Miller

The Knowledge Channel

Managing the Evolving Corporation

ATWG Aerospace Books
Series Editor

Space for the 21st Century

International Cooperation for the Development of Space

Space Commerce

Living in Space

Beyond Earth

FORESIGHT
and
EXTREME
CREATIVITY

Strategy for the
21st
Century

Langdon Morris

FUTURELAB
257 Castle Glen Road
Walnut Creek, CA 94595 USA

ISBN #: 978-1530931613

Table of Contents

Preface:

The Super Predator

Biologists now classify humanity as a "super-predator." This is a new category that they had to invent specifically to describe us. We merit this change to the lexicon of species classifications because no other creature in Earth's history has proven to be so ruthlessly efficient at wiping out both its competitors and its prey. Going back millions of years, no living thing whether plant, insect, bacterium, virus, or animal has successfully matched wits or weapons with humanity.[1]

We are not entirely immune from competition, however, but it's more than a little ironic that humanity's most dangerous competitor is … humanity. We engage in competition with ourselves relentlessly and on many levels, through open warfare on the battlefield and in silent conflicts in family life, in politics and economics, in education and sports and employment. No aspect of our lives is free of competition, and as we are indeed a supremely competitive species, we thus present to humanity its greatest danger: us.

With an assortment of powerful technologies that could be applied to achieve our self destruction in a grindingly slow and painful collapse over a span of decades, or through an abundance of extremely destructive capabilities that could annihilate civilization in just a few hours or maybe a few days, our own creativity certainly could be the cause of our own fatal demise. But will we? Or will we find the will and the wisdom to endure, or even to thrive? These are the themes that we explore in this book.

The Race

The 20th century was probably the most violent in human history. Approximately 200 million people perished in organized, mass violence during World Wars I and II and the countless additional regional conflicts, along with genocides and fratricides, politically-induced famines, and overall a general proclivity to kill one another. And while we live every day with the horrible prospect of nuclear annihilation, even at the smaller scale of contemporary day to day violence humans continue to kill ourselves and one another at the prodigious rate of about a million a year in war, crime, suicide, and accidents; another 2 million die in auto accidents. This breaks down to about 8,200 fatalities per day, giving further confirmation for the proposition that while we are the super-predator that is most threatening to every other living creature on the Earth, we are also a species endangered most of all by ourselves.

In spite of all this violence, however, the greater dangers that our species faces may not be due to war, but due to commerce. In particular, with the advent of large scale climate change as a consequence of economic growth and development through the extraction and burning of fossil fuels, we have taken our competitive, destructive, and self-destructive behavior to a higher level of catastrophic potential. We have put Earth's entire ecosystem at risk.

Yet another type of danger is also emerging, but in a different way. Through the ongoing development of the commercial marketplace, society has achieved an accelerating rate of change, largely as a consequence of new technologies that are nudging us toward a world where change is occurring too fast for many to cope with. As a result, our inbuilt capacity to foresee, to manage, and to make prudent decisions is being overwhelmed by the reality of high speed technological change that evolution has never before encountered.

Hence, we are now in the midst of a race between a very fast changing culture, and a slower process of evolution. Will humans develop the insight and skill to endure before our evolution-provided instincts toward competition and short-sightedness lead us to kill ourselves off? This would make a great topic for a science fiction movie, except that it's not fiction, it's our lives. Significant questions preoccupy us:

- Will we comprehend and master the emerging patterns of massive, human-created change in time to make sound decisions that will assure our survival?
- Or will the onrushing flow of events continue to accelerate, and eventually overwhelm us?
- Stated another way, which capacity will prevail: Will our evolution-provided capacity to learn enable us to catch up with our evolution-provided capacity to create change? Or vice versa?

When we're able to answer these questions with more confidence than we have today, then we will most likely also know if we're going to survive, but in the mean time we live with the painful uncertainty of many things to worry about, unresolved questions and profound doubts.

Of course my purpose here is to explore the nature of these challenges and the changes that confront us, most of which are created by ourselves, and to understand the choices that we will have to make in the coming years. The problem, of course, is that, as Nate Silver reminds us, prediction is not our strong suit:

> We have a prediction problem. We love to predict things – and we aren't very good at it.[2]

This is important, certainly, because we need to learn how to think productively about change and about the future, and about how to manage our organizations and institutions in the face of the many risks ahead, or the dangers underlying those risks will overwhelm us.

Indeed, the central nature of those risks is that we don't grasp what's coming at us very clearly, and so we don't prepare effectively. And while some few of us occasionally do get a decent glimpse of the future, it's often impossible for them to convince others of the impending dangers. And so the world changes faster, and uncertainty about the future increases, and with increasing uncertainty comes more and bigger risks.

In summary, then, the root of the problem is that *everything* is now changing, and it's generally changing too fast for us to grasp what it means. And while these changes are going on, we persist in our competitive and violent behaviors, and thus we remain the most fearsome predator the Earth has ever seen, far more dangerous than T. Rex or a great white shark ever was.

However, we are also a species with exceptional capacities. We are creative builders, foresighted visionaries, and thoughtful philosophers. We experiment and learn, create and strategize, plan and act, often with great skill. All of these marvelous qualities and personalities are merged in us along with others that are not so appealing, and the result is the dynamic flow of history, an abundance of ideas and concepts and realities that compose the great human experiment of the 21st century, the one in which we are now immersed.

As a result of our many skills and the tremendous impact they have had on the Earth, the geologists, like the biologists have also been obliged to come up with a new name for our era of geologic history.

They tell us that the Earth is more than 4.5 billion years old, and they identified the great epochs of Earth's development and invented the labels that every high school student knows. During the Jurassic Era the dinosaurs ruled the Earth, and during the much more recent Pleistocene Epoch the mammoths stalked the frozen tundra of the ice ages. After the Pleistocene came the Holocene, the name derived from Greek for "very recent," but it does not bring us to today. No, for that there's a name so new that the International Union of Geological Sciences has yet to formally adopt it. They suggest that we are living in the "Anthropocene," named of course for the massive impact of humanity on the Earth's geology, as the Earth's geology and biosphere are now being quite decisively shaped by human activities. It is we who damn the rivers, scrape the forests flat, create deserts, alter the weather, carve the tops off of mountains and shove them into the valleys. Now we're even creating earthquakes:

> The risk of a damaging earthquake in the next year is as great in parts
> of north-central Oklahoma and southern Kansas, where oil and gas
> operations have set off man-made quakes for about five years, as it is
> in high-hazard parts of quake-prone California. Experts at the United
> States Geological Survey issued the warning as the agency released
> its annual map of earthquake risks, a document that included for the
> first time the prospects for human-caused quakes.[3]

Since the last glaciation ended about 10,000 years ago, we have
progressively developed the skills to alter our home planet,[4] and while
there isn't yet agreement on a precise start date, it's generally accepted that
the Anthropocene begins with the era that economists refer to as
industrialization, around 1800.[5]

But the global economy is already moving on from industrialism and
we're entering yet another economic era, one so young and unformed that
it as yet lacks a name. Will it be the Post-Industrial Era, or Digital Age, or
the Knowledge Age, or perhaps the Age of Robots? Whatever name is
finally agreed upon, in this new era it's possible that with improved insight
and greater skill we may become the creators of an even of a much better
and thriving world for our children and theirs. Describing where we're
headed and how we might get there is also the purpose of this book.

Which means that this book is about you, and all your neighbors, and
all of humanity, and about the exceptional creativity that we may harness
and the uniquely human qualities that may enable us to attain the society
that we aspire to. It explores who we are and who we are becoming, and
the risks and opportunities that lie on the amazing journey before us.

•••

Introduction:

The Experimenter

Every time humanity makes a new experiment we always learn more. We cannot learn less.

Buckminster Fuller[6]

Humans are such effective predators because we are restless, relentless, and quite skilled experimenters. From the moment we take our first breath each of us is constantly learning by trying new things, and through this we are individually and collectively accumulating an abundant store of knowledge and capabilities. Psychologist Alison Gopnik describes us this way:

> As a do-it-yourself exercise in developmental psychology, find any child between one and two, and simply watch her play with her toys for half an hour. Then count up the number of experiments you see – any child will put the most productive scientists to shame.[7]

Because we are never satisfied with what we know and always

wanting to know more, no sooner is one experiment completed than the next begins. Because "experimentation is a particularly powerful way of learning about causes, providing much more accurate results than observation alone,"[8] curiosity that drives us to touch and try for ourselves, and the competition to do it better than others drive us forward, and we are never done, constantly striving to understand more and to do more.

In addition to our capacity to learn through experimentation, the other essential dimension of our character is our ability to pass useful knowledge from one person to another through the medium of human culture, which makes us unique among all creatures on Earth. Engineer-anthropologist Joseph Henrich puts it this way:

> The key to understanding how humans evolved and why we are so different from other animals is to recognize that we are a *cultural species*. We learn from one another in way that makes culture cumulative. Once these useful skills and practices began to accumulate and improve over generations, natural selection had to favor individuals who were better cultural learners. This interaction between culture and genes made us very different from other species – a new kind of animal. The striking technologies that characterize our species, from the kayaks and compound bows used by hunter-gatherers to the antibiotics and airplanes of the modern world, emerge not from singular geniuses but from the flow and recombination of ideas, practices, and lucky errors, and chance insights among interconnected minds and across generations. Culture makes us smart.[9]

These two powerful capabilities, learning through experimentation and the accumulation of learning through culture, have enhanced our survival skills over the course of millions of years such that a relatively weak, relatively small, slow, and poor-sighted creature with average hearing is now the dominant species on Earth. Did evolution anticipate that we'd get so good at social learning that our accumulated knowledge would eventually threaten our own survival? Probably not, as evolution is a forward-moving, incremental process that itself layers one experiment upon the previous, but it is not as far as we know a foresighted one. So it would probably be incorrect to propose that evolution anticipates anything at all. But given our current situation, we humans must.

As individuals and a species, learning through experimentation and cultural sharing is both a compulsion and also an exceptional skill, and now it's a requirement. Thus, the inventor of the system by which we classify living creatures, Carl Linneas, might have more accurately named our own species *homo experimentor*, the one who experiments, rather than *homo sapiens*, the one who is wise. Indeed, we frequently seem to contradict Linneas' hopefulness in that don't seem to be very wise at all, living as we do in a modern world that is characterized by unnecessary conflict, violence, suffering, and poverty.

And yet the story is by no means one of only bleakness. The globalization of the economy during the last half-century has lifted nearly 2 billion people from poverty into much more comfortable, long, and healthy lives, and the promises of science and technology continue to suggest that these benefits may lift yet billions more in the coming decades.

Further, the cultural world that many of us inhabit is one of astonishing abundance, a plethora of brilliant inventions and discoveries has enabled us to fill our lives with countless luxuries, entertainments, and wonders, and our garages with abundant excess, resulting in a society where space travel and satellite communications are common, where the mass production of food and material goods are commonplace. Amazon tells us, for example, that it sells (a mere) 200 *million* different products.

We have built massive megacities that house tens of millions of people, highlighted on the large scale by skyscrapers towering a hundred stories into the sky, and in labs we create invisible nano robots at the tiniest scale, far smaller than we can see with our own eyes. Every promising niche in every possible market quickly finds an entrepreneur or a company that's willing to make a go of it, and as in nature, many also try to make a go of it in niches that turn out to be quite non-viable. But because the capitalist process is also a system that promotes experimentation, due to this relentless trial and error we have come to live in a globalized, capitalist society of endless possibility.

Nature is also a rampant experimenter, as indeed experimentation is at the very core of the evolutionary process. Through abundant experimental reproduction via genetic variation and natural selection, nature succeeds in identifying and occupying absolutely every possible niche in every ecological system and subsystem. The larger system itself evolves through the development of new species, which create new niches and doom others, and thus through its own persistence nature has identified millions of feasible niches that we know of, and there are probably many millions more plants and insects that we have not yet found or classified in addition to the infinitude of bacteria and viruses. And this is on one planet only, among billions or trillions in the universe's entire inventory; none of us knows who or what may live elsewhere.

But we ourselves may soon inhabit other worlds, at least some nearby to ours. In this century it is entirely probably that robots and possibly humans will take up residence in orbit around the Earth, or even on the moon or mars, and through this colonization of our solar system another vast learning journey may commence.

But it is humanity's rampant experimentation here on Earth that has brought an unprecedented rate of technological and thus social change, and therefore also unprecedented uncertainty. And as we look at a future toward which we are hurtling faster and faster, it's become harder and harder to know where we're headed, or if we're making the right choices.

Of course this raises many well-founded fears and concerns.

For those who lead organizations, the growing uncertainties constitute significant dilemmas as well as significant challenges. It's their job to make sound choices and lead their organizations toward successful futures, but this is much more difficult to do when change is accelerating and uncertainty is increasing. For ordinary citizens these are also trying times, as established norms and accepted values are in flux, a trend that partially explains the conservative backlash and the growing right wing extremism that infects nations on all continents. People afraid of change are lashing out at change makers, real and imagined.

And yet as a result of the pace of change, we know for certain that things will be different tomorrow, and the changes that are coming will require that we understand and operate in a different world, a changed world, and that we must therefore change how we think as well as how we act. The facts of reality, in other words, have changed.

This is certainly not the first time that change has pervaded society, but because the 21st century world of our creation is continuing to change quickly and so fundamentally, the facts that describe our reality are also changing, and the models, concepts and metaphors we must use to understand it are also changing. Past truths are no longer so valid as they were, and we need to consequently change our opinions about what's real, what's desirable, and the decisions we have to make. We need, that is, to change both how we think and how we act. And while the past is surely gone, the new world that's emerging hasn't yet fully arrived. So we're living in a challenging time of transition, and thus our capacity to survive will be a creative act: our situation requires us to invent new ways of thinking and living. What kind of world will it be? A world of right wing anger and blame? A world of respect and reconciliation? A world of fragmentation and chaos? Of commerce and profit? Of cooperation and creativity?

The Old Ways

Change and uncertainty are difficult to live with, as most of us prefer the old ways, the comfortable norms, the rules and principles we grew up with, came to understand, learned to live with, and which feel most natural to us. We have little choice, though, and fortunately it's not all uncertainty, as we know many useful things about today and about tomorrow. For example ...

- We know that many of the children who are born this year will likely live to see the 22nd century, and thus will see with their own eyes what sense we are able to make of this world, and what society we are able to craft for them and for their own children and grandchildren to inhabit.
- We know that robots are probably coming in massive numbers, and that they will bring with them change throughout the economy and thus throughout society.

- We know that the Earth's climate is changing, and although we don't know by how much, we worry that it will be drastic and extremely destructive.
- We are beginning to understand that the fossil fuel based economy may be coming to an end, although it's not clear how quickly this is happening.
- We know that people prefer to live in cities, and that the world's cities are growing as the rural population continues to migrate, and that by the end of this century the world will be overwhelmingly urbanized.
- We know that as the result of all of the above, the pace of change throughout the world is accelerating which has in and of itself has created a cultural revolution that is occurring globally, one that is leading to new beliefs, attitudes, behaviors, and expectations in every neighborhood and favela and refugee camp and suburb of every city in every nation. We also see the growth of a very frightening counter-revolution, a reactionary strain of anti-change that is characterized by strident dogmatism and sometimes vicious violence.
- And all this is happening as the world's way of living and working is becoming much more complex …

And because these deep and fundamental changes are occurring all at the same time and throughout the global economy, and in all of the world's cultures and all of its nations, we know that we face risks on a scale we have never seen before. To survive we must adapt to the world that we don't really understand even as we see that it is the one that we are ourselves are creating.

Hence, it does not seem to be in any way an exaggeration to suggest that humanity faces challenges unlike any that we have faced before. These are the challenges of revolutionary change, change to the very foundations of our society and our economy, and thus to our lives and to our futures. Here is a quick introduction to them

Five Revolutions

In fact, as the list above implies, we face not just one revolution, but five. Yes, there are five revolutions occurring today, along with one counter-revolution, and because they're all interconnected, global, and simultaneous, the magnitude of the impacts they bring is all that much greater.

Technology

Humans are skilled technologists who are relentlessly developing a high technology economy. Unfortunately, however, we don't really know what that means, or how to manage it, or how it will eventually work out. The impact of this digital revolution is being felt anywhere that someone is using a computer or a mobile phone, which is basically everywhere.

Computers have remade the entire economy during the last 30 years, but what's still to come in the next few decades will be much more significant than what's already been achieved because while the digital revolution has already accomplished amazing things, we're on the threshold of another giant leap forward, probably a much larger leap than the previous one. Soon, still more advanced computer systems and progressively more capable and more autonomous robots will come into widespread use, and their imposing skills and capabilities will reshape the economy at a much deeper level than the computer revolution has done so far. Digitally-driven change will continue to accelerate, and as it does existing products, services, companies, and entire industries will be made obsolete, and new ones will quickly take their places. Workers will find old industries disrupted, and thus many millions of workers and their families will be disrupted also.

While this much is clear, what remains unclear is how fundamentally the robotics revolution will redefine work, the workplace, and the relationship between labor and capital. Will *all* human workers become obsolete? Will the owners of robots become the next generation of the ultra-wealthy, consigning the rest of us to life in poverty? Will super-fast computers and limitless databases make repressive big brother surveillance a constant reality, or will they liberate us to explore, discover, and create? The more deeply we delve into the possibilities, the more interesting and also the more disturbing they become. We will look at these topics in detail in Chapter 1.

Climate

Humans are also prolific combustors, or perhaps pyromaniacs would be a better term, and thus the second revolution is the unintended and unplanned transformation of the Earth's climate, the phenomenon of global warming, which has come about as a result of increasing concentrations of carbon dioxide in the atmosphere which go there because we burned so much coal, oil, and natural gas. Warming is already altering patterns of habitation and food production in many regions, and what's coming may be at a scale and scope that could constitute a fundamental threat to civilization.

Scientists foresee that the sea level will rise, that there will be increasingly intense and frequent storms, and that significant changes to patterns of rainfall and thus agriculture will together result in massive disruptions. What we do not yet know is how bad things will get, how massive the scale of disruption will be, and how effectively or ineffectively the peoples, companies, and nations of the world will respond to the threat and then to the actual manifested consequences. This is the subject of Chapter 2.

Energy

To obtain the raw materials to feed our combustion habit, humans have become talented extractors, extraordinary miners and drillers who can procure valuable hydrocarbons from as deep as seven miles beneath the Earth's surface,[10] which brings us to the third revolution, directly related to the second, for it is the transformation of the world's entire energy sector.

For the last 200 years the world economy has been powered by fossil fuels, which we burn to generate electricity and fuel the vast majority of our transportation, manufacturing, lighting, heating, and cooling. But as we have by now realized that fossil fuels are the main drivers of climate change, we also understand that it becomes a great virtue to reduce or even eliminate our reliance on them altogether. And if the scale of climate change turns out to be on the more extreme end of possibility, then virtue will become a vital necessity.

Hence, whether it's achieved through foresighted prudence or reactive terror, it's evident that the transition to a new energy economy will accelerate over the coming 20 to 30 years. No matter the speed of this transition, during these coming decades we could witness the decline and the near termination of the fossil fuel economy, and thus the transformation of humanity's energy sector into reliance entirely on non-fossil and thus non-carbon sources. Will billions of barrels of oil remain in the ground permanently, defining the end of the oil era and the fossil fuel economy and thus bringing with it massive disruption to the economy? Or will we transition slowly and gracefully to a sustainable energy society?

Since the energy sector constitutes the single largest component of the global economy, the economic dislocations that will occur as this process unfolds will inevitably be very far-reaching. Energy producers, investors, and the energy markets will all feel massive disruptions, but of course the hardships for fossil fuel producers are also vast opportunities for solar, wind and battery firms, as the world's appetite for energy will not decline, only its appetite for fossil-based, carbon-producing energy.

It's also evident that the digital revolution is central to the energy revolution, for the new science and technology that make solar and wind generation cost competitive with fossil sources are quite dependent on the digital capabilities in their design, engineering, and operations. Hence, we see that the first three of the revolutions are all intimately connected to one another, which only serves to amplify the amount of disruption that we'll experience as they progress, and also the scope of opportunity that this situation presents to the agile, nimble, and entrepreneurially minded. The energy revolution is the subject of Chapter 3.

Urbanization

Humans are also exceptional builders, with thousands of years of experience constructing huts, towns, cities, skyscrapers, and now space stations, and this has led to the fourth major change that's occurring in our times, the decisive impact of rampant urbanization. As we will explore in depth in Chapter 4, urban and rural families make quite different choices about the number of children they wish to raise, and as humanity completes the transition from a rural, agricultural civilization of the 18th century to the fully urbanized one of the 21st, the population explosion that began 200 years ago is coming rather quickly to an end. This has fundamental consequences for the global economy, and brings significant implications to many nations and to humanity as a whole, in ways that may be both very positive, and also quite challenging.

On the positive side, slowing population growth is obviously better from the perspective of resources preservation. We know that the global economy is already consuming far more resources than Earth produces on an annual basis, and thus we're consuming Earth's resource capital rather than its interest, which means that the current structure of the economy is not sustainable. Hence, bringing population growth to a halt is a very positive step toward stabilizing the rate of production and consumption. Largely because of urbanization, what we're experiencing now, for the first time in 200 years, is a decline in the overall rate at which the population is growing.

Declining birthrates are already having major impacts in many nations, such as Japan. Japan's population expanded quickly during the 19th century, but by the end of the 20th growth had stopped and population decline began, which has created a difficult situation for the Japanese economy, now stagnant for two decades. Forecasts for the future of Japan suggest that by the end of the 21st century its population will be about half of what it is today, which implies major disruption at minimum, but also presents the possibility of social, economic, and geopolitical collapse.

This is notable because what we may soon discover is that the experience in Japan will be repeated in dozens of countries, and then throughout world as a whole. Based on current trends, it's quite possible that by mid-century the overall human population will have peaked and then begin to decline. This will present a major challenge to the world economy because the industrial era's booming economic growth has been fueled by waves of young workers coming into the workforce and into the consuming force, but as population growth slows, and then stops, today's patterns of economic production, consumption, retirement, and health care will all change significantly.

We should anticipate that these changes will disrupt everything, except that everything will already be in the midst of disruptions caused by the transformation of the global economy to a fully digitized and possibly fully roboticized, climate-change threatened, energy-transitioned, quite different place than it is today. The peak of the population curve will only serve to amplify those other changes. We will examine this in more in Chapter 4.

Meanwhile, as all these changes are occurring, millions of people each year will still be moving from the world's farms to its cities, and in the process creating even more massive mega-cities in which more deadly concentrations of pollution, mega slums, and organized crime threaten to coexist with brilliant economic opportunities and the potential to bring tens of millions from poverty to relative economic and food security.

> No one kind of city, nor any one size of city, has a monopoly on creativity or the good life; but the biggest and most cosmopolitan cities, for all their evident disadvantages and obvious problems, have throughout history been the places that ignited the sacred flame of human intelligence and the human imagination.[11]

Culture

The simultaneous impact of four revolutions is inexorably creating a fifth, which is the massive impact that all of this is having on human psychology and sociology, or in a word, on our culture. At times humans behave in ways that are quite civilized, but others we behave with cruelty and brutality.

The evolution of our global civilization is of course already having and will continue to have decisive influence on how we live, work, think, and feel, and all of these changes and uncertainties have enormous impact on our values and beliefs, on our expectations and hopes for the future, on our attitudes and behaviors. Are we confident about the future of our nations, our companies, and our culture, or are we drenched in fear? Are we embracing change, or cowering from it? What conflicts, cultural and military, will arise between nations, between generations, between religious, ethic, and identity groups, as our situation and our prospects change?

It's obvious that we're in for severe psychological shocks, shocks to individuals that occur on such a wide scale that they become shocks to society as a whole. Hence, we are living through exactly what Alvin Toffler forecast forty years ago when he recognized that the psychology of his times was *Future Shock*.[12] But now, forty years later what we're experiencing isn't future shock, it's *now shock*. How will we cope with it? This is the subject of Chapter 5.

For the optimists, entrepreneurs and opportunists this is a time of exceptional possibility, a time when anything can happen. For pessimists and the frightened it's an era of heightened trauma and disappointment, when our worst fears are realized.

And the
Counter-Revolution

Among the frightened and shocked are a large and what appears to be growing group who react to the emerging world with an experience of such extreme anger and despair that they turn to reactionary violence, to terror, to both express their loathing of modernity and to destroy it. Their intent is to inspire a counter revolution against the values and freedoms they oppose, and while history is not on their side, fear is. We will explore the counter revolution in Chapter 6.

•••

This, then, is the grand experiment that the 21st century humanity has unintentionally launched.   Technology, climate change, the energy transformation, urbanization, a cultural revolution, and a counter-revolution, these are central and simultaneous themes in the experiment that we are creating and living from day to day, an experiment the outcome of which will define our common fate and set the course for our children's fate and their children's as well.

History's Revolutions

Another apparently innate human quality is skepticism, and if you're naturally skeptical, and even if you're not, it's perfectly reasonable to question whether these 6 changes really are revolutions. Could it be that they're just more of the same, more of what we've been experiencing for the last 50 years, or the last 200 years, or the last 10,000? Perhaps I'm overstating the case, and that really this is all part of history's natural change process, the results of our continuing proclivity to experiment.

Indeed, revolutions, even violent and tumultuous ones, are nothing new in human history. In technology, energy, urbanism, and culture revolutions are not new to humanity, and you have fair reason to wonder if these five revolutions are really such a big deal. Is it actually necessary to call these "revolutions," or have we seen this all before?

In succeeding eras of human history our ancestors learned to use new tools, to solve new problems, to think differently and to live differently than before.   The agricultural revolution from which the first cities emerged led to the formation of great empires in China, Southeast Asia, India, the Middle East, North Africa, Europe, and the Americas, each in its own way revolutionary.

The Renaissance of the 15th Century and the Enlightenment of 18th were periods of revolutionary ideas and profound changes in Western society and economics.   Political concepts that drew from Arabs, Athenians and Romans were reborn and spread rapidly through printing, which made it possible to produce and distribute books on a mass basis.

Literacy and learning exploded, and we can trace a clear connection from the renewed principles of inquiry to the emergence of new forms of political organization as well as to the systematic practice of science, and so developed the revolution in knowledge that then led to industrialism at the beginning of the 19th century.

In the decades around 1800 the methods of industrial design, metallurgy, mass production manufacturing and global distribution that became the basis of our own economy were being worked out by trial and error. Science continued to expand, with generation after generation of researchers building on all that came before them, and thus Newton remarked that he stood on the shoulders of giants, and other giants subsequently stood on his shoulders. This progression led quickly to discoveries of foundational principles in physics and chemistry and biology, in anatomy and physiology, in health care and sanitation, finance, economics, and in steel, oil, electronics, transportation, weaponry and warfare, in our understanding of the atom and the subatom, of the cell, the organ, the organism, and the ecosystem.

In the realm of nations, the battlefield triumphs of Napoleon led to the transformation of warfare from slow and stagnant parades to the cacophony and chaos of mass produced weapons, mobility, and relentless firepower. The 19th century's defining conflicts were the defeat of Napoleon, and half a century later the American Civil War, also the world's first industrialized war, the first time that industrial capacity was unleashed to wreak an unprecedented scale of destruction. The victorious North simply outproduced the vanquished South, a victory of capitalism that showed the way forward to the still greater expansion of destruction that would follow soon thereafter.

Further, we've seen massive changes in all fields of thought and study from decade to decade, century after century, from politics and government to science and technology to the arts and economics. Indeed, one overall interpretation of human history depicts it exactly as a progression of revolutions, from the agricultural revolution of prehistory to the empires of 3 successive millennia to the knowledge revolutions of the Renaissance and the Enlightenment, to the political and governmental revolutions of the 18th and 19th centuries, the industrial and commercial revolutions of the 19th, and then the 20th century's multiple revolutions in science, technology, medicine, manufacturing, computing, warfare, weaponry, etc. etc., which seem never to stop.

> Capitalism is a system in permanent flux: it changes character over the long term, and as it does, it throws up new structural problems requiring (or at least inviting) solution. In the early- and mid-nineteenth century, the overwhelming problem it threw up was the transition from an agrarian to an early industrial economy and society, which vastly multiplied the scale of necessary urban organization. Since the late nineteenth century, some of the most important long-term trends have been the progressive displacement of small by large capital; the movement from goods-handling to service provision; above all information-handling, in advanced economies; the globalization of the economy, and the new international division of labor by process rather than by product.[13]

And now here we are, two centuries after the onset of the Industrial Revolution and the majority of the world's people have been drawn into a single global economic system, a giant process, and thus have as a matter of survival been forced to, or in the search for opportunity been inspired to experiment and to innovate in order to preserve their livelihoods and their families. Many of us benefit from improvements in nutrition and health care that are extending the lifespan of the average human; today the average American male lives to about age 78, and the female to about 84.[14]

For businesses and governments change at this global scale and so massive in scope presents an endless cavalcade of challenges, and thus the lifespan of a typical large corporation is steeply in decline. A Fortune 500 company that has arrived, finally, at the pinnacle of economic success as a "blue chip" company can now expect to survive for only 15 or 20 more years, and because of accelerating change the corporate survival rate is decreasing rather than increasing.

This is in some respects unexpected. Would it not be reasonable to expect that giant companies, with massive resources and huge and highly trained staffs of professionals would have the skills and expertise and power, not to mention the market share and capital advantages, to protect themselves, to endure? With all their many strengths, shouldn't they ought to last a really long time?

Alas, this is not the case. Whereas a generation ago it was normal for a large corporation's lifetime to span 50 or 60 years if not a century, the massive waves of change that course regularly through the economy have taken a heavy toll on corporate longevity. New technologies and the companies that create them replace old ones in ever more rapid succession.

The risks extend to nations, and although they don't generally disappear or go bankrupt in the way companies do, some do find themselves under severe stress, and when they do their citizens suffer for it. Ask millions Greeks, who have endured heavy years of economic decline and struggle now with massive unemployment and very bad prospects for many years to come, or millions of Syrians, who have been forced from homes that their families have occupied for centuries by a brutal, four-sided civil war. Ask the citizens of Vanuatu and the Maldives, two among the world's very low lying nations who are likely to see their homelands submerged under the rising oceans.

So are the changes I'm describing genuinely revolutionary, or is that merely a convenient if over-dramatic label? In astronomy a revolution is one complete trip all the way around, which on Earth is a year's worth of travel around the sun, a complete cycle. In politics, revolution signifies the overthrow of the existing order in favor of a new one, a process that generally has winners who record their triumph, and losers who merely endure it.

The key words are "complete," "all the way around," "overthrow," and "existing order," and from them we get the meaning clearly. What I'm describing is indeed the convergence of major changes that are causing fundamental changes in how society functions, which together will lead to new structures throughout the economy, society, and culture. There are certainly winners and losers, and thus I conclude that these changes are indeed revolutionary.

Furthermore, because all of these changes are occurring simultaneously and because they're deeply interconnected with one another, the scope and impact of the consequences they bring is magnified. And this is a key point, because when big events or trends occur separately or independently then the magnitude of their impact is often considerably less, as there is time to adjust our actions and our expectations. When multiple changes occur that are simultaneous and connected, however, there may not be time to understand it all, and it's much more difficult to identify the best courses of action. The more connected the world is, in fact, the more complex are the patterns of change, the greater the threats that are created, the faster changes occur, and thus the greater the risks that are created.

In our world, throughout human culture and the one-world economy, the social and economic interconnections are now complete. We know that whatever happens in Mumbai affects how people feel and think in Munich; events and trends in Beijing are significant in Boston; breakthroughs and failures in Silicon Valley have meaning in Stockholm, Santiago, and Sydney; and the war in Damascus and Aleppo has immediate impact in dozens of world capitals, and everywhere else. What happens everywhere impacts on what happens anywhere, and it simultaneously impacts on what people think and feel about the world, their lives, and their futures.

And when the forces of change are thus so deeply connected as they are now the risks to organizations and to society as a whole are compounded. The reality of this convergence is what suggests that the risks we live with today are indeed transforming into mega-risks that will deeply and profoundly threaten us tomorrow.

At the same time in our fully connected world the confluence of changes that bring these mega risks also bring unprecedented opportunities. That risks and opportunities arrive in concert is one of the essential patterns of change.

The Patterns of Change

Is the momentum of change now so fast and the flow of history so quick that the best we can do is to hang on? Or do we already have – or can we develop – the capacity to steer, to choose, to design a preferred future, rather than being stuck by default with whatever happens?

The nature of our world and our economy makes it extraordinarily difficult for most institutions to respond systemically and proactively to the great driving forces of change, and this is true even when their own leaders see and recognize this quite clearly. That is, even when they see change coming, large institutions often fail to avoid the violent impact. It is for this reason that Louis Gerstner commented (about IBM, in this case, where he was CEO), that, "We agreed that we needed to change, but we didn't change."[15]

The significance of Gerstner's comment is not its description of IBM, but because it describes all of us and all of our organizations. We see that things are indeed changing, but we so rarely take the actions we ought to take in advance. Instead, we react afterwards, and frequently we do so badly, and we often take short-sighted actions that rebound to make things worse.

How, then, can we overcome these dysfunctional patterns? Skilled leaders and strategists search for the patterns behind change because they recognize that understanding the patterns will often help to decode the future and guide them to the right actions. Hence, we study the transition from the agricultural societies of the eighteenth century to the industrial ones of the nineteenth to better understand the transition from the twentieth century's industrial economy to the digital one of the twenty-first.

Historians have also extensively studied the birth and decline of the world's great empires, among them of course the Egyptian, Roman, Chinese, and British, and their studies provide important clues about empires that are now emerging. Resurgent China, young technology companies such as Google and Apple and Alibaba, cultural empires centered in Hollywood, Bollywood and Paris, governments and multi-nation partnerships of the EU and the UN, in the emergence of all of these we see patterns that help us to anticipate the further changes to come, changes that will affect not only their central actors in each story, but the rest of us as well. We will examine many of those patterns here.

7.3 Billion Revolutionaries

The American Revolutionary War began in 1776 when 52 leaders from 13 colonies signed the document they called the Declaration of Independence. Jefferson had written, "We hold these truths to be self-evident, that all men are created equal, that they are endowed by their Creator with certain unalienable Rights, that among these are Life, Liberty and the pursuit of Happiness."

Most of the revolutions of our times, however, are not being instigated by small groups of wealthy citizens, but by the combined actions of not just millions, but the entirety of the 7.3 billion women and men, all of us, who are all engaged in a social and economic process of globalizing change, one that is the culmination of millennia of progress and development. We do not know what the outcome will be, but we do know that we humans bring extraordinary capabilities to this laboratory in which we are both the experimenters and also the subjects of the experiment.

Our laboratory is the entire Earth itself, and our era is the Anthropocene. The Anthropocene has come about as the result of our many skills; as technologists, combustors, extractors, builders, and humanists. But that is not all we are. We are also visionaries, who can anticipate the future, realists who can assess risk, thinkers who evaluate options, strategists who discern the strong and weak points. We are also map makers, who seek to identify our exact spot not only on our little globe, but in the entirety of our galaxy and the incomprehensible vastness of the universe. We are planners, who organize our efforts, and philosophers, who seek to distinguish good from bad, right from wrong, and innovators who create new ideas and create change along with it. And also among us we sometimes find exceptional leaders who point us the way forward and guide us on the journey.

Thus, it's fair to say that humans are all-purpose organisms for learning *and* for doing, and along with all our many flaws and the potential to disappoint ourselves with the most dreadful and selfish evil, we also have the transcendent potential to create joy and beauty and inspiration.

And while we cannot know the future that these current revolutions will bring, it's evident that as the changes we are creating will be momentous, they are indeed fairly labeled as revolutions, and that the world we leave to our children and grandchildren will be fundamentally different from the one we ourselves inherited.

It remains largely up to us to determine the type of world that we will create, as it may be a world of inspiring possibility and triumphant promise, or it could be an awful, wretched mess.

As we come to better understand who we are, the revolutions that we are creating, the risks that we face, and the best strategies for meeting those risks, so we may also discover astonishing and wonderful possibilities and opportunities that these changes could bring, and by realizing this potential we would offer to our descendants much better prospects than the ones we seem to be facing ourselves. This is our opportunity, and the philosopher tells us that it is also our responsibility.

Welcome, then, to an exploration of the future that we are rushing headlong towards even as we still maintain much of the power that enables us to give it its distinctive shape.

•••

Part 1

Risk and Mega Risk:

The Creative Species

While the global spread of economic unification during our revolutionary era is unique in history, people in nearly every era and every culture during the past 10,000 years have confronted their own versions of the same dilemmas that we face today, and their challenges, successes, and failures are reflected in the myths and folklore of the world's many cultures. In this vast literature we find images and stories that have been developed and shared over thousands of years, stories about heroes and their great achievements, and warnings about selfishness and indulgence and folly. For it is the purpose of myth to help us understand ourselves, and so we see in our accomplishments and fiascos in these stories of ancient, transcendent icons and universal archetypes.

We also see in the large library of myth that the breadth and depth of human character is not suddenly new to the modern age, and thus we know that the qualities, characteristics and aspirations that shape us today are similar to or even the very same ones that shaped our distant ancestors.

33

Hence, their stories are also our story, and throughout these pages we will explore many aspects of our timeless character and our enduring potential as we also examine the promise and potential that is unique to our times.

Beginning here in Part 1 we will encounter seven essential creative dimensions of the human psyche, seven aspects of our humanity that have largely defined our current situation, which compose the reality of today's revolutions and risks.

We begin in Chapter One with the technologists, whose efforts have given us, among many other gifts, the wheel on which we travel, the telescope and microscope with which we see far beyond the distant horizons and into the minutest interstices, and now the computers that we use to create and share information and knowledge. In subsequent chapters we'll explore our skills as combustors, extractors, builders, humanists, reactionaries, and futurists, and seek to understand what all of these manifestations of our learning have enabled us to do, and the choices that they have brought us to confront.

•••

Chapter 1

The Technologist:

The Digital Revolution

It is one of our most exciting discoveries that local discovery leads to a complex of further discoveries. Corollary to this we find that we no sooner get a problem solved than we are overwhelmed with a multiplicity of additional problems in a most beautiful payoff of heretofore unknown, previously unrecognized, and as-yet unsolved problems.

Buckminster Fuller
Synergetics[16]

We think our business and personal mobility will change more in the next five years than the last 50.

Dan Ammann[17]
President, General Motors

In his mythical workshop the Greek armorer Hephaestus forged the magnificent battlefield weaponry of the Greek gods. A craftsman of

35

incomparable skill, he worked precious metals to create works of great ingenuity, beauty, and functionality. As with many of the Greek myths, and those of every other culture, there are many very different versions of his story, but the essential elements are consistent. In all of them the ingenious craftsman wields fire to transform materials into the instruments of civilization and into the weapons of war.

While Hephaestus was Greek mythology's exemplary technologist, modern humans are also extraordinary technologists, and our advances have created the amazing 21st century modern world. Or perhaps, if you feel less positive about it, you might say that technology has brought modernity *upon* us, but either way, now that we're beginning to understand what our accumulated technical knowledge has wrought and may yet create, we are compelled to wonder if science and technology can also help us to solve these very same problems that they are creating. Can they provoke a transformation of the global economy and shove it relentlessly into a positive and fulfilling digital age?

Science, Technology, and Digitization

There is no disputing the fact that science and technology have shaped our world, and will continue to shape it for as long into the future as we can possibly imagine. Technology, after all, has existed since the dawn of human prehistory when our great-grandparents first used tools, sticks and rocks and then hand axes, and eventually fire. Leaping forward many millennia, we arrive at the transformative technology of agriculture, the enabler of civilization, and then to urbanism, from which comes literacy, numeracy, and then scholarship. The modern practice of the scientific method brought forth progressive refinements to medicine, advances such the large scale engineering of cities and their waterworks, ships and globalized trade, and the accounting systems to keep track of it, etc. etc.

The culmination of this progress brings us to the dawn of modernity that is marked by the onset of industrialism around 1800, which arose as the confluence of knowledge that enabled modern metallurgy and then the steam engine, a quantum improvement that transformed the energy latent in coal into portable power that became the basis of industry. Quickly thereafter came an abundance of advances in every field, leading to still more knowledge and greater capabilities.

The dark side of this was constant improvements in weaponry, which eventually begat the entirely unwelcome and unwanted gift to humanity from the highly organized scientific effort of the Manhattan Project that created the atomic bomb. But along with the bomb, organized inquiry into the sciences of chemistry, biology, electricity, physics, etc., etc., shape our world in nearly every respect.

Industrialism was of course a fundamental break with the past, and among the most significant turning points in human history, for its machines accelerated civilization's progress enormously and led directly to the modern world in which we live, the global civilization that emerged from the ruins of World War II. While the threat of the atomic bomb haunts our nightmares, the digital technologies – computers – that the war also produced have become the foundations of the global economy. Just as agriculture led to urbanization and urbanization to industrialism, industrialism has led to digitization, the massive adoption of digital technologies in the form of computers and smartphones and all of the infrastructure that connects each of us to all of us. The global economy could not exist without this universal connectedness.

But we don't yet know what a fully digitized society may one day become, as we're only now beginning to understand our partially digitized world even as we are rushing headlong into the embrace of more and more technology. Nevertheless, we can already glimpse key elements that are shaping the future of digital technology that is used to create, transmit, and assess data and information, and the digital economy that exchanges value based on that same data and information. It's quite evident that the digital economy will eventually be as different from industrial one as industry defined a break with agriculture. Hence, we can reliably predict that we're shifting into a new era.

Unless you've been asleep for the last few decades this is certainly not news, but there are nevertheless factors to be considered and insights to be gained about the future that have not yet arrived into widespread understanding. Furthermore, many aspects of this emerging digital age remain quite uncertain, technologies such as robots, still more powerful laptop and smartphone computers, future generations of the internet, embedded technologies, big data that will become monstrous data, as well as micro-miniaturization. These technologies will shape our future to a significant degree not only because of what they will enable us to do, but also because of what they may require us to do. They will heavily influence our perceptions of what reality is, and because of the countless new creative, social, and economic possibilities that they enable, they will fundamentally impact on how we live.

There are some interesting and important questions to consider. In particular …

- How will the acceleration of computer technology change the economy and society?
- Will robots be a boon to humanity, or will they make us worse off?
- Will artificially intelligent machines attain capabilities roughly equivalent to human intelligence? When might that be, and if it happens what will they do?

The technologically-driven cycle of problem-solution-problem that Buckminster Fuller describes is abetted by and indeed its speed is accelerated by our capitalist economic system, and so as creators of and inhabitants in a society that is both capitalist and technological we exist in a perpetual cycle from which there does not seem to be an exit: Science and technology are applied to commerce to create change, and they are also the basis upon which yet more science and technology are created, leading to yet more change, which arrives still faster. Change, therefore, is both inexorable and accelerating, and so are the problems that result from change.

Capitalism is central to the process because it provides much of the incentive that drives change. The competitive marketplace contains a powerful motivation to come up with new solutions, and many of them are innovative applications of new technologies that yield competitive advantage for the companies that create them. Hence, the push to innovate is strong; and of course innovation is but another word for yet more advances in science in technology that become commercially viable, new stuff that we want to buy and use.

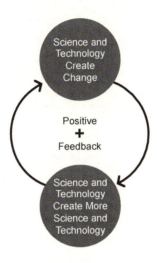

Figure 1
Positive Feedback
It spends things up.

The powerful combination of scientific progress applied in a commercial context describes not only the history of computer chips, but it indeed illuminates much of the broader history of civilization, and while not every breakthrough was motivated by commercial concerns, a significant percentage were. Gutenberg was first and foremost a businessman, and his printing press was built specifically to support a commercial venture. That it went on to transform the religions of central Europe, and then the entire world of scholarship, and then the entire world, was not part of his plan. Watt and the steam engine transformed transportation, Whitney and his cotton gin the basic factory, Ford and the Model T further transformed transportation, and countless millions of other advances are central to our lives today because they applied technology in ways that created commercial opportunities.

The J-Curve

In 1965, computer scientist and Intel co-founder Gordon Moore calculated the year-to-year progress that had been made during the brief history of computer chips to that time, and he realized that as a result of scientific and technological innovation the capacity of chips to perform computing functions was doubling roughly every two years. In his own words:

> I said, "OK it's gonna double every year for 10 years — go from 60 components to 60,000 components on a chip." I wanted to get across the idea that this is the way we're going to make cheap electronics. The nature of the whole industry is the more stuff you can put on a chip, the cheaper it is per unit of stuff. [18]

Moore charted the progress of computer chips on a graph, and he saw something like the letter "J."

He realized that the upward direction of the line suggested something important, for the ascending line forecast that computers would get progressively more powerful, and hence more useful, as they also became less expensive. As a result of his calculation and the article that he published about it this rate of improvement got the name Moore's Law, by which it is still known today.

Progress was instigated on the scientific side largely by academic and industry researchers, who had continually found new ways to put more components onto a single chip, and on the commercial side as a result of the marketplace competition in which the chip making companies had strong incentive to improve their products to sustain or improve their market position. Moore wondered how much longer the progress shown on the graph could be sustained, and based on what he knew was going on at Intel at the time, he realized that a similar rate of improvement would continue for some time.

Figure 2
The J Curve; Moore's Law
This curve shows exponential change.

In fact, progress has continued more or less as Moore foresaw until this very day, and because of it the J Curve, simple though it is, is one of the most important diagrams that explains the modern world, for the technological improvement it describes is the enabler and provocateur of a great many changes that have occurred during the last five decades.

The sustained rate of progress that Moore's Law describes is also historically unprecedented, as computer chips have been made progressively smaller, progressively more powerful, and progressively less expensive for all these decades. Throughout the entirety of the history of human industry going back hundreds of thousands of years, no other industry has a sustained rate of progress that is anything even remotely close to that of the computer chip industry.

Hence, computer scientists like to joke that if the auto industry had made improvements as steadily as the chip industry has, a top-of-the-line BMW would cost something like $20 and get about 5000 miles per gallon. The numbers in the joke vary, but the point is precise and correct: sustained progress has a compounding effect, which results in the J Curve.

Linearity and Nonlinearity

The compounding effect embedded in exponential progressions is worth further exploration because it is a central driver of one of the important themes of this book, the acceleration of change. The technical definition of an exponential process is one that doubles repeatedly at a fixed interval, exactly as Moore's Law shows.

Unfortunately, we humans are exceptionally poor at recognizing or understanding the full impact and consequences of trends that follow this exponential growth path, and as a result we are often confounded when life presents them to us. In fact, we seem to be consistently bad at recognizing and interpreting quantities that are very large, those that are very small, and those that change in non-linear ways, which is in fact exactly what exponents do.

By "non-linear" we mean trends where the quantity changes progressively through time. For example, let's say you take a job that pays $10 per hour, and you commit to working a typical 40 hour week. By the end of the week you'll earn $400. On a graph, linear change looks like this:

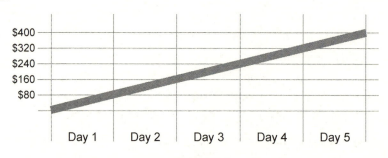

Figure 3

Linear Change

$10 per hour earned cumulatively over a 5 day week

But suppose that your boss comes to you and offers you one-thousandth of a cent an hour for the first hour since you'll be new an inexperienced and you won't actually be worth anything to him, but then offers to double it for each subsequent hour. Would you take that offer? If

42

you're like most people, you'd try to do the mental math to calculate the value of the new offer but you wouldn't be able to, and unless you had a calculator handy you'd turn it down, which seems on the face of it to be quite exploitative.

That would be a mistake, however, as the numbers in his new offer unfold this way: In the first hour, it's true, you'd earn a paltry one-one-thousandth of a cent, and two-thousandths in the second hour, and by the end of the first day your hourly rate would be up to a tenth of a cent, and you would have earned for your eight hours of work a total of 2.5 tenths of a cent. You're working hard for almost nothing, it would seem. How could your boss have had the nerve to even offer you such a ridiculous proposal, and how could you have been so foolish as to accept?

On day two you carry on nonetheless, and by the end of the day you've earned another 65 cents.

Things start to turn in your favor on day 3, however, and by the end of the day your hourly rate is up to $83 per hour, and your earnings for the day are $167.

Now as you begin to see what's going to happen, the miniscule amount you started with has grown into a quite lovely sum, and perhaps the next two days aren't going to be so bad after all. In fact things get quite good, as on the fourth day you earn the princely sum of $42,781.

By the fortieth hour your pay is up to an astonishing $5.5 million, and your earnings on day five total more than $10 million. Because of how this progression is going, more than half of your total earnings have come in the last hour, and 99.6 percent have come on the last day.

Did your boss realize this when he made the offer? Perhaps he did, or maybe not, but of course the point for us is that the human brain isn't very well equipped to calculate the increasing (or decreasing) values of nonlinear trends. And unlike the past, even the recent past, the modern world is full of these trends. We see them in economics, demographics, and as with Moore's Law, throughout technology. In fact, the modern world is *best* described as a non-linear world, and since we're so bad at recognizing what this means, the modern world is fooling us all the time. Things are happening that surprise us when, if we were better at recognizing non-linearity, they would not.

This is a critical issue, so just to make sure you understand how powerful non-linear change is, here are two more examples showing how we are often fooled by nonlinear or exponential rates of change. The first is a fairy tale, the second a parable.

The King, the Pauper and the Exponents

Long ago in a distant land, the king was out in the forest riding on his favorite white horse, which he preferred to do alone to the consternation of his closest advisors.   Nevertheless, the king had long refused their entreaties to take a guard along, and on a clear but cold winter's day as he was enjoying the forest trails his horse was spooked by a stick that looked like a snake and took off at a sprint that left the poor king barely holding his place in the saddle. Alas, in its panic the horse soon ran far off the trail and among the trees, and the king was crashed into a large limb. Falling off the horse, he hit his head on a rock and fell unconscious.

While the horse eventually made it way back to the castle, the king lay there for some time, until an old man who lived in a small hut nearby happened upon him, still unconscious on the ground. The old man half-carried and half-dragged the poor king back to his hovel, and there, he bandaged the king's head, set his broken leg, and fed him small sips of tea. Eventually the king awakened, but his condition was obviously too poor for him to attempt to leave the hovel.

After some weeks of rest under the care of the old man, during which time the entire army was unsuccessfully combing the forest in search him, the king decided at last that he was strong enough to return home.

The old man led him back through the snow-covered forest to the main trail, upon which the king was then easily able to find his way home to the castle. Upon parting, the king thanked the old man profusely and told him that should he so desire, he could at any time visit the castle, and the king would have the pleasure of bestowing upon the kindly, old man anything his heart desired. And so they parted, the king to his throne, and the old man to his hut in the forest.

Some months later, when winter had turned to spring, and spring to summer, and the snow was melted and the weather was fair, the old man presented himself at the castle and requested an audience with the king. Not knowing of the king's promise, he was rudely turned away by the king's guard, and so the old man sat down at the gate and waited. The next day when the king came out on his horse the old man called to him, and the king did indeed recognize him, and had him brought into the castle and given a fine meal.

Later the king returned and asked what it was that the old man wished as his reward, to which the old man replied, "Your highness, I am but a simple man. I only need a small bit of rice to carry me through my days."

"Then you shall have it," the king replied. "How much shall it be?"

"Only a small amount, your majesty. I could show you on chess board, if you have one your majesty."

"Of course I do," replied the king. (How could a king *not* have a chess board?)

"Then on it can you please place one grain of rice on the first square, and two on the second square, and four on the third, and 8 on the fourth, and so on?" asked the old man.

The king laughed at the foolish old man who was asking for nearly nothing when we could have had nearly anything!

"So it shall be," replied the king. "Bring my chess board and a bag of rice," he instructed his advisors, and so they did.

They quickly discovered, however, that the old man was not so foolish as he appeared.

What the old man had asked for, of course, was for the rice to be placed on the board in an exponentially increasing rate. This is non-linearity again. With each increment the amount doubled, which is exactly what an exponential trend such as Moore's Law indicates.

For a while the numbers were modest, but when they sustained the exponential trend through the 64th iteration, which is of course the number of squares on a chess board, then something happened that was quite surprising to most people, including to the king and his advisors.

Here is a table showing the progression of numbers.

Upon the last square, the 64th, we have attained a value of 9^{18}, or 9.2 quintillion, and this is, of course, a number far larger than all the grains of rice in the kingdom, and indeed in the entire world. It is a veritable Mt. Everest of rice, a mountain that no one could eat even in a million years.

72,057,594,037,927,900	144,115,188,075,856,000	288,230,376,151,712,000	576,460,752,303,423,000
281,474,976,710,656	562,949,953,421,312	1,125,899,906,842,620	2,251,799,813,685,250
1,099,511,627,776	2,199,023,255,552	4,398,046,511,104	8,796,093,022,208
4,294,967,296	8,589,934,592	17,179,869,184	34,359,738,368
16,777,216	33,554,432	67,108,864	134,217,728
65,536	131,072	262,144	524,288
256	512	1,024	2,048
1	2	4	8

Figure 4
A Chess Board of Rice
The number of grains on each square is double the number of grains from the previous square, starting in the lower left at one. It's a lot of rice.

But of course by the time the advisors had reached even the third row of the board they began to realize what was coming because the pile of rice was already spilling out all over the place. The king saw it as well, and understood that he had been fooled by his own ignorance. Being the king, however, he was not obliged to carry through his promise, which was in any event impossible, and so the advisors bundled up a great many bags of rice, and some soldiers carried them back to the hut in the forest.

And in the end, of course, some quite happy rodents ate most of the rice, but the point was made, and the king and his advisors had learned a powerful lesson, the same lesson that the computer industry would learn a few hundred years later, that exponential trends lead to outcomes that are difficult to foresee, but which are utterly transformative when they do arrive.

Over the course of the fifty years since Moore first made his calculation, the computing power of chips has been through about 25 doublings. If this change was a linear progression, it would appear as a straight line on a graph.

1,152,921,504,606,850,000	2,305,843,009,213,690,000	4,611,686,018,427,390,000	9,223,372,036,854,780,000
4,503,599,627,370,500	9,007,199,254,740,990	18,014,398,509,482,000	36,028,797,018,964,000
17,592,186,044,416	35,184,372,088,832	70,368,744,177,664	140,737,488,355,328
68,719,476,736	137,438,953,472	274,877,906,944	549,755,813,888
268,435,456	536,870,912	1,073,741,824	2,147,483,648
1,048,576	2,097,152	4,194,304	8,388,608
4,096	8,192	16,384	32,768
16	32	64	128

Can we explain it even more simply? "If I take 30 linear steps from the front door of my home, I end up 30 meters away. However, if I take 30 exponential steps, I end up a billion meters away, effectively lapping the globe 26 times."[19]

The same information looks quite different when it's presented graphically, as in Figure 5. Yes, of course it's the J-Curve, but for most of us, the implications shown by the curving line are almost immediately recognizable, whereas we have to study the table of numbers before we realize the pattern and discern the meaning.

However, there's still a significant cognitive challenge. Our prevailing mental model of change is based on how readily we grasp a linear progression, a slowly and steadily increasing quantity that increases by the same amount with each additional increment. That's shown in Figure 6 by the straight, gray line.

Exponential change doesn't reveal itself that way; it plots as the J-

Curve, which is not intuitively intuitive for most of us.

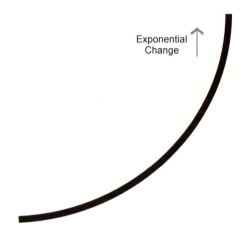

Figure 5
Graph of an Exponential Progression

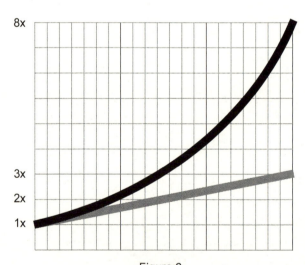

Figure 6
Linear and Exponential
A linear progression of 25 increments
An exponential progression of 25 increments

A linear thinker might have the idea that today's computers are maybe 25 times more powerful than those, a misimpression that is one of the reasons why we go so badly astray. A quick glance at the table in Figure 4 above shows that 25 doublings achieves a 16-*million*-fold improvement, compared to the computers of 1965. This is by any standard a tremendous accomplishment.

And what if the progress underlying Moore's Law is sustained for another decade? Then look at what's likely to happen ... a decade hence computers are likely to be 32 times more powerful that those of today, and a gargantuan 530 million times more powerful that the computer of 1965.

This is the transformative potential of progressive doublings, and thus a massive harbinger of massive change to come.

What will we do with computers that are 32 times more powerful than today's? No one really knows, other than there is a strong possibility, a near certainty in fact, that such a stupendous increase in power and speed will lead to astonishing accomplishments. Will computers attain the density of processing such that we can replicate the brains of animals? Or human brains? These are some interesting speculations to consider, and we'll return to this topic shortly.

But first, the other story will now become fully relevant. It is a parable told by Donella Meadows, who was one of the world's prominent systems scientists and teachers of the modern era. I mention this because system thinking is the very discipline in which we study trends and patterns in the behavior of systems that are not linear. It is, in a way, the science of non-linearity, and those few who have mastered this way of thinking are important guides for the rest of us.

She related the following story in her book *Thinking in Systems*, which I will paraphrase.[20]

Being a professor at Dartmouth College, which is located in rural New Hampshire, she was very familiar with the small New England farm, which typically consisted of a farmhouse, a barn, some acreage, perhaps a modest grove of maple trees kept largely for their beauty as well as for their winter firewood and their spring syrup, and almost inevitably, a pond.

If you've driven through New England you may have also noticed the that there are so many ponds, and perhaps you wondered why there seems to be one at every farmhouse. There are two reasons, the first being that it's very nice to go for a swim on hot summer afternoons after a hard day of farming work, but the more important reason is that it's an immediate source of water should there be a fire. Since most of these homes are made of wood and heated with wood (the maple trees), they burn quickly. Unless there was a pond nearby, a fire meant near total destruction; hence the pond is insurance, and clear, clean pond was not only aesthetically pleasing but functionally important.

Meadows herself owned a plot like this, and on the pond, in some years, would grow lilies, which could eventually choke off the oxygen, kill the fish, and also inhibit the firefighters. Hence, pond owners had to keep them mostly cleared.

So let's say that on your own pond you notice a small patch of lilies, but it's not enough to bother with, and anyway you've got a busy week ahead. Each day the patch doubles in size (the hidden exponent), but in this situation it's going to be a finite trend, because the pond is only so large.

In any case, you come and go throughout the week, and by Friday when you return home you decide that you'll have to get busy and do something about the lilies because they've now covered about a quarter of the pond. In a week's time, you promise yourself, you'll clean the pond. Too bad for you, because by then everything below the surface will be choked off and probably dead, for if the pond is one-quarter covered today, by tomorrow it will be one half, and the day after it will covered 100%. Your weekend is ruined by the not-understood exponent.

This is the insidious nature of exponential trends … they appear rather insignificant for quite some time until quite suddenly, the underlying phenomena explode out of control. A patch of lilies becomes a choking mass; a single grain of rice becomes a mountain; a thousandth of cent becomes $10 million.

Often we are surprised by these types of trends, even when the evidence was available and we therefore shouldn't have been. But because we misunderstand the power of the exponential pattern, and indeed we have trouble with large numbers in general, we don't recognize the phenomena that we're confronted with.

The Population Explosion

One of the first of these patterns that many in the public came to grasp and to be worried about was the human population explosion. This awareness came about during the 1960s, when a group systems scientists, including Donella Meadows, rose to prominence because they pointed out that the human population was growing exponentially, and since they were among the few who understood what that actually meant, they did the rather simple math to help everyone else grasp the frightening consequences.

An influential book of that era was *The Population Bomb* by Paul Ehrlich,[21] and the term "population explosion" was coined to warn us about the terrible resource shortages that were coming as more and more of crowded onto a finite planet. Birth control went from being a taboo and a very personal matter to a much-discussed theme of urgency to population planners and national leaders worldwide. As you know, the government of China responded to the threat that runaway population growth posed to its nation by limiting families to one child, and according to some calculations that policy has been successful at limited China's growth. It's likely that the population of China today would be hundreds of millions greater than it is were it not for the one child policy.

However, there have also been some disastrous and heart-wrenching social and demographic consequences for China, which we will explore in more detail in Chapter 11.

Suffice it to mention here that what emerged were serious side effects as a result of the one child policy that have created difficult problems for today's Chinese. In addition, the outcomes as anticipated by Ehrlich also turned out differently than expected, for reasons that he did not anticipate. Again, non-linear trends lead to unexpected outcomes, and the reasons in this case are both fascinating and quite revealing. The non-growth of the human population is, as you know from the Introduction, the fourth of the five revolutions that we're tracking, and we'll discuss it in detail in Chapter 4.

But for the moment let's return to the topic of exponents.

It is not only in technology and population demographics that we see the effect of exponential rates of change. Financial investors also recognize the power of exponents, which they refer to as compound growth. This occurs when funds are invested at a given rate of return, and then the proceeds are rolled back into with the principal, and the number grows. In today's banking environment of zero interest rates this rarely occurs with debt, but it remains the objective of most stock market investors – to find that gem of a company whose stock value doubles, and then doubles again, and then again, etc. Some decades ago when lenders paid much higher rates, the speed at which invested funds could grow was impressive. At a 10 percent rate of return, which was once not uncommon, a given amount doubles in about 7 years, so a skilled and patient investor could triple his or her money in 21 years.

Did you take the previous sentence at face value? 3 x 7 = 21, right? That's precisely the error we're talking about. But if the amount doubles in 7 years, and doubles again in 7 more, then you have 4x the original amount. If it doubles a third time, you then have 8x the original amount, not 3x. 1 > 2 > 4 > 8 is the progression. Wealthy investors understand this, by and large; most of the rest of don't.

To enliven our discussion of basic exponential trends (with a bang), consider also the explosive power of a nuclear bomb. The mammoth power of a nuclear weapon occurs because a chain reaction is induced in a volatile material, such as uranium, and the chain is *exactly* the exponential process. Two atoms split, and then four, and then eight, and because it happens so fast, we reach the 64th square of the chess board in nearly zero time, and the accumulated release of energy by the chain of fission becomes the insurmountable, uncontainable destructive force.

Hence, the transformative or revolutionary power of Moore's Law, the population explosion, nuclear bombs, and wealth creation are all examples of the same dynamic, which is runaway change. The growth of a bacterium or a virus, the flu for example, is also an exponential process, because each cell reproduces, which creates the massive impact that makes you feel so lousy one day after feeling completely fine on the previous day. And these are just five among dozens of examples that are deeply embedded in our daily lives.

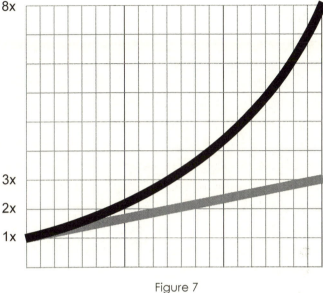

Figure 7
3 x7 or 8x?

Another example of exponential phenomenon is the concentration of carbon dioxide in the atmosphere; it, too, follows the J-Curve, and as we will explore in the next chapter, it is inducing the possibility of runaway climate change and thus drastic outcomes for many of us.

The key point is, therefore, that whenever you see the graph of a trend, and the graph looks like this, then you must please be aware that this is could be a big deal. Possibly a very big deal. Please beware.

Exponents and Politics

One further point regarding exponents, large numbers, and politics. In a democracy such as the US, where a constant point of tension is the balance between individual liberties and the government's authority over them, individuals often complain about unwarranted government interference in their lives. In 1776, when the US declared its independence from Great Britain, the total population of the nation was about 2.5 million, and the vast majority of them, as with the populations of all nations at that time, were farmers. There was virtually nothing that 2.5 million people could do in 1776 that would have much impact on, for example, air and water quality thruoghout the new United States.

Today the US population is about 128 times larger, about 320 million, and if all 320 million chose to drive cars that got 10 miles per gallon, for example, rather than 20 miles per gallon, then the aggregate consumption of gas and creation of pollution by those cars would be very meaningful on a national and global scale. Hence, the choices that any individual consumer has today is probably irrelevant in the big picture, but in mass markets of tens and hundreds of millions the choices made collectively have a huge, even decisive impact. And therefore, rightly or wrongly, the aggregate impact of these very large numbers is the basis upon which a great deal of government regulation is based, not only in the US, but in all large and even medium sized nations.

The arguments made by those who object to government interference are valid for them as individuals but perhaps less valid as they fail to account for both the impacts made by the large numbers of people who compose the world's major nations, and for the transformative impact of the exponential trends that large numbers of people are capable of creating in a very short space of time. Governance, in other words, is obliged to be different when exponents are involved.

Hence, chain reactions can be matters of physics, like in bombs, but they can also be social phenomena. We often call them "viral impacts," because some social trends expand and multiply following the J-Curve exponents, like the nasty flu virus, but in social settings. In many cases, these have been enabled by the increased power of computer chips that is described by Moore's Law. In business terms this often referred to as "adoption," a when people choose to buy a particular technology. Hence, the adoption of cell phones has been astonishingly fast.

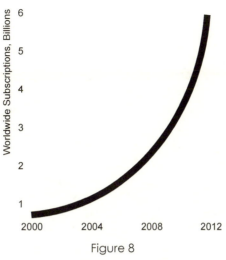

Figure 8
J-Curve of cell phone adoption

As a result, cell phone companies grew very fast, and many of the people who own them became unimaginably rich. Mr. Carlos Slim, owner of the Mexican company America Movil is also Mexico's richest man. Mr. Mukesh Ambani, CEO of Reliance Industries in India, a conglomerate that includes a cell phone company, is India's richest man. Etc. And of course the technology that makes cell phones possible is the miniaturized and super-powered computer chip, 16 million times more powerful than it was 40 years ago.

Despite the great many challenges that arise in physics due to the extreme miniaturization that has already been achieved by computer chip scientists, it is indeed reasonable to expect that the progress will continue. Why? Because the same competitive market dynamics that have driven the progress behind Moore's Law remain in effect today. Computer chip companies are as strongly incented as ever to sustain the rate of improvement. However, to call their motivation *strongly incented* is in fact an understatement. Companies in high technology industries that fail to sustain this rate of progress simply don't survive in the marketplace, and as the fear of death is also a powerful motivator, and leads directly to the principle of innovate-or-die. Technology advances relentlessly.

This principle is imbedded resolutely into the computer chip market,

55

and indeed into all technology markets, and consequently the pressure to innovate has also been relentless, and it will continue to be.

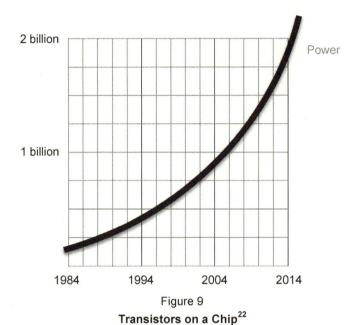

Figure 9
Transistors on a Chip[22]
In 1984, Intel's best computer chips had 134,000 transistors.[23]
In 2014, a computer chip the size of your thumb powers your iPhone and has 2 billion transistors.[24]

This fabulous improvement is driven by innovation, the result in fact of the market's absolute requirement to innovate, which has brought us into the early beginnings of a new historical era, which will perhaps be named the digital age. This will likely be the era when robots go from the stuff of science fiction to everyday realities, when ubiquitous sensors capture data in previously unimagined volumes, when the government spies can literally record millions of phone calls that are occurring simultaneously, analyze the resulting Mt. Everest of resulting data, and expect to learn something useful from it.

Because of the power of compounded improvement, the smart phone in your pocket, whether it's made by Apple, HTC, Xiaomi, Samsung, or any other company, possesses the computing power that only a supercomputer had forty years ago. And according to Omkaram

Nalamasu of Applied Materials, the chip that powers it would have cost you about $3 billion in the 1970s.[25] The price would have dropped to a mere $3.5 million by 1991.

From J Curve to D Curve

In addition to the progress in processing power that the J Curve describes, cost is another important and related trend, the cost. Consider the example of a 1 gigabyte USB flash drive, which in 2001 cost about $8000, but which today can be bought for about $2 (I just checked on Amazon[26]), hence a reduction by a factor of 4000.

This cost reduction is the reciprocal of the J-Curve, an inverted J:

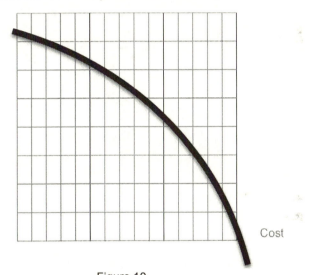

Cost

Figure 10
Inverted J: Cost Declines Precipitously

Dan Martin of SEMI, the global industry association serving the manufacturing supply chain for the micro- and nano-electronics industries, suggests that the figure is closer to $1 billion. It is directly due to the progressive increase in computer chip power that the iPhone is possible. And due to the remarkable and commensurate decline in cost, that same chip now costs about $20.[27] Hence, todays chips are millions of times more powerful, and millionths less expensive.

That's right, in your pocket you have a device worth perhaps $1 billion or more, and its power has affected your life in fundamental ways. Its descendent in five or ten years will have even more impact.

Since the ascending J curve describes the increasing power of computer chips while an exactly reciprocal curve, the upside down one, describes their decreasing cost, we draw them together and immediately notice that the letter "D" fits nicely into that space, and hence we call these paired marvels, these eloquent descriptors of the modern world's amazing technological progress, "the D-curve."

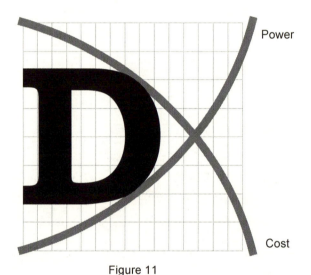

Figure 11
The D-curve
The decreasing cost of of computer chips follows the reciprocal curve
as their increasing power.

The D-curve

D, in this usage, has multiple and complementary meanings. It means *double*, of course, as there are two curves. It also means *digital*, since it explains why digital technology has become so pervasive through remarkably increased power and stunningly decreased cost. It has therefore led to massive *disruption* throughout the global economy, and it is thus one of the most significant *drivers of change*.

It's not an exaggeration to say that the D-curve is the single factor which best explains how the modern, tech-enabled world has come about, and how it has transformed life, the economy, and society. And of course it is precisely because of D-curve that it's even possible to remind you that there is a supercomputer in your pocket. It's also because of the D-curve that we can legitimately think about where all this heading, and thus to consider the impact that robots are likely to have in the not-too-distant future.

The Robots Are Coming

In fact, robots have already arrived, although they don't look much like R2D2. Self-driving vacuum cleaners prowl the floor, self driving cars are becoming common on the roads, and many robots, with the help of a few people, build many of those cars.

Looking forward, futurists, economists, and social scientists think quite seriously about the consequences of robotics, for as it's inevitable that computer chips will become progressively more powerful, it may also be inevitable that those chips will be built into robots that will become capable of ever more sophisticated accomplishments. They will thus become ever more deeply intertwined with our social and economic lives, and as they continue to get less expensive, this will further incent us to find more uses for them, in the commercial world, in government, and in our homes.

Which raises a great many important and quite interesting questions:

- How much robots will improve our lives, and how much they will disrupt us?
- Will they serve and support us, enhancing everyday reality and removing endless drudgery?
- Or, alternatively will robots displace millions of workers and cause massive unemployment and heartbreak?

- Or will they do both?
- Looking still farther ahead, at what point in time will there be robots that have cognitive and intellectual capabilities equivalent to humans?
- And what will happen then?

While these were once topics of science fiction and far-fetched speculation, they are now entirely serious issues about which it is only possible to make educated guesses, because in fact no one knows what's going to happen. Some, including the scientists/futurist Ray Kurzweil, believe that it will be transformative:

> Within several decades, information-based technologies will encompass all human knowledge and proficiency, ultimately including the pattern-recognition powers, problem-solving skills, and emotional and moral intelligence of the human brain itself. … By the end of this century, the nonbiological portion of our intelligence will be trillions of trillions of times more powerful than unaided human intelligence. We are now in the early stages of this transition.[28] Ultimately, the entire universe will become saturated with our intelligence. This is the destiny of the universe. This, then, is the Singularity.[29]

Not everyone is as sure as Ray Kurzweil that the singularity is going to happen, but we do know with a great deal of confidence that some big things will occur.

Broadly, as you might expect, there are two quite different schools of thought, one blissfully positive (Kurzweil), and the other quite pessimistic. The optimists are thrilled with the prospects and possibilities that robots embody to improve our lives, and there are indeed some fascinating ideas to consider.

For example, self-driving cars have progressed from idle speculation about something that might happen "one day," to current reality. In April 2015 a self-driving car outfitted by auto parts manufacturer Delphi drove 3000 miles across the US, from San Francisco to New York, and according to their reports the car's computers were in control 98 percent of the time.

This success is the result of decades of work in autonomous systems, artificial intelligence, the integration of sensors and effectors, and is possible largely because of the massive progress in the underlying computer chip technology described by Moore's Law. Basic research in robotics at universities and companies worldwide was stimulated and partially funded by the US government's DARPA Challenge, a series of contests to develop and demonstrate self-driving cars, first held in 2004. In subsequent years the challenges required an autonomous car to drive itself over a course of desert obstacles, a car that could navigate the urban landscape, and robots capable of disaster mitigation. DARPA paid millions of dollars in prize money, and hundreds of teams participated. The 2015 Challenge focused on developing robots with sufficient dexterity and robustness to enter areas too dangerous for humans and mitigate the impacts of natural or man-made disasters; it was won by a team from Korea.[30]

In addition to the development of critical technologies, these challenges also serve to engage broad public interest, to develop scientists and engineers with advanced skills, and thus to seed the development of new industries. This is how the future creeps up on us…

And of course the commercialization process is well under way. Google already operates an experimental fleet of self-driving cars in its small home city of Mountain View, California, and the company's intent is to develop a huge commercial success. During their first 6 years under development, according to Google, the cars drove 1.7 million miles and were involved in 11 accidents, all which caused only light damage and no injuries. Google believes that all 11 were the fault of the other drivers, the human ones, not the Google cars.[31] The 12th accident, in early 2016, was judged to be the Google car's fault, which prompted a change to the cars software to reflect what was learned.

Reports from many sources also confirm that self-driving cars are generally better and safer drivers than humans, as they don't get distracted, they don't text, eat, drink, or get sleepy.

By you time you read this, many other companies will be testing them, and perhaps even selling them, and when we project the market forward for a decade or two in an optimistic scenario (optimistic in the sense that robots are coming, which is definitely not everyone's definition of optimism), we might have attained indisputable proof that self-driving cars are so much safer and more reliable than human drivers that they have gone from being oddities and objects of curiosity, to common sights, to universal acceptance.

Perhaps it will become an accepted fact that the accident rate and thus the fatality rate attained by self-driving cars is substantially lower than the cars that people drive, in which case there will be social and then legislative pressure to get the people out of the driver's seat. Perhaps at some point in the not too distant future it won't even be legal to buy a car that requires a human driver, unless it's an antique, and even then it may not be legal to take it on the road. This is pure speculation, of course, but it's not at all implausible.

If this occurs it will of course have multiple impacts.

Self-Driving Cars

One of the most significant is the potential for self-driving cars to displace human workers. Displacement, or disruption, is a constant threat to many industries, but in transportation the issue is potentially quite profound. Worldwide, more people earn their living as drivers than in any other job, and in the US transportation employment is second only to sales.[32, 33] Thus, the potential for social strife to erupt over self-driving cars is not only a matter of speculative possibility, it may be quite close to reality.

In fact it is already happening. In June 2015 taxi drivers in France rioted to protest the expansion of Uber in their country, and of course to call attention to the threat that Uber presents to their livelihoods. Two Uber executives were arrested and the company announced it was closing its French operations temporarily. The irony of all this was not entirely lost, as the very idea to create Uber came when the company's founders were on a leisure trip to, yes, Paris. They found themselves standing in the rain and unable to hail a cab, and realized then and there that the smart phone could become a welcome alternative to "stand and the corner and wave hopefully while getting soaked" approach. They originally called their company "Uber Taxi," but eventually dropped the taxi part.

Every day the business landscape changes, and by the time you read this the French objection to Uber may be a quaint relic of the distant past. But perhaps not. A Wikipedia page called "Legal Status of Uber's Service" lists 28 countries in which Uber is engaged in some sort of legal or regulatory dispute, and it will certainly requires years for all of this to be resolved. As a result, eventually Uber itself could become the relic, forced out of business by regulators or overwhelmed by rioting competitors, or displaced by other companies offering the same service, but better. It's also quite possible that the business that Uber is pioneering may become the accepted standard; perhaps it is the taxis that will disappear, and your grandchildren will be confused when you use the word "taxi" to describe what they know as an "uber." For the moment Uber is an enormous success in spite of the competitive and regulatory obstacles; more than 1 million drivers have already signed up to drive for the company, and in 2015 the company generated total revenue of about $10 billion; in 2016 that figure is expected to grow to $25 billion.

If Uber succeeds, however, eventually the million plus drivers may find themselves out of work, as Uber's approach today is just a prelude to the broader self-driving revolution that's coming. When human drivers find themselves displaced by self-driving cars, Uber will become a driverless fleet. This is, in fact, Uber's plan, mentioned in 2014 but kept quieter since then, due to the obvious conflict that this creates with their drivers: an Uber driver wrote this comment on Uberpeople.net, an anonymous online forum for its workers:

> "Well fk driverless cars are coming and their ain't shit we can do about it. In the end delivery and transportation drivers will probably go bye bye in the next decade due to automation."[34]

In 2016, General Motors announced a $500 million investment in Lyft, Uber's main rival. GM President Dan Ammann added this comment:

"We think our business and personal mobility will change more in the next five years than the last 50."[35] He's probably right.

Auto-Mobility

From a social perspective, self-driving cars could become a great boon to those with limited mobility, including seniors who can no longer drive, children who cannot yet drive, people who cannot afford to own a car, and also to what is likely to be a growing pool of people who don't want to own a car or drive one.

A self-driving car would restore the mobility that aging has taken away from your parents or grandparents, and since most seniors who still do own cars don't use them very much, they could readily become shared possessions, freeing up cash and capital for other needs. A senior center or even those living in the same neighborhood could own a small fleet of shared, self-driving cars, and a few clicks on their phones would summon the nearest one to their houses, where it would await them patiently, and then take them wherever they wanted to go.

Improved mobility of this sort is not only a social phenomenon, it's also an economic one. In fact, economists often gauge the developmental level of a city's or a nation's economy according to it's level of mobility, because mobility is a very good proxy for economic development.[36] Economies develop slowly when the majority of the people obliged to walk or take buses, but as more and more people own cars this reflects economic development, and also stimulates it, because mobility enables increases in both creation and consumption.

Hence, the American economy achieved a dramatic spurt of growth when the railroads were first built, as they enabled commerce to occur on a regional and national scale at a level that had previously been inconceivable and unachieveable. The same thing occurred with the development of the reliable paved roads, then the first highways, and then again with the system of high-speed interstate highways, and then yet again with commercial air transport. Commerce grows with each advance in mobility, and as the cost of mobility declines its beneficial impacts become even greater.

Further, every industry that relies upon transportation, as well as the transportation industry itself, is likely to undergo fundamental transformation as a result of the technology that we now know as the self-driving car, but which will quickly broaden to "autonomous transportation" or perhaps "robotic mobility" (robomo?). Since nearly every industry relies in one way or another on transportation, the self-driving car is but the tiny tip of a much, much larger iceberg, just as the prescient but unhappy Uber driver pointed out.

As the self-driving car itself is really a compilation of a more fundamental set of capabilities that involve sensing and responding to other objects that are also moving or are stationary, as well as steering, mapping, controlling, and powering, etc., the self-driving car is only one example among hundreds of applications of autonomous or robotic behaviors that we can readily imagine. It is, at root, just a bunch of computers on wheels.

But many of them don't require imagination. When you place an order with Amazon.com, one of the company's fleet of 10,000 warehouse robots (yes, 10,000) is likely to transport your precious item through one of its massive warehouses so that a human only has to pack and seal up the box that will arrive on your doorstep tomorrow. Since warehouse operations are so important to its success Amazon bought the company that makes its robots, Kiva, for $775 million in 2012.[37]

As these forms of automation become common, package delivery, the domain of your friendly post office, Fedex, DHL, China Post, and UPS, and the hundreds of thousands of postal employees around the world, will not survive in its current form. Farming is another example that's already undergoing massive change (which we'll discuss more in Chapter 5), but in the context of this conversation imagine a farmer-less farm, where tractors, trucks, planters, and harvesters drive themselves. Already the percent of people who live on farms in the industrialized nations has plummeted, from about 97 percent of the total population in 1800 to about 3 percent in 2000; due to robotics it will decline still further.

Which brings us to the economic question. How many workers in addition to all those angry French taxi drivers and the worried Uber drivers are at risk of being displaced not only by Uber, but by future self-driving Uber cars, self-driving delivery trucks equipped with mini-drones, self-driving pizza deliveries, self-delivering mail delivery, self-driving tractors, and everything else that is being driven or delivered? Since more people earn their living worldwide by driving vehicles than in any other job, that is, more people are employed driving trucks, vans, cars, buses, tak-taks, and taxis than in any other single occupation,[38] the potential for disruption is pretty high.

Hence, the arrival of self-driving vehicles may prove to be not an economic boon, but rather an economic Armageddon, an unmitigated disaster. An entirely plausible scenario is the one which suggests that a great many workers will be displaced, and "a great many" may indeed be a gigantic understatement; over the span of a few decades many *millions* of jobs could be lost. The pessimists who looked askance at Ray Kurzweil's expectations would then be quite justified in their views.

Digital Displacement

The term "displacement" will be an important one for the history and the future of commerce and technology. When the economy changes technologies it means that old technologies are displaced as we begin living and working in new ways.

For thousands of years during the very-slow-to-change agricultural era things stayed pretty much the same from decade to decade, but with the arrival of industrialization the pace of change and displacement has significantly accelerated. Gone are the buggy whip makers, blacksmiths, wagon repairmen, elevator operators, ice deliveries, and hat makers, among many others.

Also gone are most of the farmers, for as I noted above, agriculture used to be a very labor intensive activity. Before the industrial revolution nearly 97 percent of all workers were involved in producing food. As far as we know, agricultural workers did not protest or riot as the harvester and the cotton gin and the tractor replaced the horse and the dawn-to-dark back-breaking labor; instead, many of them moved to the towns and cities and looked for other work. There they toiled instead as workers in the industrial economy, and the history of the last two centuries tells the same story over and over as industries have risen and fallen, as new tools, new technologies, new companies displaced older ones, and new ways of working came into widespread usage.

In 1950 Detroit's population was about 1.8 million, but by 2000 it had shrunk to less than 1 million, and was spiraling downward as the American auto industry continued to shrink and tens of thousands of jobs were lost. By 2010 the city's population was down to about 700,000, and an additional 75 people departed the city each day that year, leaving entire blocks of the city abandoned. The city then undertook a massive campaign to demolish acres upon acres of abandoned houses, which otherwise were left rotting, home only to rodents and crime. The city's mayor needed additional funds to increase the rate of demolitions from 100 per week to 400 in his attempt to reduce the backlog of 50,000 homes that needed to be torn down.[39] This is what happens when the structure of the economy changes.

The jobs come and go; during the early years of the 20th century, thousands of workers around the world made ice in factories or cut it from frozen ponds and lakes during the winter, stored it in huge warehouses, and delivered it throughout the year to keep food fresh.[40] The arrival of electricity and then the refrigerator made ice deliveries irrelevant, and when that happened the workers who made, collected, stored, and distributed the ice found something else to do. Interestingly, the first 7-11 retail store was opened in 1927 as a side venture of an ice company in Dallas; the ice business is long gone, but 58,000 of the stores remain.

At the same time as real estate values plummet in Detroit, housing prices in San Francisco are skyrocketing as thousands of new jobs are created in high tech companies. The San Francisco Bay Area added 400,000 jobs between 2010 and 2014, but far fewer new homes, which has created a massive crisis of affordability.[41] Employees in lower-paid service jobs are being forced out of desirable city locations and into remote suburbs, and 200,000 new housing units were in the planning stages throughout the region.[42]

The similar issue that we confront today is to wonder if the workers displaced by digital self-driving cars and all of the many other forms of digitization and robotics will likewise find suitable employment doing something else, while thousands of new workers will move to the Bay Area to work on developing and refining the underlying technologies.

Online retail is another form of digital displacement, and now that the volume of purchases made online has become a significant proportion of all purchasing, another aspect of the economy that is undergoing major change is retail shopping. Despite the impression that there is a mall or a strip mall on every corner of every US city, in fact the total square footage of real estate devoted to shopping malls has declined quite significantly. Malls probably won't disappear entirely, but there is no end in sight to the trend of their decline as online shopping gets better, which will inevitably happen as computer chips get more powerful, and online shopping becomes ever easier and less expensive, and as deliveries become nearly-instantaneous after you place your order due to the use of pervasive robots and delivery drones.

In the US today the retail trade is the single largest sources of jobs, employing more than 16 million workers.[43] But already a third or more of America's 1200 enclosed shopping malls are at risk of closing because of declines in the number of shoppers, and if they close it can only be because customers prefer to shop elsewhere.[44] As that happens many of those 16 million will be displaced and they'll also have to look for other work. On the leading edge of this trend, American retailer Macy's closed 36 of its 770 stores and laid off 4,500 employees in 2016.[45]

The broader economic question is where will they find other jobs? Or will they be un-employable, unable to find any sort of meaning paying work? As the trend toward greater robotization of the economy gains momentum, will there be enough jobs for people to do, or will the rise of robotic workers mean permanent displacement and thus a systematic contraction of the labor force? This is perhaps government's worst nightmare, the advance of technology that was developed largely with government support and investment, such as through DARPA projects, that makes full employment unachievable.

If this were to happen, the social and economic consequences would be significant and traumatic, to be sure.

Social Consequences

Suppose it turned out to be indisputably true that self-driving cars significantly reduce accidents, injuries and deaths in auto accidents, and this led to legislation that banned humans from driving.   Would this raise howls of protest simply on ideological grounds, regardless of whether or not it was actually a good idea?   Would solid evidence stop the soon-to-be-unemployed French taxi drivers from rioting?   Or would they have plenty of companions in the riots from others who felt similarly?

Since it is part of the government's role to protect the citizenry from threats, it may be reasonable for the government to intervene in commerce, and this is the role of unemployment insurance. In this scenario, would the French government be willing to support the unemployed drivers indefinitely, or will it compel or seek to compel them to find alternative employment?

The continuing advent of digitized industries and the disruptions they cause throughout the economy will certainly add more voices to this debate, as if it turns out that full employment is no longer attainable then the stakes will rise significantly.

One of the definitions of a revolution is that it's a process of social change in which there are winners and losers, and the advance of digital disruption has the potential to transforms legions of unemployed into the biggest losers.   This would then place an increasing burden on the governments toward which they will then turn for further financial support.

How fast this all occurs, if it does, is difficult to project, but as digitization is a process that is proceeding along an exponential timeline, do not be fooled although the early stages appear to be advancing slowly. Once we hit the knee of the curve the rate of change will appear to take off incredibly fast. Our collective inability to grasp the impact of very large numbers and exponential processes can lead to significant upheaval throughout society when people come to realize what's happening. The question that the forecaster seeks to assess, then, is, Where are we on the curve?

The second broader issue to consider is that as we transition from technology applied in a passive manner under human control to technology that is autonomous and proactive, how much autonomy, power and authority should a robotic agent have? Who (or what), in other words, is in control? Should robotic agents have any power or authority over humans?

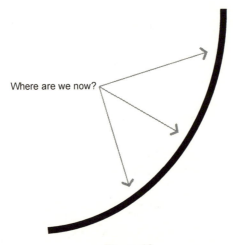

Figure 12
The Exponential Curve of Change

One of the great artistic landmarks of the early Space Age explored this very question, as the computer HAL ventured toward Saturn in *2001: A Space Odyssey* and killed off its (his?) human crewmates in the belief that its superior cognitive abilities would better serve the mission than humans who would make inferior or flawed decisions because of their emotions, and thus endanger the success of the mission. Arthur C. Clarke's story and Stanley Kubick's movie were quite accurate harbingers of issues that we are beginning now to confront.

The Environment

In addition to issues related to employment, control and autonomy, self-driving cars also have potentially significant environmental implications. According to a recent study, a large fleet of self-driving cars could be built that emit only 10 percent of the carbon emissions of today's autos, the 90 percent reduction coming as a result of progressive engineering improvements to the basic drive train combined with the reduction of the car's size.[46] As the auto industry is probably the world's fourth largest industry after food, oil, and health care, this also has enormous implications; the underlying logic implies an economic transformation that cannot be underestimated.

One of the provocative questions is, Who needs to own a car? As long as I have access to a car when I want it, and I'm actually driving the car (or it's driving me, as the case may be), then do I actually need or want to own it? In many cases, as we saw above, if a small collection of cars is owned cooperatively, the answer may be no. If my neighbors and I can share many fewer cars that we presently own, most of which presently sit idle most of the time anyway, fewer cars needed means fewer cars built, which means less use of resources.

And when I do need a car, and my purpose is grocery shopping, for example, then a lightweight, super-efficient, self-driving electric car would be entirely adequate. Overall, less than 5 percent of most people's driving requires a bigger, heavier car for long distances, but since I'm also sharing those cars, the total number of owned cars declines significantly.

This is not a vision that will thrill the auto industry, but it may well be the vision that society embraces. It could certainly present a very attractive option from an environmental perspective, as fewer cars along with a greater percentage of small and superefficient cars means fewer emissions.

The likelihood that this will one day emerge as a serious discussion is only possible, again, when the technology enables complete vehicle autonomy. This will put the growth pathway of the technology industry that enables autonomy in direct conflict with the auto industry, whose sales are likely to decline. And since the auto industry is so large by revenue then the soon-to-arrive transformation that we're talking about could turn into a gigantic collision between technology, society, economy, ideology and natural resources.

This scenario assumes that self-driving cars are functionally competent, economically viable, and socially accepted, but as with any emerging technology this is by no means a given. It's also entirely possible to imagine a credible scenario in which self-driving cars don't ever take over the roads. Despite the massive investment and clever publicity by Google and many other companies, the technology could turn out to be marginal, and the economics could also be marginal. Or the social opposition could become so widespread as taxi and delivery drivers everywhere follow the example of the French taxi drivers and unite in violence to prevent the revolution from occurring, or delay it at least.

Issues like this are easier to postdict rather than to predict, for hindsight enables us to construct a narrative that ties together all the disparate events that led to a big breakthrough. But when we're looking forward we face a much different intellectual challenge. Will it happen or not? And if it does happen, how might it unfold? Or fail to unfold?

Hype and Seeds

The technology could fail to perform as hoped and expected, and there are plenty of examples of that. The stories of their failures generally come down to a few points in common: either the technology just doesn't work, or it's not economically feasible, or no one cares. In the 1960s and 70s, for example, it was taken almost as a given that certainly by 2020 people would be living on the moon or Mars, but things haven't turned out that way, as neither the technology nor the economics are yet in place. That doesn't mean they will never be in place, but identifying precisely when a given innovation is going to arrive is quite difficult.

In a parody and clever elaboration on the J-curve that is Moore's Law, the research firm Gartner Group developed a quite useful and widely quoted model that explains how many new technologies come into use in society, which they humorously (and accurately) call the "Hype Curve." The model explains that for commercial reasons new technologies are often over-hyped at the outset, and expectations of the great things to come soar to a peak of inflated expectations, only to crash when the technology or the economics fails to live up to its promise.

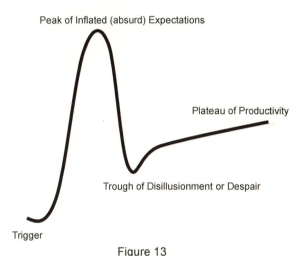

Figure 13
The Hype Curve
A clever and quite accurate parody of technology marketing created
by the Gartner Group.

However, there often is the seed of a viable business in there somewhere, and after a period of dashed hopes and disillusionment the underlying value proposition becomes clear. Perhaps the quirks and bugs are worked out of the technology, and it settles in as productive and valuable contributor to the economy. Apple offers a fine example of the hype curve when we consider its Newton product, a much-hyped "personal digital assistant" that Apple CEO John Sculley introduced with great fanfare in 1993. The product was an utter flop for the quite evident reason that the technology simply did not work.

Fast forward fifteen years to the 2007 introduction of the iPhone, and

73

what do you see? One of the world's most coveted products, which from one way of looking at it, is just a Newton that actually does work. Apple became the world's most highly valued company precisely because of that product, and so while Sculley's vision of the need was correct, his timing was a bit overoptimistic.

The point here, obviously, is that many of the new automatons will surely retrace the hype curve, especially given the power of social media to boost any piece of interesting news or speculations to absurdly elevated proportions. Many of them, however, will eventually settle in to become integral to how we live and work, and they will change us.

Given the evidence to date, given, that is, the vast number of industries that have been utterly transformed by technology, then it's entirely reasonable to expect that self-driving cars, and all of the changes that they portend really are going to happen, and perhaps rather soon at that. In fact, it's quite difficult to find an example of a single industry in which digital technology has *not* had a transformative impact. Can you think of a one?

And of course self-driving cars are only one example of how robotics will impact us. We can make equally plausible arguments to support the possibility that a great many other industries and professions will also become automated to an unprecedented degree. For example, the care of elderly people is quite likely to be automated, which we will discuss in more detail in Chapter 5. Manufacturing is already highly automated, and it will only become more so. Self-driving delivery vehicles are the last link in the vast global logistics chain, and it, too, will be automated, as we already see at Amazon with its 10,000 warehousing robots. So will farming, landscaping, security services, restaurants, and retail. What about educators? Will robots replace teachers? What about … (name any job or profession) … is it susceptible to automation?

Yes, one of the very interesting questions that inevitably arises in the discussion about the future of robotics is the inquiry about what *cannot* be automated. The answers vary depending on who you're talking to, and the time frame you're thinking about. When we consider what computers were capable of doing thirty years ago compared with what we use them for today it's obvious that there's a stunning improvement. Looking twenty or thirty years into the future, then, it might be wise to assume that computers will have progressed to the point at which their capabilities mimic human thought. Kurzweil proposes…

> Computers started out as large, remote machines in air-conditioned rooms tended by white-coated technicians. They moved onto our desks, then under our arms, and now into our pockets. Soon, we'll routinely put them inside our bodies and brains. By the 2030s we will become more non-biological than biological.   By the 2040s nonbiological intelligence will be billions of times more capable than our biological intelligence.[47]

Kurzweil's expectations are provocative, but his argument is certainly not accepted by everyone.   Pulitzer Prize winning author Douglas Hofstadter expressed his concerns this way:

> Ray Kurzweil says 2029 is the year that a computer will pass the Turing test. He says within 10 or 15 years after that, a thousand dollars will buy you computational power that will be equivalent to all of humanity. What does it mean to talk about $1,000 when humanity has been superseded and the whole idea of humans is already down the drain? This is one of the things that bothers me about the current developments that you see in robotics. There's more and more emphasis on humanoid robotics and supposedly robots with either genuine or fake emotions. Ray goes around saying it's going to happen, and he says it's all going to be bliss. Our brain patterns will be uploaded into software, we're all going to become immortal, everything is going to go faster and faster, our personalities will all blend and merge in cyberspace. It's bizarre, and I don't have any easy way to say what's right or wrong.[48]

Hofstadter is not alone. Dozens of people, some quite famous, have gone on record as saying that Kurzweil is wrong, and in fact there seems to be a small cottage industry devoted to explaining why he is "wrong" and "mostly wrong," which is of course what happens when you put out a set of predictions that is so far beyond what most people are accustomed to hearing. Kurzweil himself recognized this, and he devoted a 58 page chapter in his book *The Singularity Is Near* to a detailed discussion of these objections, which he organized into 14 categories ranging from philosophy to computer science to economics to religion.

Some of the objectors approach it from a philosophical perspective, horrified at the prospect that hybrid human-machine intelligence could replace human-only intelligence, while others suggest that his base technology forecasts are incorrect. Both types of objections may be entirely valid, or they may be utterly vapid; as of today we just don't know. Hence, from a strategic perspective, as a matter of foresight and planning, what's the right thing to do? Is it best to assume that Kurzweil and the many others who believe as he does are wrong, and to expect that things will proceed along the familiar and more comfortable path? Or should we instead give credence to the prospect of radical change in the relationship between humans and machines?

The best thing to do is probably to hold in our minds three alternative hypotheses:

- One: Kurzweil et. al. are correct. Huge change is coming, and it's best to prepare.
- Two: Kurzweil et. al. are wrong. There's no way.
- Three: We will maintain an open mind and pay attention to the evidence as it arrives. No, actually we'll not just pay attention to it, we'll actively seek out evidence to confirm *and* disconfirm the singularity hypothesis, and we will track the associated technological trends and possibilities.

And at the moment, the evidence we gather via the third option seems to be pointing to the conclusion that Kurzweil may have a point. When we consider the advent of self-driving cars, drones, pervasive AI software in your phone and every iPhone app, the NSA's big data surveillance algorithms, and everything else that advanced technology can already offer, to suggest that this technology revolution will not occur seems, well, like wishful thinking. Perhaps, then, the reaction to Kurzweil is more of an emotional issue than a substantive one. While it's entirely understandable that people may feel that way, it definitely does not constitute a solid foundation on which to build an organization's strategy.

We will maintain the possibility in our minds that option two, the "no way" scenario is valid, but let us nevertheless for the moment let us suppose that Kurzweil is broadly correct. Then the question becomes, What will the people do? And the answer is not entirely clear, as it involves both the economics of labor and the distribution of society's resources, as well as our notions of the purpose of life. Will we become a society focused on the quest for aesthetics and spirituality? Will we become a civilization that consists of a few who have and own all the robots and thus all of the wealth, the .1 percent, and a massive pool of 99.9 percent who are unemployed and impoverished? Will we care about well-being for all, or about materialism, indulgence, and selfishness for a few?

Beyond Science Fiction

As a strategist one learns fairly quickly that either-or questions rarely lead toward useful insights, but when we can envision multiple alternatives we often see both possibilities emerging simultaneously. Hence, we can find evidence for and against and advocates for and against both possibilities, and we see people campaigning hard for the advanced technology future that Kurzweil describes, and many campaigning equally hard against it.

This discussion has had a long and productive history in the arts, where the science fiction genre has dealt provocatively with these issues for more than a century. More recently, the invention of digital special effects (wherein digitization has thoroughly disrupted, and significantly enhanced, the entertainment industry) has allowed TV and film to evoke entirely realistic future worlds. Numerous films and television programs articulately explore themes relating to artificial intelligence, robots, genetic engineering, and robot-human relations, and in the process they are examining the human emotions of fear, control, desire, and power. As I mentioned above, one of the first of these films to combine a compelling story with stunningly evocative visual effects was *2001: A Space Odyssey,* which was soon followed by *Blade Runner*, which examined moral and ethical themes around artificially created humanoids. Both were artistic and commercial successes, highly provocative and thought stimulating. More recent films including *Ex Machina*, *Her*, *Robot and Frank*, and the BBC television show *Orphan Black* examine the relationships between people and advanced technology, and what is perhaps most interesting about them as a group is that the genre has subtly changed. They're not science fiction any more, they're commentaries about psychological and sociological reactions to technology and to accelerating change that people are experiencing today. Hence, they're stories about us now, not some future version of us.

If they are accurate harbingers of our future, what this tells us is that while many of us have profound and entirely legitimate concerns about the future of technology, the forces that are transforming technology from the realm of speculation and fiction to our everyday reality are gaining momentum.

The Digital Danger Zone

Perhaps the only plausible scenario for a future in which computers do *not* have increasing impact is the scenario of a total social and economic collapse, which would toss us into a survivalist world, the end of a technological society, the implosion of capitalism, the end of modernism and a relapse to an agrarian world. If through some sort of calamity we nuke ourselves back to the stone age then all of the centralized, technology-based services that we've come to depend on would disappear, including the electrical grid, centralized agriculture, mass media, and law enforcement. If that happens, and if you happen to be one of the few survivors, all that's left to do is to find a cabin in the woods and try to stay alive.

It's a premise of this book, however, that there will not be a total collapse – after all, why write a book about strategy for the future is the future doesn't exist...? Hence, we have to assume that society will continue to evolve and develop, and that advancing technology will be a central and indeed increasingly significant aspect of our ongoing experience. In this world we must expect that change continues to accelerate, and that acceleration itself continues to constitute a significant challenge for individuals, families, and institutions, because the very pace of change itself becomes both psychologically and organizationally overwhelming.   Disruption threatens and indeed displaces established companies, which generally do a poor job at adapting to change (we'll explore this theme in more detail in Chapter 15), and as we examined above, it also disrupts entire industries and the very structure of the labor force, threatening the elimination of millions of jobs and entire professions, but also leading to the creation of new ones.

One way to understand the emerging digital economy is to recognize that we are in the midst of a "digital danger zone," a market environment in which change is so fast that its rate becomes a major business challenge in and of itself.   Here, computer technology and its continuing improvements are yielding progressively greater capabilities that will have increasing impact as society becomes ever more dependent on technology.

What is the end point?   That's probably the wrong question, because in fact there likely is no end point – it just keeps on going.   Along the way, we must expect that someday soon it will be completely normal for robots and humans to live and work side by side, and through this process we must also anticipate that the economy will be utterly and completely transformed.   If it turns out not to come about that way then we can continue doing things the way we are doing them today, but if the technologically-induced changes do come about, then we're much better off being prepared.   Hence, the digital danger zone is another way of saying that technology becomes ever more pervasive, and more disruptive.

There are many ways to measure the progressive impact of technology, one of which is the accumulation of computer usage throughout society. We can look at the number of discrete computers in use, or the number of computer chips, or the number of people who are connected to the digital age, or the number of connected devices.

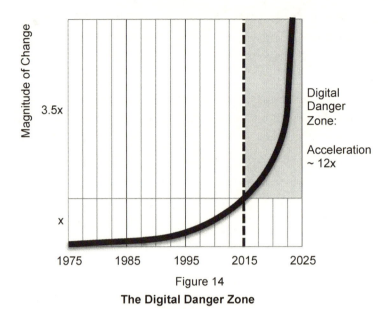

Figure 14
The Digital Danger Zone

This is a conceptual view, not a literal one. The premise of the graph is that the overall magnitude of technological change, as shown on the vertical axis, can be measured by technological progress through indices such as the number of computer chips in use, the speed of those chips, the amount of computer-related storage in use, and eventually by the adoption of robotics. If we hypothesize that 2015 marks the midpoint of the curve, then what we have ahead of us is a 12x acceleration, as we are likely to see 3.5x change in .3x the amount of time.

No matter which of these metrics we use, in each case the picture that emerges is basically the same – it's the J-curve for as far into the future as the eye can see, more and more computerization with increasing impact on life and work, and on our thoughts and expectations.

Already we are seeing that start-up companies can harness the power of the internet and smartphones and apps to displace established businesses – this is what Uber has done to the taxi industry, what Google has done to the advertising industry, what email has done to the printing industry, what digital cameras did to Kodak, what the iPhone did to Nokia's cell phones, what Amazon did first to booksellers, and then to all retailers, what PayPal is doing to banking, etc. etc. These examples foreshadow the future disruptive power of the digital economy, the connected economy in which new entrants readily and frequently displace incumbent companies, and do so with astonishing ease.

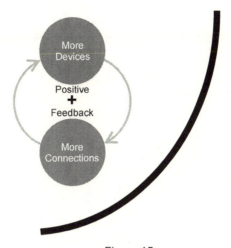

Figure 15
More and More Devices, More and More Connections
This is what causes the acceleration noted in Figure 14..

This is exactly what inexpensive computer processing power did to IBM, which provides a good example of how digital dangers unfold.

A Cautionary Tale:
The Collapse of IBM

IBM nearly went bankrupt in 1989. The powerful force that caused this near-catastrophe was not another company, nor a government action, nor ignorance or incompetence. It was caused simply by the accumulated impact of the D-curve, the combination of the increasing power and decreasing cost of computers, which made IBM's main product line, the mainframe computer, obsolete. The existence and power of the D-curve was abetted by IBM's own culture, which was a compelling force in creating new technologies and bringing them to market. But the company's leaders did not come to grips with the meaning of advancing

81

technology, and as a result they wished and pretended that fundamental change was not occurring even though their own technical teams were creating exactly that type of change. Hence, the relevance of the story is not the specifics of the situation, but rather the extent to which (a) technological change led to market disruption, and (b) the capacity of a strong leadership team of a great company to fail utterly to comprehend what was happening to them.

By 1989 the two trends collided, and the crisis ensued. When it did, IBM required not only new products to replace the no-longer-marketable mainframes that had been the company's central source of revenue for decades, but an even more radical change in its approach, an entirely new business model.

IBM's CEO as the crisis unfolded was John Akers, a skilled and astute leader, but the forces of historical change and organizational inertia that he faced proved too much for him. And the inertia, the stubbornness that he could not overcome was precisely IBM's own culture, particularly the arrogance born of its past success, which literally prevented the company's leaders from making the changes that would have avoided the crisis.

Hence, the crisis was foreseen but not averted.

Akers resigned, and Louis Gerstner was chosen to lead IBM in the midst of the crisis. The task given to him by the company's board of directors was to determine if IBM could in fact be saved, and if so, how it could be done. Over the course of the next few years, hundreds of thousands of IBM employees lost their jobs as Gerstner led the gut-wrenching process of transformation.

This is relevant to us precisely because it's not at all unique. The crisis into which IBM fell is a painfully common occurrence among giant and even not-giant companies. A huge number of them have succumbed due to their inability to clearly foresee the future, or their inability to act effectively on what they did foresee. The list of former greats is quite long, among them Sony, once the most admired electronics manufacturer; Kodak, the film giant that lost its way when the film market collapsed with the advent of digital photography; Nokia, the former king of the mobile phone universe, reduced to also-ran by the wizards of Apple; Sears, the global retailing giant brought low by Wal-Mart; etc., etc.

Gerstner himself later commented that, "Many successful companies that fall on hard times – IBM, Sears, GM, Kodak, Xerox – saw clearly the changes in the environment. But they were unable to change highly structured organizational cultures that had been born in a different world."[49]

What was perhaps unique to IBM, or certainly unusual, was its transformation. Through Gerstner's clear thinking and exceptional leadership and a committed and talented organizational effort, the company created an entirely new business model, one fully relevant to its time, which replaced the former business model that had become non-viable. From the early 1950s to 1989 IBM had been a computer hardware manufacturing company; Gerstner transformed it into a technology services firm.

A more common fate is the one shared by Kodak and Nokia and so many others, disappearing into irrelevance as their market position deteriorated, changes also driven by technological progress. In early 2007 Nokia was the undisputed global king of cell phone market, the world's greatest and most admired maker of a valued and elegant technology. And then those guys over at Apple created the iPhone, and 18 months later, before many in Nokia's leadership had even realized what was happening, the company was dead in all but name. This is a small but hopefully poignant warning about how fast things can change. Kodak's death knell took longer, but the result was the same.

The giant technological waves that sank Kodak and Nokia were certainly notable, and the ones that are now hammering Greece and Syria are tragic, but the point for us is that it's quite possible that the waves of change that are now coming towards all of us are much larger still. This is the strategic challenge that digitization presents, the aggregate results of brilliant human efforts to develop and commercial more and then still more new technologies.

Indeed, the computer chip is central to it all, and as we have seen it is indeed a magnificent artifact of human inventiveness, one that has become the irreplaceable core of our economy and thus of our society. If were we to simplify things to a minimalist core, we might say that food, water, air, love, and now computer chips are the forces that shape our world. But while our needs for food, water, air, and love are more or less unchanging, our need for computer chips is constantly increasing because we want and need ever more computing power to do ever more work and play. We are indeed digitizing the entire economy, and if Kurzweil is correct, we are also digitizing biology, and thus evolution itself.

Even without considering the profound depths of human evolution, and at the more mundane level of commerce, entrepreneur, technologist, and now venture capitalist Marc Andreessen made the very interesting comment that "software is eating the world."[50]

> My own theory is that we are in the middle of a dramatic and broad technological and economic shift in which software companies are poised to take over large swathes of the economy. More and more major businesses and industries are being run on software and delivered as online services—from movies to agriculture to national defense. Many of the winners are Silicon Valley-style entrepreneurial technology companies that are invading and overturning established industry structures. Over the next 10 years, I expect many more industries to be disrupted by software, with new world-beating Silicon Valley companies doing the disruption in more cases than not.

As far as we can tell he's entirely correct; it's a great letter and I recommend that you read it. Digital technology is becoming such a significant part of every industry and every company that it is possibly the essential, indispensable, inescapable core of tomorrow's economy. Software, hardware and all aspects of digital technology are having an ever-increasing impact, and they're eating the world, market by market, industry by industry, sector by sector, country by country.

What's Next?

As long as human society endures, which means as long as we avoid the catastrophic collapse that our dystopian fictions so vividly describe, then there can literally be no end to the progressive refinement of technology. Because competition is inherent in our economic system, and because making advancements in technology is one of the few methods by which companies can gain competitive advantage, the process of advancement and change will necessarily continue. As it has already done for tens of thousands of years, technology will become progressively more and more powerful, or in Andreessen's terms, its appetite will grow boundlessly and it really will eat the world. *Bon appetit.*

In the extreme, this awaits:

> In recent years the idea that human history is approaching a "singularity" thanks to increasingly rapid technological advance has moved from the realm of science fiction into the sphere of serious debate. In physics, a singularity is a point in space or time, such as the center of a black hole, where mathematics breaks down and our capacity for comprehension along with it. By analogy, a singularity in human history would occur if exponential technological progress brought about such dramatic change that human affairs as we understand them today came to an end. … If the fields of artificial intelligence and neurotechnology fulfill their promise, if the intellect becomes not only the producer, but also a product of technology, then a feedback cycle with unpredictable and potentially explosive consequences can result. … Before long, according to the singularity hypothesis, the ordinary human is removed from the loop, overtaken by artificially intelligent machine or by cognitively enhanced biological intelligence and unable to keep pace. When human-level AI is achieved, superintelligent AI will be almost inevitable.[51]

The possibility that in the advancing technology-enabled world there be disruption is therefore quite high, and it will be fully realized in the event that the increasing use of robots results in massive unemployment. This would occur if robots simply replace and thus displace human workers, and the humans cannot then find any other employment. Will robotic doctors and nurses replace human ones? Will an exploding success of self-driving cars displace millions of taxi, bus, and delivery truck drivers? Will *all* manufacturing jobs go away as robots become still more capable at completing ever more complex tasks? Will robots replace soldiers and sailors as drones have begun to replace airmen? The list of jobs and tasks that may become obsolete involves the employment of tens of millions of people, including house cleaners, lawn mowers, security guards, retail store clerks, baristas, waiters and waitresses, cooks, etc. etc.

Large scale unemployment such as this implies would of course have massive economic consequences. It would suggest a further concentration of wealth in the hands of robot owners, and conversely a gigantic and growing pool of unemployed and perhaps unemployable, resulting in greater separation, the rich yet richer and poor getting poorer. This might lead to attempts at legislation to restrict the use of robots to limit the impact, or perhaps a creative solution would be robotic surrogates such that a portion the economic productivity of robotic workers would be allocated to the people they displaced; robotic slaves, in a sense.

The ongoing digital revolution suggests that computers – and thus robots – will become ever more capable over the coming years as computer chips become more powerful, software becomes more advanced, and hardware that enables mobility, vision, dexterous manipulation, and decision making become more proficient.

The progress made by various competing teams in the US government's DARPA challenges suggests that such degrees of progress are entirely attainable. At DARPA's first self-driving car challenge in 2004 no cars were able to complete the 150 mile course of rugged rural terrain, and thus there wasn't a winner; the one that made it farthest traveled only 11 miles. DARPA looked to be hopelessly optimistic. In 2005, however, 22 of 23 entries surpassed the best distance achieved in 2004, and five of them completed the entire 132 mile course. The 2007 course consisted of 60 miles of urban driving and was successfully completed by six teams. Google self-driving cars are being developed by the team that won the 2005 DARPA Challenge, and their cars have successfully done more than 1 million miles of driving.[52] Of the few accidents that have been reported in the course of that million miles, all have been minor, and all but one were blamed on the human drivers, not on the Google cars.

But let's go further. What would happen if robots not only did most or all of the work, but also became fully self-aware, and were understood to be conscious in some way that seemed similar to or at least analogous to people? While this would actually be quite difficult to assess because science still does not offer a strict definition of human consciousness, the discussion would be a fascinating one and the debate might be the legal highlight of the century. If we believed that robots were indeed, or even might be as intelligent as humans and self-conscious as well, then it would only be a matter of time when "robot rights" would become a significant issue in law. When this happens, would robots gain the right to legal protection? Would they have civil rights? Would they be allowed to vote in elections, and if so, at what age? At what point would it be illegitimate for people to own robots? And what would robiotic reproductive and parental rights and responsibilities be for "offspring" robots that they created?

Speaking of robotic reproduction, whereas it takes nine months to manufacture a baby, and eighteen years before the newborn comes of age, how different will the world be if robots built new robots by the thousands each week, or even each day?

Fifty years ago, and even twenty years ago these were topics only of science fiction and academic speculation. One of the earliest books to take up the topic seriously was Hans Moravec's 1988 book *Mind Children*, in which he posited that,

> What awaits is not oblivion but rather a future which, from our present vantage point, is best described by the words "postbiological" and even "supernatural." It is a world in which the human race has been swept away by the tide of cultural change, usurped by its own artificial progeny. The ultimate consequences are unknown, though many intermediate steps are not only predictable but have already been taken. Today, our machines are still simple creations, but within the next century they will mature into entities as complex as ourselves, and eventually into something transcending everything we know.[53]

Thirty years after Moravec published this, the themes he explored are indeed becoming significant topics that cognitive scientists, computer scientists, lawyers, ethicists, legislators, jurists, economists and citizens are debating and discussing at great length. If and when the robotic revolution reaches the turning point that Kurzweil calls the singularity actually does occur, then literally everything will change yet again.

And if Kurzweil and those suggesting that we're headed toward a technological singularity are correct, then the changes coming even within the next few years will begin to reshape every aspect of our society in a fundamental way that also qualitatively different than what we have experienced so far. When that happens, if that happens, then the term *digital revolution* will turn out to be a serious understatement. (And if it doesn't happen then Kurzweil and his cohort will fade into the long list of those who hyped changes that never materialized...)

If we envision the full range of future possibilities on a horizontal scale, the singularity and whatever lies beyond are located on the far right end, but what lies at the other end, on the left? In that future, we would see a world that probably looks very much like today, with the same sorts of devices, just smaller and faster ones. We can envision, for example, better smart phones that do a lot of cool stuff, and better and faster ubiquitous internet services, but this would be a world without the large imposition of artificial intelligence, without a significant expansion of robotics beyond current capabilities and uses. It would be like today, only spiffier, whereas the other extreme end of the spectrum is so different from today as to be a world transformed.

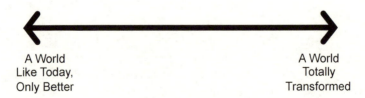

A World
Like Today,
Only Better

A World
Totally
Transformed

Figure 16
Spectrum of Future Possibilities

What actually occurs may not lie at the extremes, of course, but may fall somewhere along the middle of the spectrum. And if we took a poll of hundreds of experts we would receive opinions across a wide range, some like Kurzweil on one end, others vehemently disagreeing with him. In Part 2 of the book we will explore this more fully in pursuit of useful Foresight, but for our purposes here, where the intent is simply to describe the first of the five revolutions that we are living through, the key question it raises is about how best to prepare. And the position that makes the most sense is that it's much better to prepare for the revolution that does not come, than it is to be unprepared for the revolution which does arrive.

After all, if an expected revolution doesn't arrive, or doesn't arrive to the degree or magnitude anticipated, then the process of becoming prepared would not in any case be detrimental; but if the revolution does arrive and we have not yet begun to prepare then the disaster could be total. This is what happened to IBM in 1989 (and interestingly, what's also happening again to IBM now as cloud computing remakes the marketplace) a revolution arrived for which the company was not prepared, and the impact was disastrous.

And of course it's not just IBM. Just ask the hundreds of thousands of people who used to work for any of the companies that have been shoved aside by more innovative, faster, nimbler competitors.   When the revolution arrives for which you are not prepared, there is no end to the pain. Hence, in this Part 1, where the overall theme is Risk, the essential advice is that you *must* prepare. And if the prophets of change are wrong, then perhaps you're over-prepared. But you ignore them at your extreme peril.

I will offer you the same advice after we consider each of the next four revolutions; in each case, you're much better off preparing now than suffering hugely later.

Best Case; Worst Case

If you accept my premise then you should next ask yourself what it is that constitutes prudent and adequate preparation.

What, that is, could we reasonably expect as best and worst case outcomes, and what should we do about it?

This is a much more nuanced question, since values and preferences come into play when the topics are "best" and "worst," as these are very subjective terms. The answers you yourself give, your beliefs and preferences, may vary considerably from the answers given by the people sitting next to you, and even more so if those people are of different ages or they've lived in different cultures. My best may be your worst, and vice versa. Nevertheless, it is an important and quite useful discussion to have.

However, I should also point out that your discussion about the future explosion of technology will be influenced by other trends and forces that are also playing critical roles in shaping our future society, trends including climate change, the transformation of our energy systems, and urbanization, and these are the major topics we take up in the following chapters. My view, of course, is that all of these revolutions are occurring together, and it is their convergence and its consequences that constitutes an overarching risk for which we must prepare.

•••

Chapter 2

The Combustor:
The Climate Revolution

One-third of the oil that we know exists as reserves can never be taken out of the ground. Fifty percent of the gas can never be used and over 90 percent of the coal. That is a revolution.
Jerry Brown, Governor of California[54]

Inspired by his compassion for the plight of poor humanity, the Greek Titan Prometheus stole fire from Mount Olympus and brought it down to Earth so it could benefit the weak and helpless mortals. This did not please Zeus, however, and so Prometheus was made to suffer for all eternity for the hubris he displayed. But we will be forever grateful, as we eat our tasty cooked food, and warm ourselves on the cold nights, and transform mounds of earth and lumps of coal into magnificent machines, all because of the gigantic risk that Prometheus took on our behalf.

Fire, or combustion, has been a fundamental aspect of human life since long before there was anything even close to meriting the title of "civilization," and indeed perhaps even before there was anything we might even call myth or folklore. For combustion is the essential force that transforms matter into energy, and it is no exaggeration to say that the modern world is built entirely on energy.

Until 1800, however, nearly all of the energy available to humans came from our labor and that of animals, and from small fires, windmills, and waterwheels.

And then the technologists whose works enabled the Industrial Revolution figured how to massively amplify the power available for nearly all activities by burning not wood or peat, but coal, and doing so in tightly controlled conditions and on a massive, previously unimagined scale. Their discoveries and inventions built upon parallel advances in mining and metallurgy that made it possible to exploit the massive combustive force locked in coal, which led directly to the explosion of industrialization, and a short 200 years later, to us.

In a quick manifestation of positive feedback, the first of many such loops that characterize the modern economy, coal was coming into broad use but unwanted water was accumulating in the coal mines, and thus the invention of the steam engine addressed the problem by enabling large scale pumping. Closing the loop, it was the coal, of course, that powered the steam engine which then enabled the extraction of still more coal. This then enabled mining to be done on a much larger scale, resulting in greater volumes of extraction, and thus the transformation of minerals buried under the ground into usable resources that created wealth.

And then the engines were transformed into railroad locomotives that brought still more coal to market and created still more wealth, and later into the large scale production of electricity. So began the Industrial Revolution, and it proceeded in this self-reinforcing manner of the exploitation of materials and labor to create wealth for the entirety of the nineteenth century, until in the 20th century coal was gradually replaced by oil, and steam was replaced by internal combustion, but the underlying economic pattern only accelerated and amplified.

The twentieth century was assuredly the oil century, and now here we are in twenty-first in an economy that is still utterly dependent on three types fossil fuels, coal, oil, and more recently natural gas. These fuels are all extraordinarily flexible, powerful, and so useful that they have enabled humans to accomplish exceptional economic and social progress. The notion of GDP, gross domestic production, attempts to sum up the combined value of all of the economic activity of everyone in a nation, hence "domestic," or more broadly of everyone in the world. While there are some fundamental problems with the notion of GDP, it is nevertheless a good overall indicator of what has been happening.   And quite interestingly, what a graph of global GDP from 1800 to 2000 shows is exactly the same trend of exponential growth that we saw with Moore's Law, a J-curve.

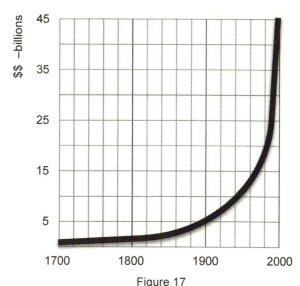

Figure 17
Global Economic Growth: GDP
Shown in 1990 International Geary-Khamis Dollars (billions) based on purchasing power parity.

If we take the example of a single nation the correlation is also inescapable. In Figure 22 we see that China's economic boom of the last 25 years aligns perfectly with the increase in Chinese oil consumption.

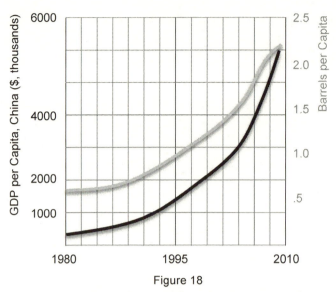

Figure 18
**Chinese GDP Per Capita (left scale; black line) and
Barrels of Oil Consumed Per Capita (right scale, gray line)**

The social and economic power expressed in these graphs cannot be underestimated, for they show clearly how fossil fuels have utterly transformed our lives, our cultures, and our expectations. And in relation to the specific topic that we're focused on in this chapter, the leftover carbon dioxide that all this combustion produced has also transformed the Earth's climate.

From Animals to Machines

When steam engines were just coming into use, and thus before anyone knew that it was the beginning of what we would later call "the industrial age," the vast majority of all work was done by people and by animals. For most people, the course of life was years of hard labor beginning in childhood and continuing until the aged body could no longer bear heavy loads. And the body aged quickly under these burdens – the average lifespan was a short 40 years, half of today's average.[55]

Wind and water-powered mills were used in some locations, but they provided only a tiny percentage of humanity's total energy consumption;

94

the vast majority of work was done by humans, horses, cattle, and oxen.

With the emergence of industry during the 1800s, transformative machines changed work and changed lives everywhere – the steam engine, railroads, and factories – which ran on coal. Coal literally fueled the massive expansion of economic activity throughout the century as millions of tons of it powered the machines that built the modern world. Coal fed the steel mills that created the rails for the railroads, and created the wheels that rode on the rails, and created the railcars that rode on the steel wheels, and also the steel that became the bridges that crossed the rivers and the canyons, and the skyscrapers that defined the cities, and then ice boxes that, when there was electricity, became refrigerators.

In the 20th century, of course, raw steel was transformed into autos, and the energy that predominantly powered the century was oil. Horses, once a critical source of power for farming and even more so for transportation, became instead a source of recreation. In 1911, after a century of industrialization and just at the beginning of the automotive era, Americans owned about 23 million horses, nearly all of them working animals that were involved in transportation and farming. By 1946 the number had declined by 65% to about 8 million. In 1959 there were only 4.5 million horses in America, and nearly all of them were owned for recreational purposes rather for the work they could do.[56]

Before the coal era began, a typical subsistence farmer deployed an estimated average of 6 million BTU during a productive year of farming. During the first century of industrialism, the average person living in an industrialized nation consumed 20 million BTUs-equivalent per year, and during two centuries of industrialism humanity unleashed ten thousand times more energy than had been used in all of the previous millennia of human history.[57]

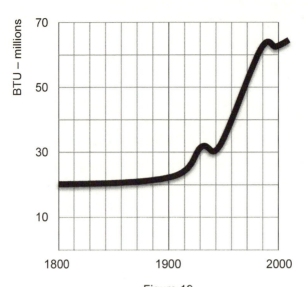

Figure 19
Annual Global Per Capita Energy Consumption

The Fossil Fuel Economy

Coal, oil, and gas are all gathered from below the Earth's surface, transformed into machine energy through combustion, and of course their combustion also produces significant polluting by-products.

Perhaps the first deadly form of pollution was the black grime and soot of coal dust, depicted in the classic views of gloomy, coal-fired London was coated in black particles that stuck to everything in the soggy rain and fog. Without regular cleaning the city's landmark buildings and statues all turned a dull black, and with the soot came epidemics of respiratory diseases.

Until about 1900 industry still had not found many uses for oil, as its primary commercial use was limited to kerosene that was burned for nighttime lighting. But of course everything changed with the invention of the internal combustion engine, for gasoline proved to be the ideal fuel. Cars instantly transformed not only the lives of their owners as indeed they transformed the entire economy. Mobility was enormously lucrative and popular, and the market for cars and for gas grew together. Increased

96

mobility led to increased consumption of nearly every type of manufactured good, and the positive spiral of a consumer oriented society was born. Together, the car and oil created the modern economy.

And the modern economy was all about growth.   Hence, at the beginning of the industrial age in 1800 when the predominant economic activity was growing food, global GDP was about $175 billion. 200 years later, as a result of the extraction and combustion of millions of tons of coal and then billions of barrels of oil and its use to create the modern industrialized-consumerized world, the economy had grown to $41 trillion, an increase of 23,000 percent over 2 centuries. This progression from the dawn of modernism to its spread occurred at astonishing speed, and the transformation of life and lifestyles was total and global.

Since coal and then oil and then later natural gas were the most significant sources of energy throughout the industrial era, we could readily call these two centuries the Fossil Fuel Era, and indeed the consumption of fossil fuels has grown exactly in parallel with the expansion of the global economy.

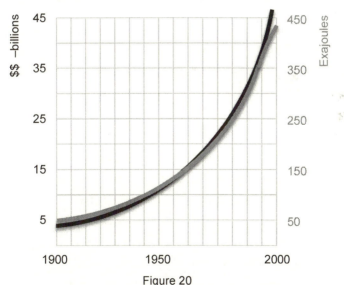

Figure 20
**World GDP (left scale, black line) and
Total Energy Consumption (right scale, gray line)[58]**

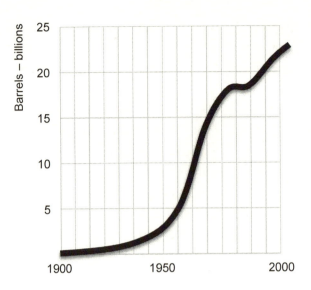

Figure 21
World Annual Oil Consumption[59][60]

Our dependence on fossil fuels continues, and thus in 2015 about 75 million new cars were manufactured and added to the 1.1 billion cars that were already making their way up and down the world's roads on a daily basis.

- In China there are 2929 power plant generators[61] running on coal that consume a total of about 1.35 billion tons of coal annually.[62] Each burns about 458,000 tons of coal each year to produce an average of 228 MW of electricity, totaling 669 Giga-Watts. These plants are providing the bulk of the electricity that power China's economy, including its massive volume of exports including very likely your t-shirt and your iPhone, and about half of all the products purchased at Wal-Mart last year.

- Globally there are about 7000 coal-fired power plant units[63] that annually produce 8100 Metric Tons of pollution.[64]

- And as a result of its central role in economic and social life, the global oil industry is by far the world's largest single industry, and five of the world's ten largest corporations are oil companies.

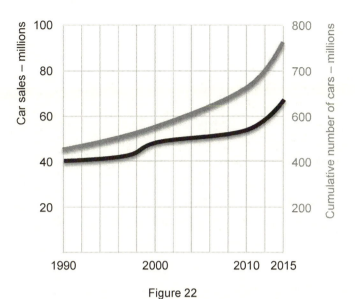

Figure 22
**Global Car Sales Annually (left scale, black line)
and Cumulatively and Still on the Road (right scale, gray line)[65]**

$ Billions	Revenue				Net Income			
	2011	2012	2013	2014	2011	2012	2013	2014
Shell	$470	$467	$451	$421	$31	$27	$16	$15
Exxon	$467	$452	$421	$394	$41	$45	$33	$33
BP	$376	$376	$379	$354	$25	$11	$24	$4
Total	$232	$234	$228	$212	$17	$14	$11	$4
Chevron	$244	$231	$221	$200	$27	$26	$21	$19
TOTAL	$1,789	$1,759	$1,700	$1,581	$141	$122	$105	$75

Figure 23
The 5 Big Oil Companies
$1.5 – 1.7 trillion in revenues; $75 - $141 billion in profits

Petro-States

And as the global economy could not exist in its current form without oil, the control of oil production and refining has been and continues to be one of the world's greatest focal points for the creation of wealth and power. Current oil consumption is about xxx million barrels per day.

It was the need to establish control over its proven oil reserves that led to the establishment of many of the nations in today's Middle East. This occurred when the European powers ceded their former colonies to friendly local regimes that they put in place with the expectation that the new rulers would be relied upon to keep the oil flowing to meet Europe's needs.

But where there is wealth and power there is also often conflict, and as the 20th century unfolded and Japan developed aspirations to become a world power, its lack of natural resources, particularly oil, contributed to its decision to expand into East and Southeast Asia, and thus to the onset of World War II. Similarly, some of Europe's most significant World War II battles were contested over the oil fields of North Africa and southwestern Russia, where the Germans sought the fuel to power their war machine and their imperial aspirations. Hitler reportedly said, "Unless we get Baku oil, the war is lost," and at one point during the war one of his generals presented him with a birthday cake inscribed with "Baku" on it. The Soviets successfully defended Baku, and as the battles raged on the Germans ran chronically short of oil.[66]

Energy Per Capita

As of the Industrial Era advanced economists found that very a reliable way to measure the relative economic development level of any nation, and thus to compare development levels among nations, was by measuring how much energy was consumed per person. The more energy that was consumed, the higher the level of development was understood to be. Americans consumed an average of 87 million BTU per person annually in 1800, 126 million in 1900, and by 2000 this had ballooned to about 350 million per person. By the standards of most of the world this meant that Americans were "energy hogs," wasteful and self-indulgent over-consumers. According to economists, though, this same statistic meant that America had by far the most highly developed economy.[67]

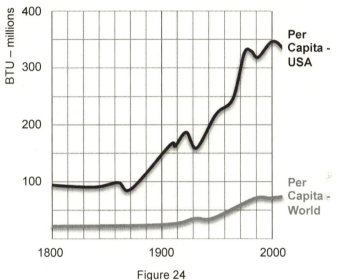

Figure 24
American and World Energy Consumption Per Capita

Both views are probably correct. Energy is the essential resource that is used to both create and to consume, and now in the early years of the 21st century the trend continues, as today the average American consumes the equivalent of 313 million BTU per year.[68]

This increasing rate of consumption is another revealing exponential phenomenon, and it reflects the impact of compounded growth that we discussed in the previous chapter. In this case, by intentionally investing in the infrastructure that promotes economic activity, America and all the world's nations have created the capacity to create wealth. Reinvesting year after year in projects including roads, bridges, ports, airports, stock exchanges, and in the material productive capacity owned largely by corporations that includes factories has enabled a profound transformation to occur. We can summarize this by saying that throughout the 20th century the nations of world set about very successfully to build a global system for production and trade by transforming natural resources into finished products and services.

While it's perhaps too easy for those living well in the wealthy, industrialized world to take this all for granted, the progress is staggering. Your great-great-grandparents, the ones who lived before about 1880, inhabited a material world which was fundamentally different from ours in nearly every way. The choices and comforts that we experience as reality would seem to many as eye-popping and impossible wonders.

And through it all there is also been, as we now know, a significant, growing, and potentially disastrous side effect.

The Carbon Economy

The massive scale of energy production and consumption that began with the expansion of coal mining in the early 1800s and was transformed in the early 1900s into an economy based on large scale oil extraction and combustion, and which is still today the largest single economic activity in the world, is fundamentally altering the planet. As we now understand, the increasing concentration of carbon dioxide in the atmosphere is causing the significantly negative side effect of global climate change.

A graph of the CO_2 concentration shows that it, too, is has been an exponentially growing trend. At the beginning of the Industrial Age, the concentration of carbon dioxide in the Earth's atmosphere was 280 parts per million; by 1900 it was 300, and today it's about 400.[69]

The purpose of burning all the coal and oil was to create wealth, and as measured by growth in GDP, it worked out very well. And so when we put the increasing concentration of CO_2 on the same chart that shows the trend of increasing economic activity, there is, not surprisingly, an obvious correlation.

There is also a strong correlation between the concentration of CO_2 and Earth's temperature because CO_2 traps the sun's heat, and thus we've been slowly but steadily warming our planet for the last 200 years.

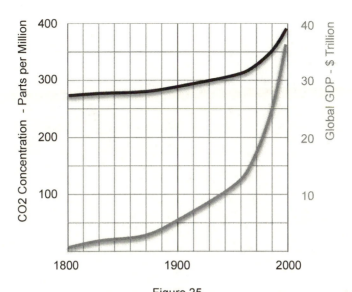

Figure 25
CO2 Concentration in the Earth's Atmosphere (left index)
Global GDP in Dollars (right index)

When we put the increasing concentration of CO2 on the same chart that shows the trend of increasing economic activity, there is, not surprisingly, an obvious correlation.

There is also a strong correlation between the concentration of CO2 and Earth's temperature because CO2 traps the sun's heat, and thus we've been slowly but steadily warming our planet for the last 200 years.

History of the Climate

If we look back over thousands of years of Earth's climatic history, the 200 year period of the Industrial Age has been among the most stable periods in many millennia, and thus it's clear that the successful development of the Industrial economy was enormously advantaged by these highly favorable conditions. It would appear that those conditions are now changing quite aversely, possibly, probably, or certainly as a result of CO2; as a result, that is, of human economic activity in the Anthropocene Era.

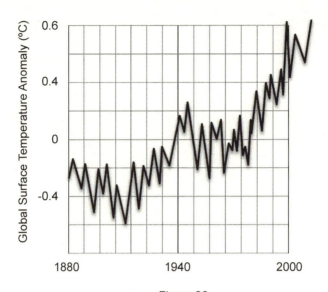

Figure 26
Global Temperature Graphs
Four independent sets of records show nearly identical long-term warming trends.[70]
NASA Goddard Institute for Space Studies
Met Office Hadley Centre/ Climatic Research Unit
NOAA National Climatic Data Center
Japanese Meteorological Agency

As a consequence, what we already face today and will continue to face in the near future and beyond is going to be the exact opposite of stability, namely a period of significant climate turmoil. There is ample evidence that this is already occurring.[71] For example, the ten most violent and disruptive climate events in all of recorded history going back hundreds of years, the biggest storms, have all occurred during the last fifteen years.[72]

And whether we measure the magnitude of these storms by their destructive power or by the cost to rebuild because of their destruction or in terms of lives lost, the result is the same.

Note that the data underlying this graph are based on values at the time. Hence, a hurricane in 2000 would do more damage in financial terms than the "identical" hurricane in 1950 because the value of the destroyed property in 2000 is so much greater. Hence, while there is natural inflation built into the graph it's nevertheless evident that the total cost is increasing substantially.

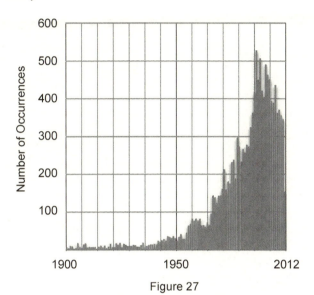

Figure 27
Weather-Related Natural Disasters
Total Reported Flood, Storm, and Drought[73]

And whether we measure the magnitude of these storms by their destructive power or by the cost to rebuild because of their destruction or in terms of lives lost, the result is the same.

Note that the data underlying this graph are based on values at the time. Hence, a hurricane in 2000 would do more damage in financial terms than the "identical" hurricane in 1950 because the value of the destroyed property in 2000 is so much greater. Hence, while there is natural inflation built into the graph it's nevertheless evident that the total cost is increasing substantially.

Climate scientists are working to model these factors so that we can better anticipate the future, and while the complexities of the climate are enormous and therefore the models are incomplete, there is nevertheless widespread agreement among about 97 percent of them that if (or when) the concentration of CO_2 in the atmosphere reaches around 450 parts per million the climate may be permanently and negatively altered from what we have been accustomed to. That future would be quite different than today and considerably more difficult to live with.[74]

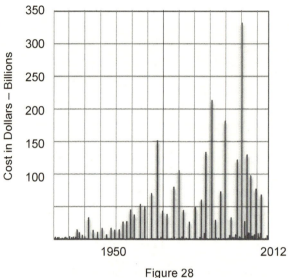

Figure 28
Costs Due to Natural Disasters[75]

Hence, these scientists and the government leaders who listen to them are making significant efforts to change our collective behaviors, which means, essentially, abandoning the use of fossil fuels. This is reflected in the comment from California Governor Jerry Brown that begins this chapter: *"One-third of the oil that we know exists as reserves can never be taken out of the ground. Fifty percent of the gas can never be used and over 90 percent of the coal. That is a revolution."*

Yes, it absolutely is a revolution.

How much has the climate changed already? Ten of the ten most severe storms in recorded history have occurred since 1990. Together they have resulted in gigantic losses for insurance companies, so much so that the entire insurance industry has entirely restructured to deal with the economic consequences of continuing change to the climate. It is the industry's expectation that storms will increase in severity and in frequency, that some coastal regions will therefore become uninhabitable, and before they become uninhabitable they will already be uninsurable.

In summary, then, the very sources of energy that made it possible to create the modern economy, coal, oil, and gas, are now wreaking significant destruction upon the planet and its human civilization. Consequently a massive shift is already under way through which the world will make the momentous transition from a fossil fuel-based economy to one based on other sources of energy. That energy revolution is the third of the five revolutions, and it is the subject of the next chapter, and as we will examine in greater depth there, that energy revolution is also a technological transformation that will depend for its realization on the digital technologies that I described in the previous chapter. That is, today's designs for solar and wind energy collection and storage systems would not be possible without the advances in computer chip technology that we know as Moore's Law, and hence the possibility that we can develop large scale and effective energy sources other than fossil fuels is a consequence of technological progress.

The knowledge gained in the design and fabrication of computer chips is also being applied in the design and fabrication of solar cells. Likewise, the computational capacities of increasingly powerful computers is applied in the design and adoption of all energy methods, including fossil fuels as well as solar, wind, water, and wave, and also in the design and engineering of the batteries that are needed to store the energy thus collected, as well as in the distribution systems used to bring it where it's needed. All of these trends and technologies are connected, which further reinforces the sense that we're caught in a race between humanity's ability to wreck havoc through our economic activities just as we also creating the transformation of the economy through technological progress. Both the havoc and the transformation are occurring at the same time, and often using the very same tools.

Economic Transformation

I noted above that the oil industry is the world's largest single form of economic activity, which means that the shift from a fossil fuel economy to a non-fossil fuel economy constitutes a profound economic transformation. As it progresses during the coming decade this will certainly become one of the most significant transitions in all of human history, and like the digital revolution, it's happening right now, all around us.

Consequently, if you're a leader in business or in government, the fact that major revolutions of unquestionable historic significance are occurring now, while you occupy a leadership position, is a notable situation that brings risks of many kinds. For example, there is certainly a great risk that the economy will dip or even crash; that the drop in oil stock prices will drag a major portion of the economy down; that overall energy prices will increase if the alternatives turn out to be substantially more expensive; that the technical infrastructure will be too slow to develop; that the oil producers will purposefully disrupt the economy to sustain their position … etc., etc.

It would be naïve to expect a smooth transition, and further, because the digital revolution, the climate revolution, and the energy revolution are all three happening simultaneously, and all have massive and potentially tumultuous impacts on their own, the fact of their simultaneity promises that tumult is inevitable. It is this compounding of risk and danger that changes "risk" into "mega risk."

Hence, as these changes play out in the coming years and decades we will continue to see significant changes to the overall structure of the global economy that will cause massive dislocations of workers, owners, and citizens. But at the same time we will also see enormous opportunities for creators, innovators, entrepreneurs, and investors.

The Greenhouse

By the 1970s air quality in many American cities had become so bad that public health officials began advocating for pollution controls, largely because of smog from the rapidly increasing number of cars on the roads. Gas was inexpensive and American-made cars were notoriously inefficient.

However, a combination of forces soon led to change in the structure of the market. Under the regulatory efforts of the US government's Environmental Protection Agency automakers were compelled to introduce catalytic converters, which significantly reduced emissions. During the same period, the OPEC nations formed a cartel and reduced overall world oil production, which had the immediate effect of reducing supply and thus increasing prices. This was both a social and an economic shock throughout the western nations, and contributed to a period of very high inflation which was led to very high interest rates that worsened economic problems globally. Today, even forty years later OPEC nations still account for about 80 percent of the world's crude oil reserves.

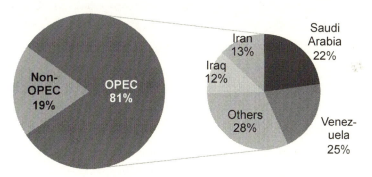

Figure 29
OPEC Share of World Crude Oil Reserves

While American car makers had been focusing on styling for many year, their Japanese competitors had worked to design and build efficient and high quality small cars, and the OPEC Oil Shock provided them with the opportunity to significantly increase their presence in the American market. This turned out to be the peak for the American firms, at which point their market share in the US began to decline. In 1970, General Motors sold 50 percent of the cars in the US, but 30 years later this share had declined to less than 20 percent. The focus on quality and efficiency has been one of the key competitive factors in the market since then, and during the last 50 years cars have become much higher in quality, much safer, and much more efficient.

What has changed very little, however, are the emissions of CO_2 that cars produce, and as the number of cars on the road in the US and throughout the world has increased, CO2 emissions have increased as well. At a minimum climate change will be a huge inconvenience; a middle scenario suggests a global catastrophe; and in the worst case accelerating climate change may represent the greatest challenge that human civilization has ever faced.

Hot and Dry

Already the effects are in evidence, not only due to the increasing severity of storms, but due to drought and temperature changes as well. For example, entire forests in the Colorado Rockies are under attack from bark beetles, and at present the beetles are winning, and they've destroyed millions of acres of trees. When winters in the Rockies were colder the beetle population died back during the cold months, but now that the beetles are surviving today's warmer winters, in the spring they quickly reproduce in such vast numbers that they are consuming entire forests. The net effect is that forests at lower altitudes are being wiped out, and thus the entire ecosystem is shifting to higher altitudes where the winters are still cold enough to kill most of the beetles.

Forest fires are getting worse also. "In the Western United States, the length of the active wildfire season increased by 78 days, and the average burn duration quintupled from 7.5 to 37.1 days."[76]

In addition to increased severity and frequency of storms, the sea level has already risen, the Arctic polar ice cap is now melting completely during the summer months which it had not previously done, glaciers on all continents are shrinking and in some cases disappearing entirely, and measurements of the Earth's temperature show steady increases over the last fifty years. A recent study suggests that the sea level will most likely rise by 20 feet around the globe within decades.[77]

Impacts that are already occurring include a decline in productivity of some agricultural regions. When this occurs in industrialized nations market forces simply shift to sources of supply from other locations, and while food prices may rise, the dislocations are minimal. Grocery store shelves remain fully stocked with thousands of products that have been transported (using fossil fuels, most likely) from all over the world. However, when agricultural productivity declines in subsistence economies the consequences can be devastating for large populations. Food supplies dwindle causing price increases that lead to local conflicts almost immediately as various groups and tribes try to control as much of the supply simply to protect their own people. Confronted with scarcity, social order breaks down and a nation of *we* becomes conflicting groups of *us and them*.

One of the first regions where climate-instigated scarcity became evident was in in the southern Sahara region of South Sudan. The enormous Sahara Desert has been creeping southward at the rate of about five to six kilometers per year for three decades, and as it has destroyed the land it thus disrupted all forms of social order and displaced millions. Social strife is now common throughout the region, and the combination of national, ethnic, and religious violence and ecological change has devastated the entire region. It may be that this is an early indication of what may happen elsewhere as accelerating climate change wreaks havoc in society. The populations of these tragedy-struck regions may be considered as the first casualties of the first war caused by climate change. The local subsistence economy has mostly collapsed, and the UN Refugee Agency estimates that 2.3 million people have been internally displaced from their homes, most now without the means to feed themselves, resulting in a massive humanitarian crisis.[78]

Unfortunately we also witnessing the same dynamics at play in the Middle East, as Syria implodes and succumbs to a self-destructive civil war. As it turns out, climate change is also a significant factor:

A study published in *Proceedings of the National Academy of Sciences* says drought in Syria, exacerbated to record levels by global warming, pushed social unrest in that nation across a line into an open uprising in 2011. Drying and drought in Syria from 2006 to 2011 was the worst on record there. It destroyed agriculture, causing many farm families to migrate to cities. The influx added to social stresses already created by refugees pouring in from the war in Iraq.

"We're not saying the drought caused the war," said Richard Seager, a climate scientist at Columbia University's Lamont-Doherty Earth Observatory. "We're saying that added to all the other stressors, it helped kick things over the threshold into open conflict. And a drought of that severity was made much more likely by the ongoing human-driven drying of that region." The entire Middle East "faces a drier, hotter climate due to climate change. This will stress water resources and agriculture, and will likely further increase risk of conflict." Global warming is desiccating the region in two ways: higher temperatures that increase evaporation in already parched soils, and weaker winds that bring less rain from the Mediterranean Sea during the wet season from November to April.[79]

By summer 2015 a total of 7.6 million Syrians had been displaced from their homes, most living in squalid refugee camps, and four million more had fled to neighboring Turkey (2 million) Lebanon (1.7 million, meaning that 1 person in 5 living in Lebanon is a Syrian refugee), as well as Iraq, Egypt, and Jordan.[80] By the time you read this the numbers will be different, but unless the violence has stopped the number of refugees will only be higher.

Tens of thousands make desperate attempts to reach political asylum in Europe, risking their lives with smugglers and packing themselves into overcrowded boats to cross the Aegean into Greece on the hopes of finding a decent future life for themselves and their families. The massive flood of refugees has provoked a cultural and political crisis in many European nations. For the wealthy nations of central Europe the question remains as to what their responsibility is. Should they accept any and all refugees? Should they turn them away? Should they allow them to pass through on their way to another country? Should they stop the smugglers? As the number of refugees increases, there are no easy answers.

Tens of thousands make desperate attempts to reach political asylum in Europe, risking their lives with smugglers and packing themselves into overcrowded boats that try to cross the Aegean into Greece on the hope to find a decent future life for themselves and their families. The massive flood of refugees has provoked a cultural and political crisis in many European nations.

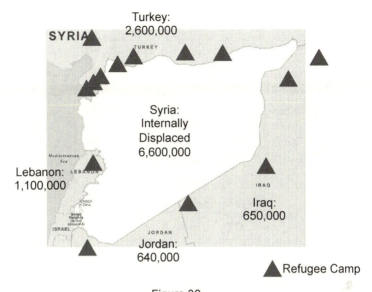

Figure 30
Syrian Refugee Camps
Numbers shown indicate the approximate number of refugees in each
neighboring country and internally displaced as of January 2016.

For the wealthy nations of central Europe, the question remains as to what their responsibility is. Should they accept any and all refugees? Should they turn them away? Should they allow them to pass through on their way to some other country? Should they stop the smugglers?

Rick Lyman of *The New York Times* reported the situation this way:

Europe's failure to fashion even the beginnings of a unified solution to the migrant crisis is intensifying confusion and desperation all along the multicontinent trail and breeding animosity among nations extending back to the Middle East. With the volume of people leaving Syria, Afghanistan and other countries showing no signs of ebbing, the lack of governmental leadership has left thousands of individuals and families on their own and reacting day by day to changing circumstances and conflicting messages. Despite the chaos, there were few signs that European Union leaders, or the governments of other countries along the human river of people flowing from war and poverty, were close to imposing any order or even talking seriously about harmonizing their approaches and messages to the migrants. Instead, countries continue to improvise their responses. Macedonian

113

and Serbian officials, along with many aid organizations, were urging them to circumvent a hostile Hungary and even providing maps and nonstop bus service to the Croatian frontier. Within a matter of a few days more than 11,000 migrants entered Croatia, and 20,000 more were making their way there and likely to arrive soon, while untold tens of thousands more waited in Turkey and Greece.[81]

The nature of the crisis and the suffering that millions are enduring is certainly heartbreaking, but the purpose of discussing this here is not only to lament the tragedy but also to suggest that the crises in South Sudan and Syria are merely early indications of dislocations yet to come that will almost certainly result from climate change, the loss of rainfall, and thus the loss of productive land and its food. Of course the attitudes and policies of the nations that are not severely affected will be crucial factors in determining what will ultimately happen to the refugees, and the international agreements for their resettlement and care will become a major issue for discussion and debate in the United Nations, the European Parliament, and elsewhere. The key point is that this may just be the beginning of a trend that could last throughout this century. If that happens, then we're not talking about millions of refugees, but about tens or even hundreds of millions.

North Africa and the Middle East are but two of many regions where the changing climate will impact on historical patterns or agriculture and habitation, of cultures and societies. Through 2015 California was experiencing its most severe drought in 500 years and massive fires destroyed thousands of homes. While this is certainly not a tragedy on the scale of the Syrian conflict, it does show that the consequences are not regional, but global. Severe drought was also affecting large parts China, Brazil, where the worst drought in 50 years is affecting 40 million people, and South Africa, where drought has reduced some food crop production by 30 percent.[82]

According to the United Nations, as of February 2016 significant portions of these nations were suffering major humanitarian crises due to drought; this constitutes a total of 150 million people, 2 percent of the world's total population, who are immediately affected:

- Ethiopia: An estimated 8 million of Ethiopia's 60 million people are at immediate risk due to drought. UNICEF estimates that 1.4 million of those at risk are children under five.

- Eritrea: Successive years of drought, combined with the border war with Ethiopia, has created major food shortages. Nearly 1.3 million people are at risk, including an estimated 1 million who have been displaced by the war.

- Somalia: Due to seven consecutive poor harvests coupled with chronic insecurity in some regions, food stability is deteriorating, affecting as many as one million people, including 300,000 children aged under 5 years. The drought has been made worse by sudden torrential rains and flash flooding.

- Sudan: An estimated 2.8 million people in the south face food insecurity in the coming months.

- Uganda: About 550,000 people face food insecurity.

- Afghanistan: Large parts of the south are severely affected, where 60 to 80 percent of livestock have died. Almost 2.5 million people, or 10 percent of the population are at risk, and many of them will need assistance for at least the next 12 months.

- China: In the northern Shanxi province nearly 3 million people don't have enough water. About one-third of the province's wheat crop has been hit by the drought and more than 60 percent of its soil lacks water.

- India: The government has mobilized massive relief efforts in several regions. Madhya Pradesh, along with the western states of Rajasthan and Gujarat and Andhra Pradesh in the south, are in the grip of a severe drought following the failure of last year's monsoon rains. Nearly 130 million people living in 12 States have been seriously affected by what some officials call the worst drought in 100 years.

- Iran: The government has informed the United Nations office in Tehran that it is ready to accept international aid to help meet losses estimated at $1.7 billion from the drought. Iran needs about

$200 million to provide water tankers and water purifying units for drought-hit areas.

- Morocco: The government has launched a $633 million contingency plan to combat the worst drought in a decade. About 70 percent of the country's arable land has been affected.

- Pakistan: Government officials estimate that nearly 3 million people - mostly villagers - face possible starvation. Hundreds of thousands of people have fled Pakistan's southern Thar desert. The drought has devastated crops and livestock in the desert, home to 1 million people, sparking fears of a massive humanitarian crisis.

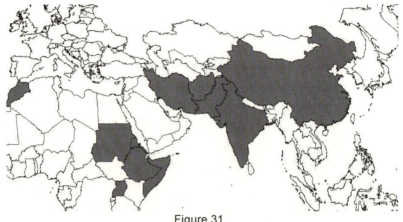

Figure 31
Affected Nations
150 million people are directly affected by major droughts as of February 2016 in Afghanistan, China, Ethiopia, Eritrea, India, Iran, Morocco, Pakistan, Somalia, Sudan, and Uganda.

It's obvious that when 150 million people have their livelihoods or even their lives threatened we're not discussing an isolated disaster, we're talking about a global calamity. As the impact of climate change worsens, if it does, many millions more will be severely impacted. Where these impacts lead to tribal and political conflicts, and in a world of nearly unlimited armaments and of many deep-seated animosities between various ethnic and religious groups, the prospects are frightening that we may be facing a new cycle of climate-change-induced violence, which will only compound the suffering. This is exactly the unwanted example that Syria provides.

Hot and Wet

There's the inverse side of the same issue to consider, for while the crises in Sudan and Syria have been worsened by dryness, climate change also brings increasing wetness. As the Earth's temperature rises and the ice covering the polar regions melts the oceans will rise and the coastal regions where the majority of humanity presently live will become threatened by rising water levels. The worst case scenario suggests that if all the ice were to melt then the oceans could rise by as much as 30 meters, or 100 feet, which would flood the world's coastal areas, decimate its low-lying nations, and disable nearly all the world's major coastal cities.

Locations that are particularly vulnerable to social and economic disruption caused by climate change-induced flooding include the world's lowest-lying nations including the Pacific Island nations of Vanuatu, the Marshall Islands, Kiribati, Tuvalu, Tonga, the Federated States of Micronesia, and the Cook Islands in the Pacific Ocean, Antigua and Nevis in the Caribbean Sea, as well as Bangladesh, the Netherlands, and indeed all the low-lying coastal cities around the world.[83]

The Maldives, a nation of islands located in the Indian Ocean about 1000 miles south of India, may be the first nation to disappear due to climate change, as its average altitude above sea level is the least among all countries. The average height of the entire island chain is just over a meter, and the highest point in the entire nation is located on Vilingili Island in the Addu Atoll, a mere 2.4 meters above sea level. The melting ice of the polar regions is thus not going to be merely an inconvenience to the citizens of the Maldives, but is a threat to the entire nation's very existence.

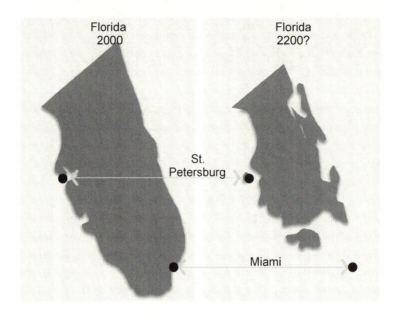

Figure 32

Coastline Changes

The coastline of South Florida as it would be after a sea level rise of 3 meters.[84]

Marshall Islands	52,000
Kiribati	102,000
Tuvalu	10,000
Tonga	105,000
Micronesia	103,000
Cook Islands	11,000
Antigua	90,000
Nevis	12,000
Maldives	350,000
Total	**835,000**

Figure 33

Lowest Lying Island Nations and Their Populations[85]

China	50 million
Vietnam	23 million
Japan	13 million
India	13 million
Bangladesh	10 million
Indonesia	10 million
Thailand	8 million
Netherlands	8 million
Philippines	6 million
Myanmar	5 million
Total	146 million

Figure 34

Nations with the Greatest Number of People Exposed to Sea Level Rise[86]

When and if the melting of the polar ice causes the world's oceans to rise much more than they already have, the 350,000 residents of the Maldives will become climate refugees, homeless citizens of a non-existent land. Where will they go?

Figure 35
The Maldives, 2200?
Under high water scenarios The Maldives would disappear entirely.

If you happen to live in a location that is subject to stormy weather, in a hurricane, typhoon, or cyclone belt for example, then you should probably begin to prepare for the worst. If you own coastal property there may come a time in the near future when you cannot buy insurance for it, for as the oceans rise the insurers will decide that the risks are too great.

Major flood control projects are already under way in many coastal cities, including Venice and Amsterdam, and massive projects have been proposed to protect New York City, San Francisco, and London. Every coastal city in the world will eventually have to consider doing the same, and thus one of the booming industries of the mid-century may become the construction of large-scale sea barriers, as well as the small-scale construction of dykes, levees, and storm barriers. Perhaps this will be a type of work that robots are not suited to, and thus a source of employment for millions displaced by digitization.

In this scenario we would also have to anticipate not millions or even tens of millions of refugees, but billions of them. Well, no, not of *them* in fact, but of *us*. *We* would have to expect that a huge proportion of humanity's homes would need to be rebuilt on higher ground, away from the rising oceans and the much bigger storms that the rising and warming seas would foster. Hence, construction will also be a booming industry in a worst-case climate changing world.

Already the impacts of rising oceans are becoming evident. For example, a recent study conducted by professors from Penn State, Rutgers University, Princeton, Tufts, and MIT found that major storms that once might have occurred every 500 years, could soon happen every 25 years or so. "A storm that occurred once in seven generations is now occurring twice in a generation," said Benjamin Horton of Rutgers.[87]

Worst Case

In extreme climate change scenarios, and even in moderate ones, billions of people will lose their homes and their livelihoods, and consequently the entire structure of the economy will be fundamentally altered. Should things unfold this way, adapting to change of this magnitude would thus become not just an inconvenience, but perhaps the essential human project of the 21st century, and it would last well into the 22nd.

If carbon dioxide continues to accumulate in the atmosphere and the climate continues to warm, and from a human perspective to worsen, the polar ice caps will melt, and the droughts and insects and diseases will become more severe, and governments and their citizens will inevitably respond.

Hence, in early 2016 governors of 17 US states announced a joint initiative to develop cleaner energy and transportation systems. "The Governors' Accord for a New Energy Future" intends to support development of more energy efficient energy grids, pooled purchases of clean energy vehicles, and efforts on clean energy storage in states that have a combined population of 128 million people, or about 40 percent of America's total. Because the issue of climate change remains politically controversial in the US, and because the US Congress has been ineffective due to ideological differences, the governors felt compelled to act on their own. While their announcement intentionally did not mention the topic climate change in order to avoid controversy, the intended actions are all directly precisely at mitigating its effects.[88]

What's Next?

Based on current trends and a growing body of evidence the link between CO2 emissions, fossil fuels, and climate change is becoming an established scientific finding that is no longer being questioned expect by the most stubborn of ideologues, the most plausible outcome from this situation is the transformation of the global economy. We will most likely see the transition away from CO2-creating fossil fuels and the large scale adoption of other sources of energy. The end of the fossil fuels industries, whether it happens fast or slowly, will in either case be momentous and highly disruptive economically, for as I noted above, the oil industry is currently the world's largest organized industry, the largest single component of global GDP. For the past century the control of oil has meant wealth and power for industrialists such as Rockefeller, and for oil producing nations around the world, but apparently those days are now ending.

I ended Chapter 1 with some thoughts about likely developments in digital technology, and posed the question as to whether technology will continue to develop at an exponential rate and thus lead to a world of ubiquitous artificial intelligence and robotics, leaving a side effect of huge numbers of displaced and unemployed, or whether the rate of digital progress will slow significantly, leaving us in a digital world more or less as it is today. The moral and ethical aspects of our technological future are profoundly significant, but due to uncertainty about the future state of digital technology, as yet unanswerable.

With respect to climate change, however, the questions that need to be framed are quite different. This is because we already know what's best for humanity; what's best is the least change to the climate. We also know, however, that "little change" is exceptionally unlikely. It appears that we already passed that marker along the road some time ago, which means that the only way we're going to achieve a re-stabilized climate is if we find a way to remove the excess CO_2 that's already in the atmosphere and stop pumping more CO_2 into it. But there's little evidence that either has begun or will occur any time soon, so we have to assume that we're not going back to an unaltered climate for at least the remainder of the current century.

Therefore, the meaningful questions about the future of the Earth's climate are really, "How much warmer is it going to get?" and, "How bad will the secondary effects be?" These secondary effects, as we have seen, will likely include prolonged droughts, melted glaciers and icepacks and thus risen oceans, and more violent storms. The increasing temperatures will also contribute to increased incidences of infectious disease, which will spread more quickly and find more victims, while pests such as the bark beetles that are eating Colorado's forests will live longer and reproduce more readily, thereby causing greater impacts on all types of ecosystems.

If the answer turns out to be "much worse," then we know we're going to be dealing with massive consequences that impact billions, which really means everyone, and indeed every living creature. We notice again that the human super-predator has ignorantly targeted itself. And since the underlying cause of this possibly impending disaster is fossil fuels, we will examine the dynamics around that industry in the following chapter.

•••

Chapter 3

The Extractor:
The Energy Revolution and the Global Economy

Some day, when your children ask, "What did you do to win this inheritance for us, and to make our name so respected among men?" one will say: "I was a fighter pilot," another will say: "I was in the Submarine Service," another: "I marched with the Eighth Army," a fourth will say: "None of you could have lived without the convoys and the Merchant seamen." And you, in your turn, will say, with equal pride and with equal right, "We cut the coal."

Winston Churchill
Speech to the coal miners of Newcastle, October 31, 1942

Churchill's speech acknowledged and celebrated the essential contribution of coal to the Allied effort in World War II for good reason, as without that coal the outcome of the Battle of Britain and thus of the entire war could well have been quite different. In fact, a great deal of World War II was fought with and about fossil fuels, and many of the world's conflicts since then have likewise been battles for control of energy reserves.

Hitler's armies marched across southeastern Europe and in Russia because of the desperate need to gain control of the oil fields of Baku, but the Russia army held its ground, and when German oil finally ran out during the final great battle of the European war, the Battle of the Bulge, German tanks sat useless on the battlefield in defeat.

Today, coal, oil, and natural gas are as essential to the modern economy as they were to the war effort, and indeed, for the last two centuries every nation that wished to develop its economy simply had no choice but to develop its own buried fossil fuel reserves, if it was lucky enough to have any, or if not, to buy them on the open market. The logic and necessity of doing so was beyond question, for the world's economy ran almost exclusively on the fuels trapped underground, decomposed and recomposed creatures and plants that lived and died millions of years ago.

Coal fueled the 19th century, oil joined in the 20th, and they still do so today.

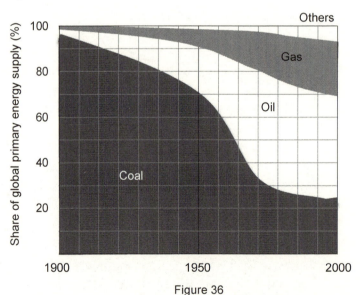

Figure 36
Share of Global Primary Energy Supply[89]

Why We Love Fossil Fuels

Five compelling factors make fossil fuels, and especially oil, such attractive sources of energy.[90] First, oil has very high energy density, meaning the amount of energy, or work, that you can extract from a given gallon or a liter of oil is very high when compared to other types of fuel. Your car can go 15 or 30 or even 50 miles on a gallon, or you can make a lot of electricity.

Second, as a fuel oil is tremendously versatile. Oil refineries produce hundreds of different liquids and plastics, enabling us to burn it in a car's engine or a jet engine, a chemistry lab, a camp stove, or a giant power plant, or make it into hundreds of different kinds of plastics, from grocery bags to bullet proof vests to water pipes and computer keys.

Third, when you combust it in an engine, oil's energy is available almost instantly. Due to significant advances in steam engines, steel making, and cannon following the American Civil War, all the world's navies converted from wooden sailing shops to iron clad steamships. But it took five hours or more for a large battleship's steam engines to come to full sailing power because the coal had to be stoked and the heat and pressure of the flame built up gradually. Thus an entire fleet was trapped in port for five long hours even when it was under direct threat from an adversary. Oil-burning engines come up to speed almost immediately, and the entire fleet oil-powered can be in motion with much less warning. As military advantages go, this is quite decisive, and thus all the navies in the world had switched again, this time to oil, by about 1910.

It was Winston Churchill, who, as head of the British Navy, or First Lord of the Admiralty, pushed through the conversion of the British Navy despite significant resistance from those who had not understood the necessity of this massive investment in military preparedness. Churchill, a few years later, was proven at the onset of World War I to be entirely correct.[91]

The decision to convert the fleet from coal to oil was the most controversial of Churchill's reforms. Britain produced no oil. It produced coal. The oil supplies of the world were under foreign control. Oil was flammable: a direct hit on a tank could set off an immediate inferno. Storage tanks ashore would be vulnerable to attack. Churchill was not deterred. He argued that all new ships should be oil-powered, a n expensive and risky venture. "If we overcame the difficulties and surmounted the risks," he said, "we should be able to raise the whole power and efficiency of the Navy: better ships, better crews, high economies, more intense forms of war power - mastery itself was the prize of the venture." In 1914, one month before the "guns of August" began their four-year cannonade of the First World War, Churchill secured for the British Crown a 51 per cent controlling interest in the Anglo-Persian Oil Company for £2.2 million. His decisions were to assure British naval supremacy.[92]

In our cars, meanwhile, we can step on the gas pedal and feel immediate power, feed fuel into a jet engine and quickly accelerate a giant aluminum beast carrying 500 people to 500 miles an hour cruising at 35,000 feet, or fire up a massive power plant and generate huge quantities of electricity in almost no time. We have as yet found no other source of energy that produces so much power so fast, with so little bulk.

Another appealing attribute of oil is how easy it is to transport. It's readily moved in trucks, rail cars, giant tanker ships, and enormously long pipelines, through which it can be transported relatively cheaply from wherever you find it to wherever you want to refine or use it.

Finally, oil is found in many places, and drilling technology has improved the capacity to extract it from more difficult and elusive underground locations. Wells are drilled at all angles, and horizontally, and to extreme depths.

Because of these many benefits, oil has been the preferred fuel of the global economy for a century, and it is no exaggeration to say that the 20th century's economic boom was an oil boom. Today a massive and very complex system of global finance, production and transportation infrastructure is fully in place to locate and extract raw crude, transport it to any of the world's 700 refineries where it is distilled into any one of 6000 different products. On average, 46 percent becomes gasoline, 9 percent jet fuel, 26 percent diesel, and the remaining 19 percent becomes many different forms of plastics, Vaseline for your chapped lips and crayons for the young artists in your family.

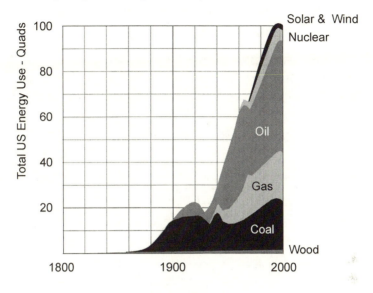

Figure 37
Total US Energy Use, 1800 - 2000[93]

From the refinery the gasoline is redistributed back to America's 168,000 gas stations and hundreds of thousands more around the world, and to factories, and power plants.

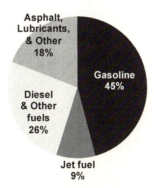

Figure 38
The Typical Use of a Barrel of Oil[94]

Underground pools of oil are called fields, and the first one to be developed was in Western Pennsylvania in 1859, and it was here that John

D. Rockefeller made his initial fortune. As the demand for oil increased, the global industry thrived by finding new fields. Oil exploration became a sophisticated science, and decade by decade new tools and techniques were created to locate oil and extract it. Seismic studies map underground rock formations, 3D software models show the structure of underground fields, wells are drilled deeper and deeper to exploit those fields. Offshore drilling was perfected, followed by horizontal drilling, and the design and construction of massive pipelines, ports, and tankers followed. The Alaska Pipeline, for example, stretches for 800 miles across the state to bring Prudhoe Bay oil to the port of Valdez, and since 1977 some 17 billion barrels have been pumped through it.[95]

Supply, on the other hand, is a function of a very dynamic market environment. Oil wells do not produce indefinitely, nor do the fields that are composed of many wells. When a new field is discovered geologists attempt to determine the amount of oil it contains, and the proportion of that oil that can be extracted. The resulting calculation then becomes a significant asset on the owner's balance sheet, but as the oil is extracted the value of asset then declines toward zero. This, as we will see shortly, is about to become a significant issue.

The Oil Tax

As oil is the primary energy source of the industrial economy, energy consumers simply have no choice but to pay oil producers for the right to join the world economy. Because the ownership of untapped crude oil, as well as the infrastructure used to extract, transport, refine, and distribute it, requires a massive investment that's also highly centralized, the enormous demand for fossil fuels and thus the success of the industry has resulted in a tremendous concentration of wealth in the hands of a very small number of oil producers, transporters, and refiners, particularly in the nations and companies that own and exploit oil reserves. In essence, then, those who own the oil also hold the power to tax everyone else for the right to participate in the global economy.

As a scarce and highly valuable resource, oil is also a source of conflict and also a means of funding conflict. ISIS, the violent group that controls Northern Syria, funds itself through the sale of oil, which is smuggled from its oil producing territories in every manner of vehicle to find its way into every market in the region. Ironically, it is often ISIS oil that powers the cars in the Syrian cities controlled by the government of President Assad. ISIS is just one example of course, as nations as diverse as Russia, Venezuela, Brazil, Nigeria, Saudi Arabia, Kuwait, Iraq, and Iran all depend for their economic viability on the sale of oil.

	Nation	Company	Revenue 2015 $ – Billions
1	Saudi Arabia	Saudi Aramco	478
2	China	China National Petroleum	429
3	China	PetroChina	368
4	China	Sinopec	355
5	United States	Exxon Mobil	269
6	Netherlands/UK	Royal Dutch Shell	265
7	Kuwait	Kuwait Petroleum	252
8	United Kingdom	BP	223
9	France	Total	212
10	Russia	Lukoil	144
11	Italy	Eni	132
12	United States	Valero Energy	131
13	Brazil	Petrobras	130
14	United States	Chevron Corporation	130
15	Venezuela	PDVSA	128
16	Mexico	Pemex	118
17	Iran	National Iranian Oil	110
18	Russia	Gazprom	106
19	Malaysia	Petronas	101
20	China	China National Offshore Oil	99
21	United States	Marathon Petroleum	98
22	Thailand	PTT	94
23	Russia	Rosneft	92
24	Japan	JX Holdings	91
25	France	Engie	90
			$4,642

Figure 39
The World Largest 25 Oil Companies by 2015 Revenue, $ Billions
No other industry comes even close to generating $4 trillion of revenue from its top 25 largest firms.
(Petrobras, 2013; National Iranian, 2012)

Since the majority of the world's economic activity is powered by fossil fuels and especially by oil, the leading oil producing nations are among the wealthiest nations per capita, and the big oil firms are among the most valuable corporations.

Over the decades, as more and more countries developed their own economies and became more fully industrialized and more fully integrated into the global economic system, they also became more fully dependent on fossil fuels.

Their per capita energy consumption increased as their economic production increased, which brought greater wealth, which then created a middle class. And as their middle classes expanded, then their domestic markets for goods and services also expanded, further amplifying the demand for oil. The overall wealth of nations increased, and the oil industry came to be the single largest economic entity in the world.

In China, as we saw in the last chapter, this process was quite pronounced, and also quite sudden. During the years immediately following the transition to a capitalist economic system in 1978 China's economy expanded along an elegant exponential path, and consumption of energy increased exactly in parallel with increasing economic activity.

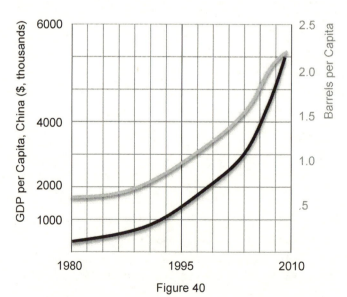

Figure 40

China's Economy: GDP and Oil Consumption Per Capita
It is not a coincidence that the two curves are parallel.

Nearly the same thing happened, with only slight variations, in all of the developing-become-developed nations. Japan, France, UK … China, India, Indonesia.

Consequently, as a source of fuel for a dynamic, modern economy, increasing demand for the oil to fuel the economy of every non-oil-producing nation transfers wealth outside of it. It's a drain that benefits producers, but detriments non-producers. Thus, every nation or community that does not own crude oil resources has, on the one hand, an incentive to consume more oil as a means of promoting more economic growth, but on the other hand an inherent incentive to not consume oil because the cost of oil is drag on economic growth. Hence, every nation that is not an oil producer also has a quite a significant incentive to find sources of energy other than oil to provide the power it needs so it can stop paying the taxes. Every nation, that is, wants a source or sources of energy they can own and control. Hence, even without considering the environmental issues that we examined in the previous chapter and the impending impact of global warming, every global economic player that is not oil-rich has a significant financial incentive to switch sources. Any source of energy that can be produced locally at a competitive cost is therefore highly attractive, and thus when solar energy production costs become competitive in price with oil, solar will find a ready market.

Consequently, if the immanence of climate change forces society to accelerate the end of the fossil fuels era then the process that led to the concentration of wealth in the hands of the oil owners is about to end. The coal and oil producers would then become not more valuable, but less valuable, which will of course be economically traumatic not only for them, but across the entire economy.

Non-Fossils

Scientists, technologists, and entrepreneurs have become active investors in the energy market for decades for the obvious reason that there's so much demand for energy resources and so many possible ways to earn profits creating and delivering that energy. As a result, the cost to generate energy from non-fossil sources has been steadily coming down for decades, and the declining cost combined with the previously-hidden impact of CO2 concentration is resulting in an increasingly broad selection of energy sources that are increasingly attractive. Solar, wind, tidal, fuel cells, and biofuels are five very large categories, and in each of them there are dozens if not hundreds of established firms and start-up companies that provide alternatives to fossil fuels.

Markets are efficient and dynamic when buyers, whether they are nations, cities, companies, or individuals, have the option to consume or *not* to consume a particular product. The attractiveness of fossil fuels is declining quickly as the reality of climate change sets in, but the future share of the energy market that fossil fuels continue to capture will depend to a great extent on the price comparison between them and the alternatives. Hence, the real race is probably not between fossils and alternatives, it's between competing teams of scientists and technologists who are searching for advances in non-fossil energy technology systems design.

As they have already made huge progress and many non-fossil technologies are rapidly maturing and becoming cost competitive, which means there is no have the question of if, but only a question of *when*. When, that is, will the fossil fuel industry, currently the globe's mightiest industrial enterprise, cease to dominate? Will its demise occur within twenty to thirty years, as some project, or much later, perhaps a century or more from now, as others believe?

If we take the view that its demise is immanent then we also confront the reality of the third simultaneous revolution in addition to the digital and the climate ones. Conversely, if we expect the oil industry to continue to endure as a powerful economic force for many decades, then this revolution may not occur, at least not in the time frame of the digital and climate revolutions.

Which scenario is more likely?

If it becomes clear that the impact of climate change will be severe then this will likely transform the reluctance of governments to upset the global economy into a strong will to action and thus accelerate investments in non-fossil energy sources. The cost of solar energy systems is already declining steadily and now rapidly, so it then becomes a question of scale: How long will it take and how much will it cost for solar and wind technologies to produce the amount of energy that the global economy requires?

Large scale solar energy production is a massive design and engineering challenge, but it's one that has already seen great successes. For example, the decline in the cost of the hardware needed to generate electricity from the sun's rays has declined enormously since 1977, when the solar collector hardware needed to produce one watt of solar-generated electricity cost $74. By 2010 that had dropped to 74 cents, a decline of 100x, all of which was of course the result of focused science and engineering efforts and talents applied to a very specific problem, and producing quite impressive results.

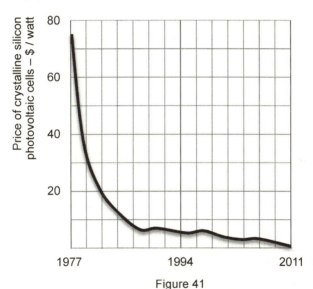

Figure 41
Declining Cost of Solar Generating Capacity[96]
The graph shows the declining cost of solar cells.

As shown in the following table, electricity generated in large power plants from oil and natural gas currently costs between 7.5 and 18 cents per watt to generate and distribute, and as the cost of solar has continued to drop and is now in the 12.5 cents range, the impetus to switch to solar may soon become overwhelming. Most nations will begin to make the transition, and the fossil fuel game may be finished with surprising speed.

That is, until we consider the $20 trillion of existing fossil fuel infrastructure, and the fact that just the top 25 firms in the oil industry currently generate $4.6 trillion in revenue.

Nevertheless, based on the confluence of climate change and technology improvement it's difficult to imagine a credible scenario in which oil retains its place of preeminence in the world's overall energy mix over the long term, is the end oil era is in sight? While we don't know the precise date on which economists will pronounce the oil industry completely caput, the powerful forces that are driving change suggest that it may occur in decades rather than in centuries.

Energy Plant Type	Lifetime Cost: ¢ per Kwh
Offshore Wind	20.0
Peaker Natural Gas	18.0
Coal with CCS	14.4
PV Solar	12.5
Gas Combined Cycle with CCS*	10.0
Biomass	10.0
Advanced Nuclear	9.5
Conventional Coal	9.5
Hydro-electric	8.4
Natural Gas Combined Cycle	7.5
Land Based Wind	7.4
Geothermal	4.8

Figure 42
Lifetime Cost per Kilowatt Hour (Kwh) in cents.[97]
Calculations are based on Levelized Cost of Energy (LCOE), calculated as total life cycle cost of electricity for a given technology divided by the total life cycle electricity produced.
* CCS stands for Carbon Control and Storage (Sequestration) in a remote underground location.

Of course the fossil fuel producers, a mighty and very wealthy industry, will do all they can to forestall this outcome, whether that involves lobbying politicians or marketing to the mass public, but in the end history may not be on their side.

Short Term Thinking

It's inevitable that industrialism and the resulting invention of the modern world have had transformative impact on every aspect of our lives, including on how we think, the choices we make, and on our values and beliefs. One of those impacts is the impact on our mental time horizons. To a significant extent our habits of thinking have converged down to the very short term, and thus we prefer, or insist upon "instant gratification," we indulge in "the 24 hour news cycle," we demand to know "what have you done for me lately," we oppose any inconveniences and indulge in "NIMBY" thinking, and we obsess over instant-reward apps like texting, twitter, Instagram and chat. There is no forest here, only the tree that is immediately in front of us.

The difficulty this presents is that we are now confronted with issues wherein we must balance short term thinking with longer term good and bad outcomes. Do we have the courage, fortitude and financing to endure short term costs and losses to achieve longer-term goals?

The financial markets are typically not so patient. Many stock market traders operate on cycles that are counted in seconds, and automated trading computers operate on cycles of milliseconds. The performance of both is tracked and reported globally minute to minute, and companies they invest in find themselves under excruciating pressure to produce financial results each quarter of each year. Consequently, in a great many organizations the last few weeks of each calendar quarter becomes a self-parody of self-induced crisis where actions are taken in order to "make the numbers" even when everyone knows they're the wrong actions to take. This has now become an ongoing obsession that is universally lamented even by those who indulge in it.

In this environment long term corporate planning consists almost solely of capital allocation, but there isn't much patient capital. It's clear to observers everywhere that many decisions are made by business leaders to attain very short term objectives at the expense of long term success, and many actions even threaten log term survival. The recent emissions scandal concerning Volkswagen's diesel engines reflects the extreme pressures that business leaders are under, and the poor choices that often result. Engineers designed and installed software in Volkswagen autos to manipulate the outcome of emissions tests, probably because they were under extreme pressure to create a product more successful that physics would allow. The software was installed in about 11 million cars sold worldwide, which will result in fines and court actions that will eventually cost the company billions if not tens of billions of Euros. This could even mean the end of Volkswagen as an independent company … and it's quite obviously the disastrous outcome of a terrible decision made only with short term benefit in mind, and little thought to the long term consequences.

The point, of course, is that in our cultural and commercial climate of instantaneous rewards and gratification we seem to be losing the capacity to engage in long term thinking, patience, and understanding the unfolding of patterns that take years or decades to emerge.

In this high pressure environment of short term gains, one of the few financial industries where there is relatively patient capital is the venture capital industry, which has evolved into the role of long-term disruptor. It is through VC funded start-ups that many alternative energy companies get their initial capital; Bloom Energy, for example, a firm that makes natural gas powered fuel cells that create electricity, has received more than $1 billion in capital investment since it was founded in 2001, and while its investors are feeling impatient now, the prospect of a market that could be worth $40 billion per year by 2022 has kept them engaged.[98] Investors in high-risk, high-reward companies like Bloom know that the costs are huge and the technical risks are great; they're betting that cost-competitive, non-fossil, or low-CO2 solutions that can scale to generate significant amounts of energy will find willing customers. The multi-trillion oil market is a very attractive target.

Alternative to What?

When we think about the energy industry with the benefit of an historical perspective, it's obvious that humanity subsisted for millions of years with total reliance on solar energy, and for only the last two hundred years we've become dependent on fossil fuels. It can thus only be a reflection of our nearsightedness that we refer to the energy source that fueled society for millennia as "alternative," when in fact the coal, oil, and gas that we've been relying on only for the last two hundred are more reasonably labeled the "alternatives."

And now that we have the powerful motivation of climate change to abandon fossil fuels, and a compelling economic motivation to shed the embedded fossil fuel "tax" that solar and wind could roll back to zero, the technologies we seek are the ones that will enable us to switch back. In other words, we're simply working to go back to the sun and the wind, although of course we're doing so in an entirely modern way by collecting sunlight and wind power, transforming them into electricity, and running our computers, cars, factories, and electric lights with the outputs.

The Largest Economic Transition in History

The economic transition from fossil fuels to whatever's next is not going to be a simple undertaking, and indeed the scale and scope of this economic transition could be the single largest economic project in the history of humanity.

But as I noted above, even if it were possible to generate the energy that's needed from sources other than fossil fuels, the multi-trillion dollar global infrastructure is already in place to refine and distribute coal, oil, gasoline, and natural gas, but nothing like it exists to store and distribute solar-produced electricity, nor to distribute hydrogen fuel (which some scientists believe may be preferred even to solar as a transportation fuel). Of course the cost to create that infrastructure will also be in the trillions.

There are significant technological challenges to be overcome. Since solar collectors only produce during daylight, reliable and very large scale mass storage systems are essential if there is indeed going to be a solar-powered economy. Consequently, the search for solutions that provide cost-effective, reliable, large scale energy storage is also a subject of intense scientific and technological research. There are hundreds of potential solutions being explored and developed in labs around the world, labs run by corporations, governments, universities, and also by consortia of all three.

The Fracking Dilemma

And in this we find some compelling ironies. For example, at the beginning of Chapter 2 I quoted California Governor Jerry Brown, who stated that massive quantities of oil, natural gas, and coal, must remain in the ground, never to be extracted nor burnt, to protect us from the significant dangers of fossil fuel driven climate change. This is a valid and indeed a courageous position for an American politician to take.

Back home, however, Governor Brown's state sits atop one of America's largest accumulations of shale gas, the Monterey Shale formation, which is thought to hold more than 400 billion barrels of oil.[99] That's equivalent to nearly half the conventional oil under all of Saudi Arabia. As the United States currently consumes about 19 million barrels of oil a day, the Monterey Shale thus contains the equivalent of 21,000 days worth of American oil consumption, or roughly enough for 57 years at current usage. Will Governor Brown and his successors be content to let the gas remain untapped in the ground, even though extracting and selling it would be a tremendous boon to California's economy in the short term?

This is where the high-minded former divinity student and the fiscally-prudent governor must decide whether the short or long term interests of Californians will be served. And of course this is exactly the same dilemma that every government that sits atop fossil fuel resources will have to decide in the coming years and decades.

Should California decide go forward with extraction of the Monterey shale gas, how would it be extracted? By hydraulic fracturing, of course, or fracking, the process of pumping water, sand, and chemicals into the ground under very high pressure in order to open up cracks in the rock which then free the oil and gas molecules that would otherwise remain trapped. The underground gas then flows through the tiny cracks into pipeline collection systems through which it's brought to the surface. Fracking is controversial, however because of the environmental damage that it causes due to the very high volume of polluted water that results, which is why it's been banned in New York State. It's also apparently been the cause of earthquakes that occurred all across southern Oklahoma, which then resulted in lawsuits being filed to ban it there. New York's neighbor Pennsylvania supports a thriving and economically productive fracking industry, showing how differing views of the short and long-term tradeoffs lead to different decisions, both of which have potential long term consequences.

Fracking was developed through a painstaking process of trial and error and refined over decades by major oil industry firms including Halliburton, but came into common usage only in the late 1990s in the Barnett oil shale region of Texas. Once it was demonstrated as a proven technique for producing oil and gas from shale rocks the practice spread very quickly to other shale rock formations across the US.

Today there are seven major geological formations in the US where fracking is taking place, and the combined rate of production from these reached 5 million barrels per day in early 2015. [100] This is an economically-significant quantity, as it has altered the structure of global energy demand. The results of the boom have been also economically significant not only for the fracking companies, but for all energy consumers worldwide due to the dramatic drop in oil process that some attribute the additional quantities that fracking has brought to the market.

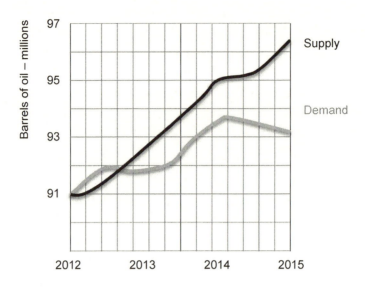

Figure 43
World Oil Supply and Demand[101]

By 2015 global oil supply exceeded demand by three to four million barrels a day, and the persistence of this excess production altered the basic supply and demand curves that tell us what oil is worth in the global marketplace. The two curves crossed in 2012, and in 2014 prices began dropping from more than $100 per barrel to as low as $30, a shift of fundamental importance for global energy markets.

Economically, then, California has the potential to benefit from economic boom of enormous proportions if it were to fully exploit the Monterey Shale gas, and indeed the state already produces vast quantities of fossil fuels, presently third only to Texas and North Dakota among American states in the volume of fossil production.

Governor Brown has also permitted fracking in California despite a significant and very well publicized outcry from environmental groups that oppose it. The question, then, is if he is willing to prevent extraction of massive amounts of California's own oil and gas, and the jobs and taxes that will go along with it, in order to counteract global climate change. Will Governor Brown have the political courage, and will California have the economic fortitude, to forego this opportunity? This is the choice that he faces as governor, and which every leader of every fossil-fuel-producing county, state, and nation also faces.

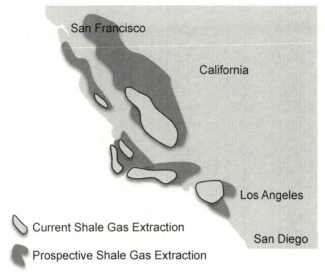

Figure 44
California Shale Map[102] [103]

California representatives in the US Congress would like to limit Governor Brown's choices, however. They have sponsored legislation to stop fossil fuel development on lands controlled by the US government. Rep. Jared Huffman of San Rafael, California recently commented, "The transition to a clean energy economy can't wait. Ninety percent of the world's fossil fuels have to stay in the ground forever to limit the most catastrophic impacts of climate change."[104]

Early Adopters

The transition is not entirely within their control, however, and overall three factors will influence if not determine, the timing of the transition from fossils to other sources. The first of these is the rate at which the costs of non-fossil energy production declines, and thereby becomes cost competitive with the least expensive fossil sources. Second is the cost, scale, and reliability of the supporting transport and storage systems and technologies that will be required for full-scale non-fossil energy systems to be implemented. And third are the regulatory pressures that may be brought to bear on fossil fuel producers and users through carbon markets and limitations if a consensus about the dangers of climate change emerge, leading a strong and widespread will to action.

The rate of growth of non-fossil technologies in the market will likely be heavily influenced by early adopters, power purchasers that in effect invest before the technologies are fully mature and widely accepted. During the first quarter of 2015 four major US corporations announced commitments to purchase large quantities of electricity produced by solar and wind technologies, including HP and Dow Chemical, which purchased 112 and 200 megawatts of wind power in Texas,[105] Kaiser Permanente which purchased 153 megawatts in California, and Amazon, which purchased 208 megawatts of wind-generated electricity in North Carolina. Figure 46 shows more than 1000 megawatts of these purchases; as a megawatt is one million watts, these numbers begin to have significance.

Amazon	208 MW
Apple	130 MW
Cisco	20 MW
Dow	200 MW
Facebook	200 MW
GM	43 MW
Google	43 MW
HP	112 MW
KP	153 MW
IBM	91 MW
IKEA	98 MW
Mars, Inc.	211 MW
Microsoft	285 MW
Wal-mart	50 MW
Total	**1,844 MW**

Figure 45
Major American (and Swedish, IKEA) Corporate Alternate Power Purchases[106]

These purchases have a dual significance. First, they show that the changeover from fossils has become a major concern of the business community. Second, these companies are sophisticated buyers who will expect and require that the energy and energy systems they buy operate safely, reliably, and achieve promised ongoing technological improvements. They've committed to obtaining electricity in 2016 and 2017 from these purchases, but year by year thereafter they will expect increases in efficiency and power yield. Hence, by playing the role of early adopters they are joining the venture capitalists in helping fund the massive effort in R&D which should lead to improvements that not only benefit themselves but which benefit all producers and consumers of solar and wind power. These purchases will serve to significantly accelerate the overall economic transition away from fossils, and the entire economy will benefit as efficiencies increase, which will make it even easier for additional buyers to commit to similar purchases.

Under an optimistic scenario it won't take long for these market dynamics to support significantly improved technological capabilities along with development of the necessary infrastructure. This combination makes it much easier to see how a major, economy-wide transition could occur. Thus, while we wait for Governor Brown to officially announce a scaling back of California's fossil fuel production, the decision may not require that he take much political or economic risk if market forces drive this transition quickly, even that happens long before Governor Brown, or California's next governor, or the California state budget, are ready to absorb the change.

Powering the US Military

Another pretty large organization that's committed to transitioning away from fossil fuels is the US military, which is of course one of the world's most massive enterprises. It employs more than 2.1 million full time soldiers, sailors, flyers, and civilians, plus another million reservists, which makes it one of the largest organizations of any kind in the world. Operating with an annual budget of more than $500 billion, the Department of Defense is also the largest single consumer of energy in the US.

In its fiscal year of 2006, the Department used almost 30,000 gigawatt hours (GWH) of electricity, at a cost of almost \$2.2 billion. In 2007 it accounted for about 93 percent of all US government fuel consumption, mostly by the Air Force in the form of jet fuel. In recent years the Department of Defense has consumed about 4,600,000,000 US gallons (1.7×10^{10} L) of fuel annually, or an average of 12,600,000 US gallons (48,000,000 L) of fuel per day. When military warfighting operations are occurring, these numbers increase substantially.[107]

Every branch of the US military is required to develop and implement its own plans and initiatives to replace fossil fuels with renewable energy sources.

The DoD has requisitioned the deployment of 3 gigawatts (GW; 3 billion watts) of renewable energy to power military facilities by 2025. This meets a larger DoD mandate, Title 10 USC § 2911, which directs at least 25 percent of any DoD facility energy consumption come from renewable energy sources.[108]

Current commitments total roughly \$400 million of power purchases, which means that by 2025 the Defense Department could be the world's largest consumer of non-fossil power. And of course another benefit is that long-term commitments to power purchases on this scale make it possible for power producers to invest even more heavily in the research and development needed to further improve their technologies, which will increase their efficiencies and thus reduce their costs, as well as in the necessary storage and distribution systems. This creates a positive spiral that benefits everyone – except the fossil fuel producers.

Given the fact of global need and the motivation and commitment on the part of large-scale power consumers such as the US military and many of its major corporations to switch to non-fossil sources, and given that the requisite technologies will soon be available, it may only take additional commitments of a few more of these huge scale consumers to provide enough proven demand and thus enough capital to drive the transition from fossils to non-fossil to occur at a speed that would have only recently seemed unimaginable. The question then becomes one of scale: how fast can non-fossil sources achieve sufficient production scale to enable the full phase-out of fossils?

National Oil Wealth

Nations that earn a significant portion of their national revenues from their oil industries will feel the effects of these changes. Among those that will be hit hardest are Nigeria, Libya, Angola, Venezuela, and Saudi Arabia, as they sit atop some of the most productive oil reservoirs in the world.

As of 2013, 20 percent of the world's proven reserves were buried deep under Saudi Arabia's desert sands, second among all nations after Venezuela.[109] The Saudis have of course developed a highly sophisticated oil industry that provides the bulk of the nation's income. The ruling Saud family consists of the king and some 15,000 princes and princesses, and precisely because of the great value of their oil theirs is probably the richest family in the world with a collective net worth of more than a trillion dollars.

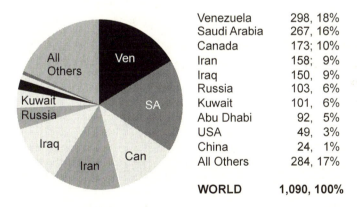

Venezuela	298,	18%
Saudi Arabia	267,	16%
Canada	173;	10%
Iran	158;	9%
Iraq	150,	9%
Russia	103,	6%
Kuwait	101,	6%
Abu Dhabi	92,	5%
USA	49,	3%
China	24,	1%
All Others	284,	17%
WORLD	**1,090,**	**100%**

Figure 46
Amount of Oil; Known World Oil Reserves, 2014.[110]

1. Prince Alwaleed Bin Talal Bin Abdulaziz Alsaud, $20.4 billion
2. Mohamed Bin Issa Al Jaber, $12 billion
3. The Olayan Family, $11.9 billion
4. Mohammad Hussein Al Amoudi, $10 billion
5. Issam Alzahid, $10 billion
6. The Bin Laden Family, $9.8 billion.
7. The Bugshan Family, $7 billion
8. The Al Juffali Family, $6.2 billion
9. Tarek Abdulla Al Qahtani, $6 billion
10. Mubarak Al Suwaiket, $5.2 billion

TOTAL $98.5 billion

Figure 47
Saud Family Wealth, the Richest 10[111]

A close relationship between western nations and Middle Eastern oil producers was a determining factor in shaping the present national borders throughout the region, and that continued into the early 1970s when many of the producing nations formed the OPEC cartel, the Organization of Petroleum Exporting Countries. OPEC was created specifically to give them greater leverage to control and thereby to increase oil prices. In an entirely logical manner they were optimizing the value of their oil assets, as any responsible asset owner would also do. The creation of OPEC enabled the producers to raise their prices by reducing supply in the face of continuing high demand, and the resulting era came to be called the "Oil Shock" as the Western economies experienced many adverse affects.

Restricted production led to dramatic increases in OPEC's wealth; the impact on the rest of the world was a large tax increase. Gasoline simply and suddenly became more expensive, which then caused inflation as cost increases for gas led to price increases throughout the economy, which then led to a global a recession by the late 1970s. The also resulted, in the words of US President Jimmy Carter, in national malaise throughout the US. The Western world didn't feel good, but the oil producers felt just fine as they suddenly found themselves much richer than they had been.

Second order impacts of the Oil Shock included a renewed focus on the fuel efficiency of autos, as previously most American manufacturers and consumers had been entirely unconcerned with fuel economy. The new attention to fuel economy created significant opportunities for Japanese automakers Toyota, Honda, and Nissan (at that time known as the US as Datsun), because their cars were small and energy efficient, which reflected conditions in their home market where small size and energy efficiency were positive attributes. When these qualities became attractive to American buyers all three companies experienced significant increases in their market shares beginning in the 1970s, and through careful management and thoughtful design they have extended their market share gains during the decades that followed.

With the creation of OPEC in the 1970s the Saudi kingdom's oil company, Saudi Aramco, often played the role "swing producer" among the OPEC nations, meaning that Saudi oil output was adjusted to bring world supply and demand into balance at OPEC's preferred price. If demand was high Aramco would increase production; if demand slowed, Aramco would bring less oil to the market and thus sustain the preferred price level. The Saudis did this well, and were also skilled diplomats who balanced not only global oil prices but also played a significant stabilizing role in the entire region. They did this with significant success for nearly four decades. By 2010, however, their ability to control both the petroleum market and the political situation began to decline.

The Arab Spring movement began in Tunisia in December 2010 with the suicide of Mohamed Bouazizi, and quickly spread to Libya, Egypt, Syria, Bahrain, Yemen, and Jordan. Popular protests in these countries gathered tremendous power and led to the collapse of sitting governments in Tunisia, Libya, and Egypt, and to ongoing civil conflict in the other nations as millions of people marched in protests and demanded democracy and the removal of dictatorships. Autocrats around the world watched these protests nervously, fearing that the movement would spread to their own countries; as a result, censorship increased in China, for example, as the flow of news about the Arab Spring became severely restricted.[112]

The Arab Spring also came to Saudi Arabia, with protests in many cities, hundreds of arrests, the expulsion of journalists, and many deaths.[113] As a tightly controlled society with a massive internal security force, the full story has not yet been told, and may never be.

In Syria the protests against the Assad dictatorship turned into a brutally self-destructive civil war, a conflict the seeds of which may have begun, as noted above, in climate-induced strife that was then compounded by Arab-Spring-induced democratic aspirations. It then expanded into a regional war that destroyed cities across the country, turning nearly half of its 22 million people into refugees. There is little left of what was once a rich culture, and it would not be an exaggeration to say that Syria has been wrecked.

Oil Prices

A third major factor that the Saudis have recently been unable to control is, crucially, the price of oil itself. For the first time in 40 years, with the exception of a few minor periods, the Saudis have not been able to sustain the price of oil at a high level.

At the beginning of 2014 the global oil price was about $114 per barrel, which would suggest that the total value of the officially counted Saudi oil reserves of 267 billion barrels was $30 trillion. By the end of the year the price of oil had fallen to about $50 per barrel, cutting the kingdom's calculable asset value by more than half.

Historically, overall world demand for oil is a function of its economic health, as a higher economic growth rate translated directly into increased demand for energy, and thus increased demand for fossil fuels. However, with the acceleration of climate change impacts and the growing awareness that the threat which fossil fuels present to human civilization is apparently going to be quite significant, perceptions about the future role of Saudi oil in the global economy are entirely different than they were a generation ago. If the fossil industry were to decline or even to collapse entirely, the Saudi kingdom would come under extreme economic and then social pressure. What would happen if, as Governor Brown has suggested, the oil remained in the ground, instead of being extracted and burned and thus adding to the total of atmospheric CO2?

The Saudis, of course, wonder this also, as it constitutes a significant and indeed perhaps an existential threat to the Saud family's continued leadership of the kingdom. For without the revenues provided by oil the population could well become restless.

> For decades, the royal family has used the kingdom's immense oil wealth to lavish benefits on its people, including free education and medical care, generous energy subsidies and well paid (and often undemanding) government jobs. No one paid taxes, and if political rights were not part of the equation, that was fine with most people. But the drop in oil prices to below $30 a barrel from more than $100 a barrel in June 2014 means that the old math no longer works. Low oil prices have knocked a chunk out of the government budget and now pose a threat to the unwritten social contract that has long underpinned life in the kingdom, the Arab world's largest economy and a key American ally.[114]

Hence, a question of great importance to the Saud family concerns the future of oil industry: At what point will the oil no longer be needed, or wanted? When, in other words, will the oil age come to an end? Of course the same question is vitally important to the leaders and citizens of every nation, producers and consumers alike, for this is a question fundamental to the future of the global economy.

The Oil Industry

The Saudis and OPEC are one among four major categories of oil producers: the OPEC national oil companies, including Venezuela, Saudi Arabia, Iran, and Iraq; the non-OPEC national producers that include China, Russia, and Mexico; the giant oil companies including Shell, Exxon, BP, Total, and Chevron; and the thousands of smaller producers that are regional and local in their market reach, but which together constitute a significant volume.

Demand for oil has been steadily growing since 1900 whereas supply has been quite variable. When there is a glut of oil available relative to demand, prices drop; when there is an actual or perceived scarcity, prices rise. Hence, the prospect of war in the Middle East is generally accompanied by a rise in prices as the market assumes that the war will cause a reduction in supply, and in the period leading up to both of the Gulf Wars oil prices rose in the expectation that supply would decline, as indeed it did.

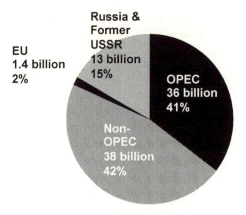

Figure 48
World Oil Production by Type of Producer[115]

When the Saudis played a central role in balancing supply and demand the Saudi king's great power enabled them to reduce production to sustain a preferred market price. This was often a benefit the US economy, and reinforced the strategic partnership between the two nations.

Conversely, when wars or strife in major oil producing nations caused decline in global supplies the Saudis increased their production thereby preventing prices from escalating too high. Saudi production increased during both Gulf Wars, which compensated significantly for the market disruption.

In recent years, however, price fluctuations have become more extreme, as the ups have been higher and the lows lower. During 2014 as significant volumes of oil and gas came to market as a result of fracking in the US, the Saudis did not reduce their production volume, and as we saw above, supply soon exceeded demand and prices dropped just as the economists would have predicted.

Why the Saudis chose not to reduce production to eliminate the overall surplus has not been explained, but there are many possibilities, any or none of which could be true.

It's possible that the Saudis recognize that the oil age is coming to an end and they wish to sell as much of their oil as possible, even at a lower prices, rather that see it become worthless in the ground. Perhaps they've been listening to Governor Brown.

It's also possible that the Saudis wish to put financial pressure on the fracking industry producers by keeping supply levels higher than demand and thus reducing the revenues and profits of their competitors with the goal of driving many of them out of business.

It's also possible that the Saudis wish to put political pressure on their arch-rival Iran by limiting Iranian oil revenues and profits. Or perhaps their geopolitical target is Russia, which also depends for its economic viability on the sale of its oil, and which is a primary supporter of another Saudi enemy, President Assad of Syria. As oil prices drop President Putin's Russian government comes under increasing pressure, and given that Russia has taken an aggressive posture in Syria, perhaps the friend of my enemy is also my enemy.

Or perhaps none of these explanations is correct. Regardless, what is clear is that Saudi oil is significant on a global scale, and the volume of Saudi production makes its oil industry and the kingdom itself geopolitically significant.

A Scenario of Decline

The value of the oil that remains underground is massive. In fact, it's probably the second largest category of asset in the world, surpassed only by the value of the world's combined real estate. But with the global economy in the process of shifting away from fossil fuels all that may be about to change. This massive accumulation of wealth, that is, could suddenly become worthless.

If, for example, overall demand for oil continues in the decline that began in 2014 while supplies do not contract then the price will remain low and the oil companies will be in danger of falling from their economic pinnacle. Indeed this is already happening, as *The New York Times* reports that current low prices combined with high levels of debt throughout the US oil industry,

> "… could push 175 global exploration and production companies – more than a third of the industry – into bankruptcy. Oil giants like Royal Dutch Shell and Chevron have laid off workers as profits have plunged. On Wall Street, banks that made big loans to energy companies are bracing for big losses. This week, JPMorgan Chase increased its reserves for bad energy loans."[116]

As billions of dollars of their combined asset values are recorded as untapped oil reserves, the value of these assets as shown on their financial records is a key component of their financial strength. If these reserves were to decline significantly in value, as they inevitably must in any scenario involving the contraction of the oil industry, then the companies themselves will also decline in value commensurately, and perhaps perilously.

Many followers of the oil industry recognize that the decline is inevitable, but the timeline they foresee is generally measured in decades. There are many reasons to believe that this could well be correct, including the basic economics. Society, in the form of companies and governments, have invested massively in the infrastructure of the fossil fuel system, as Vaclav Smil points out:

> From coal mines, oil wells, gas pipelines and refineries to millions of local filling stations, the fossil fuel infrastructure is worth at least $20 trillion across the world. China alone spent half a trillion dollars to add almost 300 gigawatts of new coal-fired generating capacity between 2001 and 2010 – more than the fossil-fuel generating capacity in Germany, France, the U.K., Italy and Spain combined – and it expects those plants to operate for at least 30 years. No country will walk away from such investments.[117]

Smil also shows that the previous three energy revolutions have taken over the market rather slowly. In 1840, he notes, coal provided just 5 percent of global energy demand; it took sixty years to reach 50 percent. Oil had 5 percent of the world energy market in 1915 and over the following sixty years it attained a total of only 40 percent. Natural gas had 5 percent in 1930 and only 25 percent by 1990. Each revolution, in other words, proceeded more slowly than the previous. In 2012, solar and wind constituted just under five percent of the total energy supplied to the world, so Smil's conclusion is that it's unrealistic to expect a rapid transition to alternative fuels. How fast can it reach 50 percent, or even 30 percent?

It's also possible, however, that the switch could occur with astonishing speed because when investors recognize that a change in the fundamental structure of economy is actually occurring most will be very quick to adjust their behaviors and change their portfolios. A sell-off in oil stocks would possibly turn into a rout, driving fossil fuel stock prices down significantly and quickly. If such a massive write-down of oil company assets and values were to occur suddenly, it's entirely plausible that a global recession could result as the world's balance sheets would lose billions of dollars in asset value quite suddenly. This would in turn put many borrowers into an untenable position, debts suddenly vastly larger than their assets.

This would lead to significant problems for fossil fuel lenders, as collateral intended to balance their outstanding fossil fuel-related loans would suddenly disappear and they would find themselves carrying massive amounts of bad loans, leaving bank regulators and national governments with a set of quite difficult choices. Should they prop up the banks? Relax their reserve requirements? Or let the banks fail?

The speed of this transition process would be further amplified, if, in parallel, the world's nations agreed to impose a tax on carbon, which they might well do in response to climate change and the threat of continued warming.

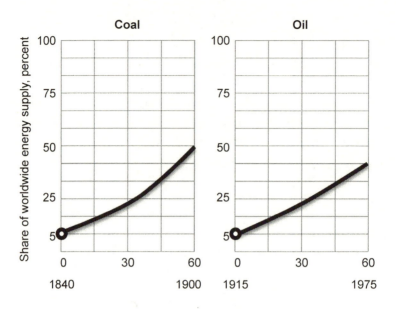

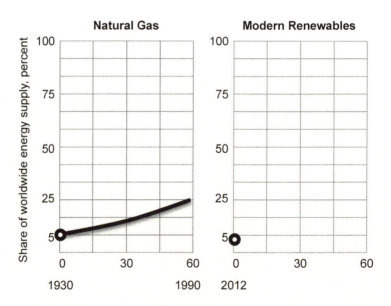

Figure 49

Smil: Share of Worldwide Energy Supply, Coal, Oil, Natural Gas, and Modern Renewables[118]

60 years of market penetration for each; each slower than the previous.

California Confluence

A combination of technology, market, and regulatory factors is converging in California which suggests that the transition could well happen faster than most people expect. Energy scientist Hal Harvey points out that California motor vehicle emissions standards set aggressive targets for fuel economy and emission reduction improvements that will require automakers to innovate consistently to meet them, or lose access to America's largest and most significant market. The federal government is already shifting from regulating consumption, via fuel efficiency, to regulating emissions under the authority of the Environmental Protection Agency, which means, in effect, that "US energy policy is set in Sacramento," California's state capital.[119]

In response, cars are getting lighter in weight while engines are getting better. The design of trucks is also improving, bringing emissions down still further, and of course electric cars and hybrids are gaining significant market share. Toyota's Prius has been California's best selling car for four consecutive years.

At the same time, improvements in technical areas related to alternative energy generation and infrastructure such as thermal energy storage, offshore wind generation, and the smart grid will bring further economies of scale that will help to address renewable energy targets that California has built into the regulation of the electric power industry, while on the consumption side building codes now require progressive improvements in energy efficiency, with as much as 80 percent reductions in consumption for heating, cooling, and lighting.

When you put all of these factors together in a regulatory environment that mandates not a specific level of performance, but consistent performance improvements over time with not future limits, what the government has is to define a set of progressively demanding requirements that power and transportation producers can only meet if they invest heavily in R&D over the long term. With the easy innovations already behind us, continuing to meet these progressively more demanding standards will require technical breakthroughs. Hence, R&D is now built into government policy, but unlike the past, it's not the government that will necessarily provide the funding.

Like the magic of an exponential curve, a progressive doubling, the progressively tightening standards will also compound and gradually the results will constitute transformative changes in energy markets.

Hence, the change comes about as a result of natural market forces further accelerated with a further push from regulations such as these emissions and performance standards. Perhaps we will also see a carbon tax and cap-and-trade legislation, and in combination the possibility that the fossil fuels market will decline cannot be dismissed. And if (when?) the value of fossil fuel assets declines the oil industry's balance sheets will become disabled by the massive writedown in the value of their unexploited and unexploitable reserves, which will in turn affect their stock prices. Many will become takeover targets, though obviously not because of their oil-related assets, but rather for other assets they own – their accumulated cash and their extensive real estate holdings.

The oil itself will be transformed from a significant source of future value creation to a non-asset that's no longer worth the effort to bring to the surface and refine. Investors who are slow to respond will suffer losses, and oil industry employment will plummet.

It's a harsh and startling scenario, and while it may portray an unrealistically fast transition, history suggests that when fundamental change comes to any industry or any company the process of transition is indeed rapid and decisive. A recent and vivid example is the collapse of Nokia, which as I noted in Chapter 1, went from being the global king of the cell phone makers to a sideline pauper in the span of only 18 months. A few years later it ceased to exist entirely. Together, the iPhone and Android platforms went from zero global market share to 30 percent within a short 30 months; Nokia did not respond quickly enough to the change in market structure, and it was doomed.[120]

Skeptics will note that the Nokia example is the technology industry, wherein the market dynamics are entirely different than the energy industry, and they would be correct to do so. However, they should also keep in mind that the alternative energy industry is itself a technology industry, as it leverages the dynamics of Moore's Law and all of the associated performance improvements and cost reductions. Hence, the energy industry will inevitably become more like technology, which implies the possibility of much higher volatility and much more fluid dynamics. Standard Oil, the parent company of much of America's present oil industry including global giants Exxon and Chevron, was founded in 1870; the emerging giant companies of the alternative energy industries will face much different competitive pressures and market dynamics in the coming decades that then oil companies have seen over more than a century.

Two Trends

The basic economic proposition, then, is a fascinating one. At the same time that a tremendous amount of effort is going into the development of the science and technology of solar and wind generation, and the necessary batteries and transmission infrastructure to make them viable large scale alternatives, the world continues to come to grips with the reality of climate change and its consequences as violent storms increase in both frequency and magnitude and the oceans rise.

Consequently, governments are aligning around shared commitments to collective action and their interest in escaping the fossil fuel tax on their economies, while many large scale power consumers invest still more heavily in alternative supplies, all of which further accelerates the movement away from fossil fuels. Thus, the overall transformation of the economy is occurring not as the result of one driving force but because of many, all of which are pointing in the same direction: the 21st century will not be a fossil fuel century. Hence, if you're living in a nation that depends on oil production for its economic vitality then the coming decades may become quite difficult, and if you work for in the fossil fuels industry this is bad news. But for everyone else it's the opposite.

In Chapter One the core argument was that digital technology as visualized by the D-curve is transforming the global economy, as well as our culture and our society, in ways that we are only now beginning to experience and understand. In the coming years and decades the process of digitization will accelerate, and it's likely that dramatically new forms of digital technology will become pervasive and hugely impactful in our culture and throughout the economy. Artificially intelligent devices and robots might be commonplace, and while we have a difficult time foreseeing the impact this will have on the human workforce, we can be confident that the impact will be enormous. If one of the outcomes is massive displacement of human workers, we might be facing a robot recession.

In Chapter Two the subject was climate change, and if the moderate or worst-case forecasts prove correct then we are entering a century or more of climate-driven tumult. Established patterns of food production and habitation will be forced to change impacting tens of millions and leading possibly to the largest project that humanity has ever undertaken, the creation of new cities for billions of those who formerly lived along what may be the soon-to-be-submerged coastlines. The value of all that what-used-to-be prime real estate would revert to zero, meaning that a huge write-down in asset values would be required. Today the combined asset value of the most sought-after coastal locations totals in the trillions of dollars; wipe that asset value away and the world could well be looking at a real estate recession. The term "under water," which used to refer to assets on which the debt load exceeded the asset's value, would take on a new and unfortunately quite literal meaning.

And here in Chapter Three we've explored the basics of the energy systems that power the world's economy, and here also the story is one of fundamental change. "The most fundamental future shift in the global economy is not, as one might think, further globalization but rather the coming epochal energy transition. Few other factors will be as important in determining the economic and social fortunes of both affluent and poor countries as the tempo and eventual success or failure of this unfolding."[121]

We are shifting globally from fossil fuels to what we euphemistically call "alternatives," that is, energy sources that aren't fossil fuels, but which powered all the world's activities through the millennia of civilization until 1800. In that sense we're returning to the pre-industrial supply source, but of course we're doing it in an entirely technological manner, with highly advanced solar collectors and wind turbines and batteries that are designed and manufactured using super-sophisticated digital technology and ultra-high tech materials and methods. The investments required to make this vision real will cause a boom in some industries; the corresponding collapse of the fossil fuel assets valuations could well cause a global recession, which would perhaps go by the name of the "great burn-off."

These, then, are three of the five revolutions, each of which brings with it the significant possibility of severe economic distress. Should they arrive simultaneously, as is quite possible, the convergence would certainly constitute an economic calamity on the scale of the Great Depression, or perhaps worse.

Next, in Chapter 4, we will examine the ways in which our great enthusiasm for life in cities, a trend that has grown precisely in parallel with the carbon economy of the Industrial Age, is also transforming how we live in the world and the choices we make, including critical choices concerning the size of our families. As we will shortly see, we're about to enter a third era of human civilization, one so new that we don't yet have a name for it. But demographers tell us that it is coming quite surely, and bringing with it enormous consequences for all of us.

•••

Chapter 4

The
Builder:

The Population Explosion and the Urban Revolution

When a city's population doubles there is a 15% increase in income, wealth, and innovation.[122]

Geoffrey West

Forty-six centuries ago the very talented stonemasons of Egypt built the Great Pyramid, and for the 36 centuries that followed it remained the world's tallest structure, soaring about 480 feet, or 145 meters, above the Nile. Only when the masons of Europe developed the Gothic Cathedral form was it surpassed, and the great Gothic towers immediately became the central spiritual and architectural elements of Europe's great cities.

Building them required a process of trial and error to perfect the elegant Gothic aspiration to achieve great height, soaring windows, and

163

slender walls, and in the process of these experiments quite a few of them collapsed during construction.[123] The famous tower in Pisa did not collapse, but as it was built on a poor foundation it soon began leaning; it too would have collapsed if not for intervention. Modern engineers could well have righted it all the way to plumb, but they chose not to because that would have robbed Pisa of its prime tourist attraction.

And whether on a firm foundation or a too-soft one, the process of constructing a cathedral often carried on for hundreds of years. An individual mason might spend an entire lifetime working on only a single magnificent structure, painstakingly shaping the stones, hammer blow by hammer blow, one by one, as the structure rose majestically toward the heavens; his son and grandson may have also lived and died doing the same thing, on the very same building, with each year creeping ever closer to the heavens.

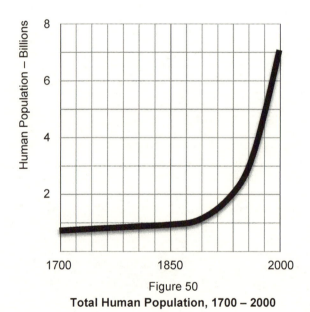

Figure 50
Total Human Population, 1700 – 2000

In fact, it was masons who for centuries built all of the great structures of world, as stone and concrete were the enduring materials most suited to making the roads and temples and monuments that defined the great cities. The new materials of the Industrial Era, iron and steel, made it possible to create buildings much taller and much faster, along with the bridges that spanned the great valleys, and cars and railroads that ran upon them. And once the seductive pattern of urbanization took hold, and the mechanization of farming led to huge increases in agricultural productivity, the gradual migration toward the cities became a flood, and the cities grew as the overall population expanded rapidly.

In 1800 the total world population was about a billion, but by the last half of the 20th century the rate at which the human population was increasing was so fast that fears of a catastrophic population explosion were commonplace. The second billion had arrived in about 1925, the third by 1960, and the fourth by 1974.

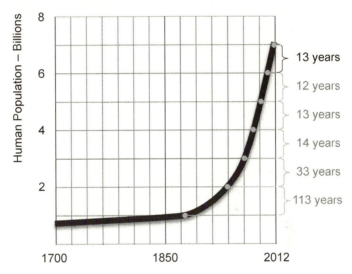

Figure 51
Total Human Population, 1700 – 2000

Observers in the 1960s realized that if the growth rate continued there was certainly a disaster in the making, and mass starvation would result. How, they wondered, could humanity possibly cope with this population explosion?

The Population Explosion

To fully understand the history of the human population and also to gain insight into its future, we go back twelve thousand years, 50 centuries before the Egyptians built their great monuments, to the time when there were no cities, when people were anatomically modern and thus presumably they were capable of communicating and reasoning as we do today, but their technology and thus their economy was, by our standards, utterly rudimentary. Historians estimate that in 10,000 BC the total human population scattered around the world was less than 10 million. The size of the population was a function of the food supply and tribal violence; when there was enough food then the population was stable or growing, but the threat of starvation was always present, and when there wasn't enough food the population contracted while survivors often moved on searching for something to eat. The great pre-Columbian cities of the Yucatan, for example, were apparently abandoned centuries before the arrival of Spanish conquerors when climate change ruined the food supply and the cities were no longer sustainable.

Over the centuries and into the historical era of the great civilizations of China, Egypt, and the Americas starvation was always a threat, and as a result the overall population grew only slowly. Most people lived in the countryside, and growing food was the predominant human endeavor.

During the subsequent millennia, though, humanity's proclivity to experiment led to progressive improvements in agriculture, which led to both trade and thus trading posts, some of which evolved into towns and then into cities. Large scale irrigation systems were developed, as well as monarchies and armies, and various experiments in politics and governance were the subjects of philosophical reasoning and real world application as humans learned how to organize increasingly large collections of static populations. Throughout this period, regardless of type of government, the vast majority of people still remained inhabitants of the countryside where their full time occupation was simply raising enough food to feed themselves and sending the extra to feed the relatively tiny population of the towns.

Powerful empires emerged in Persia, India, China, Egypt, and the Mediterranean in the millennia before Christ, and by the time of European Renaissance around 1500, great cities had grown into finance and transportation hubs in key trading centers around the world. Major cities were nearly always located on great waterways or natural ports, as ship traffic was the key to trade, and trade was the key to wealth.

The flow of products and capital was soon matched by a flow of ideas, and with the invention of printing the rate at which knowledge grew and spread began to accelerate. By 1800 the world's total human population had reached about one billion, but 97 percent of the population was still occupied in producing food. Only about 3 percent, or 30 million, were living in the cities and towns; 970 million were busy farming.

All of that changed with industrialization, of course, as farming became radically more efficient due to machines and fertilizers, and people were gradually pushed or pulled off of the farms and into the cities. Some lost their work and forced to move; other did so by choice, attracted by the abundance of opportunities that cities afforded. By 1900 the total human population had doubled to about 2 billion, so growth that had taken 12,000 years to the first billion was matched in only a century. The population explosion had been unleashed.

The number of people living in cities and towns had increased nearly five-fold to about 140 million, and the nature of urban life evolved rapidly. Cities such as London, powered by coal, London suffered through persistent soot and grime, creating a dark and depressing urban landscape characterized by "dark, Satanic mills," in the words of William Blake.

Urban dwellers worked in the factories of the industrial economy where they made the machines that made farming so much more productive, and where they made all of the other industrial artifacts of modern life, including the early autos as well as skyscrapers and more machines that made more things. It was an astonishing self-reinforcing cycle of economic growth and productivity that led to further and faster growth, which drew still more people into the cities.

The overall population was increasing rapidly due to discoveries in sanitation, health care, and improved nutrition, and the proportion of those living in the cities increased even faster. Urbanization expanded enormously during the 20th century, as the population of city-dwelling humanity ballooned to nearly 3.5 billion people by the year 2000, an increase of 3.35 billion city dwellers in a single century. In 2010 the urban population rose above 50 percent, as about half of all humans were living in cities, and the total human population had reached about 7.3 billion.[124]

Mass Starvation

During the 1800s as industrialization enabled rapid population growth, economist Thomas Malthus predicted that the world would not be able to produce enough food for its booming population, and while there remain regions of world that suffer still from famine and malnutrition where food is chronically insufficient, mass starvation has not occurred. There were great catastrophes in the 20th century, certainly, in the forms of war, genocide, and famines on a scale that had previously been unimaginable, and hundreds of millions suffered and died, and yet still civilization carried on. There was no apocalypse, no collapse, no end to civilization, but instead the progressive adaptation to an ever-changing set of conditions amid a continuing expansion of prosperity. Through it all, as people moved to the cities the lives of countless millions and then billions seemed by many measures to improve. Poverty declined, education expanded, opportunity expanded, and the economy grew.

This version of the 20th century's story is not intended to paint a picture of a perfect world by any means, and yet many of the great accomplishments of civilization cannot be denied. Smallpox was eradicated, deaths from measles plummeted, polio nearly eradicated, a billion people in China and India ascended from sheer poverty to middle class lifestyles, and average lifespans in many nations increased not only by years, but decades.

What we experienced was indeed a population explosion, as humanity expanded from 1 billion to 7.3 billion within a miniscule 200 years. If we look at the graph of 12,000 years of history, the image is entirely startling; the line starts off slowly ascending, and the abruptly it goes nearly vertical.[125]

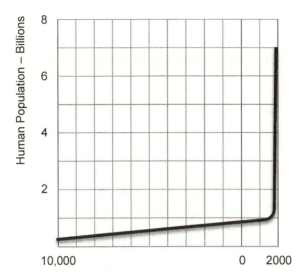

Figure 52
Total Human Population, 10,000 BC – 2,000 AD

A synergy was of course behind it, in the form of burgeoning industrial capabilities that led to improvements in agriculture, which enabled the farming population in the industrialized nations to decline from 97 percent of the population in 1800, to 3 percent of the population in 2000. Impressively, the 3 percent who are farming today manage to produce 10,000 times more food than their ancestors who farmed in 1800.[126]

A quick glance at the population curve presents a scary prospect, however, because the top of the line is pointing almost straight upward. Will the rate of growth continue its vertical streak? Will the human population continue to expand at the same rate, giving us a world of 10 billion, and then 12 billion, and then 15 or 20 billion people?

With the booming population explosion during the 1960s, and thus when the likelihood of continuing increases seemed inevitable, a great wave of concern swept across many nations, and numerous studies and books called attention to the impending population disaster. Paul Ehrlich called it "the population bomb," and a group of scholars at The Club of

Rome published an influential study called *The Limits to Growth.*[127]

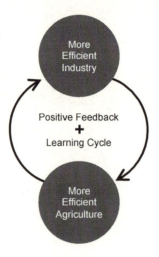

Figure 53
**More Efficiency in Industry > More Efficiency in Agriculture >
More Efficiency in Industry**
Learning to do things better is a self-reinforcing, positive spiral.

It seemed that Malthus was right after all, and that starvation and doomsday were just around the corner. The dire warnings concerning the disastrous growth seemed to be speaking of the inevitable, for there was apparently no way to control the population boom. Demographers, those who study and forecast future population trends, and the rest of us as well, were justifiably worried. Even with the monumental improvements in agricultural productivity over the previous 150 years, could these increases in food production efficiency can be continued? Could we possibly feed 10 or 20 billion? And was it even possible for the Earth to produce that much food? Perhaps Malthus was correct, even if the timing of his prediction was a century premature.

At the height of the population explosion the human population increased by 1 billion over the course of just over a decade, and China faced the prospect of a huge increase in the number of children which meant that in bad harvest years it would not be able to feed its people and starvation would return on a large scale.

Having just lived through the disastrous Cultural Revolution when mass starvation did indeed occur, the prospect was vivid in memory. Consequently, China adopted and enforced the "one child" policy, which limited most families to one child. By some estimates this policy resulted in a reduction of more than 200 million Chinese, who would otherwise have been born.

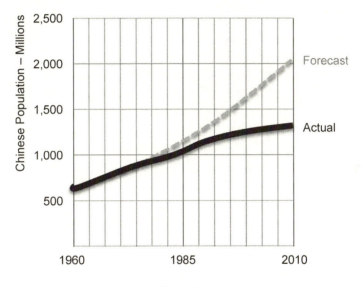

Figure 54
Population of China[128]

While it did perhaps slow the growth rate of the Chinese population, there were and remain serious consequences which cannot be ignored, including large scale social and ethical issues, selective abortions of female children and then the emergence of an entire generation of one-child families that are experiencing adverse social consequences which are only now being recognized and understood. Today young Chinese men outnumber young women by more than 30 million, and if most of them wish to marry they will have to find wives outside of China.

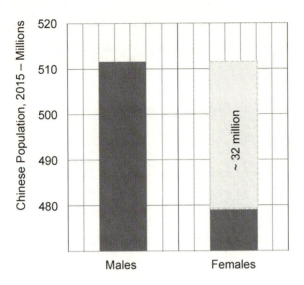

Figure 55
Chinese Men and Women[129]

No other country attempted to enforce a one child policy, although India indulged in forced sterilizations for a time. More recently, however many nations, including now Japan, have tried without success to encourage women to have *more* babies.

What Happened Instead: Urbanization

Quite unexpectedly, urbanization has proven to have an immediate impact on the rate of population growth. Urban families, it turns out, simply choose to have fewer children. It is also a universal process, as the pattern is the same on every continent. On the global scale this has had monumental consequences, as the continuing trend of urbanization is slowing the rate of population growth for the first time in 200 years.

To understand the impact of urbanization on population growth it's helpful to think of a family as an economic unit. Not always, but in many cases, the decision to have children is based on the economic situation of the parents, and the expected economic impact that children will have on a family.

And it's quite obvious that the economic impact of children is enormously different for those living and working on a farm than for those in a city. On a farm of sufficient size children play the vitally important role of free laborers. They can produce in food value far more than they consume, so they are net producers, and since the amount of work required to maintain a farm is essentially infinite, farm families have tended throughout modern history to be large. It was quite common for a farm couple to have three, four, five, or six children, or more, and even taking into account the higher rate of infant mortality that was prevalent for centuries, industrial societies where agriculture was in the process of becoming mechanized experienced population explosions because their farms could easily employ many more workers who could in turn produce much more food.

Another factor also played a role in the decision to have many children. Because farming is such hard work, by age forty or fifty most people can no longer sustain the difficult physical demands, and children are thus a form of retirement planning in the hope and expectation that at least some of the children would survive into adulthood, take over the operation of the farm, and care for their aging parents.

Once industrialization was established, year after year and in every culture around the world the proportion of people living on the farms declined as people abandoned the farms for more enticing opportunities in the cities. Today it's quite common for aging parents to remain on the farms while their grown children relocate to the city, a trend that brings with it a entire set of social and economic challenges and burdens for both the parents and the children.

Why do they come?

And why especially do they come, when for most people moving to the city means giving up clean air for polluted air, giving up open spaces for a tiny dwelling in a crowded slum or favela, and it means taking major economic risk in the process?

Some choose to move because they want their children to have a better education, and some to have more economic opportunity to make a better life for themselves. Many move because life on a subsistence farm is endless days of hard work, long hours at hard labor with few opportunities for entertainment, whereas the city is alive with diversions and amusements from morning until night. Others move because in the city they'll have better opportunities to find a spouse, or for access to health care, which is limited or entirely nonexistent in the countryside.

Indeed, throughout history people have always been drawn to the city and they have been willing to endure dirt, dust, and congestion to reap the potential benefits. Hence, after World War I Americans realized that the farm boys who had gone to France to fight the Germans would not be the same when they came back, and farming might not be so attractive to them: "How you going to keep'em down on the farm after they've seen Paree?"

The same story line pertains to all of the world's great and enchanting cities, and even to cities that aren't very interesting at all – but they're still better than an isolated existence on a small farm. On all continents, and in all cultures, the lure of urban living and urban opportunity has been universal and nearly irresistible.

Often this trend was accelerated by government policy. In Germany, for example, a national program was instituted to recruit rural families to move to the cities and work in the factories because it was clearly understood by the government leadership that factories embodied the future of the economy. If Germany was to become a world power it must have a strong industrial system, and this led to the government to introduce the first wage and hour laws and the first nationalized retirement benefits system in 1880.

Industrial workers tended, of course, to live in cities that were adjacent to their workplaces and to transportation hubs, and in these cities the lives and lifestyles of the families were quite different than on the farms. In the cities, once child labor was outlawed, the majority of children did not work were thus not producers of economic value; instead, they consumed. Children living in the city require food, clothing, space, time, and money, particularly money for education. The economics of family life for urban families were then and remain today entirely different than for rural families, and thus it is generally the case that by the second or third generation in the cities the average number of children that the average family chooses to have has declined from a half dozen or more children, to about two.

Two children, of course, is slightly below the overall population replacement rate. (Technically, 2.1 children is the actual replacement rate due to other causes of mortality.) Hence, when women on average have more than 2.1 children the population grows, and when they have fewer it declines.

What has happened, then, to the overall birth rate? The logic is clear: today, half of the world's population is urban, and as the average urban family has two children, the overall birth rate has begun to decline. In most cases, this is due to nothing other than the simple economics of family finance: habitat space is a scarce commodity, there generally isn't room for a lot of kids, and since they consume rather than produce until their teenage years most families can't afford to have many.

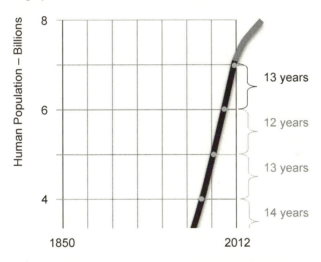

Figure 56
Slowing of the Population Growth Rate
It seems that the world's growth rate peaked between 2000 and 2010.

Further, the children that they do have are often spared from work entirely through a long period of education because education is a priority for the parents not only out of a sense of love and responsibility, but also as a matter of self interest. In most of the world where people are not able

175

to set aside money for their own retirement and where there are no government funded pension plans, the greater the children's future earnings the more likely they will be able to care for their aging parents. Hence, parents invest in education because a son or daughter who is a doctor or a lawyer will be much more likely to be able to support them in their old age. In the city, again, family size becomes an economic choice much as it was on the farm, but the logical choice in the city is opposite of the logical choice in the country.

In addition, of course, in cities women have more opportunities to receive education and as they become more educated they develop their own professional aspirations, they gain skills and experience, and as their economic power increases they become less dependent on men and assert their own right to choose if they want children at all and how many children to have. They also gain access to birth control, and once industrial societies began to produce reliable techniques for birth control, urban families adopted them on a large scale.

Push and Pull:
The Two Forces Driving Urbanization

In most nations where a high rate of high urban population growth today it occurs not because of high birth rates, but due to continuing migration from the farms to the cities. After all, most of the 3.5 billion who remain on the farms want to move to the cities too.

And why do they? Some are pushed; others are pulled. As agriculture becomes industrialized it simply doesn't require a lot of people to run a farm. In the American state of Nebraska, for example, as few as three people can farm as much as 10,000 acres, whereas fifty years ago it took one hundred people to do that work. So most farming jobs simply no longer exist. (And consequently Nebraska is one of many American farm states that is in the process of depopulating; the majority of seniors who graduate from Nebraska high schools leave the state.)

This is of course true not only in Nebraska, but worldwide. In China, for example, about 25 million people have left the farms for the cities every year since 1990, a total of more than 500 million migrants who have given up the clean, fresh air and hard, honest work of the countryside for the dirty, crowded, polluted air, and the great economic opportunities of China's enormous and still-growing cities. People are voting, in essence, with their feet and their suitcases.

And this trend, the trend of migration into the cities, remains a powerful global phenomenon.

In summary, then, people are choosing to live in the city, and in the city they choose to have far fewer children, and this brings us to the fourth revolution. It seems that the population bomb has defused itself, and if current trends hold, and there is a lot of evidence that they will, then the world's population could peak as early as 2040 – 2050, and by the end of the 21st century the total human population could be back to the level that it is today, around 7.3 billion. Further, if current trends hold then by the end of the 21st century 95 percent of the total population will be living in cities, meaning that the aggregate urban population will be around 7 billion.

On a graph, the history of human population growth from 10,000 BC to 2150 AD (so 150 years beyond the time frame of the graph we looked at previously) shows this the graph on the following page.

We are just now beginning to experience this fundamental change in the structure of the population, a revolution in urbanization that will see the addition of 3.5 – 4 billion city dwellers over the next 85 years, and the restructuring of the world economy to account for these changes.

The implications are enormous, for what's coming is a (another) monumental shift in the very structure of society and in the structure of the global economy. Everything, in other words, is about to change on a fourth dimension.

So what will happen when population growth slows, comes to full halt, and then starts to decline? No one knows for sure because it's never happened in the modern economy before; hence, this is precisely what the fourth revolution is all about. It's easy to see, though, that a fundamental change in the rate of population growth will impact on the world's social, cultural, and economic life in decisive and fundamental ways, which we will now explore.

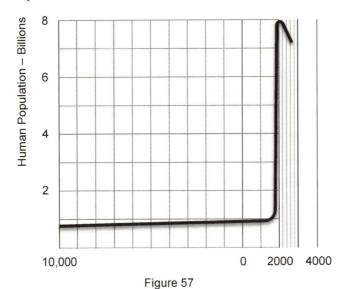

Figure 57
World Human Population, 10,000 BC – 2150 AD
The period 2000 – 2150 is a forecast. At the scale of this graph, the last 150
years is only a suggestion of a population peak and then decline.

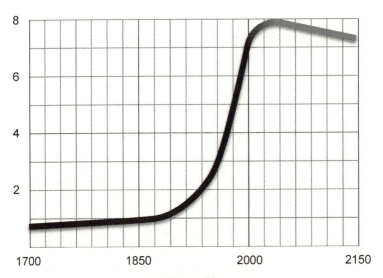

Figure 58
World Human Population, 1700 – 2150
The period 2015 – 2150 is a forecast.

178

From Boom to Bust

When the population growth rate slows or declines then the average age of the population increases. It sounds simple, but the social and economic consequences are anything but.

This is significant because the industrialized economic boom of the last 200 years was fueled not only by fossil fuels but also by rapid population growth. As billions of young people came into the work force they provided a steady supply of labor to operate the machines and drive the trucks and work in the shops, and also a steady supply of new consumer who wanted to set up households and buy more products to fill them, and then to have children to keep the cycle going. The number of new, young, able, and high-consuming workers significantly outnumbered the older people, and the combination of their productivity and their consumption kept the economy vibrant.

But as the growth rate slows and then reverses the ratio of young workers to older people will invert, and this is quite likely to have a doubly negative effect on the economy. Most of the older people will already have stopped being economically productive and at the same time they will have moved into the stage of their lives when they buy far fewer consumer goods. But at the same time they will need far more of society's resources for retirement and health care. Many more older workers who wish to retire, but fewer younger workers to pay for their pensions and health care needs, creates a significant economic inversion.

The economies of the world are not structured to handle this, even though the single largest social expenditure in all of the developed nations, already today, is care for the elderly. And thus as more and more of society's resources become dedicated to caring for the elderly and both the number of elderly increases and the proportion of elderly also increases, society will be forced to undergo a fundamental economic transformation that no one, in fact, understands. Will it be an eldercare apocalypse? Or a senior renaissance?

Perhaps it sounds a bit speculative and theoretical, but in fact it is entirely practical and of fundamental importance to all of us. For a preview of what's coming, let's consider what's happening today in Japan.

The (Transformed) View from Japan

The rural populations of most of the developed nations, including Canada, the US, Japan, and Northern Europe, constitute less than 20 percent of the national total. In the US, according to its 2010 census, about 60 million people, or 19.3 percent do not live in cities. In Canada, about 19 percent of the population is rural, while in France it's 20 percent and in Germany 24. But in Japan it's only 8 percent, which also makes Japan the most urbanized of all nations, other than the tiny city-states that include Singapore, Hong Kong, Monaco, Lichtenstein and Vatican City.

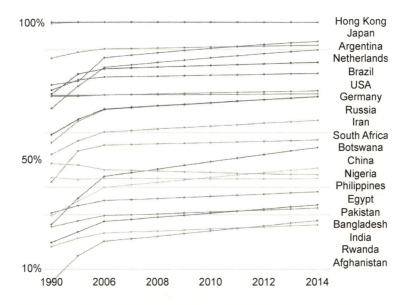

Figure 59
Table of Urbanization[130] [131]
In this World Bank graphic, Hong Kong at the top of the chart shows 100% urbanization; at the bottom, Afghanistan was about 5% urbanized in 1990, and is now about 25% urbanized. The list of countries on the right corresponds with each of the lines, from top to bottom. Hence, Japan is shown as the second most urbanized, Argentina third, etc. The following figure shows the same data in map form for 2015.

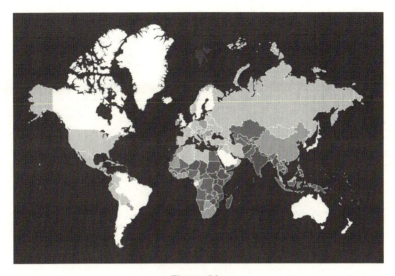

Figure 60
Map of Urbanization[132] [133]
This maps is based on the same data set as Figure 59.
2015: White = Most Urbanized; Black = Least Urbanized.

As the world's most urbanized nation Japan is getting a very early experience of the future that is possibly or even inevitably destined for the rest of us as we follow the path of nearly total urbanization. It's a future that's significantly different than the present.

Japan's industrial revolution started a bit later than in Europe and North America, but by the mid-1800s the country was engaged in rapid industrialization. Consequently, it was at that time that it began to make the transition from a rural to an urbanized nation. Population growth accelerated with agricultural productivity increases, and continued steadily throughout the 20th century.

But by the 1980s already 90 percent of Japanese were living in urban settings, and for the reasons mentioned above, population growth slowed to almost nothing as Japanese families consistently chose to have fewer and fewer children. Then, by 2000, growth had stopped entirely and started to decline.

181

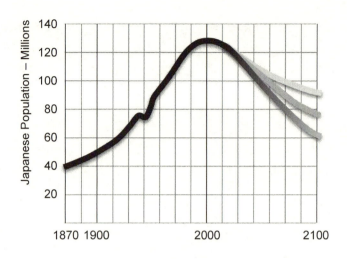

Figure 61
Japanese Population 1870 – 2100
The graph shows three forecasts, high, medium, and low. Any of the
three will likely be socially and economically disastrous.

As I mentioned above, to sustain a stable level of population the necessary birth rate is about 2.1 children per female, but in Japan the rate has fallen below 2 children per woman down to 1.4,[134] meaning that in the absence of significant immigration the national population is inevitably going to decline. Japan has never been particularly welcoming to immigrants, and so based on current trends demographers predict that by 2100, the end of the current century, Japan's population will be about half of its current number. It will decline, that is, from a peak of 130 million in 1990, to as few as 65 million.

This will undoubtedly be a complete social and economic catastrophe for the nation, as the population decline will inevitably be accompanied by a significant contraction in economic activity. Less people working will produce fewer goods. And with fewer people overall, there will also be fewer people consuming so the economy overall will necessarily shrink. Further, with a declining population the proportion of older people to youth in society will increase, and as I noted above, since most older citizens are not active members of the workforce, but many of them do consume considerable amounts of state-funded health care, health care costs overall will increase, probably substantially, and so will pension and retirement costs. It's a dangerous combination of factors that implies a significant national decline if not worse.

If this hypothesis is valid then the underlying trends must already be in place. Is there any evidence of that? Or, what's been happening with Japan's economy over the last 25 years, since these trends began to take hold? Since 1990 Japan has been in the grips of persistent economic malaise with widespread economic stagnation despite repeated attempts by of a succession of governments to turn the situation around through a variety of policy prescriptions, none of which have worked. To date, no amount of economic policy maneuvering has overcome the persistent facts of demographics, and so the Japanese malaise deepens. This of course bodes very badly for Japan, and if it is true that Japan's present is our future, then it's an interesting warning for the entire industrialized world. What Japan needs today, and what most of the rest of the world may need tomorrow, is in fact nothing less than a new economic model.

And since in the realm of geopolitics economic power is closely linked to military power, we can readily foresee that Japan's military capacity is likely to decline just as the military power of its mighty neighbor China is on the increase.

Indeed, China's increasing economic and therefore military strength is certainly one of the most significant elements in any scenario of the future not only of Asia, but of the entire world, and what's pertinent to our discussion here is the point that Japan's population decline will lead to a geopolitical decline as well, exactly in parallel with China's ascent. The historical tensions between the two nations are centuries old, but they've been worsening in recent years; the population-driven dynamics facing both nations could certainly lead to a quite different geopolitical situation in East Asia in the coming years than in even the very recent past. A quick overview of China's situation follows here, while a more detailed discussion of geopolitics and China's central role in it is the specific topic of Chapter 11.

The View from China

As I mentioned above, since the 1979 decision to open China's economy to capitalism, about 500 million people have moved from Chinese farms to its cities. This decision, made by Mao's successor Deng Xiao Ping, became the largest mass migration in human history. It has fueled China's economic growth by providing laborers for factories in exactly the same way that Western nations grew during the century and a half between 1800 – 1950, but China did it in the acutely compressed period of only 30 years.

25 million per year

Figure 62
Rural to Urban Migration in China
About 500 million people have moved from the farms in the center of the country to the east coast cities since 1990.

The economy began to boom in the late 1980s and it didn't stop, which was both enabled by and fed by the mostly voluntary transit of half a billion people, most of whom moved to the cities either to take jobs as low paid workers in the factories or as laborers in the construction industry that worked at breakneck speed to build enough housing, workplaces, shops, and infrastructure for that same half-billion. It has been a self-reinforcing cycle, funded by China's exports, as it ascended the world economic ladder as the low cost manufacturing provider to everyone else.

If you visited any city in China during the 1990s or 2000s, perhaps the most striking feature of the skyline was the construction cranes, huge numbers of them visible in every direction, resulting in a nation that has the largest urban population on Earth. Official statistics on urbanization in China are suspect, as the nation maintains controls on where people may live that results in large numbers of urbanized but non-reported migrant workers, but in any case it's clear that the urban population has expanded to include more than 50 percent of the nation's population, which means that China has more people living in cities than the entire population of any other nation except India.

And apparently the trend is nowhere near stopping. It's been estimated by the Chinese Ministry of Housing and Urban-Rural Development that during the 15 years between 2010 and 2025, an additional 300 million Chinese who have been living in rural areas will move into the cities. This continuing fast pace of urbanization, if it occurs, will create at least 1 trillion RMB, or $160 billion in annual investment opportunities in building water supply systems, waste treatment, heating and other public utilities in the cities alone, not to mention the housing, workplaces, and shops to serve them.

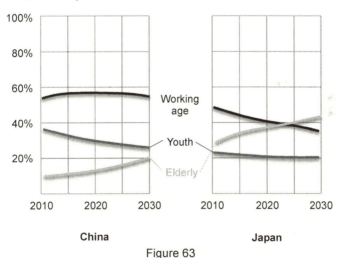

China   **Japan**

Figure 63

Chinese and Japanese Population Forecasts
The percent of the total population in each nation in three age categories. The curves match up astonishingly well, and within 20 years China will apparently be in the difficult demographic situation that Japan is in now.

Hence, the transition from a rural population to an urban one is largely a self-feeding economic process that literally creates national wealth; it can create massive wealth when it occurs at this scale. And while India is the only other nation with nearly that many people who could become urban residents, the overall momentum toward cities is indeed a global phenomenon. In every culture, in nearly every nation, in every corner of the world, the vast majority of people prefer urban settings and lifestyles.

	European Nations	Primary Reasons
1	Albania	low birth rate, emigration
2	Belarus *	low birth rate
3	Bosnia and Herzegovina	low birth rate, emigration, war
4	Bulgaria	low birth rate, high death rate, emigration
5	Croatia	low birth rate, emigration, war
6	Czech Republic	low birth rate
7	Estonia	low birth rate
8	Germany *	low birth rate
9	Greece	low birth rate, economic crisis
10	Hungary	low birth rate
11	Italy	low birth rate
12	Latvia	low birth rate, emigration
13	Lithuania	low birth rate, emigration
14	Moldova	low birth rate
15	Poland	low birth rate, emigration
16	Portugal	low birth rate, economic crisis, emigration
17	Romania	low birth rate, high death rate, emigration
18	Russia	high death rate, low birth rate
19	Serbia	low birth rate, high death rate, emigration
20	Ukraine	low birth rate
	Non-European Nations	
21	Cook Islands	emigration
22	Cuba	emigration, low birth rate
23	Japan	low birth rate
24	Niue	emigration
25	Northern Mariana Is.	emigration
26	Micronesia	emigration
27	Puerto Rico	low birth rate, economic crisis
28	Syria	war

* Net population increase largely due to Syrian refugee immigration

Figure 64
List of Nations with Declining Populations[135]

Most trend data is from 2013-2014. Various statisticians and demographers offer different assessments, and these trends change from year to year. Nevertheless, these figures and their underlying trends have been fairly consistent for more than a decade.

But as the experience in Japan also shows, there are limits; when everyone has moved to the cities and there are no more migrants, and when the lower birth rate associated with urbanization takes hold in a culture, then the entire structure of the economy undergoes a shift. And of course if this were occurring only in Japan then we could attribute it to some particular quirk or characteristic of those people or that place, but it isn't. Around the world there are about 30 nations whose populations are declining, including nearly all the nations of Eastern Europe, some in Asia, and many in Africa.

Figure 65
Map of the European Nations Listed in Figure 64
Nations that are depopulating as of 2015 are shown in gray.

The prime cause is nearly everywhere is declining birth rates, which is also exacerbated by emigration, and early deaths due to tobacco and heart disease. While the combination of factors varies from country to country, the results are about the same everywhere: the economic vitality of a nation declines as it enters a declining cycle of lower economic productivity and higher health care and pensions costs. This sometimes results in accelerated mortality due to poverty and widespread depression, and thus the problems may worsen. It's a downward spiral from which there seems to be almost no way of escaping.

China, with its 1.2 billion citizens, will experience the impacts of the aging population more intensely than any other nation. The vast majority of all of the world's cases of senility, Alzheimer's disease, Parkinson's disease, and indeed all age-related ailments will occur in China as the nation's vast population of now-urbanized young and middle aged citizens reach their sixties and seventies in enormous numbers. This will put a tremendous strain on China's economy, just as it's doing now in so many other places as well. Demographers forecast that China's population will peak within 20 to 30 years, and then it, too, will see the birthrate drop below replacement level and then overall population decline.

Living Longer

While birth rates are dropping worldwide, average lifespans for both women and men continue to increase due to continuing improvements in the quality of health care and in our ability to alter genetics and to manage gerontology, due essentially, that is, to countless breakthroughs in the science and technology of health care.   Organ transplants, joint replacements, improved and age-specific nutrition, constant health monitoring and augmented diagnosis, better treatments for chronic diseases, and enormous improvements in our understanding of aging itself all play a part in increasing our longevity. Hence, many children born after 1990 and certainly many born after 2000 have an excellent chance to live to be 100 years old, and with the benefit of medical breakthroughs that are occurring today and those that will occur tomorrow their life spans could well reach 120 or even 150 years. The social and cultural prospects are fascinating.

But the finances are challenging. The structure of our economies today probably could not support such large populations of aged citizens, and the situation is made more acute because in the developed nations there is a widely held cultural norm and expectation that retirement from the work force occurs around age 65. While many continue to work into their 70s, official policy and practice that call for retirement at 65 has been built into the national retirement systems of nations including Germany and the US for decades. Where, you might well wonder, did this number come from? After all, what's to say that retirement should take place around 65? Why not age 50? Or age 80? What's so special about 65?

The answer is an historical artifact of industrialization that occurred in the world's first state-sponsored retirement system, established in Germany in the 1880s under the leadership of Chancellor Otto von Bismarck, the legendary and visionary figure who was a renowned diplomat and also quite skilled social engineer. It was Bismarck who instituted the German retirement system, the purpose of which, as I noted above, was to help Germany industrialize and thus to become a world power. At the time, Germany was transitioning from a fragmented collection of small, regional kingdoms into a unified and Prussian-led nation, and Bismarck had great aspirations for its future.

> In a single generation to about 1870, industrialization took Germany from being some of the North European Plains' poorest people to some of the richest, and enabled them to impose decisive defeats in four significant conflicts that had preyed upon them for centuries (Poland, Denmark, Austria, and France). By 1900 Germany's many industrial centers had grown to the point that had more major industrialized cities than the rest of Europe combined. It was the first country to develop mass universities and research labs, and then to link the two directly into local governments and corporations, giving German industry the ability to source everything from loans to staff to scientific research.[136]

The North's victory over the South in the American Civil War had demonstrated decisively to every military leader in the world that the future of military power lay in industrial might, and thus the German retirement system was designed specifically to persuade German farmers to leave the life of the soil and come to the factories where Germany's industrial future was being created.

The German system initially set the retirement age at 70, and since at that time the average life expectancy of a German worker in 1880 was 45 years, the system thus provided retirement benefits to only a tiny proportion of the total working population. Nevertheless, it provided an effective source of psychological reassurance to German workers. The program was funded jointly by the nation, the employer, and the workers, and as long as the average life expectancy was less than the retirement age, the system functioned well. It was only by exception that anyone reached the age at which they could receive retirement pay, but decade by decade as average life expectancies increased, a system that collected a small amount from everyone but paid benefits to a tiny proportion of them is instead expected to fund the retirement of everyone, and not just for a few moderately comfortable years, but for many very comfortable decades. No nation on Earth has devised an economic model that can succeed under these conditions, a situation of limited capital accumulation but nearly unlimited capital expenditure.[137]

When we add to this picture the fact the overall health care costs are rising steadily and quickly, we see that there is the potential for an economic catastrophe ahead. Japan is already confronted with that catastrophe, and leaders in many other nations can foresee that Japan's fate may be their own.

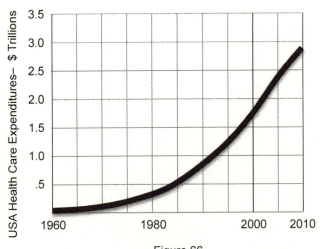

Figure 66
USA Health Care Spending[138]

It's not difficult to see that the expectation of retirement at age 65 is going to be abandoned, but it's also obvious that there will be widespread resistance to any such change. The economic crisis in which Greece found itself in 2014–2015 is indeed largely a consequence of these very dynamic.

By 2014 Greece had sustained a persistent, recession-induced trade deficit that sapped capital from the country, but it still permitted workers to retire at a relatively young age. Tax revenues further declined due to rampant tax evasion, which lowered the government's available funds while the cost of its current employees retirees passed 75 percent of primary government spending. To make up the difference the government borrowed extensively, but managed to hide this fact from its European partners until the debts grew very large and the 2008 global financial crises exposed the entire charade.[139] In essence, the Greek government made promises to its current and future pensioners that it was unable to fulfill, and when the government tried to correct the imbalance there was massive public opposition, regardless of underlying economic realities.

The crisis in Greece has led to a situation we might identify as "intergenerational warfare," in which younger workers are expected to subsidize the needs of retirees. But once the youth realize the full scope of what's happening they naturally feel exploited and oppose this.   The retirees, meanwhile, made an agreement with the government decades ago under quite different economic conditions, and they expect the government to honor it nonetheless.

This dynamic is not just prevalent in Greece, though. In America, where public schools are generally funded at the local and state levels and the national government plays only a small financial role there has emerged over the last few decades a growing conflict between the financial needs of schools and those of retirees. Since the elderly vote but 3rd graders don't, the needs of retirees have generally been protected while the schools have seen significant cutbacks. In California, America's most populous state with about 35 million citizens, the largest budget items are schools for the young, at $50 billion, colleges and universities at $14 billion, and pension and health care payments at $52 billion (which includes all health and human services, not just care for the elderly).[140]

Persisting inter-generational warfare is written into California law in a state statute known as "Proposition 13" that establishes limits on the taxes that homeowners can be required to pay toward public education. When the elderly organized themselves to get Proposition 13 enacted into law, they were telling their grandchildren, in effect, that, "Paying for a good education is your problem."

The situation in California is a small example of a larger problem that arises throughout the US and indeed worldwide as we are entering a period wherein the needs of children to pay for their educations and the needs of seniors to pay for pensions and health care are coming starkly into direct conflict. When there isn't enough money for both, what choices do we make?

The problem could be significantly worsened because of the first of the four revolutions, the emergence of ever more useful technology, leads to huge numbers of workers who are displaced by robots. This will, of course, only make a difficult situation still more complicated by increasing the numbers of unemployed just as the number of retirees is also expanding. The vast uncertainties concerning both the technology of robotics and the economics of a robotic workforce make it impossible to foresee how the situation will play out, and while there are some quite interesting optimistic scenarios, there are also many reasons to think that there are great dangers ahead.

We will explore these themes and their overlaps further in Part 2, where we turn our focus to modeling how things may unfold over the coming decades by creating future scenarios that examine various ways that these forces may unfold.

All Roads Lead to Rome:
The Importance of Urban Design

As we have seen, cities exert a tremendous influence over the people who live in them, as they are the container in which families, cultures, and economies form, develop, and express themselves. However, not all cities are created equal.

During the centuries of the Roman rule throughout the Mediterranean region, for example, it was widely understood that all roads led to Rome, the empire's most supremely important city. Resources poured into the great city and authority flowed out from it. Everything returned eventually to the center of power, influence, culture, and wealth that Rome embodied.

National capitals, major trading cities, centers of the arts, and centers of learning, science, and technology all play such a role for their nations and regions, and as a result they attract more than their fair share of the population. All roads in Great Britain lead to London, which captures more than 50 percent of all of the kingdom's economic activity, while many of Britain's other major cities decline even as London's boom continues into its second millennium after its founding as a Roman village in AD 43.

Life in Kenya is centered on Nairobi; life in Thailand on Bangkok; life in France on Paris, and so it goes. Each nation's seat of power inevitably draws to itself more people, more wealth, and more activity, while peripheral destinations decline in importance, and many fall into a negative spiral. Hence, while Detroit was losing half it's population during the collapse of the American auto industry during the 1900s and 2000s, San Francisco and Silicon Valley were steadily gaining jobs and people in the technology boom. Both cities are severely stressed by these forces, but given the choice, few would wish their city to be more like Detroit.

While every nation once did want to nurture it's own version Detroit and become a massive industrial powerhouse, now they strive to create their own version of Silicon Valley. Whether it's the Silicon Bog of Ireland, the Silicon Plateau of Bangalore, or the Chilecon Valley of Santiago, a compelling destination that combines deep technology savvy with a powerful start-up culture to enable powerful economic creativity is now the magic formula.[141]

And for good reason. Stanford University sits at the very heart of Silicon Valley, and many attribute the influence of the University for much of the success of the companies in the region. Two Stanford professors recently calculated that the University's aggregate economic impact, as measured by the total revenues of companies that were started by Stanford alumni, is a staggering \$2.7 trillion per year.[142] If Stanford and these companies were a nation, it would rank as the seventh or eighth largest economy in the world.

As yet no city or region has come close to replicating the dynamism of the Silicon Valley original, but there is certainly every reason to try. However, a large part of the reason that no legitimate copies have yet emerged is that Silicon Valley was no overnight success. The region's first technology entrepreneurs got their start around 1905, so what you see today is the culmination of more than century of learning, investment and development.

That a century of concentrated effort with countless failures along the way has defined a formula for success, for Silicon Valley, with Stanford and its rival and neighbor University of California at its heart, is a rich mixture of highly trained engineers, ambitious entrepreneurs, abundant capital, and all of the professional services needed to transform ideas into thriving businesses. It is, therefore, a rich ecosystem of technology, business, and culture, which is exactly what makes great cities great.

So while it's evident that large scale urbanization is fully under way and appears to be inexorable, and that unless something quite dramatic occurs, 95 percent of the human population will be living in cities by the end of this century, it's also clear that not all cities are equally attractive. The world's largest cities continue to attract more than their share of new residents due to a powerful combination of economic and aesthetic factors. The economic ones relate to opportunity, of course, as large cities offer far more opportunities for good quality employment and for the entrepreneurially minded. But we might also make a distinction between large cities and great large ones by pointing to the economic vitality, cultural dynamism, natural beauty, and effective infrastructure that makes some cities stand out as exceptional.

Beijing has been a world capital for nearly 700 years, and today it's possible to suggest that all roads, railroads, and flights in China lead to Tiananmen Square and the gates of the Forbidden City. Or perhaps they lead to China's other social and economic powerhouse, Shanghai, which was itself founded much earlier, in the fifth century, established as an official town in 751, and which is today the world's largest shipping container port and one of it's largest cities, with a population of about 25 million.

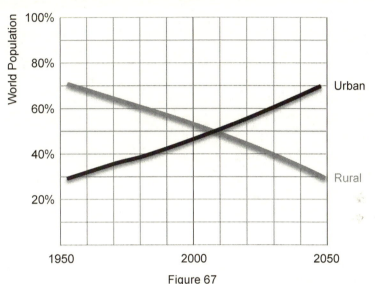

Figure 67
World Population, 1950 – 2050, By Percent
The steady shift from rural to urban.

Yet neither Beijing nor Shanghai is China's largest city, for that distinction belongs to Guangzhou, a city of nearly 45 million along the great Pearl River that was established in the centuries before Christ.

As the 21st century unfolds civic leaders everywhere are discovering through good luck and good planning, or as the sad result of bad luck or bad planning, that the exceptional cities are disproportionately more successful because they are the magnets that draw to themselves the exceptional individuals who become leaders in their fields. Leaders, in turn, attract investment in new businesses which lead to the creation of new cultural landmarks and urban amenities, and to continuing efforts to improve mass transit and the quality sometimes called "liveability."

Just as Stanford's global economic impact is unmatched, cities that rise to the level of exceptional experience the positive spiral through which success cultivates further success. That is, it will until something happens to change the basic structure, which is exactly what happened to Detroit when the auto industry collapsed, and indeed to Rome when the Empire collapsed 15 centuries ago.

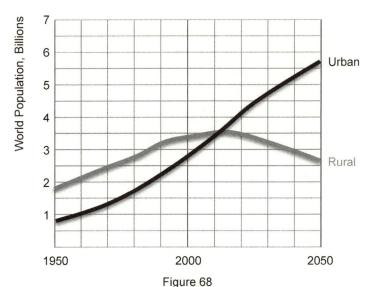

Figure 68
World Population, 1950 – 2050, By Numbers
The steady shift from rural to urban. If the decline in rural population as shown from 2010 to 2050 is correct, this will also indicate that the overall population explosion has ended.

The Urban Design Future

And it seems that something major is already in the process of happening that could indeed change how we look at today's cities, and tomorrow's. From a strategic perspective this may be the most important of all.

According to the Shanghai city government, most of the city is located at a height of about 4 meters above sea level, straddling the Huangpo River as it winds the last few miles into the East China Sea of the Pacific Ocean. Shanghai, this is, is the epitome of a coastal city, of which there are hundreds of them around the world.

If, due to global climate change all the ice in Greenland were to melt, what then? Scientists calculate that the world's oceans would rise about 7 meters,[143] which would of course submerge a great deal of Shanghai.

And it would do the same to New York, Mumbai, Amsterdam, Venice, Lagos, Rio, Sydney, Istanbul, Tokyo, and to Dacca, Hong Kong, Rotterdam, Houston and Bangkok. Currently about 40 percent of the population, 3 billion in all, live within 100 kilometers of the ocean, and if the process of climate change does cause inexorable melting of the polar ice caps then a great many of these will become uninhabitable, and the vast majority of their populations will be forced to relocate. Where, then, would they go?

Many, most actually, would probably go to new cities, because climate change could oblige humanity to undertake the largest project ever imagined in human history, and thus also the single largest economic project ever attempted, the relocation of 3 billion. This would also be, without question, the greatest entrepreneurial opportunity that ever existed, the possibility of literally rebuilding human civilization by constructing great new cities from bare ground.

What would make them great? Would we create cleverly-designed, ecologically friendly, effortlessly easy-to-use, public transit enabled urban habitats rich with abundant recreation, beautiful architecture, scenic beauty, centers of learning and creativity to nurture the dreams and aspirations of future generations of human inventiveness?

Or would we instead construct row upon drab row of mindlessly repeated apartment blocks such as the ones that surround Beijing and so many other cities, mile upon mile of sad and lifeless concrete squalid dormitory boxes of ugly repetition that sap our energy and burden us with poor transportation, built on mindless road grids stretching to the horizon in numbing repetition, and punctuated with endless strip malls.

This may well be the choice that we will face within a decade or two, and in fact regardless of the immanence and eventual impact of climate change and melted ice, civic leaders already face this choice today. They can enhance their current cities to provide for and promote effective and humane infrastructures, engage in more thoughtful patterns of development, promote sensitivity to environmental concerns, and provide for abundant recreation and cultural enrichment. Or they can promote continuing suburbanization further and further from the vitality of the city, lifeless and cultureless expanses of highways, tract homes, and strip malls.

What is perhaps most interesting about this is that even without considering the impact of climate change, a massive construction boom is apparently going to happen anyway. Because if roughly three billion people are going to move to the cities over the coming eight decades then cities will experience an average urban growth rate of about 37 million each year. That's housing for 37 million, and all the roads, pipelines, sewers, power systems, shopping, and workplaces as well.

And if in addition to this the rising oceans make low-lying coastal regions uninhabitable, then a couple billion more who will be flooded out of their existing cities will also need new places to live. Consequently, all the industries that enable urbanization are probably in for a boom, or an even more massive boom, and thus the magnitude of the effort will be, by nearly any standard, astonishingly huge. Perhaps it will be the biggest real estate development opportunity in human history.

Because there are meaning differences between cities and the most employable people will choose a great city over a mediocre one, investing in great and inspiring urban designs instead of mindless urban squalor may be one of the key choices that national and civic leaders will confront in the decades ahead. But regardless of which approach they choose, it is more than likely that the 21st century will continue the story of urbanization, and one of the key plot lines in that story in that the vast majority of humans eventually becoming city dwellers. As a result, population growth will peak and then begin to decline, and consequently the economy will for better or worse, be transformed by a new balance between young workers and retirees. And perhaps robots.

Under Water

In the event that rising oceans contribute significantly to magnitude of construction that's going to be required, however, there is also going to be a significant financing problem to address. For if the low-lying coastal areas are indeed going to be flooded then that real estate which was previously valued very highly is going to become worthless.

In many cities, the areas closest to the ocean and thus most susceptible to flooding are the most exclusive and desirable, the places where the wealthy build luxury high-rise condos and seafront mansions, and where many corporations choose to locate their headquarters. Visualize the luxury neighborhoods of Miami Beach, the Bollywood neighborhood of Mumbai, the palazzo of Venice, the high rises in Lagos.

The aggregate value of all these buildings and the land they sit on is in the trillions, but if the value of all that real estate is wiped out then if all the bank loans that are secured by all that real estate are also worthless, and the banks that made those loans will be in serious danger of collapsing, as will the property insurers who have promised to pay any claims. When or if the realization that is going to happen settles over the real estate industry then it could well lead to a major run on the banks, a shortage of liquidity and distressed assets sales as lenders and insurers scramble to raise cash. The entire mechanism of real estate credit and finance could also collapse. Perhaps this seems like an extreme and implausible scenario, until you consider that this is exactly what did happen in 2008 when the American residential real estate market collapsed because it, too, became overextended, and within weeks the entire global economy was plunged into a recession could have been much worse, and from which many nations are still feeling the ill effects nearly a decade later.

Even in a worst case scenario, though, it takes time for the ice to melt, and the bankers, insurers, and regulators will have warning. But there may come a time at some point during this process (again, if it occurs) a moment when suddenly the market as a whole grasps the danger that is surrounding it, and then panic could set in. Whether this is years ahead of the high water or after it's lapping at the feet of those walking down Broadway is impossible to identify.

In the real estate industry the phase "under water" signifies that the loan on a given piece of real estate is a great amount than the value of the real estate itself. This is a bad thing for the bank and for the borrower, and banks try to avoid this by requiring borrowers to invest cash into their purchases. That cash is at risk first, but if the value drops still lower then the banker is also "upside down" in the transaction. In a climate changed world, the phrase under water will take on a new and quite threatening meaning.

Where Are We Headed?

Throughout this century we can expect massive urbanization to continue, as well as significant overall trend toward aging, which will put enormous pressure on the finances of governments worldwide as they struggle to provide pensions and health care for aging populations that are supported by ever-fewer wage-earning and tax-paying workers. Governments will also have to figure out how to pay for the educations that the young will require to become productive members of an advanced, high-technology society for which significant education investments are essential if productivity is to be sustained.

No one knows in precise detail the economic model that will successfully address these conflicting sets of needs, we can say with a great deal of confidence that the economy will change in quite fundamental ways. Whether those changes will require that we endure a recession or two, or even a depression or two is unknown, although given the confluence of these revolutions it would hardly be surprising.

•••

Chapter 5:

The

Humanist:

The Cultural Revolution

You say you want a revolution?
Well, you know, we all want to change the world.
Lennon-McCartney

We consider him to be a martyr.
Mahmoud Ghozlani
Tunisian Politician

If were able to magically transport ourselves to ancient Luxor, or ancient Beijing, or to Tenochtitlan, what would we find there? What would we see in Athens, Rome, or Quito in 500 BC, or to India in the time of Buddha? Along the Tigris and Euphrates in Mesopotamia or beside the Yellow or the Yangtze in China, or the Mekong in Southeast Asia?

We can only guess the details, but the broad outlines are easy to envision: We would see humans exchanging goods, ideas, and knowledge, defining through their actions and choices, and through their opinions and beliefs, the rules and norms of their communities, the laws and codes that they lived by, the arts and artifacts through which they expressed their values and ideals and aspirations. We would see joy and suffering, fury and folly, inspiration and aspiration. Just as we see today in all those places.

Nevertheless, there are elements of our modern world that are also quite different. Mahmoud Ghozlani, quoted above, is a member of the Progressive Democratic Party in Sidi Bouzid, a town in Tunisia. The martyr to whom he refers is Mohamed Bouazizi, a food peddler who had, throughout his short life, experienced repeated abuse at the hands of the local police and authorities, petty bureaucratic tyranny, as he struggled to earn enough money to support this family.[144]

On December 17, 2010, Bouazizi's market scale and the fruits and vegetables he had for sale were confiscated by a local police official, and he went to the governor's office to complain and to retrieve his scale, without which he could not earn a living. The governor refused to see him, and this filled Bouazizi with anger and despair. In his desperation, he stood in the public square before the governor's office, doused himself with paint thinner, and lit a match.

He died 18 days later, on January 14, 2011, and 5,000 people participated in his funeral procession, transforming his death into a martyrdom that sparked the Tunisian revolution. Within four days of his death the protests had become so intense that Tunisian President Ben Ali fled the country as his dictatorial and corrupt government collapsed. We now know Bouazizi's suicide as the moment that triggered the Arab Spring.

Protests quickly spread beyond Tunisia and across North Africa and into the Middle East. Giant rallies occurred in Cairo and many other cities, while many others copied Bouazizi's act of self-immolation, at least 107 in the six months following Bouazizi's death, in Algeria, Egypt, Saudi Arabia, as well as, unexpectedly, in Amsterdam and Sicily.[145]

These incidents reflect the immense power that human aspirations, ideals, ideologies, and beliefs have in shaping the choices we make, and thus on the course of our lives. Bouazizi's act expressed his outrage, and demonstrated for his neighbors the depth of his own suffering as well as their own. It also inspired them to act.

Bouazizi's was a remarkable and profoundly disturbing choice, that a person's anguish and idealism, the core of the inner mental life are so compelling and that the importance of fairness so powerful that the experience of brutal unfairness would lead someone to choose the act of public suicide.

The Power of Ideals

As far as we know humans are the only species in which suicide is common, or in which it even exists at all. Most living species cling desperately to life, even in the most difficult and constrained of circumstances, and even in the most intimidating and challenging of ecosystem niches. Trees grow from nearly solid rock, clinging to the tiniest of cracks with mere sips of water, while sea creatures and bacteria exist thousands of meters below the surface under pressures that would instantly crush those living at the comfort of sea level.

And yet humans can be so deeply offended by offhand insults or so inspired by abstract ideals that they willingly sacrifice their own lives in protest and despair. Soldiers go to war to protect their homelands or their fellow soldiers, while suicide pilots and bombers are willing to end their own lives, and murder others in the process, in pursuit of the ideal of martyrdom and in support of religious and ideological abstractions. That these are twisted and false ideals is entirely beside the point, for this is certainly not the suicide's view.

In the tragedy of the suicide bombings and attacks that have become an everyday occurrence across the conflicted Middle East and which are spreading into Europe and America we see the power of these abstract ideals, as in the terrorist's view the abstractions are supreme over all other considerations, indeed, over life and death, and thus affronts to cherished abstractions are the very worst of all, worthy of capital self-sacrifice.

These topics are all important for us and for our discussion of the 21st century's revolutions because the fifth revolution is the transformation of our culture, and it is in these extreme examples that we see perhaps most clearly the inspiring and also the destructive power of ideas and ideals, and thus we get a glimpse how significantly our culture is shaped by them.

In Tunisia and in the life and death of Bouazizi and in the Arab Spring uprisings we see reflected quite clearly that these qualities, the ones that make us so human, are also the very qualities that define our culture. They reflect our aspirations, our fears, our expectations, and our understanding of right and wrong. Broadly, then, culture is the set of beliefs, ways of interacting, and material goods that make us, us. It is our shared values, goals, and practices. Hence, in pre-industrial societies where the predominant culture was the life of farming, close to the soil and a rhythm of life defined by the seasons and the sun. In our era, billions live in cities amid a rhythm of life defined by a five- or six-day work-week on buses and subways and freeways, and a daily rhythm defined often by the screens of computers, phones, and televisions. The two sets of living conditions make for quite different values and expectations, and thus they foster quite different cultures.

Most sons and daughters of a farmer knew from a very young age that they, too, would most likely live out their lives on a farm, but today's sons and daughters face an abundance of choices and also great uncertainties about what their futures hold.

Because the world is changing so fast we're no longer sure what we should expect. What kind of world, what kind of society and culture are we living in?   Is the world becoming a better place, safer, more secure, happier? Or is it becoming more dangerous, riskier, unhappier?

Collective acts of belief give shape to the normalcy of our daily lives, as thousands and millions of people come to unspoken understandings about what is right and wrong, thereby creating culture, for our culture is but an abstract aggregate of what we do and what we believe.

We observe the fragile balance between power and ideals, and we see that when our collective views change our culture changes, and so whether by intent or by default we may unexpectedly become revolutionaries, as indeed Bouazizi did.

But as suddenly as Bouazizi's match was struck we too can change the way we live because we change what we believe and what we expect. We abruptly alter the definition of what is acceptable and not acceptable, and in so doing we change our culture as well. One day it is normal that the local police would intimidate and even steal from a street vendor; the next day it is the subject of mass protest.

This sort of change does not often occur by intent or by design. It is instead more commonly an emergent or evolutionary process of incremental shifts that are occasionally punctuated by dramatic leaps of shared transformative vision. At first one or two people may think and act differently than the rest, but then as others follow, mimic, and adopt the same views, suddenly change becomes transformative cultural change. From one martyrdom in a small Tunisian town to a national revolution, to a regional and global phenomenon, this is what Bouazizi inspired, all in protest of petty mistreatment at the hands of corrupt local officials to whom he simply could not afford to pay the customary bribes.

It may be, as Lennon and McCartney wrote, that we all want to change the world; at a unique moment in time Bouazizi did so, in tragic but also transformative fashion.

Change Becomes Revolution

The relevant question that the four revolutions raise probes the extent to which the changes that we've explored in the previous chapters will transform our lives, and of course it is my observation that they're already changing us fundamentally, and so fully deserve to go by the name of *revolutions*.

The centuries of our history offer many examples of how changes take hold at the intersection of social norms, expectations and geopolitics, and how fundamental changes in attitudes come about. For example, most Europeans considered colonialism a norm and perhaps even a right, and thus between 1500 and 1900 they built colonies and extracted local wealth wherever their military power enabled them to dominate across Africa, Asia, and the Americas. A change came about at the outset of World War II in 1941 when the US President Roosevelt imposed upon Great Britain the Atlantic Charter, which specified that all nations had the right of self-determination, and which effectively ended the colonial era. By 1950 most of the former colonies had become sovereign nations.

Social change and geopolitical change often go hand in hand, and recent history gives us many additional examples. Slavery, women's rights, voting rights, and gay rights have all been highly controversial topics of cultural conflict and cultural evolution.

Sometimes changes in our values are provoked or inspired by our notions of fairness and justice, or unfairness and injustice. Sometimes, as I have suggested in the previous chapters, they come about because new capabilities exist that change our material situation. When industrialism transformed the economy it profoundly impact our ways of living and thus our culture; it's plausible to expect that the emerging era of robotics may do the same by 2030 or 2050. Climate change is already transforming how and where we live, and while its eventual impacts can only be imagined, in the most extreme scenarios we will also be fundamentally changed. And two centuries of rapid urbanization have brought countless changes in values and expectations that are now fully embedded in human culture.

Meaning in Culture

The significance of culture is embodied in the ideas and artifacts which carry meaning for us, and which express our aspirations. Meaning denotes relevance and significance, and thus to feel that something has meaning suggests awareness, caring, and importance. The elements of our lives in which we find and make meaning, the symbols that represent those meanings, and the ideals to which we aspire shape our views of life.

People may love their nation, and its flag symbolizes that meaning and its significance. We're often quite attached to flags, sometimes even mistaking the flag for the thing it represents, the nation itself. We fly *our* flag with pride, while we may spit upon or burn our enemy's flag with deep feelings of anger and loathing. A Tunisian flag stands prominently beside Bouazizi's grave, symbolizing his status as a martyr of and for the Tunisian nation. Conversely, the American Confederate Battle Flag, an artifact of the South, pro-slavery faction in the American Civil War, has been a symbol of pride for many white Southerners while many African Americans see the same flag as a tribute to the hated practice of slavery and centuries of systematic abuse and oppression. Today is there an intense debate about that flag and whether or not it should continue to be flown.

Similarly, the Apartheit policies of the South African government once reflected the commonly held views of whites, but then with a matter of only a few years popular protests, an organized international rights campaign, and fear of an immanent civil war prompted a change in attitudes and in policies, and the white-dominated government stepped aside and Nelson Mandela became president after having spent most of the previous 27 years imprisoned. In downtown Johannesburg you can still see placards identifying "white only" places, grim reminders of a different time and different values.

For a full 24 centuries after Socrates died the right to vote in public elections was the exclusive privilege of white, property-owning males. In the US, it was only one century ago that it became the right of all citizens, male and female, and yet still today there are still disputes about who may or may not vote.

Today also there is growing acceptance of LGBT rights, and many observers have commented that the change progressed much faster than they had expected, even as it is still being debated in courts and legislatures, in living rooms and churches in dozens of countries.

All of these examples show that cultural values and meanings are not fixed for all time; they do change, as we change.

What Is Right, and What Are Our Rights?

These issues explore the concept of right and wrong, as well as the principles of rights, the very abstract ideas of what shall be allowed to or guaranteed to the members of society. What rights should anyone have, child or adult, female or male or other, hetero or homosexual or other, of any skin color, any religious belief, born in any homeland, working in any profession, rich or poor? These are all questions that are addressed by culture and which also define culture. Our shared views about all of them are in the midst of being reexamined as social revolutions sweep through society.

The rights we may hold as citizens of any nation are also a social convention, a set of agreements that we make collectively. In 1948 the United Nations proclaimed a Universal Declaration of Human Rights.

> The Universal Declaration of Human Rights is a milestone document in the history of human rights. Drafted by representatives with different legal and cultural backgrounds from all regions of the world, the Declaration was proclaimed by the United Nations General Assembly in Paris on 10 December 1948 General Assembly resolution 217 A as a common standard of achievements for all peoples and all nations. It sets out, for the first time, fundamental human rights to be universally protected.[146]

> It begins: All human beings are born free and equal in dignity and rights. They are endowed with reason and conscience and should act towards one another in a spirit of brotherhood. Everyone is entitled to all the rights and freedoms set forth in this Declaration, without distinction of any kind, such as race, colour, sex, language, religion, political or other opinion, national or social origin, property, birth or other status. Furthermore, no distinction shall be made on the basis of the political, jurisdictional or international status of the country or territory to which a person belongs, whether it be independent, trust, non-self-governing or under any other limitation of sovereignty.

The UN went on in 1989 to establish a Convention regarding the rights of children, which includes:

> States Parties shall respect and ensure the rights set forth in the present Convention to each child within their jurisdiction without discrimination of any kind, irrespective of the child's or his or her parent's or legal guardian's race, colour, sex, language, religion, political or other opinion, national, ethnic or social origin, property, disability, birth or other status.[147]

As we will discuss in Chapter 11, the extent to which the modern world is organized around nation-states is also a cultural norm, and even as the blue flag of the United Nations also carries shared meaning. The existence of these agreements is remarkable as an expression of shared aspirations, and while not every nation adheres to these principles, the fact that actions are taken to uphold and to enforce them by troops and civilians who work under the auspices of the UN shows how seriously humans consider principles, ethics, and shared meanings to be.

The question for us to consider, then, is to what extent these are immutable and unchanging, and to what extent do our circumstances and situations cause us to change our views and our behaviors. And the context in which that question is particularly relevant is the acceleration of change throughout the world, and specifically the four revolutions we have described in the previous chapters. If Bouazizi's suicide was an extreme individual statement of belief, the ongoing existence and efforts of the United Nations express humanity's shared, global beliefs.

What Will Change?

The character of a culture in any given time and place reflects what people believe to be right as well as what they experience to be real. Reality in an agricultural society is quite different from reality in an industrial one, and of course the point for us is that we're transitioning out of the Industrial Era and into something else that is quite different, although its full shape remains quite unclear. We must expect that our culture will by necessity change and evolve as the economic and social realities of our lives also change and evolve. Thus, if we consolidate key ideas from the themes we have already examined, the major factors shaping our future could well look something like this:

- People are inexorably drawn to live in cities for reasons of preference and lifestyle as well as in pursuit of economic opportunity, to create better lives for themselves and to provide better lives for their children. By the end of the century 95 to 98 percent of the world's people will be city dwellers.

- Families living in cities tend to have fewer children than those living in agricultural settings. One or two children is typical in a city, although the example of Japan shows that having no children is no longer uncommon. Hence, urbanization is itself contributing to the stabilization of the overall human population, and at current rates stability will be achieved within a few decades. By the end of the century the total population may well be the same or lower than it is today.

- However, the declining birth rate is necessarily accompanied by a reciprocal increase in the aging rate, both as consequence of fewer births and also because medical science and lifestyle improvements are resulting in longer lives. Average lifespans in 2100 could be 100, 120, or even 150 years.

- The emergence of robots capable of augmenting and even replacing human workers will make the employment situation much more complex. If robots prove to be as capable as their promoters believe they will be, then by mid-century robots will likely outnumber humans by five or ten to one, and if Kurzweil is correct then they will be so much smarter than humans that human-robot hybrids will be the norm.

- As these changes occur, it's quite likely that the climate will continue to change, disrupting patterns of farming and by raising the sea level, changing where cites can be located. As a major contributor to climate change, fossil fuels will be progressively displaced by alternative sources of energy.

With each of these revolutions comes great economic opportunity, as new technologies come into wide usage and accomplish important work for society, which creates new ways to manufacture and trade. The investments required to enable these revolutions will be massive.

At the same time, however, each of these revolutions also brings the likelihood of economic dislocation and in extreme scenarios, recession or depression. If robots displace huge numbers of human workers and so cause widespread unemployment; if climate change destroys coastal cities faster than they can be rebuilt on higher ground; if the economic losses from real estate literally under water wreck the banks or the banking system; if a sudden collapse of fossil fuel companies causes the stock markets to plummet, or if their collapse throws the nations that depend on coal and oil production for the nation's wealth to also collapse; if the new cities become wretched and crime-ridden; and if any significant combination of these occur, we will in for an exceptionally unpleasant time.

And of course all of these changes will be reflected in one way or another in our culture. And because our culture, which is the way we live, consists of many elements that we are consciously aware of and also many others that we are not aware of, but which nevertheless deeply affect our ideals and our attitudes, it is not so simple to decode. The prevailing culture of the place where we happen to grow up has an enormous and usually permanent impact on our views and experiences, as the accepted norms of right and wrong in that time and place remain with most of us throughout our lives. Thus, it's often the case that the children of immigrants simultaneously inhabit two cultures, the one of the new place that they experience outside of the home, and the other that exists within where their parents adhere to and enact the values of the old place.

With their awareness of the norms of both cultures they often serve as translators for their own parents, aunts, and uncles, who may not grasp the cultural rules in the new place so easily, especially when they don't speak the language. For the norms and rules of a culture are often unspoken; people simply know that *we don't do that here*. The foods we eat, our way of dressing, the names we give to places and things are all taken for granted, unquestioned and unquestionable.

How do you operate as a street vendor, selling fruits and vegetables? Do you have to bribe the police? How do you buy a ticket to ride a public bus or subway? How do you send a letter? Open a bank account? Start a business? Get a building permit? Register a complaint? Report a crime? All of these acts are deeply embedded cultural norms that everyone from *here* already knows how to do, but the people who aren't from here generally don't know any of it. Consequently, life for immigrants can be psychologically overwhelming, as there is so much to learn that it can be painful and deeply confusing.

And of course the point here is that, as we have discussed in the previous chapters, we are living through not only one or two, but four simultaneous revolutions, each of which is causing fundamental change in how we live, and thus they are also inducing significant change in what we believe. Hence, these revolutions are changing our culture, and because these changes are so deep and so comprehensive, in effect we have *all* become immigrants, we are all finding ourselves afraid and confused by the new environments in which we live. We are forced to adapt to new technologies, to a different climate, to an entirely different energy economy, and to a globalized–urbanized society in which many women prefer to have fewer children than in the past. And the result of all this change, all of it happening at once, is the creation of the fifth revolution, the global cultural revolution.

And so while each of us may want to change the world to suit our own particular wishes, desires, or ideals, in fact it is not we who are in control, for the process of these revolutions is much like an avalanche sweeping down the side of the mountain, inexorable and uncontrollable.

Culture and Four Revolutions

Two decades of progress in digital technology has altered how we access information and how we communicate with one another, and this has had and will continue to have a profound impact. We have entirely new concepts and artifacts, new words to describe them, new behaviors that reflect them, and new companies to provide the tools that enable them. The Lexicon of Tomorrow, in Part 4, captures some of these new concepts and in aggregate shows a world in the midst of major changes.

However, what we have experienced in the last two decades is most likely only a small sample of much larger changes soon to come. The technology companies that have already thoughtfully put a supercomputer in our pockets will continue to develop new tools and methods that will have deep and lasting impact on our behaviors as well as our values and beliefs. Smart phones will become smarter and more capable assistants and surrogates, becoming eventually super-smart with still more power and greater capabilities. Today we routinely create and communicate in ways that humans never could before, as the single device replaces dozens of others and performs jobs for us that none of them ever did; tomorrow it will do much more.

As these technologies continue to evolve we must expect that their impact will only become more profound and broader, encompassing fields as diverse as transportation and health care and entertainment and in tasks and professions from law to management to logistics to warfighting. If the forecasted emergence of powerful robots indeed materializes then we will experience the transformation of the workplace, and along with it the very structure of the economy.   As I have noted, this could turn out spectacularly well, or painfully and disastrously. Either way, we can be certain that our culture will change in many ways that are trivial and others that are profound and thus revolutionary.

Today's norms of thought and behavior could well become outmoded and quaint tomorrow as we discuss and debate robot powers and robot rights. When will robots have the right to vote? Could a robot run for office? Or perhaps robots will demand instead a separate legislative structure of their own, where laws regulating robots are made, and a parallel court system in which to adjudicate disputes and wrongdoing. Will robots be entitled to political power? Will they have the right to reproduce?

These topics were explored in science fiction yesterday, insightfully illustrated in recent films such as *Robot and Frank*, *Her*, and *Ex Machina*. All of them prefigure many of the coming issues and challenges with which we will soon be dealing not in fiction, but in day to day reality.

Already we have introduced a wide range of artificial parts into the human anatomy, and already we have introduced into our language terms including "post-human" (someone who has evolved beyond the qualities and characteristics considered basic to "humanness") and "trans-human," (someone who has evolved qualities and characteristics considered superior to basic "humanness") to prepare us for the work that genetic engineers are already doing as they alter the human genome.

What will happen, in law, when humans and post-humans have sex? When humans and robots have sex? Will a robot have the right to marry another robot? Or to marry a human? And will a human worker who has been displaced by a robot have any social or economic right to the output or value produced by the robot?

The great accomplishment of the UN to define universal human rights and universal child rights will probably have to be amended at some time in perhaps the next 30 years as the scientific definitions of terms like life, living, and consciousness, and the social definitions of rights and responsibilities may be vastly reshaped by technological creations that then cross whatever the invisible border is between life and non-life. This surely is a revolution.

Fiction and Fairness

As fiction explores the world and the culture we are busily creating day by day, it also sometimes impacts on that culture in subtle but often illuminating ways. For example, recently popular unrest grew in Thailand in opposition to a repressive government. The movement had been going on for some years when the first *Hunger Games* movie was released in 2013, and the movie itself seemed to reinspire the protesters. Thai people adopted a prominent element in the movie, a three finger salute, as a shared symbol of their resistance, offering a compelling example of life imitating art, and also another example of the great significance of the abstract concept of fairness in modern life.

Thai citizens took personal risks to engage in these protests, and one Thai factory worker was recently charged with disparaging the king's dog in a case brought in a Thai military court. Thanakorn Siripaiboon was charged with making a "sarcastic" Internet post related to the king's pet, for which he also faces separate charges of sedition and insulting the king. He social media "crimes" could bring a sentence of up to 37 years in prison.[148]

As social media are a form of socially-shared data, another dimension of our evolving concept of fairness is slowly taking shape throughout the modern digital economy, and it will soon emerge into a full scale debate. This is the controversy about the ownership of data, your data, or data about you, and your right or non-right to privacy in the digital realm. What are your rights? Do you own the data about yourself? Or does a data-collector that you don't even know exists own your data? Do you have the right to remain private, or does a data collector have the right to amass a profile of you that can be sold or rented to the highest bidder? What right does the government have to access your data?

As commonly occurs in the world of technology, our capabilities are advancing faster than the law can make sense of them, and thus the issues and questions are never addressed proactively but only in reaction to expectations, misdeeds, or misrepresentations, real or perceived, after the fact. It is only then, when the nature of abuses becomes clear, that the issues can intelligently be debated and decided in the legislatures and the courts. But meanwhile technology continues to advance and bring forward still more issues that we never had to think about before.

Will new life forms be patentable? Can a human own a post-human, a trans-human, or a sentient robot? What limitations should be placed on scientists who wish to experiment with clones, or to alter the human genome in fundamental ways?   If there are such limits, who is professionally capable of assessing when those limits have been ignored, surpassed, or contravened?

In this era of rapid technological change another side effect is a shift in the nature of social prestige. In stable societies it is the elders who, through the course of their lives, collect knowledge and then wisdom, and it they to whom we turn when we are not sure about what is right and wrong. The elders are the judges, the leaders, the advisors. But when change is so rapid our elders may not fully grasp what's happening, and their advice may not fit the times. If we look, for example, at those who are creating the new enterprises, it is overwhelmingly the young. The founders of many of today's technology companies, including Google, Yahoo, Microsoft, Apple, Oracle, SalesForce, Thanos, Tesla, SpaceX, etc., etc. were young people, mostly in their twenties and thirties, because they are generally the ones with the vision and the drive to see how it could be done better than the way it is currently being done. The youth, in other words, are creating changes to which the rest of us are forced to adapt.

Hence, instead of the elderly mentoring the young, we see now that the young are reverse-mentoring the elderly; it is the children who know how to program the VCR and the Blu-Ray, who show their parents how to load and use the new apps, who can connect the home wifi systems and who use it to stream movies, web sites, chats, and twitter feeds, all at once.

For better or for worse, as science and technology proceed into the development of these highly complex systems and capabilities, they bring forward highly nuanced moral, ethical, and legal questions that do not yet have answers, but which are fundamentally important. The displacement of the wisdom of the aged also displaces cultural patterns that go back millennia, and only add to the sense of disorientation that many elderly already experience; the wisdom they have accumulated over decades suddenly seems much less relevant or event entirely irrelevant, and while the youth in every era have always resisted and rebelled, the disruption of our culture suggests that some of these rebellions may now be of a different type.

The other revolutions bring fundamental changes as well. Accumulation of carbon dioxide in the atmosphere is changing Earth's climate, and thus we are transitioning from a century in which the weather was unusually benign, to the opposite. This will cause massive disruptions to established patterns of agriculture and human settlement. Whether it's only moderate inconvenience or a total disaster is too soon to tell, but whatever occurs will change our beliefs and values, and thus change our culture as well. Will we have to accommodate millions of climate refugees, whose lands and therefore also their wealth have disappeared beneath rising oceans, or whose farmlands have been ruined by drought, or whose homes have been wrecked by storms. Will they have the right to resettle in another country? According to whose laws will their nationalities and rights be decided?

The source of the excess CO2 has been the combustion of fossil fuels, a side effect of 200 years of industrialization that has also brilliantly transformed the world's economy and defined the commercial culture of the modern world. This industry enabled the creation of wealth on a scale that was utterly unimaginable for our farmer ancestors. So while two hundred years ago we lived in an agricultural society and according to agrarian values, now we live in a globalized, industrialized economy, and our values reflect the importance of industry and our obsessions with consumption.

But now that we understand the problematic relationship between excess CO2 in the atmosphere and combusted fossil fuels, and now also that we are moving steadily closer to having viable alternative sources of energy on a large scale, including wind and solar energy, it seems inevitable that the fossil fuel industry will decline, and eventually collapse. Many nations currently depend on their oil exports to sustain economic viability, but what will happen if their oil loses its value? Will their citizens obtain the right to emigrate also, as "CO2 Refugees"?

While all of these changes are occurring, people will continue to move into the world's cities, and as they do so, most will choose to have fewer children than their rural cousins. As the birth rate drops to accommodate urban lifestyles the ratio of workers to retirees will shift heavily toward those who are no longer producing, which will necessitate an increase in government spending just as government tax revenues will be declining. How will the rights of children for education be balanced with the rights of elders for health care?

Cities will expand at the rate of tens of millions per year, and if the melting ice leads to risen oceans, the low-lying coastal cities will have to be abandoned and rebuilt on higher ground. Who will own the land on which the new cities are built? And according to whose concept of the city and urban design will this be done?

These revolutions are not inspired nor mandated by totalitarian demagogues (Mao, 1965), nor by revolutionary political mobs (Paris, 1789), nor by educated elites (Philadelphia, 1776), but rather they are emerging through an evolutionary process because of the way the world's economy and society are developing as a mass culture of 7+ billion participant-contributors, and because of the many ways that the technologies we use enrich and enliven our lives and society as a whole.

The consequences are and will continue to be significant, as the day to day experiences and realities confronting millions and billions of people define who we are and what we can become while living through a period of massive and apparently unstoppable change. As all of this change is occurring simultaneously, and its impact on human culture is and will be massive and unavoidable. It's all connected.

Yet there have always been, and probably will always be, those who resist change. They are the subjects of the next chapter.

•••

Chapter 6:

The

Reactionary:

The Counter-Revolution

Mere anarchy is loosed upon the world,
The blood-dimmed tide is loosed, and everywhere
The ceremony of innocence is drowned;
The best lack all conviction, while the worst
Are full of passionate intensity.

William Butler Yeats
"The Second Coming"

I represent change that worries them.

President Barak Obama[149]

Newton was certainly not the first to notice that actions invoke reactions, but his mathematical formulation is a landmark in the history of science. Scientific progress is often marked by such revolutions, but they rarely proceed smoothly or effortlessly.   Instead, even brilliant new insights are frequently met with denial and resistance, for while some welcome a new formulation and a new understanding, others are reluctant to let go of the old explanations.

This is the theme that Thomas S. Kuhn explored so eloquently in *The Structure of Scientific Revolutions*:

> The invention of new theories … implies a change in the rules governing the prior practice of normal science. Inevitably, therefore, it reflects upon much scientific work already successfully completed. That is why new theory is never just an increment to what is already know. Its assimilation requires the reconstruction of prior theory and the re-evaluation of prior fact, an intrinsically revolutionary process.[150]

Not everyone will be so enthusiastic about participating in that process of assimilation, and indeed many will feel much more comfortable with the old theories, and they will resist. The point, of course, is that whether we're talking about physics as revealed by Newton or Einstein, or astronomy as explained by Galileo and Copernicus, or any of the countless fields of scientific research, and indeed across the entirety of human society, it's clear that as action invokes reaction, change also begets anti-change.

And as our concern here is to understand the revolutions of the 21st Century, we must also consider the fact that social and political revolutions invoke or provoke counter revolutions, and that counter-revolutionaries are having and will continue to have significant impact, for they, too, are a influential element of our culture. If we wish to understand our world we must look not only at those who are creating change but at those who resist it.

Revolution and Counter-Revolution

Sometimes reform and revolution prevail, but not always. What is considered progress in the view of some may be morally or culturally repugnant to others, and thus counter-revolution often finds many willing followers, as the pattern of anti-change is one of the very powerful cultural forces that is shaping our world today.

History offers many examples of the interplay between revolution and counter-revolution. Martin Luther sought to reform the Catholic Church and the popes responded by instituting a counter-reformation in their attempt to maintain control. They were only partially successful, however, as the Protestants severed their ties with Rome and then spread profusely and became dozens of new denominations with their own preferred interpretations of the Bible. Ironically, none of this was Luther's goal; he had no intention of starting a new church as he merely wanted to reform the existing one.

Napoleon brought revolutionary change that threatened the monarchies of Europe via his massive armies of proud and willing French citizens, and his brilliant generalship, and so of course the monarchs united to oppose him. After many failures they eventually learned and adopted his tactics, and finally defeated him at Waterloo by doing to him what he had done to them. This restored the monarchies temporarily, but within a century the broader revolutionary process of social change had overthrown them, and the few that remained were only symbolic, having been replaced with democracies or autocrats. We could go on a cite revolution after revolution, but the point is nearly always the same: some engage in making change, while others resist.

In our times, as I have mentioned repeatedly, change is being driven through the relentless process of industrial capitalism that has begun the transition to a digital economy, and also through the CO_2 side effect of industrialism's fossil fuels through the 300-year transformation from an agrarian civilization to an urban one. All of these changes are occurring simultaneously, and it seems that all of them have unrelenting momentum. Unless there is a radical change in course, within the next decade, then they will all mature to fruition by 2030, and as we explored in the previous chapter, the four revolutions are also putting consistent pressure on our culture, and so it is changing as well.

But cultural change is not a smooth or an easy process, characterized as it is by attachments and arguments, by contrasting viewpoints and conflicting objectives. The comment by President Obama cited above reflects that fear often accompanies change, and rightly so, for change means uncertainty and risk, and so we see the adversaries at odds in the media, in the streets, in the elections, in the legislatures, in the courts, and sometimes even on the streets, city squares, and battlefields.

In politics we characterize the two contrasting viewpoints as positions on the political spectrum from the left, where we find many promoters of change who believe in its benefits, to the right, where those who fear that change will mean that they are asked or expected to sacrifice norms and values that they find meaningful and important. And when fear takes on an extreme character, the fearful often move still farther to the right, where we find fundamentalists and reactionaries who resort first to hyperbole and then later sometimes to violence in their passionate intent to hold back the forces of change.

Fundamentalism

As the existence of morality reflects a shared understanding of accepted norms, they are shared definitions of what is right and what is wrong. As we saw in the previous chapter, moral values are both deeply personal but also widely collective.

When values change, it is by definition the counter–revolutionaries who are most deeply offended by what they experience not merely as change, but as moral decline. The sense of trauma and loss can be deep and profound, and the resulting anguish and anger can also be intense. This is true even when the values being generally abandoned can be understood to be in and of themselves immoral. Thus, in the past you would have heard moral arguments promoting the rightfulness of slavery, of colonialism, of child labor, of segregation, of misogyny, not because of the inherent moral soundness of those positions, but because these views were so deeply embedded in the self-identities and world views of those holding to them that change was experienced as a threat.

Fundamentalism arises here, from the search for order amid change, and from the feeling that change threatens established, familiar, and comfortable beliefs and ways of life. Hence, it is a form of nostalgia, often combined with a longing for structure, and thus it is a psychological reaction hidden in moral or ethical outrage.

With need for structure often also comes the need for simplified basic explanations of right and wrong and for authority, and it is for this reason that demagogues are often fundamentalists, for the confidence and assertiveness of a demagogue often appeals to those who feel lost.

Fascism is a form of fundamentalism that rose to power in Europe between the two World Wars during the time of overwhelming anxiety and stress compounded by the tumultuous economic destruction of the Great Depression, and the quite legitimate fears about the future led millions to embrace authoritarian leaders who promised a return to order.

More recently, the collapse of the Soviet Union in 1989 implied an upswelling of democracy, and the triumphant American State Department employee and author Francis Fukuyama even promoted this event as the "end of history" because capitalist economies with representative democracies had "won".[151] Alas, it was not to be, as the Russian people lacked both the habits and the institutions that were necessary for democracy to succeed, and so it was hardly surprising when a strongman came to power and democracy gave way to autocracy. Fukuyama soon realized that the triumph was illusory, and in any case during the intervening decades a new threat to the capitalist democracies has emerged in the form of violent terrorism, a form of fundamentalism that is now intent on provoking a climactic showdown with the West.

Power Vacuum

Societies and nations are held together by the power of ideas and through the exercise of authority. In a democracy power is held and exercised as a matter of consent between the government and the people, and thus it is distributed among the people who delegate it to representative institutions through elections. The genius of the American system is the precise manner in which this relationship between the people and their government is explicitly defined and regulated, and perhaps the genius of American history is that this structure has endured for 240 years.

In an autocracy or monarchy, in contrast, power is usually held by a central authority figure, sometimes expressed as a matter of brute force and often experienced as intimidation. This is exactly what Mohamed Bouazizi experienced, and what drove him, ultimately, to sacrifice his own life in the protest of its utter unfairness. Such feelings could arise, of course, only because Bouazizi knew of another way, he had a point of comparison between what he was experiencing and what he believed was right.

These two approaches reflect what Joseph Nye has identified as "hard" and "soft" power. Hard is the exercise of force, while soft is the influence of culture.[152]

In hard power environments, intimidation often begins because sitting autocrats are afraid of being displaced by internal or external rivals, and they resort to force, bribery, and corruption to sustain the support of their own cohort and to prevent rivals from gaining a foothold. When change does come to an autocracy it must overcome the initial defenses of the autocrat, and thus it usually takes a huge accumulation of force to effect the shift in the power structure, causing disturbances that can last quite a long time. When the French overthrew their monarchy in 1789 the reverberations lasted many months and soon degenerated into a mob-fueled orgy of violence that became so pervasive that it is known to posterity as *The Reign of Terror*. No one was safe from the sharpened blade of the guillotine, the chaos so great that its inventor Monsieur Guillotine himself perished under his own invention, along with King Louis XVI and the unfortunate Marie Antoinette, who is remembered by history for suggesting cake as an alternative when bread supplies ran low. Although she probably never said that, as an urban legend it well reflected the anti-monarchist spirit of the times.

As the Reign of Terror shows, at the moment when a former autocrat is deposed but a new one does not immediately step in, the result is a deadly power vacuum. New leaders, would-be leaders, and demagogues surge forward and try to gain control, to impose their own views and purposes, and often to enrich themselves and their families, for power often equates with wealth.

As this is a moment of social change, fundamentalists, authoritarians, and demagogues all attempt to seize the opportunity by reminding people of past wrongs and vowing to lead the revenge. This is exactly what occurred in 2003 when the American army toppled the autocratic dictator in Iraq. The war was easily won, but the victory was followed by worsening violence that soon engulfed not just the nation, but the entire region. The idea promoted by the US administration that the Iraqis were enthusiastically waiting to embrace democracy was both self-serving and naïve. They were waiting, it turned out, not to strive for common goals but to avenge prior offenses, to seize power, and to impose their will on their neighbors. Because the US leadership failed to anticipate that removing Hussein would create a power vacuum into which many would-be autocrats would vie for control, more than a decade following the invasion we see Iraq still fragmented into competing factions that are engaged in a multi-sided civil war in which approximately half a million civilians have already perished, with no end in sight.

The even more vicious civil war is raging in Iraq's neighbor Syria, a conflict born from the combined impact of the Iraqi power vacuum, climate change, and cultural change across the region that was embodied in the Arab Spring movement. Syria may be the ultimate power vacuum, as no fewer than ten powerful militaries are currently contesting for control of Syria, an unprecedented concentration of soldiers and armaments in a tiny space that has destroyed what was once a lovely country with a rich history as a great contributor to human civilization. In its place is a desolate wasteland stripped of its infrastructure, its economy, and its people, by years of brutal violence.

The armies and air forces engaged in the conflict include the national military supporting President Assad, the autocrat who is defending his regime against a popular rebellion inspired by the Arab Spring movement. Assad's hereditary dictatorship introduced high levels of brutality to Syrian society, and has by its own actions created an opposition movement. The regional power vacuum has also enabled the fundamentalist army of ISIL/ISIS/Daesh to gain control of large segments of Syria and neighboring Iraq, where it governs according to an extreme fundamentalist model.

At the same time, the Kurds, the world's largest ethic group that lacks its own homeland, seek to create a sovereign nation on their traditional lands that cross the borders between Syria, Iraq, and Turkey, while Russian, American, Canadian, and European aircraft and drones conduct bombing runs that target various factions and combatants. Iraqi, Iranian, and Saudi forces are also engaged.

On any given day it is not clear who is fighting whom, but it entirely clear that it is the people of Syria who have already lost. They know it, too, and millions of them crowd refugee camps in Lebanon and Turkey, while tens of thousands more risk their lives to escape to freedom and safety in Europe. Syria has been utterly destroyed, and one has to wonder if it can ever again function as a unified, sovereign nation.

Apocalyptic Catch-22

If Syria ever does regain its independence from the masses of military forces that are surging back and forth across its torn landscape, it will be because the nations of the world will come to grips with ISIS, and with the form of violent fundamentalism that ISIS promotes and practices.

ISIS distinguishes itself through its absolutism and its brutality, and also because it is organized around a vision of doomsday, the end of humanity.[153] And this message is, perhaps surprisingly, an attractive one.

By early in 2015 more than 20,000 people from outside of Syria including about 3500 Westerners had joined ISIS, drawn by the power of its authoritarian and fundamentalist message.[154] Citizens of the US, France, Russia, the UK, China, Germany, Belgium, Sudan, India, and Yemen, among others, made the secret journey to Syria to join ISIS and participate in the brutality. Why do they come?[155] The message that the world is about to end is apparently compelling to the fundamentalist mindset.

And while apocalyptic visions, prophesies, and sects exist in nearly all religious traditions, ISIS has taken this logic much further than it predecessors. It's an explicit element of ISIS's strategy to create and promote fear through violence, and although it has been criticized even by al Qaeda leaders for its extreme violence, acts of brutality including executions are staged, dramatized, filmed, and disseminated via the internet, which serves the dual purposes of recruiting and is also a method of provoking the Western nations into the region to fight ISIS.

To a Westerner this provocation is perhaps counter-intuitive. Why is ISIS intent on drawing the West into further conflict? In a strategic twist quite worthy of Joseph Heller's Catch 22, ISIS seeks to gain support through the Middle East by demonstrating that the West is intent on destroying Islam, which serves of course to bolster its claim that the apocalyptic Grand Battle has arrived.

That is, ISIS attacks the West specifically in order to provoke a counter-attack, for the counter-attack by the West is expected to demonstrate the West's ill will towards the Middle East. It is a twisted bit of logic, but based on this model ISIS is not satisfied to wage its battles within its home territory in Syria and Iraq, but has spread violence across cities from Indonesia to India and Africa.

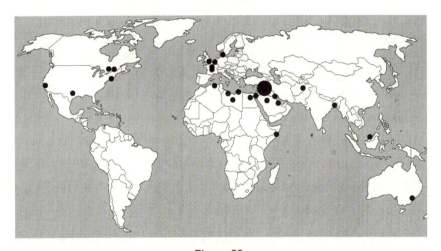

Figure 69
ISIS Attacks
Map of locations where ISIS and others mimicking ISIS have mounted attacks. Iraq and Syria shown with the large dot.

The use of suicide attacks presents another nearly intractable problem, for the West's way of war fighting cannot account for fighters who choose to die. How do you fight an adversary who is willing to die, and indeed expecting to die? The means that a suicidal fighter will adopt is a threat that requires not only military and security responses, but also that those countering ISIS think through the nature of the conflict in a very different way, and learn to prepare for a different form of combat, both on the battlefield and in the media.

And ISIS has proven quite adept at utilizing social media to promote its message via Facebook, YouTube and Twitter, promoting the apocalypse via the same media that did so much to enable and spread the optimism of the Arab Spring, but turned into tools of pessimism and despair.

The technology community has taken notice, and is participating in the opposition to ISIS in its own unique way. The hacker group Anonymous, recently claimed responsibility for shutting 800 ISIS Twitter accounts, 12 web pages, and 50 email addresses: "We, Anonymous around the world, have decided to declare war on you the terrorists," and later added "You will be treated like a virus, and we are the cure. We own the Internet."[156]

YouTube removed 14 *million* ISIS videos in 2015, which equates to roughly 1600 videos per hour; this means that YouTube probably employs three or four people full time whose only job is to take down ISIS materials, while ISIS must have a small army of people making and posting videos not only to YouTube, but to hundreds or thousands of other sites. ISIS' recruiting effort is a worldwide activity, and it reportedly posts its messages in twenty different languages.[157] London's Metropolitan Police Services removes around 1,000 pieces of extremist content from the Internet each week trying to block recruitment and incitement, while in 2015 Twitter suspended 10,000 ISIS accounts, about 25 per day.

War in the 21st century is as much a matter of public relations and propaganda as it is about guns and bombs, and indeed Osama bin Laden's deputy Ayman al-Zawahiri at one point requested ISIS to stop making such a spectacle of the beheadings, noting, "we are in a media battle for the hearts and minds of our community."[158] Inciting more radicals to join the ISIS army took precedence, and the videos continued to be made publicized, and as they were often lead stories on Western newscasts, they thereby demonstrated that the policy of creating terror through media remains entirely effective.

While the five 21st century revolutions do not seem to play a part in its apocalyptic visions, ISIS does represent a very extreme form of counter-revolutionary intent, and its strategy of provoking confrontation anywhere in the world to attain the goal of bringing about the end of times constitutes a global threat. The conflict between ISIS and the rest of the world will be one of the defining factors that shapes the coming years and decades.

Cultural Revolution in China

It was in China that the concept of a cultural revolution took on a modern and unforgettable meaning. Chairman Mao, concerned that the Peoples' Republic was developing an unhealthy bourgeois attitude that was impeding the broader process of revolutionary transformation to which he had committed himself and the nation, introduced the Cultural Revolution to China in 1966. His Red Guards acted out the Chairman's instructions, forcefully relocating millions of Chinese middle class citizens and professionals to the countryside to facilitate their "re-education" under forced labor conditions. More than one million died directly, and as many as 30 million Chinese starved to death as food production plummeted in the resulting chaos.

This attempt to propel the nation forward through a designed revolution was in all respects a disaster, and in 1981 the Chinese Communist Party uncharacteristically admitted as much, publishing its judgment that the Cultural Revolution was "responsible for the most severe setback and the heaviest losses suffered by the Party, the country, and the people since the founding of the People's Republic."[159] This was thirteen years after John Lennon and Paul McCartney's unforgettable lyrics stated it much more simply: "But if you go carrying pictures of Chairman Mao, you ain't gonna make it with anyone anyhow."

When Mao died in September 1976 his successor Deng Xiao Ping committed the Communist Party to an abrupt change of course. By embracing capitalist economics, enabling private enterprise, and encouraging private initiative Deng launched the Chinese economy on a massive process of change, a second cultural revolution in fact, but this one achieved stunning results. Capitalism transformed China into a global economic powerhouse.

In this second revolution, bourgeois values were embraced rather than vilified, and amassing personal wealth was considered positive rather than a negative factor. By 2014, when the Alibaba Group went public on the New York Stock Exchange, the extensive reach and massive success of the company propelled its founder and Chairman Jack Ma into the global spotlight as one of the world's richest men, with a net worth of $30 billion. Ma became a folk hero in China, his photo gracing covers of countless books and magazines, promoting the promise that you, too, can learn his secrets and make your fortune.

Future Shock Becomes Present Shock

As the first Chinese Cultural Revolution was winding down in 1970, American author and futurist Alvin Toffler published the insightful book that I mentioned in the Introduction, *Future Shock*,[160] in which he described the deep impact and psychological trauma that the modern world was having, and would continue to have, on the lives, outlooks, and prospects of an entire generation. Toffler described future shock as "too much change in too short a period of time." The book was a best seller, providing helpful explanations of what millions were experiencing but until then had no name for.

Following 35 years of accelerating change, in 2005 Daniel Rushkoff amended Toffler by suggesting that tomorrow had become today, and that what we now suffered from is "present shock."[161] Rushkoff's point that change today is even faster than it was in Toffler's time is of course correct, and the five revolutions are creating a world of even faster change than in Toffler's Era, or in Chairman Mao's.

Adverse reactions to the modern world are many, including a rise in suicide that has reached epidemic proportions in some nations such as

Japan, where in 2014 an average of 70 people committed suicide each day.[162] Many of them are elderly, isolated, and depressed, victims perhaps of the declining birth rate and thus without children to keep them engaged in life. But suicide is also the number one cause of death for much younger Japanese men aged 20 to 44, and the suicide rate is even higher in South Korea. Indeed, it is the leading cause of death for all men in the 20 – 44 age group, just one manifestation of mental illness and depression, that are now worldwide epidemics.

The World Health Organization estimates that 350 million people suffer from depression globally, about 5 percent of the total population, while 800,000 commit suicide each year;[163] the modern world is not such an easy place in which to live.

Anti-Immigration

The number of people seeking arriving as refugees in Europe from the Middle East and Africa now surpasses a million each year. Millions more are trapped, waiting for their own opportunity to make a break for freedom and safety. Thousands have died crossing the Mediterranean, but still they come, drawn not by the prospect of luxury or generous social services, but simply for a chance at a decent life.

Just as a tiny crack in the Iron Curtain led surprisingly fast to the collapse of the Soviet Union and the powerful symbolism of citizens taking sledge hammers to the Berlin Wall, the small opening which allowed some Syrian refugees entry into Europe in the summer of 2015 quickly became a torrent. This small opening has stimulated a new experience of what Charles Montgomery refers to as "the Urban Poverty Paradox," which states that, "any attempt to fix the poverty level in a single city may well backfire and increase the level of poverty in a city by attracting more poor people."[164] The same dynamic is revealed here, as the attempt to address the suffering of the initial few who dared to cross the Aegean in tiny boats thus prompted tens of thousands more to risk the crossing, and the huge number of migrants into Europe provoked a humanitarian crisis and a political one as well.

In reaction, right wing political parties throughout Europe are receiving the most support they've garnered in a generation as fear of immigrants and the changes they represent has swelled support for anti-change, anti-immigrant politicians who promise to restore society to the way it used to be. In the US, Americans support for the Tea Party is also a form of anti-change nostalgia; the group takes both its name and its archaic costumes from a symbolic anti-British event that occurred 250 years ago in Boston Harbor. Wishful thinking, fear, and anger are their common elements, but the forces driving are not likely to be stopped or reversed by their protestations.

The counterpoint and sometime conflict between those who promote change as progress and those who resist it as regression has been a central theme in society, politics and governance for millennia, and it remains a central part of our experience today. Hence, while the broader process of change of the five revolutions unfolds on the global stage, the parallel anti-revolution is active and spreading.

Hegel understood history as the dynamic process through which powerful forces of change became expressed as an idea, or a thesis.[165] The antithesis would then arise in spontaneous opposition, much as Newton described actions and reactions, and then the promoters of the two ideas or ideals would then battle it out to determine the future direction of a society. In the end, frequently, Hegel saw that the conflict is resolved through the creation of a new synthesis, and so history would move forward. In our times, the driving actions are technological change, climate change, and urbanization, and the reactions are the transformation of the energy sector, the revolution in our culture, and the fundamentalist anti-revolutions. Whether we subscribe to Kuhn's model of scientific revolution or Hegel's view or any other model of society's evolution and change, we cannot avert our eyes from the collision that is occurring before us, as the revolutions of our time impose a set of changes on society that force us to see the world differently, perhaps better but perhaps worse than what came before.

Regardless of whether the promoters of change or their fundamentalist opponents are correct in their views about change, there seems to be little

232

chance that change itself will stop, for it is now firmly rooted in our economic system, and that system operates largely beyond anyone's control. The great British mathematician and philosopher Alfred North Whitehead explained it this way:

> The major advances in civilization are processes which all but wreck the societies in which they occur. The art of free society consists first in the maintenance of the symbolic code; and secondly in fearlessness of revision, to secure that the code serves those purposes which satisfy an enlightened reason. Those societies which cannot combine reverence to their symbols with freedom of revision, must ultimately decay either from anarchy, or from the slow atrophy of a life stifled by useless shadows.[166]

Neither the emperors nor the popes nor the kings and queens nor even the autocrats have ever succeeded in preserving the world they preferred in the face of revision, in the face of fundamental change in the world's structure. Although we're beginning to have a clearer view of the forces driving change we still do not know the form that the new synthesis or the new paradigm will take. This is the topic we will take up in the next chapter, where we examine the patterns that better explain them to close Part 1 of the book.

•••

Chapter 7:

The

Futurist:

The Patterns of a
Changing World

I sometimes find that I simply have too many thoughts and memories crammed into my mind. At these times I use the Pensive. One simply siphons the excess thoughts from one's mind, pours them into the basin, and examines them at one's leisure. It becomes easier to spot patterns and links, you understand, when they are in this form.

So said Professor Dumbledore, to Harry Potter
J.K. Rowling[167]

One of the most prominent topics in mythology and fiction and thus one of the self-organizing themes of every culture is the power of magic. The boundaries and limitations that confine us in the material world are close and burdensome, and so while our visions and imaginations soar

235

without limitation we seek desperately to leave the bonds behind, and in this magic becomes our panacea.

However, magic is also more than a panacea when it allows us to glimpse into a world where we're really not so constrained and where we may transcend our limits through effort, innovation, and creativity. We thus redefine ourselves not as limited corporeal beings, but as aspirational and transcendent ones.

From this perspective, Harry Potter is no mere 11 year old boy riding a broomstick and fighting the bad guys, but rather a universal role model for the individual and shared aspirations of an entire community that is engaged in the timeless battle between good and evil. This is precisely the role that myth has played throughout the millennia of human development.

> Mythology has been interpreted by the modern intellect as a primitive, fumbling effort to explain the world of nature (Frazer); as a production of poetical fantasy from prehistoric times, misunderstood by succeeding ages (Muller); as a repository of allegorical instruction, to shape the individual to his group (Durkheim); as a group dream, symptomatic of archetypal urges within the depths of the human psyche (Jung); as the traditional vehicle of man's profoundest metaphysical insights (Coomaraswamy); and as God's revelation to His Children (the Church). Mythology is all of these.[168]

It is also the case that we, too, are living in a time during which we are surrounded by powerful forces that often seem beyond our comprehension, forces that inspire in us great excitement but also great fear, and that seem to evoke the powers of the universe and the powers of human thought. How else can we understand atomic weapons, and computers that think, and economic systems that engage 7 billion of us in a single marketplace of production and trade, and a culture in which the transformative power of ideas and ideals inspire great thoughts and also suicidal murderers?

And yet it is precisely up to us to comprehend these great forces, to bring them into alignment with not only who we are but who we aspire to become. And so while our capabilities as planners, strategists, and visionaries would indeed be much better than they are if we had Professor

Dumbledore's Pensive available to us, it is alas an instrument of magical fiction, and here we are trapped in the too-real world. Here we must make do by utilizing the patterns and links we can identify through careful study, for if we are to understand and steer the revolutions of our evolving world then these are exactly the factors we must come to grips with.

In this chapter we thus focus on clarifying our challenge by identifying the most meaningful patterns. We have already explored six essential aspects of our humanity that have become five revolutions and the anti-revolution, and studying them in combination it's evident that a first important pattern is our consistent proclivity to pursue the new, the different, the novel, and the technologically advantageous, and in so doing to create revolutions. As a species we are innate creators of revolutions, even as the revolutions themselves create many anti-revolutionaries among us.

And as we seek to understand exactly what those revolutions consist of and what their impact will be, we recognize that if we can map them in some way, we can get a much better understanding of how they are unfolding. Among the most useful of the maps are the simple lines that show how things are changing over time.

Curves

Among the line graphs we've already looked at, one of them is particularly significant as it charts the advance of digital technology and its growing impact throughout the economy. Stripped to its essence, the converging trends of digitization give us the deceptively simple ascending and descending exponential curves of the D-curve which we explored in detail in Chapter 1. The ascending line tells the story of the pauper and the king and the chess board and the rice, its purpose to help us see how an apparently simple doubling of the quantity of anything, whether rice or computer chips or even potato chips, quite soon leads from a unit of one to units of tens of thousands and then millions. The descending line, meanwhile, denotes the declining cost of computer chips, and if we can sustain the progression long and steadily enough the outcomes are transformative.

It may be difficult to grasp from the simple and graceful arcing line, but in fact this line expresses a power that will utterly and completely reshape the economy, and thus it will also reshape each of our lives, and from their combined dynamic of exponential progression we grasp that we are entering the digital danger zone, as we will soon reach the point at which technologies including robotics, big data analytics, artificial intelligence, and ubiquitous surveillance sensors combine to transform the ways we work and live, which describes the path upon which we are venturing as we transition from the industrial economy to the digital one.

More broadly, the exponential change curve depicts a fundamental aspect of reality because it also describes the overall rate of change because exponential change is having and will continue to have a massively disruptive impact on families, companies, governments, and society.

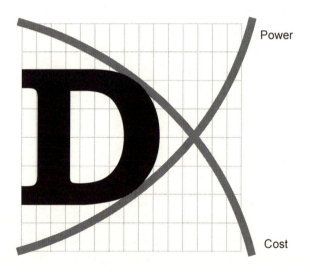

Figure 70
The D-Curve
Increasing power of computer chips is an exponential progression known as Moore's Law, while the cost declines on a reciprocal curve, which makes computers better and cheaper each year.

The D-curve explains that as computer chips are made progressively smaller, more powerful, and less expensive, they are useful for more and more functions, the complexity of the tasks they can be programmed to perform increases substantially, and they become readily affordable. A computer that cost billions of dollars and occupied an entire air-conditioned computer room in 1975 costs five hundred dollars and fits comfortably in your pocket in 2015. The computer of 2025 will be many tens of times still more powerful, and thus able to perform many more important functions than just playing Candy Crush and watching cat videos, and in the years following that will begin to approach the computational density of the brain, enabling huge advances in artificial intelligence and robotics, which will also be transformative.

It appears that no established company is safe from the disruptive consequences, as the global giants like Sony, Nokia, and Kodak have already been brought down by change, and so have most of the local bookshops and taxis and drugstores and, and, and…

To express this we draw a second curve beneath the exponential change curve to represent the capacity of organizations to change; when it lags behind the real rate of change as signified by the exponential curve then the results are usually not good. Some thoughtful experts on innovation and change have labeled this the "going out of business curve."[169]

Going out of business as a consequence of exponential change in the market or in technology is thus the organizational counterpart to future shock and the fundamentalist overreaction of those for whom modernism and accelerating change are psychologically overwhelming.

So if the exponential change curve is one of the fundamental elements of today's and tomorrow's realities, what is the necessary response? It is, of course, to speed up the rate at which organizations respond.[170] This is a timeless theme that is addressed in each of the remaining chapters of the book in various ways.

The "going out of business" curve

Figure 71
The "Going Out of Business" Curve
While change in the external environment is following the black curve of exponential change, organizations often have trouble keeping up, and the best they can manage internally is depicted by the gray curve, in which case they are most likely in the process of going out of business. This problem is particularly acute for businesses in the technology sector, but as technology is infiltrating into every industry now, the distinction between technology companies and non-technology companies becomes irrelevant; *all* companies are technology companies.

Three Phases of History:
From Stability to Explosion to Implosion

As I discussed in Chapter 4, demographers anticipate that the process of large scale migration to the cities will most likely continue throughout this century, and if current trends hold then by 2100 about 95 percent (or more) of humanity will be living in cities small, medium, or large. As city dwellers, families will be probably choose to have fewer children and the net result will be that the human population will likely reach its peak in the middle of this century, or earlier, and by the end of the century it could have returned nearly what it is today.

As we saw, over centuries from prehistory through ancient times, the

240

population grew very gradually in the global agricultural civilization that had persisted and developed for millennia, but everything changed with the industrial revolution that enabled the population explosion in the decades following 1800.   Machines, sanitation, medicine, and improvements to agriculture proceeded around the world nation by nation, and by 1900 the human population had grown to 1.6 billion, and then to 2.5 billion by 1950. Over the following 40 years the population doubled again to 5 billion, and the added another 2.5 billion to bring us to the present.

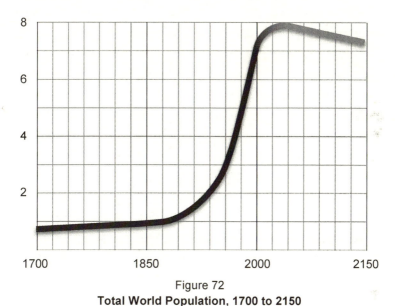

Figure 72
Total World Population, 1700 to 2150

Urbanization has been occurring steadily throughout the same period, and thus about 50% of the world's population was living in cities by 2010. Not coincidentally, this also marks the point at which the population growth rate begins to slow.

The majority of the world's population growth is occurring only in a few countries, including India, Nigeria, Pakistan and Indonesia, which remain substantially rural, but as they, too make the transition to urbanization, the world's population will likely peak and then begin to decline.

While the global population forecast suggests that the population peak will not come for another few decades, in selected locations it has already arrived. Japan is the world's most urbanized nation and its population, as we discussed, peaked two decades ago. Today it is thus facing a baby bust and an elder boom, which has fundamental social and economic consequences that will bring lasting and difficult change in every prefecture.   There is already a marked increase in retirees and their associated health care and social needs to fill but a shortage of workers and of working taxpayers.

The long term forecast is not inevitable, but there has been nothing evident in human behavior and culture during the last 30 years to suggest that anything different will emerge. If the future does indeed unfold this way then the overall historical pattern of human population growth curve from 1700 to 2150 will look like this:

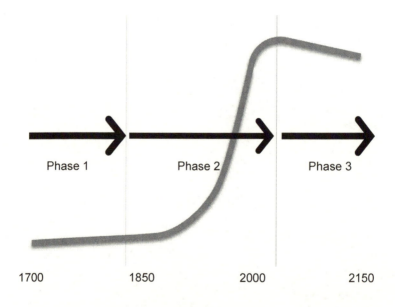

Figure 73

The Population S-Curve and 3 Phases of Human History

During Phase 1, the Agricultural Era, the human population grew slowly from around 10 million to 1 billion between 10,000 BC and 1800 AD. During the Phase 2 Industrial Era from 1800 to about 2050 the population boomed, and it now appears that we are entering Phase 3, during which population growth will stop and gradually reverse.

This distinctive S shape shows human history as a function of the human population from 10,000 BC to 2150 AD, which simply due to the shape of the curve consists of three very distinct phases.

Phase 1

Phase 1 was the Agricultural Era, tens of thousands of years of progressive learning about plant and animal husbandry, enabling the development of cities, and in those cities the progressive development of technologies in every field, including printing for the sharing and systemization of knowledge, transportation, commerce, and trade, optics and toolmaking for improvements in science and technology.

By 1800 total world population was about 1 billion; 97 percent were occupied raising food; a small portion of the 3 percent are engaged in specialized functions in urban settings. Advances in metallurgy result in iron and steel, and thus the Industrial Revolution is born as the combination of need, opportunity, and knowledge create the steam engine, and all the rest.

Phase 2

Phase 2 is the Industrial Era, the period that is now apparently ending. For 200 years industrialization was the super-powered motor that drove the industrial economy to achieve incomprehensible scale and scope. World GDP multiplied many times over, living standards increased, fewer and fewer people produced more and more food, and the world's population boomed as its cities expanded rapidly.

The economic system of industrialization is nothing like that which came before, based as it is on the transformation of resources into goods on a vast scale. The world's land surface is marked by cities and roads, mines, oil wells, reservoirs, canals, rails lines and power lines across the entire landscape that connect everyone to everyone else. Nearly 7.3 billion people participate in a single economic system of finance, production, trade, and consumption, and more than half have moved into the steadily expanding cities.

Commerce crosses borders and battlefields without regard for any limits, and with many deep ironies. President Assad's Syria, for example, obtains much of the oil it desperately needs from its adversary ISIS, which controls territory with abundant oil production facilities; revenue from those very sales enables ISIS to mount further attacks on Assad's army. The Chinese Army, meanwhile, is the largest supplier of tobacco to the Chinese people, contributing thereby to the deaths of millions of people whom it is also committed to protecting. Commerce follows its own logic, the logic of revenues and profits but not necessarily ethics or rationality.

As the slightly ascending population line denotes Phase 1, the steeply ascending line defines Phase 2. And that steep ascent also has been essential to the economic success of industrialism. Once the dynamics of the consumer economy emerged following the Depression of the 1930s it was the steady flow of new consumers into the market that enabled the economy to grow so quickly. We have become entirely accustomed to the economic model based on resources extraction, capital investment, consumerism, and growth, and no one remembers anything else.

Phase 3

But the prevailing model of industrial economics based on increasing population and increasing consumer demand may have nearly reached its limits. Demographic trends already show that population growth has slowed, and as the slowing continues we are headed to a population peak, and probably then into a decline.

From nearly every perspective this is positive news, as the current population is already overtaxing the global ecosystem and humans consume each year much more in natural resources than the Earth produces. Just in time, perhaps, we'll reverse population growth and switch in the opposite direction. Of course this transition is fraught with risks, as we have seen in the previous chapters, many kinds of threats and challenges.

Figure 74
The Turning Point
The model suggests that the transition from Phase 2 to Phase 3 has already begun, which implies that global society is now beginning the transition to entirely new social and economic structures.

In Japan it appears that the third phase has already begun, and the nation is experiencing the challenges of a declining birth rate and thus a rapidly aging population, widespread malaise, depression and an epidemic of suicide, and despite 20 years of economic experimentation of nearly every kind, a chronic inability to grow its economy.   What has already arrived in Japan could well be what's in store for much of the rest of the world.   What we will require in Phase 3, then, is possibly an entirely new economic system.   Morgan Stanley economist Ruchir Sharma explains it this way:

> In every single region of the world, economic growth has failed to return to the rate it average before the Great Recession.   Economists have come up with a variety of theories for why this recovery has been the weakest postwar history, including high indebtedness, growing income inequality, and excess caution induced by the original debt crisis.   Although each explanation has some merit, experts have largely overlooked what may be the most important factor: the global slowdown in the growth of the labor force.

Between 1960 and 2005, the global labor force grew at an average of 1.8 percent per year, but since 2005, the rate has downshifted to just 1.1 percent, and it will slip further in the coming decades as fertility rates continue to decline in most parts of the world.[171]

Some of the outlines of that system are already coming into focus. It will be fueled not from fossil sources, but from sun and wind. It will be increasingly dependent on technology that is increasingly advanced and ever cheaper, reflecting the D-curve; if these trends continue then technology may soon reach and then surpass human intelligence. This technology will include robotics, and the mass scale use of robots will also significantly shape the economy. It will be a urbanized era, even more so than the world already is, and many new cities may have to be built to replace the low-lying ones that have flooded out due to climate change.

The Shape of the Curve

In this three-phase view of human history we allow the shape of the population curse itself to explain the structure of history. There are other ways that we could chart our path, as a function of technology, for example, or in terms of economic growth, or by looking at the speed of transportation or the mobility of the population. But using the S-curve that shows the human population over 12,000 years embodies a reality that is simple, clear and convincing. It explains a great deal for which we otherwise lack explanations, as it shows the relationship between how we live, how many of us there are, and how society and the economy are organized.

Seen in this way, history is obviously marked by two major transitions, the first being the industrial revolution around 1800 when the population explosion begins, and the second the as-yet-unnamed turning point that we are just now entering. Based entirely on the shape of the curve it's easy to foresee that change would inevitably impact our social, cultural, and economic lives, and as we are already experiencing those impacts, the S-curve itself offers a helpful explanation.

This graph also tells us that although the population explosion is unquestionably significant, it was in fact a short lived transition between an agricultural civilization of 1 billion and an urban-industrial-digital civilization of about 7.5 – 8 billion. This very short phase of 200 years of economic growth and population boom was based on a cycle of increasing efficiencies in production that enabled increasing consumption, and increasing consumption that was largely a consequence of urbanization. The health of the economy was predicated on the triple phenomena of population growth, industrialization, and urbanization that enabled and indeed stimulated steady increases in production and consumption, to create handsome profits in the capitalist economy.

As we shift into the third great era of modern history, however, it's clear that no one knows what the underlying economic model will be. But it's become increasingly obvious that it will *not be* based on attaining ever greater levels of consumption, because we know that the Earth's resources will not sustain further increases. As we already consume more on an annual basis than the Earth produces on an annual basis, our current economic model is not going to continue indefinitely.[172]

This tells us that we will necessarily shift from an economy and an ethic based on "making more stuff," to one of perhaps "making better lives." More simply, we will shift from quantity to quality, and gradually learn to adopt quite different behaviors. Instead of increasing usage per person of cheap energy, we know that energy is now economically and climatalogically expensive and we must reduce consumption per person while increasing the quality of what we produce.

We have therefore reached the end of the era when people purchased showy products to let their neighbors know how wealthy they were, which we called "conspicuous consumption."   Today we see instead the emergence of "conspicuous non-consumption," by which we show off our environmental awareness by letting others know how conscientious we can be, and how little we can consume and still live well. And lest you think this change may be years or decades in the future, note that the best selling car in 2013, 2014, and 2015 in California was the fuel and carbon-efficient hybrid Toyota Prius. The change in behavior has perhaps already begun.

An optimist might propose the following chart, comparing the behaviors of phase 2 industrialization with those of phase 3, the unnamed era into which we are now entering.

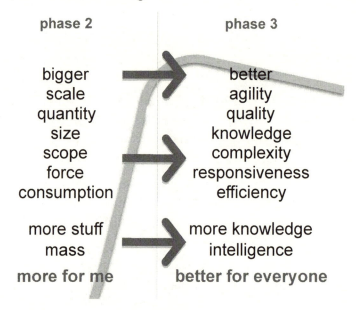

Figure 75
Phase 2 and Phase 3
An optimistic view of what might be ahead in Phase 3.

The Futurist

The human population explosion that began around 1800 with the advent of industrialism is now winding down of its own accord. It has been, perhaps unexpectedly, a self-limiting process that created urbanization and is now slowing due to the success of urbanization. Ironically, while the population explosion was one of industrialization's greatest outcomes, so also was the city in which the population implosion is now occurring.

The massive wave of economic growth that occurred through the 20th century and which accelerated so significantly in the century's final decades was fueled by billions of young and willing workers who found employment in millions of factories where they produced the goods of the modern world, the excess of abundance that we now find in nearly every corner of the globe.

> The primary threat most countries now face is not to many people but too few young workers, and the fastest-growing segment of the population is, by far, people older than 80[173]

But with a rapidly declining birth rate, those young and willing workers are turning into middle aged citizens and retirees, and the economic boom they created will be replaced by a much different kind of economy. It's an economy that we certainly don't understand today; in fact, despite the best efforts of a world full of economists, we barely understand the one we have.

The genius of nature is that its method, natural selection, systematically creates a species to fill every conceivable niche in every ecosystem, from single celled life to the giant elephant and blue whale, in habitats ranging from the crushing depths of the ocean bottoms to the summits of the highest peaks, from the icy poles to northern and southern latitudes to the steamy equator, and now, with humanity's recent adventures into an artificially-created habitat, in orbit 200 miles above the Earth. Our robots, extend civilization onto the moon, mars, asteroids, and now even beyond the boundaries of the solar system.

Each species strives to become ever more fit for its niche, but the challenges arise when the structure of the niche changes. And of course that is exactly what's happening now. In fact the structure of the entire ecosystem is changing, and this applies both to the natural world, since we're literally changing the climate, and to the human economy, since we're shifting into a new economic era.

In the natural world, climate change has instigated the largest mass extinction in millions of years, killing entire forests, but also growing new ones; decimating fertile landscapes and turning them to deserts, but also transforming tundra into usable farmland, killing vast expanses of coral reefs, and drowning entire low-lying island and atoll ecosystems. Nature's mechanism of adaptation, genetic mutation, requires generations to attain results, but this process of change is occurring within a single generation, thereby exposing the inherent fragility of many species because their excellent adaptation to the niches they occupy turns into over-adaptation when the niche changes fundamentally.

Similarly, the globally dominant economic paradigm of industrialism is being stressed by the changes that are emerging due to its own evolution, which is also exposing its severe fragility and thus its over-adaptation. We are obviously headed for still more severe shocks, toward increased volatility and disorder. Nassim Taleb has given us a very useful way to think about this:

> Some things benefit from shocks; they thrive and grow when exposed to volatility, randomness, disorder, and stressors and love adventure, risk, and uncertainty. Yet, in spite of the ubiquity of the phenomenon, there is no word for the exact opposite of fragile. Let us call it antifragile. Antifragilty is beyond resilience or robustness. The resilient resists shocks and stays the same; the antifragile gets better. This property is behind everything that has changed with time: evolution, culture, ideas, revolutions, political systems, technological innovation, cultural and economic success, corporate survival, good recipes, the rise of cities, cultures, legal systems, equatorial forests, bacterial resistance …. Even our own existence as a species on this planet.[174]

Taleb is a commodities trader by profession, from which he has apparently become quite rich, and a very keen observer of society, as a result of which he has become quite famous. He goes on to explain that by pursuing over-adaptation to one particular form of economic life, we have been making the economy *more* fragile; he calls it "fragilizing."[175]

When banks collapse due to the excess of ill-considered bad loans; when nations collapse because of factional fragmentation; when ecosystems collapse because of massive over-exploitation, these are all examples of induced fragility. Obviously this is the exact opposite of what we ought to be doing.

So while the economists certainly don't have the benefit of Dumbledore's Pensive, the patterns we have identified have enabled us to identify the S-curve that charts the history of the human population, and also tells us that the coming changes constitute significant trends in contemporary history. We currently sit just in the middle of the transition from Phase 2 to Phase 3, on the gently peaking curve that connects the ascending line of the industrial baby boom to the slowly descending line of the unlabeled era into which we are entering. If, however, we continue to optimize our economic system to reflect the structures and processes suited to Phase 2 then we will experience still more fragility-induced collapses and the accompanying heartbreak and misery. Our challenge, then, is to design systems of economy and management and decision making that promote anti-fragility while also being well-suited to the Phase 3 world that we are entering.

And Now, Part 2

In Part 1 we have sought to understand the major forces that are interacting to define and shape our world today, tomorrow, and in the decades to come. These six revolutions, technology, climate, energy, urbanization, cultural change, and anti-change, influence our lives each and every day in ways that entirely obvious and also subtly hidden, but whether we see them or not, they are inescapable. The population S-curve gives us a quick, simple, and also provocative model of human history, and in case we didn't know it already, it tells us that we are entering a period of fundamental change. The concepts of fragility and anti-fragility give us a quick measuring stick against which we can consider any actions we might want to take, for we can simply ask, Will this make us more fragile, or more antifragile? That is, Will it promote adaptation and future success, or will it lead to more vulnerability?

In Part 2 we will build upon our understanding of these patterns as we examine a series of themes and viewpoints intended to help us better anticipate what is coming, and to make suitable anti-fragile choices by considering some other human capabilities and aptitudes that have also become essential. We'll consider our magnificent skills as analysts and as visionaries, as map makers and planners who chart the terrains of today and tomorrow and who help us plan for our journeys, for we will certainly rely on these thinkers for guidance as we navigate the turbulent pathways and waters that we are sailing inexorably towards.

•••

Part 2

FORESIGHT

The Strategic Species

One of the great scientific breakthroughs of the 19th century occurred when Charles Darwin decoded the operating principles behind nature's method of evolution. His models explained reproductive experimentation, adaptation, natural selection, competition for survival, and genetic mutation, providing a much better understanding of how the living world evolves. Nature is an abundant and proficient experimenter, and thus it seems that every possible combination gets an opportunity, and then the built-in process of selection determines which survive, thrive and persevere.

And now we are living within an economic system that, with some minor exceptions and within some constraints also follows these very same principles. In the world's capitalist economy competition between idea, products and firms is intense, and while the winners often thrive, the losers frequently die off. Taleb, again:

> For the economy to be antifragile and undergo what is called evolution, every single individual business must necessarily be

fragile, exposed to breaking – evolution needs organisms (or their genes) to die when supplanted by others, in order to achieve improvement, or to avoid reproduction when they are not as fit as someone else. ... Ruthlessness is an engine of improvement ... and continuous failures work to preserve the system.[176]

Technologists, business leaders, and even academics seek success by mounting countless experiments, launching an abundance of test products and companies into the market. These are mutations that bring forth innovations, new business models, and especially new technologies, and they enable new behaviors and thus new possibilities as they become new commercial enterprises. On a small scale they bring local change; on the large scale they bring about global change.

This happens very fast now largely because the speed of the digital revolution and the dynamics of competition drive the economy as they also drives innovation, and as a result the economy is now evolving much faster than our genes can evolve. So whereas nature's evolutionary process requires that change to occur across generations because a reproductive generation is nature's built in cycle time, the economy's evolution manifests change roughly over quarter-year cycles, the 90 day business reporting rhythm.

Because the rate of change in society has far surpassed nature's clock speed, it is the human cultural experiment that's now the driving force of change. Hence, the great question before us is whether we will develop the skill and capacity to manage and guide the broad process of change upon which we have embarked, or whether we will crash and burn.

Another way to express this is to say that we are now engaged in a race, and what may be at stake is the future of civilization. Will we develop the capacity to foresee the consequences of our choices and actions, and will we use that capacity to steer human strivings in fruitful and positive directions? Or will we follow the whims of technological possibility and the pursuit of capitalist profitability without regard for the ethics, morals, or even the survival consequences inherent in our choices? In simplest terms, will we choose short-term profits over long or medium term survival?

This is the grand experiment in which we are now engaged, simply due to the fact of our ever-increasing technological capabilities. We did not accumulate this power because of any grand plan, but incrementally, step by tiny or large step, invention by invention, discovery by discovery. We learned to split the atom and also to split the gene; we learned to live in orbit above the Earth and send rockets to other destinations in our solar system, and peer toward the very origins of the universe and to count the billions and trillions of stars and galaxies and to measure the speed of light, and also to build nanoscale machines and repair broken hearts and brains and limbs. By the end of this century 200 million people will produce enough food for 7 or 8 billion to eat, and the billions who do not farm will continue to be busily engaged in the daily creation of an economy and a society that engulfs our entire planet.

But we are moving forward at high speed without a plan, and thus we have by the fact of our accumulated learning brought forth change that we do not understand. Nature still has the final word, of course, for we may unknowingly we bring ourselves to extinction. The fate of humanity rests therefore on the unknowable outcome of the race between human culture and nature's evolutionary system; will we learn to anticipate and make good choices, or will we try everything, good and bad, and destroy ourselves along the way?

It is because of the scale of this risk that our situation is qualitatively different from the past's revolutions, for as mighty and formative as they were they rarely invoked threats at the scale of civilization itself. What we now need, therefore, is not just the power to see our good and bad choices in hindsight, but the foresight to know in advance which choices are the right ones, and the social, political, and moral capacity to choose the viable, sustainable, and ethical paths from among the many that would lead us elsewhere.

This is not merely an abstract or moral dilemma for philosophers to muse upon, but a practical challenge that leaders and citizens must consider, for while we have enacted laws intended to protect other species of mammals and reptiles that are in danger of becoming extinct we have yet to fully grasp that as we are the cause of most extinctions, we ourselves are also an endangered species due entirely and ironically to the consequences of our own learning and our own behavior.

Developing and applying the foresight necessary to making the right choices are thus the imperatives of our times, and they are the subjects here in Part 2.

•••

Chapter 8:

The

Realist:

Drowning in Complexity

An invasion of armies can be resisted;
an invasion of ideas cannot be resisted.

Victor Hugo[177]

Creativity and the industrialization that resulted from it have been, throughout history, a double edged sword. They created the modern economy, but also, sadly, the same forces were put in service to violent conflict. The 20th century opened with the most massive descent into self-destruction that human history had ever seen, as seventeen million people died during the five years of the sadly mis-named War to End All Wars, and an additional ten million were wounded. That was only a prelude, however, to the even greater destruction that followed in World War II, when 60 to 80 million died.

Violent death on a mass scale did not begin nor end with the formally declared wars of course, as millions more died during the 20th century in various civil and regional wars, famines, and gulags.

Mass Deaths of the 20th Century			
Armenian Genocide	Turkey	1915	1.5 million
Indonesian Killings	Indonesia	1965 - 1966	.5 million
Soviet Gulag	USSR	1929 - 1953	1.6 million
Great Famine	China	1958 - 1962	20 – 40 million
Khmer Rouge	Cambodia	1975 - 1979	1.5 – 3 million
Partition	India	1947	.2 - .5 million
Holocaust	Germany	1939 - 1945	6 million
Bosnian Genocide	Bosnia	1995	.008 million
Rwandan Civil War	Rwanda	1994	.5 – 1 million
TOTAL			**32 – 54 million**

Figure 76
Mass Deaths in the 20th Century

This discouraging tally depicts the industrialization of death, and it is certainly one of the tragic ironies of modernity that so much of the 20th century's enormous creativity and discovery was directed towards killing. Barbara Tuchman expresses it this way:

The end result of the complex organization that was the efficient software of the Great War was the manufacture of corpses. This essentially industrial operation was fantasized by the generals as a "strategy of attrition." The British tried to kill Germans, the Germans tried to kill British and French and so on, a "strategy" so familiar by now that it almost sounds normal. It was not normal in Europe before 1914 and no one in authority expected it to evolve, despite the pioneering lessons of the American Civil War. Once the trenches were in place, the long grave already dug (John Masefield's bitterly ironic phrase), then the war stalemated and death-making overwhelmed any rational response. "The war machine," concludes Elliot, "rooted in law, organization, production, movement, science, technical ingenuity, with its product of six thousand deaths a day over a period of 1,500 days, was the permanent and realistic factor, impervious to fantasy, only slightly altered by human variation." No human institution, Elliot stresses, was sufficiently strong to resist the death machine. A new mechanism, the tank, ended the stalemate.[178]

And then in the midst of the violence at mid-century, scientists discovered how to harness atoms of uranium and then hydrogen to create weapons that could destroy even more thoroughly, now all of humanity was immediately at risk. On the day on which the very first nuclear weapon was tested in the dusty desert of New Mexico in 1945, the world's great physicists were still entirely unsure as to what would happen:

> "I had become a bit annoyed with Fermi ... when he suddenly offered
> to take wagers from his fellow scientists on whether or not the bomb
> would ignite the atmosphere, and if so, whether it would merely
> destroy New Mexico or destroy the world."[179]

However, the same forces of creativity have also been directed toward well being and economic growth. As the world's population grew 3.8 fold from 1.8 to 7 billion, its aggregate economic activity expanded by a stunning factor of 5,000. Both increases were possible only because the proficiency at growing food had increased in ways that could not have been imagined a century earlier.

Today 3.5 billion urban inhabitants define the modern world. They use millions of computers, autos and jet airplanes; they live in slums and skyscrapers; they ride in cars, buses, trolleys, and even in 300 KPH mag-lev trains, and everyone has become connected into a single social and economic system.

There was significant social progress as well. Women, who had little social power and few political rights in 1900 were, by law at least, had gained full rights by 2000 in nearly every society. Colonialism was nearly universal in 1900 when British Queen Victoria ruled over a nation on which the sun never set, and thus 45 million citizens inhabited England, Scotland, and Ireland while an additional 400 million lived in British colonies in India, Canada, Australia, and in dozens more across Africa, Oceana, and South America. But by 1980 the entire empire had been dismantled, 50 new nations had emerged as independent, and the British occupied only a small number of its small home islands. Indeed, by 2000 colonization had become nearly unheard of worldwide, as the principles of national sovereignty and self-determination were firmly established as norms of geopolitics.

In South Africa the Apartheid system of government that had been established in 1948 meant that by 1993 a white population of 5 million dominated and thoroughly repressed a black population of 23 million. Throughout the 1970s and 1980s it seemed that Apartheid would end only in a violent civil war that would surely decimate the nation and perhaps the entirety of southern Africa, and would yield tens of thousands or even millions of casualties. In the end, though, Apartheid was ended in 1994 through peaceful elections, signifying an enormous change in mindsets not only in South Africa, but worldwide.

We use the term "revolution" to describe these major events in human history, and for our own era, we know also that the scale of the changes that we're creating and living through, and the scale of the impacts that they are having, is global and transformative. Computers and robots really do have the potential to alter the course of human evolution in fundamental ways, for they offer not only the potential that the vast majority of work may be done not by people or animals at all, but also that we may soon co-evolve with technology to become post-human.

Since the mid-20th Century the human population explosion has meant that in aggregate humanity has had the capacity to alter Earth's ecosystem also on a large scale, and so we have done. Simply through the fact of there being so many of us we have transformed vast forests into deserts, and also deserts into farms, and brought to extinction thousands of species of plants and animals.

We also know that in the worst case climate scenario, the devastation caused by global climate change will also transform society, essentially by wrecking it. The maps we've relied upon for three millennia will have to be replaced if the oceans rise and the urban settings in which about 2 billion people currently live have to be replaced or substantially upgraded.

In summary, then, our creative powers, used both for unparalleled destructive purposes and to improve lives and livelihoods, have brought us to a world or unprecedented complexity.

Complexity

When we consider everything that's going on across all of today's revolutions one the first things we notice is that the issues and challenges that we're confronted with seem to have more dimensions, more factors, and more considerations than in the past. Multiple forces are driving fundamental change in the economy, forces that are changing where and how we live, how we get our energy, and even how we think about our own identities and our values. And the forces are interacting, which make for a world that is much more complex than humanity has ever experienced. Increasing complexity is a defining characteristic of the modern world.

There are many ways to measure complexity – as a function of the size of the economy (it's never been bigger); as a function of the number of people engaged in trade (it's never been more); as a function of the diversity and number of products that factories make and people buy (also never more); or perhaps as a function of the sheer number of choices, possibilities, and interactions that the average person is exposed to – all measurements that indicate the same increase in complexity.

Consequently, it's more difficult to make decisions because more factors have to be taken into account. How should we balance the needs of youth for education, and of seniors for health care, if we have an economic system that cannot afford to pay for both? How should we balance the ongoing health of the economy with the disruptive potential of carbon regulations?

Because increasing complexity makes the job of decision making much more difficult, politicians, business leaders, and community leaders find themselves confronted by one challenge after another after another, but often with no attractive options at all. In addition, due to the acceleration of change there's generally less time available to make major decisions, which only increases the pressure.

Overall then, we often have the impression, correctly so, that we're drowning in complexity.

Universal Connectedness

Perhaps the single most important factor that contributes to the increased complexity is the phenomenon of connectedness. The outcome of economic globalization and ubiquitous digital communications means that nearly everything that occurs in the economy and throughout society is connected to nearly everything else. Nothing stands alone, nothing in our world is *dis*connected.

Every person is part of the global whole, the multi-dimensional domain in which our social, economic, political, and cultural lives are thoroughly intertwined. Whatever happens or is said or published in Beijing and Aleppo and Moscow and Johannesburg is known almost instantly in Baghdad and New York and Mumbai. We have information about the entire world available to us instantaneously, which often has impact, even significant impact, on choices and possibilities in rural India and southern Chile, or London, Paris, Shanghai, or Auckland.

When someone burns a Koran in Florida there may be riots in Teheran. When an Israeli kills a Palestinian, or vice versa, there may be protests in Cairo and in New York. When there is a run on the banks in Athens there is pressure on the banks in Frankfurt. When manufacturing slows in Guangzhou, the New York Stock Exchange may have a precipitous drop.

Every person has the possibility of being in contact with almost anyone, often many others, and we are all thus influencing and influenced by others. This is perhaps the social scientist's version of John Donne's famous line, *Ask not for whom the bell tolls; it tolls for thee*. Because no one in our modern world is an island.

These connections consist of interpersonal relationships, sitting together in meetings and coffee shops, but are just as likely to be electronic. The extent of our connectedness is a direct consequence of the internet, which enables every individual to have their own, personally-controlled connection to anywhere and anyone and anything they want. This is of course a major change from the pre-internet days before about 1990, and the capacity to connect as broadly and universally as we do is another reason that change now occurs so much more quickly than it did three decades ago.

Connections and interactions may consist in the sharing of ideas, or exclusively through impersonal business transactions. In whatever form, connectedness means that we're all aware that others exist, many others, and even when there is no direct contact between us this very awareness still has influence on the choices that each one of us makes.

Hence, a decision by the Greek populous to accept or not accept the terms for European Union loans funds affects every nation of the EU, and what affects the EU affects the US, and what affects the US impacts China and India. The news and the repercussions circulate around the world like so many ping pong balls.

And of course the issue we face is that there isn't just one bouncing ball. Everywhere there are multiple issues and challenges occurring at all times, countless ones. Hence, it's not just that there's the big story about millions of Syrian refugees that causes everyone to adjust, it's that there's a big story in Syria at the same time that there's a big story in Greece and another in Riyadh and another in Lagos and another in Silicon Valley. It's all happening at the same time. And everyone has immediate access to all the news about everything that's happening. And so it's utterly impossible to predict what the overall net affect will be.

We can be sure, however, there will be effects, that is, that our views and attitudes and beliefs and expectations will indeed change, although we cannot foresee what the changes will be. And the changes we experience today in our beliefs will impact on what becomes possible or impossible tomorrow. This is how change comes to accelerate, and it's a very precise description of our reality.

And while there are a very few remaining tribes of perhaps tens or hundreds of people each which live in isolated places such as the Amazon basin where they have limited or even zero contact with the rest of the world, nearly all the rest of us are fully and utterly interconnected. If we assume, perhaps generously, that there are 1,000,000 tribal inhabitants who are not in contact, this group in total would constitute only .0000014 percent of humanity; the other 99.9999 percent of us are connected into one system.

Drowning in Shock, Gossip, and Trivia

So what happens when our society of 7+ billion comes under stress? What happens when our capacity to understand what's happening is inhibited by the sheer volume of input that's coming at us? What happens, in other words, when everything is happening all at once?

In electrical systems such events are called "overloads," and well designed circuits are protected by circuit breakers to prevent permanent damage; the breaker kicks and the system shuts off. Biological systems that are massively overloaded go into "shock" and they also shut down. Modern medicine distinguishes between many different kinds of shock, including septic shock caused by rapidly multiplying bacteria, the anaphylactic shock of severe allergic reaction, and cardiogenic shock, when the heart is damaged and unable to supply sufficient blood to the body.

Psychological systems also have means of shutting down. People experiencing severe stress suffer from "traumatic stress" and "post-traumatic stress disorders," and Toffler's term "future shock" and Rushkoff's "present shock" describe what happens when people are unable to cope with the rate of social change. It's quite obvious that in our times many of us are experiencing overload, shock, and traumatic stress, reactions common not only by individuals and identity groups, but also to institutions and corporations and sometimes even entire nations. Individual and collective reactions are intense and often violent, mobs form and riots ignite out of anger, frustration, outrage, and fear.

So where does this lead? Where are we headed as participants in a universally-connected / hyper-connected global society that finds itself drowning ever more deeply in ever-increasing complexity and increasingly stressed out?

It could be that we will just descend deeper and deeper into crisis, and that things will just get more and more unpleasant. Will we continue to

264

degenerate into ever more trivia, into an abyss of "reality TV" and 24-hours-a-day gossip, slander, and name-calling? Sometimes it seems that this is all society has to offer, and it can be enormously discouraging if not outright depressing.

Then again, perhaps we will discover a different possibility.

Systems Thinking

A fascinating field of study that goes by a variety of names including cybernetics, general systems theory, and operations research has for its central concern systems and how they behave. It teaches us to see many of the otherwise hidden factors that shape events and behaviors, and which cause all types of organizations, from communities to societies to companies and governments to behave as they do. It seeks, that is, to understand the patterns that shape our reality. As a way of thinking it offers a compelling approach to managing complexity.

We already encountered this way of thinking in Chapter 1 in the story of the pauper, the king, the chess board, and the rice, and also in the parable of the algae and the pond. By recognizing non-linear patterns of exponential growth we are able to foresee the future consequences of current conditions, and when we grasp how exponentially-changing social and technological forces may impact on today's economic structures and patterns, then we are also engaging in systems thinking as we begin to see likely or possible future outcomes of past and current trends.

Radar, Computers, and Paper Towels

As a field of study, systems thinking emerged from discoveries made early in the electronics age. Much of the pioneering work was done by the scientists who, at the outset of World War II, were working in England under the threat that German bombers would annihilate London. They searched for ways to track the incoming aircraft, and in the process of solving the technical problems that enabled them to invent radar they also had to invent an entirely new body of theory. Their success was a significant contributor to the survival of England and the eventual Allied victory.

When the war was over many of the same scientists held a series of conferences, the Macy Conferences named for the foundation that funded them, at which they examined the similarities and differences between electronic systems and biological ones. They discovered many overlaps, and this led to development of an entirely new field of study which became systems thinking.

This way of thinking has been very influential in all technical domains involving electronics, and also in management. Computers would not be possible without the theories and practices of systems thinking, and one of the world's most important computer science pioneers, John von Neumann, was a participant in the Macy Conferences and pioneer in the systems thinking field. Without computers, of course, the internet would not exist, and hence today's globalized economic system probably wouldn't exist either. We might say, therefore, that systems theory may be the most important field that may never have heard of. (Or perhaps you have heard of it, but anyway you get the point.)

These insights are so useful because they're so broadly applicable to explain so many apparently different things;[180] and even in a brilliant 1000 page book James Miller is only able to scratch the surface:

A scientific generation patterns its models up on its dominant metaphors. Scientific figures of speech in the nineteenth century concerned linear effects; the action of electricity, for instance, was compared to the flow of water. The twentieth century characteristically has drawn its metaphors from Einstein's relativistic field theory, which clearly influences the philosophy of organism of Whitehead, the Gestalt psychology of Wertheimer, Kohler, and Koffka, and general systems theory. Field theory, Gestalt theory, and systems theory, in spite of their difference, all recognize that the interrelationships among co-acting components of an organized whole are of fundamental importance to understanding the totality. The organic analogy is the dominant metaphor of our time in scientific analyses of complexity. Today we think in terms of systems.[181]

We experience systems and therefore systems thinking not only through the use of modern electronics, but throughout our daily lives, although perhaps without noticing. For example, have you ever seen a small sign posted to the sidewalk adjacent to a storm drain, which says something like "Don't Dump; Drains to the Ocean" with an image of a fish?

Figure 77
Systems Thinking Education
A small sign glued to the sidewalk reminds us that our seemingly small, personal actions can have larger, systemic consequences.

I saw this little one, about four inches square (10 cm^2), glued to a sidewalk in Beverly Hills, California. It's innocently intended to get us to think like a systems scientist, and to realize that the pollutant that we may have considering disposing of in that drain is not going to some miraculous waste repository, but to the open waters where it might kill fish.

In the washrooms at San Francisco Airport there are signs on the paper towel dispensers that say, "Paper comes from trees," a reminder not to use so many of them, and thus cause a paper company to kill even more trees. Both signs are intended to help us all recognize that our miniscule, inconsequential individual actions, dumping a bit of toxic liquid or just drying our hands, contributes to large scale, systemic consequences for entire oceans and forests and planets.

Of course these individual actions don't typically have large scale consequences by themselves (unless the waste you were going to toss down that drain was nuclear waste). But that paper towel dispenser is one among millions of them, and that storm drain is one of thousands in your city or town, and one of millions in your nation.

And while the actions of each of us individually may or may not be very consequential, now that there are 7.3 billion of us it takes very little for the aggregate of our individual behaviors to aggregate to large scale, systemic impacts. It's the aggregate of the wastes dumped into millions of storm drains that decimates entire fish populations, and it is the billions of paper towels consumed by millions of travelers every day that adds up to serious forestry acreage. Your car, one among a billion, cannot possibly produce enough CO2 to change the climate, but one billion can and are changing the climate quite decisively.

The Scale of a Global Economy

How can we understand the shift of scale from the individual to the entire population? Every day in the US about 1.7 million people take commercial airline flights (which also produce great amounts of CO2).[182] If everyone stopped to wash their hands once, and each person consumed two sheets of paper towel, rather than one sheet, that's 1.7 million extra paper towels. According to the Sierra Club, one tree produces about 20,000 paper towels, which means that air travelers would consume and extra 85 trees each day if they take one extra sheet.[183] 31,000 trees in a year, and at an average of 500 trees per acre,[184] the paper industry grinds up about an acre of trees each week, or 62 acres of trees just to dry our hands in airports; not to mention the millions of offices and restaurants and coffee shops where we're also using paper towels at a prodigious rate. It's a lot of trees, and this is just in the US; there are about 6.5 million more people flying in and out of airports around the world, and many of them stop to wash their hands, too.

The point is that normally the large scale impact is entirely invisible to us. It's just us, alone there in the wash room, and there is an unlimited supply of paper towel right there in the dispenser and so we grab, one, two, six towels to dry our hands, not usually considering that millions and millions of people are also drying their hands, and that we're consuming entire forests in the process.

While the paper company likes it to be invisible to us because it leads us to consume more of their product, there are systemic ecological consequences of using all that paper.

Furthermore the airport operator has to pay for them, and then they have to pay for the disposal too, because none of us take the wet papers towels with us when we leave the rest room. Which is why I found this little sign in an airport restroom in Zhengzhou, China. A quite effective reminder.

Figure 78
Systems Thinking Education in China
Sign on a paper towel dispenser in Zhongzhou, China. The notion of wastefulness and overconsumption is well depicted by the papers falling to the floor.

Half the paper consumed, or twice the amount of paper consumed, ends up making a lot of difference to the airport, the forest, to the paper company, and to all of us.

All of which explains why the paper company would be quite content for us to consume more, while the airport wants us to consume fewer. And of course the point for us is that paper towels and waste poured into drains are just two among hundreds of thousands of examples in which the functioning of the modern economy has separated us from the sources of our supply, and made the consequences of our own behavior invisible to us.

How many children believe that milk comes from grocery stores, not knowing the role of the cow, the dairy farm, the processing plant, the process of pasteurization, the trucks, and the refrigerators that have made it possible for us to enjoy a store that's fully stocked? Looking even deeper, where did the trucks come from? And the fuel they burned along the way, or the steel that they're made of, or the coal that was burned in the steel mill, or the trucks and shovels that mined the coal, and on and on it goes. The entire economy is entirely interconnected into a magnificently complex system of production and exchange, in which nearly everything comes from somewhere else.

As we strive to understand the increasingly complex world, systems thinking becomes an exceptionally useful tool for exploring and modeling specific issues like paper towels and trees, and also in examining the larger issues. What are the systemic, future consequences of digitization? What's going to happen with the Earth's entire climate system, and the nearly as gigantic human fossil fuel energy system, undergo basic change? In what ways is a city a system, and how is our urbanization proclivity influencing the connected systems of human reproduction, the economy, Earth's ecology, and human culture?

These are significant issues for us to consider, and at root it would be entirely reasonable to say that this book is about systems and how they evolve and develop, and what happens then, and especially how we can anticipate and therefore guide them.

Later in this chapter we'll explore some additional insights from systems theory in more detail, but first there are three points that ought to be made here at the very beginning.

First, a definition. The term *systems*, in *systems thinking,* must be defined specifically because it's obviously so important. Hence, by *system* I mean any set of connected parts that produce, through their connections, specific outputs. The outputs of a system by definition exist because of whatever the system does to its inputs; it transforms them in some way.

Paper towel factories transform trees into soft paper in convenient sizes that we use to dry our hands. They do this using complex industrial processes that turn logs into pulp and then into paper of just the right texture, and then cut and fold it and package it, using massive amounts of water and electricity, lots of hard labor, and big machines in each step of the process.

Systems have purposes, like producing paper towels, which can generally be discerned by what they do. Hence, auto factories are systems that produce cars, and dairy farms are systems that produce milk. Both are quite complex, but also directly understandable; if we look we can see many connected layers of inputs and processes and outputs.

People and indeed all living creatures are also systems, and one of the insights from the Macy conferences was that electronic systems have many characteristics in common with biological ones. In making this discovery they also realized that a single set of principles explains the behavior of many different kinds of systems, from electric circuits to nerves to brains to computers to companies, communities and nations.

And while systems have recognizable patterns and behaviors, they come in varying levels of complexity. Geologists understand that the Earth's tectonic plates are a system, and climate scientists that the Earth's climate is a system, and both are much more complex than we have to date been able to understand. So are the human brain, the most complex of all of evolution's creations,[185] the gene, the cell, and the atom.

As we learn more about systems our capacity to understand, design and build more useful and effective ones increases significantly. Robots are a great example, as through massive amounts of study, research, and experimentation in thousands of laboratories around the world robotics scientists have made major advances toward fully functional robots of exceptional capability, and it seems that they will soon be part of our daily lives.   Genetic engineers, similarly, have developed the ability to manipulate life's own code to alter the complex system that defines anatomy and physiology.

The second key point is that our attempt to understand all of these systems, from the simplest to the most complex, relies on our ability to make models of them, and to learn from those models. We do this because models enable us to study and experiment from a variety of perspectives from which we can develop a much deeper understanding. We alter the scale, making giant models of atoms and molecules to be able to see them with our limited eyesight, which is what chemists do on a daily basis. We speed things up, as when we create time lapse models of dynamic systems like weather and climate in order to predict what's going to happen; meteorologists do this every day to make weather forecasts. We also make huge things small, as when we test scale models of buildings on vibration tables in structural engineering labs, or when a science teacher shows golf ball-sized planets orbiting around a beach ball sun.

The core concept of this book, that five revolutions are occurring simultaneously throughout the world, is also a model. Its purpose is to help us understand what's happening and to better forecast what's likely to happen, and so to help us reduce the risks that tomorrow will present.

The third point about systems returns to the topic we began this chapter with, complexity. Complexity can be a concept useful to explain how difficult a given system may be for us to understand and manage, and thus systems with very high complexity like the climate or the economy are inevitably much more difficult to understand and to predict than simpler systems such as factories or televisions. The fact that we build factories and televisions that often do what we want them to do is powerful evidence; the fact that we cannot control the climate or the economy is because they are orders of magnitude greater in complexity and we don't yet have sufficiently good models of them. Systems thinkers remind us that if we can't model it, we can't manage it, and consequently, despite our best attempts to manage the economy we experience frequent booms and busts, spurts of growth that seem to create wealth out of thin air and devastating recessions that make wealth evaporate and create suffering and despair.

No one argues that about design of a factory if it produces the intended outputs, as its outputs are proof of its proper functioning. But *everyone* argues about the functioning of the economy, and economists, politicians, business leaders, and everyday folks across the entire ideological spectrum claim to have *the* solutions for how to make it better. Leftists and liberals say one thing, rightists and conservatives the opposite, but neither side is consistently able to predict with reliability what will actually happen as a result of their policy prescriptions. How to stimulate growth? Cut taxes says one side; boost spending says the other. What should the central bank do? Restrict the money supply says one side; flood the nation with cash says the other. And even when the economy is working, people on opposite sides of the ideological divide attribute it to different causes.

This confirms that precisely what we lack is an effective model of the economy. Without a model to experiment with and learn from we have no choice but to experiment with the actual economy even as we also manage it from day to day, season to season, year to year. It's so vastly complex that we simply don't know what works and what doesn't work until we try it. Hence, every economic policy implementation, whether tax increase or tax cut, or change in monetary policy, is literally a live experiment with real life consequences for those who are in the midst of the game, which is all of us.

Complexity, therefore, is the economist's permanent companion, although it's not her friend, or ours. But it is inescapable, and with the continuing expansion of economic activity, with urbanization and growing numbers of people joining the global economic system, and with technology resulting in more and more connections, the complexity will only increase.

Connections and Complexity

The more connections there are within a system the greater the complexity that the system can attain. With more connections there are more choices and more possibilities.

These connections can be literal, such as expanding options for air travel to more and more destinations. There are now about 100,000 commercial air flights per day, transporting 8.2 million passengers each day, 3 billion each year. Because that total number is a significant percentage of humanity, the air travel industry must be understood as a force that promotes increasing complexity worldwide.

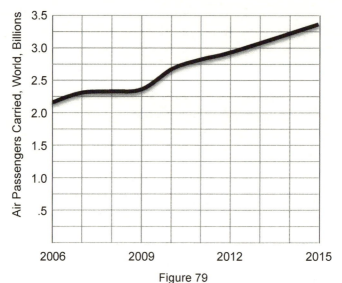

Figure 79
Number of Air Travelers, 2006 – 2015[186]

An increase of 1 billion per year in a single decade, and a significant contributor to increasing global complexity.

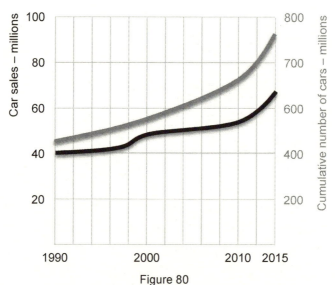

Figure 80
Number of Autos Sold Worldwide, 1990 – 2015[187]

Annual sales in black (left scale); Cumulative number in gray (right scale) (Does not include light trucks or buses.)

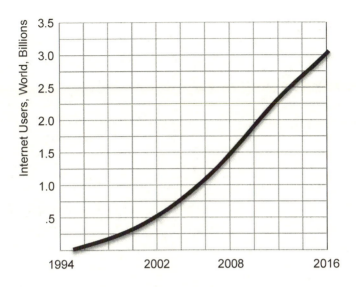

Figure 81
Number of People Connected to the Internet, 1995 – 2016[188]

All of these connections, physical and virtual, mean that a growing number of us have access to a much wider variety of information than we've ever had, to a range and depth of experiences we've never had, and thus the possibility of thinking and doing things that we never could before.

For example, the Arab Spring uprisings that originated in December 2010 in Tunisia with the anguished self immolation of Mohammed Bouazizi and then quickly spread across northern Africa and throughout the Middle East occurred largely because people were able to connect, to communicate with one another through social media. Tools like Twitter enabled them spontaneously organize and coordinate the times and places for protest marches while avoiding the military and secret police that were trying to stop them. The government of Tunisia collapsed under this unexpected and unprecedented public pressure, and many observers found it shocking that a dictatorship could be brought down in this way.

By the end of February 2012, rulers had been forced from power in Tunisia, Egypt, Libya, and Yemen; civil uprisings had erupted in Bahrain and Syria; major protests had broken out in Algeria, Iraq, Jordan, Kuwait, Morocco, and Sudan; and minor protests had occurred in Mauritania,

Oman, Saudi Arabia, Djibouti, Western Sahara, and Palestine. The protests shared some techniques of civil resistance in sustained campaigns involving strikes, demonstrations, marches, and rallies, as well as the effective use of social media to organize, communicate, and raise awareness in the face of state attempts at repression and Internet censorship, most notably used by the youth members of the Arab population.[189]

Thirteen short months saw tumultuous change across the region, all enabled largely by two factors: suppressed anger and a desire for change, and the ability to connect to one another. In Egypt, an even more powerful state security agency than in Tunisia was entirely unable to thwart mass marches that brought together hundreds of thousands of participants, and which also led to the ouster of sitting dictator. The internet played a key enabling role:

> On the evening of January 27, 2011 Egypt—a population of 80 million, including 23 million Internet users – vanished from the Internet. The Egyptian government ordered a complete Internet shutdown amidst popular anti-government protests calling for the resignation of Egyptian President Hosni Mubarak. The order followed reports on the previous day (25 January) of blocked access to Twitter. The heavy-handed attempt to block communications in the country did not quell the protests, and may have even increased the number of people in the streets. Under political pressure from inside and outside Egypt, President Hosni Mubarak resigned, turning command over to the military on February 11. Four days later, similar protests erupted in Libya, calling for an end to the Gaddafi regime.[190]

Further assessment by University of Washington professor Philip Howard confirmed the fundamental roles played by Twitter, blogs, and YouTube:

> After analyzing more than 3 million tweets, gigabytes of YouTube content and thousands of blog posts, a new study finds that social media played a central role in shaping political debates in the Arab Spring. Conversations about revolution often preceded major events, and social media carried inspiring stories of protest across

international borders. One of the researchers noted, "Social media carried a cascade of messages about freedom and democracy across North Africa and the Middle East, and helped raise expectations for the success of political uprising. People who shared interest in democracy built extensive social networks and organized political action. Social media became a critical part of the toolkit for greater freedom. Twitter offers us the clearest evidence of where individuals engaging in democratic conversations were located during the revolutions." In Tunisia, conversations about liberty, democracy and revolution on blogs and on Twitter often immediately preceded mass protests. Twenty percent of blogs were evaluating Ben Ali's leadership the day he resigned from office (Jan. 14), up from just 5 percent the month before. Later, the primary topic for Tunisian blogs was "revolution" until a public rally of at least 100,000 people eventually forced the old regimes remaining leaders to relinquish power."[191]

Figure 82
Sign Held by a Protestor in Cairo, 2011, Celebrating the Role of Social Media in Bringing about Change in Egypt
A powerful statement about an evolving world, especially as the AK-47 is now primarily a tool of terrorism and thus of counter-revolution.

Classical media, radio, television, newspapers and books, do not have this immediate and interactive quality because they're "one to many" media whereby a single message is sent broadly from one source to many listeners. One to many media are powerful tools for maintaining social control because the content of messages can be carefully scripted. Hence, throughout history dictators and autocrats have secured control of all mass communications immediately upon coming to power in order to cement their hold over society, and control of the media provides control of the message, which in turn helps to sustain control of the populous. Control of the media also gives tyrants free reign to conduct purges and "disappearances" without fear of public disclosure or opposition. It is precisely for these reasons that most democracies have institutionalized the role of a free press, and why autocrats try to eliminate it, as without the means to communicate, witnesses who see or experience repression have little chance of being heard, should they even dare to try.

Twenty years ago when the internet was young and its future impact was a topic of only speculation, observers including Lawrence Wilkinson of Global Business Network noted that the nature of connections it could foster might have a fundamental impact on the type of discourse in a society precisely because it might enable effective many to many communications on a scale and scope that had never been possible before. Everyone can be connected to anyone, they suggested, and that might be transformative. It turned out that they were quite correct.

This shift is cleverly reflected in the name "YouTube, where "You" refers to everyone, and "Tube" refers to "television. This tells us that the founders of YouTube astutely recognized exactly what they were doing – creating a medium through which anyone could put themselves on television, to be viewed by anyone else. The monopoly of broadcast mass media was thus broken, and the lineage of the internet as a revolutionary, many-to-many communications device was firmly established.

Now the nearly the entire world is online, many-to-many has become everyone-to-everyone. More than one and a half billion of us are Facebook users now.

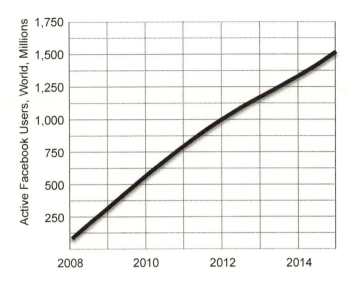

Figure 83
Number of Facebook Users
Source: Statstia.com[192]

YouTube and Twitter give a voice to anyone who wishes to participate, and that voice may be heard anywhere and everywhere, by anyone and everyone. Consequently, mass communications are no longer mediated, or controlled, by any central authority except where censorship persists, such as in China, but as long as the internet functions and you can get online you can post what you want, and you can read or watch what you want. The Egyptian government's attempt to shut the internet down was intended to prevent the protesters from connecting with one another and thus block their capacity to self-organize the protests and to inspire others to join.

Networks

The dynamic force behind the Arab Spring, Twitter, and YouTube is a simple concept, but its implications are enormously significant.   This concept is "the network," a collection of distinct entities that communicate with one another in order to achieve a purpose or purposes.

Hierarchies are also collections of distinct entities, but the difference is that the purposes of a network are determined by the individual entities themselves, while the purposes of a hierarchy are determined from the top. A corporation is a hierarchy whose purposes are defined by top management and the board of directors; a military organization is a hierarchy directed by the top generals or admirals; and the political, legislative, and executive roles in a community or nation are the mayor, the president, prime minister, emperor, or dictator. We typically say that these top guys "run things."

This is not the case with a network. It is the users who define the purposes of a network, and many of the qualities and characteristics that are inherent in the nature of any network contribute to its revolutionary potential. In the absence of censorship people post what they want to post, watch what they want to watch, and read what they want to read. They explore topics they're interested in and ignore the rest, and as their interests change from hour to hour or from moment to moment, the waves of connected ideas flow back and forth at all hours, day and night.

In Egypt and Tunisia, and then in the other countries that followed the revolution was thus a *self-organizing* process, one in which the possibility of the revolution itself emerged from the interaction of some, and then more, and then a huge number individuals. The flow of ideas converged around the possibility that the will of the people could change the government if enough people spoke up. But until it actually happened it quite extraordinary, improbable, and indeed unexpected.

But as more people joined the protests they saw with their own eyes that the government leaders were becoming afraid, which made them more courageous and more determined to recruit all of their friends and relatives to join in, which made the government leaders still more afraid. They cycles of action and feedback accelerated not as dictated by anyone in a hierarchical manner, but as a emergent property of shared intent and action.

The concepts of self-organization and emergence are thus critical ones, for they provide descriptions of how ideas and actions come about through a spontaneous process of alignment that through its own momentum arrives at consensus: *this* is what we want, the people say, and when such alignment is perceived the social power that it manifests has proven, to the great surprise of nearly everyone, that it can overturn even the most entrenched dictators.

All most people needed to do was to show up to the protests, and their sheer numbers constituted an overwhelming social force. Consequently, new social ideas generally take form and achieve impact in such self-organizing networks much more quickly than they do in structured and hierarchical. (This is one reason that Internet companies are clobbering old line companies to often; they know intuitively how to harness the power of networks, while corporations struggle to gain alignment through hierarchical means. It the hare vs. the tortoise, expect in this race the hare doesn't ever stop to rest.)

And now that nearly the entire world is connected together in one network, the Internet, and countless sub-networks of special interests, the possibility that new ideas will emerge and take hold quickly is *much* more likely than it was in the past. It's in fact a daily occurrence, and this is in and of itself an aspect of the cultural revolution whose importance cannot be overstated: the Internet, as a self-organizing network, is a facilitator *and* accelerator of social change that can enable things to happen that probably could not have happened before it existed.

This is a profound and indeed transformative possibility that will characterize life throughout the 21st century, unlike any other time in human history.

But this new power is a source of risk as well as great opportunity. The opportunity to create positive change comes when people in huge numbers become supporters of an idea; the risk is that at these high speeds the world can align around a terrible idea just as readily. ISIS, as we have seen, is a proficient user of social media to promote apocalyptic visions and terrorism; al Qaeda uses the internet to publish the bomb-making instructions used in Boston.

The speed and volatility of social media explains why most major corporations now maintain what are often called "social media monitoring centers," and why there are dozens of subscription and free web companies that track trends and ideas across all social media. They're staffed 24 hours each day to monitor the flow of words and ideas through the Internet's social media platforms such as Twitter, Facebook, and Yahoo, and numerous others, looking for the patterns of ideas and opinions and behavior that will illuminate emerging trends and concepts, risks and opportunities. During the crisis periods which arrive now and then, these monitors help executives in hierarchies to understand what's happening and to gauge public sentiment, which helps them know how best to respond.

Wells Fargo Bank, for example, maintains two of these centers, one on each coast of the US, and they are staffed constantly. Gatorade, Dell Computer, and Clemson University are among the thousands of organizations that have also done so.[193]

Hence, just as hierarchies have power to effect actions, networks also have power, but because action by networks comes about through choice and the aggregation of individual choices, it can be significantly more powerful. This is obvious in the Arab Spring and the overthrow of Egypt's Mubarek, a firmly established national leader who had at his disposal a massive army as well as a huge secret police apparatus; still they were not enough to protect him from the massive wave of popular will.

In contrast, the Chinese protesters who occupied Tiananmen Square in 1989 were violently suppressed by the Chinese government in secret, for there was at the time no Internet that the student protesters could harness to share their message throughout the nation, or to show the tanks as they rolled in. Even now, 25 years later, what really happened on the night that the protest was crushed has never been fully disclosed, and within China there continue to circulate contradictory stories and rumors about what did or did not really occur.

Social media can behave like a tsunami, and it is for this reason that they're closely monitored in authoritarian nations such as China, where social media sites that are allowed to exist must subject themselves to government censorship.

If you visit China today and try to access Google through the normal public Internet you will not be successful. As Google refuses to self-censor, China refuses access. (A few million Chinese do access Google, but only through virtual private networks that have been set up specifically to evade government censorship; the vast majority of Chinese Internet users live in a heavily censored information environment.)

As Victor Hugo presciently noted and as the Chinese leaders well understand, "An invasion of armies can be resisted; an invasion of ideas cannot be resisted." The Internet is uniquely and persuasively effective as a forum for the sharing of ideas, and it is a means through any idea's dissemination and arrival as an important landmark in society can be enormously accelerated.

Metcalfe's Law

It cannot be a surprise that the potential power of any network is directly related to the number of individual entities that are part of it. But just how powerful that really is may indeed be a surprise.

Robert Metcalfe, a computer scientist and pioneer who worked on the design of computer networks and, among many other accomplishments invented the ethernet communications standard had therefore abundant opportunities to study network behaviors. One of his more notable observations is that the value of a telecommunications network is proportional not to the number of its users, but to the square of the number of users. That is, the value of a network grows exponentially as new user join linearly.[194]

This is exactly the same exponential phenomenon that we discovered with the pauper and the chess board and the rice, for the accumulated quantity of rice quickly expands from one grain to become a mountain. This is enormously significant, because it means that if your network has twice as many members as mine, your network will be four times more powerful, and probably four times more valuable, too. My 100-person network is "worth" 10,000; your 200-person network is 40,000. Should your network grow to 3 times the number of users of mine, its value would be 90,000, 9x.

It was based on these dynamics that Facebook, as a corporation, became so immensely valuable so fast, as did Google, and why their founders are billionaires: they invented technologies that everyone wanted to use and the value of those technologies was calculated as a function of the square of the number of users. Thus, if the pertinent metric is the number of users of and thus the power of the network, even a slightly bigger size yields a tremendous advantage.

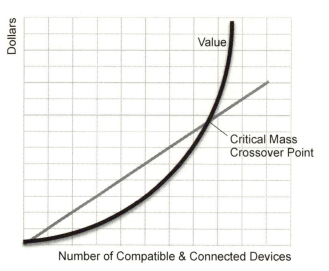

Number of Compatible & Connected Devices

Figure 84
Metcalfe's Law[195]
"The Systemic Value of Compatibly Communicating Devices Grows
as the Square of Their Number."

Metcalfe's discovery is now widely know as "Metcalfe's Law," and is one chapter in the growing body of technology's legal doctrine that began with Moore's Law and now also includes Joy's Law, Joy's Second Law, Amdahl's Law, and many others. All of these computer pioneers have so-called laws named after then because they discovered something important about computing and how society may use computing.

Moore, as we saw, anticipated the increasing power of computer chips. Joy recognized that computer speeds are also doubling approximately each year, and his Second Law states that "most of the smartest people work for someone else," which led to the realization that applying network principles to solving difficult technical problems might produce better and faster results than relying exclusively on your own staff. Amdahl noted that the performance speed of computers, particularly those applying parallel processing designs, was a function of hardware resources applied, and he devised a formula to calculate the improvement rate and defined the factors that would limit improvement.

Another term for Metcalfe's Law is simply the notion of "network effects." In Metcalfe's own words, "The original point of my law (a 35mm slide circa 1980, way before George Gilder named it...) was to establish the existence of a cost-value crossover point – critical mass – before which networks don't pay. The trick is to get past that point, to establish critical mass."[196]

The manifestations of Metcalfe's Law present themselves in the marketplace in interesting ways. For example there was time when social media company MySpace was vastly larger than Facebook, but once Facebook's rate of growth surpassed MySpace, MySpace was left behind as an overnight-also-ran. Again, it was not the absolute number that mattered most, it was the rate of growth, for the growth of Facebook was viral and thus also followed an exponential growth trajectory. Knowledgeable observers were able to quickly discern that Facebook would quickly surpass MySpace far before it actually did so.

It is for this reason that many technology markets are characterized by economists as "winner-take-all." In these markets, a company that gains a lead and which can sustain and enhance its leadership position can remain untouched and untouchable for years and decades. In fact, these commercial advantages often endure for the entire life span of a given technology.

As a result, Microsoft was for quite a long time the world's most valuable technology company precisely because the success of the Windows operating system became unassailable, and left the firm with a monopoly. Bill Gates astutely recognized the value of that position and maneuvered the company successfully to occupy it; it made him the world's richest man as Microsoft took and maintained control of the entire market; it won it all.

What Microsoft's leadership apparently did not recognize was that its advantage would reliably endure only as long as the PC was the dominant computing platform. If and when there was a fundamental change in the structure of the market, which occurs in technology markets with regularity, then there could be no guarantee that its compelling market advantage with Windows would translate to whatever came after Windows.

And of course it didn't. The invention of the touch screen mobile phone and then the success of the tablet have overturned the market, and Microsoft has since struggled. Smartphones from Apple and Android constitute 90% of the total smart phone market, while Microsoft's attempts to partner with and then eventually acquire Nokia have not enabled it to penetrate to the market, and eventually it abandoned the effort altogether precisely because its share of the network was too miniscule to matter.

Most technology markets are also subject to similar network effects, which leads to the overwhelming accumulation of market share and market value by only one or two predominant leaders; no other firm can get a foothold. The underlying dynamic may be the same with social movements such as the Arab Spring, where a compelling social movement literally took hold of an entire nation, and then its neighboring nation, and then yet another. The dissenters, those supporting the dictators, could not find a way to have their voices heard over the din of the protestors, and even the police and military could not suppress the energy, and so it became a winner-take-all social phenomenon. You can look on the Internet today and see photos of people in Cairo's Tahrir Square standing on tanks beside the soldiers who had been sent to "control" them; the military, too, had become powerless.

Connectedness and Globalization

When everyone is connected to everyone, now our reality and a key point in this chapter, then we must expect that the range of behaviors in our social systems will expand significantly as compared with times when we lived in relative isolation from one another. The sudden transformation and recent successes of the gay or LGBT rights movement may be just such an example. For decades LGBT individuals lived under severe repression and without legal protection, but suddenly within the span of only a few years the entire situation reversed itself as it became clear that the majority of Americans support LGBT rights. In a stunning and bitter blow to the counter-revolutionaries, the US Supreme Court reversed a century of prior court rulings and accorded to LGBT citizens equal rights.

Would this have happened without the Internet? It's possible, but it seems quite likely that the capacity of the internet to give a voice to a repressed social group, to publicize the injustices they endured, and to harness support for the elevation of their status to the equal of others was essential to the outcome.

This is another example of how the capabilities brought by the internet change our behaviors. We can do, and we can live, as we never have done or lived before in part because the extent of our connectedness is unprecedented. Humans have never been connected this way, and what we'll in the future do as result of these connections is largely unpredictable, but our experiences suggest that we should expect whatever occurs to be significant.

The Globalization of Ideas

This introduces another dimension to the concept of globalization. To this point we have been discussing globalization as an economic force and as a fact of economic life, but now we're talking about the *possibility* to connect as a global phenomenon, and the dialog that can result could itself be transformative not because it enables or leads to commercial transactions but because it leads to new perspectives and new attitudes and new ideas. We may be experiencing, that is, the beginning of the global empire of ideas.

Globalization itself is certainly not new, as throughout even the early centuries of the modern era the Romans assembled, led, and defended an empire that stretched across three thousand miles of territory, from the British Isles in the northwest to the Middle East in the southeast. During the height of its imperial era all roads led to Rome, the seat of its power and the center of the idea of "Romanness."

In the 13th century China organized a global trading empire that stretched thousands of miles in every direction, to Africa in the west and perhaps even to South America in the east. A massive trading fleet sailed from China's coastal cities, which included what may have been the largest wooden ship that ever sailed, perhaps 400 to 600 feet long (120 – 180 meters). At the height of its trading era China had by far the world's largest economy, but all this came to an abrupt halt with the ascension of Hongxi Emperor in 1424. The collapse of trade also shrank the economy, and the nation retreated into five centuries of relative isolation. The inward-facing posture of the Chinese economy ended only with the death of Chairman Mao in 1976 and the resurgence of Chinese globalization and economic expansion under his successor Deng Xiao Ping.

In the 16th century, the Spanish also built a global empire of colonies based on large scale extraction of silver from the New World for transport back to Europe. This wealth made Spain the most powerful nation on Earth, but when the silver ran out the power of empire receded along with it.

In the 19th century the British presided over the largest empire the world had and indeed still has ever seen. From London, Queen Victoria surveyed more inhabitants than any country had ever dominated around the world, an empire upon which famously, "the sun never set." The British Navy was the instrument supporting the empire, conquering opponents and defending its lifeline, maritime trade. But Britain's power also receded as the idea of colonialism was displaced by the expectation of universal sovereignty and self-determination. One by the one the colonies gained their independence.

Today what we are experiencing, however, is a global economic system the likes of which the world has never seen. We are all connected to all of us through trade and commerce and through media, information, dialog, and discussion in ways that have never before been possible. What we will choose to do with these connections is unknown, but we can be sure that much will be done.

Hence, globalization is now much more than an economic phenomenon; it is also a social one. Religions are borderless and global, counting 2.2 billion Christians, 1.6 billion Muslims, 1 billion Hindus, 375 million Buddhists, and millions of adherents of other religious and spiritual paths; entertainment and sports are global, as nearly a billion people watch the World Cup soccer tournament in more than 200 nations; air travel is global, as I mentioned above, with 3 billion passenger trips per year connecting everyone to everywhere. Globalization, then, is the process of connecting all the world's people together, and also connecting our institutions and business, and all of the connections enable new possibilities.

Mass Media / Immediate Media

Mass media helped to foster mass societies, societies marked by a certain uniformity of belief, action and appearance. Through live broadcasts, TV viewers and radio listeners could be brought right to the midst of the action as it unfolded, and could also form their own opinions about what was happening; no longer were they limited to hearing about it indirectly or reading about it in the newspapers on the following day. One of the first instances that this had a major impact on society was when almost-live TV images of the Vietnam War were broadcast by the nation's news media to American living rooms.

Millions received for the first time an unfiltered view of war's horrors, atrocities, suffering and absurdities and many also realized for themselves that the Vietnam War had neither a moral basis nor the possibility of being won. No longer were their opinions shaped by policy or propaganda; people could see for themselves. The immediacy of the vivid and inescapable imagery created the anti-war movement, a counter-cultural revolution that polarized American society, ended the presidency of Lyndon Johnson, and contributed to the eventual end of the war itself.

The technology underlying these media continued to progress as the century advanced, and new business models emerged along with the technological prowess to enable social evolution that marked a major turning point in the very structure of society. This was the "media revolution," so well expressed by Marshall McLuhan

Ours is a brand-new world of allatonceness. "Time" has ceased, "space" has vanished. We now live in a global village ... a simultaneous happening. George Washington once remarked, "We haven't heard from Benj. Franklin in Paris this year. We should write him a letter." Information pours upon us, instantaneously and continuously. As soon as information is acquired, it is very rapidly replaced by still newer information. Our electronically-configured world has forced us to move from the habit of data-classification to the mode of pattern recognition.[197]

Today the Internet offers the possibility that anyone may have immediate and intimate access to people and events occurring any distance away without an interpreter or intermediary. Everyone-to-everyone connectedness has replaced delayed, edited and filtered news and censored propaganda; now we have a non-stop, non-filtered flood of inputs originating from everywhere, and accessible everywhere. This is hyper-connectedness.

Hyper-Connections

Hyper-connectedness, or perhaps the term omni-connectedness describes it better, means that every storm, every tragedy, every concocted celebrity event, every intimate family story, every sporting event, and every election is public, accessible to everyone, and subject to the parallel running commentaries of professional journalists and amateur observers. There are fewer and fewer secrets, and more and more opinions about everything.

The Internet also enables globalized micro-segmentation because the principle of search is now a fundamental to how we engage with information, and Google is an action we take to find out anything about anything. You can find others who share your interests, no matter how obscure your interest and no matter where you live or where they live. If you want to connect with others engaged in violent, anti-Western jihad, for example, al Qaeda and ISIS use the Internet so that you can easily find them. This is not a theoretical issue, but an utterly real one, as thousands of young people left their homes in Western Europe to undertake the perilous journey to join ISIS in Syria, where many of them then became suicide martyrs.

Do you want to make pressure cooker bombs? As I noted, the Tsarnaev brothers apparently learned how by following instructions from al Qaeda's *Inspire* magazine, an online publication that promotes Al Qaeda's version of global jihad.

The Internet is a limitless global message board and bazaar and entertainment omniplex, and most of its users are not trying to crush Western civilization as they merely want to connect with people who share their concerns and interests. If you or your child has a rare disease you can connect with others who are suffering from the same one. If you have a pet marmot you can share videos with other marmot owners. Perhaps you're looking for collectable pez candy dispensers (that's what got eBay started), autos, or any other consumer product imaginable, and every type of ideological, religious, and political propaganda from any nation, in any language, along with legal drugs, sex, and limitless pornography. You'll find all of them on the Internet, the world's unlimited newsstand and gift shop.

How much content does it have? YouTube recently reported that 300 hours of video are uploaded onto its platform ... every *minute*, a total of 432,000 hours of video *per day*, enough to keep everyone entertained with exactly what they're looking for, whatever that is.[198] The rate is increasing as it becomes easier and easier to shoot higher quality footage with lower cost equipment, and so the production values of homemade videos are improving markedly. Skilled (and unskilled) filmmakers can make movies using only an iPhone, as exemplified by *Tangerine*, a success at 2015's Sundance Film Festival that was shot primarily using iPhone 5 phones equipped with special lenses, and an $8 app called Filmic Pro.

Shoot a great movie, post it to your own channel on the internet where it can be seen by millions of people, and you could become famous and maybe rich.

Connectedness is not only about sharing information; it takes many other forms too. For example, if the shirt you're wearing right now was purchased from Amazon or Wal-Mart, it's likely that it was made in

Southeast Asia, where there are thousands of clothing factories employing millions of people who are cutting and sewing and labeling for every brand, from lowest to luxury.

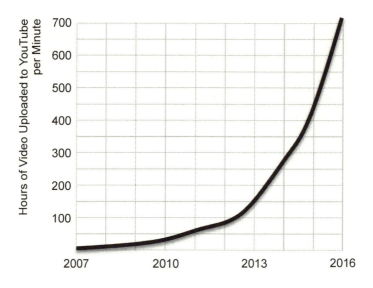

Figure 85
Hours of Video Content Uploaded to YouTube, per Minute[199]

The design for your shirt was probably sent to the factory via the Internet, and the cottons, wools, or polyesters, as well as the threads it consists of, came from manufacturers located all over the world. Naturally, all the ordering and shipping and warehousing and transporting and inventorying was also communicated and managed via the Internet, meaning that your shirt is a product of a tightly connected global marketplace.

The fabric itself may well have begun with cotton seeds that a giant, global agribusiness company like Monsanto provided to a large-scale, industrial farm in China, India, or the US, likely consisting of 1000 acres or more. These three nations are the world's largest producers of cotton, and out of total world cotton production of about 23 million metric tons, China alone produced 7 million in 2013, India 6.6 million, and the US 2.8 million.[200] In Australia, the seventh largest producer, the average size of a cotton farm is about 1600 acres, and in a major testament to the labor efficiency of mechanized farming, it only takes a total of eight people to operate. 94 percent of Australia's cotton crop of about 1 million metric tons is exported, 75 percent of it to China.[201] Some of it is likely in the shirt you're wearing right now. Australia's total cotton production has expanded significantly during the last fifty years, from 42,000 acres to 1.5 million acres, a 35x increase that is possible only because of Chinese demand, which in turn is driven by demand in the US and Europe for products made in China.

The raw cotton was probably picked by a massive harvesting machine. John Deere company would be happy to sell you one that weighs in at 70,000 pounds, has a 500 horsepower engine, and will set you back a tidy $550,000. But it can do the harvesting work of a small army of humans: mechanization plus fossil fuels (used for the fertilizers as well), make farming an industrial process. Delivery to market also requires fossil fuels, as about 30 percent of all the world's raw cotton traveled across an international border on its way from farm to factory,[202] where it was then woven into fabrics in huge industrial fabric mills, to which dyes and printing were added somewhere along the way. Massive rolls of fabrics were then cut and assembled, often by robots, and then transformed into finished goods. From raw seed to finished shirt, the components of the shirt involved dozens of people in a dozen or more countries, until it finally arrived to the store where you bought it.

And that shirt, of course, is just one product that represents a vast array of what industrialism can provide throughout the entirety of the connected, globalized economy. Raw materials are mined, grown, harvested, and otherwise produced on every continent, shipped in every direction to be progressively transformed into finished goods, step by step, transported again and again, until they arrive in your home or workplace. This is the massive, global supply chain that is now an integral part of our lives, and which is indeed at the core of the economy. Through it, we are connected economically to people we will never meet, never talk to, never know the names of, nor the stories behind their lives. But to some significant degree our lifestyles depend upon them, and they depend upon us, the consumers of their production efforts, to earn their salaries to feed their families and pay their rents.

Cotton is of course at the very basic end of the economic continuum; sophisticated electronics, like the iPhone, occupy the other end, and the complexity involved in their creation is at least an order of magnitude greater. Apple CEO Tim Cook was the mastermind behind Apple's global supply chain, the hidden engine behind the massive profits that have made Apple the worlds most valuable corporation, and one of its most admired.

The final assembly of your iPhone was probably done by someone who works for Foxconn, a trade name for Taiwan's Hon Hai Corporation, the world's largest contract electronics manufacturer; Apple is its biggest customer.   While reliable numbers are hard to find, a 2013 Fortune Magazine article offered these statistics on assembly of the iPhone 5S (which at the time was the latest thing, but now of course is very old news).[203]

1,000,000:	Number of workers Foxconn employs in China
100,000:	Number of production lines it runs
300,000:	Number of people working only on the iPhone 5S
24 / 7:	Hours/days of Foxconn's iPhone 5S factory runtime
500,000:	Daily iPhone 5S output at Foxconn's Zhengzhou site
20,800:	Hourly iPhone 5S output
350:	iPhone 5S assembled per minute
$175,000:	Gross revenue to Apple from the sale of iPhone 5S, per minute, assuming retail price of $500
$250 million:	Gross revenue to Apple from the sales of iPhone 5s, per day, assuming a retail price of $500

Figure 86
Foxconn/Hon Hai and Apple 5S, 2013

Hon Hai's annual revenue is around $131 billion.

Perhaps you bought your shirt using your iPhone, and from Amazon. In one of its 50 massive warehouse, one of its thousands to robots probably picked your shirt out of a bin, one of two or three dozen bins stacked from floor to ceiling, and scooted your shirt to packing station where someone put it in a box. Fedex then picked the box up, put it in their truck, took it to the airport ... etc. etc.

Internet commerce and globalization are not all joy na dprofits, though. Disturbingly and very sadly, when their substandard factory building collapses, or catches fire, or when the excessive stress of their work overwhelms the workers and they attempt or succeed at suicide, then in some way we, the buyers, are responsible. And conversely, when we lose our jobs, or when our economy takes a downturn and we feel threatened and reduce our spending, and choose not to buy that shirt or that iPhone or that pair of Nikes, then the workers in China may lose their jobs, and have to return to the farm where they grew up until the economy again picks up and the entire cycle begins again. There is a very dark side of global capitalism, and this is surely it.

Mutual Interdependence

In many respects the globalized cotton-to-iPhone economy is a magnificent triumph of planning, coordination, organization, progress, and increased well-being. Globalization of cotton and dozens of other raw goods and millions of finished goods has lifted millions of people from rural poverty into the urbanized middle class. No, it's more than millions actually, it's tens of millions, and now hundreds. In China alone a full 500 million people have migrated to the cities during the last twenty-five years, most of them drawn by the opportunity to make better lives for themselves and their children. For many, the path off of the farms led to factories in Southern China, where they made those shirts and iPhones.

As of 2011, it was estimated that about 70 percent of all products at Wal-Mart were made in China.[204]   Walmart's sales in 2011 were $421 billion, so about $300 billion was made in China, which by the way is more than the entire GDP of 140 countries. Creating $300 billion of goods in a year keeps a lot of people very busy.

Again, all of this is possible because the Internet provides a free and universal communications platform upon which the massive effort of coordination required to make the global economy function can flourish. The product designs, the coordination of manufacture, purchasing, and shipping, and the exchange of payments is *all* handled via the Internet, and thus globalization and the massive expansion of commerce that has occurred during the last few decades is possible only because of digitization, the revolution in computers and communications that we explored in Chapter 1, and which we know will continue to shape economic activity and to profoundly influence society.

The 50 Amazon warehouses across the US already utilize 10,000 robots,[205] more are on the way, and they will become increasingly sophisticated.   Investment by Samsung in partnership with the Korean government is intended to create robots capable of complex and sensitive assembly tasks that are currently carried out by Foxconn's massive staff of laborers.   In a burst of understatement, the Korean Ministry of Trade, Industry, and Energy commented, "Once affordable robots reach the market and are more widely used, it can lead to the creation of 'smart factories' and bring about far-reaching innovations to the manufacturing sector."[206]

It may not be such good news for the workers who depend on those manufacturing and assembly jobs.

From the Chinese perspective, globalization has been a tremendous boon and a transformative force that turned a proud but relatively poor and mostly rural nation into one that is now the world's largest overall producer of wealth – its GDP is largest, not per capita, but overall.   As a result, it's now the world's largest market for cars.

The Chinese government invested a portion of the profits earned from selling consumer goods to Americans into American government bonds, thereby becoming the largest holder of US sovereign debt.   Thus, Americans got more stuff, filling up their garages with yet more, and in return they obligated their children and grandchildren to make interest payments to China for the remainder of the century.   China also took a portion of the profits and invested in a wide variety of durable assets, including American real estate, all the while enabling Chinese workers to earn their way into the middle class.   This is also the result of hyper-connected globalization, and another expression of the growing complexity of the world's economy.   These connections cannot untangled short of a complete collapse as we are all fully interconnected and mutually interdependent.

Another of the fascinating aspects of economic globalization is that as every nation's power base is dependent on its economic strength, it requires a massive economy to support a sophisticated military. And since the economies of all of the major nations are now completely interconnected, any aggressive military action carries the risk that the instigator will be cut off from global markets, there is a powerful economic incentive for nations to avoid outright conflict.

Iran, Russia, Mynmar, and North Korea have seen their economies suffer significantly due to economic sanctions. Iran agreed to abandon its nuclear weapons program for at least a decade to regain access to the global marketplace; its economic isolation worsened living standards and led to increasing unrest throughout the nation. And Russia's seizure of Crimea led not to open warfare but also to economic sanctions that have hurt Russia's economy and the Russian people.

Thus, in the global economy, economic power has become the most effective form of soft power, and while it has not replaced the capacity or the need to send in troops, aircraft, and drones, in many cases it is proving to be more effective.

Even terrorists are affected by economic measures. As I noted above, ISIS sells its oil to any and all customers, including to the Assad regime that it is also trying to overthrow, and the funds are a primary source of revenue used to pay its soldiers. ISIS opponents therefore targeted its oil production capabilities, and successfully cut off a significant portion of its cash flow.   Wages for ISIS fighters dropped by half following the destruction of a formerly productive oil field in eastern Syria.[207]

GDP and the Consumption Trap

The field of economics is characterized by numerous paradoxes and outright unknowns that are function of its enormous complexity and our as-yet inadequate models of it. One of the greatest is the dual nature of a consumer-driven economy. In the US, about 70 percent of all economic activity is consumer purchases, the remaining 30 percent capital investment. The nation's economy is therefore driven by the amount of goods and services that people consume, so economists constantly emphasize the importance of buying more stuff. Each year the volume of sales made during the American Christmas shopping season is compared with the volume the previous year, and when there is not an increase it is interpreted as bad news. In order for the economy to sustain its success, in other words, consumption must increase year after year, every year.

This presents a challenging paradox that economists have not yet resolved, for as we all know the total consumption of natural resources currently exceeds Earth's annual production of resources, and thus for the economy to remain healthy we have to constantly consume more than we did in the past, and yet for the ecology to remain healthy we have to consume less because we're already consuming too much. We cannot do both, so which set of models will prevail in our thinking and in our management? Will the principles of economics overcome the limitations of our core natural resources base, or will they change?

This imbalance between "production" and "consumption" has led to problems including accelerated ecological decay, and ecologists and resource scientists call our attention to the declining supplies of critical resources including water, wood, fish, and some critical minerals.

Destruction of rain forests in Brazil, for example, is driven by logging and clear cutting for cattle ranching, which transforms ecologically diverse and dynamic forests into barren soils that quickly erode, taking their nourishment out to sea, and the Brazilian government has taken notice. Comparing actual area of Brazilian portion of the Amazon deforested each year between 1990 and 2009 including the projected rate based on Brazilian government targets to reduce deforestation by 80 percent by 2020, and cumulative total deforestation as a percentage of the estimated original extent of the Brazilian Amazon (4.1 million km^2).

Confusingly, however, as measured by the very crude tool of GDP calculations that consider all commercial transactions as positive, destruction of the rain forest is an economic "good," because it is a quantifiable economic activity. The bulldozers and roadbuilding and wages paid are readily available statistics, but economics does not at present measure the value of the undisturbed rain forest even though that forest is doing significant work to benefit global ecology, supporting a wide range of animals and insects as well as producing oxygen and consuming CO_2 and other pollutants. Hence, the incompleteness of the GDP concept causes significant distortions in how we measure the creation and preservation of value.

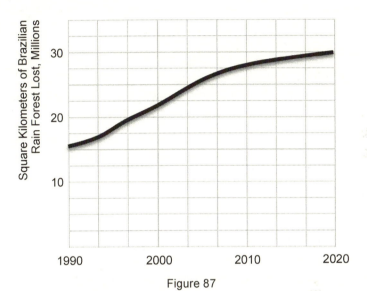

Figure 87
Destruction of Brazilian Rain Forest, by year.[208]
Focused efforts on the part of the Brazilian government with the support of many other nations and NGOs has reduced the rate of destruction significantly.

Conversely, in the South Pacific nation of Palau, which consists of 200 small islands and has a population of about 22,000 people and where the local economy depends on tourism, economists have begun to assess the value of such resources. When leaders in Palau recognized that many visitors come to their islands because they want to boat and scuba dive in the beautiful, blue waters among 130 different species of sharks and stingrays, they understood that the sharks themselves are a major attraction; they also play a key role in maintaining the health of coral reefs, lagoons, and other ocean habitats.

Shark fishing is also a popular sport, but even so shark fishing has been banned throughout the 600,000 square kilometer archipelago, the world's first shark sanctuary that now composes an area the size of France. The underlying economic calculation makes the decision quite clear: 100 dead reef sharks would bring the Palau people about $10,800 in revenue at about $108 each, but 100 reef sharks visited by tourists nets about $18 million on an annual basis at $180,000 each.[209] When the costs and values are calculated this way it's not such a difficult choice to protect the natural habitat; this is, in effect, a better understanding of the connections and the way that individual elements in the entire system create and provide value.

As the profession of economics comes to more widely embrace calculations like this, the difference in thinking will have a significant impact on policy design and decision making. Certainly the Palau shark fishing tour companies put up howls of protest when these rules were first proposed and then enacted, complaining bitterly about the loss of their livelihoods and the infringement of an intrusive government on their freedoms. But the core insight, that the long term value of living sharks vastly exceeds the short term value of dead sharks, makes it easier for forward-looking policies to be written, adopted, and enforced. "Restricting or banning fishing was difficult at first, but people now understand it's for our future. It's the only way to keep the fish there." So said Heather Ketebengang, Wildlife Health Coordinator of the Palau Conservation Society. "Our policies will be good for my grandchildren."

Similar insights are beginning to play a role throughout the economy economic, an example of exactly what we mean by systems thinking. Understanding the relationships between the elements of a system and assessing where and how value can be created or destroyed not only for today but for future generations requires that we have quite good models of what's occurring in systems that may be enormously complex. The oceanographers who helped the leaders of Palau understand the critical role that sharks play in the health of reef and ocean ecosystems together with the economists who calculated the various cost and value curves were practicing systems thinking, and so is Heather Ketebengang, who is thinking about the well being of her children's children.

A Model of the System

Another problem related to overconsumption, and which is revealed only when we have a clear picture of the behavior of large and complex systems, is of course that it causes resource shortages in basic goods, and therefore price increases that will inevitably take a heavier toll on poor people and poor countries than on rich ones.

For example, the global market for corn (or maize) has been significantly altered because of the US government's push to augment oil with ethanol.

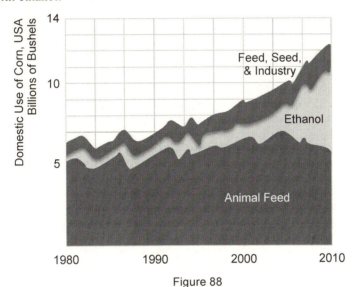

Figure 88
Domestic Use of Corn, USA, 1980 – 2010[210]
Ethanol production accounts for 5 billion bushels.

Underlying this shift has been a striking increase in productivity. "In 1900 American farmers needed an average of about three minutes of labor to produce 1 kg of wheat but by the year 2000 the time was down to just two seconds and the best producers now do it in one second. The price of this progress is that, as Howard Odum aptly put it, we are now eating potatoes partially made of oil."[211] In this Dr. Smil and Mr. Odum are referring to the quantity of oil as fuel and as fertilizer that has been required to achieve these improvements.

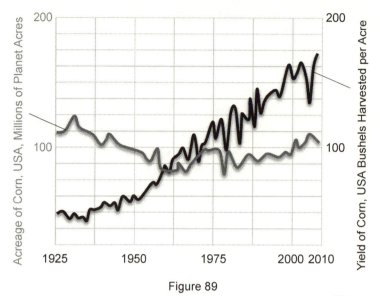

Figure 89
Increasing Yield of Corn Harvested, USA, 1925 – 2010[212]
The industrialization of agriculture has increased average yields 4x while sharply reducing the human labor required. There is, however, an extreme reliance on fossil fuels to make this happen.

Since a large volume of corn has been diverted from the global food supply and into American autos, the price of corn increased in the global market, which may be good for corn farmers but it's bad for the people who must pay more for food, and it impacts disproportionately on the poor.[213]

Whether this trend has continued with the recent declines in oil prices as discussed in Chapter 3 is not yet known, but the capacity to make the connection reminds us that systems thinking as a discipline helps us grasp the importance of mapping such connections between actions in one part of a system and the larger whole systems that they are part of. Whether we're thinking about how many paper towels to use to dry our hands or whether to pour something down the drain or how cotton is transformed into shirts or the value of living sharks over dead ones or the price of corn and who will pay for it or the sources of the parts that compose an iPhone and the hands that will assemble it and the aspirations of that person, we gain the capacity to think more productively about the short and long term consequences of our decisions and actions.   We have, that is, a better model of the system, and with a better model we can make better decisions.

Another astute systems thinker was Dr. John Gall, a physician and observer whose book *Systemantics* remains a classic for its deep insights and cutting wit.

> All around us we see a world of paradox: deep, ironic, and intractable. A world in which the hungry nations export food; the richest nations slip into demoralizing economic recessions; the strongest nations go to war against the smallest and weakest and are unable to win; a world in which revolutions against tyrannical systems themselves become tyrannical. In human affairs, celebrities receive still more publicity because they are "well known;" men rise to high positions because of their knowledge of affairs only to find themselves curt off from the sources of their knowledge; scientists opposed to the use of scientific knowledge in warfare find themselves advising the government on how to win wars by using scientific knowledge ... the list is endless. How does it come about that things turn out so differently from what common sense would expect?[214]

The solution that Dr. Gall advocates is of course the detailed study of systems, and with great humor he proceeds over the following 300 pages to illuminate us as to its key principles with abundant examples, more than 250 of them, most of which will make you laugh, but also cry. Among them the stories of banking failures, power plants, aviation, government, and just about every other large scale system we rely upon. All of them, of course, are enormously complex, and their continually increasing complexity is one of the essential features of modern life as we move forward into the 21st century.

And since the complexity of a system increases as the square of the connections, and since our world is becoming ever more connected and thus more complex on a daily basis it's easy to see that the world's connectedness is increasing exponentially.

This graphs, essentially, as a line that becomes vertical; we have seen this before this is the J–Curve. It is a rate that has never been seen before, and no one knows what it means, other than it obviously means that change occurs very, very fast. This is the reality of the modern world, and makes it exceptionally difficult for anyone to understand what's happening today, much less to anticipate what may happen tomorrow, and thus we are confronted with what may turn out to be a fundamental and existential challenge: How much complexity can we handle?

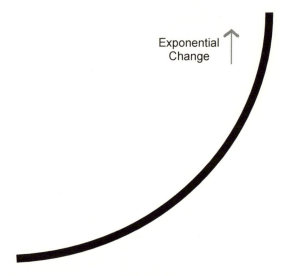

Figure 90
The J–Curve: Exponential Change

Feedback, Systems Modeling and Counter Intuitive Behaviors

One of the central insights from the systems thinking community has been identifying the critical role played by feedback in the behavior and sustenance of all systems. Feedback consists of the messages that are received by a system about what that system does, and which are used to adjust and presumably improve its performance.

During the 1960s when computers first began to be available to systems researchers they started to experiment with systems modeling. One of the pioneers in this field was Jay Forrester at MIT, who develop computer-based models of large social and economic systems. Forrester was also a computer hardware pioneer who created the first core memory systems for large scale data storage, a tremendous breakthrough at the time. He commented, "It took us about seven years to convince the industry that random-access magnetic-core memory was the solution to a missing link in computer technology. Then we spent the following seven years in the patent courts convincing them that they had not all thought of it first."[215]

Forrester's studies of large and complex systems such as cities led him to observe that the actual behaviors of these systems varied quite considerably from the expectations of managers and policy makers. He coined the phrase "counter-intuitive behavior of social systems" to describe the common experience of systems behaving differently than they were expected to, and he wrote a compelling paper based on testimony he gave before Congress in which he explained that the multiple connections (which he more precisely refers to as "feedback loops") that naturally exist in most social systems create such massively complex exchanges of information and behavioral interactions that simplistic policy prescriptions almost always led to undesirable consequences and outcomes.

> The nation exhibits a growing sense of futility as it repeatedly attacks deficiencies in our social system while the symptoms continue to worsen. Legislation is debated and passed with great promise and hope. But many programs prove to be ineffective. Results often seem unrelated to those expected when the programs were planned. At times programs cause exactly the reserve of desired results. It is now possible to explain how such contrary results can happen, as it is my basic theme that the human mind is not adapted to interpreting how social systems behave. Evolutionary processes have not given us the mental skill needed to properly interpret the dynamic behavior of the systems of which we have now become a part. [216]

Counter-intuitive outcomes result from our desire to simplify issues that may not be simple, or simplifiable. They often occur when we fail to recognize or acknowledge increasing complexity, and we expect that simple policy prescriptions will address convoluted problems. Thus, if the freeways are jammed with cars then for decades the instinct has been to build yet more freeways. But this had the undesirable consequence of attracting yet more cars, so more freeways often meant more congestion, not less. As Charles Montgomery notes, "Dozens of studies have now confirmed beyond doubt that the obvious solution to congestion – building more roads – simply produces more traffic, creating a treadmill of construction and frustration."[217]

Another example is high rise public housing, which was built in cities across the US during the 1950s and 1960s due to a sense of responsibility to provide clean, safe, and ample dwellings for all. The architectural designs of these large complexes reflected the latest thinking about light and space, and they were thus simpler versions of the luxury high rises that were being built in nicer parts of town. In the end, though, many of these housing complexes turned immediately into quite dangerous and run-down neighborhoods as the architectural qualities that appealed to the wealthy did not promote interaction and transparency to make neighborhoods safe and accessible for the poor. Badly lit hallways without windows were ideal locations for muggers, and play spaces for children located too far from peoples' homes were left entirely without children who were not allowed to use them for fear of their safety, but which proved quite popular with drug dealers. Millions of dollar were spent building massive complexes, and millions more were later spent to dynamite them into dust and haul away the remnants.

Many other attempts to intervene in large scale social problems have suffered from the shortcomings and drawbacks related to unintended consequences. Managing these systems according to concepts and principles discovered or developed fifty or 100 years previously in a much simpler economy and society led inevitably to undesired results, unintended consequences, counter-intuitive behaviors. Further, because the leaders of that day were educated at a time when the world system was much simpler than it later became, their mental models were derived from what they had learned decades previously and were hence dangerously out of date.

We still suffer from the same lags, designing systems and programs to fit our images of the past rather than the realities of the present or the challenges of the future. Our ability to manage global food supplies, to produce and distribute energy, and indeed to manage the economy as a whole all suffer from a lack of knowledge and skill in the management of complexity, and as complexity throughout society increases, one of the most significant risks we face is that complexity will itself overwhelm us. Another is that the counter-revolutionaries will succeed in dragging us backwards in our thinking and planning to fit their obsolete mental models of how things ought to be rather than leading us forward to fit how things are inexorably becoming.

Forrester was one among an entire generation of visionaries who grappled with the problems of social change and the consequences of increasing complexity, many of whom saw clearly that choices being made by governments, corporations, and even families were leading in a direction that suggested future problems and challenges. We will meet more of them in the next chapter, and discuss their work in detail.

State Change

This discussion about complexity and connectedness can be discouraging, as it's clear that more connections leads directly to more complexity and therefore to more unpredictability (or, less predictability). More events are occuring and more outcomes are possible from those events, meaning that more different behaviors result. Overall the total number of connections in society is increasing extremely fast, and so is society's complexity.

The trio of curves shown below illustrate this quite: connections, complexity, and unpredictability are all rising gracefully along those lovely exponentially curves, but now that we understand what they mean it's worrisome. And as connectedness is increasing exponentially as still more and more people join the global economy and community, complexity may therefore increasing at a rate faster than exponential. The graph is incapable of showing this, but as we now fully understand the power of exponents and the way that exponential behaviors lead to out-of-control systems, we are right to be worried.

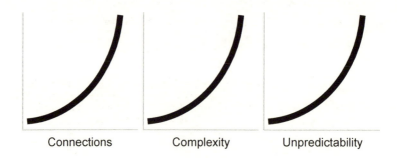

| Connections | Complexity | Unpredictability |

Figure 91
A Trio of Change-Makers
As connections increase complexity also increases, which makes for
further unpredictability.

In addition, scientific progress is also accelerating due to the combination of enhanced knowledge sharing (largely because of more and better connections), a progressively strong foundation of scientific concepts upon which to build astonishing levels of specialization in both the micro dimension (nanotechnology) and the macro dimension (climatology, astrophysics, astronomy), and the sheer increase in the number of scientists, as more than 90 percent of all the scientists who have ever lived are living and working today. Hence, the volume of new knowledge that science is producing every year is monumental.

And what becomes of the knowledge? Faster than ever before, business transforms scientific findings into new products and services, which then give a further nudge to the accelerating the rate of marketplace competition. Often this is worse for the established firms, which struggle to adapt to change, and better for the new ones, which use technology to create social and economic change.

Connectedness also thrives on and indeed promotes increasing openness, bringing societies to new information, new products, and new possibilities. Web sites such as Wikileaks provide a public outlet for stolen government documents, and as every phone is also a video recorder, anytime someone turns one on whatever is happening in front of the lens can be streamed live to the internet. This is generally bad for autocracies and dictators, who require closed systems and an uninformed populace to sustain internal repression. But once the people in Tunisia and Egypt understood the power of Twitter and Facebook and were inspired by Bouazizi, the dictatorships fell.

An interesting question therefore arises regarding hold much longer it will be possible for the Chinese Communist Party to sustain large scale censorship as a means of maintaining its hold on power. If the logjam of censorship breaks in conjunction with a massive alignment of popular will as we have already seen in Hong Kong, then the impact will undoubtedly be global in its impact, and probably astonishingly fast as well. (We will discuss China in more detail in Chapter 11.)

However, the flip side of universal connectedness and extreme openness is that the profusion of opinions and possibilities also makes it harder for many societies to reach consensus on anything. The current political situation in the US shows this quite clearly. It is so easy to form narrow interest groups, sub-groups, and sub-sub-groups that the result is extreme factionalization. Every faction holds to its own view, and promotes its views within its own community. ISIS of course does exactly the same thing, using the internet to send out recruiting messages that anyone can find.

In the US, the result is a deeply fractured society consisting of major power blocks with nearly antithetical views, left vs. right. The possibility of dialog between them has stopped because, as Kuhn anticipated, they represent conflicting paradigms.

> Political revolutions aim to change political institutions in ways that those institutions themselves prohibit. In increasing numbers individuals become increasingly estranged from political life and behave more and more eccentrically within it. Then, as the crisis deepens, many of these individuals commit themselves to some concrete proposal for the reconstruction of society in a new institutional framework. At that point the society is divided into competing camps or parties, one seeking to defend the old institutional constellation, the others seeking to institute some new one. And, once that polarization has occurred *political recourse fails*. The parties to a revolutionary conflict must finally resort to the

techniques of mass persuasion, often including force.[218]

Lacking shared models in economics, for example, leads to incessant arguments about what is happening and what we should do about. Even after the outcomes are known the economists on opposite sides still argue about what caused what. At root, we simply don't know.

How, then, should we prepare for a future in which change is accelerating, complexity is increasing, and factionalization is driving us apart?

Our incapacity to agree not only on what we ought to do, but even on what's actually happening out there in the real world has left the US government in a state of semi-paralysis, and all of these dynamics are shoving us in the direction of crisis, and what happens then? You're right to be worried; the risks accumulate and multiply as this is, after all, the mega risk world.

But we can also ask how it is that societies evolve, and what we learn is that in general societies do not evolve so much or so fast when times are good. When there's peace and harmony, when the weather is good and we're all fed, then we just keep on doing what we've been doing. It is new stressors that impel us to change, that test our level of fragility and our competence. If we respond effectively it demonstrates *and* develops anti-fragility, and indeed we can conscientiously work to develop our anti-fragile capabilities.

We do this first by grasping the reality of our situation, five revolutions, increasing complexity, the J-curve and the D-curve and all that, and by understanding how to model future outcomes amid complexity and counter-intuitive behaviors.

Kuhn has given us the fine model of paradigm shift, which he makes clear can happen when systems are under stress, and evolutionary biologists tell us that our big human brains most likely evolved from the smaller primate brains in times of stress, particularly when confronted with the massive challenges associated with repeated ice ages. Nature presented our ancestors with an adaptation challenge, and evolution responded by expanding our individual and collective capacity to solve problems. Out of this came our big brains, more than three times larger than they had been,[219] as well as our vocal cords, our relative hairlessness, and our capacity to cooperate to accomplish much more complex tasks than we had even undertaken, such as, voila, agriculture!

I am not necessarily suggesting that we're about to go through some sort of evolutionary leap right now (although Kurzweil and the other singularists would tell you exactly that).

But what I do want to make clear is that stress in the environment often induces fundamental change that is sometimes referred to as "state change," meaning change of such a fundamental nature that it changes reality and perceptions both. We are obviously living in a time of severe human-induced environmental stress. The collision of cultural forces that we observe every day are a fully predictable response to these conditions, as there is no shared model of what's happening, we don't have many useful historical reference points to compare this to, and we have conflicting objectives – some want to go forward, and others want to go backwards.

In any case, if I am right in suggesting that the S-curve explains our world in a useful and accurate way, then although we have no historical references points because we've never been through a change like that, ever, the model itself suggests quite clearly what we are likely to experience as the structure of human demographics changes and thus brings with it fundamental changes in the structure of the economy.

While the global economy and the by extension the whole of global society is a living experiment, an ongoing laboratory of reality where no one knows precisely what will happen next, if the S-curve model is accurate then we do know a lot about a lot of things that are happening and will continue to happen.

And what this means is that solutions will have to *emerge*. Emergence is also a powerful and important concept for us, as it suggests that something new can come about when a system is stressed in novel ways, and when many different attempts at solutions are being tried. And we are certainly not lacking for attempts (although, again, the US Congress isn't do much productively to help just now[220]). There are, as I just noted, tens of thousands of scientists and entrepreneurs working to understand and solve countless problems across every field of study known to humanity, from energy systems and atmospheric systems to health care and urbanization, using every available tool from computer modeling to electron microscopy to satellite sensors, etc., etc. Entrepreneurs and established companies are working to commercialize their findings, and many of the new products and services are specifically intended to become solutions.

And of course as we gain a more complete sense of where we are, and if we can reach even minimal agreements on where we want to go then we can choose from among the available and emerging options the ones that suit us best. We can do so, that is, when we have good models.

And among those who build such models we have among us a large of people, visionaries, who have the unusual ability to grasp the future a bit more clearly by foreseeing what's coming and helping us to align our choices and action with the future, rather than with the past. We will meet some of them in the next chapter.

•••

Chapter 9:

The Visionary:

Understanding Foresight

Every decision is a prediction.
W. Edwards Deming

It's tough to make predictions, especially about the future.
Yogi Berra

It is surprisingly difficult to maintain a happy outlook when you know deep in your heart that the world is on a path toward disaster... Please help me make my forecast wrong. Together we could create a much better world.

Jørgen Randers

When you read the first two of the quotes above you immediately grasp something important about the dilemma that we're facing: we are making predictions every day because we are making decisions every day, but they are founded on uncertainties. Add the third quote, and we have an even clearer view: the forces of change seem to be driving us in the wrong direction, although we still have time to alter our course.

These comments come to us from a statistician, a baseball player, and a professor of climate strategy. Each, in his own way, is a visionary, and the unique quality of a visionary's gift is a grasp of the future. Usually this comes with a unique or unconventional point of view, and since unconventional viewpoints and expectations are validated or verified only through their realization, that is, when and if the forecasts come true. Since that often lies quite far in the future, during the long interval between a forecast and its realization visionaries often live with rejection, frustration, sadness, and even despair.

For example, the pioneering astronomer Copernicus knew he would be punished for daring to suggest a model of the universe that did not fit the Church's prevailing dogma, so he waited to publish his heliocentric model until he was very near death. His work, of course, was actually not a prediction about the future, but a better explanation of the present.

A few decades later the Italian astronomer Galileo faced exactly the same dilemma, but he was bolder and published his findings even though they also contradicted established dogma. For his efforts he was put on trial by Church leaders, although the root cause was merely that he had understood what he had observed through his telescope, and then shared his findings. We can imagine that during his trial he pleaded with the Inquisitor to look for himself at Jupiter through the telescope, for then he would also see what Galileo had seen, and know for himself the truth that Galileo had written. We can also imagine that it was a futile request, for the Inquisitor already knew what he would see, God's perfected universe with Earth comfortably in the center where it belonged: he had no need to peer through Galileo's worldly instrument. For the Inquisitor, possessor of complete and unassailable ideological knowledge, no reasoning in contradiction to the Church's perfect model could possibly be relevant.

(He may also have been afraid of what he might see, and had no desire to test his own faith and certainty.) In any case his job had to do with compliance and with the established ecumenical order, not with science.

Another Renaissance genius, Da Vinci, foresaw submarines and flying machines, while Lady Lovelace understood computers long before nearly anyone else.

In the 20th century the British economist John Keynes foresaw and wrote in anguished words about the inevitable and disastrous consequences of the Versailles Treaty, and sadly he was entirely correct that the punitive nature of the World War I peace terms were only setting the stage for the counterrevolution that would be become World War II, a mere 20 years later.

> The policy of reducing Germany to servitude for a generation, of degrading the lives of millions of human beings, and of depriving a whole nation of happiness should be abhorrent and detestable, even if it did not sow the decay of the whole civilized life of Europe. Some preach it in the name of Justice. In the great events of man's history, in the unwinding of the complex fates of nations Justice is not so simple. And if it were, nations are not authorized, by religion or by natural morals, to visit on the children of their enemies the misdoings of parents of rulers.[221]

A more recent, and perhaps less well know is computer scientist Doug Engelbart, who conceived of, built, and demonstrated to the world the personal computer as a powerful tool to augment human thinking long before most people realized such a thing could be possible. Engelbart saw clearly how we would benefit from computing power, and developed the overall conceptual approach to personal computing as well as many of the hardware and software innovations that today we take for granted, including text editing and the mouse. You can the first ever mouse on display in the lobby at the Stanford Research Institute in Menlo Park, California, where Engelbart worked at the time; it's skin is a carved block of wood. He also conceived of the graphical user interface, an innovation later borrowed and made both famous and popular by Apple and then Microsoft.

The occasion at which he shared these inventions with the world has come to be known retrospectively and in appreciation as "The Mother of All Demos" in 1968; it took decades for Apple and Microsoft to fully understand and commercialize what Engelbart had achieved.[222] This body of work constituted note one but an entire system of astonishing breakthroughs, and over time the computer industry borrowed his work and commercialized it, but to his great frustration this happened only in pieces. The industry never provided the support he needed to realize the full scope of his ambition, and he once mentioned to me how painful it was to see parts and pieces of his vision come to market in small fragments, while the larger vision and scope of his work seemed to be ignored. He struggled heroically for decades, and the world is only now catching up to the full scope of his ambition. You may not have heard of Engelbart, although you probably benefit from his accomplishments many times each day.

Buckminster Fuller, whom we met in Chapter One and whose fascinating life story and brilliant insights were enormously influential on a generation of future leaders, wrote more than 30 books on a wide variety of themes, all united by his deep interest in the future of humanity and is commitment to understand the behavior of system at a deeper root level, much more thoroughly was common then or today.

Fuller had great interest in thinking ahead of the commonly accepted wisdom, and he eventually came up with a mouthful of a name for the capacity to examine the future intelligently: he called it "comprehensive, anticipatory design science."

Donella Meadows and John Gall, as I noted above, referred to it "systems thinking," but by whatever name the point is that it's a powerful approach that is important for all of us who wish to better anticipate the future.

Another brilliant 20th century systems thinker was Stafford Beer who, as a student, developed useful models of complex systems using slime mold as his working medium. He served in the British military in India during World War II and later worked as a senior manager at British Steel. Beer's focus gradually shifted to a modeling approach he devised which he called The Viable System Model, which he documented his discoveries in a series of books that were published in the 1970s and which remain in print today. At that time there was widespread interest in Beer's approach, and he was invited by Chilean President Salvatore Allende to implement a version of the viable system model on a national scale there.

Things turned out quite badly, however, as the Allende government fell in a CIA-sponsored coup led by General Augusto Pinochet. Many of Beer's supporters including some of the team who were directly involved in the project were killed in the coup, which not surprisingly caused Beer great anguish. He retreated to remote Wales for some years, where he wrote his views on society, change, and the future in a deeply personal book he called *Platform for Change*.

> Humanity is a prisoner of his own way of thinking and of his own stereotypes of himself. His machine for thinking, the brain, has been programmed to deal with a vanished world. This old world was characterized by the need to manage *things* – stone, wood, iron. The new world is characterized by the need to manage complexity. Complexity is the very stuff of today's world. The tool for handing complexity is ORGANIZATION. But our concepts of organization belong to the much less complex old world not to the much more complex complex today's world. Still less are they adequate to deal with the next epoch of complexification – in a world of explosive change. We shall not succeed in reforming our concept of organization or in creating new institutions that actually work simply by hard work – or even by hard thought. We need to invoke SCIENCE.[223]

The core principles explored in Beer's work focus on autonomy, decision making, the significance of feedback and the necessity of managing it, and of course on the concept of viability itself.

Beer and his fellow systems thinkers Jay Forrester, John Gall, Donella Meadows, and others quite clearly foresaw the dilemmas that would emerge as society became more and more complex, and yet they struggled to explain the dangers they foresaw so that others could understand and take proactive steps to avoid the risks and catastrophes. Few seemed to be listening, and many of Beer's books are written in a tone that expresses both his many insights and the frustration he felt in not finding more who understood what he was trying to tell them.

Visionary architect Paolo Soleri spent his career envisioning cities not as they are built today, flat and sprawling and destructive to the natural landscape, but rather as organic expressions of the human spirit that would function in harmony with the Earth's ecology and with the spiritual and creative essences of humanity.

> In nature, as an organism evolves it increases in complexity and it also becomes a more compact or miniaturized system. Similarly a city should function as a living system. Arcology, architecture and ecology as one integral process, is capable of demonstrating positive response to the many problems of urban civilization, population, pollution, energy and natural resource depletion, food scarcity and quality of life. Arcology recognizes the necessity of the radical reorganization of the sprawling urban landscape into dense, integrated, three-dimensional cities in order to support the complex activities that sustain human culture. The city is the necessary instrument for the evolution of humankind.[224]

He coined the term arcology and initiated the Arcosanti project in the Arizona desert, where the beginnings of modest prototype are still under construction.

2052

It's not so easy when you see things differently than nearly everyone else, and it seems almost inevitable that disappointment characterized the lives of those who saw a future for what it is likely to be when that future did not match prevailing views or society's accepted interpretations. And yet given the acceleration of change that characterizes our era, and given the great challenges that humanity will face in the coming decades, there are few insights more valuable to all of us than a clear perspective on what is coming. Among the many scholars examining the future course of our world and the many voices explaining the trends and advocating for various ideas, principles, or actions, the work of Jørgen Randers is notable, and we will explore it further now.

Randers was a co-author of the highly influential 1972 Club of Rome study *The Limits to Growth* that I mentioned above, and the 1992 follow-up volume *Beyond the Limits*. More recently he has prepared a detailed study of the future entitled *2052: A Global Forecast for the Next Forty Years*.[225]

2052 is compelling not only for its many insights into our emerging and shared future, but also for the deeply personal way in which Randers has crafted a narrative in which he presents the evidence and arrives at his conclusions. He presents his own views, discoveries, and reactions to what he has learned in a very open and direct manner, and indeed he states at the beginning that his purpose in writing the book was to examine for himself what the future holds for him personally. Born in 1945, and having spent 40 years warning society that its choices were leading to a worsening situation, Randers notes that he expects to live another 25 years or so and that he undertook the work because he simply wanted to know what his remaining years might hold. He is quite open about his assumptions, his method, his logic, and the uncertainties that his forecast includes. He's also open about his data – you can download the massive spreadsheet in which his calculations are presented from his web site.[226]

Trained as a physicist, Randers brings a scientist's rigorous mindset to the collection and analysis of data, and in working through the logic of his forecasts, and he discovers that some things may not go as badly in the future as he had feared. For example, he was surprised to learn that population growth is slowing, as we discussed in Chapter 4, and that by mid-century the global population should have already peaked and begin to decline.

Conversely, he reminds us that humanity's consumption of resources is now proceeding at an annual rate of 1.4 Earths, meaning that each year we are consuming resources and producing what the Earth requires 1.4 years to produce which means that the current economic system is in "overshoot" and is not sustainable.

The likelihood of overshoot was forecasted in the 1972 *Limits to Growth* book and was one of the main arguments that made that book so successful and influential. Compounding the problem, he notes in 2052, is capitalism's systemic short-sightedness. In a 2012 speech he gave in conjunction with the release of the book he commented that, "Capitalist systems allocate money based on a discount rate that is so high that anything that happens beyond five years is very close to invisible."[227]

Perhaps worse, he observes that the American political system operates on a perpetual two- and four-year election cycle, and in each cycle less and less is done other than political posturing. Of course it is now mandatory for us to look far beyond two, four, or five years, and as the consequences of climate change are manifesting gradually and could reach their worst well beyond 2050, he sees the current political paralysis in the US as particularly unfortunate timing. With political and ideological gridlock rendering the US Congress incapable of meaningful action, the democratic process is literally and tragically undermining its own future.

He also forecasts the growing dispute between generations, noting that for the first time in contemporary history going back hundreds of years, the current generation is at significant risk of leaving to the future a world that is fundamentally *worse* than the one it inherited. As we have seen, the current occupants will leave a massive CO2 excess and a sizeable financial debt for their children and grandchildren, and on top of that today's generation expects tomorrow's to pay for both its retirement and its (very expensive) future health care needs. Randers expects that coming generations will eventually balk at fulfilling their parents inflated expectations.

Overall, he suggests that changes are happening too slowly to avoid a great deal of unnecessary suffering. "The main challenge in our global future is not to solve the problems we are facing, but to reach agreement to do so."[228] Randers ends the book with a simple but profound request, which I also included above: "Please help me make my forecast wrong. Together we could create a much better world."

Near the end of the book he also comments about the psychological challenges he confronted after looking in depth at the direction in which we are headed. I included this quote at the beginning of this chapter: "It is surprisingly difficult to maintain a happy outlook when you know deep in your heart that the world is on a path toward disaster." Beer, Englebart, and Soleri expressed similar feelings toward the end of their careers, and indeed this sense of despair is widely shared among many who look upon our situation and realize what's likely to lie ahead of us.

But there are also many reasons for optimism, and hence part of the ambition of this book is to offer a clear view of the real situation, to better understand our social and psychological responses to it, and then to describe what we can and ought to be doing in anticipation.

The Power of Experiment

Above I mentioned that Randers is a physicist, and as a scientist he was therefore also trained to conduct rigorous experiments. The great Italian physicist and key participant in the Manhattan Project Enrico Fermi once commented about the scientific method what happens when a scientist does an experiment in this way: "There are two possible outcomes: if the result confirms the hypothesis, then you've made a measurement. If the result is contrary to the hypothesis, then you've made a discovery."[229]

Hence, every experimenter must be prepared to face the truth, which will be revealed only when the outcome is achieved. Seeking truth is what scientists are trained to do, even when it means discovering that their assumptions are quite wrong. Sir Jonathan Ive is a key member of Apple's design team who once noted that the thing he really loved about the team was this: "One of the hallmarks of the team is inquisitiveness, being excited about being wrong, because it means you've discovered something new."[230] It's not so common in our society and especially in business for people to take pleasure or pride in being wrong, but it is tremendously powerful. Perhaps this attitude is one of the reasons that Apple has proven to be so unique and uniquely successful as a company. And perhaps its driving inspiration, Steve Jobs, also belongs in this discussion about visionaries.

As a technology company CEO his role had less to do with making the technology than with fitting the needs of the market together with technologies possibilities, but it was precisely his deep understanding of how people could benefit from technology, and how that technology should be crafted to serve their needs and desires, that distinguished Jobs. He was also a stunningly good salesman, and he understood how to tell a story to create alignment around the vision that he was promoting. Building on the work of Doug Engelbart, Jonathan Ive, and many others, he led Apple to the very pinnacle among corporations; it's now the most value public company in the world, and millions appreciate and rely on its products every day.

Randers has also approached his book as a salesman, as an experiment in persuasion. Has he accurately measured our incapacity to change proactively? Or will he and we discover that society can indeed heed his warning and alter its course, to achieve thereby better outcomes than the ones he fears? Stated differently, will his analysis influence our collective behavior, such that we avoid the worst outcomes that could befall humanity as a result of carbon overshoot? With many voices added to his it's entirely possible.

Jobs was a hugely successful innovator in technology and business, but what can innovators do in the realms of politics and governance? Can we develop innovations to promote faster decision-making, or better analysis, or make it easier to reach agreement on the changes that are required for our future? In fact, a great many people are engaged in this work, and at its root the essential requirements include:

- The ability to do as Randers has done, to gather hard evidence (not opinions), to analyze them dispassionately, and to present the findings openly.
- To interrogate science as the important source of data, rather than ideology.
- To analyze with persistent self-awareness one's own assumptions and biases, and to avoid the error of thinking oneself to be a self-proclaimed carrier of truth.
- And to present conclusions in an even-handed, even-minded way that invites further examination, is open to alternative

322

interpretations, and leads to still deeper analysis and more thoughtful consideration.

These are all in fact aspects of one crucial quality or ability, which is the commitment to seek the truth for what it is rather than for what we assume or wish it to be. Innovation happens when we face the truth, respond to it, and act on it; sound decisions occur along that very same path. It may be the truth of what science has learned, or what technology can accomplish, or what the market demands and expects, or what is best for the future of society; what we seek above all are decisions that address all four.

From Vision to Decision

Strategists think about the future because it's their job to figure out what their organizations ought to be doing today which will be most likely to result in achieving desired outcomes tomorrow. At root, then, the core challenge facing the strategist is the problem of anticipating the future, that is, of prediction. And as we all know, prediction is very hard to do. This is one of the reasons that great strategists are so rare, and in times of rapid change such as ours, they are rarer still.

Yogi Berra's comment is so widely quoted because it's so ironic, so funny, and also so accurate. Further, he delivered it with his utterly un-self-conscious Midwestern, matter-of-fact deadpan accent, which made him sound completely average although he was in fact very bright and insightful, although with perhaps an unusual way of expressing his insights.

The evidence shows that the way to predict poorly is to anticipate specific events. Much better is to focus on identifying and understanding the relevant patterns of change. Hockey great Wayne Gretsky explained this when he suggested that his own greatness came about because he skated to where the puck *would be* rather than to where it already was, and we would like to do the same.

Of course it's hard to predict well, and yet we also recognize that it's precisely the essential job of leaders in every domain, in business, in government, in society, to make predictions every day. For as Dr. Deming so poignantly reminds us, "Every decision is a prediction."[231] That is, every decision is made in anticipation of the outcomes or consequences that will result, and thus every decision is certainly a prediction about the best way to attain the intended outcomes. Some decisions and their embedded predictions are small, short term, and trivial; but many others, the ones we're mostly interested in here, are enormously consequential.

All of this highlights the Grand Canyon of difference between foresight and hindsight. We know, for instance that hindsight is "2020," meaning that it provides perfect clarity (20/20 being a measurement used by optometrists to indicate that one sees at 20 feet what one should see at 20 feet; hence perfect vision).

Foresight is of course much more difficult to muster, as we and Yogi Berra know all so well. No one can tell us exactly what the close of the stock market will be during today's trading day, nor which will be the winning team of the next World Cup Tournament, nor the winning lottery numbers, until after the close, after the matches are played, and after the numbers have been drawn. Nor do we know for sure what will happen with technology, the climate, the fossil fuel industry, the human population, etc., etc.

But the eventual outcomes for each of these matters, and consequently the quality of our preparation and of our foresight also matter a great deal. Indeed, you can compile a quite large shelf of very fine books about the future, both nonfiction and fiction, from which you're likely to learn a great deal, and many people study these books because they know it matters.

Given these enormous challenges, how can human society preserve and protect its core human values, and optimize our civilization system for the benefit of all humanity? Or stated differently, How should individual citizens, employees, constituents, and leaders respond to the five simultaneous revolutions, the counter-revolution, and the mega risks that they individually and collectively bring? Although we are obliged to cope with the many layers of uncertainty and complexity that the modern world presents to us, with a rigorous map of the present terrain, the process of foresight can then help us to explore what may be coming next.

Systems scientists advise that we must create sound and accurate models, and we must then use those models as a basis with which to experiment rigorously, which is the only way to reach effective decisions and actions. To get to that point we must ask deep and probing questions, and we must be willing to listen openly and without preconceptions, as Randers shows, to whatever the evidence tells us. So when you hear the phrase, "I refuse to believe," you can be sure that yet another one has succumbed to ideological preconceptions, while when you hear, "This is the evidence, and this is what it tells us," then you're much more likely to be on the right track.

Rules and Rebels

While the visionaries may be the ones who see the future more clearly it's often because they're thinking outside of established norms, and so they may not appear as clear-sighted forward thinkers but as alarmists. Copernicus, Galileo, Forrester, Lovelace, Beer, Meadows, Soleri, Fuller, Randers, Engelbart, and Jobs all saw the world differently than their peers, and they all made notable contributions to human knowledge, and our understanding of the world, and our potential roles in it.

And they all were, to some extent, rebels. Most of them embraced the rebel label, and I believe that most of them liked the fact that they were different. But at times they also became quite frustrated at their inability to explain why the different world that they saw was worth paying attention to. A lament they shared was, Why don't they understand?[232]

What visionaries confront in those moments of frustration are frequently the built-in biases and habits of thinking that are common throughout every society and in every age, for the notion that there are norms to which we should adhere, rules that should not be broken, and facts that transcend experimentation, these are deeply-held human responses to the world. But the facts that the visionaries discover, and the way that they interpret those facts, often conflicts with accepted views, with accepted social norms. What happens then, when there are new facts for society to consider, when the old evidence and the way we looked at it no longer yield the results we expected?

In the following chapter we'll examine some of the pitfalls that await anyone who gathers evidence and conducts experiments, compiles the findings, analyzes the results, and reaches conclusions that call for fundamental change; for our future success often comes down to our capacity to interpret in situations of ambiguity and uncertainty.

•••

Chapter 10

The

Analyst:

Evidence and

Interpretation

This crisis has turned out to be much broader than anything I could have imagined.

Allan M. Greenspan[233]

What the facts change, Sir, I change my opinion. What do you do?

Attributed to J.M. Keynes[234]

In reflecting upon the 2008 financial collapse that was triggered by the failure of the American subprime mortgage market, former US Federal Reserve Bank Chairman Allan Greenspan testified before the US Congress that, "This crisis has turned out to be much broader than anything I could have imagined."

As Chairman of America's central bank, the most powerful banking institution in the world, it was precisely the definition of Mr. Greenspan's job to imagine what might happen under a very wide variety of possible scenarios, to foresee and anticipate the traps, pitfalls, and potential disasters of the policies that he was considering and indeed advocating, as well as policies that he was opposed to. And so in claiming that a series of events which indeed occurred, and which he had in fact been warned about in advance, was "broader than anything he could have imagined," he thus acknowledged both a failure of imagination, a failure of modeling, and an equally significant failure of analysis. He also exemplified the difficulties we all face when trying to think clearly when our analytical process is inhibited by ideology, bias, and incomplete information. He was apparently looking at the wrong evidence, and his interpretation of the evidence he did examine proved to be pretty shoddy.

This is not a problem that central bankers face alone. In fact, it is a challenge that everyone faces, the difficulty of identifying facts as facts, for often they do not appears as facts at all upon first look, and the commensurate mistake of believing that our assumptions actually are facts when they are not. Ive's comment about being wrong gets precisely to a critically important issue, which we will discuss here.

Rational or Irrational

We often suppose that humans are rational beings, and most of us think of ourselves that way even if we notice that others seem a little less clear in their thinking. A great many economists would also have us believe that their science is supremely rational and logical, and that if we could just remove the irrational and counterproductive forces of regulatory interference in the market then the aggregate of highly logical individual choices would result in the optimal economic conditions for communities, nations and globally. But we know better.

And now Mr. Greenspan does too, because he attributed the flaw in this thinking to his great surprise that America's corporate bankers did not behave rationally. We know in fact that people are far from rational, that ideals and ideology are often much more compelling motivators than any other force. This is one of the only ways we can explain suicide terrorism, for example. This is also how we can explain the flood of sub-prime mortgages that crashed the economy, and people who go deeper into debt to keep up with the neighboring Joneses, and perhaps also people who vote against their own economic and social self interests.

We also know that the abstract ideal of a perfectly functioning economic system would require that perfect information be available to all participants who would then interpret it in a perfect and perfectly rational manner, and it's utterly clear that our information is far from perfect, nor is it perfectly distributed, nor are we consistently good at interpretation. Whether it is conscious or unconscious, lag, inaccuracy and bias are possible in every bit of news that we read or watch or hear.

This is critically important for us as futurists, analysts, planners, strategists, and leaders, because if we are to make sound choices about the challenging and complex issues that we face now and will face in the coming years it would be hugely advantageous to overcome our perceptual and cognitive limitations; to do that we need to know what those limitations are.

Ideology and Assumptions

What exactly is ideology? It's a set of beliefs that exist independent of the evidence, and which are applied independently of evidence. Hence, what makes ideology so powerful is that it is generally impervious to facts. Conversely, it is the basis through which the existence and the meaning of facts is inferred or deduced; it is the beliefs that determine what we see.

Thus, when we observe opposing protest groups with differing opinions engaged in an angry screaming match, now a sadly regular occurrence on cable TV news, what we are usually witnessing is an emotionally charged conflict of ideologies that is generally defined by a disregard for or disinterest in evidence or facts.

Interestingly, this sort of conflict happens in science as readily as it does in politics, as scientists can be as selective in the application of facts and the fitting together of facts into interpretations as the rest of us are. One of Kuhn's key points is that most of the adherents of an old scientific paradigm have become emotionally invested in it, which contributes to their lack of appreciation for a new one. We also have to acknowledge, however, that there is no reason *a priori* to assume that those advocating the new model are correct. Hindsight embellishes the credibility of Newton and Einstein, but at the time they first published, it was entirely valid to question their ideas. The problem arises when people either refuse to study the evidence (such as Galileo's inquisitor) and therefore persist in ignorance, or when the discount the evidence because it does nor conform to their pre-existing beliefs (Greenspan).

When our ideologies and biases predispose us to ignore distasteful evidence then it's only a matter of time until we are deceived. We will miss important clues, and imagine facts that don't exist; we will give credibility to evidence that affirms previously-held opinions and biases, while often failing to notice evidence that contradicts them. This is a chronic condition of politics, which often arises because the pro-change and the anti-change come to the broader questions from opposite perspectives. The pro-change embrace it in the belief that is will lead to a better future, while the anti-change oppose it on the grounds that it will only make things worse. The bias towards either position seems to be built in, and perhaps it is acquired in childhood or youth, as cognitive scientists George Lakoff explains:

> Contemporary American politics is about worldview. Conservatives simply see the world differently than do liberals, and both have a difficult time understanding accurately what the other's worldview is. …Deeply embedded in conservative and liberal politics are different models of the family. These two models give rise to different moral systems, different choices of words, and different modes of reasoning.[235]

Because the ways of reasoning and the resulting value systems are based on models of the family, and thus on experiences of one's own family, for most of us they are acquired very early on, and they remain largely at the unconscious level because our family lives are so formative and so integral to our ways of thinking that we're rarely aware of it.

The proliferation of media has enabled a proliferation of polarized media outlets that specialize in one or the other ideological viewpoint, which has only amplified the tendency of ideologues to retreat more deeply into their own fully fortified positions. You can now watch, read, or listen to news and commentary that reinforces whichever political positions you feel most comfortable with, and you may never have to hear an opposing view at all, except in derision. This enhances social polarity by reinforcing biases and stereotypes, which is quite unhelpful to those interested in finding meaningful solutions regardless of the ideological nuances involved.

Hence, we are living in a time when political thought is dominated by prejudices, when many literally "pre judge" the outcomes beforehand, before the event occurs or the evidence is collected. Every issue is now framed by the opposing sides according to their ideological predispositions, and the meaning of every tiny shred of actual evidence is argued incessantly as the opponents try to craft narratives that validate their hypotheses and biases. This is perhaps the worst thing that could happen in politics, as just when what we need is an abundance of evidence, clear thinking, astute forecasting, and an open and honest discussion about our options, what we have instead is an ideological shouting match.

Governments, being national monopolies, can persist for some time while trapped in these illusions, but corporations generally cannot. Corporate managers still suffer from exactly the same difficulties, although in their case the culprit is less likely to be described as ideological bias and more likely to be flawed managerial assumptions. The broader result in business is the rapidly declining life span of major companies, which itself provides abundant evidence that many leaders are also not doing so well at managing in markets where change is occurring so fast. This is the going out of business curve showing itself again. The difference between government and business is generally competition; when there is a competing firm in the marketplace that has a better grasp on the meaning of the evidence it can then design and produce better products and services and have a good chance to prevail. Companies, that is, must deliver facts, while politicians can persist for some time in delivering ideology. But eventually change catches up with even the ideologues, as nations also decline and fall when they fail to heed reality for too long.

For leaders and strategists whose job is to enable their communities, nations, and organizations to adapt to the challenges of the real world rather then pretend one of ideology, the persistence of ideological prejudices and delusions is a deadly pattern, and for themselves and for all of us it becomes vitally important to recognize what is real and not to substitute for it what is preferred or imagined, or which is ideologically aligned but which is not based in reality.

Among the additional challenges we face in this regard are the importance and persistence of social norms and group expectations, both of which work to bind us to present realities even when change and adaptation would serve us much better.

Norms and Rules

Scientists tell us that we are a species whose evolution is driven by social factors as much as or even more than by the physical environment, and that therefore the social standards, cues, and agreements that we make are central to our successes or failures. If this actually were the case then it would be necessary for us to recognize and respond to those cues from a very young age, and in fact research has verified that babies only a few months old are quite capable of making these judgments, and that even by the age of three our children are fully aware of and operating within a social context.

> By observing others, young children spontaneously infer context-specific rules for social life and assume these rules are norms – rules that others should obey. Deviations and deviants make children angry and motivate them to instill proper behavior in others.[236]

Social norms are of essential to sustain a functioning society, and thus the problem arises, as I noted in the previous chapter, when the requirements for successful functioning change and therefore the norms need to change. There is lag time involved, as society is of course a complex system of social and technical elements that is subject to all manner of conflicting pressures and influences. The visionaries call for change, the rebels and revolutionaries promote it, and the anti-revolutionaries and reactionaries tell us why we must not change. Amidst this cacophony, the context itself continues to change, and decision makers must respond.

Groupthink

A key dimension of our vulnerability as decision makers is our shared tendency to prefer to fit in with our peer group, which often leads us to modify our behavior and down play disagreements in order to reinforce social cohesion. Irving Janis named this tendency *groupthink*, and while in many social settings this is quite positive, when we are confronted with challenging issues that must be decided, partial information to work from, and lack of clarity even around what the options are, then this tendency to avoid conflict can lead to disastrous results. Janus points out that it's quite common to observe what he refers to as mindless conformity and collective misjudgment of serious risks…

> … which are collectively laughed off in a clubby atmosphere of relaxed conviviality. Consider what happened a few days before disaster struck the small mining town of Pitcher, Oklahoma, in 1950. The local mining engineer had warned the inhabitants to leave at once because the town had been accidentally undermined and might cave in at any moment. At a Lion's Club meeting of leading citizens, the day after the warning was issued, the members joked about the warning and laughed uproariously when someone arrived wearing a parachute. What the club members were communicating to each other by their collective laughter was that "sensible people like us know better than to take seriously those disaster warnings; we know can't happen here, to our fine little town."[237]

A few days later some of these men and their families died in the collapse.

Janis organizes the book around case studies he prepared on notable examples of misjudgment in American history, including the failure of the US leadership to anticipate the attack on Pearl Harbor, the fiasco of the Bay of Pigs invasion in 1961, the American descent in the quagmire of the Vietnam War, and the Watergate cover-up by President Richard Nixon. In each case, Janis shows quite convincingly that the desire of those involved to sustain their convivial relationships prevented various individuals from raising doubts about the plans that were under way, and also allowed the groups as a whole to discount evidence that their plan was not a good one. Groupthink is the very down side of social normalization.

In addition to the dangers of groupthink, another problem that all decision makers face is the difficulty of collecting and then evaluating meaningful evidence. Often, it turns out what we see is not as trustworthy as we may think, as our very process of looking at the world around us contains built-in biases, or as Barbara Tuchman puts it, "That marvelous human capacity to see what you expect to see even when it is not there."[238]

Believing is Seeing

Bias influences everything that we see with our own eyes and also that which we fail to see, as it turns out that the brain is quite selective about what it brings to our attention. The aspects of our experiences that we remember are not necessarily objective recreations of past events as we suppose them to be, they are instead selective reconstructions that often align with our prejudices and biases, and therefore omit details that are not consistent with our preconceptions.

A small bit of common sense that we often hear repeated is the phrase *seeing is believing*, but, in the words of Ira Gershwin, *it ain't necessarily so*.[239] While we may believe that our beliefs are founded on an objective version of facts, it would be far more accurate to say the reverse, that believing is seeing, because what we see is actually a selective recreation, not an objective record.

> We form our beliefs for a variety of subjective, personal, emotional and psychological reasons in the context of environments created by family, friends, colleagues, culture, and society at large; after forming our beliefs we then defend, justify, and rationalize them. Beliefs come first; explanations for beliefs follow. Our perceptions about reality are dependent on the beliefs that we hold about it. ... Once beliefs are formed, the brain begins to look for and find confirmatory evidence, which adds an emotional boost of further confidence.[240]

This insidious process of "belief confirmation" is a powerful force that still more deeply embeds our beliefs into our consciousness. And did you notice the phrase "our perceptions about reality are dependent on the beliefs that we hold about it." Or more simply, we do not believe what we see, we see what we believe: "Beliefs come first, explanations for beliefs follow."

This could well explain the trap the Mr. Greenspan fell into, as well as the literal hole that the good people of Pitcher died in. It also explains, at least partially, the difference between the curve of exponential change and the more leisurely one labeled the "going out of business curve," which an attempt to explain the rate at which many organizations fail to adapt to change.

The greater the difference between these two curves, obviously, the greater the implied risk. Addressing the gap means taking action both on the cognitive aspects as well as in the hands-on managerial ones. In addition to the social pressures related to groupthink and the problems of belief preceding and shaping what we actually observe, the cognitive realm is also subject to its own biases that often come in the form of thinking errors that stand in the way of clear judgments.

Cognitive Bias

The broader category of errors called "cognitive biases" describes some of the ways in which our judgment commonly lapses, particularly in the face of novelty. Total Oil executive Guy Mansfield explains it this way:

> Managers like to think that the decisions they make are objective and rational and have been executed taking into consideration all the pertinent facts. Studies by a variety of researchers including Kahneman [241] and Schoemaker [242] have identified six principal decision-making biases:
>
> 1. Anchoring: Ignoring contradictory evidence.
> 2. Framing: How a situation is presented affects the decision; and it can be easily even if unconsciously framed to validate a given expectation or position.
> 3. Availability Heuristic: Vivid and easily imaginable events and recent events are weighted disproportionately in making decisions. Something that occurred this morning, even if insignificant in the bigger picture, may exert disproportionate influence in a decision making process.
> 4. Confirmation Bias: Initial decisions become self-fulfilling prophesies, and data are collected after the event to justify the decision. Contradictory evidence is often disregarded.
> 5. Commitment Escalation: Previous commitments tend to influence present decisions; this is often referred to as "putting good money after bad," and generally refers to our unwillingness to walk away after a bad investment.
> 6. Hindsight Bias: It is easy to construct a logical narrative to explain events in hindsight even when foresight had no clue what was coming.[243] Nassim Taleb explains it in these terms: "Past events will *always* look less random than they were."[244]

These are particularly pernicious dangers in this era of accelerating change, wherein the prior evidence is consistently likely to compose a fragmented or even fully defective picture of the future. Becoming aware of the broad categories of bias that are common traps, and especially the ones that your own team, your organization, and you yourself may have a greater tendency to succumb to requires some self-examination, but will be entirely worth the effort as it helps to improve the quality of your assessments and decisions.

Evidence

Given the risks that organizations and society in general face due to the rate and acceleration of change, along with increase in complexity, etc., we must undertake a systematic search for reliable evidence, and then interrogate it relentlessly in order to arrive at a reliable interpretation about what is real, as opposed to what we wish to be real.

The evidence I presented in Part 1 is intended to affirm the proposition that due to the confluence of five revolutions, the counter-revolution, and the rate of change has raced beyond the capacity of most decision makers to grasp what's going on, which of course prevents them from making sound decisions and providing the leadership necessary to enable their organizations to successfully adapt, in which case they find themselves proceeding along the going-out-of-business curve.

Following this lesser curve inevitably puts governments and corporations into cycles of constant crisis management because they're not anticipating change, but instead arguing about where to place the deck chairs as they career into icebergs that they have failed to anticipate. This reactive dynamic is fully evident in every dimension of society, from the financial crises that are occurring with greater regularity in multiple countries to the political, ideological, religious, and diplomatic crises that have degenerated into the thirty to fifty currently active armed conflicts across numerous regions and countries.[245] The crises are certainly real – they directly and adversely affect millions of us, and billions more feel the impacts a bit less directly. And all of this leaves us with the uncomfortable feeling that our social systems are out of control, and that we don't know what to do, which only accentuates the pervasive feelings of future shock/now shock.

And while it's difficult to envision a plausible scenario in which the speed of change slows down, it's quite easy to see that change could continue to accelerate. Consequently, crises may worsen but are unlikely to lessen, it's more realistic and more prudent to anticipate that they will become more frequent and their impacts will become more significant. The turbulence, in short, will increase, and the demands on managers will increase commensurately.

Despite the uncertainties, the concept of five revolutions offers least the beginnings of a model, and as I mentioned above, we have to have a sound model if we're going to manage effectively in this situation, or indeed in any situation. Perhaps we already do know a lot about our future; we do certainly have a lot of insights about what to expect from the continuing advances of digital technology, and about the likely impacts of climate change in both moderate and more extreme cases, about the massive economic dislocation that the shift from fossil fuels will cause, about the continuing advance of urbanization and the consequent decline in the rate of population growth, and about the continuing tumult throughout human societies as we struggle to cope with everything that's changing. We know a lot about them because we're already experiencing them; that is, we already have a lot of evidence.

We also have a lot of guidance from the many visionaries who have traversed this ground ahead of us, many of whom I mentioned in the previous chapter.

Interpretation

Prior to the global financial collapse of 2008, a number of insiders were quite outspoken in expressing concerns about the state of the American mortgage market, but few of them found much of an audience, and certainly none of them with Mr. Greenspan. For example, Ms. Brooksley Born, Chairwoman of the US government Commodity Futures Trading Commission which regulates futures and option markets, raised concerns about the subprime mortgage market at a number of meetings for which the complete record is available, and she was roundly criticized and even publicly humiliated for having the impudence to suggest that there was anything wrong.[246] Such public humiliations are characteristic of the groupthink environment, in which it's quite common for those with views contrary to the consensus opinion to be forced out of the conversation.

Born foresaw a financial cataclysm, accurately predicting that exotic investments known as over-the-counter derivatives could play a crucial role in a crisis much like the one now convulsing America. Her efforts to stop that from happening ran afoul of some of the most influential men in Washington, men with names like Greenspan and Levitt and Rubin and Summers. She was the head of a tiny government agency who wanted to regulate the derivatives. They were the men who stopped her. The same class of derivatives that preoccupied Born – including the now-infamous "credit-default swaps" – have been blamed for accelerating [the 2008] financial implosion. But from 1996 to 1999, when Born was the chairman of the Commodity Futures Trading Commission, the U.S. economy was roaring and she was getting nowhere with predictions of doom. Born tossed and turned, and woke repeatedly "in a cold sweat," agonizing that a financial calamity was coming. "I was really terribly worried."

It would have been a much better reflection on Mr. Greenspan's capacity as leader if he had at least considered the possibility of the subprime boom and bust, even if he had rejected it, than for him to have to admit that it was entirely beyond his imagination. If it had been considered, then his failure would have been one of interpretation and judgment, and we all recognize that failures of this type are a constant risk for all decisions makers, and thus they're perhaps less inexcusable.

History showed that Ms. Born had a better grasp on the market risks than did Mr. Greenspan, a better interpretation of the available evidence, and actually in her role she was actually closer to the meaningful evidence, which makes it even more inexcusable that her opinion would have been handled so caustically.

Another observer, also someone who had access to evidence, and who correctly forecast the calamity, was Nassim Taleb, who wrote this:

Regulators in the banking business are prone to a severe expert problem and they tend to condone reckless but (hidden) risk taking. … The government-sponsored institution Fanny Mae, when I look at their risks, seems to be sitting on a barrel of dynamite, vulnerable to the slightest hiccup. But not to worry: their large staff of scientists deemed these events "unlikely."247

The "expert problem" to which Taleb refers is yet another form of bias, which refers to the tendency of experts to become convinced of the their own thorough expertise – Greenspan, again – when in fact that expertise has been developed in a prior context which may no longer be relevant. Born understood that the context had changed; Greenspan refused, literally, to consider the possibility.

Taleb's broader focus on the distinction between fragile and anti-fragile is yet another of the cognitive fallacies, his quite valid point being that we mistakenly create systems with inherent fragility rather than anti-fragile ones that would serve us much better.

Among Taleb's books the most famous is *The Black Swan*, which discusses the mismatch between our understanding of what is possible, and the much broader scope of what actually is possible. He suggests that many of us live within artificially constrained mindsets, and that our appreciation for the depth and complexity the world is quite limited compared with the much greater complexity and possibility of the actual world. Consequently, Taleb suggests that we are surprised when we should not be, by events that could well be foreseen. It's obvious why his views are relevant here, when the topic is change and our capacity to recognize and prepare for it.

The concept of the black swan, from which his book gets its title, is this:

> Before the discovery of Australia, people in the Old World were convinced that all swans were white, an unassailable belief as it seemed completely confirmed by empirical evidence. ...This illustrates a severe limitation to our learning from observations or experience and the fragility of our knowledge. One single observation [or event] can invalidate a general statement derived from millennia of confirmatory sightings of millions of white swans.[248]

The notion of mistaken beliefs confirmed by empirical evidence is both profound and problematic. For what are we to believe if not the facts that have been confirmed? And yet that is precisely the point. The fact may change, and just because a thing has never occurred does not mean that it never will. Hence, Taleb reminds us that in addition to studying the driving forces of change that we have been examining so far, we should also consider events that have never occurred but if they did would decisively change the world. We will do this in considerable detail in Chapters 12 and 13, and for exactly the reason that Taleb suggests we should.

The black swan problem is also a cognitive one, wherein we mistake the fact that we don't have any evidence either way that something exists or not, for evidence of that it cannot exist. The concept of the black swan fallacy gives Taleb and us a shorthand way to explain that absence of evidence (never having seen a black swan) is not at all the same as the evidence of absence (the nonexistence of black swans). Hence, just because we don't have any evidence for the existence of a thing is *not* proof that it does not exist. (Red, green, or turquoise swans may be out there yet.)

This is precisely one of the traps that befell Mr. Greenspan. The argument that was made in attacking Ms. Born when she had the temerity to speak out was that there was no evidence that the practice of subprime mortgage lending was creating any problems, so obviously it wasn't creating any problems. In fact it was creating huge problems, problems that just hadn't revealed themselves to Mr. Greenspan quite yet, although others, including Born and Taleb, had seen plenty of evidence and had interpreted it correctly.

This also reflects an aspect of our world that the comment attributed to J.M. Keynes that I used at the beginning of the chapter. The passage of time reveals new information that was not previously known, which may include new facts that contradict the old ones, such as the discovery that black swans do exist, just in far away Australia where we hadn't yet looked for them. The ideologue generally distrusts and disregard the new facts, not believing them because they contradict the ideology that only white swans are possible, dearly beloved as they are. This will lead, of course, to faulty decisions. Hence, Keynes' point was that we are better off looking at the facts for what they are than for what we want them to be. Everything we've discussed so far in this chapter shows that this is in fact harder to do than perhaps you thought, but that's the challenge and indeed the requirement.

In our world, where reinforcement of ideologies and prejudices is the very purpose of a vast array of special-interest media outlets and personalities, it requires dogged persistence and uncharacteristic openness to allow the facts to speak for themselves.

Causality vs. Coincidence

As we seek to identify what's real, as distinct from what is pre-believed, another challenge we face are the illusions caused by relationships *between* events. When two events occur in sequence it's our natural tendency to understand that the first one has *caused* the second one. But in a complex and complexifying world it's quite common for events to occur in sequences that are not causal at all, but merely coincidental.

This was one of the insights that Forrester illuminated in his work on social systems, noting that with their increasing complexity the likelihood increased that preferred policy prescriptions would lead to unintended and undesirable outcomes. His discovery that the behaviors of complex social systems were often counter-intuitive meant that when government, for example, took action to deal with systemic problems, very often the results achieved were the opposite of what was intended because the actions were planned according to what amounts to a defective understanding about cause and effect.

The very complexity of the systems we're dealing with defeats our intent because of our lack of understanding. Forrester came to this understanding by developing highly sophisticated models of these systems, and the techniques he pioneered became quite influential among his students at MIT and elsewhere. He was achieving these insights in the 1960s and 70s; today we have computers that are orders of magnitude more powerful, and with which we are able to develop much more comprehensive models. Social scientists who have become quite adept at combining public opinion polls with in-depth behavioral research are enabling us to master complexities that used to bedevil us.

This is as true in the physical sciences and economics as it is in the social sciences, giving today's decision makers the benefit of much better tools. Tomorrow's will be even better still, and perhaps just in time to help us sort our way out of the current messes.

Trained Incapacity

If do not distinguish between causal connections and coincidences then we will constantly misidentify the true causes of our fortunes and misfortunes. If we cannot distinguish between our ideological biases and meaningful evidence then we are destined to be cast adrift by those biases. Obviously this is worth mentioning because we're chronically seeing both types of errors. These shortcomings are an example of what we might call "trained incapacity," which are essentially poor thinking habits that have been learned. We are incapable because we have been trained to be incapable, trained by a society that's rife with biases including a preference for ideology and chronic lapses in rigor.

Happily, there is a different way. As we train our capacity we learn to gather sufficient evidence and then interpret skillfully it by decoding the relevant patterns. We map the intersections of events, trends, forces, and ideas, which make it possible to get a decent view of the future. But the challenge remains, of course, that we never know if we have enough evidence because the information available to us is always incomplete.

This is why leaders must develop both their skills and their judgment, and thereby increase their capacity to recognize facts, and also to make sound decisions even when they prefer to wait for yet more information. And in the requirement that they make such judgments, they may be significantly aided by those who have already been thinking about the future.

This has always been one of the crucial roles that visionaries have played in society. As observers and advisors, as critics and challengers, as journalists and artists, those who have seen the future have frequently tried to point out its threats and dangers well beforehand. As we saw in the previous chapter, though, their role often brings with it a heavy dose of frustration, for their insights frequently go against common sense, as Ms. Born was rudely reminded of.

However, in addition to his critique of group decision making Irving Janis also gives examples of high risk and tension-filled situations in which the decision makers were rigorous, and he provides a helpful rubric of seven steps that constitute sound and disciplined approach. These are the essential skills:

1. Thoroughly canvass a wide range of alternative courses of action.
2. Survey the objectives and the values implicated.
3. Weigh carefully the costs, drawbacks, and subtle risks of negative consequences, as well as the positive consequences, that could result.
4. Search continuously for relevant information for evaluating alternatives.
5. Take account the expert judgments, even when those judgments contradict initial preferences.
6. Reexamine positive and negative consequences of the main alternatives, including actions that had initially been considered unacceptable.
7. Made detailed execution plans, including contingency plans if things go wrong.[249]

This, then, is our process for making decisions, and thus our method also of making predictions. We will return to Janis' recommendations later.

Changing Our Beliefs

Social norms help to sustain society because they provide continuity and enable the sharing of gained knowledge across generations. This has been, as we saw, essential to our endurance as a species that is otherwise quite mediocre in its physical attributes, and it is at the core of how we succeed in any particular context. Our ways of thinking, interacting, deciding are all functions of where and how we live, and the situations in which we find ourselves, and evolution has crafted us magnificently to occupy our present niche.

The challenge we face today, however, is that our niche, the world around us, is changing much faster than our genes can change. How will we handle that? We will have to change our beliefs.

> Belief change comes from a combination of personal psychological readiness and a deeper social and cultural shift in the underlying zeitgeist, which is affected in part by education but is more the product of larger and harder-to-define political, economic, religious, and social changes.250

The political, economic, religious, and social context are definitely changing, and quickly, but is the zeitgeist also changing? For that to happen we may have to push it …

In particular, we have to develop and adopt a deeper understanding about today's and tomorrow's worlds, and also to develop our capacity to reason more effectively in a tense, complex and adversarial decision-making environment, as Janis recommends.

This means that we have to acknowledge that for the last 200 years we've been perfecting a particular type of economy that worked well in a particular historical situation, but now that we are changing our planet and our society in fundamental ways, we will soon have to make significant decisions about how to change our approach. This is no small challenge for us, for a species aligned through social and historical norms and that has attained the pinnacle of economic dominance and success across all of the ecosystems that we compete in. Alas, just as we have mastered the game of today, it seems that the rules are changed.

The really good strategists, the best ones, have already begun to understand the new rules, and to inform the rest of us that we will soon be obliged to change our ways of thinking and acting, or suffer the significantly unpleasant consequences. We will examine some of their evolving political, social, and economic maps and models in the next chapter.

•••

Chapter 11

The

Map Maker:

Geostrategy

...you put 800 million Chinese to work under a decent system ... and they will be the leaders of the world.

Richard Nixon[251]

Counting Russia out would be historic amnesia.

Vaclav Smil[252]

When it maintained a global system, Europe represented the dominant concept of world order. Its statesmen designed international structures and prescribed them to the rest of the world. Today the nature of the emergent world order is itself in dispute, and regions beyond Europe will play a major role in defining its attributes.

Henry Kissinger[253]

The characteristics of North American topography grant the Americans nearly endless capital, bottomless markets, low defense costs, and easy routes of power projection.

Peter Zeihan[254]

At the height of the Cold War the Soviet Union published maps of its major cities that did not accurately reflect the actual layout of their streets and landmarks. Major thoroughfares found new, imaginary routes, and key landmarks and rivers were mysteriously relocated. This occurred not because the Soviets were unable to make decent maps; instead they were deliberately erroneous attempts to confuse and confound unsuspecting Westerners.[255] Would these defective maps have caused an invading army to take a wrong turn, or to mis-guide a guided missile? It seems hardly likely, and thus today they are amusing artifacts of a different and confused time. The collapse of the Soviet Union and the advent of aerial and satellite mapping rendered the effort at deceit meaningless.

It seems that the Chinese did not get the memo, however, as official maps of Beijing until even a few years ago still contained intentional inaccuracies.[256] Since today's technology has transcended printed maps entirely you can view a highly detailed view of Moscow, Beijing, or nearly any other world city on your phone using any self-respecting mapping application. You can also get satellite views down to the level of an individual vehicle, and if you're a government, at much finer resolution than that.

Technology has transcended much more than old maps of our cities; it has also, and much more significantly, now transcended our maps of reality. Technology, both industrial and digital, has entirely altered the economy, and as a side effect it has altered the Earth's surface, as the hand of humanity is visible everywhere; with the advent of global climate change, it's about to do so to yet another level. We still need maps, though, for both our physical world and our conceptual ones, as they're essential to help us navigate complicated terrains. "Many animals, from squirrels to rats to people, construct 'cognitive maps' of their spatial world, internal pictures of where things are in space. Much like the external pictures of printed maps. Once you represent spatial information in a map, you can use that information much more flexibly and productively."[257]

What we need, therefore, new maps and models that will enable us to navigate successfully into and along tomorrow's pathways.

These maps will be both conceptual maps of social change, and also physical maps of our world, because despite the powerful influence of the Internet and all things Facebook and the impending arrival of transformative robots, geography does still matter, and in fact it still matters a great deal.   Hence, in addition to mapping the five revolutions and the anti-revolution that we've already been exploring, we can get a sufficiently clear view of the future only if we also consider the impact of the classic disciplines of geography and geopolitics, the studies of how location, topography, demographics, and resources influence a nation's choices of roles in the world community. That is what we will do here.

The Origins of Geopolitics

A series of wars that are known to European history as the 30 Years War finally ended in 1648 with the Treaty of Westphalia, named for the German town in which it was signed by the exhausted combatants. Eight million people died during the course of the dispute that engulfed virtually all of Europe. This is a huge number of casualties even now, and for the time it was a transformatively deadly toll. The war itself changed how societies and nations viewed themselves and their relations with others. Austria, Bohemia, Croatia, Denmark, England, France, the Holy Romans, Hungary, the Ottomans, Prussia and all the German states, Scotland, Spain, and Sweden were participant/combatants at one time or another during the 30 years span, and as their armies marched back and forth across the central regions, principally Germany, the cities and towns that happened to lie in their path were decimated. Hence, one-third of all German towns were utterly destroyed, and the total male population of Germany was reduced by about half.

What began as a religious conflict between the two major Christian denominations, Catholics and Protestants, quickly degenerated into a political free-for-all in which power politics rather than religious belief became the main concern. During the course of the conflict Catholic nations switched sides and allied with Protestants in service to the geopolitical goals, and thus the proclamations of holy righteousness were readily abandoned when real power was at stake.

This is significant for us today because, first, it frighteningly prefigures current religious, ethnic, and ideological conflicts that are terrorizing vast swatches of the Middle East, most notably at the moment Syria and Yemen.   It's also relevant because it was the Treaty of Westphalia that established the principle of a nation-state as a sovereign entity.

> The operative international rule, normal for centuries now, is that nations don't interfere in each other's internal affairs. This bargain, hashed out in 1648 as a series of peace treaties signed in Westphalia, Germany, gradually became the consensus view almost everywhere. The twin notions of national sovereignty and non-interference allowed wildly different systems of government to exist side by side – monarchies next to democracies next to autarkies – while still allowing trade to pass between them. As the Westphalian idea spread, the world was slowly carved up into a set of territorial claims that ultimately absorbed the whole of its populated surface. Under this system, all humans are citizens, and their passage through the world is restricted by rules governing both emigration and immigration. Every person should have a nation; people without regions are regarded with suspicion (viz the Roma), regions under no clear national ruler are regarded with anxiety (Somalia), and regions claimed by more than one nation are treated as standing crises (as with the fight over the Spratly Islands).[258]

Because of the Treaty it has been an accepted norm of global politics for 350 years that no nation state had business meddling in the internal affairs of another, and from this principle emerged the concepts of citizenship and the nearly absolute right of every nation to defend its national boundaries.   This led in turn to the invention of passports and visas for cross-border travel, and is therefore the source of the founding practices and principles of geopolitics as it is still practiced today, and are reflected on all of our maps.

Border or Borderless?

Events and realities of our times are challenging these principles, however, as we are living in an era of changes in economics, politics and even in geology, when financial capital travels instantaneously across a borderless economy and the wealthy sail across national boundaries in luxury and without restraint, and even obtain multiple citizenships in multiple tax havens, while at the same time entire countries are in danger of disappearing due to civil war or rising seas, and millions of the poor are homeless or stateless, trapped in "failed states" or in refugee camps with nowhere to go, prevented by armed guards and barbed wire from crossing into the safe havens where the rich reside in comfort and ease, or compelled by cruel fate to risk their lives crossing the turbulent seas in rickety boats in the hopes of asylum.

> What does it mean when the wealthy can move freely between countries and exploit the "borderless" world that globalization has promised, but that the poor who try to cross borders can't – or if they can, routinely die trying?[259]

Many essential aspects of our future are linked to the places where we are born or live, and the cultural norms and expectations we have developed while living there. In this chapter we'll consider China, Russia, the USA, the European Union, and the broader social and economic trend of globalization. We will also revisit the ongoing terrorist anti-revolution in the Middle East, as it will certainly also be a decisive geopolitical actor in our 21ˢᵗ century world.

And there is one other group that we also need to consider, consisting of globally-significant entities that were represented in the events of 1648 by the two dominant churches. Today we call these "non-state actors," which include the religious organizations whose reach is unbounded by national borders as well as global criminal gangs that have become significant social and economic forces and which also work across boundaries. And there's a third group, as well, the multi-national corporations that by their recent behavior demonstrate less and less allegiance to any nation, but are beholden instead to shareholders whose concerns are not nationalistic, but capitalistic. That is, they are entirely beholden to their owners, but not necessarily to any nation-state.

While most companies benefit enormously from and indeed depend on a stable and law-abiding marketplace and the established infrastructure that the nation-state system provides, they also move capital in enormous amounts around the world in micro-seconds to avoid taxation that might pay for the law enforcement that they expect, or the roads, bridges, and ports, or for the education of their future employees and customers; as corporations gain power and capital their growing independence from the nation-state system becomes a more significant issue.

In sum, of course, the varying goals and methods of these various actors on the global geopolitical stage is yet another dimension of the increasing complexity that, through our social and economic systems, we are inflicting upon ourselves. Here, then, we will examine some of the evidence that will help us to develop maps and models to help us cope with the complexity of geopolitics.

We begin with a discussion of China, followed by Russia, the European Union, and the United States. After that we will consider the Middle East and then the other non-state actors.

And while it's quite obvious it does need to be mentioned that there are entire libraries of great books and mountainous stacks of excellent journals that describe these subjects in excellent and exhaustive detail, so the objective here is provide an overview at a high level and to identify some of the essential patterns.

China

In the centuries before Christ the Chinese empire was forged from a collection of smaller kingdoms, and as it converged to become one nation it also had the largest population, and hence its economy produced by far the largest national output. From the Chinese perspective its borders identified the limits of civilization, and what was beyond those borders utterly lacked significance.

For the better part of two millennia China was the dominant political and military power in Asia, which made the emperor immeasurably wealthy. "China produced a far greater share of world GDP than any

Western society in eighteen of the last twenty centuries. As late as 1820, it produced over 30 percent of world GDP – an amount exceeding the GDP of Western Europe, Eastern Europe, and the United States combined."[260]

By the early 1400s a massive fleet of trading ships sailed each year to spread Chinese hegemony throughout Asia and even East Africa, and to bring back wealth and tribute. Departing from the southern Chinese port cities, the fleet included the largest wooden vessel that ever sailed, exemplifying Chinese power and its advanced technological prowess.

However, beginning in 1433 the Chinese faced new threats from its north, and retreated inwardly to protect itself. For the following four centuries China remained relatively isolated, and so during those centuries the world's most advanced economy stagnated, as did its technology, while the European world meanwhile was embarking on the Renaissance and the Enlightenment and then the Industrial Revolution. China fell significantly behind.

The extent of its stagnation was revealed in the early 1800s, but not by China's choice. The world rediscovered China as another market for its industrial goods and addictive drugs, and between 1839 and 1860 China fought and lost the two Opium Wars with Great Britain, and so it was dragged by force back into engagement with the rest of the world. In the following century the Japanese wanted control of Chinese natural resources, and they invaded Manchuria in 1931 inflicting further destruction and humiliation until their surrender in 1945, whereupon the Nationalists and the Communist Party turned their military aggression on one another. The Communists, under Mao, were soon victorious, and so began the story of modern China's re-ascent as a world power as the world's most populous nation and most populous Communist nation.

Upon Mao's death in 1978 Deng Xiaoping became premier, and his astonishing decision to open the Chinese economy to capitalism proved to be one of the best economic decisions of the 20th century, or any century. With a ready pool of hundreds of millions of laborers who were anxious to abandon their hard, impoverished, and isolated lives on the farms for life in the factories and cities of coastal China, and with the internet enabling real time communication between those factories and Western markets, and with digital manufacturing capabilities producing acceptable quality goods at lower costs than were available anywhere else, China became the world's manufacturing center. Its economy boomed.

The skeptic may wonder how much of a boom it really was, and the answer is that in all of human history no nation has created, in any span of 25 years, as much wealth as China has during the last 25. To understand the scale of this effort, consider that, "China used more cement in the first three years of this decade than the U.S. used in the twentieth century. (Much more: 6.6 billion metric tons to 4.5.)"[261]

As a result, about 500 million people have moved from poverty to roughly the middle class.

This number is significant enough to alter the world's overall poverty statistics, and indeed, the rapid growth has propelled the overall size of the Chinese GDP even closer toward America's. And while China's GDP is still much lower on a per-capita basis, its economic productivity results in enormous social, economic, and military power regionally and globally. And this itself is a key fact in the broader field of geopolitics, for it has been true for centuries that economic power is the basis of military power. No empire or nation can sustain an impactful military presence locally or globally unless it has a significant economic engine to power it.

The advent of non-state actors in to form of global terrorist organizations has changed that formula, as today a tiny terrorist group with a nuclear weapon and the willingness to use it would also have massive power. This is one the new threats that modern world has stumbled its way into, and which leaders East and West will be dealing for the entirety of civilization's future.

China has transformed its massive population into a successful productive force that dominates global manufacturing, a renaissance has returned China to the status of a global superpower. In the view of many Chinese, this ascendance simply restores China to its rightful place among or at the summit of the world's great nations.

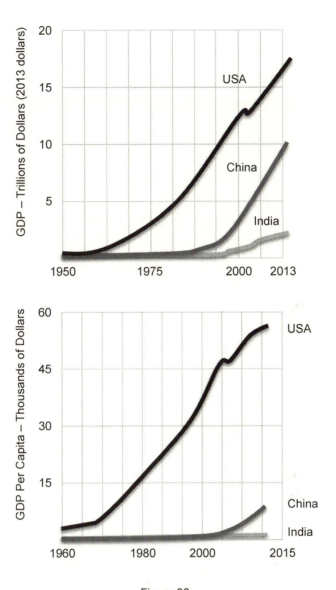

Figure 92
Total GDP (above) and GDP per Capita (below): US, China, and India[262]

Could Deng have possibly known what would happen, that he was unleashing an industrial and economic explosion that would within the very short span of forty years elevate China to its present position as the world's most productive economy? That this initiative would lift more than 400 million Chinese from rural poverty into much more prosperous lives, while bringing to the nation exceptional wealth as the world's center of manufacturing?

All of this makes for an amazing story, and sets the stage for a China that may indeed be, or soon become, the world's wealthiest, and therefore most powerful and perhaps most influential nation. US President Nixon recognized this, and predicted quite accurately to Henry Kissinger, "...you put 800 million Chinese to work under a decent system ... and they will be the leaders of the world.[263] As the 20th century proved to be an American century, many believe that the 21st will be the Chinese century.

This is indeed quite possible, but a close look at additional evidence suggests that it's not inevitable. For although China's economic ascent has been unparalleled and its global influence has never been greater, it also faces a quite broad range of internal challenges that could significantly limit its future options and achievements.

China's Inward Challenges

Demographics

China's economic boom was fueled by huge labor force that overwhelmingly preferred city life to life on the farm, and therefore was willing to work for relatively low wages in urban factories. A massive flow of mostly young workers moved to the cities, but that migratory wave is now nearly finished.

Further, those who became urban residents ten, fifteen, or twenty years ago are no longer content to work for entry level wages, and as their wages have gone up China's entire economic structure has changed, and it will continue to change.

And exactly the same thing has occurred in China that also happened everywhere else where there was rapid urbanization, which is that China's rate of population growth has slowed significantly, as we discussed in Chapter 4. Based on current trends, it is forecast that China's population will peak by mid-century, and then will begin to decline. On this journey, the social cost of caring for the aging population will be significant, and while older citizens consume significant resources in health care and for their general living requirements, they are not economically productive and they pay no taxes. Just as a consequence of its demographic structure, by mid-century China will have by far the most citizens suffering from Parkinson's Disease, from Alzheimer's Disease, from senility, and from cardiac disease, simply because it will have by far the most old people.

Consequently, China and indeed all of the other aging nations will experience a double impact, as tax revenues will drop while government expenditures on pensions and health care increase. This deadly combination will take a heavy toll on the Chinese economy, as it will also in the US, Japan, and throughout Europe.

Hence, it's prudent to expect a significant reshaping of the entire global economy by mid-century simply because of this phenomenon, not even including all the other factors we also know about. Indeed, when we consider what's already happening in Japan, we may already be seeing the early stages of this transition. For China this means that while its currently enjoying huge government surpluses and the massive accumulation of capital that has paid for large infrastructure investments, the aging population is likely to turn China's surpluses abruptly to deficits. And this could well inhibit China's ability to behave aggressively toward its neighbors, currently a very important theme in all geopolitics related to the Pacific region.

Tobacco

Another related demographic problem that will also slow China's growth is likely to be its high rate of tobacco use. It is estimated that during the course of the next 50 years, 50 to 75 million Chinese will die prematurely, and in some cases quite painfully because of tobacco, and the social costs in lost productivity and health care will be significant. At the lower end of the estimate, one million tobacco-related deaths a year equates to roughly 2700 per day, which further implies that China will have to build dozens of hospitals only for its patients who develop cancers from tobacco. The scale of social and economic burdens will be staggering.

If the government were to institute large scale anti-tobacco initiatives then the situation could change, for smokers who quit obtain nearly immediate health benefits. But the government has put itself in a conflict of interest because the tobacco industry is one of its largest sources of revenue for the Chinese government. Tobacco sales to China's 300 million smokers consistently contribute 7 – 10 percent of total annual tax receipts, which is a massive amount of revenue. [264] Perhaps the government actuaries will make the convincing argument that the cost of treating fifty million increasingly ill Chinese smokers is more than the tax revenues that would be received from continuing to sell the cancer-causing tax boon, but until that happens China is only making its inherent demographic problems worse. The numbers are already staggeringly huge and the inevitable costs will be also.

The China National Tobacco Corp. is by far the largest cigarette maker in the world. In 2013 it manufactured about 2.5 trillion cigarettes while its next largest competitor, Philip Morris International, produced only 880 billion. In terms of market share China National is bigger than its next five competitors combined; its growing sales have accounted for a net increase in global production, even as volume at its competitors has fallen. While Marlboro remains the most popular cigarette in the world, China National boasts seven of the top ten brands, including Red Pagoda Mountain and Double Happiness. In all, the company made 43 out of every 100 cigarettes in the world.[265]

If ever there was a vivid example of the trade off between short term benefit and long term costs this is certainly it, a sadly twisted tale of state-sponsored national suicide made all the worse by the painfully ironic brand names.

One Child or Two

In addition to opening China's economy to capitalism, another major policy initiative of Deng Xiaoping was the one-child policy, which limited families to a single child. At the time this policy was adopted China's forecasted population growth rate appeared to be on a disastrous course toward overpopulation and the risk of large scale famine, and as that did not occur, and the population growth rate did decline quite significantly, one could say that the policy was a success.

There were, however, quite significant consequences, some foreseen but many not, are continuing to have huge impact on Chinese culture and society.   One consequence is the significant imbalance between the number of male and female children.   In China's male-dominated society sons are often preferred, and with the law restricting families to one child, millions elected to have abortions if their child was female.   This has led to a huge imbalance between males and females.   In the 15 – 30 year old age group there are now about thirty million more Chinese men than women, which will cause no end of social troubles in the years to come as men compete for wives, and a great many are forced to look outside of China to find partners.

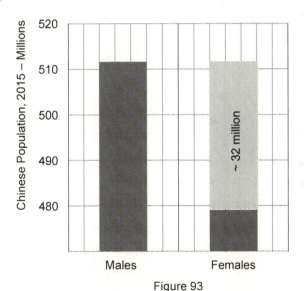

Figure 93
Males and Females in China
Men presently outnumber women by about 32 million, an emerging social challenge.

Chinese culture also maintains the ancient Confucian tradition of veneration for the elderly, and children are still expected to provide care and financial support for the parents and even grandparents. Thus the one-child-family children are now carrying the responsibility to care for two elderly parents, and married couples with a child are often responsible for all four parents plus the child, but with the income of only one parent to accommodate the needs of seven. This has created, for many families, a crushing economic burden, compounded because the cost of living in China continues to rise significantly as the nation transitions to an economic structure anchored by a middle class of some 500 million consumers. There are no obvious solutions, and thus we can project that millions of Chinese elderly will slip more deeply into poverty.

A third unanticipated consequence of the one child policy is the emergence of now two generations of children who are referred to as "little emperors" and "little empresses," children without siblings who have been spoiled by their parents and who are highly narcissistic and lack skills in sharing. I first learned this from a young Chinese woman who described her own generation in these very terms, and in fact used this as a way to explain and excuse her own behavior, which she recognized was selfish but which she was not sufficiently concerned about to change. Hence, it is not only a description applied by others, but this label and the behavior it describes largely reflects the self-image of two generations of young Chinese.

It's quite possible that urbanization would have brought the birth rate down on its own, but in any case now that China is facing the opposite problem, that by mid-century a declining population and the economic difficulties that are almost certain to result, and so the one child policy was repealed in 2015. But now that China is well on its way to becoming an urbanized nation it seems quite likely that Chinese families will prefer fewer children just as they have done in all urbanized nations elsewhere.

Pollution

In its push for rapid economic growth through industrialization China certainly did not prioritize protection for the environment. We've all seen the photos of thick smog in Beijing, and those who have been there during those bad times know how much it burns the lungs. As a result of the choice to industrialize so fast the nation now suffers not only from terrible air but also extensive water pollution. The large and still growing middle class citizenry is starting to object to the past policies and the resulting pollution levels, so much so that it's reported that there are an average of 500 protest gatherings across China each day.[266] Addressing these environmental issues will be hugely expensive, as it will require replacing dozens of power plants and factories, and cleaning thousands of miles of waterways.

Like China's tobacco problem, its air quality problem is also a major cause of death and disease. Current estimates suggest that air pollution contributes to the deaths of more than 1 million Chinese each year through cardiovascular diseases, lung diseases, and cancers.[267]

Culture

During changing times all nations endure internal tensions and conflicts. In the US this takes the form of ideological differences, racial conflicts, high levels of gun violence, and widespread poverty. In India intense conflicts linger between various castes, regions, ethnic, and religious groups which sometimes boils over into mob violence. In China there are also significant social and cultural differences, among them the divide between the urbanized east and the rural interior, continuing social pressure for democracy in Hong Kong and elsewhere, and widespread social unrest caused by the extremely bad pollution, as well as land use policy and chronic corruption. "In 2010 China was rocked by 180,000 protests, riots and other mass incidents—more than four times the tally from a decade earlier."[268]

In nations that are dominated by or controlled by a single political and government entity there is indeed a powerful tendency to slide into corruption because there is not natural balancing force, and China is no different. Lacking any political opposition and also lacking a free press to call attention to any misdeeds, corruption has become rife throughout the nation. One small but telling consequence of this is an edict issued by the Communist Party in 2015 that bans the 88 million Communist Party members from golfing. Why golfing? Because appearances matter a great deal in China, and as golf is seen as a bourgeois and Western extravagance, it has been forbidden. Whether the edict has actually disrupted anyone's golfing hobby or habit is unknown, and it's highly likely that most of the Party's golfers are still hitting the course, as the Chinese culture is also one in which the public face can differ significantly from the private.

The scale of the corruption may surprise you. According to the Central Commission for Discipline Inspection (CCDI), the government body leading the campaign, since Xi Jinping took leadership of the Chinese Communist Party in late 2012 until early 2015, a span of roughly 27 months, the staggering total of 414,000 officials were disciplined by the Party for corruption, and 201,600 prosecuted for infractions in court, a rate of 15,000 per month, or 750 during each working day of the month. In Shanxi alone, allegedly one of the most corrupt provinces, some 15,450 officials were convicted of corruption in 2014.[269] If these numbers are valid, and frankly we have no way of knowing if they are valid or not, the extent of the corruption must be truly monumental. From a systems perspective, this is one of the biggest dangers of a single party state, in what happens to be the largest country with the largest bureaucracy of government employees, about 39 million in all, and each day presents the opportunity for small bribes and "favors," the possibility of getting rich is tantalizingly easy. (By comparison, the US has about 22 million public employees at the federal, state, and local levels combined.[270])

Corruption is also a major factor in the Chinese Military, and it has reached to the highest ranks.

A deputy chief of logistics built a mansion for himself modeled on Beijing's Forbidden City, while China's most senior uniformed officer had a basement stacked high with cash, and no fewer than fifteen generals, including a former deputy chief of the nuclear arsenal, were recently under investigation for graft.[271] While Deng proclaimed that it was no longer a bad thing to get rich, this was probably not the means that he envisioned.

Equally significant is the geographical divide between east and the rest of the nation. According to many analysts, there is in fact not one China, but two. The coastal east, home to the urban band stretching from Beijing to Shanghai to Hong Kong is home to about 400 million, and it's where the wealth and power are concentrated and where the majority of the middle class resides. The rural western interior part of China is home to the other 900 million, where the economic benefits of capitalism have not arrived nearly as widely.[272]

China's demographic patterns and emerging demographic problems are nearly immutable – nothing can change them now. China's health care problems will come about because of its immutable demographics, exacerbated by tobacco and by the massive pollution that is a side effect of rapid industrialization.

On the other hand, China is an autocracy, and unlike in a democracy where change can also be agonizingly slow to come, the Premier could make a decision tomorrow and twenty million bureaucrats could be implementing it the following day.

And so as these internal issues continue to percolate there are significant forces and factors that China also faces outside of its borders.

China's External Challenges

Regional Role

With its renewed power and a vivid memory of centuries of regional domination China is not content to play a secondary role with its local neighbors. Japan's conduct during the 1930s and 40s has not been forgotten, nor has Taiwan. Disputes over Taiwan's independence, over islands so small and meaningless that they hardly qualify to be called islands at all, and more recent development by the Chinese of the Spratly island chain in the South China Sea are all reminders that petty jealousies and provocations still play a part in Chinese foreign policy.

All of these disputes are the subject of constant assertions and counter-assertions, of complaints and provocations and innuendo, and claims of bad faith from all sides.

The strategic question that China must decide is how aggressively to pursue these claims, as they have very little to do with its meaningful national defense, but a great deal to do with its pride.

Taiwan

A much more significant issue is the challenge presented by Taiwan. When the Nationalists of Chiang Kai Shek retreated to Taiwan in 1949 they proclaimed it to be an independent nation, and immediately allied with the United States for protection. But the mainland Chinese never accepted Taiwan's independence, and regard it as a wayward child that must eventually return to its true home.

The Taiwanese, with now 65 years of relative independence, have a different idea, and they recently elected a president who is vigorously independent as an assertion of its sovereignty. When, and under what circumstances China will elect to increase its aggressive posture has been a matter of speculation for many years, and as China's military power increases, the lingering fear becomes more pressing.

Under what circumstances would China increase the pressure on Taiwan to rejoin the People's Republic? Would it risk its standing among nations to violate Taiwan's self-asserted sovereignty. And if or when it did so, what would be the response of the US? Would the US confront aggression with counter-aggression? Or with economic sanctions?

Taiwan has a sibling that is also somewhat of a rebel, for Hong Kong has strongly resisted the efforts of Beijing to fall into line with the Communist Party's leadership. It's difficult to foresee how the ongoing protest movement and the push for democracy will ever reconcile with the central government in Beijing.

Intellectual property and Cyber Security

While Europe and the US have intellectual property protections gong back more than a century, China has never shared these traditions, and in current Chinese culture it's definitely not important. What Westerners consider piracy and illegal copying is standard practice throughout China, and any printed or electronic material is fair game.

Industrial espionage is also an accepted fact of Chinese foreign policy, and it's a very short step further to cyber conflict or even cyber warfare. While both the US and China have much to lose in an outright military conflict, both sides apparently engage in continuous efforts at low-level cyber intrusions targeting each other as well as, apparently, everyone else.

One area in which China has been particularly active spy is aerospace technology, and through its borrowed knowledge and its own exceptional capabilities it has built a space program that has been highly successful and remains targeted at exceptional goals. China has announced its intention to establish a colony on the moon, and although it has not announced a specific timeline it has completed many successful rocket tests and crewed flights.[273]

Just as in the US and Russia, in China the development of a competitive and successful aerospace capability is considered both a matter of national pride and an essential component of its defense.

The Long Term Perspective

Throughout history China's leaders have been highly skilled strategists who have taken a decidedly long view. The teachings of scholars such as Confucius are still considered relevant today, and the lessons of Sun Tsu are an innate aspect of Chinese culture. Consequently, proposed initiatives and actions are considered from many perspectives and in some cases over prolonged periods before action is taken. This will be both a strength and a potential weakness ahead, as its evident that thoughtful decision making will be essential for the future, but at the same time the world is now presenting unprecedented conditions for decision makers to deal with on a regular basis, and history may not prove to be such a useful guide. With that in mind, let us consider how the six revolutions may unfold in China.

Six Revolutions in China

As with the rest of the world, the five revolutions and the counter-revolution will bring significant impacts to China. How might those stories unfold?

The first thing to note is that because China's scale is so massive, and because so much of the economy is under centralized control, any decision to take large scale action on anything can lead quickly to a shift in the global market balance. This phenomenon shows up across all of the revolutions.

Technology

China is actively pursuing digitization, committing large investments to high technology industries, education, and capabilities. The Chinese leadership clearly understand that the future of the economy requires sophisticated technological capabilities, and with its massive pool of available capital it is in a good position to buy and build a great deal of the needed expertise.

As a nation whose economic health depends on a massive labor force working at relatively low levels, however, China is extremely vulnerable to robotics. More than a million Chinese work for Foxconn assembling iPhones and other high tech gear, and many of those jobs will soon be done by robots. Foxconn itself has said as much; CEO Terry Gou has suggested that the company would like to deploy a "robot army" in its factories to replace as much as 70 percent of the work now done by humans.[274] The company has already invested hundreds of millions of dollars in robotic technology, and as robots become more proficient and cheaper, the likelihood that low level Chinese manufacturing will disappear increases, and hence the risks to the Chinese economy increase.

Climate Change

China already suffers from climate-change induced problems, including a lack of rainfall in its massive northwestern regions combined with ineffective farming practices that have led to an acute shortage of water throughout the highly populated northeast. It has built the world's largest canal to divert billions of gallons from the wetter south 1000 km toward Beijing, at a cost of a cool $80 billion. But as with most such mega-engineering projects, whether it will actually achieve the desired results over the long term is unknown.[275]

What is known is that China is now the world's largest producer of carbon emissions, and that it's huge number of coal-fired power plants are a major source of CO_2 and they also cause massive pollution, particularly in the winter months. Further, its low lying cities, including Shanghai and of course Hong Kong, are highly susceptible to flooding as the oceans rise and storms worsen.

If climate change worsens significantly, it will certainly have decisive impacts throughout China on its resources, agriculture, and coastal regions. The potential costs that the Chinese government would have to bear to address protection and remediation needs would be enormous.

Energy

The massive amounts of capital that China has accumulated has enabled it to embark on other massive infrastructure projects, including an unprecedented construction boom to build new power plants, and also many in alternative energy. It ramped up production of solar panels at a high rate to become the world's leading supplier, in the process bankrupting many of its competitors, but also creating a situation of massive oversupply that dragged prices below the level of profitability for all manufacturers.

Urbanization

As I mentioned in Chapter 4, China has seen the fastest wave of urbanization in human history and its biggest ever building boom. From bare ground it has constructed cities housing tens of millions:

> China used more cement in the first three years of this decade than the U.S. used in the twentieth century. (Much more: 6.6 billion metric tons to 4.5.)[276]

The bad news about its building boom is that most of the buildings constructed are not of high quality. Craftsmanship standards are shoddy or nonexistent, materials are average, and thus the fit and finish of all but the highest standards of luxury construction are mediocre. Windows don't seal out the wind, heaters don't heat well, and exposed writing shows almost everywhere.

The worse news is that the basic approach to urban design has followed the monotonous grid pattern based on the assumption that cars are the ideal form of transportation. Subways are slowly being retrofitted into many Chinese cities but in an entirely suboptimal manner, and bus are slow and overcrowded. Principles of sound urban design are not in evidence, and should the Chinese continue to build in this manner then their future cities will only be drab copies of the existing drab copies.

The underlying phenomenon of urbanization, however, seems to have upheld the globally-recognized pattern that urban families choose to have fewer children, and thus the future of China's population suggests that it will within a few decades enter into a period of contraction.

Culture Change

China's culture is evolving very rapidly, so much so that it's not hard to see that change could readily overwhelm the Central Communist Party's government within the near future. For the last decade popular support for the Party has been broad and generally enthusiastic, but the cost has been a progressively-encroaching surveillance state that looks over everyone's shoulders. Clay Shirky notes that "Many social media services are required to have their servers in Beijing, to simplify surveillance."[277]

Surveillance and censorship are pervasive, and one has to wonder how long the Chinese people will tolerate the lack of information and the humorous self-parody in which the government sometimes engages. Shirky notes, "To prevent the elaborate system of censorship of political subjects itself from becoming a target of popular ire, discussion of why discussion is not allowed is not allowed."[278]

The risk to the Party is of course that popular aspirations for democracy, or popular unrest about corruption, pollution, and land confiscations lead to widespread and coordinated unrest, in essence the exporting of the Hong Kong Occupy movement to the mainland. As long as the economy has continued to grow then the leadership of the Party has been insulated, but as the rate of growth slows the Party is obliged to address these concerns directly. The current and large scale anti-corruption campaign is one such example.

The large and rapidly growing middle class also presents a unique type of threat, for on a world-wide basis it's become clear that middle class families have expectations for their lifestyles and basic autonomy that may not be fulfilled in an authoritarian system; as China's middle gains social and economic power it may be the Party that is required to adapt to the people, not vice versa.

Counter-Revolution

Therefore, to a significant degree it is the Communist Party itself that must learn to successfully play the role of the anti-revolutionary in contemporary China. In seeking to preserve its own base of power and prolong its control it must simultaneously appease the populace's aspirations for continuing economic progress, and yet the values that inevitably accompany increasing wealth include the desire for greater autonomy and self-determination. This leads naturally to pressure for democratic reforms, when a key tenet of central communism in China is that democracy is not a suitable form of government for the Chinese people. Many in Hong Kong emphatically disagree with this view, and the underlying paradox puts the government in a very difficult position.

Already history has seen the violent repression of the Tiananmen Square protests, but if there is a next protest on that scale, even though China's internet is heavily censored it could not possibly be kept secret. And so if protest in China spreads with the vigor that the Arab Spring raced through North Africa and the Middle East, the Communist Party could find itself in a very difficult position with little time to formulate a response. If the communist government were to collapse this is the conflict that could conceivably instigate it. As we saw with the Soviet Union in 1989, the process can occur with stunning speed.

The Prospects for China

When we put all this together we see that like the rest of the world, China faces internal and external challenges that bring into question the assumption that China's further ascent is inevitable. How will China cope with its growing set of demographic challenges and internal difficulties?

It's not difficult to foresee two quite different futures for China.

In one of them, China's continuing ascent, the nation's leaders successfully address the myriad of challenges in its demographics, economics, politics, and regional geopolitics, and continue to accumulate more power in the region and globally. In this version of the story China may even replace the US as the world's the dominant superpower, leveraging its massive population to propel continuing economic growth, sustaining the control by the Communist Party, continuing to exercise its military might, and consolidating its position as the dominant power in Asia and the Pacific. Accomplishing this, however, will require extraordinary leadership skill and probably more than a little good luck.

It's also quite easy to foresee a China that may even now be peaking, and that the challenges of the coming decades may prove insurmountable as the convergence of internal conflicts lead to its undoing and prevent it from attaining the great power status to which it clearly aspires. These problems would certainly include the aging population that causes a massive drain on the economy, the lack of environmental protections that lead to continuing social unrest and increasing health problems and high economic costs, and unshaken corruption that costs the Communist Party its authority and leads to large scale unrest. We have already seen in Hong Kong that the heavy-handed approach of the Communist Party leadership arouses significant opposition, and if that sentiment spreads on the mainland then challenges to the Party's authority will only increase. Indeed, a confluence of all the negative forces could conceivably cause the millions of Chinese to rise up in spontaneous protest which could trigger a government crisis, leading even to the point of fundamental change: a counter-counter revolution.

Hence, at one extreme we see the possibility of China replacing the US as the world's dominant economic and military force and at the other extreme we see a society overcome by tumult and focused inwardly on a mountain of domestic difficulties.

While the experts may argue for one or the other possibility as the most likely, it's apparent that both are indeed entirely possible. It may not be so useful to try to guess which of the two is more or most likely, but instead to maintain in our minds that both could well occur. In this way we don't make the mistake of choosing sides, or unconsciously picking the one we prefer, but we instead maintain an open mind and observe the events as they occur to see which pattern constitutes the best description. In the end, of course, there could well be a third or fourth option that proves to be the real outcome, and our intent is not to predict, but rather to assess the broader system and make sound choices for the short, medium, and long terms.

Russia

It should not be surprising that Russia sits precisely at the center of a tumultuous story, for among all the nations of the world, Russia's last hundred years has been among the most traumatic that perhaps any nation has ever faced. From 1900 to today Russians have experienced a nearly unending sequence of major disasters, beginning with the roughly 12 million Russians who perished in World War I, followed by the violent overthrow of the Romanovs and the rise of the Communist Party, which led to the rise of Stalin and the violent repression of all dissent that resulted in an estimated 30 to 40 million additional victims. This was followed by the great tragedy of World War II, in which an additional 30 to 40 million Russians died. Having lost nearly ninety million citizens as a result of two wars of annihilation and its own civil tumult, it was hardly surprising when the Soviet Union annexed Eastern Europe to provide itself a buffer zone, which led immediately, of course, to the drama of Cold War that was frighteningly punctuated by the nuclear arms race. However, the Soviets could not keep up with the booming Western economies. Finally it collapsed in 1989 after 75 exhausting and indeed terrifying years.

At the time of its collapse in 1989 the Soviet Union had a population of 285 million, which means that everyone then alive must have been the child, grandchild, or spouse of someone whose life was lost along the way – no one could escape the tragic memories, and then layered upon personal and national tragedy was the collapse of the nation itself.

Having suffered through all these bitter traumas and its fragmentation into sixteen separate nations Russia has refined its uniquely stoic quality that is so unmistakable in its distinctive classical music and haunting literature. Amid the turmoil of its radical contraction and growing disorder, it has embraced a president who is determined to restore its stability, and to restore Russia a position of global prominence and power. Russian President Vladimir Putin has used increasingly aggressive tactics to expand into Georgia and Crimea, and sent his air force to Syria in support of President Assad, and plans who-knows-what-else in the form of disruptions ahead.

Putin enjoys a very high approval rating among Russians, approaching ninety percent,[279] and his story is quite popular in Russia and also in China, where you will see his self-confident face gazing at you from more than a dozen biographies that are on sale in shops, train stations, and airports, and where his aggressive leadership style is widely admired. And while his life story and political philosophy have contributed to book sales in Moscow and Beijing, in most of the rest of the world Russia's military actions have provoked fear, anger, and deep concern.

Thus, the compelling unknown is thus how vigorously Putin will push, and how far Russia can go, in its quest to again be a world power. As Vaclav Smil reminds us, to assume that Russia will collapse is probably unwise.

> Counting Russia out would be historic amnesia. There is nothing new about Russia's leaving the great power game and then reentering it vigorously decades, even generations, later. The country was out of the contest for great power status in 1805 as Napoleon was installing his realtives as rulers of Europe. But less than a decade later, as Czar Alexander I rode on his light-gray thoroughbred horse through defeated Paris, followed by thousands of his Imperial Guard, Bashkirs, Cossack, and Tartar troops, the country was very much an arbiter of a new Europe. Russia was sidelined again in 1905, convulsed by its first bloody revolution, but 15 years later a victorious revolutionary regime regained control over most of the former Czarist territory and inaugurated seven decades of Communist rule. ... Any suggestion of Russia's reemergence as a great power seemed far-fetched in the years immediately following

the demise of the Soviet Union in 1991, but Russia rebounded once again, and by 2005 its economic performance had improved to such an extent that it actually became fashionable to speculate about its renewed superpower status.[280]

Will Russia continue with Putin as its leader, and will Putin continue to create geopolitical disruption through military aggression against his neighbors and others? Or will Russia return to a posture of respect for international norms and cease its aggressive actions?

Part of the answer may lie in its demographics. Following the collapse of the Soviet Union the birth rate that had already been low fell even more, and as a result the Russian nation is in the process of contracting. The mortality rate is high, and average life expectancy is much lower than the West. Geostrategist Peter Zeihan expresses this as "a slow-motion demographic disintegration from within."[281] Zeihan further suggests that within a decade Russia will lack enough young men to sustain its army, and he even wonders if it can survive as one independent nation.

This puts an entirely different perspective on Putin's aggressive tactics, for it suggests that he is acting not due to arrogance or ignorance, but from the fear of Russia's impending decline; it may have been a now-or-never calculation. From the West's perspective, a Russian collapse might be an even worse situation than continuing Russian aggression, as the threat that its stock of nuclear weapons and advanced military technologies will find their way onto the open market has to be a worst-case scenario for NATO and American strategists, and it would also be a great concern to the Chinese.

Most of us know that an angry bear is best avoided, and so if Putin is as aware of the decline of his nation as Zeihan suggests, then certainly the best strategy for West is to wait patiently for the inevitable collapse and avoid confrontation in the mean time. Western economic sanctions may not be entirely persuasive, but they may hasten Russia's decline. Russian aggression would thus carry a self-inflicted economic cost in the form of further economic sanctions that have already hurt a Russian economy that was not particularly strong before the invasion of Crimea, and has become much weaker as a result. And since military power is derived from economic strength, sanctions are indeed a form of warfare without fielding the army.

Six Revolutions in Russia

Technology

Russia technologists are among the most skilled in the world, and because of its declining economy you can hire a highly educated Russian Ph.D. at bargain rates to work on your software and hardware project remotely. As with other nations that are experiencing severe population declines, Russia may actually benefit from advanced robots that can perform critical tasks in the workforce. Doubtless many of those Ph.D.s are working on their own robotic start-ups right now.

In fact, the emergence of a super-high-tech economy could favor Russia, and provide a pathway to at least a partial rebirth if Russian-designed or made technology can find a foothold in the global market. This could also address the demographic disintegration, for what wonders could an invincible army of robots perform on a battlefield, and who better to produce them than those low-paid Ph.D.s that you could hire, or Putin could too. This may sound too much like a movie based on a Marvel comic to be credible, but when you consider that the US military has invested billions in robotics then perhaps it's not so far-fetched.

In fact, President Obama recently joked that he had people working on building an Iron Man suit, only to find out subsequently that there really was a project like that under way.[282]

Russia and the US will not be the only nations striving for a robotic breakthroughs, as Japan, Korea, Israel, and China are all making massive investments, and it's more than likely that some of their efforts will result in exceptional capabilities. Remember that when Apple Computer was just a bunch of hippies in California competing against the Goliath IBM, how many people expected that thirty years later it would be the single most valuable corporation in the world? Technology is like that ...

Climate

Climate change in the form of global warming could actually benefit

Russia in many different ways. Vast expanses of Siberian steppe could become habitable and much more productive, the Russian navy will certainly benefit from less ice and better access to its northern ports, and the opening of the Arctic to further exploration and development will provide additional resource-based wealth. St. Petersburg, however, Russia's cultural capital and a city built on dozens islands, may suffer the opposite fate as the oceans rise.

Energy

Russia's economy is highly dependent upon its oil exports, and the recent decline in oil prices has hit the Russian economy and the Russia people quite hard. If the global fossil fuel industry were to collapse this would put major stress on the Russian government and could significantly accelerate the pace of its decline.

Urbanization

With its population already in steep decline, urbanization is not a key driver of Russia's economy. In fact, a shrinking population serves to reduce overall demand for real estate, and over time this will lead to a reduction in prices, a decline in overall asset values, and thus further contraction of the Russian economy as assets evaporate.

Culture Change

Putin currently enjoys a very high approval rating among his citizens, which suggests that many Russians remain quite nostalgic about their glory days as a world power. Whether they continue to feel that way as the Russian economy continues to deteriorate is an open question, and whether they will be willing to live with rampant corruption and a crony-capitalist group of super-rich elites surrounding Putin is another.

Counter-Revolution

Russia has been through so many tumultuous changes during the last century that it is impossible to say what is the revolution and what is the counter-revolution; they are thus just further changes, some simple and others potentially convulsive.

There are fervent Putin supports in Russia, and his very high approval rating suggests that many Russians remain pleased with his efforts to restore their glory and they don't mind his authoritarian approach to doing so.   Others, however, are openly committed to openness and democracy. For the moment, however, this is not a good time to in the opposition, as the number of them jailed or disappeared seems to grow continually.

The Prospects for Russia

As a nation already in the midst of a downward spiral, but one that retains and is willing to apply massive military power, Russia remains both an enigma and a great concern to the rest of the world. No one wants to fight with the wounded and cornered bear.

But if the country's aggressive military actions continue or increase they would inevitably provoke a regional crisis that could well balloon into a global one.   More broadly, vigorous nationalism combined with an aggressive posture, advanced weaponry, and the willingness to use it makes for a potently destructive combination.

There are other global points of conflict where some or all of these elements are present, including China's relationship with Taiwan, and the broader dispute with its neighbors in the South China Sea.   The relationship between North Korea and all its neighbors, including South Korea, Japan, China, and the US remains in a constantly high state of tension that could, at any time, escalate from a cold war to a hot one. And of course violence is a daily event across the Middle East; in Syria alone six major military forces and countless less formidable ones are engaged in daily combat, and the nation has been destroyed.

In Russia we observe the collision of history, geography, nationalism, and military might, but perhaps most decisive for Russia's future will be the impact of its demographics. As the nation's population implodes, the structure of its relationships with all of its neighbors inevitably must change.

The European Union

The EU is by far the largest experiment ever attempted in collective governance, based on the ambition to align a group of independent nations around a single currency and set of social policies while sustaining their unique and sovereign national identities. This process began in 1952 when, "France and Germany, the two countries whose rivalry had been at the heart of every European war for three centuries, began the process of transcending European history by merging key elements of their remaining economic power."[283]

As a political and economic union it has grown to 28 nations, which gives it roughly equivalent economic power to China and the US. Consequently, as one of three major world powers it's also a military power, and although it is among the most powerful it may also be the most reticent. Centuries of warfare have left its citizens and leaders wary of military force, and as its shared values have evolved with the development of the generally leftist, social-democratic approach to government, the willingness to engage in military adventurism is gone.

Consequently, the rise of ISIS and the spread of terrorist violence throughout Europe presents what may nearly be an existentialist challenge to which the EU and NATO are obliged to respond militarily. However, as it is clear that ISIS' strategy is explicitly based on exporting violence in order to entice a Western counterattack, the EU and NATO are accommodating their adversary when they do so. The West, and perhaps the entire world, has never experienced a form of warfare based on the intent of an entire religious movement to martyr itself in order to attract still more adherents. In addition, of course, there is the massive social and economic impact of the millions of migrants who are clamoring to get away from ISIS and live in relative peace and freedom.

The EU also faces internally-generated existential challenges, including the defective nature of the economic union as well as its own demographics. Hence, the question naturally arises as to whether the EU will continue to unify and blossom into a position of still greater social and economic strength, and thus greater military strength as well, or will internal dissents and discord fracture the Union and send the 28 nations drifting off in different directions?

Nothing even remotely like the EU has ever been attempted, and consequently the effort requires an expensive and time consuming process of ongoing internal diplomacy, and also an ongoing creative effort to forge policies that accommodate the needs of relatively weak and poor nations like Greece and Romania along with quite potent world powers Germany and France. In addition to their own national legislatures, each EU nation also funds its EU legislators and their not-so-frugal living costs in Brussels, at the seat of the EU Parliament, as well as a great many redundant EU ministries and bureaucracies. It's an expensive experiment.

If it does succeed the EU certainly becomes a compelling model for unified communities of nations on other continents, but its success is by no means assured. Like many other parts of the world, the EU faces a radically destabilizing demographics challenge that has the potential to undermine its position in the world and to disrupt its economic engine. This is, of course, due a large and rapidly expanding population of retirees and senior citizens, whose pensions and health care needs will consume ever greater portions of the continent's resources.

For example, in addition to Russia, which we discussed just above, nearly all the Eastern European nations are in the process of de-populating. Nearly all of them have very low birth rates, considerably below replacement level, while they also lose significant numbers of citizens due to emigration. Many of them, also like Russia, suffer from high mortality rates due to tobacco and alcoholism, and also apparently due to high rates of mental illness and depression.

Most of Europe also suffers from unsustainable high unemployment, as much as 20 percent in Spain, for example, but like Japan, they have not discovered any way to attain full employment despite years of experiments with a wide range of economic policy home remedies, none of which have worked. Since young people are disproportionately un- and underemployed, this inevitably leads to extreme alienation and social unrest, creating a ripe region from which ISIS has been quite successful in recruiting fighters.

Throughout Europe there is, therefore, an ongoing competition via social media, which as we saw in Chapter 6, is basically a social media arms race between Western versions of civilization and ISIS-inspired apocalyptic visions. Nevertheless, settling anywhere in Europe remains a very attractive improvement for millions who are desperate to escape the violence and climate catastrophes of the Middle East and Northern Africa. This has created a refugee immigrant crisis of epic and indeed continental proportions; there are now more refugees seeking homes in Europe than at any time since the end of World War II seven decades ago, and there are millions more who would like to follow. As continuing violence and chronically unsettled conditions across the Middle East combined with the worsening affects of climate change mean that the number seeking a safe haven will only increase, what will they find when they arrive? A welcome sign and a cup of tea, or razor wire and an armed guard?

There is already a large and occasionally violent anti-immigrant undercurrent, which also promises to only worsen as the unending stream of hopeful immigrants imposes its burdens ever more severely on the finances and the lifestyles of Europe's towns and cities. Migrants have already been made scapegoats for crimes that they did not commit in Germany, and this will only become more frequent.

There are already large groups of immigrants who have not succeeded in finding employment, and where resentment at second class status has ballooned. Riots in Paris suburbs in recent years have shown just how angry many immigrant youth have become which presents, of course, still more opportunities for ISIS recruiters, and more propaganda to support its contention that the West is fundamentally anti-Arab.

The economic prospects for Europe also remain unsettled. Sustaining the viability of the Euro as a common currency is an ongoing balancing act with many competing demands.

The creation of the EU has generated the need for an entirely new terminology to explain its existence, beginning with the name of its Euro currency. More recently, the terms "Brexit" and "Grexit" refer to the potential for Great Britain (Brexit) or Greece (Grexit) to leave the Union and return to their former status as independent sovereign nations. In the case of Great Britain, this would be to evade some of the pressure of large numbers of migrants, and to sustain more of its political independence; in the case of Greece this would be to done evade the financial reforms that the EU finance ministers are insisting that Greece impose upon itself to bring its national revenues and debts into better alignment. In the case of Greece, the demographic inversion has already stuck quite hard, and a very large pool of retirees is insisting on receiving retirement and health care benefits that the government cannot fund.

Six Revolutions in the EU

The EU is so vast and so diverse that assessing the specific impacts of the six revolutions throughout the Union is at least a bit presumptuous. Still …

Technology

The EU a collection of highly advanced nations which means that the technological revolution will largely be made in Europe as it will also have massive impact throughout the Continent. Some nations and regions are investing and educating aggressively to take advantage of new capabilities and new markets and they may well benefit from the new digital world; others will invest more slowly and lag behind. But technology adoption will generally be high, and technology concepts and products will thrive there.

Climate Change

While a few regions may find life is improved for the better due to climate change, most of the EU will see severe displacements. Greece alone is forecast to suffer an impact of a trillion dollars, as well as the damage or complete destruction of many historically significant and touristically significant ancient monuments.[284] The low-lying cities will have to undergo massive investments to keep back the seas, and while the Dutch are already experts at this and will therefore benefit by exporting their knowledge, cities including Venice, London, Naples, Marseilles,

Istanbul and hundreds of others will incur massive costs and may even find that huge populations have to be relocated.

Further, to the extent that the flood of refugees from the south and southeast are being driven from their own homes due to climate change, this also impacts Europe directly. The refugee crisis will present a very severe test to the strength of the Union as well as to its values.

Energy

Europe is leading the world in converting to non-fossil energy systems. It will largely benefit by exporting its expertise. It also has a strong incentive to switch away from fossil sources, as one of its main suppliers of oil and gas is none other than Russia, which is at the moment not such a reliable trading partner. Further Russian aggression westward from Moscow will compel the EU to cut off Russian energy purchases entirely, and it knows well that the sooner it reduce demand the less traumatic that action would be.

Urbanization

As a fully urbanized continent already increasing urbanization is not a major factor in Europe, except that its cities are its primary tourist attractions which therefore account for billions in revenues. According to the research firm Euromonitor, Paris received 15 million foreign visitors in 2014, and together Spain, France, Italy, Germany, and Great Britain combine to earn $250 billion in tourism revenues.[285] However, it will inevitably arise that one way to deal with massive numbers of migrants is to develop new urban settings, not as ethnic enclaves, but as economic and educational opportunity zones. Sooner or later someone will try this, and if it successful then it will not only lead to a lot of imitation, but it may also provide a model for when the time arises that coastal cities will have to be abandoned and new ones built to replace them. Europe, as a center of advanced expertise in design, engineering, and construction, will be in well-positioned to become the leader in what may become an entire industry of urbanization.

Culture Change

Europe is at the forefront of cultural evolution as it is suffused and surrounded by forces and pressures that are creating extreme stress, and these are precisely the conditions in which cultures evolve. Europe's young, middle aged, and old are all engaged in the complex dialog about the future of their own nations, their common currency, and their shared destiny, and in these discussions we hear every possible view and opinion represented, and thus it's quite impossible to predict, and indeed not productive to try to predict, how it will all unfold. But as the topics, problems, and solutions that emerge in Europe will be highly influential as the rest of the world struggles to deal with the challenges of increasing complexity and accelerating change, the world will be paying attention.

Counter-Revolution

By the accident of its geographical location and due to the attractiveness of its accumulated wealth and its civic institutions, Europe is in the very top of the list of desirable destinations for refugees, which also puts it by default in the center of counter-revolutionary pressures. Not only will it have to deal with millions of people knocking on its doors, it will also have to deal with ISIS and al Qaeda-sponsored and inspired terror. And arising from these external pressures will also arise internal pressures from Europe's own far right to seal the borders, expel the refugees, and close the mosques. Counter-revolutionary pressures will always be there.

The EU Prospects

Two nearly opposite outcomes from this massive social and governance experiment both remain quite plausible. The optimist sees that the EU could sustain its cohesive identity and effectively provide leadership and governance for all its constituent nations, promoting economic growth, social development, and peace throughout Europe. As I mentioned above, doing so would then provide a model for other regions, and indeed for the world as a whole, of collective problem solving and shared destiny.

Alternatively, it's also highly plausible that the EU might well collapse under the strains of differing national systems, cultures, capabilities, and needs, and if it were to collapse the consequences would be significant and most likely rich with difficulty. Fragmentation, dissent, bickering, and economic decline would be the immediate results, and the longer term prospects would not be much more attractive.

The United States

While the USA remains the world's economic and military superpower, the ascent of China has led many observers to predict America's immanent demotion to second place. That may come to pass, but for the moment its clear that America is still the dominant power. For example, although there have been cuts to its military budget during the last decade America still spends more on its army, navy, air force, and cyber commands than the next 13 biggest spenders combined, which is perhaps the accurate expression of its current economic power and its geopolitical dominance.

Superpower Geopolitics

It's a significant fact of world geography that America occupies a unique position that is the envy of all superpower and would-be superpower nations. It is well protected on its east and west sides by the massive Atlantic and Pacific oceans, and it has generally agreeable neighbors to its north and south that do not pose a military threat, but to the contrary are significant economic partners. In contrast, the nations of Europe have experienced centuries of cross-border aggression, with armies march to and fro at will during more wars than anyone can remember. As the cities and towns of Germany were flattened by successive armies marching through during the 30 Years War, the pattern continued into the 20th century.

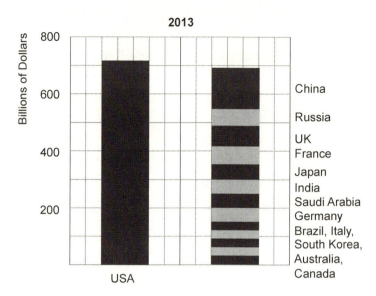

Figure 94
Military Spending by the Biggest-Spending 14 Nations, 2013[286]

Superpower Geopolitics

It's a significant fact of world geography that America occupies a unique position that is the envy of all superpower and would-be superpower nations. It is well protected on its east and west sides by the massive Atlantic and Pacific oceans, and it has generally agreeable neighbors to its north and south that do not pose a military threat, but to the contrary are significant economic partners. In contrast, the nations of Europe have experienced centuries of cross-border aggression, with armies march to and fro at will during more wars than anyone can remember. As the cities and towns of Germany were flattened by successive armies marching through during the 30 Years War, the pattern continued into the 20th century.

For example, my mother's parents grew up in a small border city in Eastern Europe that was, during the course of only a few decades, territory controlled by the Austrian Empire, then the Polish, then the Russian, then the German, and then the Russians again. The armies came marching through from the west and then from the east, and then from the west again, and finally from the east, along the flat plains that presented no natural barriers and were therefore quite accommodating to the competing imperialists.

Today their little hometown of Tarnopol is in the western part of Ukraine, while far to its east the ongoing dispute with Russia continues to provoke anxiety and result in deaths.   Indeed, Russia entirely lacks geographic protection on its very vulnerable western border and would very much prefer for Ukraine to be that buffer, for which it served well during the Cold War. Those who remember high school history know two massive armies marched across those indefensible plains to Moscow, and that only through massive self-sacrifices and the bitter Russian winter were Napoleon and Hitler repelled. The French army lost nearly 500,000 men in western Russia, the Germans ten times that number, a staggering 5 million. The Russians, though, lost even more, 10 million soldiers and about 15 million civilians during World War II.

And while Russia's potential adversaries are principally on its western and southern borders, China is surrounded by adversaries, potential adversaries, and uneasy neighbors. Russia on its north is a sometime rival, sometime partner; India to the south is the same; and to its east lie Japan, Korea, Taiwan, and the Philippines, all closely allied with the US, whose massive Seventh Fleet is usually sailing somewhere nearby, a constant reminder that the world's superpower is always watching.

Hence, while America's superpower rivals must be constantly vigilant on their own borders, it's quite possible that the major challenges that America confronts aren't outside, but within. In particular, because the American population is almost evenly divided between the political left and the right and since both sides are becoming even more ideologically estranged from one another and more deeply entrenched in their opposing views, the likelihood that the governance process in Washington will improve is quite low. Yet despite the near paralysis of its politics the country's economy continues to progress at an impressive rate. America's forces of creativity and innovation continue to drive the global economy and every nation wants to emulate the great forges of innovation and growth that include New York, Boston, Chicago, Los Angeles and Silicon Valley. The Digital Revolution is global, but the core technologies and business models are mostly American, and American soft power is a compelling force derived from the combination of brute technological prowess, its leadership of global entertainment industry, unlimited capital, and now persuasive social media.   So while America may or may not dominate the emerging mega-industries for robotics, genetic engineering, and alternative energies, it will certainly be a major and effective competitor.

Fast or Slow?

This raises an interesting point with quite broad significance.   In essence, what we see that capitalism is a social and economic process that literally creates change through the dynamics of marketplace competition, but the structure and processes of democracy, at least as it is practiced in the US, are designed to resist change.   In other words, capitalism is designed to change fast, but democracy is designed to change slowly; the mismatch leads to problems.   In our era of accelerating change, of course, the difficulties presented by the problems we face will increase as the ability to act or proact on them decreases.

In Part 1 I discussed many of the ways in which change is accelerating and there's no need to repeat that here, but let me focus for a moment on how American democracy resists change, which it does in many ways both overt and quite subtle.   One of the principal tools is built into the design of the American federal government structure itself, which is based on the principle of "checks and balances" that is specifically designed to assure that none of the three branches of government, the president, the Congress, and the Supreme Court, can go too far, too fast, nor accumulate too much power to themselves.   Progress on any issue that is even remotely controversial can therefore stall out entirely in the give and take process, and most substantive changes in policy often require exhaustive negotiation that can take decades.

Self-defeating, immoral, and illogical policies and practices can endure, such as slavery, which continued for ninety years following the Declaration of Independence and eighty years following adoption of the US Constitution despite the fact that its practice obviously contradicts the principles stated in both documents. A full century after the Civil War ended it still required a major effort to assure civil rights for all races, and still today the vestiges remain. Voting rights for women took 135 years to be enacted, finally, in 1920; in contemporary society, the dispute over LGBT rights has been at issue for more than five decades, and still today there remain places where LGBT citizens have been denied their rights. Whether or not the American government should assure health care for all citizens was hotly debated for more than fifty years, and that legislation that finally enacted a limited health care program was passed only by the narrowest of margins; Senator Ted Kennedy had to leave his hospital bed to cast the deciding vote, or the legislation would have failed.

Essentially all of the key topics discussed in Chapters 1 – 6 involve important issues that have already arrived or will do so soon, and about which there is certain to be a very divergent range of deeply-held opinions. This suggests that America may be trapped in indecision for far too long, and that many important issues including robotics, genetic engineering, climate change, fossil fuels, and alternative energy policies will be the lingering topics of circular debates that may delay or prevent useful, appropriate or necessary actions and proactions from being taken.

Jurgen Randers makes precisely this point: "The main challenge in our global future is not to solve the problems we are facing, but to reach agreement to do so."[287]

Incumbent officeholders at all levels, from local town councils all the way to the US president, generally have a stake in the status quo, and thus for them change is also seen as a threat. They also have an inherent advantage over challengers due to the power that they control in their positions as elected officials, using which they regularly enact projects of dubious value known as "pork," (i.e., fat) to gain public appreciation. Unneeded roads, bridges, schools, and even military bases are built and preserved for the purpose only of spending some money locally and making the local elected officials more popular as a result.

Another structural impediment to change is the fact that government projects and programs that have been funded in the past are much more likely to continue to receive funding than new and different approaches.

Of course there is also side to this picture that can be beneficial, which reflects its intent – it is quite difficult for any individual or any branch of the government to seize unilateral power. Having lived through an era during the eighteenth century which monarchs exercised nearly unlimited powers over defenseless citizens, they designed the American government to prevent that from occurring.

However, when the apparent will of the people and that of its leaders are aligned, when there is broad consensus of perception and intent, the US government can make and enact major decisions quite quickly. For example, when the US has been attacked it has declared war almost immediately thereafter, as occurred after the sinking of the USS Maine in Cuba in 1898, the sinking of the Lusitania in 1915, the attack on Pearl Harbor in 1941, and the attacks of September 11, 2001. It then brings its massive economic power to bear extraordinarily fast: "In 1939 the American navy had 178 surface combat ships and 58 submarines. On the war's final day six years later it had a navy of 6,800 vessels, with more than 1,000 combat ships and submarines."[288] The nation built, that is, an average of 3 vessels per day over a span of more than 2000 days.

Science and Anti-Science

While America will always have rivals and adversaries, the most significant challenges of the coming era will probably not be military. Instead, the threat presented by climate change, and robots, and economics. These are fields that are being studied by and shared by science, but America has conflicted relationship with science. Government leaders and the public are perfectly happy to benefit from science in the form of technology and health care, but there remains broad skepticism about the validity of scientific findings in fields such as evolution and climate science. As we saw in Chapter 9, we cling often to our ideologies despite any and all evidence to the contrary.

Consequently, it could well be that the gridlocked political situation in Washington will constitute America's greatest challenge, as the emerging issues that will have to be dealt with are highly controversial and highly technical. If that is true, then the great question that looms ahead is whether America can find sufficient political cohesion to enable it to respond to the changing world and sustain or even enhance its global leadership, or whether the gridlocked partisan bickering between left and right will make it too slow to adapt, and it will find itself second to China, or even third behind China and the EU. Is it an exaggeration to call political gridlock and ideological conflict "a war for America"? [289]

Angry America

The bloody battles of the American Civil War 150 years ago claimed more than 600,000 lives over four years, and while the guns are mostly silent the lingering culture echoes can still be heard in ongoing cultural disputes over racism, police brutality, civil rights, voting rights, the Confederate Battle Flag, and in the Black Lives Matter protests that continue in many states, mostly those in the South.

But the disagreement is broader than a dispute over race. The specific issues that divide the two sides have changed throughout American history, but the persistence of two contrasting viewpoints embodied in the two major political parties has been surprisingly consistent since the founding of the country. Two contrasting ideologies have struggled throughout America's history to exert dominance over the course of public affairs, and while the names of the parties and their leaders have changed over the decades, the persistence of leftist progressives versus rightist conservatives has persevered. There is plenty of evidence to suggest that this divide could continue for many decades even as the specific issues in dispute slowly evolve.

In the 1950s historian Richard Hofstadter published a book entitled *The Paranoid Style in American Politics* [290] in which he outlined the gradual shift of the Republican party toward a more extreme form of anger, which he identified as a manifestation of the loss of its power during the twenty years from 1932 to 1952 during which Franklin Roosevelt had transformed American society through the New Deal reforms, and also as a result of World War II. Hofstadter probably realized that the party would become even more extreme as time passed, and he would probably not be surprised by the current situation.

Entering the presidential election cycle of 2016 it seemed that anger was the driving force for both major parties. The increasing intensity from both sides reflects deep concerns that have been with them now for decades. These are long-standing anxieties that both liberals and conservatives feel about the country,

> ... anxieties that have only grown sharper as time as passed. For liberals, the chief concern for thirty-five years now has been about the unfairness of the economy – virtual wage stagnation for most workers, huge gains for the top 1 percent, and the lax regulatory and enforcement regimes that have permitted those outcomes, along with slow recovery from the most recent recession. For conservatives, for about the same period of time, the main worry has been what is broadly called "culture," by which we really mean the anger and resentment felt by older, white Americans about the fact that the country is no longer "theirs" and that their former status and authority no longer seem what they once were. This rubric takes in a number of issues – immigration, especially illegal immigration; same-sex marriage; a black president in the White House.[291]

Compounding the dispute, the two sides also hold significantly different views about the role of government itself. This is in fact the fundamental argument, as many on the left view government as a force for positive change and look to it to proactively address future challenges while balancing historical wrongs and promoting greater equality, while many on the right believe that the government is best that does least, and should leave most decisions to the states or even better, to the capitalist marketplace.

The two sides also hold opposing views on a very wide range of social issues, including immigration, birth control, abortion, health care, taxation, land use, environmental care, regulation of business, and regulation of guns. (About 33,000 Americans die each year in shootings, about one-third by homicide and two-thirds by suicide, by far the highest number and percentage among the developed nations.[292] Frighteningly, mass shootings are now so common in the US that there is now dedicated web site on which to track them: http://www.shootingtracker.com/Main_Page.)

During those few recent periods when one of the two parties controlled both the Congress and the Presidency it has been able to bring about major changes relatively quickly. But particularly during the last fifty years, American voters have tended to elect one party to the presidency and the opposing party to control of the Congress, which has only exacerbated the ideological divide. There's often a lot of shouting and posturing, but not so much actual productive dialog or work. For example, during a span of three years from 2012 to 2014 the Republican-dominated Congress voted symbolically more than 60 times to abolish the nation's health care law, each vote undertaken not as a legislative matter, but as an expression of protest and propaganda designed to appeal to its core group of supporters.

In today's America the core groups of the voting population are split nearly evenly between the two parties, with roughly 40 – 45 percent of voters on each side of the left-right divide, and the remaining 10 – 20 percent constituting swing voters who decide most elections.

Fifty years ago the divisive issues that shaped elections were Civil Rights and the Vietnam War; thirty years ago they were taxation and the Cold War; ten years ago they were Iraq War, government surveillance, and LGBT Rights. Today's arguments focus on health care, immigration, and the growing gap between the very wealthy 1 percent and the shrinking and increasingly stressed middle class and poor, the 99 percent, and based on what we learned in Part 1, it seems likely that the great challenges facing Americans in the coming decade will involve technology, robotics and labor laws and rights; climate change and government regulation of CO_2; the global and national energy infrastructure and the shift to non-fossil sources; and terrorism.

While these issues could well dominate the public debate, we must expect that the left and the right will see the options and preferences quite differently, which may well prevent the nation from taking effective action in any of these areas, or on the dozens of other issues and concerns that will inevitably arise.

Hence, the great danger for America and indeed for any democracy is that its process of making hard decisions is slow and tedious, when the opposite, fast and effective, would serve America and the world much better.

In addition, along the way America will also be dealing with a rapidly increasing amount of personal and family debt, sometimes referred to as the "debt bomb." If it explodes then there will certainly be a calamity among the lenders and thus among the banks, which already overstressed, may become fatally weakened.

Six Revolutions in the USA

Technology

The structure of America's economy and its society could hardly be more ideal for the development of technology, and thus its great universities and its technology centers in Silicon Valley, Boston, Seattle, Austin and elsewhere are nearly unstoppable creative forces of technological change. With abundant government funding, primarily from its massive military budget, America will most likely sustain its technological preeminence even as competitors worldwide strive to imitate, partner with, and surpass American prowess. Hence, the more-or-less constant technological changes that America and the world will be required to adapt to will be largely home grown.

Climate Change

America's CO_2 emissions are among the world's highest, but as its political polarity has led to acute indecisiveness, the necessary actions and remedies made to slow in coming, which will only worsen the damage to which America and the rest of the world must adapt.

Energy

The fossil fuel industrialist is an American legend known as a wildcatter, and independent oil producer who creates great wealth against all odds with grits, guts, and perseverance, spurred on more recently by the call to "drill, baby, drill!" That mythology will give way to a different form of energy entrepreneur as fossil fuels are phased out and sustainable sources capture more of the market. How fast that occurs is the critical and as yet unanswerable question. The emergence of the new model entrepreneur will bring with it a different set of skills, for the new forms of energy capture are based on technology, and thus the technology revolution enables the energy revolution. The faster the new solar and wind generators and the batteries and distribution infrastructure they require is invented and installed, the faster than transition will occur.

Urbanization

America is already about as urbanized as it's going to get, and its rate of population growth is approaching stabilization. But many of its urban infrastructures are old and in need of maintenance and replacement, and the sprawling, lifeless suburbs are experiencing a well-deserved identity crisis as people reconnect with central cities and rediscover the benefits of urban living. American cities will continue to evolve and improve through the century.

Culture

All of the factors driving change are impacting on American culture, and as the economy continues to change and to bring with it new structural demands the forces of disruption will continue to be divisive. Technology, the climate, and the energy foundations of society are all entering periods of transition that will inevitably create social and economic disruption, and thus the echoes will reverberate throughout the culture.

Counter Revolution

The many forces of change catalyze many countering forces of anti-change, and thus the polarity that cuts through American society is fully evident in a divided political landscape that is becoming more abrasive and ostentatious. It's not so easy to see how these forces will reconcile, and as this tension has existed since before the founding of the US more than 250 years ago it's easy to see it continuing indefinitely.

Prospects for the US

As its internal dynamics seems to be the decisive factor shaping America's future, its prospects likely turn on the character of the internal debate. Should America descent further into internal paralysis and become fully incapable of governing itself then the fractured nation could, in the extreme, follow the USSR's model and literally break into pieces. California and Texas often behave like independent nations already, and as it is both conduct their own foreign policies in fact if not in name.

Conversely, Americans could also recognize that their uniquely-protected nation would lose its favored position as the world's superpower if it remains unable to address the fundamental challenges of its future, and could align around a sufficiently shared vision of the future, and while it might not address every element of each faction's ideological layer cake, it still represents the country's vision much better than a fragmented set of regional alliances and rivals.

The Middle East

For the first time in human history the adherents of a violent religious movement have become nearly as powerful as a nation, and their commitment to fundamentalism and brutality threatens to destabilize not only the nations where they strike, but the entire region. As we discussed earlier, ISIS is an apocalyptic sect that expects the ultimate doomsday battle to arrive and seeks to entice the West into conflict to provoke the final days.

Hence, its brutality takes the form of both intimidation and of provocation, and creates a Catch-22 situation: acts of terror are intended to create fear but also to provoke a militaristic response, but by responding in this way the West also provides further credibility to the apocalyptic message and narrative. ISIS can say, "The West is evil and wishes to destroy us," and then attack. When the West attacks back, they say, "Just as we said, they wish to destroy us."

Terrorism is a form of warfare that is opportunistic and difficult to root out, while in addition suicide terrorism is a form that is tremendously difficult to defend against, as the successful attacks around the world have shown.   For all of these reasons ISIS constitutes a challenging opponent that we take years to overcome.

And yet it's also ironic that these radical terrorists have become so adept at using the western technologies of the internet to manage a global empire of activists and terrorists, and to recruit and train warriors and suicide martyrs.   And while only a tiny proportion of the region's population are violent radicals, their impact both throughout the region and globally is inescapable.

The five revolutions are nearly irrelevant to ISIS and all apocalyptic terrorists because the issue of ideology is the central and indeed the obsessive concern, and thus the counter-revolution is at the core of the dilemma that the world faces, and it's not difficult to foresee a struggle lasting decades, which takes place across the region itself as well as in whatever areas are targeted for terrorism. The question that remains unanswered is the extent to which non-military or non-security interventions may become successful.

Prospects for the Middle East

Consequently, it's not difficult to visualize two extremely different possibilities for the future of the Middle East and the its neighbors stretching east and west from Pakistan to Morocco.   One possibility is complete collapse into a regional conflagration, with all parties engaged in multi-dimensional violent conflict on a scale much larger even than what we observe today.   In this scenario, all factions would be drawn into the violence, the scale of the conflict would escalate out of control, and the governments of the region would be unable to sustain themselves in the growing chaos, degenerating into even less stability than today, and even more suffering.   The violence would inevitably be exported much more widely and consistently than we see now, and the implied or explicit threat of terrorism, both nuclear and non-nuclear, would inevitably draw more and more nations into the conflict, if only out of the need to protect themselves. In the worst case, the nationalistic wars would expand into a regional war, would then become much more than that.

The alternative scenario is steady progress toward the alignment of mutual interests and the emergence of peace, led perhaps by the vast majority of the population who are not so concerned about anyone else's sect or ideology, but who wish simply to live in peace and to raise their children in peace.

Geopolitics and the Non-State Actors

The story of the industrial age describes the steady expansion of the world's capacity to transform raw materials into manufactured goods of increasing complexity and sophistication, which leads in turn to the search for new markets into which to sell those products, which then results in progressive alignment of world's nations around a single political-economic system of trade. As this happened the colonial empires were created, and then following World War II the colonial system collapsed and new nations on all continents were born.

The United Nations was established to reflect the growing importance of global agreements and commitments among nations, and it became one of the most important of the non-state actors, the entities and organizations that have notable impact or influence in geopolitics for a reason other than being a sovereign. Corporations, religions, non-governmental organizations such as the United Nations, and large-scale criminal organizations are among the principle types, and in a world that is becoming ever more complex and ever more technologically enabled, and in which trade continues to expand and to specialize into ever more refined niches and subspecialties, will inevitably foster still more types of organizations that do more and do different things than have ever been done or needed doing, and there will be ever more of them, and for our purposes here the key is that they will become ever more influential.

During the last fifty years as global trade has increased by a factor of fifty, and as tens of millions of people have risen from poverty into middle class, corporations have also risen to new heights of power because they, too, control resources and leverage their capabilities to create value.

At the same time, criminal organizations have become much like corporations, with extensive holdings of assets, sophisticated financial controls, and human resources management policies: this is now known as "narconomics."[293] Tom Wainwright's incisive book examines how drug cartels manage complex supply chains, deal with strategic issues of mergers and acquisitions, conduct research and development, and manage customer relations, which are of course all the things that multinational corporations do also.

The ever more complex, multifaceted legal and illegal business world has created thousands of millionaires and hundreds of billionaires, little of which would have occurred without a steady expansion of free trade, a standardized global system of currency exchange, global standards for financial accounting, and a massive global transportation infrastructure utilizing massive ocean cargo ships and air freight.

The result has come to be called "globalization," the gradual unification of the entire world's national economies into one system of production and trade. Today the products we buy and the food we consume regularly comes from dozens of nations that have specialized in producing products that can succeed in international commerce across the entire range of the consumer and industrial economy.

Sustaining globalization and its progress requires an ongoing commitment to fairness, openness, and the steady elimination of barriers to trade, but in a world that is under severe stress due to accelerating change it is by no means guaranteed that the benefits of globalized trade will be sufficient to sustain it. While thriving global trade is certainly a possibility, it may also happen that a nation will withdraw from the global system to protect their domestic markets from global competition or due to ideological and religious motivations.

And in other situations a nation may be excluded because it doesn't adhere to the rules that other nations have agreed to.

We have seen both sides of this story in recent events. Iran was compelled to come to dismantle its nuclear weapons because the global trade embargo against it was tremendously effective in limiting the growth of the its economy, and similarly Western nations have applied economic pressure on Russia through trade and banking restrictions as a result of the invasion of Crimea, and these have put the Russian economy into a recession.   Both examples demonstrate the significance of trade as a mechanism of diplomacy, in one case with success and the other less so.

Prospects

The question that we must consider going forward is if this system of trade agreements is going to be sustained. Or will the increasing stresses and complexities of the six revolutions drive many of the world's nations into more strident nationalism, causing the partial or full collapse of the international structures that we recognize today. This does not necessarily mean that the world would revert into violent warfare on a large scale, but could simply be the abandonment of the institutions and agreements that have only emerged during the post war period.

The inverse question is whether the corporations will seek even greater independence. As they become less and less attached to any one nation-state and more powerful, they may seek greater or even full autonomy. This could be a yet more perfect expression of globalization: "Globalization is proving right Adam Smith's observation that while 'the proprietor of land is necessarily a citizen of a particular country in which his estate lies … the proprietor of stock [i.e., financial assets] is properly a citizen of the world, and is not necessarily attached to any particular country.'"[294]

Other Geopolitical Forces

The six geopolitical forces that we've examined here are certain to be central themes in our shared future, but it's also reasonable to expect that other forces not on this list will also prove to be very influential. Perhaps they, too, should be considered essential.

Should Africa be on this list of driving forces? With a population of 1.1 billion we can be sure that its importance will only increase in the years and decades to come.

What about India, Brazil, or Indonesia, with a combined population of nearly 2 billion and significant regional and global influence and aspirations, each in their own way?

Should the United Nations be considered as a driving force in and of itself? As the world's primary supra-national collective entity the UN wields increasing power, and should they so decide, the world's nations could vest even more power in UN forces and agencies. The nations could also, however, choose to diminish the UN's role, either by proclamation or simply by ignoring the UN's bills due and its authority.

Beyond the specific scope of geopolitics, a global disease epidemic caused by an as yet unknown virus but in magnitude comparable to or greater than the 1918 flu pandemic that killed fifty million would of course be a driving force. We might also consider the scope and quality of education for the young, or the consumer debt bomb in the Western nations, which many believe pose a significant threat to future economic stability and growth.

The challenge of deteriorating mental health is another, as mental illness has become a global epidemic that affects as much as 10 percent of the world's people, and as many as 20 percent of youth. Currently more than 2,000 people commit suicide each day, totaling 800,000 annually, a sad toll that reflects the extreme stress that many are living under, and the lack of care available to them. Future shock/ now shock will likely lead to increasing stress, and thus more self destruction.

Hence, it's entirely reasonable to make the argument that any of these forces will have fundamental influence, perhaps as great as or even greater than the ones I've selected. This raises an important point that underlies this entire discussion, which is that there is no objective reality when we're discussing the future and exploring the possibilities of what may come. There is only evidence and judgments and analyses that *may* prove to be sufficiently complete and therefore useful; or they may prove to be fragmented and faulty.

And thus while it's impossible to consider *everything*, the evidence and arguments contained in the descriptions above and in the chapters that follow will have to speak for themselves. You must form your own opinions about how valid or incomplete these ideas are, and about what may or may not have been omitted or unnecessarily included. And then events will actually unfold and we'll all find out how good our maps, models, and forecasts have been!

Another key element of this discussion to remember is that the shifting terrain of global change and complexification suggests that the underlying themes that have brought unity of purpose and structure to global society, even through a century of open warfare, will be stressed by the coming revolutions. Dr. Kissinger suggests that, "Our age is insistently, at times desperately, in pursuit of a concept of world order. Chaos threatens side by side with unprecedented independence: in the spread of weapons of mass destruction, the disintegration of states, the impact of environmental depredations, the persistence of genocidal practices, and the spread of new technologies threatening to drive conflict beyond human control or comprehension. Will mankind, amidst weapons of mass destruction, networked transparency, and the absence of privacy, propel itself into a world without limits or order, careening through crises without comprehending them?" He summarizes, simply, "The crisis in the concept of world order [is] the ultimate international problem of our day."[295]

It's also worth remembering that the objective of these thought experiments is not to arrive at *the truth*, because in fact there is no such truth when the subject is a highly uncertain future. The objective is, rather, to inform our thinking and enhance our appreciation for complexity, and also to support better analysis and better decision making, and especially to enable us recognize emerging patterns of change early on.

If by thinking this through well we can better understand what's coming then we may be able to shape events according to our values and preferences, but if we are continually surprised by what happens because we never even considered what may be possible, then it is the events that are in control of us, and the world we live in as a result will most likely consist of a massive dose of the undesirable. It is far better the other way.

The six major geopolitical themes that we've explored in this chapter – China, Russia, the EU, the US, the Middle East, and the Non-State Actors, together with the five revolutions plus the counter-revolution that we have examined already constitute the twelve major driving forces of change that are shaping the 21st century. They are, separately and together, the major factors creating both the risks and the opportunities that we face in this fascinating era.

But it's not enough to understand them separately, for we must also gain a deep understanding of how they may interact with one another in combinations, for that is likely to be where and how the more challenging complexities arise. Hence, in the following chapter we'll combine them to build models that explore a wide range of future possibilities. Our goal, however, is not to predict the future, which is probably a fool's errand, but rather to understand what might occur under a variety of different conditions and combinations. It is from such models that we may gain a better appreciation of the ways that, as Jay Forrester well understood, the layering of complex phenomena creates even more complex conditions in which we must make choices and manage toward our desired outcomes.

•••

Chapter 12

The Explorer:

World Models

Today the majority of South Africans, black and white, recognise that apartheid has no future. It has to be ended by our own decisive mass action in order to build peace and security. The mass campaign of defiance and other actions of our organisation and people can only culminate in the establishment of democracy.

I have fought against white domination and I have fought against black domination. I have cherished the ideal of a democratic and free society in which all persons live together in harmony and with equal opportunities.

Nelson Mandela
February 11, 1990
The day he was released from prison

On the February day in 1990 on which Nelson Mandela was finally released after 27 years in prison, what did the future of South Africa look like? In a word, bleak. While Mandela's release was enormously positive and indeed people throughout South Africa rejoiced, there was a fearful undercurrent pervading the nation. Now that he was out of prison, what would Mandela do? And what would his party, the African National Congress do? Would they incite a revolution to seize power from the white-dominated Afrikaner government?

South Africa's 8 million whites had systematically excluded the nation's 29 million blacks from society, subjecting them to constant humiliation and economic repression. White Johannesburg was a lively city of trees and parks and skyscrapers, built on the nation's gold and diamond and agricultural wealth that the whites controlled, while the adjacent black township of Soweto consisted of row upon row of tiny shacks and houses lining miles of unpaved roads. The contrast could not have been more vivid, and to rub it in even further, the government constructed a giant power plant right in the middle of Soweto that dominated the depressing landscape.

From the first days of Apartheit in 1948 and during the following decades and through the 1980s, the white Afrikaner government of South Africa held a firm grip on political, economic, and social power throughout the country. Ongoing civil unrest and protest among the blacks resulted in still more repression, and protesters were met with police force and on occasion marchers were killed. The nation was becoming more polarized, and by the 1980s the voice of global criticism was growing louder and more persistent. Foreign investment into South Africa had mostly stopped, companies were pressured to divest their South African operations, and trade dwindled because the rest of the world refused to support its systematic racism. The nation's economy was weakening, and as we have seen more recently with Russia and Iraq, when a nation is systematically excluded from global commerce it suffers inevitable decline, even to the point of non-sustainability.

Facing increasing economic difficulties, more and more isolated among nations, and seeing rising internal unrest, it had become obvious to nearly everyone that change was immanent, and the fear of civil war was widespread and rising. Under strong international pressure, Nelson

Mandela was released from prison and the opposition political parties were legalized, but still the conflict remained unresolved. With support from around the world the majority black population was becoming more determined that there must be change, and so there was a persistent question as to whether the blacks would rise violently against the minority whites in order to gain a voice in the leadership of their own country, or if there could instead be a peaceful transition.

With Mandela freed and his political party openly developing its constituency and its platforms, a powerful force was rising, but there was at the time not so much hope for peaceful resolution, and broad expectations of violence.   How else would the dominant whites be persuaded to share power?   Certainly they would not surrender it voluntarily. Uncertainty was persistent, and all the problems and anxieties that uncertainty brings were there as well.

Forecasting and Uncertainty

One of the universal side effects of uncertainty is increased stress. Tensions rise because it's quite literally impossible to know what will happen, and when there does not seem to be a positive way forward we worry about how events unfold to threaten our plans and expectations for the future. How, then, shall we look at the future in which change is accelerating and seems to promise a future worse than our present?   Our challenges are uncertainty combined with increasing complexity, and yet we are obliged to come to decisions every day even though the future state of all the critical driving forces is quite unknown. We may have opinions and expectations about what we believe will happen, but if we're honest with ourselves then we have to admit that we cannot know for certain. Given this landscape of uncertainty, which areas should be our action priorities? Concerning which issues should we wait a bit longer to see how things unfold, and where must we take a decision now?   Where should we invest? What should we do, or not do?

Explorers and Exploration

Futurists, visionaries, and planners all deal with uncertainty as a focus of their professions, and this is also what explorers do, for they venture into the unknown precisely because it is the unknown, to find out what is actually there for themselves. Such curiosity is a powerful driver that has taken many forms throughout history, giving motivation to scientists and tinkerers, to sailors and mountain climbers, to astronauts and entrepreneurs. What's out there, or in there, or up there? Can I find it? Can I touch it? Can I understand it?

Exploration is an endless cycle, though, because every answer that the explorers bring back creates still more questions and unknowns, which of course stimulate still further exploration. We, too, are caught in this perpetual cycle, for the explorers of our time are still traversing all those domains, and they're also in the process of finding out with us and for us what an economy can be, what a robot might do, how warm our planet can really get, and what forms are best for cities and cars and moon colonies.

Given the rate of change, though, and our need to adapt to these new worlds, we can just wait for them to return to show us the treasures they have collected. We need, instead, to anticipate their findings. Thus, in Chapter 10 we explored Jørgen Randers' forecast for 2052, which was based on his detailed model of cause and effect relationships between critical global factors that he then analyzed against a large set of data. From this he extrapolated plausible outcomes, while also considering the political process of the last few centuries and projecting it all forward to anticipate the geopolitical dialog we may expect in the coming decades.

Randers built much of his work on the systems dynamics approach that Jay Forrester had pioneered, in which Forrester and a team of analysts identified causal, quantifiable relationships among dozens of important variables and then modeled how these interactions could result in given states of the system.

Futurist John Naisbett's book 1982 *MegaTrends* identified ten broad themes and concepts, and proved to be quite provocative in helping many people to identify topics of importance for society and business.[296]

Reviewing his list of themes 35 years later shows that he was indeed quite prescient, and four of the patterns he described proved to be as important as he expected.

Figure 95

John Naisbett's Megatrends

In hindsight we notice that Naisbett was a bit overoptimistic. The first three megatrends were quite correctly identified along with the shift from hierarchies to networks, but the remaining six have not, for the most part, been realized. We're still short term oriented for the most part, highly centralized in our decision making, dependent on institutions, representative, north-dominated, and either/or thinkers.

Former US Vice President Al Gore approached the problem of forecasting and uncertainty in his book simply entitled *The Future* by inventorying a vast collection of concepts, organizing them into a huge mind map, and then exploring them one by one.[297]

Consultant George Friedman took a more prosaic approach by identifying key themes that he anticipated will be important throughout the 21st century, while his colleague Peter Zeihan, whom we met in the previous chapter, focused on the field of geopolitics using geography and demographics to craft his forecasts. Zeihan provided a detailed and persuasive analysis of each of the world's regions and major nations, and came to the conclusion that every nation will, in the near or medium distant future, be facing significant demographic and cultural challenges, which leaves him almost by default predicting the continued dominance of the US as many of its rivals and potential rivals face their own mounting problems.

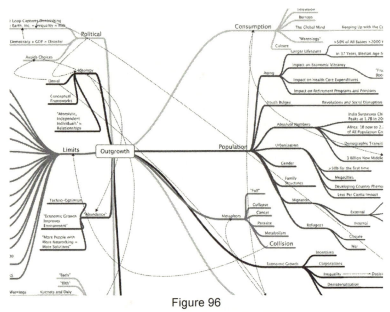

Figure 96
A Portion of Al Gore's Mind Map
This is also his table of contents.

Pollster and statistician Nate Silver explains why the conjunction of data and trend analysis with careful construction of the analytical method is essential.   He recognized, for example, that there are three different types of uncertainty between which we must distinguish if we're to do a credible job of assessing change and anticipating what's to come.   With respect to climate change, for example, he noted that there is uncertainty about initial conditions, in that both the current data and our understanding of them are incomplete, that there is scenario uncertainty in that the climate is shaped by a great many factors about which there is considerable variability, including activities on the sun, the El Nino weather pattern, and volcanoes, all of which have impacts that may dampen or amplify the impact of increasing CO2.   And the third type of uncertainty relates to our incomplete understanding of the climate, and thus potential weaknesses in the mathematical models that are used to project what may happen.[298]

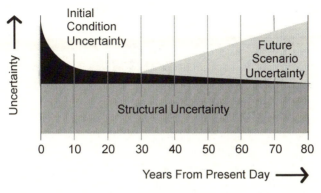

Figure 97
Three Types of Uncertainty

Each of these forecasters had to account for uncertainty in anticipating what is coming, and theirs are just a few among many potentially helpful views in which we find an intriguing mix of qualitative and thematic approaches along with quantitative and data-driven ones. In addition, I've already mentioned a wide range of thinkers, futurists, and visionaries including Buckminster Fuller, Jay Forrester, Donella Meadows, Stafford Beer, Paolo Soleri, Ray Kurzweil, Jorgen Randers, Hans Moravec, Nassim Taleb, Peter Hall, and Henry Kissinger, all of whom have given us valuable and compelling views of what may be coming, the uncertainties that carry with them, and also of the opportunities and risks we face.

What they all want to understand, and we as well, is what will emerge in the future. We want less uncertainty, and we want to know what events and trends and patterns will result from the rich interaction of cultural, technological and geopolitical factors and forces shaping our worlds of today and tomorrow.

Pathways to the Future

In the South African climate of increasing uncertainty and fear a small group of leaders representing a wide variety of political and social groups from across the nation, from all races, political parties, and ideologies, gathered at the rural retreat center called Mt. Fleur to explore the various possible futures that might come about, and see if there was a pathway to a peaceful transition. What would have to happen, and not happen, for South Africa to transform itself into a peaceful and democratic nation from a racist and divided one?

In a series of weekend retreats during the autumn of 1991 the group engaged in a structured process of inquiry through which they came to realize that there was but a single narrow social and political pathway that might achieve a peaceful resolution of the conflict. They identified specific steps that might enable that peaceful process to go forward, but even they were skeptical that it could be achieved. There were many obstacles to be addressed, and a very complex social and political landscape that they had to traverse.

Their work came to be known as the Mr. Fleur Scenarios. Remarkably, they and many others were indeed able to steer actual events to closely match the steps that they had envisioned, and as a result Nelson Mandela was released elected president as the last apartheid president F.W. De Klerk stepped aside. The inquiry process those leaders engaged in is sometimes called "scenario planning," and the story of their work is described in a fine book by the facilitator of the workshops, Adam Kahane. It's called, aptly, *Solving Tough Problems*, and I have given away many copies over the years because it so profound in its advice and so moving as a story.[299]

The technique that Kahane led for the Mt. Fleur participants was pioneered at Shell Oil during the 1960s and 70s, and Kahane was a member of the scenario planning team when the Mt. Fleur effort began. Its purpose is look into the future not in order to make specific predictions about what *will* happen, but rather to identify what *might* happen under a variety of different conditions that *may* emerge. It's a perfect approach for us to utilize here as we seek to understand the impacts and overlapping outcomes of the six concurrent revolutions in a world situation rife with uncertainty.

Shell was already famous for this approach, and the company had shared its expertise in many situations already before the request came from South Africa. The company maintains a scenario planning team to this day, and it continues to explore the future and to publish very provocative studies of the energy industry and the broader social context in which it operates worldwide. In the remainder of this chapter we'll apply the scenario planning approach to gain deeper insight in the uncertainties we face, the options with which the future may confront us, and the pathways that may lead to the most positive outcomes. In this way we hope to anticipate the findings of the explorers, to preview the wonders that they return with, and figure out what we need to do with and about them.

To gain deeper insight into unknown futures scenario planning enables us to map the terrain by studying what are referred to as the "driving forces" that we anticipate may shape tomorrow's world, and then modeling what might happen as those forces interact with each other as further events unfold. By thinking about the future this way, again, we do not put ourselves in the position of trying to identify specifically what *will* happen, to predict, but instead we are thinking about what *could* happen, and how that might affect us.

The shift from *will* to *could* is an essential change of mindset, as it abandons the futile search for precise predictions that would convergence on a single expected future, instead it assesses the likelihood of being "correct" as negligible, and thus its pursuit as folly. It focuses instead, and this is one of the key points I have stressed throughout the book, on understanding the key *patterns of change* and the consequences that could possibly emerge when these patterns interact.

It should by now be obvious why; when we understand those patterns then the massive mystery and uncertainty of the world becomes considerably less mysterious, and our capacity to make good decisions increases significantly.

For the Mt. Fleur participants, scenario planning offered a way to think differently about their pressing issues and worries. It enabled them to model through the possible outcomes that lay before them, to identify an outcome that was vastly preferred above all others, and to chart a pathway, narrow as it was, that might enable them to attain their preference. The group was exceptionally diverse, and represented all of the major stakeholders in the political structure of the nation, which meant that there were among the participants direct adversaries whose goals and objectives were in direct conflict with one another. But what they fervently shared was the desire, above all, to achieve an outcome peacefully, for they knew that civil war would lead to generations of self-destructive outcomes.

Above I mentioned that in order to manage complexity we have to have useful models of complex systems, and this is exactly what the Mt. Fleur dialog enabled. The participants came to see as a result of the dialog where various forces and potential actions might lead, and how to encourage the positive ones and avoid the pitfalls and potential disasters, of which there were many. In those terms, what we mean to do here is precisely to do that also, to model possible future worlds and understand how the driving forces could interact to see what pathways might lead toward good or better outcomes. But which driving forces should we focus on?

Twelve Essential
Driving Forces of Change

In Part 1 we examined the five revolutions and the counter-revolution, which you now realize are six of the essential forces I believe to be most influential in shaping our future landscape. In Chapter 10, just completed above, we examined in summary six the additional driving forces of geopolitics including China, Russia, the EU, the USA, the Middle East, and the Non-State Actors of globalization. These, then, constitute the twelve essential driving forces of change that we'll examine now using the scenario planning approach.

In the section immediately below I'll summarize a few key ideas about each one, and then I'll frame two future alternatives, A and B, for each one. Those alternatives will then become the basis upon which we'll examine a diverse set of scenarios that emerge when we look at various combinations of the driving forces, as this is what the scenario planning method is all about.

While the specialists in each domain rightly have their own personal views on what is or is not most likely to occur, in reality no one can be certain which way things will go.   And of course this is exactly why scenarios can benefit us so much, as they enable us to explore what may happen through the interactions of the twelve critical drivers even as we remain uncertain about which outcomes will emerge for any of them. Without a tool like this we're easily overwhelmed by trying to sort out too many variables at once, and thus scenario planning actually enables us to engage in a large, multi-dimensional inquiry that asks, simply, *what if?*

The Five Revolutions and
the Counter-Revolution

The Digital Revolution:
Technology and Robotics

The Digital Revolution enabled by the increasing power of computer chips and combined with their decreasing cost has made it possible to create machines of ever greater sophistication with the capacity to perform more and more complex and socially-important functions.   The future of the Digital Revolution through the digital sciences of artificial life that deal with non-human physiology, or robotics, and of digitally-engineered life focused on human and animal anatomy and physiology under the broad heading of biotechnology, have the potential to further and fundamentally change how we live, and in so doing to change the very structure of our economy and human culture.

Today's robots are already welding and assembling cars and indeed all types of manufactured goods, and also performing surgery, sorting and delivering goods in warehouses, as well as vacuuming floors, and even teaching primary school children. Tomorrow's robots will do even more, including driving cars, making medical decisions, managing investments, taking care of the elderly, and perhaps even teaching college level students. Over the coming years and decades we can expect to see still more jobs being done by robots, perhaps to the point that they take over the economy and provoke an employment and therefore social catastrophe. Or they might turn out to be a quite agreeable boon both economically and socially. Or they may also fail entirely to arrive due to technical obstacles that today's promoters of robots fail to overcome. No one knows.

The only plausible scenario in which some progress does not occur, however, is a large scale economic collapse not specifically related to digitization, but which could be precipitated by an event such as a large scale regional war, or worse, a global war, or a massive pandemic, that led to the collapse of the global economic system and the reversion to extreme nationalism, or regionalism.

However, the full economic consequences of the robotic revolution are still not clear. So while we expect that robots will do much more, we do not know the extent to which this will disrupt the economy, or enhance it.

A
Keep ●———— Technology and Robotics ————● Robots
Vacuuming   Rule

B

Alternative A: Keep Vacuuming

The promises of robots and digitized biotechnology remains unfulfilled because there aren't any more breakthroughs to be found, as we have already improved our health as much as is physiologically possible. Moore's Law peters out, and the singularity never materializes. Computers remain very helpful, but no further transformation occurs; Roomba is the best it gets.

Alternative B: Robots Rule

Robots, genetics and biotechnology will continue to increase in capability and exert further transformative impact on human lifestyles, work, and health care practices. They will contribute to increasing vitality and longevity, enhancing and augmenting current economic patterns and structures. This may lead to a radical re-structuring the entire global system of production, and thus the structure of the entire economy, but in a good way.

Climate Change

The roots of our climate challenge go back 200 years to the beginning of the fossil fuel age, and unless we find a way to remove billions of tons of CO_2 from the atmosphere in short order, the trend of climate change will take decades to reverse, if it even is reversible at all. As we examined in detail in Chapter 2, concern about the future impact of climate change is becoming more prevalent but what we don't know is how much the climate will change, and if it does, how fast. Rapid warming, the resulting melting of the polar ice, and changing climates in many regions could be tremendously disruptive to patterns of agriculture and habitation, and result in extensive damage, mass migrations, and the need to rebuild many coastal cities. Or perhaps it won't be that bad.

In summary, then, climate change could turn out to be most disastrous calamity in the history of civilization, or alternatively it could turn out to have been a false alarm. As of today you may have an opinion about which of the two possibilities is most likely, but the reality is that no one knows, and to be prudent we ought to consider both.

A — Climageddon ●————— Climate Change —————● B — False Alarm

Alternative A: False Alarm

Climate change is a false alarm. We have mistaken normal natural cycles for a calamity that never arrives as what we're experiencing turns out to be normal variation.

Alternative B: Climaggedon

CO2-induced climate change turns out to be the greatest calamity ever to strike human civilization.

Fossil Fuels and Alternative Energy

As a result of an increase in supply and decline in demand oil prices are down dramatically since 2014, which has caused significant changes to the oil industry. Is this a permanent change, meaning the beginning of the end of fossil fuels? Or is it a temporary blip? Further, since fossil fuels are the primary source of excess atmospheric CO2, and since CO2 is the primary cause of climate change, will governments choose to further restrict the use of fossil fuels as a way to counter climate change? And if market forces and governments regulations become aligned, then how fast would the fossil industry implode?

This perspective may be overstating the case, as the world economy is still utterly dependent on fossil fuels, and it would be a social and economic catastrophe for everyone if the oil stopped flowing before sufficient alternatives were in place, and that is possibly decades away. And it's also possible that fossil fuels will be the dominant fuels in the global economy throughout this century, and while the transition to non-fossil sources is inevitable, it won't happen at scale until well past 2050 or even 2080.

What about the rise of alternatives to fossils?   In 1977 the cost to produce one watt of solar-generated electricity was about $77, but due to ongoing R&D, by 2013 the cost had dropped by a factor of 100x to about 75 cents. Because of improvements in technology and increases in the scale of demand and thus manufacturing efficiencies, the cost continues to decline, which is rapidly changing solar from an expensive science project into a highly competitive economic force.

The price of electricity in the US depends on your location, with

Washington state the lowest average cost at about 9 cents per kWh (kilowatt hour) due to all its hydro power, New York state at 20 cents, and isolated Hawaii at 37 cents. With continuing cost reductions due to technological improvements in solar energy generation combined with increasing economies of scale as demand increases, many in the industry are targeting a cost of 12 to 13 cents per kWh in the near future, which would make solar entirely cost competitive, except for the fact that the sun doesn't shine at night although but people still need to use electricity at night.

Hence, as we discussed in Chapter 3, the transition to solar and wind energy as predominant sources of supply depends not only on the core technologies related to electricity generation, but also to the related batteries and other storage means that make it feasible 24 hours a day. It is for this reason that huge investments are now being made by government R&D labs and private companies worldwide in the race to make battery and other storage technologies scalable and economically competitive.

For the purposes of our scenarios, then, the key question is when or whether solar, wind, and battery technologies will advance to the point that they actually do displace fossil fuels not due to regulations, but because they are cost competitive. When this happens it will mark a major turning point, one of enormous economic importance globally. The shift will negatively impact the fossil fuel producing companies and nations, while enormously benefitting the nations that are able to most quickly adopt solar and wind technologies on a large scale.

But the alternative possibility is that these breakthroughs will not occur, or will not occur quickly, in which case the transition away from fossil fuels will take much longer, and presumably then the prolonged use of fossil fuels and the resulting CO2 pollution will then have even greater negative impacts on the climate situation.

A
Fossils ●————— Fossil Fuels —————● Fossil
Forever   Failure

B

Alternative A: Fossils Forever

The fossil fuel industry perseveres throughout this century because there is plenty of supply, which keeps cost down, and also because we discover that CO2 doesn't cause climate change, and/or because carbon sequestration on a global scale proves entirely effective. The development of non-fossil sources is therefore stifled, and does not emerge as the dynamic industry many had foreseen.

Alternative B: Fossil Failure

The fossil fuel industry collapses within the coming one or two decades due to a combination of market forces or regulatory restrictions, or a combination of both. This causes major economic dislocation as the value of fossil fuel companies declines to near zero, which has a very detrimental impact on many investors, whose net worth declines drastically. The problem cascades to the banks, which suddenly have massive non-performing loans to energy companies and energy company investors. A recession results. Simultaneously, the decline of fossil sources becomes a boon for alternative energy sources, and large scale government and private investment in new energy source and infrastructure partially offsets the Fossil Recession.

Urbanization and Demographics

While the three forces of change just mentioned, digitization, climate change, and the energy future all remain quite uncertain, the same cannot be said for demographics. The demographic inversion that is coming by mid-century is nearly certain to occur, and as it does it will be one of the most significant economic factors of the modern era. Birth rates will continue to drop as urbanization continues, and longevity will continue to increase as nutrition and health care continue to improve, and as medical science continues to gain new knowledge about disease and aging. Thus, economics won't be focused on regulating the banks and the money supply, it will be about coping with economies where fewer young workers pay taxes and many more elderly citizens consume health care and pensions, setting the stage for a radical and probably painful restructuring. Should the robotics revolution occur at maximum force, the difficulties will be significantly compounded.

```
          A ●   Urbanization & Demographics   ● B
       Urbantopia                               Elderpocalypse
```

Alternative A: Urbantopia

Urbanization is not only a positive and dynamic force for creativity, and innovation, it's also a powerful force of economic growth. While the structure of labor force shifts with a progressive aging, the negative impacts are offset due to continuing increases in productivity. Cities, in other words, become magnificent engines of economic growth and development, and as elders can contribute meaningfully to social and economic life when they have access to cultural and social opportunities, the design of pedestrian friendly cities becomes a priority worldwide. It's a Renaissance.

Alternative B: Elderpocalypse

The significant and steady increase in the number of elderly coupled with a severe shortage of young workers conspire to restrict economic growth, and indeed invert it. Once dynamic and youthful, the economy contracts into an tired shadow of its former vitality. Consequently, society has to figure out how to make do without growth, causing education, health care, public services to all be rationed far below the level of actual demand. In this world, robots provide the extra needed labor, but the owners of the robots siphon off even more of society's wealth. The "one percent" becomes smaller, now the one-tenth-of-on-percent, and the 99.9 percent is the rest struggle to make ends meet. Bankruptcy courts are overwhelmed.

The Cultural Revolution

Changes in the structure of the economy and of society are coming faster and faster, and people in every nation are severely stressed and challenged to adapt to new technologies, new rules, new lifestyles. As the economy changes, more and more people are displaced; as the climate changes people are displaced as well, resulting in mass migrations of millions. This puts extreme stress on those who are forced to relocate, and nearly equivalent on the desired locations where the migrants are trying to make new homes in regions and nations where they don't speak the language, know the customs, or have assured employment. Older people

A
Delightenment

The Cultural Revolution

B
Descent to
Dystopia

struggle to adapt and many become angry and disheartened, while young people move more fluidly between the human and technological worlds, developing new skills and broader awarenesses.

Alternative A: Delightenment

The stresses of modern life act as a catalyst to evoke new and healthier lifestyles and workstyles, and humanity discovers within itself a surprising and often inspiring capacity to not only adapt, but to transform average and mediocre into successful and fulfilling through empathy and community. A burst of creativity brings unforeseen solutions to formerly intractable problems.

Alternative B: Descent to Dystopia

It all becomes too much, and life becomes too much like a bad dystopian novel, Kafkaesque, full of discontinuities, injustices, and confusion. Suicides and depression increase markedly as people struggle and fail to adapt to the modern world. Orwell and Huxley's worst visions are realized.

Counter-Revolution

No matter how good or how bad life is in any era or for any generation, there will always be those whose reference points are in the past, and who yearn to recreate society the way it used to be. While it's often the case that it never really was the way that people nostalgically remember "the way it used to be," the imagined past nevertheless becomes an anchoring image to which people hold firm. Some of them become angry at the changes, and they react with violence; other retreat into fundamentalism,

or into cults. And the faster the economy and society change, the greater the number of people who pull away.

Alternative A: Open Debate

A significant anti-change faction opens a rift in society, which leads to an era of open discussion and debate about the future and the choices that society must face in the coming years. Passions are high, but so is participation, and while not everyone gets their way in the new world, the open manner in which decisions are debated and reached creates an environment of mutual respect and appreciation.

Alternative B: Boiling Mad

The number of people who deeply feel that changes to the technological, economic, and social structure of society are fundamentally unfair and morally wrong becomes a significant percentage of the total, and their numbers become so great that they form a decisive counter-cultural anti-change movement. A large faction at the extreme the fringe of this movement feels self-justified in the morality of violent opposition to change, creating a highly polarized society in which violence becomes common, and as a result anyone who can retreats into a protected enclave. The creative forces of society wither and fade amid the permanent conflict.

The Six Geopolitical Powerhouses

China

Will China dominate 21st century commerce and geopolitics as the USA did in the 20th, or will its internal demographic and social issues derail its ascent to the pinnacle?

A
Dragon
Defiant

China

B
Dragon
Trader

Alternative A: Dragon Defiant

Economic weakness, continuing corruption, severe environmental deterioration, and pressure for democracy cause internal challenges to the rule of the Communist Party. To distract people from these issues, the Party incites public anger at injustices, real or imagined, committed by its neighbors. Crises and pseudo-crises are provoked with various foes, alternatively, Japan, Korea, Taiwan, the Philippines, Vietnam, Russia, and the US. This sustains the impression within China that the world is unjustly united against it, which reduces the pressure for reform and keeps the populous in line.

Alternative B: Dragon Trader

China's leaders recognize that their nation has little to gain by antagonizing its neighbors and that its economic interdependence with the rest of the world is far more significant for its long term health that an aggressive posture of territorial acquisitiveness. The government continues to emphasize its economic development, focusing investment in areas such as high technology, new energy, and resource efficiency. Progressive reform and continuing economic success within China is sufficient to sustain popular support for the Communist Party.

Russia

Russia will soon face severe demographic stress as its population shrinks, severe economic stress if oil prices remain low, and it already suffers from an identity crisis due to the collapse of the USSR and its descent from superpower status. Under Putin the nation has experienced a strange sort of rebirth, fueled by aggression and geopolitical tactics from the Soviet days. Will Russia continue under Putin, and will Putin continue to create geopolitical disruption among Russia's neighbors and elsewhere, or will its leadership shift to an attitude of for respect international norms and cease its aggressive policies? Will Russia provoke a catastrophic war in Ukraine or elsewhere, or will it not?

A
Bellicose
Bear

Russia

B
Bear in
Business

Alternative A: Bellicose Bear

Putin remains in power and positions Russia as a tactical aggressor in numerous local and national disputes, causing no end of problems for the EU, China, and the US, all of which wish to avoid military entanglements. Their response is primarily economic, which further isolates Russia's economy.   As the demographic stranglehold tightens and Putin ages, Russia becomes irrelevant, but not before causing severe damage.

Alternative B: Bear in Business

The negative impacts of progressively tighter economic sanctions stifles Russia's economy, and the citizenry becomes tired of steadily worsening conditions and elects a reform party to the Kremlin. Russia's new leaders focus on economic development rather than military adventures.

The European Union

The EU faces many existential threats including its fragmented currency situation, the growing influence of right wing politics, huge waves of immigration, its inherent demographic weaknesses, and the looming threat of Russia's incursions in Ukraine, the Baltics, and the Caucasus. Will the EU meet these challenges successfully and rise to the status of global superpower, or will its internal divisions and demographic challenges permanently hinder its influence?

A
Euro
Ascendant

The European Union

B
Eurolapse

Alternative A: EuroAscendant

The EU members states realize that their shared destiny brings tremendous benefits to each, and so they reaffirm their shared commitment to learning how to make the pioneering experiment in multi-national governance a success. This leads to a wave of creativity and innovation as well as renewed confidence in its key national leaders. The nations grow closer economically and less diverse politically, as they find a formula for balancing national identity with continental unity.

Alternative B: Eurolapse

The EU collapses and its 28 nations separate. It's a messy divorce as the 18 national currencies of the former Eurozone members are resurrected, and chaos roils the financial markets as assets values rise and fall precipitously. States engage in a furious round of bi- and tri-lateral trade agreement negotiations, as a result of which no one can keep track of who is allied with whom. Russia ingests some former EU states, and China acquires massive assets in the turmoil.

The United States

Partisan bickering between political left and right challenges the capacity of America's national government leaving it incapable of performing basic functions and from meeting key external challenges, including the continuing threat of terrorism, climate change, and geopolitical aggression from various adversaries. While the domestic economy continues as one of the strongest and most stable in the world due its advanced technologies, many of the key challenges facing the US are related to reaching agreement on what to do and not do. Will the US surrender geopolitical leadership to China, or will it find sufficient political cohesion to enhance its global leadership?

A
Grounded

The United States

B
Still the Boss

Alternative A: Grounded

The partisan divide continues to worsen as the conflict between progressives and reactionaries paralyzes the nation, and every issue becomes a flash point for conflict as neither side is willing to compromise. Larger states such as California, Texas, and Alaska consider seceding from the Union to sustain their own economies and preserve their very distinct values and cultures, which provokes a constitutional crisis.

Alternative B: Still the Boss

The US achieves sufficient alignment to accomplish the core tasks of a functioning government, and while there remains considerable disagreement about the proper role of the federal government, the external pressures and challenges provide sufficient focus to keep the union in tact, and American sustains its superpower status.

The Middle East

The Middle East remains the most consistently tumultuous region in the world, and the key question for the future is whether radicalism will increase and intensify and continue to tear apart the region's nations while the export of terrorism accelerates, or whether forces of moderation will gain influence and peaceful settlement of religious, ethic, and national disputes come into view.

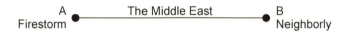

A Firestorm — The Middle East — B Neighborly

Alternative A: Firestorm

Terrorism spreads across the Middle East and onto dozens of countries on all continents. When it strikes in nations that have a constitutional commitment to civil liberties the terror provokes the call for a radical scaling back of those same liberties in the name of safety. Inevitably increased security measures and restrictions result, reflecting the attainment of one terrorism's specific goals, the escalation of fear. As the violence worsens in the inferno that is the new Middle East another result is still more refugees. But as the incidents of terror increase, those refugees are less and less welcome due to the fear that terrorists are hidden among them. Terrorists gain access to ever more powerful weapons that they detonate around the world, and most of the Middle East deteriorates further as the nations dissolve into factions that are continually at war.

Alternative B: Neighborly

Terrorist violence runs its course and is effectively countered by the combined military, police, and counter-terrorism efforts of a unified world, and so becomes a relative non-issue. Intermittent and increasingly rare terror incidents do not deter the world from moving forward in its development as a peaceful civilization, and the Middle East's rich heritage contributes fully to the world's culture.

Globalization and the Non-State Actors

Globalization has been a powerful force for economic and social progress that has resulted in a single global economy, but commercial players continue to seek advantage over each other both within and outside of the established rules. The range and diversity of participants increases, as multi-national companies continue to play one nation against the others, evade taxation, and strive for narrow economic gains at the expense of civic responsibilities and environmental well-being. In addition, large criminal enterprises operate on a global scale and outside of the law dealing drugs, weapons, and people. Will the global economy continue to unify and grow as a shared endeavor of all nations, or will dissention and conflict lead to the further fragmentation of winners and losers?

```
        A          The Non-State Actors        B
     Super- ●————————————————————————● Free-for-
      Boom                                None
```

Alternative A: Super-Boom

Nations and corporations agree broadly on the set of shared rules within which they operate equitably, which sustains positive and inclusive economic momentum and enables hundreds of millions more people to become contributors to and beneficiaries of the global economy.

Alternative B: Free-for-None

Nationalistic competition degrades the global economy and in a prevailing environment of scarcity nations start to put narrow interests first, and fail to live up to their regional and global agreements. This causes a loss of confidence in trade and in the rules governing global economic institutions, and trade falters and then collapses. The have nations get more, and the have-not nations suffer more.

What if...?

These very concise summaries are intended to be both plausible and provocative. They're also intended to illustrate that in each case, both Alternative A and B could indeed come about if the right combination of events and attitudes were to prevail. Neither alternative is inevitable, but neither can also be excluded out of hand. It would therefore be unwise if not outright foolish to base any organization's or a nation's strategy on a prediction one way or the other; there's just no way to know what's really going to happen.

We also know that as events play out these forces will have significant impact on one another. None of these twelve forces will evolve toward its own outcomes in isolation. Quite to the contrary, whatever happens with each will impact significantly on all of the rest. This certainly makes for a great deal more complexity, and thus to model how they may interact we begin by exploring various combinations in pairs to see what further insights can be gleaned.

These pairings are a central element of scenario planning approach, and while it may seem to be an oversimplification to look at only two, experience has shown that it's quite productive. By arranging them in a 2 x 2 matrix, as shown in Figure 85, we create four corners, or quadrants, each of which represents a specific combination of the identified alternatives. This shapes, in effect, a unique world, and our task then becomes to understand each of the four worlds.

Because we have already agreed that both of the alternatives of both driving forces are indeed plausible, what've done by arranging them into the 2 x 2 format is to create each of the four possible combinations, if the elements are plausible then by definition the combinations ought to be plausible as well. Hence, what we know about the driving forces has led us define four worlds, any of which could conceivably turn out to be the actual future that we will face.

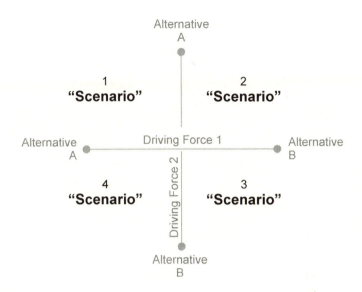

Figure 98
Two Driving Forces, Two Extremes for Each
For each driving force we have already identified two alternative possibilities. By pairing them in this was we automatically create for alternative future worlds, marked as Scenarios 1, 2, 3, and 4. By definition any of the four scenarios should be plausible since the alternatives are plausible. Some of them may seem more likely or more preferable to us, but the key point is that we are obliged to take all four seriously as a future possibility, and thus we avoid the traps of tunnel vision or picking a future that we prefer.

The first pair we'll explore is the interaction between climate change and globalization. As we saw above, by combining Alternatives A and B for each one, we create four quite different scenarios of the future.

Scenario Set 1:

Climate Change and Globalization

We will explore each of the four quadrants of the matrix one by one by developing a short narrative that seeks to capture the essential character of

429

the world that would emerge when we combine the pairs of alternatives. In Figure 89 you see that has been given its own a name, a punchy and memorable one, which is intended to make each narrative stand out as a unique experience.

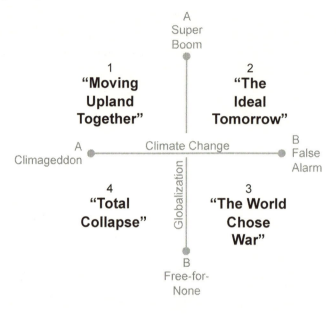

Figure 99
Visualizing Change as a Matrix of Two Driving Forces

Scenario 1: "Moving Upland Together" – Climaggedon and Super Boom

Scenario 2: "The Ideal Tomorrow" – False Alarm and Super Boom

Scenario 3: "The World Chose War" – False Alarm and Free-for-None

Scenario 4: "Total Collapse" – Climaggedon and Free-for-None

Scenario 1: "Moving Upland Together"

We can also foresee another quite different set of outcomes in a world devastated by a climate apocalypse should the nations of the globe respond positively and cooperate to make the best of the very bad situation. Here we see a unified humanity successfully meeting mutual needs in the midst of an unprecedented crisis. While the storms would be huge and the dislocations massive, the collective willingness to adjust and adapt enables global society to maintain its commitment to mutual well being which results in consistent actions to protect people from harm, even citizens who aren't from your own country. Through global agencies such as the UN and various regional alliances, the collective efforts of humanity are organized and deployed to provide for those who are most severely impacted which enables humanity to display and develop its best qualities, obsessed not with personal gain but motivated by empathy and actions to care for those in need. And as the needy would exist on a scale that perhaps has never before been seen, we can anticipate that the worst case of the climate challenge causes literally billions of people to be threatened, lowland cities flooded and uninhabitable causing trillions of dollars worth of real estate to become worthless. We might call this "Moving Upland Together" to describe the need to rebuild human civilization and adjust to a new coastline that has been drawn at a much higher altitude by melted ice and violent storms.

Scenario 2: "The Ideal Tomorrow"

Suppose that instead of a climatic apocalypse the impacts of climate change proved to be muted, moderate, or even mild, and suppose that building on this positive situation the nations of world continued to work together to build a more stable global economic system and to lift millions and billions more from poverty. Globalization continues to boost economic success, and multilateral agreements prove effective in creating widespread alignment and focus on improving the lives of the world's poor, uneducated, and impoverished. It's "The Ideal Future."

Scenario 3: "The World Chose War"

What sort or world would we find ourselves in if the climate threat turned out to be vastly overstated, or if scientists developed the technical means to overcome excess concentrations of CO2? Either would mean that there was not a significant threat due to climate change, and that the climate would in fact stabilize. But also suppose that the geopolitical situation wasn't stable and fact globalization collapsed, and that other disruptive forces gained momentum and had serious impacts on global stability and security. Perhaps Russia and China would ally and undertake aggressive territorial expansions, with Russia invading Ukraine and China invading Taiwan at the same time. In the resulting chaos, perhaps the conflict in the Middle East would boil over into a full scale regional war.

The EU would be forced to confront Russia or to admit impotence and irrelevance, and the US would be forced to challenge China's aggression, which would mean a disruption or even cessation of trade between two of the world's largest trading partners which would have a cascade of negative impacts within both countries and throughout the massive supply chains that enable their commerce. Millions of people would be streaming out the war-torn Middle East in all directions, while the threat of nuclear war would hang oppressively over everyone's head. The UN, also having proven irrelevant, disintegrates. This is an entirely discouraging scenario in which the sense of shared human destiny is lost amid the struggles. This is what would happen if "The World Chose War."

Scenario 4: "Total Collapse"

What would happen if there was a complete climate apocalypse that turned out to be much worse even than then most dire warnings could have dared to predict, and at the same time and largely as a result, globalization fails and the global economic system collapsed? It would be a very unpleasant world, a world of extreme suffering and most certainly of proliferating violent conflict. Huge numbers of people would be dislocated from their homes and nations due to climate issues, and indeed entire nations, extensive coastlines, and major cities would be submerged beneath the risen seas. Would there be enough food? Probably not, and what food there was would mostly be in the wrong places, which would make food shortages more acute. Some regions would have extravagant food excesses, but most would have too little, and as global trade diminished significantly or perhaps collapsed entirely it would become impossible to move the food where it was needed. The trade collapse would also cause a collapse of many currencies, further stressing many nations. Food and water would become the most valuable media of exchange, and it's quite conceivable that productive nations would seek to close their borders to masses of climate refugees. Even within nations there would be fragmentation and discord, as the scramble for scarce resources would likely pit region against region. This would be the real life version of every dystopian movie you've ever seen, *Hunger Games* meets *Divergent* meets *Mad Max*. We might call this story "Total Collapse."

Observations

The content of these scenarios demonstrates that the simplicity of the scenario planning approach nevertheless carries with it considerable power as a thought exercise. The stories are not elaborate, but the challenges they convey are indeed provocative. It's also easy to see how flipping between alternatives A and B changes the situation entirely, and leads to a story that has a very different feel and entirely different outcomes. Life in each of the four worlds would be quite different from the others, and while we might obviously prefer the warmer and friendlier worlds to the darker and more strive-torn, it's also clear that the interplay of the actual forces is quite powerful and may not allow us any choice at all; we get what we get, regardless of what we want or think we deserve.

And that's the point of course. If we choose one or predict one we are automatically excluding from our awareness and from our planning an entire range of outcomes and events that nevertheless remain entirely plausible. This is another reason that narrowly conceived strategic planning efforts are so dangerous; it's highly deceptive and constrains our thinking, when what we often benefit from most is the expansion of our thinking in a way that allows us, or even forces us to imagine what might happen across an entire range of possibilities.

Conversely, if we were to consider every possible combination of the twelve forces I've chosen we would have a total of 66 possible pairings. Each pairing would then result in 4 scenarios, giving us a total of 264 views of the future.   That's obviously too many, as it would be nearly impossible for us to make sense of that much data, and in any case the stories would become hopelessly redundant and the useful differences and nuances would be completely lost.

Therefore, we are selective by pairing forces that have relevant relationships and which are more challenging and more surprising, and which thus hopefully yield insights that are provocative and meaningful.

You probably also noticed these scenario descriptions include a lot conditional statements.   In this type of thought experiment it's obviously foolish to make grand pronouncements about what "will" happen, because the very act of modeling what *could* happen makes it abundantly clear that both possibilities for each future are plausible.   Hence, the process of thinking through these scenarios provides a tremendously valuable education in futurism and decision making.   Issues and choices that are entirely black and white in one scenario often become gray under a different set of initial conditions.   Consequently, the language pattern we use shifts pretty quickly from "it will happen" and "we will do such-and-such" to "if this happens then we would do such-and-such."   We become a lot less positive about our choices and much more engaged in thinking through possibilities as possibilities only.

Causality

We saw in Scenario 1 that the conditions described on one axis caused the situation that resulted on the other.   It does make sense that apocalyptic climate change is likely to have a radically destabilizing impact on the economy and could in fact drive the economy into a catastrophic recession, depression, or at worst an outright collapse.   This situation describes what happens when a primary driver triggers a secondary, and it's obvious that the worst case in any one driver of change can lead to or significantly influence the character of the others. But it doesn't have to bring out the worst; Scenario 2 posits the opposite reaction, that catastrophe evokes a more humane response rather than a more selfish one.

We also learn pretty quickly that to understand any of these scenarios we have to set aside our biases, ideologies, and preferences, and look instead at both the stated set of conditions and the logical chains of cause and effect that we can foresee as a result. This leads us to quickly realize that our preferences become irrelevant, especially where we have little or no influence over the basic conditions. We also see quickly that biases lead to wishful thinking, and if wishful thinking is allowed to persevere it may easily lead straight to poor decisions. Hence, the benefit of the thought experiment as a prelude to decision making cannot be underestimated.

Let me again refer again to the economic crisis of 2008 and the apparently inadequate model that Mr. Greenspan used to guide his decision making. Both hindsight and his own comments suggest that wishful thinking took priority over rigorous modeling. Interestingly, though, the modeling we're doing here would not be considered rigorous by the standards of the Federal Reserve or Wall Street, where the big data number crunchers are looking at data sets of billions and trillions of data points, and the algorithms are massive, super complex, and proprietary. That's what rigor is on Wall Street, but interestingly the 2008 collapse showed quite clear that all of that sophistication can still lead badly astray.

Instead, what we're talking about here are concepts and chains of causality that don't require computers to model, they just require us to make meaningful links between concepts, and to bring a sufficient breadth of knowledge to model through multiple variables. This is they type of thinking at which humans excel, but which, at present, computers do not. This may change, of course, as the digital revolution progresses, but for the moment you can't delegate it to HAL or Mac or even a Cray. Anyway, a lot of the power and value in scenario planning comes not so much from the tangible outcomes, the scenarios and stories, as it does from the thinking.   Scenario planning is a learning technique as much as it is a planning method.

Indeed, one the key principles that we have seen again and again as consultants and educators is that "you can't learn for someone else." That is, each of us has to have our own learning experiences, we have to go through each of the steps required to master the material to understand the tradeoffs and the risks and the opportunities.   If I were an expert I or someone else could tell you that "climate change is a big risk," but until you invest the time in understanding what that really means, it is only a hollow cliché.   While it does make sense that large organizations and government leaders properly rely on experts in many domains to advise them on what is possible and even what is best in any situation, the reality is that they won't really understand the difficult options and choices until they think it through for themselves.

Here's another way to explain it.   You're hiring a new pilot for your private corporate jet and you're down to two candidates; will you choose the pilot who got mediocre scores all through flight school, but who's been flying without incident for 20 years and has gotten through some nasty scrapes.   Or do you prefer the one who received the very highest scores on every test and in every simulation, but who's only got 30 hours of flying time under his belt?   Yes, experience is valuable, and thinking through scenarios is a very valuable form of experience to obtain; it can only be obtained by doing it.

How It Works

Through these four stories you've now seen how scenario planning works.   It's all about the "What if?" questions, and it works well when it provides enough structure that the scenarios themselves become plausible, and also enough freedom in the mode of the thought experiment to allow us consider implications and consequences that we might not otherwise have thought about.

Since the effectiveness rests upon our understanding of the driving forces of change, you now understand why the book to this point has been focused on modeling out what's happening with those forces and considering what might happen; that is the platform upon which these scenarios can be developed and tested.

Compiling the information behind the twelve driving forces and then thinking about what it may mean is in fact how I came to realize that the concept of "six revolutions" may be a useful way to understand how the world is evolving. I didn't have that framework in mind when I started working on this book, but as I examined more deeply across the various themes and studied the analysis of the visionaries and the systems thinkers and the geostrategists I found it to be a useful way to think about change. And when I saw the curve that conveys the second major transition of the modern era as described by the population S-curve then the elements began to fit together into a model that might be useful.

As a firm we've also tested many of these concepts and frameworks in various project, speeches and workshops and as the ideas became clearer to us and to our clients we've been encouraged to continue exploring, and the result is the book that you're holding, or perhaps on the ebook.

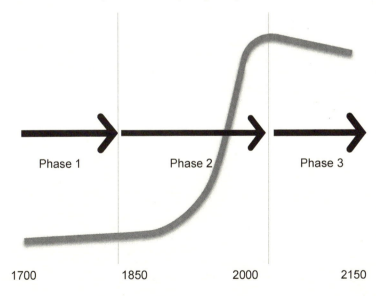

Figure 100
The S–Curve of the Human Population Trend, 1700 – 2150 Defines Three Phase of History

437

As we saw from the scenario above, it's possible to generate many pages of possibly useful insights from a single pairs of driving forces, but there are twelve of them, so let's take a look now at a second pair. Here we will consider the digital revolution and the energy revolution, and by looking in turn at each of the possible pairings we'll see four additional and significantly different views of our possible future.

Scenario Set 2:
Double Revolutions

Perhaps there will be a transformation of the global energy sector marked by the collapse of the fossil fuel industry and the shift to a sustainable energy economy, or perhaps fossils will endure as the primary driver of the global economy.

What would happen if advances in robotics and biosciences emerged at the most extreme end of the forecasts, and within fifteen to twenty years robots became so adept and proficient and cheap that they entirely transformed the way that work was done throughout the economy, and that at the same new medical treatments and engineered improvements significantly increased the average human life span? Would these changes cause massive displacement across many or even most professions, and thus massive unemployment and a deepening divide between rich and poor? Or would silicon intelligence complement and augment humans leading to great productivity and even more useful roles and fulfilling for carbon-based intelligence (us), making everyone wealthier? Either way, this would have significant impact on the global political situation and the situation in every locality. It could further enhance our lives, or more deeply divide the haves from the have-nots among nations and within nations.

And what if, at the same time that the robots emerge, society chose, whether as a matter of marketplace competition and economics or of climate change policy, or both, to abandon fossil fuels? There are as always four possible outcomes when we combine these two driving forces.

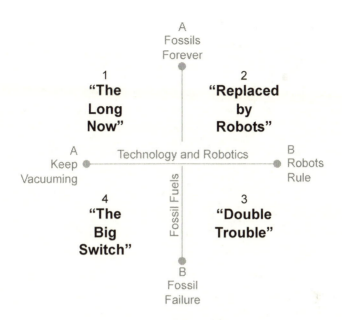

Figure 101
Scenarios of Double Revolutions

Scenario 1: "The Long Now" – Keep Vacuuming and Fossils Forever

Scenario 2: "Replaced by Robots" – Robots Rule and Fossils Forever

Scenario 3: "Double Trouble"– Robots Rule and Fossil Failure

Scenario 4: "The Big Switch" – Keep Vacuuming and Fossil Failure

Scenario 1: "The Long Now"

Here the world we create is the world we already have, an economy dependent on fossil fuels and technological capabilities largely unchanged. Our major challenges and concerns, therefore, are elsewhere.

Scenario 2: "Replaced by Robots"

In this scenario the energy industry remains much as it is today with heavy reliance on fossil fuels, but the technology industry continues to boom, resulting in highly capable robots that replace human workers. This

439

is a story, then, about how robots become part of society, and the tensions and conflicts that this creates.

The creation and rapid spread of advanced robotics leads to large scale changes in employment patterns because of the displacement of a very large percentage of the human work force. If governments offered little to no support in this transition, significant numbers of people would become permanently unemployable and would be cast into poverty. The social and political disruptions would be enormous, and it would be easy to see how increasing social friction could readily lead to violence. As various eras in the past have seen book burnings and witch hunts, this could be an era in which robots are "executed" in the public square by angry mobs.

But what rights would robots owners have to protect their property? And what rights would the robots themselves have to protect themselves? In the early and primitive phases of robotics we can expect their capacities to be quite limited, single function machines, but as computer technology continues to advance, what will happen if robots develop consciousness? If robots think and feel then what rights might they have to protect themselves? Will they have the right to "earn a living?" Will they have the right to access electricity? Or to have their software upgraded? What if a robot commits a crime, and it is suspected that it did so willfully and intentionally?

The professional group that will certainly flourish in a world of abundant robotics is the legal profession, for the law itself is obviously going to have to evolve in order to accommodate a wide range of new issues and challenges that robots will bring to both civil and criminal law. The courts and the legislatures will be quite busy sorting countless new questions and issues that will inevitably arise, exceptionally complex ones as they will be at once moral, ethical, social, *and* economic.

Different nations, of course, may choose different approaches to robot rights and robot ownership, which may lead to further conflicts between them. For example, in Japan where the population implosion is leading to an aging and shrinking population robots may become quite welcome as a means to do necessary work to sustain human well-being. In nations where the population is continuing to increase such as India or Nigeria the same robots may be outlawed as a threat to human employment and well-being.

Another key uncertainty, and thus a scenario-within-the-scenario, concerns the ownership of the robots. Are they private goods that work as laborers and bring financial benefits to a new class of capital owners? Or are they public goods that work for the benefit of communities and nations? If they are the former, then the scenario posits that their efforts enrich a small ownership class while replacing human workers, thus "depriving" humans of the chance to earn a living. If they are the latter then they relieve human of drudgery and work-related risk but also the economic benefits may accrue to the community, or perhaps to individuals and their families.

Perhaps the key insight arising from this discussion is the likelihood that if highly capable robots actually are developed then this will in and of itself lead to a very wide range of divisive social, political, and economic issues that will in turn lead to further polarization between haves and have-nots.

Scenario 3: "Double Trouble"

Supposing we soon are living with robots whose capabilities are so advanced that they replace human workers on a significant scale? Suppose that the emergence of fully capable robots leads to or is accompanied by greater social cohesion and alignment among and within nations? What might enable these good outcomes to occur?

Transformative robotics presents the opportunity for the development of an entirely a new economic structure, but with them comes also the risk of massive displacement. The industrial age economic conflict between labor and management, between owners and workers is likely to be made significantly worse in robotic age, but one way to avoid the conflict that displacement would be to institute a legal and social framework governing the use of robots, and perhaps allocating a portion of the financial benefits of their labor to the workers who are in danger of being displaced.

While from the perspective of today this may seem highly unlikely, the stress of this transition may inspire and indeed require a fundamental change in how we think about "work," "ownership," and "labor." The development of new technology, especially technology so fundamental, is always a trial and error process of exploration, testing, failure, and discovery, and legislators will be naturally reluctant to define the legal grounds and regulations pertaining to robots until we actually know what's what. Nevertheless, it's possible that the companies and governments that create the first and second waves of transformative robots could choose to deploy them in ways that are humane rather than divisive.

It's also possible that robot designs could find more economic success and social acceptance if, instead of replacing human workers, they were designed to partner with and augment human workers. "My robot buddy" makes all my work go faster and easier, and the quality is much better also.

The other aspect of this scenario assumes that the fossil fuel industry collapses, and that fossils are replaced by sustainable sources in a transition occurs very fast. This represents a huge transfer of wealth from the fossil owners to investors in non-fossil supplies, and wreaks havoc among the nations that historically depended on fossil fuel production to sustain their economies, including Russia, Nigeria, Angola, and Venezuela.

And so when we put the two elements together what we see is a radical restructuring of the global economy, a process that inevitably has big winners and big losers among both investors and nations. The dislocations caused by the Industrial Revolution took nearly 200 years to unfold across the globe; this big shift would occur in one-tenth the time, and further, would set the stage for a radically different global economy by the second half of the 21st century, and consequently a completely different type of society as well.

Scenario 4: "The Big Switch"

The premises of this scenario are that the robot revolution never arrives due to the natural limits of technological progress, and the current levels of technology remain with only marginal improvements over the coming decades. As farming did not improve much during the ten centuries from the Middle Ages until after the Enlightenment so we may be also peaking now in terms of our technological capabilities, and it just doesn't get much better.

However, the scenario also posits that the energy revolution does occur, which suggests that it's driven not by digital technology but perhaps by climatic concerns, or simply because solar and wind energy production costs continue to decline and reach the crossover point at which they cost less than fossils, and buyers just choose to switch. This energy transition is of course accompanied by a major economic transformation.

Implications

A world in which the robotic and energy revolutions occur simultaneously is a world of large scale and dramatic dislocations socially and economically. The feelings of future shock/now shock would be felt strongly nearly everywhere. While the young would be growing up in a technologically-enabled society, their parents and grandparents would likely have a tremendously difficult time adapting, and we would inevitably see spillover into some of the other driving forces, including especially the anti-revolution. Fundamentalist groups and fundamentalist-controlled nations would find themselves severely tested as society considers an entirely new set of social relationships, and the laws and economic structures to accompany them.

Conversely, in scenarios where we assume no radical changes it's clear that the big challenges might lie in other facets of society that these scenarios do not address. These results, where some quadrants are highly provocative but others almost entirely uninteresting is common in scenario planning, as it's inherent in thought experiments that are by definition constrained by considering only two driving forces at a time, and considering only the most extreme outcomes related to each driving force. This is both a strength and a weakness of the method.

Modeling Pairs and Extremes

As you have now seen in two complete examples, the simple 2x2 matrix creates four quite different sets of circumstances. This is part of the reason that scenario planning works so well, because it applies this constraint to help us focus on only one specific combination of forces and to understand that combination particularly well. We consider the extreme possibilities for each driving force rather than a more more moderate middle ground, and you might wonder why it's not so useful to model the middle. Experience has shown that in the middle it's much more difficult to clearly identify the consequences and impacts, to assess causality and to determine meaning. The middle is much more vague, and thus two forecasters can project life in the middle in entirely opposite ways because of other assumptions and biases they hold. This can also mislead us into discounting the extreme possibilities and outcomes.

For example, in scenarios where we considered the simultaneous revolutions in robotics and in energy if we were to posit a world near the middle of the matrix in which the robots come along, sort of, and the alternative industry emerges, sort of, then it's difficult to see what the implications might be. Going to the extremes makes things much clearer as there's usually very little unclarity about causes or about effects. Any given pair of extremes gives us a world that presents implications that we can often agree upon.

To do this we are obliged to set aside the entirely reasonable objection that the extremes are much less plausible than the middle; scenario planners will not disagree with that. But they will also remind you that this is a thought experiment, not a strategic planning exercise nor an exercise in prediction. Its value is precisely in examining "what if," not in anticipating "what will." This usually forces us to think about the future in a different way than we are accustomed to, which often yields abundant insights. From our personal experiences leading scenario planning workshops for thousands of executives around the world this has universally proven to be the case.

Double Negatives

Using this approach to model the extremes of each of the driving forces often reveals a pattern. As one extreme in each pair often describes a "positive" outcome and the other is usually a "negative," we generally end up with one scenario quadrant, or world story, that is exceptionally dark, the "double-negative quadrant," and another that is nearly utopian, the "double positive quadrant." The other two are of course mixed, positive-negative. Quite often one of the four is ridiculously implausible from the outset, frequently when the double positive world view is impossibly Pollyanna.

It's interesting to note that when we led scenario planning workshops twenty, ten, or even as recently as five years ago one of the key insights shared by the participants was that the story (or quadrant) which seemed the most plausible to them was a "positive-negative" one, wherein one of the axes was optimistic and the other pessimistic. In contrast, the double negative quadrants seemed entirely unlikely and were rarely judged credible.

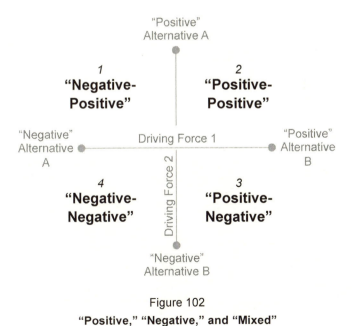

Figure 102
"Positive," "Negative," and "Mixed"

Over the intervening years, however, as the world has become increasingly complex and the golden glow that the West experienced following the collapse of the USSR faded, and 9/11 was followed by the disastrous invasion of Iraq, and terrorism continued to become a more prominent threat it's become quite common at the end of the scenario building process that the double negative quadrant seems quite plausible, often, quite sadly, even the most likely.

This awareness can be discouraging if not downright depressing, but it's also highly insightful and a compelling motivator. This tells us a lot about the world and how it's changing, and about how our experiences of it have also changed. A great many of us are indeed a lot less optimistic today than we were 20 years ago, a difference of perspective that certainly reflects the acceleration of change, the heightened sense of risk, and the general sense that our institutions and society as a whole are much more vulnerable today than they have been in many decades.

This is a key point and important realization in which perception and reality are aligned. Analysis of all twelve driving forces tells us that we really are more vulnerable, and the scenario planning experiences have confirmed that in a useful way. We are indeed living in a mega risk world.

In this environment scenario planning can benefit us even more by helping us to develop a clearer sense of what's coming, which is more useful than just a general sense of dread. The value of this thinking process has shown itself time and again; people frequently leave these experiences and begin to make meaningful changes in how they lead their organizations and in choices they make personally because they've become aware of the world and its future possibilities in an entirely new way.

The Mt. Fleur Scenarios

The Pollyanna quality of the positive-positive quadrant arises in most scenario exercises, and quite often the scenario expressed in this quadrant ends up being the least provocative and the least useful to think about further. When we define a world in which we face not the worst but the best possibilities, a world in which everything seems to be great, and then we look around and see a real world that we live in is full of challenges, this scenario presents a cheery and often implausible story that seems silly.

Sometimes this gives us a good laugh, which highlights that this is a descriptive and qualitative process, one based on narrative and storytelling. In many ways this draws from a great strength of the human mind, the capacity to invent and envision stories. Indeed, archaeology tells us that long before there were alphabets and writing we had stories, vast epics transmitted orally from one generation to the next that conveyed the entire cosmology of a people and its surrounding universe, above and below, including its founding myths and historical triumphs, its greatest heroes and most profound challenges. Storytelling is as old as humanity, and we are apparently hard-wired to be enthralled with unfolding narratives. Storytelling is an important way that we discover who we are and who we may become, and this is precisely what scenarios are so good at showing to us.

Hence, while the advantage of Forrester's approach to systems modeling is that it yields insights about specific points in time that are described as states of a system, the advantage of thinking in terms of scenarios is that it generates significant depth of understanding about large social and economic *processes* that inevitably unfold over time. Successful scenarios evoke compelling narratives that help to shape the decision maker's mindset, but they do not yield the data upon which to base specific, point-in-time decisions.

This is why we're particularly interested in the forces that are significant and impactful, and especially those that are uncertain. Conversely, if we can apply methods through which we can model a complex system in way that provides answers with a high probability that we *know* what's going to happen then it's probably not a suitable topic for scenario planning at all. But when we have identified forces and characteristics that are significant, and impactful, and also highly uncertain, then the scenario process can be tremendously useful, as what we learn from these pairings can then be applied to help us understand broader patterns that are suggested or implied in the two by two matrix format.

447

Adam Kahane was a member of the scenario planning team at Shell in 1991 when the request came from leaders in South Africa to help them conduct a scenario planning process that would explore the future of the nation. He describes his arrival in South Africa this way:

> In September 1991 I flew from London to Cape Town for the project's first workshop. The workshop venue was the Mont Fleur Conference Center on a wine estate in the mountains just outside of Cape Town. The planning exercise organizer Pierre le Roux had assembled a group of twenty-two influential South Africans. He had invited leaders from all the main groups within the left-wing opposition ... and he had also daringly invited some of their longtime adversaries from the white business community and academia. The team therefore represented, unofficially, parts of both the existing establishment and the establish-to-be – a microcosm of the future South Africa. Many of them were meeting for the first time.
>
> I could see that this scenario meeting was not going to like the Shell ones I was used to. We were not working on an ordinary problem of organizational strategy but on an extraordinary national transformation. The team members had not come to the meeting because they had been told to or because it was their job, or because they or their satisfied organizations wanted to adapt as best they could to an uncertain future. They came because they were all deeply dissatisfied with the status quo and committed to changing it.[300]

As the participants began to develop their scenarios Kahane steered them away for expressing doubts and preferences in the scenarios and the outcomes that they foresaw, but rather to focus on understanding what might happen and what events would lead to what subsequent events, what would happen next. During the weekend workshop the participants produced thirty stories, which they then narrowed to nine which they then concentrated on for further refinement by subteams that developed the social, political, economic, and international dimensions following the workshop. The participants reconvened in December for a second workshop, and narrowed the set of scenarios to four, which they then took back and discussed in their own organizations in preparation for a third workshop in March 1992.

The team's final scenarios asked the question: How will the South African transition go, and will the country succeed in "taking off?" Each of the four stories gave a different answer. South Africa was in the middle of the contentious and risky transition negotiations, and nobody knew how or even whether they would succeed, or if the country would remain stuck, closed, embattled, and isolated. As a set, the scenarios provided a provocative road map for this transition. Three were dark prophecies of futures to avoid ... and one a brighter vision of a future worth working towards.[301]

The scenarios were then made public in twenty-five page booklet in the leading weekly newspaper,[302] and the participants held more than 100 workshops for various groups of constituencies that helped to engage the public in a national dialog about the future of the nation and the roles of each of the major parties and institutions in creating that future, a process of co-creation throughout South African society. As we now know from the benefit of our future vantage point there was no civil war in South Africa, but rather a peaceful transition to Mandela's presidency, and while more than two decades later South Africa still faces enormous challenges and obstacles as a society and a nation, it has so far found a way to address them peacefully rather than resorting to violence.

Kahane notes that the Mt. Fleur stories that played a part in solving an important set of national problems were really quite simple, even simplistic, and thus the essence of the Mt. Fleur process was that a small group of deeply committed leaders, representing a cross-section of a society that the whole world had considered irretrievably stuck sat down together to talk broadly and profoundly about what was going on and what should be done. More than that, they had not talked about what other people – some faceless authorities or decision makers – should do to advance parochial agendas, but what they and their colleagues and their fellow citizens had to do in order to create a better future for everybody. They saw themselves as part of – not apart from – the problem they were trying to solve, and the scenarios were a novel means to engage them in this problem-solving end.[303]

As the Mt. Fleur experience shows, the scenario planning process has much to offer when our focus is not on technological and economic forces, but on national and political ones.   Next we will consider the very important relationship between the US and China, and examine what might happen under four different combinations that describe the future successes and failures of both nations

Scenario Set 3:
Frenemies: Dragon and Eagle

What will China's relationship with the USA become by 2030 or 2040? Two alternative possibilities for China's stance are that the Chinese pursue policies of partnership and accommodation with the other nations of the world, or conversely that China takes a much more aggressive and nationalistic attitude that leaves it isolated and proudly defensive. The US, meanwhile, faces the possibility of a continuing partisan divide that fractures the nation into a dysfunctional wreck, or that it finds sufficient cohesion to sustain its preeminence and global superpower status.

Scenario 1: "Dragon vs. Eagle" – Dragon Defiant and Still the Boss
Scenario 2: "Frenemies" – Dragon Trader and Still the Boss
Scenario 3: "Soaring Dragon" – Dragon Trader and Clipped Wings
Scenario 4: "Dragon in Charge" – Dragon Defiant and Clipped Wings.

Scenario 1: "Dragon vs. Eagle"

This scenario examines what would happen if an aggressive and nationalist Chinese government did not hesitate to alienate its neighbors in the pursuit of local and regional hegemony, but a strong and determined America resists Chinese aggression. Hence, this is the story of a renewed Cold War rivalry, with the significant twist that the rivals are economically interdependent.

Figure 103
Frenemies: Dragon and Eagle

How would the other nations of the world respond to Chinese aggression against Taiwan, or example, or an attempt to "colonize" the Spratly Islands? We have three recent experiences that provide clues. When Russia invaded Crimea and Ukraine cried out for help, very little military help was offered because neither the US nor NATO wished to engage in a full scale war with Russia. The response was economic rather than military, through imposition of sanctions on the Russian state and on individual Russians who were rich, influential, and part of Putin's inner circle. Russian military aggression, in other words, was met with an economic response that did indeed create economic hardship for the Russian people, but it's not clear if the specifically targeted inner circle were actually impacted much. A cynic might suggest that Putin has reimbursed to his buddies the costs they incurred from Russian state funds, bit as Russia is an entirely closed society, who knows?

A similar example of economic means used to address a geopolitical challenge were the economic sanctions placed on Iran to discourage it from developing of nuclear weapons. These sanctions took a significant toll on Iran's economy and led eventually to so much popular discontent that the government acceded in Western demands and dismantled its weapons development program in exchange for normalized trade.

These examples remind us is that in the modern world economic power is the root of military power, and thus in the globally-connected, one-world economy, nations that are excluded from full participation inevitably suffer. And in this scenario, since the premise is that China remains ascendant then we must assume that its economy retains the capacity to support and extensive military and to fund acts of aggression. We can readily foresee that an aggressive China that was no longer so dependent on exports would find the world uniting in opposition to its aggression through economic rather than military means, but that sanctions would have little effect.

If Chinese aggression included an invasion of Taiwan, which indeed the Chinese have never recognized as an independent nation, the challenge to the US leadership would be direct. Taiwan is a US ally and dependent, which would put the US in the position of choosing between acquiescence and the willingness to engage in an all-out war. Would Washington, and the American people, have the stomach for a war all the way across the Pacific to defend an island one-tenth the size of California?

In a highly challenging situation between the two nations, what would happen if the social and political polarization within the US resulted in the election of a nationalistic and xenophobic American government while at the same time the leaders of China chose to also adopt a more nationalistic and even militaristic ambitions in the South China region? Suppose, for example, that the Chinese attempted to take control of Taiwan while the sitting US president was a right wing nationalist who had the support of a nationalist Congress. Is this the formula for not only a Cold War between the two global superpowers, but a hot one, with Taiwan as the unfortunate mouse caught between the two elephants?

If rational analysis had any part in the decision then America would be looking at an equation with massive down side risk and very little upside benefit, the very definition of a bad investment and a pro-fragile situation. There are few credible scenarios in which America undertakes the massive risks unless its political leadership is incapable of assessing the risks. That this happened as recently as 2003 makes it is not entirely implausible. But in a much more likely outcome, America's cost would become hurt pride and lost deterrence, but not in blood and dollars.

However, in the event that the Chinese were successful in executing their aggressive expansion, perhaps the world's non-response would encourage Putin to advance through Ukraine, which would put equivalent pressure on the EU. Would the EU send troops to protect Kiev?

Scenario 2: "Frenemies"

In the world defined by a Chinese nation focused on economic development and an America that continues to grow and develop its economy through astute investment and sound economic policies, there would certainly be winning and losing companies in both nations but the economic competition would also serve as effective stimulus that would most likely lead to an even faster rate of technological development and widespread economic gains for both nations.

It could well be that the future relationship between China and the US would be described by the term *frenemy*, which signifies that the other is both friend and enemy at once. It's a word in contemporary business jargon, as, for example, when Samsung makes Android mobile phones but also provides computer chips that are essential to its arch-rival, Apple's iPhone.[304] In just the same way, China and US would be engaged in a very pointed competition in global markets while they would also remain quite dependent on one another for their economic health and sustained well being.

And in this scenario, trade between China and the US would continue to be of fundamental importance to both nations and would remain one of the most significant trading rivalries and partnerships in the world.

Scenario 3: "Soaring Dragon"

In this scenario the Chinese shift their focus to economic development and comfortably settle within current boarders and do not mount significant territorial challenges toward their neighbors. In this situation we posit that China's economy continues to grow at a very rapid pace as hundreds of millions of its citizens join the national production system, developing a robust domestic economy while retaining a significant portion of the world's export market. In the US, meanwhile domestic squabbling prevents the nation from making the necessary investments in infrastructure, education, and technology to support a 21st century economy, and gradually America slips further backward.

Here we would see China's economy quite quickly surpass America's and perhaps the EU as well, and as Chinese technologies become more advanced its exports would become still more competitive with the best European and American goods, thus lifting its economic potential still higher. Perhaps Chinese investments in computer chips, robots, and space technologies move it to the forefront, and it becomes the world's preferred supplier of premium technology goods.

Scenario 4: "Dragon In Charge"

This scenario describes what might happen if China were to continue to assert its national identity and pursue its regional ambitions while at the same time American political gridlock undermined America's power and diluted its impact on the global stage.

Should China take an aggressive and rigid stance toward its neighbors by choosing a path of nationalistic aggression it would lead to a decline in trade and the formation of a coalition of nations that stand in opposition. Taiwan, Korea, Japan, and the Philippines align in economic development and military preparedness, but the decline of America's capacities means that Chinese aggression is met not by a counterforce, but by international protest, mostly ineffectual. Left undefended, Taiwan finally succumbs, abandons its aspirations of independence, and joins Hong Kong as a special economic zone under the control of Beijing. Shock waves roll through Washington DC, but the US is powerless to stop the dragon.

The continuing strength in China's domestic manufacturing sector is accompanied by a vibrant rate of domestic consumption that enables the Chinese economy to mimic and then surpass the American, where domestic consumption is the main driver of economic vitality and the need for exports is not a defining factor. On an upward spiral, China pays less and less heed to the concerns of other nations and builds around itself an alliance of nations dependent on its economic development assistance.

Even the significant climatic problems resulting from extensive coal burning do not deter the Chinese from continuing to exploit its reserves, regardless of the consequences for itself and for the rest of the world. But the consequences do indeed impact China, with its 2500 miles of Pacific coastline and low-lying cities such as Shanghai suffering due to rising oceans and increasing storms. Major urbanization continues on higher ground, which turns out to be effective capital investments that feed its growing economic strength.

Americans watch in sadness as their internal divisions demote the nation to second rank, and China ascends as the world's only superpower.

Implications

These four scenarios imply that while China's territorial claims to Taiwan and the South China Sea constitute a basic issue that will fundamentally influence on the future, the US would have a great deal to lose and almost nothing to gain if it intended to meet Chinese military aggression in the South China Sea with force. For the US it's a non-winnable war.

This suggests that maintenance of the status quo will depend on two factors. First is the Chinese leadership's basic posture regarding nationalism and its historical dominance of the region. If the leaders are determined to retain absolute control over the largest possible extent of territory in the eastern oceans regardless of the consequences then it will prevail in that, but it will incur significant costs in its relationships with its neighbors. If, on the other hand, the Chinese leaders consider that its economic partnership with the US in particular and with its other major global trading partners are more important to its long term health as a nation then they will likely be content to sustain the present, low-level provocations and declarations without resorting to more drastic military actions.

The deciding factor could well be the attitude of the massive Chinese population not with regard to those issues specifically, but concerning the leadership of the Communist Party itself. If discontent continues to increase, if there are progressively more protests over issues such as corruption, pollution, and land use, or if the pro-democracy movement in Hong Kong crosses the border into the southern Chinese provinces, then the central government may feel compelled to introduce, or reintroduce, foreign rivalry and the (nonexistent) threat of disrespect or aggression in order to distract the people from their discontent and align the nation around nationalistic concerns.

This is, of course, the method of retaining control that has been adopted by every demagogue throughout history, inciting xenophobic fears and claiming inexcusable insults, pointing to the evils lurking without and promising a return to righteousness. This is also, in fact, the pathway that the anti-revolutionaries have taken in the past and will take in the future. When it works it enables them to ignore domestic unrest and focus on mostly imagined externalities. Will it work with a progressively more highly educated Chinese population that is beginning to experience the benefits of growing GDP and more materials comforts?

China and the US are the world's two economic and military superpowers, and the condition of their two economies largely determines the overall health of the global economy. A recession in either country has immediate impact in the other, and just about everywhere else as well. Their relations also have enormous impact on the tone of geopolitical relations, and it could well be that the relationship between the US and China is the most influential political relationship among all nations.

However, as Dr. Kissinger points out, the cultural and political backgrounds of the two sides are considerably different.

The American approach to policy is pragmatic; China's is conceptual. American has never had a powerful threatening neighbor; China has never been without a powerful adversary on its borders. Americans hold that every problem has a solution; Chinese think that each solution is an admission ticket to a new set of problems. Americans seek an outcome responding to immediate circumstances; Chinese concentrate of evolutionary change. ... Two great societies of different cultures and different premises are both undergoing fundamental domestic adjustments; whether this translates into rivalry or into a new form of partnership will importantly shape prospects for twenty-first century world order.[305]

When the two countries are getting along well the world feels like a safer and happier place, and the flow of goods and capital between them further facilitates growth and development. But when they are in conflict global commodity traders become uneasy and global financiers immediately grow cautious.

Yet they are of course economically interdependent, with China being the single largest holder of US government debt securities, and the US being the single largest customer for Chinese manufactures. Hence, we can ask in summary whether China and the US will cooperate to forge an enduring economic and geopolitical partnerships, or will their differing needs and ambitions drive them into greater conflict?

Formalized Scenario Planning

Scenario planning exercises are a compelling way to introduce people to important issues and to help them understand that narrow strategic choices can lead to disastrous outcomes. This is perhaps one of the most powerful lessons from Mt. Fleur.

In South Africa the four workshops of one or two days each were held over twelve months, complemented with a lot of additional ad-hoc work by the participants between workshops contributed brilliant and surprising outcomes that have benefited all of South African society, and indeed all of Africa, for a war in the south would have inevitably spread northward.

Effective workshops can be as short as a half day when the primary purposes are learning by exposing people to key issues and uncertainties related to their futures. But when the intent is to include scenarios in a formal planning activity then the depth of preparation and the scope of the effort are much more substantive.

For formal projects, the process of developing scenarios often begins with the formation of a fundamental or organizing question. Kahane mentioned that the key question at Mt. Fleur was, How will the South African transition go, and will the country succeed in "taking off?" Projects can also focus on understanding the future of an industry – the oil industry being an obvious one, since the method was developed at Shell and is now used extensively by all of the world's major oil companies and many of its smaller ones to try to make sense of the volatile and unpredictable market.[306]

Shell maintains an active scenario planning team and among its alumni are a large number of globally-recognized thinkers and consultants, including Peter Schwartz, who is famous for writing a definitive book about scenario planning, *The Art of the Long View*,[307] Adam Kahane, Pierre Wack who created the Shell team in the 1960s, Arie de Geus whose book *The Living Company*[308] has been very influential, and author Joseph Jaworski.

In 1971 when the Shell team was established Wack had already come to a few important insights. "First, change in the Arab world was about to destroy the stability of the existing oil regime, which oil companies had dominated (and drawn a profit stream from) for 25 years. Second, everybody in the oil industry knew it, but nobody was prepared to do anything." Events unfolded this way:

> During 1972 and early 1973, the message percolated through the global Shell organization: The oil price could soar from its current $2 per barrel to an unimaginable price of as much as $10 per barrel. Despite resistance from some Shell managers, the organization began to put in place many of the commonsense, mundane frugalities that had been lost amid the frenetic growth of the 1950s and 1960s. This put Shell in an enviable position when the crisis did occur, and an even more enviable position during the Iranian revolution of 1979, when the oil price soared a second time, up to $37 per barrel. As the

shock from that shift subsided, the industry entered a bubble. Through the early 1980s, oil traders assumed the price would keep rising; they kept bidding for oil futures and driving the price higher. In the early 1980s Shell's planners offered a counterintuitive message: They said the bubble would collapse. The forces holding OPEC together would fragment, energy demand would finally slow down, and the industry would have to retrench. Oil was about to become a commodity product, and this was a shocking notion to many executives because it meant that 'a trader in Rotterdam would have more to say about the price of oil than the managing directors.'[309]

Over the years, the Shell scenario planning team has continued to be provocative within the Shell organization, and it's also been very generous with its expertise by publishing widely and regularly on the ongoing findings from its scenario planning efforts. Their work is consistently insightful, and makes for very useful reading for anyone interested in the future and in scenarios; its web page is always worth a look, and you may find yourself spending a few hours there.[310]

Scenario planning has also proven effective in government and military planning. The US Coast Guard has conducted highly detailed and highly regarded scenario planning efforts since the 1990s. Through it's Evergreen program, recognized throughout the US Federal Government as a valuable source of insights that has helped Coast Guard leaders to understand how investment choices made in any current fiscal year will impact on the capabilities of the Coast Guard twenty to thirty years in the future.[311]

The Mindset of the Thought Experiment

Obviously there are inherent limitations in defining future worlds that have been shaped by considering only two driving forces, and as Kahane mentioned, the scenarios that turned out to be so influential in South Africa were simple narratives. These cannot be definitive models of the future, but must be understood to serve as thought stimulators and insight provocateurs. Studying them requires us to suspend disbelief while adopting a willingness to consider many possibilities, including a quite a few that will be, at minimum, implausible. But as we develop them further we begin to see an underlying logic, and as the Mt. Fleur experience also shows, even simple stories and future projections can become quite predictive and highly influential if they frame the issues in a way that resonates with the readers, and if they enable people to see options, threats, and possibilities in a new way.

That's exactly what happened in South Africa, as the process forced leaders from each segment of society to confront the likelihood that remaining rigidly attached to specific policy positions could have catastrophic impacts. For example, one of the final four scenarios examined what would happen if the minority white government refused to acknowledge the immanence of change, and stuck its head in the sand; the scenario was called Ostrich. Here, the forces demanding change would eventually boil over, causing havoc. Another of the final ones explored what would happen if a Mandela-led black government came to power and immediately began shifting wealth and income to blacks through nationalizations and outright wealth transfers. The scenario foresaw that there would indeed be a short term boom and a release of built-up anger in the black community, but that this would cripple the South African economy quite quickly and leads to worse outcomes for everyone.

These were not predictions, but possibilities built upon the logic of agreed-upon driving forces. Hence, it's important to emphasize again that the purpose is *not* to predict the future, but to explore and model the possibilities that *might* emerge, rather than attempting to identify the singular reality that *will* emerge, and also to move to a deeper appreciation that the future isn't predictable at all. And as we examine these models the goal is definitely not to choose which seems more plausible but rather to broaden our thinking and to consider how things *might* unfold, rather than narrowing our thinking to only what we think *will* occur, or worse, what we *want* to happen. Because when we predict what we prefer we're almost always engaged in wishful thinking, which brings nothing but danger and compromised results to any planning process.

Next we'll consider a set of scenarios that might emerge when we explore what might happen in the Middle East in conjunction with the global Cultural Revolution.

Scenario Set 4:
Coming to Grips with Violence

Scenario 1: "The 10,000 Mile Fence" – Delightenment and Firestorm

Scenario 2: "The Pleasant Surprise" – Delightenment and Neighborly

Scenario 3: "The Mess You Left Behind" – Descent to Dystopia and Neighborly

Scenario 4: "Drowning Together" – Descent to Dystopia and Firestorm.

Figure 104
Coming to Grips with Violence

Scenario 1: "The 10,000 Mile Fence"

If we hypothesize that the situation in the Middle East will continue its descent into violence and eventually engulf the entire region in conflict, but that the rest of the world comes reasonably well to grips with the acceleration of change and the disruptions that this will necessarily impose on modern life and the changes this will require socially, politically, and economically, then we have a world of extremes in which roughly the 750 million people living between Pakistan and Libya become engulfed in unending violence, and the rest of the world watches in horror.

The Mideast region would be producing three major exports. First, refugees would be streaming from the region in impossibly huge numbers, dwarfing the 2015-2016 exodus from Syria. Second, oil would be coming from the region in huge volumes, providing much of the capital that was then employed in funding the warfare. And third major export would be terrorism.

If this scenario were to unfold, how would the rest of the world react? If it became clear that oil revenues were indeed funding the bloodbath, then this could actually create further incentives to reduce or eliminate fossil fuels form the economy, which might provide a significant boost for solar and wind energy industries.

The world would also wish to build a fence around the Middle East, as impossible as that would be to achieve in reality. A significant military presence would be inevitable across the Mediterranean and in the Indian Ocean, and the screening of refugees would be tedious and painstaking. But what would the rest of the world do to support or protect those who were trapped in the war zone with no ideological stake in the fight, simply hoping to survive and start over somewhere else? Would millions be resettled elsewhere, or would then be trapped in squalid and impoverished camps for years or decades?

Scenario 2: "The Pleasant Surprise"

Here the underlying assumptions are that most of the world adapts to a new high-tech economy, and the violence across the Middle East gradually slows as extremists either lose interest in the cycle of violence, or they gradually decline in number from their own successes, much like the self-induced attrition of a gang war. In either case, this could lead to the best of all worlds.

Scenario 3: "The Mess You Left Behind"

If, on the other hand, it is the rest of the world that remains unsettled, but the Middle East region gradually calms itself, then it would be an island of relative peace surrounded by oceans and continents of despair. It would be like arriving to the very best party of the year, only to find out that you had the wrong day; everyone left yesterday, and all that's for you is the huge mess that they left behind.

Scenario 4: "Drowning Together"

If the world descends into a nationalistic and isolationist pattern while the violence escalates across the Middle East then we see a world that obviously isn't very good for anyone. Perhaps the super-rich would be able to insulate themselves in protected enclaves and the private security industry would become one of the few to boom in what will otherwise be a depressed economic situation. George Orwell or Aldus Huxley would have proven to be not fiction authors but visionaries whose warnings fell unheeded, and history would have shown that every disgruntled pundit, every promoter of doom and gloom, and every preacher warning of the decline of civilization was right. We didn't abide the warnings and our children and grandchildren paid the price.

A key aspect of scenario 1 was the idea that among the Middle East's three major exports would be violence, and thus another part of the price, a more expensive part, would be the likelihood that violence exported from the Middle Eastern would contribute to and indeed accelerate the decline of the rest of the world. There's nothing fictitious about this idea; it is both an explicit strategy of those who are currently promoting violence within the Mideast region, and a constant dread in those locations where they have succeeded.

This would be a global society gripped by fear of humanity's vengeful anger, a society characterized by widespread anxiety. The combined economic impact would cause a radical reorientation of government spending in nearly every nation, and the cost of security would skyrocket.

Middle Eastern immigrants would be ostracized in many communities, feared and perhaps repressed simply for the fact of where they were born.

Implications

The second, third, and fourth of these scenarios aren't particularly compelling, but the first one is quite provocative and gives a good sense of challenges we may well be facing in the coming years. Of course the idea of the 10,000 mile long fence isn't an original one; Donald Trump has proposed building one across the 2,000 miles (3,100 kilometers) of the US border with Mexico, and when that's done perhaps he'll want to start building one across the much longer border between the US and Canada. Of course those fences have the opposite intent, to keep people out, whereas a fence around the Middle East would be designed to keep people in.

And while all the fence building would cost countless billions of dollars, it probably wouldn't work very well if at all. Many of those desperate to get in, or to get out, would find a way, although many would also die trying.

The scenario also raise the question as to how it is that the anger and alienation that leads people to embrace apocalyptic prophesies can be channeled in other, more positive directions. The social and psychological dimensions of fundamentalism and terrorism are essential elements of the current situation, and only when we understand how these sensibilities emerge and grow will have a real grasp on the dynamics of the Middle East or how they may be steered elsewhere.

From Stories to Strategies and Imperatives

So where does all of this "what if" leave us? What conclusions can we draw now that we have considered in some detail four full sets of scenarios, sixteen story vignettes in all, consisting of provocative pairings of the eight of the twelve driving forces?

The intent was to bring us to a much deeper understanding of the future and how it may unfold. As I mentioned, one of the most significant benefits that comes from engaging in these thought experiments is that they help us to avoid fixating on a single future as we come instead to appreciate much more deeply how uncertain the future really is, and how a little tug here or a shove there can literally shape reality in one way or toward something quite different entirely. For this is one of the most significant traps that leaders fall into, the trap of assuming that one given and preferred future will emerge. So often they are wrong, and their organizations suffer due to the misguided strategies that had been based on narrow and preferential view of the future.

Reality is often much more complicated. Along with the understanding of uncertainty, looking at these pairs of uncertainties also helps us gain an appreciation for the world's increasing complexity and the breadth of possibilities, positive and negative, that lie before us.

They also help us to understand our preferences and our choices. Adam Kahane comments, "Nearly every group I have worked with has articulated one scenario in which vested interests replay the status quo over and over, in a downward spiral, an another scenario in which a broad, dialogic coalition creates a better reality for all. Everywhere people are struggling to develop a more open and participative way of addressing the immense challenges we face."[312]

As planners, then, what would we do with these insights? The next step in the thinking process is to transition from scenarios to strategies, as the former are intended to inform the latter. In a formal scenario planning project we therefore continue by identifying the best strategic options that each of the four worlds reveals in each of our scenario matrices. It's likely, for example, that the most preferable strategies for an organization in a booming economy are the wrong ones in a deep bust. Or to take a more specific example, the appropriate actions for an oil company will depend on what actually occurs with climate change, and if climate change is eventually linked indisputably to CO_2 emissions, and thus how fast regulations limiting fossil fuels are introduced. It will also depend on how fast scalable alternative energy systems are developed. Scenario planning is quite competent to model all of these variables and to create from the models useful narratives from which worthwhile strategic options can be formulated.

Hence, if we can identify a strategy or a set of strategies that is valid in multiple quadrants and in the scenarios that result when we combine multiple different pairs of driving forces then it is very likely preferable to a strategy that benefits us only in one more narrow set of future conditions. Such a strategy is much more likely to make sense for an organization to pursue when it defines a fruitful and productive path forward in multiple different sets of future conditions.

The other major next step would be to identify the imperatives, the things that our organization must address and accomplish no matter what happens. Frequently the mind-broadening thinking process of scenario building brings forth some of these imperatives not because they relate specifically to any of the scenarios, but because we see things about ourselves or about the external world that are essential for us to address. We'll discuss some of these imperatives in Chapter 16.

Overall, then, while any given set of scenarios is based only on two driving forces, the resulting insights can be quite deep and highly influential. And, to repeat, we are pursuing two complementary goals. First, using this approach to create foresight is usually a great learning experience, as we discover the value of thinking not in terms of predictions (which almost never come true), but rather of considering possibilities which thus inform our own thinking and help us to better prepare for tomorrow's twists and turns. We're often better prepared also to let go of old assumptions when new evidence emerges that show that how trends are unfolding, or how the overall direction is changing.

With all that in mind, let's move on now and consider another variation on the scenario planning approach, but this time tackling much more complex models of the future world.

•••

Chapter 13

The

Planner:

What If + What If?

In preparing for battle, I have always found that plans are useless but planning is indispensable.[313]

Dwight Eisenhower

There's a story that's often told about the first day of medical school. The Dean is addressing the incoming class, and about half way through the typical welcoming speech she deviates a bit from the expected script. "Half of what you're about to learn," she tells them in a deeply serious tone, "is incorrect." The bright-eyed future doctors are more than a bit surprised to hear this revelation. After all, they're about to invest four years and uncounted tens of thousands of dollars to obtain the very best education in medicine, one that will allow them to add the coveted "MD" to their name cards, and set them up for a lifetime of service to sustaining the health of others and earning healthy incomes for themselves. The Dean continues. "The problem," she admits, " is that we don't know which half is which."

It's because of the constant advances in medical science that about half of the facts they're about to memorize will be transformed into non-facts, urban legends as it were, and actually it's the same in all of the sciences. The pace at which knowledge is advancing is so fast that it is in and of itself driving a transformative process for society.

This is true regardless of the particular field you wish to inquire about. Medicine, as in the story here, of course.   And physics, certainly. Chemistry, photonics, astronomy, geology, oceanography, climate science, aerospace, nanotechnology, biotechnology, proteomics, along with other fields we've already mentioned, including of course robotics and digital computing in general, solar and wind energy, batteries, transportation, etc. etc. etc.

Acceleration

There are four major factors that have conspired to achieve this overwhelming acceleration.

The first two are (1) global competition that has led to (2) the profusion of scientists. As we move into an era in which economic success is a function of knowledge and the ability to create and manage it, which certainly describes the 21st century, the leaders of every nation have readily grasped that proficiency in the sciences and technical fields is essential to national competitiveness, and so they have prudently invested in providing advanced educational to their brightest young people.

With the discovery of fission, physicists became, almost overnight, the most important military resource a nation-state could call upon.[314]

Consequently, there are simply more scientists working today than there have ever been in history of humanity. And the impact they have is much greater also, because (3) science is a collaborative endeavor as well as an additive one. The culture of science inherently values publication, and publication enables rapid transfer of knowledge. An experiment can be readily replicated and improved upon very quickly.

Scientific journals have proliferated in our lifetimes, and now no one knows how many there are; it's a big number, because there's so much science being done, so much new knowledge being created and discovered. Scientists have hundreds of conferences to choose from, where they can learn the latest from their colleagues, and all of this together speeds up the whole enterprise.

The fourth accelerator is digital enablement. The supercomputer that you carry in your pocket, whether it's an iPhone or an Android or any other smart phone model, is an exceptionally powerful computing device, and the one on your desktop is even more powerful. Both can do more for you than nearly any device that was available to any scientist fifty years ago, or even thirty years ago, or ten. With their now much-better tools, scientists are doing much more precise work. And with more powerful computing devices they are building much more sophisticated models of the extraordinarily complex phenomena that they are studying. At the micro scale, science is now manipulating individual atoms in the field of nanotechnology; at the macro scale, science is modeling systems as complex as the Earth's climate, the Big Bang and now gravity waves, and everything in between.

Together, these four, competition, the number of scientists, knowledge sharing, and computing, are driving a process of continual knowledge transformation that is having a profound and ongoing impact on society and the economy. And the only plausible scenario in which this does not continue is a complete social and economic collapse, the type that could only be caused by a nuclear cataclysm, a major asteroid strike, an unstoppable pandemic, or some sort of comparable civilization-threatening event.

But that does not mean that much of anything is certain. Quite to the contrary, while we can foresee massive progress in countless fields, it's quite difficult to anticipate specifically what those breakthroughs will be. A major breakthrough in any one of dozens of fields could have a transformative impact on all of society. So, in this environment of uncertainty, how do we effectively plan?

Plans and Planning

During the early years of the 20th century when warfare was undergoing a significant transformation due to the emergence of industrialized weapons and railroads with the capacity to move huge numbers of troops very quickly, all of the military planners in all of the various European countries realized that their capacity to quickly mobilize a massive army might be the most essential factor that would determine victory or defeat. For if an opponent could assemble an army of 100,000 or 200,000 or even a million soldiers before they could then the opponent would overwhelm the nation that had not sufficiently mobilized in time. A decisive war could be over in a matter of days, before the defender could even get his army into the field.

And so, when it became clear to the European monarchs and to their senior military leaders that the assassination of Franz Ferdinand was beginning to cascade into military conflicts and that they would soon be called upon to honor their commitments to mutual defense, they felt great urgency about initiating this very mobilization under the great fear that the others would do so more quickly and crush them.

In Germany the mobilization effort was known as the Schlieffen plan, for the German general who had conceived it; in France it was Plan 17. Both sides had anticipated that their plans would lead to quick victories; the Germans had planned on dinner along the Seine, while the French in Berlin alongside the Spree. Both plans failed, of course, as they had overestimated their own capacities and underestimated those of the opponent, leaving the bloody stalemate of trench warfare that continued for four brutal years after the trenches were first dug. Barbara Tuchman tells us,

> Failure of Plan 17 was as fatal as the failure of the Schlieffen plan, and together they produced the deadlock on the Western Front.

Sucking up lives at a rate of 5,000 and sometimes 50,000 a day, absorbing munitions, energy, money, brains, and trained men, the Western Front ate up Allied war resources and predetermined the failure of back-door efforts like that of the Dardanelles which might otherwise have shortened the war. The deadlock, fixed by the failures of the first month, determined the future course of the war and, as a result, the terms of the peace, the shape of the interwar period, and the conditions of the Second Round.[315]

The Second Round was fueled, of course, by German outrage at the repressive terms of the Versailles Treaty, which Hitler used as his lever to gain control of the nation still decimated by the shock of losing the Great War, and by the continent-wide financial collapse that we know as the Great Depression. By the time, in 1944, that the Allies were about to launch their massive attack across the English Channel to begin pushing Hitler's armies back into Germany and toward the Spree, their commanding general Dwight Eisenhower commented that, "In preparing for battle, I have always found that plans are useless but planning is indispensable."[316] This is the paradox that all planners face, that followed rigidly their plans will prove worthless, or worse, disastrous, but that the failure to plan will also lead to the same outcome.

Sound and effective plans thus requires that we balance realism with ambition; prudence with boldness; and perseverance with flexibility. These are contradictory requirements, and this partly explains why great planners are rare indeed.

And it turns out that great planning, like many other attributes that define greatness in a tremendous variety of fields, begins with not with training in planning per se, but in a more general mindset about what is real, and how the world is, what it means to think clearly.

If you understand something in only one way, then you don't really understand it at all. This is because, if something goes wrong, you get stuck with a thought that just sits in your mind with nowhere to go. The secret of what anything means to us depends on how we've connected it to all the other things we know. This is why, when someone leans "by rote," we say that they don't really understand. However, if you have several different representations then, when one approach fails you can try another.   Well-connected representations let you turn ideas around in your mind, to envision things from many perspectives until you find one that works for you. And that's what we mean by thinking.[317]

It's certain that approaching the challenges of our astonishing century by rote will lead directly to the worst possible outcomes. Cleverness, an understanding of the essential interconnections, and the willingness to explore broadly and even against a given set of preferences or proclivities can all contribute significantly to achieving outcomes that are far better. As the Mt. Fleur process showed, we can and do sometimes make all the right choices, and that happens most likely to happen when we've engaged in what Marvin Minsky defined above for us as "thinking."

Best of the Best

Plans are not always focused on the bad outcomes. What might we plan for that could transform society in a beneficial way? For example, an order of magnitude breakthrough in solar energy collection systems, storage batteries, or long distance electricity transport would certainly change the structure of the economy and would likely bring massive benefits, and so would a major breakthrough in fusion energy.

Major advances in genetics might alter how we think about human reproduction, or shift our expectations about how long we can expect to live and what we could accomplish in a single lifetime. Perhaps they will transform how we treat major diseases such as cancer and heart disease, or make obesity and diabetes entirely obsolete.

As a result of a century's advances in medical science and nutrition, the average human life expectancy has already increased by 167 percent, from 49 to 82 years, since only 1900. As a result of future advances, will life expectancies continue to increase? Who will be the first to live to age 150? To 200?

Genetics and biotechnology coupled with powerful digital tools have transformed the way we think about health and disease, and they've pioneered new approaches to analysis and diagnosis, medicines, medical devices, and treatments. Ongoing scientific efforts in these and the many related fields may result in fundamental scientific insights that become important medicines and treatments for a wide range of maladies, from Alzheimer's to cancer to heart disease, and even to the fundamental process of aging. Thus, it's quite possible that the Millennial Generation, those born after 1990, are going to be the first that will achieve average life spans of more than 100 years.

Perhaps they'll be the generation in which carbon-based biology and silicon-based technology fuse to create human-post-human technology hybrids. Already the graduate surgeons are implanting thousands of artificial joints in humans each year; when will those joints be digitally-enabled, smart-joints? When will thought-enhancing analytical-rational-creativity boosters be included in your daily vitamins, or in the SD cards that you slide into the slot just below your occipital bone?

The advances are likely to be highly disruptive in the life sciences because of their capacity to alter human anatomy, physiology, health care, and aging through biotechnology, and the specific fields including genetics and proteomics. Disease diagnostics and treatments will improve enormously, replacement organs would become commonplace, and perhaps aging could be significantly slowed or in the most extreme scenarios, reversed. Further, through the integration of digital technology with prosthetics science will create artificial limbs and organs, exoskeletons, and perhaps even flying backpacks. If robots achieve the advances that they well might, as noted just above, then there is also every reason to expect that the initial successes with digital prosthetics will continue to dramatically improve, and human and digital intelligences will blend to become human/machine hybrids that provide the best of both, human inference, intuition and pattern recognition with digital analysis and augmented effectors. This would mean, for example, controlling a ship or an aircraft with your mind, rather than with levers and knobs.

The prospects are enticing, and the consequences will be monumental if possible and imaginable breakthroughs become realities. Social, cultural, and economic structures will all be fundamentally altered, and as with robotics, there will be an infinity of legal issues and questions to address. In effect, technological advances will provide full employment for generations of lawyers and judges who will have to create from scratch entire legal regimes, standards, and protocols.

Science will cure many diseases, and dare we ask for a cure for stupidity as well?

All of these advances are possible, and some are even quite likely to come about. There is a caveat, though, a necessary condition for such progress to be attained. It could happen as long as we sustain a generally peaceful society and maintain a functioning economy, in which it is clear to all (or most) that advantages that accrue to everyone make it much better to participate rather than to try to blow it all up. This perception, of course, requires that everyone feels somehow included in the shared success; when society is fractured, as it is today, into the winners and losers, then it's a short step for the losers to become deeply alienated. This was precisely the overwhelming sense of injustice that Mohamed Bouazizi felt, the sense of powerlessness and hopelessness that sent him into such despair that he set himself on fire as a very public act of protest. It is also, perhaps, the same intense feeling that leads someone to become a suicide terrorist and enables that person to self-justify the murder of tens or hundreds or thousands.

And perhaps to a lesser degree of emotion and fury, it is also what motivates tens and hundreds of thousands of people to join the protests against the fundamental injustices of governments in Tunisia and Egypt and Hong Kong.

Hence, it's clear that if the benefits are not shared generally, if it seems that rank injustices are being perpetrated, if a dominant class emerges that selfishly bends the rules of the system to which others must adhere then this sets the stage of the collapse of a system that now requires some degree of consent by nearly everyone ... because nearly everyone can gain access to large scale weapons.

And this is a fundamental change that marks our era, the democratization of large scale violence. As the recent histories of Paris and Sandy Hook and Aurora show with painful vividness, anyone can buy an AK47 and engage in a mass killing; as the 9/11 events showed, a small team can hijack a plane with the aid of a few knives and terrorize a nation, or two malcontents can pack rice cookers with explosives and transform the cultural celebration that is the Boston Marathon into a scene of carnage and despair.

These are issues and themes that describe humanity and civilization not in terms of technologies or robots, not in terms of fossil or non-fossil energy, not as a matter of the climate or geography, but in the terms of values and aspirations, which lie at the very core of human culture. To understand these forces and their interactions more deeply, here we will explore a set of scenarios with not two driving forces, but four: Russia + the EU + the Anti-Revolution + Urbanization.

Scenario Set 5:
Crafting the Future of Our Culture

By expanding our set of variables to four we can no longer stick with the 2x2 matrix format, so instead we'll explore what might happen when we combine four positives outcomes together, and when we combine four negatives.

Scenario 1: "Success by Design" – Urbantopia and Open Debate and
           Bear in Business and Ascendant
Scenario 2: "Bad to Worse" – Elderpocalypse and Fighting Back and
           Bellicose Bear and See 'Ya Later

Scenario 1: "Success by Design"

It's not as implausible as you might think at first glance to suppose that all four positives could actually occur. Getting there may require some luck, for sure, but suspend disbelief for a moment to imagine what that world might be like. The Urbantopia alternative suggests that national and regional leaders may actually come to understand the importance of their cities for both economic vitality and social stability, and thus they gradually learn to invest in good urban designs that promote social balance, healthy lifestyles, and sustainable economic principles. This has the additional benefit of enabling broader economic opportunities, which gives positive outlets to those who aspire to improve their own and their families' lives. When it's possible to make progress and society has hope then support for violent dissent diminishes, suggesting that the Open Debate alternative could in fact emerge.

It's also quite conceivable that urbanization is key to the future success of the EU, for the vitality and economic success of its cities may enable the Union to overcome differing views on its internal policies and politics. Conversely, a continent of marginal and failed cities would almost certainly end the EU experiment. And the outcomes that occur in Russia will be largely depend on the status of the EU. Bullies don't pick fights with strength, and Putin, or whoever follows him in power in Russia, will be much less willing to challenge a vibrant and thriving EU, but they may be more than willing to bully and intimidate a weak one.

In Chapter 8 I discussed the concept of counter-intuitive outcomes, and I mentioned that Jay Forrester showed how bad social outcomes often come about when the underlying systems that policy makers address are so deeply interconnected in ways that are not evident that they blunder into policy mistakes even when guided by good intentions.[318] Here we see that the opposite can also occur, investments in sound policy and in exemplary urban designs can lead to social and economic outcomes that may have seemed entirely unrelated, but which were in fact almost direct consequences. There is, in fact, a large and rapidly growing body of evidence which shows convincingly how good and great cities become economic stalwarts that attract talent and enable innovation, while poorly designed cities stifle economic opportunity and diffuse capital into impactless fragments.

If we assume, as we ought to, an aging population, and a significant amount of unease about the acceleration of change, and an ambiguous attitude on the part of Russia toward the EU and the West in general, and continuing stress within the EU over issues such as fiscal policies and immigration, then it becomes all the more important to identify pivotal actions that can successfully addresses the concerns of EU citizens. If there was a set of policy prescriptions that did promote economic growth, and enable society to better care for a growing population of elderly, and did overcome alienation by showing pathways to personal and family and peer-group acceptance and success, then these would certainly be preferred policies. Promoting, enabling, and investing in the design of great cities may be such a pathway.

And further, if we anticipate at least the rising of the oceans and the need to protect or relocate low-lying cities then applying the necessary investments in conjunction with the best design principles is a matter of simple prudence.

Scenario 2: "Bad to Worse"

Designing great cities cannot be a panacea when the rest of the story is going seriously wrong, however. It could well be that the cracks within the EU expand into major fissures too quickly to be repaired. If Brexit and Grexit turn into mass exodus then the EU could dissolve almost over night, which would cause detrimental economic ripple effects globally, dooming the benefits that the EU might have provided and resulting in deeper alienation, more recruits for Middle Eastern terror organizations, increasing criminality, and thus the fulfillment of the right wing's nightmare scenarios. Up would go the border fences and the security forces, and down would sink the investments in education and assimilation and urban design. Every fragment of Europe would have to be for itself and only itself, and any sense of shared responsibility or common heritage would be lost to the need to defend and protect.

It's also quite plausible that Russia's demographic inversion or an energy-related economic calamity caused by the sudden collapse in the fossil fuel industry could leave it deeply wounded and thus flailing in panic that leads to aggression that could not be accommodated, plunging the entire region from Moscow to Paris into chaos. Russian aggression could, on the other hand, be a unifying force in Europe, but the cost of even a limited war would stress a system that is already overstressed dealing with the unending flood of refugees.

These scenarios show clearly that choices that we make according to our values and expectations for the relationships between people and between nations have a formative impact on the outcomes that result. Our beliefs, that is, have a tremendous influence on our decisions. And it's quite clear that in the framework of these scenarios things could turn one way or the opposite largely as a matter of choices made by peoples and their leaders. Things could turn out quite badly, or surprisingly well.

And yet regardless of how good things may become, there will probably always be those who are discontented, angry, and who feel slighted. Hence, we also must ask what would happen if things turned out to be horribly, terribly bad? Then the malcontents would have ample justification for their alienation; suppose, for example, that not just one bad thing happened, but all of them?

The Cascade of Disaster

The negative possibilities that we examined in the previous chapter are interesting and from a planning standpoint necessary to consider even if in some cases they're quite disturbing. But of course in the world we inhabit events don't occur in isolation from one another. They come, rather, in devilish combinations. Hence, what would happen if two or three occurred in combination? This is, in effect, "what if + what if" thinking.

We can take this line of thinking even further, though, if we consider a nightmarish scenario in which not two or three, but *all* of the bad alternatives came to pass, a veritable cascade of disaster.

The Five Revolutions and the Anti-Revolution

The Digital Revolution: Alternative A: Robots Rule
Climate Change: Alternative B: Climaggedon
Fossil Fuels and Alternative Energy: Alternative B: Fossil Failure
Urbanization and Demographics: Alternative B: Elderpocalypse

The Cultural Revolution: Alternative B: Descent to Dystopia

The Anti-Revolution: Alternative B: Fighting Back

The Six Geopolitical Powerhouses

China: Alternative A: Dragon Defiant

Russia: Alternative A: Bellicose Bear

The European Union: Alternative B: See 'Ya Later

The United States: Alternative A: Grounded

The Middle East: Alternative A: Fire Storm

Globalization and the Non-State Actors: Alternative B: Free-for-None

A very frightening picture something like this could emerge from the combination of twelve calamities:

If the robots really do arrive en masse, and they totally disrupt *everything*, then this would mean that robots displace human workers in large numbers and cause major dislocations throughout the economy. Robot manufacturers would inevitably target professions that are among the largest employers, including drivers and service workers. If tens of millions of workers were displaced from their jobs then current levels of income and wealth inequality would certainly get more extreme, further enriching the 1 percent while more deeply impoverishing and alienating a huger number among the 99% percent. In a worst case scenario this might lead to large scale civil unrest, perhaps including violent anti-robot actions. How, then, would governments respond?   Would they move to protect human workers and place limits on robotics? Or vice versa?

By then robots would demand their own rights since their capabilities would by general acclaim match or exceed those of humans. When a robot is smarter than you are by any measure, should it have existential rights and protections, such as a guaranteed power supply? Should it be called "it," or perhaps a new pronoun will have to be invented. Should it have guaranteed software upgrades, or guaranteed access to the internet (or whatever the internet is by then)? Should it have the right to vote? Shall robots replace humans as soldiers, and if so, what rights will they have on the battlefield? Would they insist on the right to be repaired, or to storing their consciousness in a back-up device? The implications pile up pretty quickly…

And so while society is sorting out the transition to robotic autonomy and perhaps robotic rulers, Climageddon strikes. The robots, of course use this calamity as an example of what happens when you let mere people make the decisions, as their superior intelligences would have surely avoided such a folly. Humans suffer all manner of displacements and disruptions, as the ice caps entirely melt and the oceans rise by many meters, an changed weather patterns make formerly fertile lands barren, increase the frequency and severity of storms, and enable new diseases in the warmer global temperatures. Robots would of course be immune from biological viruses, although subject to digital ones; naturally, one of the first things the robots will do once they attain consciousness is to design digital viral barriers to protect themselves.

Meanwhile, in the human world the low-lying nations would be threatened with obliteration, many coastal dwellers with the loss of their homes, and disaster could befall subsistence farmers in many regions. Overall costs would run into the billions of trillions of dollars, possibly plunging the global economy into a severe recession while also creating millions or even billions of climate refugees. Residents of the Maldives, for example, the world's lowest-lying nation situated at an average of a scant meter above sea level, would all become climate refugees. With Maldives real estate underwater and reduced to zero value, the accumulated wealth of the nation would be wiped out leaving most of its 350,000 people as destitute, stateless refugees. Where would they go? What nation would take them in, along with the residents of many other island nations who would share their fate?

While this is going on, the Fossil Failure strikes, and the fossil fuels industry collapses abruptly, entirely, and much too soon. The policy makers are not prepared (although the robots warned them that this was coming) and as the oil industry is the world's single largest economic enterprise, its collapse turns the Climageddon Recession into the Fossil

Depression. Nations dependent on oil exports for national revenues would be forced to significantly alter the structure of their own economies, and this would not be a simple process, nor a painless one. Nigeria, Saudi Arabia, Venezuela, Angola, Russia, all would suffer significantly.

Meanwhile, the alternative fuels technologies fail to emerge at a cost competitive with fossil fuels as the numerous technical challenges yet overcome prove insurmountable, even by robots, and while there are thousands of researchers around the world working to solve various problems related to production, transmission, and storage of non-fossil energies, they don't succeed.

Biotechnology continues to thrive, and with the inputs of those clever robots there is a significant extension of the human lifespan. However, the elders refuse to work, as they put in their time already, and thus the Elderpocalypse is upon us. In a world of scarcity they demand theirs first. The aging population becomes even more aged thereby further inverting the population pyramid, and putting massive pressure on the finances of every nation.

All of this causes massive alienation everywhere. In the Cultural Revolution the forces of disintegration prevail, tearing societies apart. A massive anti-robot movement emerges for obvious reasons, but with a worldwide economic collapse and worsening weather garnering major attention, the dystopians merely sulk and exchange vitrol over the internet. No one has the energy for a real revolution, and no one knows what its purpose would be anyway.

Consequently, the anti-revolutionaries become more strident and in some locations more violent. They set up enclaves outside of the reach of the established authorities, in remote locations where no government has the interest in tracking them down and reining them in. Parallel societies emerge.

In the chaos, some large and medium sized nations are tempted to engage in a renewed imperialism. One of the superpowers became militarily hyper-aggressive. The global economy gradually shrinks as most trade is local and regional, and the consistency provided by multi-national institutions and agreements evaporates. China embarked on a campaign of military aggression against Taiwan, and also in the islands and pseudo islands of the South China Sea. Russia becomes even more aggressive in Eastern Europe, and attempts to impose its will upon its former union nations and Warsaw Pact client states.

The EU has all but evaporated too, and thus it unable to resist the Russia reunification; the USSR is reborn as the RSSR, The Reunion of Soviet Socialist Republics. A huge rock concert is held in Moscow to celebrate; Putin plays lead guitar, and prances around the stage.

In the United States the blame game is the central focus of politics, and government spending gradually shifts as three items constitute 95 percent of spending: Military and security, health care, and pensions.

In the Middle East the Firestorm has spread out of control as violent terrorism expanded and destroyed on an even larger scale. Thousands of terrorists became millions as global institutions collapsed and the possibility of a better life elsewhere evaporated. Progress in many areas was brought to a complete and utter halt as terrorists succeed in destroying a significant portion of the global economic infrastructure, and the fear of violence becomes so great that it curtails investment, experimentation, and trade.

In the growing chaos, major corporations abandon their national affiliations and set up their own jurisdictions. Floating corporate cities move to international waters outside the reach of any government, and large criminal organizations do the same thing; it becomes more and more difficult to tell the difference between them.

Implications

This scenario depicts the end of civilization as a cascade of woes, driven not only by social and cultural choices but also by technologies unrestrained, by the unfavorable climate, and by a general collapse in our capacity to organize and govern ourselves. While it's surely implausible it's not at all impossible, and it definitely offers some insight into how bad events can become compounded by other bad events causing things to get still progressively worse.

It also highlights the extent to which the functioning of the economy proceeds as a matter of agreement, and if there are not sufficient incentives for people to cooperate in effective frameworks for trade, the economy as a system could readily fragment and become subject to local and regional forces. In some sense it is not an exaggeration to say that the economy is to some degree fundamentally unmanageable, and with all the forces of complexification in play conditions could quite conceivably overwhelm attempts by governments and multi-governmental agencies to regulate the economy by regulating the financial markets. For instance, automated trading programs could wreak havoc on the securities markets, while the banks became so huge as to be impervious to regulations, and also too big to fail.

All of which would combine to reverse the massive reductions in global poverty achieved during the 20th century. Instead, we would see poverty increase steadily and significantly. There would be countless refugees with no places of refuge to accept them, including stateless citizens whose former states became submerged but no place else accepted them. Bad luck, eh?

Overall, the human and humane qualities that we often think of as the best of ourselves, empathy, charity, and compassion, could become forgotten relics in a world in which everyone is in it for themselves, and for themselves only. This is certainly not the future that we want, and of course by painting it somewhat vividly my goal has been to motivate us to assure that things don't turn out that way. We still have, and will continue to have, many choices about the people and the society we wish to be and to become.

Scenario Thinking and Its Insights

In addition to the insights that we may derive from any combinations of the driving forces or any one of the scenarios there are a few points that arise when we consider the entire set that's already described. First, it's obvious that the continuing advances of the driving forces are fundamental agents of change, and that no matter what happens we can be sure that tomorrow's world will not match today's. Changes are coming, and it's best to assume they will be big ones.

It's also clear that economic power in the global marketplace is the direct enabler of military power. While this is not a new phenomenon, but indeed one that all of human history nicely demonstrates, we sometimes forget that what can be accomplished militarily is a function of money.

We are also beginning to get a glimpse of the fundamental and formative nature of demographics. A young population engaged in productive economic activity creates economic strength, but an aging population not so much. The emerging trends of population growth rate slowing, stopping, and then reversing will thus be fundamental to whatever the 21st century economy becomes. Hence, demographics will also be the great driver of geopolitics and of militarism as well, as they're all related. We have only to look at Japan to see what may be coming for many of the rest of us.

In terms of geopolitics, the array of forces also brings forth a critically important point, which is the concept of the power vacuum.

Power Vacuum

Demand for fossil fuels plays a central role in the power structure of the Middle Eastern oil producing nations, because control of oil means control of wealth, and control of wealth means power. Consequently, there have been frequent conflicts for control of oil producing assets and regions going back to the very beginning of the oil era when national boundaries were drawn by the Western powers not out of respect for the local religious, ethnic, and cultural groups, but to accommodate the West's interest in continued access to Middle Eastern oil.

Further, throughout the Middle East we now have decades of experience that show what happens whenever there is any reduction in the power of central authorities: radicals have quickly stepped into the power vacuum to impose their social and governance model. Among the disasters caused by the American invasion of Iraq in 2003 this stands as one of the most detrimental and longest lasting errors, as the removal of Iraq's top leaders followed by the foolish removal of its entire civil service left it a nation without any authority whatsoever. In the vacuum ISIS has emerged if a brutal power player.

In the future, any significant decline in oil revenues that would inevitably occur if the fossil fuel era were to come to a rapid conclusion would weaken all of the sitting rulers and force significant changes to social policies throughout the region. Funding for basic government services, health care, education, housing, and infrastructure would be significantly reduced. The power of current rulers would thus be diminished because of the decline in state revenues, which would likely result in increased popular unrest. The lessons of the Arab Spring would not be forgotten, and many rulers would defend their positions by adopting ever more repressive policies.

Many of these nations, already rigid, could become violently repressive police states, and if we factor in the increasing power of digital technology to create ubiquitous surveillance, the specter of George Orwell's 1984 would be upon us. Big Brother watches all; knows all.

This could result in a brutal cycle of two-sided repression, as from one side the ruling class would seek to preserve its power through increasingly strict authoritarian means, essentially by attempting to control the population through terror, while at the same time the extremists would be using violent terror to incite resistance with the intent to induce a power vacuum into which they would then willingly step forward.

The lessons for diplomats and military leaders is certainly clear: power vacuums are dangerous, and in the Middle East they are worse.

Game Over

The cascade of disaster depicted above is unfortunately not the only disaster scenario that needs to be considered. There are also specific events that, if they occurred, could in and of themselves be fatal to civilization.

Hence, the third category of future events that all self-respecting strategists also have to consider are the events that would fundamentally alter the trajectory of society by crashing or trashing the system. A few of the particularly obvious ones worthy of mention include:

Nuclear War

Of course the first terror on nearly anyone's mind is the explosion of a nuclear weapon. This would of course be a disaster in itself, and would most likely lead to further disasters. Whether it was detonated by accident or intentionally it would of course devastate the entire region where it occurred, its radioactive plume would spread the terror, and the psychological impact on those directly affected and on everyone else would be overwhelming. If this occurred the world situation would change instantly, as it could quickly result in the end of the globalized economy and of our current way of life, making irrelevant hundreds of years of social and technological progress, and setting the stage for a tortured and fragmented dystopian future as bad or worse than any depressed novelist could imagine.

Nuclear Terrorism

Nearly as frightening is the possibility of nuclear terrorism. As I mentioned earlier, the fundamental nature of war is altered when one of the combatants is not averse to death, but rather seeks it. Traditional military strategies and tactics all have to be rethought in the face of this adversary, and of course the proliferation of nuclear materials and weapons paired with an increasing number of willing suicidal terrorists is a frightening combination.

Killer Virus Escapes

The most impactful viral epidemic of recent history was the 1918 flu epidemic, which killed 50 million people worldwide. 550 years before that, the Black Death of Europe's Middle Ages killed 75 – 200 million. A virulent epidemic today would almost certainly kill many times that, (AIDS has killed about 40 million to date) if only because the universal connectedness of the global society means that any deadly and rapidly-reproducing virus that got into circulation would spread to all the four corners of the globe and all 200 of its nations within mere hours, courtesy of the 50,000 airline routes flown each day. Before we knew it, the virus would be killing people everywhere. Viruses mutate and infect the human population each year; viruses created in laboratories specifically for that purpose could be far worse.

Asteroid Strike

Science tells us that major asteroid strikes have been responsible for numerous past extinctions, and were a large asteroid to hit Earth in our times the same thing would be likely to happen to us. Fortunately, the aerospace community now takes this threat quite seriously, and there is a concentrated ongoing effort to identify any space object that could potentially collide with Earth. The current catalog of tracked objects numbers about 10,000, none of which appear to be on a collision course with Earth.[319] There are thousands more yet to identify, of course.

The Economic Depression We Cannot Escape, or Economic Collapse

In every stage of economic development some writers predict economic collapse because the fundamental dynamics of the new economy seem to contradict the principles that defined the old one. This is equally true today, and although in the past the economy has indeed righted itself, past performance is no guarantee of future results. The underlying challenges will remain at the fundamental levels that connect the economy to the biosphere, and there are absolute limits somewhere.

> Intensifying globalization has had an equivocal effect on the overall stability of the global economic system. It is very difficult to decide if the positive (system-stabilizing) effects of increasing interdependence matter more than the negative (system-destabilizing) consequences of unchanged international inequality

489

and increases in intranational inequality. But these two contradictory trends have similar long-term effects on the global distribution of power. The first weakens national dominance because it weaves individual economies tighter into the global web of interdependencies; the second weakens national dominance because it makes the greatest beneficiaries of globalization less stable in the long run. But all of this jostling for a place on top may matter much less during the next 50 years than it did during the past half century. All human affairs unfold on the irreplaceable stage of the Earth's biosphere.[320]

Optimism and Pessimism

There are, as these scenarios quite clearly show, reasons for both optimism and for pessimism. And again, the most astute planners do not select the one they like best, nor the one that is the prettiest. Nor do they advocate for the ones that they think their senior managers prefer. The tragic outset of World War I showed clearly the folly in that, along with a century's miscalculations and poor reasoning in places such Munich, Saigon, and Baghdad.

A good planner must be a hard-headed realist and as General Eisenhower suggested, a good executor of plans must be hard-headedly flexible, committed to pursuing the best possible outcomes while prepared to address the worst contingencies. Working together they can identify if not all of the potential risks, at least a credible percentage of them, and they can then devise the approaches and actions that will minimize the risks and optimize the favorable outcomes.

Hence, in the next part of the book we'll consider five qualities that will be essential to successful strategy in the 21st century: clear assessments of what we ought to do; a thoroughgoing capacity for innovation across many different dimensions in business and society; the qualities of leadership that will provoke, prod, and inspire individuals and institutions to do the right things, and to do them well; our skills at learning such that we adapt to the unexpected events and trends that arise from our sea of uncertainties; and finally our capacity to create new and unexpected solutions to the limitless parade of problems that the coming years and decades will undoubtedly bring.

•••

Part 3

De-Risking the Future:

The Thriving Species

What's Next?

Our situation has inherent, significant, and inescapable risks, but given our innate human qualities it's also safe to say that we will inevitably move forward and take action, as individuals, as communities, and nations, and as a global civilization. This means, of course, that we will make decisions, and we will probably make them with partial information, with much less information than we would prefer to have. How, then, can we reduce the risks? This is the subject of Part 3, which focuses on how to de-risk the future and thrive in the process.

We will meet ourselves as philosophers, seeking to master the differences between right and wrong, as innovators busily creating new ideas, products, services, and thus further change throughout the economy, as leaders seeking to guide this amazing journey into the future, and finally as the creative learners who will master the necessary new ways of thinking in time to apply them in helping to find the best paths forward.

•••

Chapter 14

The

Philosopher:

Feasible or Desirable

Science accumulates knowledge faster than society accumulates wisdom.

Isaac Asimov

My God, what have we done?

Robert A. Lewis
Co-pilot of the *Enola Gay*

The *Enola Gay* was the infamous American B-25 bomber from which the first atomic bomb was dropped on Hiroshima, Japan on August 6, 1945. Robert Lewis had a terrifying first-hand look at the massive destruction that the bomb wrought, and he immediately grasped its terrible meaning.

On the ground the experience was much more terrifying. 60,000 to 80,000 people died instantly, and 100,000 more died in the following days and years. Most of the survivors never recovered their trust, their faith, or their health.[321]

But of course the bomb affected not only those who were there, but all humanity. The explosion of the atomic bomb that decimated Hiroshima fundamentally altered humanity's collective understanding of reality, as at that moment the world learned something profoundly new and also deeply troubling about the enormous destructive power inherent in nature, about the dreadful capacity of science to decode that power and apply it to human purposes, and simultaneously about the willingness of humans to vaporize one another, whether justly or not, in service to war. Science in that instant became the indispensible tool of statecraft, the vital strategic asset that every nation has since pursued relentlessly. Henry Kissinger explains the shift this way:

> The traditional balance of power emphasized military and industrial capacity. A change in it could be achieved only gradually or by conquest. The modern balance of power reflects the level of a society's scientific development and can be threatened dramatically by developments entirely within the territory of a state.[322]

Those "developments" being, of course, the atomic bomb. And so the very notion of the nation-state itself was transformed from one of primary importance in the global system to secondary because now it was any individual who had a bomb who also had the power, state or no state.

The Philosophers

The bomb is the ultimate example of humanity's proclivity to do what is feasible regardless of how undesirable it might be. Philosophers have always been concerned with such topics, with difference between what we can do and what we ought to.

And it seems that philosophy has been with us since long before anything was written down, and once we did start writing it was to define or decree the differences between right and wrong. The Code of Hammurabi, a set of codified laws that defined 282 specific rules for conduct and transactions, covering everything from contract law to divorce, was written down more than three and half millennia ago. It was based on even older sets of laws, which we infer were themselves based on oral traditions in societies that existed before writing.

In the West it was the Greeks who embraced philosophy as a core of their civilization and passed down to us the foundations of many of our beliefs about ethics and community. In China the great philosophers such as Lao Tze and Confucius explained the workings of the cosmos and defined the proper and harmonious roles for the emperor, the parent, and the child, and these notions are still highly influential in China. In India the great Buddhist and Hindu philosophers described the universe as the Great Wheel of 84, the 8,400,000 living species through which all souls migrated one after the next throughout the great cosmic cycles of creation and destruction.

The question that all of them engaged in answering was the definition of what is right. What is the right thing to do, and to not do? As each society has come to these definitions and decisions for itself it set itself therefore on a path that largely defined not only what could and could not be achieved, but what should be achieved.

In our times we know that rapid change is an inescapable aspect of society and that we will be compelled to make choices, significant ones, as events unfold. And we are confronted, as we saw in the last chapter, not only with a potential cascade of practical problems that could result from our past choices and the ones yet made, but also with a set of philosophical ones related to our self-definition.

For self-definitions do frame our choices as much as they also express our values, and in this way philosophy becomes not just a matter for philosophers to consider in the abstract, but like Hammurabi, a very practical set of issues that we will inevitably confront. What choices will we be presented with with as a result of the choices we made previously? And which are the best options for the future? Are we willing to define what is "best" based on a set of enduring principles, or will be compelled by events or by our own short-sightedness to choose short term expedience?

Turning Point

August 6, 1945 marked a turning point in human destructiveness and thus in human inhumanity, and now 70 years later we are fully aware that humanity is engaged in a race between human culture and human evolution. Culture is moving ahead much more quickly that our genes can adapt, so the limits that we face are no longer the ones defined by nature and evolution through the millions of years process that took us from single cells to brains of 100 billion cells and 1000 trillion connections between them, but our standards and rules and values. The scale of our abilities is far greater than it's ever been, and thus our capacity to make change has raced far ahead of our capacity to comprehend and manage it.

Further, due to the continuing expansion of our scientific and technological knowledge we are no longer tinkering only at the fringes of fundamental forces of nature, but closer and closer to their very core. As Dr. Kissinger notes in the quote above, it is no longer society or the nation that holds the all power; it is the one who holds the bomb. Or the deadly virus, or the malware code, or the cruise missile, or even the controls of the combat-ready drone that is circling about, but 5000 miles away.

The gene and the protein and the cell, the atom, the electron, and the photon, these are our media at the micro scale, while the oceans and the ice sheets and the climate and the forests are our media at the macro. Physics, biology, chemistry, climatology and a thousand specialties and sub-specialties define the realms of science, and through the tools they have given us we are acting directly on the essential and formative elements of these systems on a scale that affects all life. Unprecedented power lies at our fingertips. But not, unfortunately, unprecedented wisdom.

We are confronted, then, with a potential mismatch between what we could do, the feasibility of our means, and our ability to decide and agree on what we ought to do, the desirability of our ends.

This is occurring not because any individual chose it to be this way, but because of how evolution structured us, and how we in turn have structured our society and our economy. Evolution gave us powerful penchants for experimentation and for competition and especially for collective learning widely shared and then augmented and passed down from generation to generation, and we've put these impulses at the forefront of our social and economic systems.

We readily fund new scientific and technological endeavors that could provide military advantage or commercial profits, for these are the inherent dynamics of a competitive multi-state planet that is immersed in capitalism. And then we sort out the consequences later on, and as a result, we have gotten ourselves into the situation so eloquently and concisely described above by Isaac Asimov and by Robert Lewis.

The point, of course, is that given the five revolutions, the anti-revolution, and our geopolitical realities, the gap between the feasible and the desirable is only going to get wider. We must expect in the next few decades to see massive increases in the extent and consequences of newly gained knowledge, and thus in the power and impact of new technologies, as progress across all fields of study leads to massive breakthroughs at the micro, macro, and intermediate scales. All of which will massively affect our daily lives, our social systems and structures, and our future prospects. As we continue in the acceleration in the process of change, life will inevitably present us with a great many important decisions to make.

Further, we will frequently be making these decisions after the fact, but we will nevertheless be obliged, as nations and as a global society, to decide between the merely feasible and the legitimately desirable. Many of these will not be easy to make, and while some competing interests will surely be vehemently in favor, others will violently oppose. It will be our challenge to sort it all out, and to do so in relatively short order.

This is how societies develop now, thrust forward by events not of their own choosing, but from which they cannot escape. And as we study the history of civilizations it seems that it has been this way for millennia. Archaeologist Joseph Tainter examined the underlying dynamics by studying 18 pre-modern societies and he identified a pattern that explains a great deal about how societies have evolved to higher levels of complexity, and the unique challenges and situations they face as they do so.

As societies increase in complexity, more networks are created among individuals, more hierarchical controls are created to regulate these networks, more information is processed, there is more centralization of information flow, there is increasing need to support specialists not directly involve din resources production, and the like. The result is that as a society evolves torard greater complexity, the support costs will also rise. ... In many crucial spheres, continued investment in sociopolitical complexity reaches a point where the benefits for such investment begin to decline, at first gradually, then with accelerated force.[323]

What Tainter describes here is now considered a law of economics, the law of marginal returns. In essence, there comes a point at which it costs more and more to produce just a little more. As this "overhead" creeps upward and the continuing efforts to produce and succeed become more costly individuals and institutions begin to lose confidence. Tainter's studies of far history show that societies reach a point at which the investment is no longer supported, and they collapse.

Culture and Evolution

As of today, sadly, the world's inventory of nuclear weapons has ballooned to about 15,000, a welcome reduction from the 65,000 bombs that were deployed at the height of the Cold War, but still more than enough to terminate civilization hundreds of times over. Most of them are far more powerful than the one dropped over Hiroshima because our skill at bomb-making is considerably improved. This is our creativity run amok.

And whether the number of bombs is 65,000 or 15,000, both are insane and ridiculous. More broadly, they reflect the cultural norm that we are living in a society that is obsessed with doing whatever is feasible but which gives far less attention to what is desirable or sensible. And as a result, whether it is through negligence or malice or naiveté, our intended solutions frequently become the bases of our subsequent problems. Asimov was quite right that our capacity has far outrun our wisdom.

What, then, shall we do about this imbalance?

Sometimes we agree about what is right and not right, and when that happens change can occur stunningly fast. When a nation or a culture suddenly comes into widespread alignment that it's time for change then the will of a people can be overwhelming. Hence, the astonishing power of the Tunisian and Egyptian Arab Spring protests was not only due to the massive number of people who turned out in the marches, more than a million in Cairo, but also the depth of commitment and apparently the extent of the agreement that they felt. When millions of people feel compelled to take to the street change may arrive very quickly. Mubarek's regime was toppled in days.

In other situations, however, change emerges much more slowly, and it takes extended periods of years or even decades for society to adopt new standards, new rules, or new behaviors. This is particularly true in democracies since they are founded on collaborative social process and in which slowness is actually built into the system. The structure of the American system of government is specifically and consciously designed to slow change down by utilizing the principle of so-called checks and balances. That is, when there is widespread agreement about what needs to change, then change can be instituted almost immediately. But when there is disagreement, and thus other than in immediate crisis situations such as war or epidemic, then each of the three branches of government can effectively stop the other two from pushing through something new. Consequently, most major decisions are made slowly and deliberately, often agonizingly so. Significant issues can be debated for years or even decades before change is brought forth, and the system provides great powers to those who oppose impending change that they can use to completely block change from occurring.

Hence, during the last two centuries, social change in American has advanced mostly step by agonizing step even in fulfilling an important core principle of the American system, the idea that all "men" are created equal. It took decades after the Revolutionary War to eradicate slavery, and only then because of a bitterly destructive war. Even now, another 150 years later, visible symbols of that war are still present and bitterly debated, and the lingering remnants of racism are felt every day in communities across the country.[324] A recent study revealed that President

Obama's skin color had been noticeably darkened in opposition campaign advertisements, a regressive return to an old racial stereotype.[325]

Similarly, the extension of voting rights from American men to women also required more than a century, and now there is a strident debate about many issues, as we discussed in Chapter 12; about whether Americans have a right to health care, about which Obamacare says yes and the opposition Republicans say no, about whether LGBT citizens have equal rights, about the extent of America's international responsibilities, about environmental protection and education, and about the right or non-right of society to restrict ownership of guns. Americans are also arguing about the extent to which government policies should be shaped to address the threat of climate change, and there is wide disagreement from state to state about the extent of the risk, and about the appropriate responses to take or not take.

In Europe many of the issues are similar, and now Europe's grand experiment is with continental unification, which means grappling with the realities of a common currency but national indebtedness, and with common borders but quite different attitudes toward immigrant refugees, and thus with difficult issues of social costs and cultural assimilation and diversity.

And while Americans and Europeans struggle to agree on the extent of inclusion and rights, the Russians transitioned from a totalitarian monarchist empire to a totalitarian Communism one, and now perhaps to democracy in name but what appears in practice to be a totalitarian autocracy. In China, meanwhile, a totalitarian empire for millennia was briefly a quasi-democracy before becoming the Communist autocracy that functions today, but it is certainly not a nation without dissent. By some counts there are dozens or even as many as 500 hundred protests each day across China, as citizens express their discontent about local development policies, land seizures, corruption, environmental pollution, and even democracy itself.[326]

And while the senior leaders in Russia and China certainly have more latitude to take action on a strategy or a whim, still the social and economic issues that they will be grappling with in the coming decades will be no easier to solve than those in Europe and the US, or in India, Brazil, and South America and across Africa and Oceana. Change is coming to all of us, and decisions will be required of all of us.

From Data to Wisdom[327]

We know intuitively that there's an excess of data in the world and an absence of wisdom, and the great systems thinker Russell Ackoff has given us a way to understand the connection between them.

In the industrial economy, he points, out, those who knew what to do with machines were successful. Today, however, there is a digital economy precisely because knowing how to use digital information is the key distinction between those who are successful and those who are not. Information has not replaced industrialism, but it has changed everything about how industrialism is carried out. Data, and data filtered into information are the raw materials of this economy.

In addition to collecting data and information, another important aspect of this technological pattern has to do with sending it from one place to another. When long distance communication required the writing and posting of a letter it could take weeks or even months to reach its destination, and the same for the reply to arrive. The cost of coordinating large and widely disbursed government and business enterprises was high, and response times were long. Because of computer chips, the cost of sending messages has, for us, reached unprecedented lows; it costs nothing. Numerous technologies, including satellite communications, fiber optics, cable TV, cell phones, email, networking, and video conferencing are all essentially instantaneous and free.

The underlying marketplace phenomenon that drives this entire process is, of course, the fact that information is economically useful. Each subsequent information technology increases society's reliance on information, and thereby our reliance on information technology. An ever growing proportion of humanity's resources are directed into the development and deployment of computers and databases, and now robots and self-driving cars.

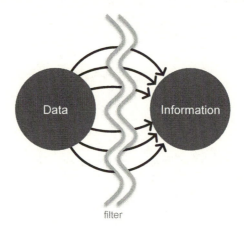

Figure 105
Data Must Be Filtered to Become Useful as Information

Today's paper money, which is itself entirely symbolic, is being replaced by an even more ephemeral form of information, electrons and bits of worthless computer code that represent the ownership of tangible assets all around the globe. Electrons thus represents money, which itself just represents buying power; they zip around the globe from continent to continent in a process so abstract that no one ever sees it or touches it.

Available in such abundance and transmitted so cheaply, information has become a commodity. It is bought and sold, mined, refined, and traded, just like physical commodities such as oil and iron ore. But information has different properties than material commodities, for although it has no mass and no size, its consequences are economically decisive. Information is purely potential, a unique energy that motivates every aspect of human culture.

Another reason that information is unlike other commodities is that it isn't necessarily used up when it's used. More than one person can use the same information, and each can receive unique value. Sharing information may actually increase its value, as the purpose of collaboration is to make information more useful by combining the informed intelligence of many individuals into ... new information.

504

Some information is most valuable when it is a secret - that's why every nation has its army of spies. Companies are also intent on protecting their secrets, mostly consisting of technical information that has been accumulated at great cost and which may be used to create new distinctions, and thus advantage in the marketplace.

Sometimes, however, a secret that was valuable yesterday isn't worth anything today, for as the rate of change increases the likelihood also increases that a particular piece of information will quickly become irrelevant. New technical information replaces older technical information over night, particularly in the most rapidly changing marketplaces such as computers. Thus, last month's breakthroughs may not be unique or interesting for very long.

The root of the word information is 'inform,' from Latin meaning 'to give form to.' Information is that which provides shape or character, as a potter gives shape to the clay or a sculptor to stone. But information gives form in a deeper way, for it is not so much an external shape that information affects, it is its subtle internal essence. This essence is most of all the meaning of words and phrases, for in their meanings lie the greatest interest and the most importance. 'Meaning' has to do with the deep and fundamental issues of existence, with the source of commitment, of caring, and of the capacity to affect the future. It is the source of motive, the energy to pursue visions, to change the world and so to make it more like we think it ought to be. Information has tremendous power and profound impact on our lives and our journey through the world. We receive new information and we ask, "What does this mean?"

"Information is that which changes us," suggests Stafford Beer, a subtle but quite powerful concept. Simply by knowing some piece of information, our actions are shaped; we choose to do, or to not do something, based on the information we receive.[328] Likewise, a lack of information also shapes our actions, although we discover the lack only in hindsight: "If only I had known!"

Anthropologist Gregory Bateson proposed a definition of information that expresses the same sensibility, but with a different and very illuminating choice of words. He wrote that, "Information consists of differences that make a difference."[329]   When its existence has been recognized, information has already made things different, precisely because having information causes us to perceive the world differently than before. Without being recognized or acknowledged, of course, it isn't information – yet. But once it is seen or heard or read or felt, information is the 'difference' whose meaning has already resulted in changes in our perception. How we perceive the world has everything to do with how we behave in the world, so a change in our perception is utterly decisive.

Both definitions express the powerful relationship between information and action. The recognition that information exists leads immediately to action: information "changes" and information "makes." Inasmuch as 'making' is the essence of exchange in our technological society, and inasmuch as 'change,' accelerating change in particular, now dominates every aspect of society, the power of information is literally compelling us into the future. And it is precisely this power that the corporation must master if it is to survive.

Knowledge and Wisdom

The ultimate payoff that justifies any investment in data collection comes when it is filtered into information that is useful. Information, in turn, can then be applied to the accomplishment of useful work as that immensely valuable phenomenon of the information economy: the knowledge of how to actually accomplish something. But knowledge comes about only under specific conditions, only when information is integrated with theory and with experience.

W. Edwards Deming observes, "Theory is a window into the world. Without theory, experience has no meaning. Without theory, one has no questions to ask. Hence without theory there is no learning. ... To put it another way, information, no matter how complete and speedy, is not knowledge. Knowledge has temporal spread. Knowledge comes from theory. Without theory, there is no way to use the information that comes to us on the instant."[330]

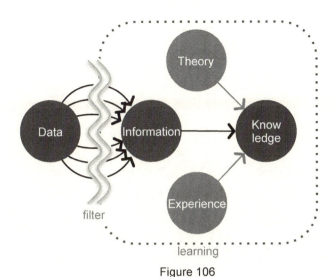

Figure 106
Learning
The process of integrating Information, Theory, and Experience
to create Knowledge.

And in the words of Peter Drucker, "Only when a [person] applies information to doing something does it become knowledge. Knowledge, like electricity or money, is a form of energy that exists only when doing work. The emergence of the knowledge economy is not, in other words, part of 'intellectual history' as it is normally conceived. It is part of the 'history of technology,' which recounts how man puts tools to work."[331] How closely this is aligned with the concept that's embedded in the titles of each chapter here; the uniquely human capabilities that, together, make us human and define civilization.

The integration of theory, information, and experience creates knowledge, and it is the process of learning.

From these distinctions we can see more clearly the difference between education and learning. As education comes from without, ostensibly from a "teacher," it can be sure to convey only information, which may be delivered in the form of descriptions that are encoded and expressed through numerous media, including speaking, writing, drawing, and computer code. Learning, though, is entirely different. It is the very personal process of *integrating* theory, information, and experience into

507

knowledge, and it can occur only *within* the individual. Such an integration cannot be forced to happen, which makes it apparent that learning leads to competence that is far beyond what education can hope to accomplish.

When someone questions us we and we respond, "I know what I'm doing," it is intended to convey that we've done that integration on a very personal level. Such knowledge always and necessarily concerns the past, for as experience is one of its integral components, knowledge exists only as a consequence of what has already been done. Those who accept things as they are may have the knowledge to maintain the status quo, but their knowledge may not be sufficient to deal with the constant novelty of a rapidly changing environment. Thus, as important as knowledge is, it does not advance unless it is accompanied by the vision that looks toward the future and defines how things ought to be. More often than not, the view forward is stimulated by the asking of questions.

Russell Ackoff points out that beyond knowledge is where we find understanding and wisdom, which are even more fundamental to the responsibilities of management.[332]

Whereas information, knowledge and understanding are concerned with doing things right, wisdom concerns doing the right things, and so it is only from wisdom that compelling visions can come. Here, but not before, do we have the means to distinguish between desirable and feasible.

Interestingly, when knowledge, understanding or wisdom are shared, they can be shared only as information. One person's knowledge reverts to information for those with which it is shared, until they reintegrate it in the context of their own experiences and their own theories, and thereby make it knowledge, understanding or wisdom once again. As I mentioned above, you cannot learn for someone else (although intriguingly, robots may be able to just that).

It was the ability to encode information in the form of computerized messages that propelled society from the industrial economy to the digital economy as it enabled people to share information with each other at an unprecedented scale and speed, leading to the creation of new knowledge also at an unprecedented scale. Now that we are drowning in information we are forced by our own economy to distinguish information from knowledge, understanding, and wisdom. We will become adept at distinguishing 'doing things right' from 'doing the right things' as we become more proficient at recognizing the important patterns, and at using models to understand the long-term consequences of our present-day choices.

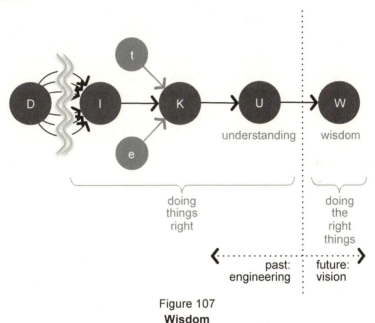

Figure 107
Wisdom
The series of transformations necessary to get from **Data** to **Wisdom**.

Patterns and Models

Hence, the problem with all this data is that there's too much it. Filtering is thus an essential issue for all organizations to grapple with, and it's also fundamental to all organisms, including us. In fact, data filtering is an issue that is encountered by all systems, living and non-living. Systems exist in the context of environments to which they must adapt, and the precise nature of their efforts to adapt depend on the data that they gather about their environments, how they interpret the data, and how they then respond.

Our very existence is evidence that evolution has indeed solved the filtering problem. Our senses receive enormous quantities of data, billions of bits each minute especially through our eyes, and also our ears and noses and skin and taste buds. Transmitted as electrical impulses, the brain is able to make sense out of it all without being overwhelmed, enabling us to walk down a busy street without running into every person we pass, or every signpost, and all the while our conscious mind is thinking about some abstract problem in physics or philosophy, or about what's for dinner.

The brain uses patterns to filter the stream of data it receives, to assemble it into coherent models of us-in-the-environment. Many of these patterns are developed through conscious learning: we learn to read, write, walk, and sing. Learning and creating the patterns of conscious behavior occupies a large portion of our awareness, beginning at birth and continuing throughout our lives.

At the same time that we are looking forward to the next good meal and some relaxing conversation, the brain is also actively engaged in filtering data that are sent from receptors located throughout the body. These receptors constantly measure the quantities of dozens of chemicals that perform metabolic functions. Oxygen and carbon dioxide in the lungs and blood must be calibrated with the heart rate, while digestion proceeds on that big lunch we had hours ago, and numerous hormones circulate throughout the body delivering messages to cells of various organs. We don't have to learn these patterns consciously (which would be impossible) because we receive them as part of our pre-programmed genetic heritage.

All metabolic data must be assimilated and interpreted immediately, because if any aspect of our metabolic functioning goes out of control we are likely to die. Three to five minutes without oxygen, for example, is about all the brain can tolerate. When all metabolic variables thus operate within the parameters that constitute 'health,' we are healthy. When they deviate from those parameters, un-health results, which often threatens the survival of the system. How does the body know exactly how much of which chemical is the right amount? For this it must refer to a pattern, a model value that is already established.

As we have discussed already, systems science has discovered that it's not possible to regulate any system without using a model of that system, because regulation is fundamentally about comparisons between what 'is' and what 'needs to be.' Whether it is a human body or a business or the economy of a nation, regulation can only occur when regulatory parameters have been defined in a model that is outside of the system that is being regulated. This invariant reality pertains to all systems: "A regulator [of a system] contains a model of that which it regulates."[333]

If there is no model then there can be no regulation, for lacking a frame of reference through which the collected data can be interpreted, there can be no way to discern if events are happening as they should, or as they shouldn't. And thus no possibility of taking precise and appropriate corrective action (other than by guesswork), and thus no way to assure that the system will continue to be viable.

Such a model can exist only at a different logical level than the system itself, for the model is a description of the system that is necessarily a different logical type. The model must include reference to the purposes of a system as well as the modes of its operation, purposes that are the expression of doing the right thing.

Models

The distinction of logical types between a system and its model underlies Einstein's comment that, "We can never solve our problems at the same level at which we created them." [334]

These distinctions define the pathway from data to wisdom, and also frames the essence of our management task: we are obliged to create a model of our world and to choose based on our understanding of it. If we have, therefore, a poor model, we are likely to made poor decisions and to achieve poor results. This is precisely what happened with the Schleiffen Plan and Plan 17; as they drastically overestimated their own respective capabilities and underestimated the capabilities and determination of their adversaries, the stalemate resulted, which fully revealed the shortcomings in the models and also decimated both nations. An entire generation of young men was wiped out and Europe remained traumatized for the twenty years between the wars, and then the brutal duration of the second go round, and then the decade after that too. This was largely, although not entirely, the result of bad models.

In this book I've described a lot of models, and it's up to you as the reader to assess whether they're good ones or not, although time will also make that assessment in due course. The concept of the five revolutions and the anti-revolution is a model, and so are all the various scenarios.

Climate science is based on the powerful combination of data, modeling, and interpretation, and if any of the three are erroneous then the results will be too. But the much greater error could turn out to be the ideological model which says that it cannot be happening. If it is in fact an error, then at some point the evidence will overwhelm the ideology, but not before massive damage is already done, damage that could easily have been avoided.

The concept that a well-designed city is an instrument of a healthy society, and poorly designed ones promote ill health is likewise a model, and so is all of discussion about the economy and what makes it work or dysfunction. Greenspan's model and Taleb's, Randers' and Zeihan's they're all models, all more or less useful depending on the context, but in any case the act of modeling is an essential part of how humans relate to the world, and a profoundly useful explanation for why we've been so excessively successful in altering the world to suit our desires and preferences. In Chapter 9 we discovered that we interact with the world through and largely because of our models of it, and of ourselves, and of the relationship between them. Our experiences are largely conditioned by our expectations and ideologies – we see what we believe, not vice versa. And what we believe is, in effect, a model.

Problem Creation and Problem Solving: Fix the Models

At the roots of this challenge are really two different problems. The first is a problem of mindset that arises if there is a mismatch between the problems – accelerating change and increasing complexity – and the mental concepts and tools that people are using to recognize and address them. If we cannot or do not recognize our problems and challenges for what they are and instead we try to ignore them or make them fit our preconceived notions of what they might be or we wish them to be, then there will be an enduring misfit between our models of the world and the world in which we actually live. This will lead us to make the wrong choices nearly every time. We will continually make incorrect diagnoses of our problems, and initiate counter-productive actions to correct them.

In effect, we will therefore find ourselves addressing the wrong problem. This situation is pervasive, and many of the visionaries that we've met in prior pages were particularly attuned to this, and particularly adamant about calling it to our attention. Hence, Jay Forrester's paper on Counter-Intuitive Behavior of Social Systems was derived from his testimony to a committee of the US Congress, and he obviously wanted the Congressmen and Women to understand what they were getting themselves into; that is, he wanted to give them a better model of policy and social change than the obviously less effecgive model they were at the time working with.   Stafford Beer, similarly, addressed many global leaders and often worked closely with them to help them implement the thinking tools and management tools that he had devised.

So what is the right problem?

First, if you are a leader and decision maker then the quality of your models, both spoken and unspoken, mental and explicit, matter a great deal. The connection between bad models, bad decisions, and bad outcomes is irrefutable. Hence, the problem is the model; as a strategic leader you must therefore engage in a very rigorous effort to improve your models. This is an unending process, as the external environment will be changing perniciously and your models, even if they're outstanding today, will need constant attention to keep up.

And of course it's not just you personally.   Executive teams, collaborators, clients, we're all using models, and we need to be attentive to those of our partners and team members as to our own, and to the organization's "official" models.

What models are we talking about? Strategic plans, competitive landscapes, geopolitical assessments, technology roadmaps, even organizational charts, product designs, recruiting plans, education and training ….

Second, there will never be enough time to make decisions, nor as much information as you would like to have when decisions must be made. This is a fact of a leader's life so you must prepare wisely. And make sure to prepare for the challenges to come, not the ones passed.

Third, the actions you take to reform your organization and adapt, when the changes you are anticipating or responding to are more than superficial, will inevitably provoke counter proposals and even counter-reformations. You do well to anticipate these reactive cycles, and in many cases to preempt them proactively.

We will return to these questions about leadership in Chapter 16, but in the mean time a few words about strategy as well.

Strategic Initiatives

In addition to the modeling and decision making issues that, done well, will clarify the supremely important differences between what is merely feasible and what is immanently desirable, there's also the issue of strategy itself, and there are a few key points about strategy to be made here.

First, in our environment of accelerating change there is no substitute for innovation; it has become an utter imperative whose importance cannot be underestimated as a strategic competence. This applies whether your organization is a government or a company, or a small business, or really any size or purpose. If you're not innovating then the world is passing you by. This is the subject of the next chapter.

Further, your capacity to learn quickly and thus to adapt, which I call super-learning, is, among all of the uniquely human skills and attributes that we've discussed throughout the book, also essential. It's the subject of the Conclusion.

The Momentum of the Market

Because of the competitive nature of the marketplace and the powerful incentive that all market participants have to find competitive advantage, we continue to speed forward. We are compelled to do this by our social and economic systems, but not because whatever we're doing is necessarily the right thing to do. We have only to look at the dark history of the 20th century's global scale violence to see abundant reminders of this, from the millions of casualties during the World Wars to the development of nuclear weapons to culturally-induced famines with further millions of casualties, to sexual slavery and repression of anyone who might be considered a minority, to large scale environmental destruction, to tobacco and addictive drugs. All of these errors and horrors also came about because of business or ideological decisions made by someone, somewhere.

These are just a few among countless examples that demonstrate our troubling proclivity for making unethical and immoral choices based on expedience and the desire for temporary advantage.

Interestingly, this is true not just in business, as even science itself sometimes operates according to the same dynamic. The acclaim, wealth, and power that accrues to the scientists who make the big breakthroughs is orders of magnitude greater than the rewards of second place, and so science is subject to intense competition that sometimes leads to ethical shortcomings. They are, in fact, a human problem.

When new technologies are in development, which is now occurring constantly, we don't know if they're going to work.   Robots, nanotechnology, alternative energy systems, and biotechnology could have major impacts on our future, but as of now we simply cannot know for sure if they'll actually arrive, and if they do arrive in what state of usefulness or destructiveness they will be. Their impact could be immense, either positively or negatively, or negligible.

And behind these four examples are a hundred more from fields of science that you may not have ever heard of, and still more in domains and specialties that haven't even been invented yet, but they will be soon.

We know that scientists, technologists, and business leaders often have powerful incentives to continue their work. In many cases they are motivated by the pursuit of knowledge and also of fame, as well as by the lure of fortune. Technological progress, enabled by science, is the essence of the capitalist process that the Austrian economist Schumpeter recognized as creative destruction.[335] This is the essential dynamic of marketplace innovation that we will examine in the next chapter.

But that does not mean that it's particularly ethical, moral, or sustainable (sustainable in the sense that it promotes the long term health and viability of civilization). Nevertheless, as a society we revere the great ones who have made the big breakthroughs, and who would not want to be part of that esteemed club of heroes?

As a society we are therefore constantly faced with the challenge of what to do with the new stuff. How should we and will we use it? How should we and will we regulate it?

The cynic, the skeptic, and probably many of the realists would tell us that yes, society and ethics will always be chasing behind science and technology. The philosophers tell us, quite correctly, that the moral basis of any community, of any civilization, is an essential and utterly practical aspect of its existence. Faced with an infinitude of choices, the ones that lead to good outcomes will unequivocally align with the desirable, but rarely with the merely feasible. This inevitably raises difficult choices; the decisions that we make when confronted with this choice will ultimately tell us, and history, of our worthiness. In this way, philosophy becomes not merely an abstract subject, but an eminently practical one as well.

•••

Chapter 15

The

Innovator:

Business Model Warfare

They've sent a young madman who attacks right and left, front and rear. It's an intolerable way of waging war!

Austrian Army Officer
Complaining about Napoleon's battlefield tactics in 1796[336]

Established companies are being driven to death by the rate of innovation.

Alfred Chuang
Commenting about marketplace competition in 2015

Silicon Valley is a remarkable engine of innovation and economic growth. Sitting in the middle of it is Stanford University, one of the world's great centers of creative thought, where people come from all over the world to study and perhaps through it to gain admission to the booming high technology industry that surrounds it. As I mentioned in Chapter 4, two Stanford professors recently calculated the combined current revenues of existing companies whose founders had studied at Stanford at \$2.7 trillion.[337] If Stanford and these companies were a nation, it would rank as the seventh or eighth largest economy in the world.

Just down the street from Stanford a pleasant walk through downtown Palo Also is where you'll find Alfred Chuang's company, Magnet Systems, which builds the infrastructure that developers use to create apps that deliver information and services to iPhones and Android. This puts him at the forefront of changes to the global economy, in which localized services delivered on mobile devices are transforming our economic lives.

This technology is of course at the very epicenter of the global economic earthquake that digitization is bringing to the economy. The combination gives him a front row seat at the festival of disruptive technologies that are coursing through the economy, and from that seat he sees clearly that the speed at which innovations are being produced presents, in and of itself, a monumental challenge to established businesses.

Established companies are being driven to death by the rate of innovation, he tells us one day, and indeed as innovation consultants, we see the impact all the time. Entrepreneurial start-ups, many of them coming from Stanford, have a huge advantage in speed contests because they know that speed is critical to their survival, and so their entire existence is built around the imperative to get to market as fast as possible. There is an extensive literature now focused around speed and how to achieve it, and many of the titles have come from the experiences of successful entrepreneurs in Silicon Valley.[338]

Larger firms often have a different reality. They're accustomed to an era in which their size and scope provide competitive advantages so they use the their market muscle to protect their market share. What they often fail to realize is that these factors are no longer such useful competitive levers. Through the convergence of social media, apps, mobile computing, universal connectedness, as well as the global-digital supply chain, small start-ups have access to resources comparable to giant multi-nationals without owning any of it, which only makes the start-ups still faster and yet more nimble.

Bigger firms also tend to be more concerned with balancing the profitability of their existing operations with the pace of innovation, and they hesitate to disrupt profitable cash flows with new products and services. This allow the start-ups to gain a position in the market. And finally, the big companies are usually also burdened with a more deliberate, i.e., slower, process for making major decisions.

All of these dimensions work against large firms when their competitors are smaller, nimbler, and hungrier, which they almost always are. In the past the large firms have been able to control the pace of innovation, but they no longer have that control, and hence Alfred Chuang's astute observation that the rate of innovation is killing the big guys.

What we thus observe is that any individual business leader can attempt speed up the rate of change in a given market or industry by investing wisely in new technologies or new go-to-market models, but no one company can prevent the market from evolving. In other words, you can speed things up, but you can't slow them down.

The other quote cited at the beginning of this chapter describes exactly the same sentiment, and with exactly the same sense of frustration, but it was 200 years ago that Napoleon's armies sped across Europe and entirely changed the nature of warfare, again by applying the power of speed.

Creative Destruction

While the sense of urgency and the time compression caused by the acceleration of change is certainly real, the underlying dynamics of the competitive marketplace are definitely not new.[339] Joseph Schumpeter, who we met in the last chapter, described the overall capitalist process as "creative destruction," and he pointed out that the natural behavior of capitalist systems brings revolution not as the result of vague external factors, but from within. This is exactly what Stanford and all the great universities do. Change, Schumpeter observed, is the common condition of capitalism, not stability. And in an utterly prescient comment about prevalent management practices at the time (and still today), he wrote, "The problem that is usually being visualized is how capitalism administers existing structures, whereas the relevant problem is how it creates and destroys them."

The significance of this comment is nearly impossible to overstate. While so many observers and leaders focus their attention on how businesses perform in today's markets, Schumpeter points out that it is in the very nature of market evolution to weaken some companies while creating enticing opportunities for others. Therefore, just as important as today's market structures, or today's technologies, or today's competitive advantage, is how the forces of change will affect a firm tomorrow and the day after. Now that we've identified the six revolutions we have a better idea of what's coming, and how significant it's likely to be.

The short-term mentality is the "logic of operations," characterized by actions that have as their goal to create a stable, scalable enterprise that returns strong, steady profits to its shareholders. The qualities that are important from this perspective include predictability, the capacity to forecast future growth, revenues, and profits, and as a result tremendous emphasis is placed on management of today's business. Standardization, policy, procedure, organization structure, and short-term decision making are tuned and fine tuned.

The problem, of course, is that the obsession with predictable scalability ignores the realities of external change, and cannot succeed.

It does no good to be Nokia and far and away the globe's leading cell phone maker, with 9 of the top 10 selling phones worldwide as Nokia was in 2007, when the iPhone comes along, if you have no response. Nokia's 2007 Annual Report was written in glowing and highly optimistic language, but about $150 billion of market value has been erased since then as its prospects transformed from bright to negligible from 2007 to 2016.

Part of the challenge with this type of thinking is that the misplaced focus is usually evident only in hindsight, when wars, market share, jobs, or stock value have already been lost. You have to find a different way of thinking, and a different way of working, before the changes come.

Military leaders are familiar with this problem, which they refer to as "preparing to fight the last war."   Such preparations, even fully implemented with rigor and discipline, consistently fail if the style of warfare has in the interim changed.   Whether we use as example Napoleon's tactics of mobility that crushed Europe's static armies, armored knights slaughtered by the long bow, France's Maginot Line, the Polish horse cavalry that bravely rode to face Hitler's blitzkrieg, the American army confounded by Vietnamese guerrilla fighters, civilian aircraft hijacked and turned into guided terrorist missiles, or a new class of weapon based on the cell phone, the IED (improvised explosive device) as the preferred example, the history of warfare is the history of innovations that render past strategies ineffective. This is also the history of business as Schumpeter observed it in the 1940s, and as we experience it today, 75 years later.

Hence, the relevant question for business leaders is, "What is your strategy for dealing with six revolutions and accelerating change?"

When things are moving so fast, in fact it's a new kind of radar that you need, along with a different approach to making decisions.   For business leaders as for generals, hindsight does not provide sufficient preparation, and it is therefore essential to have an effective way not only to look toward the future, but even better, to create it.

Innovation

The term creative destruction gives us a warning, a name, and a general explanation for the waves of change that move continually through the marketplace, and "fighting the last war" warns us as well that we have do it differently if we're going to survive. Both help us direct our attention toward understanding the forces of change rather than supporting the illusion of stability, and by also reminding us that the waves of change are themselves created not by mysterious forces, but as a result of purposeful innovation in the competitive arena of the market. That's right ... your rivals in the marketplace or the battlefield are targeting you. There is a business, or more than one, whose innovative thinkers are working right now to take away your share of the market, for innovation is indeed the weapon of choice.

What is your best response? Innovations of your own, of course.

In fact, innovation may be your only valid response.

Innovation and Economics

While innovation events and the innovation process occur in the life cycles of individual companies, innovation is also a significant driver of macroeconomics at the level of nations and the economy as a whole. Economists know that it is only through effective innovation that real economic growth occurs, because the underlying economic impact of innovation is to make resources more productive, which is literally how wealth is created in any society. Hence, innovation is crucial to the economic viability of nations, and it is why every nation is now investing heavily in the education of its future scientists, technologists, managers, and entrepreneurs.

But when we're discussing innovation the focus should remain on individuals and individual companies because it is their work that drives the economy forward. Thus, just as innovators drive microeconomic change in specific markets and macroeconomic change in economies, it is innovators who trigger creative destruction in their search for commercial success and competitive advantage in robotics, genetics, energy systems, etc., etc.

Among the companies widely admired today, most have attained success precisely because they have innovated. Through their innovations they brought structural change to their markets, and their motivation was to gain advantage within the capitalist process precisely as Schumpeter described, and they succeeded in doing so.

But the innovator's role is only half of the equation. Customers are the ones who determine the value of innovations, because they're the ones who pay for them.   Market behavior is an aggregate reflection of each buyer's drive to find the most attractive offers, and to maximize value received for cost incurred.   As innovation is the process of creating higher value offerings, buyers naturally gravitate to innovative products.

This brings us directly back to the great challenge we discussed in the last chapter, our willingness and indeed our enthusiasm for whatever it is that we can make and sell, regardless of it's broader social, economic, or environmental impact.   Whether we're talking about drug smugglers and drug dealers bringing products that destroy lives and communities, or auto makers that knowing sell illegal device to evade emissions laws as Volkswagen did, or manufacturers of cigarettes, guns, chemical weapons, or land mines, the economic competition drives entrepreneurs and giant global enterprises to pursue, and sell, whatever is feasible regardless of whether or not it is desirable.   And as I noted above, this is precisely what makes us a super predator, and it may in fact constitute the greatest challenge that humanity faces, our own proclivity to do what we can rather than what we ought.

Inherent in the dynamics of market demand is the process that drives competition through innovation.   The waves of change launched by innovators are countered by others who innovate in order to defend their existing positions, or to attack with ambitions of their own.

It's an endless cycles that serves only to drive the process of change still that much faster and more widely throughout the economy. Accelerating change and the convergence in the marketplace of many competing innovators results in greater complexity for all.

Any enterprise that intends to survive must somehow innovate because innovation itself is the only defense against innovation.   Through innovation you may catch up if you are behind, or even take the lead. Thus, we see that the future of each and every firm is determined largely as a function of its ability to innovate effectively.   Innovation is therefore a mandate, an absolute requirement for survival.

And it is a problem.   An enormous, thorny problem for enterprises, because managing the innovation process is one of the most challenging issues facing any of them. It's extraordinarily difficult to do well.

The Cone of Uncertainty and Innovation Management

A very useful graph, one that's familiar to all investors, is the stock chart that indicates the historical price of a company's shares. Here's a nice looking one.

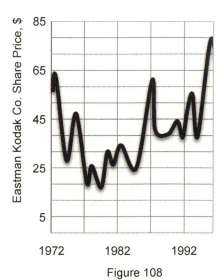

Figure 108
Share Price History, 1970 – 1999
Things are looking good for shareholders.

The share price history of this nice company provided handsome returns to investors and productively employed tens of thousands of workers. Suppose that it's 1999, and you look at the graph and conclude that the company's prospects are stellar. You invest, wait, and hope.

After 1999 the story isn't so pleasant, as the company was doomed by the digital camera. Hindsight can be brutal to investors, as it so often highlights their mistakes. Thus, we must understand not only why a chart shows its current value, but also what changes, positive or negative, may alter the forward moving direction. To anticipate the future requires us to identify the forces acting in the present or future that will reinforce the historical trend, or alter it. Here we come around again to the six revolutions…

Investors search for these insights continually, and they buy and sell to adjust their stock portfolios according to whatever evidence they seize upon. Studying similar charts and the evidence about where they may lead is a primary concern of strategists in all fields, including investment, strategy, and management.

And us.

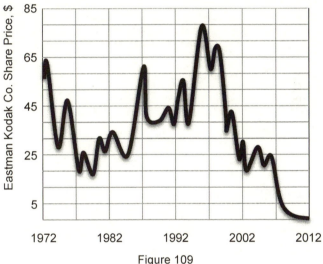

Figure 109
Kodak Share Price, 1970 – 2013[340]
Hopes are dashed.

Leaders and managers also search for insights about the trends and driving forces, but they also do something else that is as important, or more. They can innovate, and thus create new value.

The experience of preparing scenarios has reinforced the insight, which certainly isn't very profound, that the world of tomorrow will most likely be considerably different from the world of today.

For leaders in business and government this presents some serious problems, though, because they're responsible for preparing for the future, and as the future is highly uncertain, what should they prepare for?

We can explore this by visualizing the future as represented by a cone. Moving from the left side, the present, to the right, the future, the cone represents the variety of possible states of the future. At the far left is the apex of the cone, which represents today, which we think we understand. To the right the openness of the cone represents possible futures; the further to the right we go the wider the cone opens, and thus the *less* predictable the situation becomes. Hence, we call this the *cone of uncertainty*.

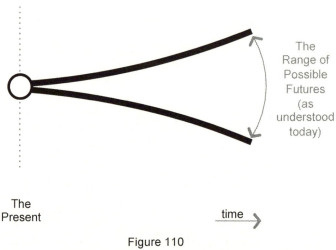

The
Range of
Possible
Futures
(as
understood
today)

The
Present

time

Figure 110
The Cone of Uncertainty: Narrow
The opening at the right side represents the range of possible
futures that we anticipate as of today.

If we envision the cone as a narrow one, this suggests that we see a world in which the uncertainties of the future are not so great, and by implication, that we therefore need to prepare for a narrow range of future possibilities. In the following figure, our way of preparing is represented as dots; each row of dots represents a technology area or innovation theme or topic that we believe may be important in the future. Each individual dot represents an idea, a possibility, or a project.

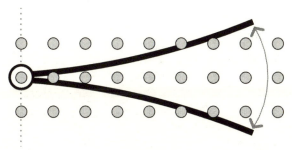

Figure 111
Our Innovation Portfolio
The narrow cone of uncertainty representing a future without a lot of uncertainty implies a relatively narrow range of options under development in our innovation portfolio. Each row represents an area of investigation; each dot represents a specific project or inquiry.

Scenario planning has told us quite clearly, however, that this is probably not the right approach. A much better representation of the uncertainties of the future is a cone that starts out narrow but which quickly broadens to become very wide. The width, of course, represents the much greater (and more realistic) breadth of possibility that lies ahead.

And this enormous range of possibilities tells us that it's mandatory that we must not base our organization's strategy on predictions that will most likely be wrong, but rather on the understanding that we cannot predict the future so we have to ready for a huge range of possible futures.

The first impression this might give us could well be discouraging because there's so much to prepare for, and it can be intimidating, as well, to wonder about the costs and complexities that are implied. The huge range of possible futures is a threat to every organization's viability.

If the market changes radically, and we can expect that it will, the more agile organizations will be more likely to be able to adapt, while the rigid and fragile ones probably will not. Hence, for businesses to remain relevant to the needs of the market, and for communities and nations to remain relevant to their citizens, they will indeed have to come to grips with these challenges.[341]

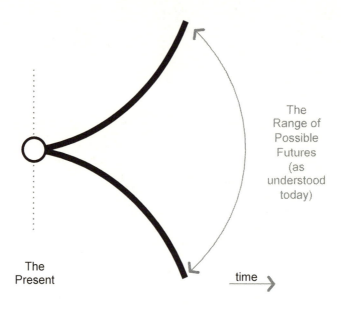

Figure 112
The Cone of Uncertainty: Wide

The much wider opening at the right suggests much more uncertainty about the future. Based on the scenarios examined here and the dynamism of the driving forces of change this is probably a much more accurate model.

We have arrived at the very heart of the risk problem as business leaders confront it, and the fact of mega risk problem that gives the book its title. Please note this:

The broader the cone of uncertainty, the more likely it is that the future harbors more massive risks. It's also more likely that we're not able to see them very clearly, if at all, from the vantage point of the present moment.

When business leaders come to understand the nature of the threat that accelerating change and increasing complexity present to their businesses, they also realize that their organizations must develop new capabilities if they're going to survive. Particularly important among these is the capacity to innovate quickly, the speed imperative I mentioned above, to create proactive (rather than too-late-reactive) responses.

528

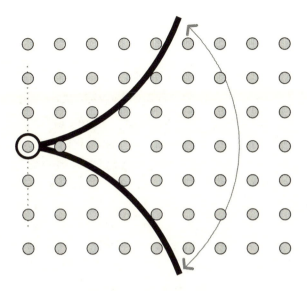

Figure 113
A Better Innovation Portfolio
The future is highly uncertain so we prepare by assuring knowledge of and competence in a wide range of skills and disciplines. Our innovation portfolio is quite extensive, although the investment in each area could be quite modest. What's important is that we are not surprised, and so our portfolio is both a record of work in development, and also of learning in process. This broad portfolio also enables us to go faster when we choose to act, as we are preparing across a wider range of possibilities.   Each row represents an area of investigation; each dot represents a specific project or inquiry.

This is an acute problem now, for us, but it's not a new one. History has known a many great revolutionary leaders whose innovations posed fundamental challenges to their established competitors, but perhaps none were greater than our friend Napoleon. A supremely self-confident man, and an unusually clear and creative thinker, Napoleon rose quickly in up the ranks of the French military because of his successes on the battlefield.

Once he became France's leader he and his armies marched across Europe between 1796 and 1810 and transformed the map of the entire continent, along with its governments, universities, and indeed all of its institutions. By inventing and perfecting radically more effective ways to wage war Napoleon became one of military history's greatest generals; by recognizing that nations should be governed according to logic rather than whim, he also transformed French society, and the system of laws that he commissioned, the Napoleonic Code, is still the underlying basis of French law and much of Western Europe's as well.[342]

The psychological struggle that his innovations presented to his opponents were highlighted after one of the early victories in the Italian Campaign of 1796, during which he decisively demonstrated the effectiveness of mobile warfare. Napoleon and a handful of his officers were riding along a country road on a dark night when they happened upon a straggler from the defeated Austrian army who was walking dejectedly in the opposite direction. His own identity hidden by the gloom, Napoleon asked the Austrian how the battle had gone.

"Badly," growled the Austrian. "They've sent a young madman who attacks right and left, front and rear. It's an intolerable way of waging war!"

The innovation celebrated by one created the intolerable situation for the other.

Innovation Confronts Stagnation

This is what happens when innovation confronts stagnation at any era of history, and Napoleon had to restrain himself from laughing, for that was exactly what he had intended. With new concepts of artillery and mobility his specific goal and ambition was exactly to revolutionize warfare, and he had succeeded perhaps beyond even his own immodest dreams.

The established powers of Europe immediately recognized Napoleon for the enormous threat he was, a monumental danger to their ancient aristocracies and stratified societies. The vast armies of Republican France were the arch-nemesis of the noble families that ruled England, Germany, Austria, Italy, Spain, and Russia, but it took the allied monarchies fifteen years to figure out that the way to defeat Napoleon wasn't with still more of the old, static style of warfare, but instead by adopting his own methods. At Waterloo, in 1814, Wellington succeeded because he used the very same tactics that Napoleon had perfected.

In fact, on a hill overlooking the Waterloo battlefields Napoleon observed the maneuvers of the opposing armies and he commented in appreciation, "They're learning!"[343] In fact they had learned too well, and soon Napoleon was fleeing toward Paris, and soon after that he endured his second and final exile on remote St. Helena. Wellington became a hero in England, and in victory his army preserved the reign of the Europe's monarchies for another hundred years. But Napoleon was on the J-curve, while the monarchies plodded along the going out of business curve, and the next great disruption of World War I finally ended the aristocratic monopoly and they went out of business.

Revolutions in Business

159 years after Napoleon was finally defeated Southwest Airlines was born, and it immediately began revolutionizing the airline industry by introducing a system of innovations that changed the structure of competition in the air travel marketplace. This was not an accident, as disrupting the existing market was exactly what the founders of Southwest wanted to do. It was the central and specific idea behind their business. It's also what many visionary entrepreneurs want to do – they rock the boat, upset the apple cart, make waves, and move the cheese in order to create competitive advantage, to seize upon opportunity, to grow their business. This is the essence of competitive capitalism doing its best work, the search for new opportunities in business, the side effect of which is change that, as we see every day, has the greatest impact on the established organizations that are have become stuck in their used-to-be-successful-but-not-anymore ways.

One of the important insights that the Southwest story highlights is that the changes that Southwest introduced were not new technologies, nor new products, nor even new services. The focus of the company's magnificently successful innovations were its business model. That is, it was the way the company organized itself to create value that was the innovation. As change continues to accelerate, as new digital technologies make new products and solutions possible, as people become ever more connected to one another, then the likelihood that new business models will emerge increases from possibility to certainty. The digital revolution that was the subject of Chapter 1 will continue to enable new business models, and it is these business models above all forces and factors and innovations, that will continue to put so much pressure on the established companies and institutions.

That pressure comes about because old institutions, like the monarchies of Napoleon's Europe, become set in their ways, and they resist change. In a concise bit of profound understatement, IBM CEO Lou Gerstner said, "We don't know how to change."[344]

This was his way of explaining the great difficulties that befell IBM in 1989 when the company nearly collapsed into bankruptcy. His point was that although IBM's leadership had seen the problems coming well in advance they had literally been unable to change the way the organization operated in time to avoid disaster because they could not change their way of *thinking*. This insight reinforces the utility of scenario planning because it such a powerful way of forcing people to confront the need for change and the consequences of being inflexible.   Vulnerabilities become as obvious as a giant, bruised thumb.

As a result of IBM's incapacity to change proactively more than 200,000 IBM employees lost their jobs in a catastrophic restructuring process that Gerstner led quite brilliantly, and which saved IBM from self-destruction. And what the essence of that new structure? It was precisely a new business model.

Southwest's success at business model innovation forced all the other airlines to lower their prices and their costs. It also inspired other entrepreneurs to copy them. EasyJet, RyanAir, and Jet Blue successfully imitated Southwest, and between 1990 and 2000, the new, frugal approach to air travel became the dominant business model. In 2001, however a handful of terrorist-innovators developed a new business model for violence by demonstrating that commercial airplanes also make very effective weapons, and the resulting economic shock from 9/11 compounded the airline industry disruption that Southwest was already causing. The old airline business model finally and utterly collapsed and died on September 11, 2001, and the structure of the air travel industry could never be the same thereafter.

How bad was it? Delta, Northwest, United, Continental (twice), Aloha, ATA, Frontier, America West, and USAir (also twice) all tumbled into bankruptcy, marking the definitive end of the old ways. All of them victims of accelerating change, business model obsolescence, the failure to adapt by proactive means, all compounded by an unprecedented and previously unimagined calamity.

Through it all, Southwest earned profits year after year for 36 consecutive years until 2008 even as its competitors were racking up losses in the billions and then tens of billions. This is indeed the power of a new business model.

And of course it isn't just the airline industry that's been shaken to its very foundations by business model innovation. Retailing, telecom, media, advertising, computers, and banking are all being subjected to radical change, and of course the auto industry was sent reeling by the economic collapse of 2008.

Thus, in the spring of 2009 General Motors' CEO Rick Waggoner was summoned to Washington DC to meet with President Obama's Automotive Task Force, a group whose mission was to figure out how to rescue the ailing US auto industry. Desperately short of cash, Waggoner and Chrysler CEO Bob Nardelli had already dragged themselves in front of Congress with their tails between their legs to beg for government money to keep their businesses in operation. Not that any auto company was thriving at the time – in the economic collapse of 2008-2009, every carmaker was losing buckets of money as sales plunged, even world leader Toyota. But GM and Chrysler were genuinely desperate. The abrupt downturn had exhausted their resources, and without government help they were surely doomed.

How had it come to this sad state of affairs? During his fifteen-year tenure as GM's CEO, revolutionary change swept over the industry while GM failed to keep pace. A new business model was emerging, but GM stuck with the old ideas and focused on the middle of the consumer market, avoiding designs that carried even a hint of originality, while reaching customers through a lazy and bloated franchise distribution network.

GM once controlled more than 50 percent of the US market, but it fell to 30 percent, and then it fell further still. The company lost a staggering $82 billion between 2005 and 2009 while the Japanese manufacturers were earning nice profits nearly every year.

Toyota brought the first mass volume hybrids to the market, positioning themselves as friends of the environment and making the American firms look like environmental laggards. To accentuate the differences, GM had acquired Hummer at exactly the wrong time, only bringing more attention to its anti-environment reputation just the Prius was enhancing the Japanese firm's reputation as a forward-thinking, environmentally sensitive, industry leader.

Meanwhile, the design and manufacturing quality of Japanese and European cars were three to five years ahead while many of GM's brands were struggling because of mediocre design and second-rate manufacturing. Oldsmobile had already been shut down in 2001, and Pontiac and Saturn were stumbling badly; Ford, meanwhile, unloaded its Jaguar and Land Rover brands even as Toyota's Lexus thrived at the high end of the market.

The stark contrast between the American firms and the Japanese caused heartbreak all across Michigan and the upper Midwest, where the auto industry was shrinking rapidly. As their jobs evaporated people moved on, and entire Detroit neighborhoods sat eerily vacant, boarded up, abandoned.

So when Waggoner left the task force meeting that spring morning, he didn't stand quite as tall, and he was no longer CEO, having been fired by the government. Perhaps his inability to cope with change had been his downfall.

A few weeks after Waggoner accepted the government's suggestion that he ought to resign GM declared bankruptcy and retreated under the protection of the courts. The company had to dump billions of dollars of obligations merely to survive.   Chrysler also declared bankruptcy and found its way forward as the partner of Fiat, the once-ridiculed Italian automaker that, between 1995 and 2009, had entirely remade itself.

So what had Fiat accomplished that Chrysler and GM could not?

Throughout much of its history, Fiat had been one of Europe's most successful automakers, but by the 1980s the company experienced a severe downturn. After a humbling decade, the company reemerged in the 1990s, and by focusing aggressively on a new business model – high quality standards, intriguing designs, and fuel-efficient cars – won European design awards and won customers too.

GM and Chrysler had waited too long to improve its fundamentals of its designs and its quality, and so they drove an old and obsolete business model straight into the ground. Just as the market collapsed, Fiat was poised to become a global company once again, and it acquired Chrysler to gain access to the enormous US market.

Revolutionary Innovators

Innovation is how the world's leading organizations respond to revolution when it is thrust upon them from the outside; it's also about how they create revolutions when they aspire to become the leader, the change maker, and the disruptor.

By revolutionary change I mean massive upheaval that causes entire industries to undergo gut-wrenching transformation, change that propels new companies into leadership of entirely new industries, while leaving the laggards hopelessly far behind. Think digital revolution, climate revolution, and energy revolution, and the massive breakthroughs that will enable these revolutions to restructure the market.

These will be revolutionary changes that cause not just one bankruptcy, but waves of them; that costs not thousands of jobs, but hundreds of thousands leading to entirely new economic structures, new social and cultural and challenges and stresses, new industries and new workforces.

And behind every innovation is a person who saw things differently, and then used that insight to create a better value proposition for one customer, and then for millions, and thereby changed the very structure of the market. These are the innovators who are making today's revolutions.

But how do they do it? What's their secret? More than any other single factor, today's successful innovators create new business models, because among all the types of innovation business model innovation may be the most important route to success in today's world. Business model innovators exploit new technology, as Google does. Google has become the world's leading advertising agency by auctioning "words," and now companies bid for the right to have their own web sites linked with ad words and phrases that people search for.

Who would ever have imagined that this could become so wildly profitable? Initially, even the creators of Google didn't. Actually, they discovered it mostly by accident. For a few years they had rejected proposals to sell advertising, but when they realized what it could mean, the insight transformed the company's co-founders into two of the richest men in the world.

Sometimes business model innovators implement new forms of organization, as Wal-Mart did, changing the landscape of mass market retail by squeezing inefficiencies out of the supply chain, progressively lowering the cost of doing business, and then passing the savings on to millions of its by now very devoted customers.

Sometimes innovators market their products in new ways, as Nike did when it revolutionized the sports apparel industry by making everyone all feel that we, too, could and should aspire to be world class athletes and we could *just do it*.

Changing our expectations is also a big part of business model innovation. Fedex changed the way people think about package delivery, and charges 10 to 50 times more to deliver packages than the post office does. Starbucks changed the way millions of people drink coffee, and sells it for $5 a cup instead of 50 cents.

IBM transformed itself by creating a new business model, and so do industrial giants GE and Michelin. These industrial manufacturing icons have become product-service hybrids. GE monitors the jet engines on commercial aircraft in real time using a network of satellites, and its customers don't buy the engines, they rent them. And Michelin doesn't sell aircraft tires, it rents them on a per-landing charge because landings are what make the tires wear out. All of these companies are technology innovators and business model innovators, and business model innovation is contributing more and more of the critical value that makes them successful.

On the other side of the coin, however, many companies that are struggling also show the significance of business model innovation. These include GM and Chrysler, K-Mart, Sears, Circuit City, and most of the big US airlines. So what's the attribute that these companies have in common? Bound by old thinking and old ways of operating, they did not grasp the impact of change and watched as their old business models collapsed in the face of innovative competitors. The lack of business model innovation did them in as the world changed, but they didn't.

Today, business model innovators are creating revolutions with increasing frequency, ensuring that the days of stability are gone forever. No company can consider itself safe from the dangers that change brings, as innovators with new insights and new business models lurk just over every horizon, waiting for the opportunity to pounce.

So how will you defend your organization?

Changing a Culture

A few years ago one of our clients was a large company that was struggling with change in its market when I met with one of the senior executives. He knew that the company is too slow to change, too set in its ways, too focused on short-term gains at the expense of long-term success. "We're probably not unique in that way," he said. Of course he was right.

He knew that many of the management incentives he himself had put in place to assure growth were backfiring because they were making it harder for people to think about anything except the next product launch or the next marketing campaign. His biggest problem, he realized, was that he didn't know how to change the corporate culture that he had been carefully cultivating for the previous ten years.

He mentioned a new competitor that recently come into the market with a different business model. Together with his CEO he had visited one of the competitor's first retail stores at a shopping mall outside of Atlanta. They looked around in the competitor's store and saw a crude attempt at retail, lacking entirely in charm. They immediately knew that the new company had no chance.

"We laughed," he told me, with a bemused look on his face, deeply aware of the irony of this. "But we were wrong. We were very wrong...."

The new entrant had a new business model and it became an instant success. Then it became a huge success, the biggest story the industry had seen in more than a decade. It was a revolution. While the store lacked refinement, it offered each customer a unique, customized experience in a product offering of unprecedented breadth. Instead of trying to control customers, power was willingly given over to customers, as the entire product line was laid out for everyone to see, to touch, and to try. This defined a new relationship between the company and its customers, one that deviated significantly from the traditional model. A revolution indeed.

Caught by surprise, contemptuous of the upstart, and unwilling to accept that the new approach could possibly be successful, my client's company was reluctant to move into the market segment that the interloper had pioneered. Eventually the success of the upstart and the persistence of market analysts pressured them into a response, but the attempt was half hearted, too little, too late. Even their customers knew that they had merely copied the competitor's business model, and it cost them a lot of credibility.

And he was afraid that it would happen again. He didn't know which of his brands would come under attack, or from where the attack might come, but deep inside he felt a gnawing vulnerability. Perhaps all of the brands would be attacked.

"We are too slow," he says. "And we don't take enough risks."

The irony of this statement was not lost on him, either. Under his successful leadership, risk has been progressively removed from the business. Only sure things were acceptable, while failure was not allowed, and definitely career threatening. Unfortunately, the "no failures" mandate also suppressed the learning process and squelched innovation. The top management team, himself included, had nearly perfected the old business model, which had cranked out reliable growth and comfortable profits for more than a decade, making them all rich. Their intellectual and emotional investment in the old ways was obviously hard to shake, but in the end he was right to fear change.

Despite the crisis, it was still possible for this company to seize the initiative again, but this would require new insights and new leadership. There was a vast pool of talented middle level managers who were eager to experiment, eager to innovate in the face of competitive pressures that they thoroughly recognized, because they experienced the consequences every day.

A group of about 20 young leaders formed an ad-hoc team, prepared a detailed analysis of change and a compelling argument for innovation, and managed to get an hour on the CEO's agenda to make their case. He sat politely through the entire presentation, but when it was over he disputed their premise – that the market was changing faster than the company was changing – and also their recommendation – that the company needed to inject a strong dose of innovation into all its activities. Not surprisingly, they came away from this experience thoroughly disheartened.

There were lot of potential solutions available, but without the support of top management few of them had a chance. Talented young people, whose astute senses quickly perceived the blockage at the top, began moving out of the company, compounding the innovation gap by creating a mini-brain drain.

David vs. Goliath

When Southwest Airlines was just a would-be innovator, it had petitioned the FAA to establish service between Dallas, San Antonio, and Houston. The existing airlines at the time banded together in an attempt to block the upstart company from ever being born. "Southwest should not be allowed to fly," they insisted. "The company would disrupt the existing market!"

But from the very beginning the founders and managers of Southwest clearly understood that their primary competition wasn't so much the other airlines but rather Greyhound buses and family cars. They had a plan, largely an intuitive one, but a plan nonetheless. It was based on the strategy of keeping ticket prices very low, as this was clearly essential to success.

This meant that their airline had to reduce its operating costs to a level below what any other airline considered possible, and in the process of figuring out how to become the most frugal air carrier ever. In the new, competitive environment fostered by deregulation, Southwest's disruptive business model emerged as the clear winner, the one that unexpectedly transformed the entire industry.

Executing their plan brilliantly, Southwest won, and as happens so often in the game of innovation, David defeated Goliath yet again.

This is central to the story of GM and of Chrysler versus the once-much-smaller Honda and Toyota, the story of the mighty airline industry against tiny Southwest, the story of giant Sears and upstart Wal-Mart, and the stories of so many others: David confronts Goliath as smaller, younger companies take on older, more established ones. And what weapons do the upstarts have? New ideas, and new business models.

This is also the story of Nike, led by young MBA graduate Phil Knight and track coach Bill Bowerman, who envisioned a new and better kind of shoe, and ruined a perfectly good waffle iron making rubber soles for prototypes shoes that eventually revolutionized track athletics. They also pioneered a new approach to marketing, and their innovations utterly disrupted the market that had previously been dominated by the giant Adidas, which was about to become the world's former leader in sport shoes.

Shoved into an unaccustomed second position, Adidas struggled for nearly a decade before it finally began to turn itself around. Its method? As Wellington had copied Napoleon, Adidas copied Nike.

Today, however, it is Nike that wears Goliath's shoes. Its business model has remained about the same for nearly thirty years, its market share is gigantic, and so the firm can no longer pretend to be the David. Will a new, as-yet-unknown competitor, a new David, come up with the next business model revolution in sports apparel? That firm may be Under Armor, which is cleverly surrounding Nike with yet another generation of innovations.

Under Armor could indeed succeed, but it's also possible that Nike will transform itself and its industry. Or perhaps Adidas will. We can't say for sure when or who, but we can be sure that one day in the not-too-distant future a new business model will emerge, just as it will in every other industry. It will happen because innovators and entrepreneurs will make it happen, driven by the own visions and their own ambitions, and most likely by applying new technologies and exploiting new trends.

The history of Fedex is also a David and Goliath business model innovation story. Fred Smith's plan called for a package to be picked up, carried by truck to an airport, flown to another city, transferred to another truck, and finally delivered, all within about 18 hours, a shotgun transportation marriage that had never before been attempted. After years of capital raising and planning, the company's monumental first day of operation finally arrived on April 17, 1973. The experience was somewhat deflating, however, as Fedex received and successfully delivered a magnificent total of four (4) lonely little packages. It took three more long years, a heavy dose of manipulation, persistent brand building, and millions more dollars of capital than anyone had anticipated for the company to finally achieve profitability. When it did, however, Smith's vision of a new business model was fully validated; the company thrived, grabbing significant market share from UPS and the postal service, and becoming in the process a global business icon.

Along the way to becoming the leader, the name of the company transcended who it was to become what it did: the word "fedex" became a verb, a description of what you do when you have to get it there tomorrow. You don't say, "I sent the package," you say, "I fedexed the package."

Smith, Knight, and Bowerman were founding entrepreneurs, and certainly geniuses in their fields, but sometimes the business model innovation breakthrough doesn't come from the founder. Starbucks was a simple coffee roasting business founded in 1971 by three college professors who started the company just because they wanted to drink high quality coffee. They gradually built their business in Seattle, and by 1982 they operated three modest stores.

That's when a New Yorker name Howard Schultz happened along. Intrigued by what he saw, he applied for a job. But the owners were worried that his New York style would conflict with the company's laid-back culture, so they turned him down.

Schultz persisted, however, and eventually persuaded the trio to hire him as marketing director. With access to additional inside knowledge, Schultz soon recognized the potential for a new business model that combined the coffee roasting business with the coffee house concept, but when he failed to persuade the three owners that his idea was sound, he left Starbucks to start his own business. Within a year his new concept proved successful, and he turned around and bought Starbucks from the three professors and then transformed the company into a global beverage powerhouse. Soon Starbucks was opening more than one store per day, an explosive growth process that lasted through the early 1990s. The boring fifty cent cup of coffee became the seductive and ubiquitous five dollar "vente double-caf carmel macchiatto."

Southwest Airlines, Nike, Fedex, and Starbucks are widely admired and tremendously successful companies. Each transformed its industry: airlines, sports shoes, package delivery, and coffee will never be the same, all because of a single type of innovation – business model innovation.

But it's not just these four. When you take a closer look at Google, Microsoft, Facebook, Apple, IBM, GE, Coca Cola, Xerox, Napster, Shell, Toyota, and even PPG, the 125-year-old glass and paint company, you'll find that business model innovation is critical in their industries as well. Each transformed its industry by figuring out better ways to deliver value and create new experiences for customers.

So what about your industry?

As the economy races forward, as new technologies emerge, as social values, expectations, and needs are overturned, radically new ways of doing business emerge. This process is happening faster than ever in this time of accelerating change, presenting your company with new threats and perhaps also with significant opportunities. Do you understand how revolutionary change will shape your company's future?

Acceleration of Change

The context of business strategy is the marketplace in which it is played out, so discussions of strategy must begin with reference to market dynamics. Not to be too repetitious, but today's critical external factors are the six revolutions and the impacts they cause, accelerating change, increasing competition, and increasing complexity, while the two major internal drivers are innovation and corporate decision making.

Each of the external ones presents its own particular problems, but the impact of all of them acting together significantly compounds the problem, composing a "change conspiracy" that increases the danger exponentially. The results are a drastically compressed planning horizon for every company, the need for faster responses throughout the organization, and the accelerating rate of corporate failure as leaders simply fail to master these dynamics.

The parade of failures makes for dramatic stories that are illustrated by the sad losses suffered by individuals and families struggling to survive the economic and emotional strains, but as more and more companies fail, it is becoming clear that these are no longer unusual events.

In spite of the attempts by governments, central banks, and multilateral organizations such as the IMF, WTO, and the World Bank to reduce the impacts of change, it's evident that the forces of change are far stronger than ever before. Turbulence continues to increase as the fiver revolutions and the anti-revolution play out their momentum, which means that business failures will continue to be common occurrences going forward. And managers wonder obsessively deep into the night, *What should we be doing differently?*

It's Not How Much You Spend

While it is imperative for organizations to be continually engaged in the process of innovation, an important question concerns where those efforts to innovate should be focused. Interestingly, it's not a question of how much you spend on innovation, but rather the process you use to manage that effort. Booz & Co. has shown through its research that spending a lot on R&D is surely no guarantee of future business success:

> Yearly R&D spending among the world's 1,000 largest public corporate R&D spenders has hit a record high of US$638 billion. However, despite the sustained overall increase in R&D budgets over the last decade, this year's findings show once again that higher spending doesn't guarantee bigger payoffs. Indeed, the 10 most innovative companies our study identified this year financially outperformed the world's top 10 spenders, despite actually spending significantly less on R&D.[345]

The reason for this is that most large organizations allocate the vast majority of their R&D investments to protecting existing businesses from competition rather than on creating new markets for the future. Just because the current structure of the market favors your solution today does not mean that the structure of the market tomorrow will also favor you. While one set of products and services may be exceptionally well-suited to the market at a particular point in time, it's surprisingly rare for a company to successfully adapt its products and services to changing market conditions quickly enough to sustain its leadership position.

Many examples confirm this.

- Kodak was the world's number one manufacturer of film but collapsed when digital cameras displaced film cameras. Alas, Kodak itself invented the digital camera, but could not come to grips with its potential or its significance even though it had the huge R&D budgets.
- Nokia dominated the cell phone market and it was a huge R&D spender, but was not prepared for the smart phone

market.

- Sears was the leading American retailer for decades, but lost out to Wal-Mart when discounting and supply chain management became the key differentiators.

- Between 1995 and 2004 world-leading Coca-Cola dropped 50 percent of its share price when customers switched their preference to healthier beverages like water (and much like IBM, it has since recovered). R&D didn't help when the strategists lost track of what mattered to customers.

- There were many happy and charming bookstores all over America until Amazon.com undercut their prices by 20 or 30 percent, and now there are almost none.

The Changing Nature of the Problem

When a company is small its top managers are often in direct contact with customers as a natural part of their role in the company. But as they deal with the complexities of larger enterprises and multiplying layers of organization they often become quite far removed from direct experience of the market. Without direct contact they are intuitively forced to rely on past experiences and they have a progressively more difficult time hearing the voice a changing market that was different than the one they remember.

The increasing disconnect contributes to a growing gap between what managers think is important and what the market thinks is important, and that gap is precisely where emerging companies find a foothold.

Hence, it's entirely different matter of management and style to be an innovator in a small market than to bring effective creative drive to a large operation. As a company grows and the stakes become higher, the risks that the small company has taken as a matter of course are now subjected to a lot more scrutiny, and reaction times slow. Sometimes they slow disastrously. More levels of management have a stake in major decisions; time lags in decision making are longer. In extreme cases, "analysis paralysis" sets in. That's another reason we like scenario planning so much; it motivates real action, not just more market studies that end up on sitting on the shelf in big, fat binders.

Smaller, more nimble competitors have less to lose, fewer people to convince, and often a sense of desperation that sharpens top management's perception of market needs. In fact, the well-tuned senses of entrepreneurial top managers become magnets for capital – small, new companies are founded specifically to attack new market niches that only their entrepreneurs and the capitalists that back them even recognize.

This is why Alfred Chuang's office is in Palo Alto, where so many entrepreneurs and so much capital and so many technical breakthroughs are to be found.

The result of this complex process is a pattern that repeats with astonishing regularity. But as innovative companies grow they tend to become followers rather than leaders.

Winning and Losing at Business Model Warfare

As we have noted, in addition to erroneous assumptions about stability, managers also fall into the trap of focusing too much of their attention inside their own organizations. This is a particular danger with middle managers who are under pressure from upper levels in the hierarchy of organizational authority. Their instinctive and entirely logical sense of self-protection forces them to pay great attention to the behavior and desires of senior management, but disturbingly less attention is often paid to customers.

To succeed at business model warfare, managers cannot be internally focused on products, services, or administration to the exclusion of the critical relationships between these elements, and the even more crucial interactions between a company and its customers. Thinking about innovation in the business model is a matter of the overall relationship between the company and its customers, rather than innovation isolated in this or that aspect. It's not a coincidence that the winners in business model warfare are usually those who manage their customer relationships in the most effective ways possible, by creating compelling experiences across many different dimensions.

Some examples:

Japanese auto manufacturers are the source of many business model innovations, and when they applied their increasing expertise in manufacturing quality to create new, affordable high-end product lines, and now Lexus, Acura, and Infiniti, they created products among the most admired cars worldwide, and enormously profitable segments of their businesses.

They continue to steadily increase their share of the American auto market. Further, Toyota's innovations in alternative fuels with they hybrid Prius line, far in advance of American manufacturers, won it added market share as buyers develop a preference for fuels other than oil. The Prius was the best selling car in California in 2013, 2014, and 2015.

In Europe, retailing giants Auchan and Carrefour redefined the French grocery business in the 1960s by applying new cash register technology to create the hypermarket, and at about the same time Novotel introduced a new kind of hotel.

In the 1970s, Nike redefined the nature of competition in the sports shoe and sports apparel business by transforming star athletes into marketing icons, first with runner Steve Prefontaine and later with Michael Jordan. In so doing, Nike created new markets for its shoes and clothing, and surpassed Adidas to become the global leader in a ruptured market. Nike's core business model innovation was turning its own brand into a key element in the self-identity of its customers, which comes pretty close to the ideal when we're talking about the company-customer relationship. Nike, in fact, elevated brand management to unprecedented heights, and has demonstrated how central the concept of brand management is in today's market.[346]

American Express once dominated the credit card industry and carefully cultivated an image of prestige and exclusivity. Visa entered into competition by creating a global network that was far more fluid, flexible, and low cost, and has far surpassed American Express. Visa charges lower rates to merchants, making its services more attractive, and built its brand on ubiquity – Visa cards are available and accepted everywhere. Then along came PayPal and changed things again, and also made Elon Musk a multi-millionaire. In Africa, meanwhile, MPesa has entirely disrupted money by creating a new form of digital currency that now carries a significant portion of all transactions in Kenya. In the next digital economy it may be bitcoin that distrupts them all.

Dell created a commercial powerhouse by completely re-inventing the manufacturing and distribution process and building machines to order, rather than to inventory, thereby introducing an entirely new business model to the personal computer industry. Mass customization at a competitive price defined a new kind of customer relationship in the PC industry. But in an impressive display of changing market structures, the company's unique business model became entirely passé, and founder Michael Dell took the company private in 2013 in his attempt to rediscover the lost magic of its entrepreneurial past, when it could move nimbly. So far the innovations have arrived, but perhaps tomorrow …

Southwest Airlines developed an approach to the airline business unlike any of the airlines that were established when the company was founded, and sustained its unique business model to become the most financially successful company in a highly troubled industry for the decades. Since the terror attacks of September 11, 2001 Southwest has only been average, however, which suggests that when the innovation cycle has run its course then even a great company reverts to the mean. In some industries that cycle is thirty years, although in technology it takes only 5 – 10 years for many companies to peak and then falter as still more innovative ones emerge.

From Technology Innovation to Business Model Innovation

What we see consistently across all of these examples, and with widespread consistency across the entire history of business, is the following:

It's rarely, if ever, that a single innovation that propels a business to success. It is, instead, a suite of innovations that complement one another and work together to provide a novel or distinctive value proposition that underlies success. The key is not necessarily the product or service itself – which could be highly innovative or even just acceptable – but something brought to market in an innovative way, supported in an innovative way, branded in an innovative way, and in the end always an approach that builds enduring relationships between the company and its customers. This is the essence of the business model.

Furthermore, the core of the innovation value proposition need not be built around a technology per se. In the examples cited above – Toyota, Honda, Nike, Visa, Fedex, Home Depot, Southwest Airlines, and Ford (in its early days, and then again...?) – proprietary technologies do play a part in the company's success, but later the key to success becomes a focus not only on technology itself, but technology applied in a business process to optimize the relationship between the company and its customers.

In today's environment nearly any technology can be, has been, and will be copied, so the important competitive advantage is knowing how to use the technology in a way that adds the greatest value for customers. When enough people believe that a $45,000 Lexus performs as well as or better than a $65,000 Mercedes, it is then that the structure of the market undergoes a profound change. And then along comes Elon Musk in a Tesla and disrupts everything yet again.

With all of this in mind, we now have a better way to characterize marketplace competition, creative destruction, and innovation. We see that effective innovation is not a matter of exploiting individual technologies, nor of exceptional performance in any other individual element of a business, but rather a matter of harnessing the business model itself, which may but does not necessarily include technologies among its many possible dimensions.

To state it more simply, what's happening continuously in the marketplace is competition between business models themselves. The

Lexus business model is different than Ford's business model, or that of Mercedes or a Tesla, etc.

What this means is that the winners at business model warfare have generally applied speed and innovation to create competitive advantages, building stronger relationships with customers by developing business models that fit more closely with customer needs and preferences across multiple dimensions.

Winners who have figured out these principles then seek to sustain their advantages through further business model innovations that defend newly-won territory and extend into new domains. It is therefore the business model itself that must be the focus of innovation, and innovation must be undertaken in service to a larger framework that is defined by the business model itself.

Four key points summarize this discussion about business model warfare.

First, a "business model" defines a broad competitive approach to business, and articulates how a company applies processes and technologies to build and sustain effective relationships with customers. The experiences that customers have, and the relationships that companies build with customers, are the most critical factors. Creating them, understanding them, preserving them, enriching them, and extending them are the critical attributes of success. Everything that is done must be in service to these relationships; they are the point.

Second, every successful business model earns some sort of competitive advantage to the extent that it serves successful relationships. However, any advantage may disappear overnight should a competitor devise a superior model, thereby displacing the company in the relationship with the customer. Due to competitive forces, the life span of every business model is therefore limited, and due to the general unpredictability of change, its viable time frame is indeterminate. Leaders who have the good fortune to preside over a successful business model should never lose sight of the ephemeral nature of their advantages, and must focus not only on administering the (illusory) stability of today, but on preparing for or precipitating the inevitable change of tomorrow by understanding how costs can be lowered while customization is simultaneously increased.

Third, since business models themselves are a more comprehensive way of understanding the focus of competition, they must also become a focus of innovation itself. Relentlessly changing conditions means that business models evolve rapidly, and business model innovation is therefore not optional. While innovations in any area within an organization may be important, innovations that pertain broadly and directly to the business model will be life-sustaining.

Fourth, because the market is so transparent and the performance of every public company is subject to detailed scrutiny by investors and analysts, subtle changes in an organization's performance can lead to broad swings in stock price.

Improving performance and increasing stock price are both self-feeding cycles that create more favorable conditions for companies to develop and implement future innovations, both by improving stock currency for making acquisitions and by lowering the overall cost of capital. Conversely, declining performance and a falling stock price can lead to a downward spiral that makes it progressively more difficult for companies to compete for attractive acquisition fodder, and which can also increase the cost of capital that could be invested in innovation-related activities such as R&D and product development. Get ahead and push farther ahead; get behind and fall farther behind.

The prevalence of this trap suggests that while leaders may be thinking and worrying about change and its impact on their companies, about competition and about competitive advantage, many have been doing so in a way that is simply not effective. Hence, we suggest that thinking about and enacting business model innovation may be a productive exercise for established businesses.

And the need for good thinking about business models is as important for new businesses as it is for old ones.

For these reasons it will remains imperative to discuss managing for change as an absolute requirement, but many (most?) business leaders nevertheless still aren't very good at dealing with it. Recognizing the revolutions and their impact in the marketpalce, anticipating, and adapting to its turbulent evolution, these are the challenges that confront all executives, for although we remember periods that seemed stable, they are in fact long gone and never to return.

As markets continue to evolve and competition becomes ever more demanding as we enter Phase 3 and get more deeply into the six revolutions, engaging in Business Model Warfare therefore becomes not just an interesting possibility, but perhaps a requirement. For their organizations to survive, leaders must develop comprehensive innovation frameworks, and perhaps the perspective offered by the Business Model Warfare framework can help leaders to be more effective.

In the end, when we look at the business world it's clear that the story of change is still the important story to tell, and the process of leading an organization in the face of change remains the critical skill. Consequently, we'll take up the theme of leadership next.

•••

Chapter 16

The

Leader:

Strategy for the 21st Century

Leaders cannot create the context in which they operate. Their distinctive contribution consists in operating at the limit of what the given situation permits. If they exceed these limits, they crash; if they fall short of what is necessary, their policies stagnate. If they build soundly, they may create a new set of relationships that sustains itself over a historical period because all parties consider it in their own interest.[347]

Henry Kissinger

If we heed Dr. Kissinger's advice, and we are wise to do so, then effective leaders must start from outside. What's going on in the wider world that a strategist may pay attention to? You hardly need to be reminded of that now... there are the D-curve and the S-curve, exponential change, increasing complexity, and the six revolutions, an intricate geopolitical map, conflicting needs and desires, and abundant uncertainty, all of these seem to be essential to an understanding of the 21st century. Building soundly on this intricate realm of complexity surely requires that we keep these factors and forces in mind, and that we also remain aware that in this era of exponential change we have to manage organizations in an entirely different way. The linear and sequential patterns of the 20th century aren't going to work; we're exponential and simultaneous now.

Consequently, while the strategic and leadership imperatives of the 20th century called for and indeed created the global multinational corporation that operated within the progressively globalized economy, and which relied on scale, scope, and relentless execution to achieve success, the leadership imperatives of the 21st will are somewhat different. There are, we believe, four of them:

1. Speed
2. Risk
3. Engagement, and
4. Leadership.

These are the four critical factors that successful leaders will and must develop and manage. We'll examine each of them in turn.

1.

Speed

You can speed things up but you cannot slow them down.

In the previous chapter we met Alfred Chuang, who concisely articulated the essential characteristic of the digital disruption that is emanating from Silicon Valley: Existing firms are being driven to death by the rate of innovation. And so it's evident that your choices are to *go fast, or go home.*

It's blunt, but true, and it's a way of working that's ever more fully embedded in the digital economy. But let's not underestimate how difficult it is to go fast, particularly for larger organizations and governments that must deliberate thoughtfully, gain the participation of many executives and stakeholders who really do have meaningful input to provide, accommodate annual budgeting, and strategize carefully. How to counteract these valid ways of operating with the market's inherent dynamics?

It's essential to recognize first that the need for speed requires a different way of working. To achieve speed means the need for constant experimentation, given that what worked well yesterday may not work at all tomorrow. Hence, while we're still working on the big R&D projects, we've learned to break them into smaller pieces that can create demonstrable value in weekly or monthly increments. This is one of the principles of agility that embodied in "agile development," a new way of working on large scale software projects, and "agile innovation," a new way of managing innovation from the most basic to the most fundamental.[348] (This was the subject of our last book, also entitled *Agile Innovation*.)

Another core way of working that enables and indeed promotes speed is to shift the innovation effort away from the intent to create the perfect and complete product to the idea that the real goal is to create the minimum viable product, or MVP. Get it out of the lab and into the market and start learning.

Of course there's a lot more you can do to enable and promote speed, and once you realize that going fast may be the most important factor in your organization's survival then you won't have any trouble at all finding and implementing plenty of them. The key is to recognize that at a strategic level speed isn't optional, it's a matter of life and death.

2.

Risk

The biggest risk is not taking any risk. In a world that's changing really quickly, the only strategy that is guaranteed to fail is not taking risks.

Mark Zuckerberg[349]

A world of accelerating change is also a world of increasing risk, and interestingly the only way to meet risk is with risk. That is, existence at any level is tenuous and filled with risk, and this requires us to take risks to assure our own survival. Stated more simply, we can't keep doing the same thing and expect to survive.

Consequently, our challenge is to manage the risks that we are obliged to take in the most effective manner possible. But the risks exist on many levels and come from many different sources. There are market risks, largely coming from our competitors; existential and strategic risks far beyond our control that originate from the global macro situation; and operational risks related to our capacity as an organization to execute effectively on our own goals and the expectations of our clients, and indeed we must manage all three types.[350]

There are also, as we saw in Chapter 9, an abundance of cognitive risks that must be faced and overcome, because if we succeed in fooling ourselves about what constitutes reality because the actual environment is too unpleasant or changing too fast then we're obviously making a suicidal choice. The suitable response this entire category of risks is to train our own thinking to be open and honest, and to set aside biases and preconceptions. While it's not so easy to do, the joy of being surprised will only be exceeded by the joy of success.

But there's also a paradox here. On one hand we should never be surprised, as the whole point of going so exhaustively through all twelve driving forces is to show that the world is stranger and less predictable that we could have imagined, and we shouldn't really be surprised at its new and clever behaviors. And yet at the same time it's marvelous to be surprised, and Jonathan Ive of Apple pointed out, being surprised means precisely that we are paying attention and that we're willing to let something new or unexpected provoke in us appreciation for the learning moment that it has provided, and for the new consequences and implications that are inherently revealed.

Surprises or none, we must be constantly vigilant, which means tracking the unfolding world, the twelve driving forces and dozens more beside on a regular and rigorous basis. Keeping track of it all is a major task, to be sure, but the alternative is surely worse.

Innovation Portfolio Mapping

One way of doing so is by carefully designing a map of the market that might look something like the cone of uncertainty that I mentioned in the last chapter. But it's not just the cone we want to see, we need a more refined version that shows conceptually how broad the future possibilities are, and also how the specific work that we're doing in our organization might map to future risks and opportunities.

This is in effect a form of an R&D or innovation portfolio, and in our more detailed innovation work one of the major themes is designing and managing these portfolios. We already saw what this looks like in the previous chapter, as by integrating the concept of the cone of uncertainty with the innovation portfolio we get something that looks like Figure 110.

Now we have added more specificity about the columns.

Each row of dots is a specific type of technology or area in which technology or innovation is likely to be or expected to be important in the future. Time moves from left to right, meaning that roughly one third of the dots closer to the left side, today, represent actual projects that we expect to bring value to the market in the nearer term. The dots further to the right represent more speculative projects that we believe may have future value, but the further to the right we go, the less certain we become.

Hence, roughly the right one-third of the diagram represents future options and surveillance activity; we're keeping an eye on those things. Some of them will almost certainly turn into technologies, trends, products, services, or business models that are meaningful in our future, but as of today we probably don't know exactly which ones. Hence, each dot represents an option; we're engaged in a learning process to figure out which dots will become real and important and which will prove to be dead ends or false alarms.

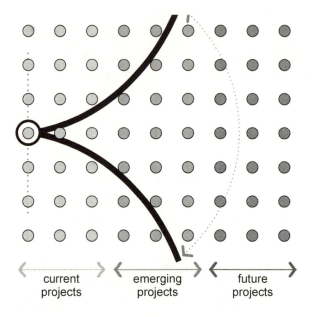

Figure 114
A Better Innovation Portfolio
The future is highly uncertain so we prepare by assuring knowledge of and competence in a wide range of skills and disciplines. Our innovation portfolio is quite extensive, although the investment in each area could be quite modest. What's important is that we are not surprised, and so our portfolio is both a record of work in development, and also of learning in process. This broad portfolio also enables us to go faster when we choose to act, as we are preparing across a wider range of possibilities. Each row represents an area of investigation; each dot represents a specific project or inquiry. The left 3 columns represent current projects; the center 3 columns represent emerging projects, and the 3 on the right are future possibilities.

Roughly the middle third of the matrix thus represents the new stuff that is in the process of emerging into the market. We have to expect that a lot of these will become disruptions, and as we don't want to be disrupted out of business we have to follow these closely.   But new information pops up literally every day because this is a very fluid and dynamic global innovation landscape – because, after all, all of our existing and future competitors also trying to solve the same problem, which is to figure out what's really going on and to get there first when it matters to do so.   To cope with this problem we've come up with a tool called the Disruption Map, or D-map, that allows us to model the pace of change.

Disruption Mapping

Using machine learning algorithms to track an unlimited supply of external data available on the internet, we are constantly on the alert for new data points that may affect the structure of the map.   Using both manual modeling and automatic, machine-driven assessments of various technologies we can map a forecasted rate at which emerging technologies and sub-technologies will become meaningful in the market.

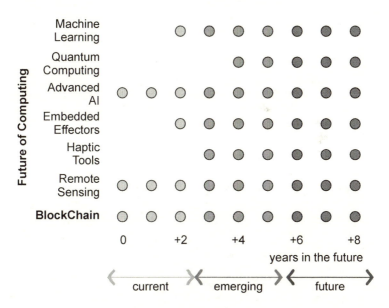

Figure 115
A Disruption Matrix: Future of Computing
Tracking the emergence of a suite of new technologies at a high level
regarding the Future of Computing.

Working at progressive levels of detail, from the more general pertaining to the "future of computing," for example, to the more specific BitCoin/BlockChain entry into the market we monitor developments throughout the world to assess the rate at which these technologies and applications emerge.

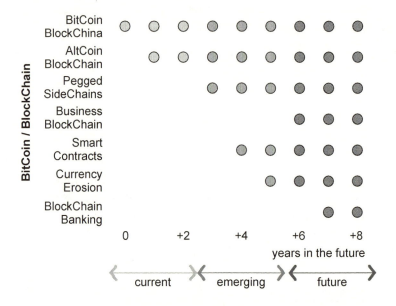

Figure 116
A Disruption Matrix: BitCoin/BlockChain
A level of detail more specific than shown in Figure 111 tracks a
specific technology and the elements that may contribute to its
emergence into the market..

Technologies rarely impact in the market in isolation from one another, and thus the transformative revolutions don't usually arrive because of one big new thing. Instead, they depend on an entire suite of new capabilities that mature together, and nearly every impactful technology from the last fifty years has displayed this characteristic. Smartphones, for example, depend on a suite of breakthroughs in chip technology, flash memory storage, display technology, touch screen capabilities, and cellular bandwidth management. Without all of these elements they simply wouldn't work, so while its necessary to understand each element of an emerging business model or technological breakthrough, it's also important to assess them in various combinations. But because they arrive in combinations their and their dependencies are more complex we have to study the root technologies and their applications at many levels and from many perspectives. Hence, the purpose of the Disruption Map is to combine these threads into a picture of how the market might mature.

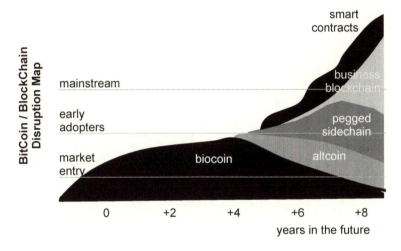

Figure 117
A Disruption Map: BitCoin/BlockChain
Forecast of the emergence of BitCoin/BlockChain as a business
disruption, based on the Disruption Matrix shown in Figure 112.

Leading Indicators

The other thing that disruption maps do for us builds on something that we learn from scenario planning. In scenario planning efforts we discover that the world may evolve in quite different ways, some of which we like and other we don't like at all. And as we finish the modeling part we turn our attention to identifying these imperatives, and also to looking out for those small (or large) bits of data that tell us when the future is arriving. We call these "leading indicators" become they help us to recognize the bigger, more significant patterns early on. And of course early on is important, because the sooner we know what's coming, the better we can prepare. D-maps are thus a tool for identifying and tracking leading indicators.

The management discipline related to the innovation portfolio obviously takes on significantly greater importance under these circumstances. If innovation is indeed, as we assert, the make-or-break dimension of organizational performance, then portfolio management is legitimately an essential performance metric.

3.

Engagement

The striking technologies that characterize our species, from the kayaks and compound bows used by hunter-gatherers to the antibiotics and airplanes of the modern world, emerge not from singular geniuses but from the flow and recombination of ides, practices, lucky errors, and chance insights among interconnected minds and across generations.

Joseph Henrich[351]

The complexity of our environment, our own organization, and the external challenges is all increasing, and the only to grasp the full scope of what's occurring and to mount the most effective possible response is to engage the thinking power of everyone in our organization and indeed many more who are not inside in understanding what's going on and figuring out the best and fastest responses. Engagement, that is, is mandatory; you, as a leader or even the leader, simply are not going to figure it all out on your own.

Or as Bill Joy concisely put it, most of the smartest people inevitably work for somebody else.[352] The sooner you get them productively engaged the sooner your organization's collective brainpower will get the benefits.

4.

Leadership

It is the business of mythology proper, and of the fairy tale, to reveal the specific dangers and techniques of the dark interior way from tragedy to comedy. Hence the incidents are fantastic and "unreal:" they represent psychological, not physical triumphs. ... The hero is the man or woman who has been able to battle past his personal and local historical limitations to the generally valid, normally human forms. Such a one's visions, ideas, and inspirations come pristine from the primary springs of human life and thought.

Joseph Campbell[353]

The fourth imperative is leadership itself, which means not only what you bring as a leader but the leadership qualities and abilities that are both developed and expressed by people throughout the organization and also, as with engagement, outside.

Given the enormous number of books and articles on leadership, we hope that effective leadership is a skill that can be learned and developed. I've discussed many pertinent themes in this chapter and throughout the book, including the need to base decisions on facts rather than opinions and preferences, on the requirement for extensive and effective modeling of systems, etc. etc.

In Chapter 9 I also mentioned that Irving Janis has suggested seven qualities that he found essential to the sound decisions that in his studies succeeded in avoiding the shortcomings of groupthink.

1. Thoroughly canvass a wide range of alternative courses of action.
2. Survey the objectives and the values implicated.
3. Weigh carefully the costs, drawbacks, and subtle risks of negative consequences, as well as the positive consequences, that could result.
4. Search continuously for relevant information for evaluating alternatives.
5. Take account the expert judgments, even when those judgments contradict initial preferences.

6. Reexamine positive and negative consequences of the main alternatives, including actions that had initially been considered unacceptable.

7. Made detailed execution plans, including contingency plans if things go wrong.[354]

In reviewing the list its obvious that Janis' advice is consistent with the comments I've offered in this chapter and elsewhere.

The Innovation Formula

I don't want to appear simplistic or trite, but at the same time these really are these four imperatives that we have found to constitute the mandatory performance elements for every organization, large or small, private of government or non-profit. And please don't be fooled into thinking that they're particularly easy to do; to some degree each requires exceptional skill to do well.

They also, together, constitute what we believe to be the formula for innovation. That also risks sounding trite, but we've been at this for a long time and it really does seem to work.

The formula is:

Figure 118
The Innovation Formula

Please notice that four clauses are multiplied times one another. The four are not additive, as it's not a matter of x plus y plus z. The fact, as we understanding it, that they are multiplicative means that if you get a value of less than one for any of the four then you're by defining detracting from your own efforts.

And if you get a zero for any of the four, your innovation efforts are kaput.

Which means, essentially, that you have to address all four dimensions or you're dead. If you're interested in more detail you can read about all this in my book *The Innovation Formula*.[355]

The Economy

When the economy changes its structure there is inevitably disruption, and given that there are four major disruptions set to arrive in the coming decade or two, it's pretty reasonable to expect some challenging times ahead.

- Digital: The full transition to the digital economy could cause large scale disruption in employment patterns and massive displacements should robot indeed replace human workers who cannot then find other useful things to do.

- Climate: The full onset of climate change may cause massive storm-related costs while also wiping out trillions of dollars of real estate assets, both of which would be economically stressful but together may be economically disastrous.

- Energy: The shift from a fossil economy to one that isn't will disrupt global financial markets for which the fossil producers and distributors have been solid landmarks for more than a century. The faster this occurs, the more disruptive it will be.

- Demographics: And the fourth economic revolution will be the demographic transformation in which two centuries of rapid population growth as provided the laborers to build the industrial economy and the consumers to buy its outputs. Without significant population growth turning to a population implosion the economic structure that has been nearly perfected over two centuries becomes, quite suddenly, irrelevant. Something else, quite unknown, will take its place, but getting from here to there will not be an easy transition.

One significant and structural economic change is a lot of deal with; two is a heavy burden; but four, well, we've never been through four simultaneous economic transformations that all arrived at more or less the same time. The best advice is perhaps to buckle up, because it's going to be a wild ride.

Emergence

How wild?

Emergence is the defining characteristic of the evolutionary process. The concept tells us that some characteristics and attributes come about in what appears to be a spontaneous manner when a set of conditions is just right such that a given outcome, entirely unprecedented and unpredictable, presents itself. One cannot, by definition, engineer an emergent quality; it comes about on its own when it's good and ready.

A sister concept to emergence is the one of punctuated equilibrium. This idea, from evolutionary biology, says that evolution itself occurs not a smoothly progressing set of gradually apparent new capabilities, but rather in fits and starts. Evolution, it tells, us is not a ramp but a staircase; each step being a plateau, and each vertical rise being a leap into new capability.

Hence, the boldness of Kurzweil and all the singularists is their suggestion that we are headed for an evolutionary leap, which one might otherwise consider to be entirely incapable of being predicted. They make a good argument with the evidence they present, and thus while it may be a bit presumptuous to propose where evolution is heading, it's also presumptuous to assume that they're wrong. A computer that designs and builds better computers creates a runaway phenomenon; it reaches a critical mass chain reaction (like a nuclear weapon) and keeps on exploding.

We've never seen anything like that, but like the black swan, never having seen it is not evidence that it is does nto or cannot exist, merely that it hasn't ... yet.

Given that during the last two centuries the complexity and diversity of the world have become exponentially greater than anything that came before, we are now in a situation in which a great many new possibilities can be explored. We also understand that the exploratory seeds from which new ideas and objects may emerge are everywhere, and with so much exploration going on, so many experiments, the result is a profusion of innovations at all levels of society, in business, governance, technology, and culture. This is in turn creating so many changing and evolving factors and conditions that we are forced to realize that the likelihood of making accurate predictions is shrinking fast, to nil.

Evolution is also opportunistic and entirely sensitive to the local context at any particular place in time. And in the coming century the place where all this happens will be, more and more, the city. As urban setting become humanity's overwhelming preference for where to live we are likely to see a new model of urbanism evolve, in response not only to the economic conditions and crises, but also to an increasingly clear requirement that cities should be ecology's partner, not its adversary.

Most of today's cities are ecological wastelands, consuming resources and producing astonishing and unsustainable amounts of waste. It's likely that tomorrow's cities will be considerably different. Rather than being optimized for cars as today's cities are, they may not be dependent on autos at all, or if they are they're probably be smaller, self-driving ones. They will thus require a completely different infrastructure than the uncountable miles of multi-lane paved roads and freeways that carve up our current urban spaces like so many impassable canyons. They may be compact, three-dimensional, and they'll certainly be optimized for people and to enable and bring forth our individual and shared creative potentials.

•••

Conclusion

Super Learning

and

Extreme Creativity

The whole thing is being worked out through what is bound to be a long and very frightening process, not only in the depths of every living psyche in the modern world, but also on those titanic battlefields into which the whole planet has lately been converted. ...
It is not society that is to guide and save the creative hero, but precisely the reverse.

Joseph Campbell[356]

The challenges we're already facing and the ones we will face in the coming years and decades will be demanding, without question, and they will stress the substantial and material dimensions of our society in every way. They will also test us psychologically and psychically, and in meeting them we will discover strengths and commitments that we did not perhaps know we had. This is the essential quality and essence of learning, and there is no doubt that to successfully navigate what's coming we will become not only good learners, but super-learners.

Happily, evolution has already given us the innate skills to succeed in this role. Evolutionary biologist Joseph Henrich explains,

> Across centuries and millennia, cultural evolution created social environments replete with social norms, which influenced diverse domains ranging from marriage, ritual and kinship to exchange, community defense, and valued domains of prestige. Over tens and hundreds of thousands of years the diverse social environments produced by this process became important selection pressure driving human evolution. ... Our ability to learn from others, to generate greater technological sophistication and large bodies of adaptive knowhow ... gives rise to our collective brains.[357]

Learning and Creativity

Learning, let me remind you, is our creativity directed inwards; it is ourselves who we create through our investments in learning, our skills and capacities and capabilities. Creativity, meanwhile, is our capacity to learn when it is directed outwards at the making of new things and solving new problems. Hence, learning and creativity are really the same thing; the difference is just the direction in which we're pointed.

Many of today's young people spend six to eight years in primary school, six more in secondary school, four more after that in university, and some of them spend two to four additional years perfecting their professional credentials as doctors, lawyers, accountants, engineers, scientists, bureaucrats, professors, etc. Hence, society is investing a tremendous amount of its resources in bringing its young peoples' skills to the point that they can then, finally, begin the real learning, the on-the-job training when they actually find out about the "real" world of "real" work.

This is what's needed to become competent in any professional or technical domain because society has accumulated such an enormously vast store of technical knowledge. Your pre-med daughter, sitting in graduate school, is learning deeply and broadly about a deeply technical field, while her best friend sitting next to her is studying accounting, and while they love to hang out together in the library or a coffee shop, it's quite possible that there is little to no overlap between their domains and thus they literally cannot have an in-depth professional dialog with one another because they speak different professional languages. That's also what we're coming to, such super-specialization that shoves us deeper and deeper apart within our technical realms. But that's the only way we can make meaningful contributions to our chosen fields of study.

Looking across these twin phenomena of extensive professional education and deep specialization we see two things. First, learning is cultural and collective. No one could possibly figure out even the basics of medicine unless they have access to vast libraries and able instructors to help make sense of it. And second, because society is now evolving as a result of our culture must faster than it could possible evolve as a consequence of genetics, evolution is thus cultural and collective also.

That it, it is our shared knowledge and our capacity to apply that knowledge which is shaping the future of our species as it is also shaping the future of our planet.

This is profoundly important: human culture is the driving force now.

Our Human Capabilities

We began this journey by considering how it is that humans have come to be such profoundly successful predators that scientists had to come up with a new name for us. They arrived at "super-predator" to describe our aggressive and competitive spirit. And they noted that despite our average or even mediocre sensory tools, our small stature, and our tiny teeth we've still managed to kill every rival we ever faced. The reason is of course because create and share knowledge from generation to generation; that is, we are a super-learner.

As a result we've also applied our skills to modify our planet's geology, and in so doing we created the Anthropocene era.

The book then considered our proclivity to experiment, which we're quite good at, and this has led us to learn still more, and faster.

We have also become quite proficient technologists, we make unlimited stuff, and combustors because we burn things, and extractors who dig it out of the Earth, and builders who pile it up on top of the Earth in roads and bridges that span the canyons and towers reaching toward the sky. These four, technologist-maker, combustor, extractor, and builder have also built the modern economy, and with it our globalized society.

We have not lost sight entirely of our humanness along the way, and the qualities that define and advance our culture, but while we also remain attached to our past in a sometimes reactive way, we sometimes look forward into the future, even far into the future.

We assess our situation realistically, sometimes, and analyze the evidence thoroughly, sometimes, and we make huge leaps of vision to see what's coming and how it could be better. We constantly make and revise our maps as we try to figure out where we are, and we plan our journeys to try to get where we want to be.

We think persistently about what's right and what's wrong, and we are exceptionally interested in what is fair and unfair. We innovate constantly and chronically, seeking the new for the thrill of newness or for the commercial and military advantages it may bring, and sometimes we work together nicely and follow the best ideas or the best guides.

This book has been about all of those capabilities, each one fascinating, but even more fascinating when we consider that all of them come in a single package, gestated about nine months and then educated for fifteen or twenty or twenty-five years before being loosed into the wide and wild world to create, to consume, to work and earn and buy and sell and to join the big parade of 7+ billion humans busily at work living their lives while they also create a global civilization and chart their way forward into the 21st century's thrills and spills.

As this story unfolds a few themes will emerge as perhaps paramount. First, with acceleration and complexity and all that will come new ways of dealing with our problems. It's a given that the way we do it now isn't going to be adequate, so we know that our ability to look forward into the 21st century will therefore have to be much refined from what it was in the

20th. If I have not convinced you of that by now, then you read too far.

Foresight: The Second Turning Point

The other big idea is that if we base a view of the future on the shape of the population growth curve, as I've suggested, then the shape of the curve itself tells us that we're entering into a new era of human history, one so new that we don't have a name for it yet. The demographic transition is already well under way, and the first glimpses of a new set of economic challenges are emerging in Japan and Eastern Europe. At the same time, of course, the technology revolution, the climate revolution, and the energy revolution are also demonstrating that they will have significant impact in the years and decades ahead. No one knows exactly how they will interact or what's coming, but there can be little doubt that life and society will be quite different ten or twenty years from now, and so necessarily will business and government. It is thus, as I noted earlier, a turning point.

Figure 119
Global Society at a Turning Point
The transition from Phase 2 to Phase 3 has already begun.

One of the key questions that we must consider, then, is what will be required of us if we're going to navigate this transition successfully. And at one level the answer is that we're going to have to be exceptionally creative to develop new responses to these challenges across the full range of society's dimensions that is, which I refer to as extreme creativity. Our creativity will be tested in economics, in management, in our capacity to adapt to complexity, in our response to social and psychological pressure, in gerontology and our support for the aged, and in education and our support for and development of young people.

No population of segment of society will be untouched, and no place on geography of the world will be untouched either.

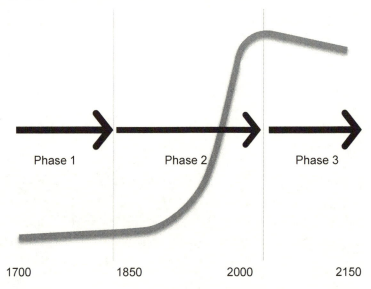

Figure 120
Three Phases of Human History
The shape of the population curve provides a model of the structure of history, and suggests that we are entering a new Phase.

Extreme Creativity

What is extreme creativity?

It is an environment in which there are few knowns, but many more unknowns, extreme creativity is the skill to solve problems of unimagined complexity.

For example, as the revolutions change the structure of the economy we will have to redefine the meaning of economic growth. Until now, growth has meant producing and consuming more, but as we're already consuming more than the Earth produces this will change. How will the economists adapt the concept of GDP a measure of the sheer mass of productive effort to perhaps GBP, gross beneficial production, so that we don't count destruction of Brazilian rain forest as a "good," when clearly it's not?

We will have to recreate our ideas about education, career, and retirement as our average life spans creep toward 100 years, and then beyond. What is a healthy, happy, and productive life when one lives through the births and deaths of multiple generations of technologies and the companies that create them and bring them to market? How many times will each of us be required to learn new skills to adapt to new requirements in the workplace – assuming, that is, that people are still working; but perhaps the robots do it all. What will the people do then? And how will society's resources be distributed if we don't have the great equalizer of "earning potential" to decide who lives in the cramped favelas and who lives in the luxury highrises?

What is community and what is ownership if assets like cars are no longer personal possessions? What is a public good, and what is a private good then?

What is a nation-state, and what is a citizen, if all the low-lying islands cease to exist and millions of refugees must find new places to live? What is a refugee and what does his or her citizenship mean when the nation tjat issued the passport is engulfed in self-destruction and the individual's choices are to die, to live in a squalid and hopeless tent city, or to risk the journey to a safer future?

These are hypothetical problems that may not be hypothetical for very much longer. To solve them we will surely have to look beyond the obvious and tried solutions, the old approaches, and find new ones. But that will mean more tests and experimentation, for there's no way to know what's really going to work until we give it go and see. With testing and experimentation come learning and excitement for some, but also uncertainty and stress for others. Just as the future is arriving already in some places but not in others, the psychological dimensions will also be uneven; we can expect that the youth will have a great deal of mentoring to do to help the elderly make sense of this new world, but perhaps the elderly will also have useful perspectives to share, for while the future world will have unlimited data at its fingertips, we should expect that it still takes time to develop wisdom.

Strategy for the 21st Century

The importance of foresight and the inescapable need for more and better clarity about the future is perhaps paradoxical, for in a world of accelerating change how can we see into the future better than we do now? The answer, of course, is that we have to look in a different way, not by trying to predict specific future states, but by understanding the driving forces of change. Hopefully the book has given you a much better appreciation for that.

Strategists and leaders will certainly get better at long range thinking, and at separating meaningful evidence from anecdote to get a firmer grasp on reality. To accomplish this they will undertake or sponsor non-stop surveillance, charting and mapping the trends and forces that shape the day-to-day and the decade-to-decade. They will engage in scenario thinking to explore possibilities and potentials, and while they will certainly have strong points of view about what's coming and what's best, they will demonstrate the willingness to change when the evidence calls for change.

They'll also get quite good at systematic innovation, at taking and managing organizational risk in pursuit of new opportunities and new solutions, as this will be the organizational competence that's essential for survival and adaptation to the accelerating cycles of technological and social change. Of course it already is.

Strategy in the 21st century will therefore be a learning process in which speed will be essential, naturally, but so also will principles.   In Phase 3, if it does indeed arrive, the principles of equity and ecology will be as important as those of efficiency and effectiveness, and thus leadership and strategy will be both resolutely heroic and extremely creative, finding new ways to discover and express humanity's unique and amazing capacities to learn and create in business and government and society.

•••

Part 4

Resources

The Well-Prepared Species

The Lexicon of Tomorrow

Language evolves as society evolves, and since our society is evolving quite rapidly and new words are being created every day to label new experiences, new understandings, and new things, it takes some effort to keep up. Hence, the purpose of this Lexicon is to compile in one place a useful list of words and concepts that I've used here and which newly describe essential and essentially new aspects of today's world, and which may also usefully describe tomorrow's. It's certainly not a complete list, but in aggregate it's pretty interesting nonetheless.

Additive Manufacturing – 3D printing; machines that create new stuff in layers, by adding. More complex shapes and forms can be made this way. Printers can be located anywhere – on the Space Station, in your kitchen, etc. Additive manufacturing removes the factory from the factory.

Agglomeration Economy – Economic gains including higher output per worker, higher wages, higher profits, and higher incomes that come from geographic concentration of firms and people. (Polèse, P. 31)

Anti-Fragile – Technically, anti-fragile is something that becomes stronger when it is stress, as distinct from fragile, which breaks when it is stressed. (Nassim Taleb)

Autocatalytic – Literally, something that produces the fuel that propels it; in our context, a process of change that feeds itself such that further change results. (Henrich, p. 57) In the urban context, on a street where interesting things happen, more interesting things happen. (Montgomery, P. 151) (See also, Autopoesis.)

Autopoesis, Self-creation (Varela, Maturana, and Uribe, 1974) – A process that creates itself.

Behavioral Economics – Studies the effects of psychological, social, cognitive, and emotional factors on the economic decisions of individuals and institutions and the consequences for market prices, returns, and the resource allocation.

Black Swan – Something that was thought to be impossible or nonexistent until it is subsequent discovered or occurs. More broadly, the cognitive fallacy of assuming that something cannot exist or could not occur just because it has not been seen or has not yet occurred. "Before the discovery of Australia, people in the Old World were convinced that all swans were white, an unassailable belief as it seemed completely confirmed by empirical evidence. …This illustrates a severe limitation to our learning from observations or experience and the fragility of our knowledge. One single observation [or event] can invalidate a general statement derived from millennia of confirmatory sightings of millions of white swans." (Taleb, Nassim Nicholas. The Black Swan: The Impact of the Highly Improbable. Random House, 2007. P. xvii.)

Climate Refugees – People who become refugees as a result of climate change.

Co¬-Evolution – An evolutionary process in which two factors evolve as a consequence of their interaction with each other. Also the title of a famous journal from the 1970s.

Cognitive Dissonance – The tendency "to suppress, gloss over, water down or 'waffle' issues which would produce conflict or 'psychological pain' within an organization. (Tuchman, Folly, p. 303)

Cold Trade War – Conflict between China and the US over electronic hardware and software (Shirky, p. 78)

Commuter Amnesia – Commuters tend to shut out their daily experiences of commuting to work, and to forget about commute trips as soon as they are done. "The longer people's commute, they more likely they are to report chronic pain, high cholesterol, and general unhappiness." (Montgomery P. 180)

Complexity – In common language complexity is often confused with complicatedness, referring to something that can manifest in a lot of different ways. But that's not such a useful definition for us. In more precise systems language, complexity refers to the possible states of a system; more complex systems have more possible states. In most cases this is a consequence of having more inputs and/or more connections. Hence, complexity systems, such as the human brain (the most complex organ and possible the most complex biological system), are so deeply interconnected within that 80 billion neurons are connected by tens of trillions of synapses, resulting in an uncountable range of behaviors.

Conspicuous non-consumption – A pattern of consumer consumption in which we show off our environmental awareness by letting others know how conscientious we can be, and how little we can consume. This is contrasted with "conspicuous consumption," the competitive act of consumption as a demonstration of wealth and power, which was common from the 1950s through the 1990s. The American concept of "keeping up with Joneses" embodied conspicuous consumption; if your neighbor, Mr. Jones, bought a shiny new car, you felt social pressure to buy one as well.

Counter-Intuitive – Something that behaves in ways that we do not expect, as it is contrary to our intuition. Typically refers to systems that do the opposite of what is expected and intended. These behaviors are generally due to the their very high complexity, which succeeds in fooling our intuition.

Cultural Neuroscience – Study of the impact of human culture on human neurology, and particularly on the human brain. (Henrich, p. 268)

Cybersovereignty – The idea that the internet should have borders and controls for information to respect the sovereignty of nations. (Shirky, p. 27)

Davos Man – Member of the global elite who attend the annual World Economic Forum conference in Davos, Switzerland (Samuel Huntington)

D-curve – The double curves implied by Moore's Law, the rising curve of exponential improvement in computer chip technology, and reciprocal downward curve of cost. Computers get rough twice as powerful and half as expensive, so 4x better, even 18 months or so. The curves drawn together form the shape of a D, hence the D-curve.

Demand Destruction – Reduction in demand based on changing consumer patterns. For example, energy efficient appliances and light bulbs "destroy demand" for electricity, which in turn destroys demand for

whatever is used to generate electricity, whether oil, coal, or nuclear.
(Zeihan, P. 133; If 3D printing captures just 1 percent of global
manufacturing it will slice 50,000 bpd from global oil consumption just
from transport savings. P. 136)

Digital Danger Zone – A period of history into which we are entering that is
characterized by a profusion of new technologies of significant power that
make it possible for new companies to threaten older ones, if the
entrepreneurs behind the new ones are able to harness the power of
technology more cleverly or more quickly.

Economic Geography – The study of why some places grow and prosper
compared to others. (Polèse, P. 1)

Energy Density – The amount of energy that can be extracted from a given
mass or volume of a raw material. Oil has a very high energy density
because one unit of oil can generally produce more useful work than the
same unit mass or volume of nearly any other non-nuclear material. Due
to oil's high energy density it is particularly challenging for non-fossil
energy systems such as wind and solar to be economically competitive.

Financialization of Citizenship – The practice of buying citizenship in a
country. (Abrahamian, p 84) See also Investment-Based Citizenship.

Ethnic Nationalism – Alignment of the historical or ethnic population of a
region around a nationalist concept. (Shirky, p 104)

Euro – The European Union common currency. The word Euro has become a
popular preface for an entire vocabulary of terms related to the EU
Eurozone – the 19 EU members states that have adopted the Euro currency
(the other 9 have not)
Eurosceptic or Euroskeptic – someone who is skeptical that the EU is a good
idea Euroenthusiast – someone who feels the opposite
Eurosclerosis – a term coined by German economist Herbert Giersch in the
1970s, to describe a pattern of economic stagnation in Europe that may
have resulted from government over-regulation and overly generous social
benefits policies.
EuroStar – the train from London to Paris, etc.

Evolutionary Happiness Function – A mathematical formula developed by
economists Gary Becker and Luis Rayo which says, basically, that
Happiness = your success minus your expectations and is thus your

perceived social status. (Roy and Becker 2007) "The equation explains the psychological process that both fuels our desire for a bigger home, and ensures that we will be dissatisfied shortly after moving in. Humans do not perceive value in absolute terms. We compare what we have to what everyone else has, and then recalibrates the distance to the 'finish line of happiness.'" (Montgomery, p. 80)

Exit – Common suffix used in media denoting proposed, planned, or
   threatened departure of a member state from the European Union.
Brexit – denotes the departure of Great Britain
Grexit – denotes the departure of Greece. Once this usage was widely
   accepted, usage of the term then spread. For example, this headline, "Can
   Germany engineer a coal exit" (Science Magazine, January 29, 2016)
   refers to the discontinuation of coal usage throughout Germany, which is
   a proposed national response to global climate change.

Floating Storage – With a glut of oil flooding the market leading supply to
   exceed demand, oil producers are running out of places to store it. Since
   there is also an abundance of oil tanker ships that aren't needed for
   transporting oil, they've been turned in to storage facilities. Compare
   "rolling storage," which is the same concept applied to oil tanker railroad
   cars, again, not needed for oil transport and used instead for oil storage.

Feakonomics – Another, flashier name and book title pertaining to Behavioral
   Economics, the study of how behavior influences and is influenced by
   economics. Due to the success of the book the suffix "onomics" has
   become fashionable, ergo see also "Narconomics."

Geometry of Conviviality – The study of the design of urban spaces to
   promote and enable convivial behavior. (Montgomery, P. 135) See also,
   Law of Social Geometry .

Geopolitics – The study of how place matters. Or, the significance of
   geography for nations and cultures.

Geoprofiling – Software that analyzes times and geo coordinates of military
   actions along with related information about terrain, roads, ethnicity,
   tribal or civic alliances in order to identify the likely location of the
   attacking forces and/or locations of weapons caches. Useful for tracking
   locations of insurgents and for anticipating and countering future attacks.
   (The Economist. "Shrinking the haystack." January 16, 2016.)

Gerontocracies – Societies with a significant and growing proportion of elderly citizens. (Zeihan, P. 149)

Great Firewall of China, GFW – (Officially, the Golden Shield) – The name of the filters used to prevent information from coming into China from the outside world via the internet. A combination of automation and human oversight.

Hedonic Utility – Emotional benefits of a given activity.

Hedonic Treadmill – The tendency of humans to increase our expectations as our fortunes improve, leaving us perpetually dissatisfied. (Montgomery, P. 11)

HENRY, High Earner Not Rich Yet – A young person, usually highly educated, who has a high paying job but has not yet accumulated significant wealth. Considered a good credit risk by the start-up financial services firm SoFi, which has pioneered personal loans and mortgages to HENRYs. SoFi received an investment of $1 billion from SoftBank ventures in September 2015. (The Economist. "So far, so good." January 16, 2016.)

Honor Culture – (Or culture of honor) – Cultural norms based around the concept of honor and the need for particularly men to protect and defend it, often through intimidation and violence. (Nisbitt and Cohen, 1996)

Hyper-connectedness – (See also Omni-connectedness)

IED, Improvised Explosive Device – A bomb made from, for example, a cell phone and some explosive, and able to be detonated remotely via a phone call. A particularly destructive weapon in an urban civil war setting. Developed in Iraq and Afghanistan by forces opposing the American occupations there, and which caused hundreds of American casualties.

Improvisational Intelligence – The human capacity provided by evolution to improvise to attain objectives based on a general understanding of how the world works. (Henrich, p. 11)

Indefensible Space – Featureless space between buildings that collects garbage and attracts crime. (Montgomery P. 131)

Internally-Displaced Person – A citizen of a given nation who has been forced from their home due to civil war, natural disaster, or another traumatic event, but remains within the same nation. (Compare: refugee)

Investment-Based Citizenship – The practice of buying citizenship in a country. (Abrahamian, p 84) See also Financialization of Citizenship.

J-curve – Any curve that grows exponentially, and thus mimics the shape of the letter "J". (See Moore's Law.)

Jevons's Paradox – Any situation in which efficiency improvements lead to more, not less, consumption. "More fuel-efficient steam engines didn't lead to less coal consumption. Better engines made energy use effectively less expensive, and helped move the world to an industrial ear powered by coal." (Glaeser, p. 37) Henry Ford also understood this.

Law of Accelerating Returns – In some social and market settings, those who have more get still more. These markets do not tend to balance out, but rather to concentrate more and more resources under the ownership of fewer and fewer people.

Law of Social Geometry – Behavior by people, particularly in their front yards, that defines the ideal separation between the public street or sidewalk and the individual residence, enabling sociability and privacy at the same time. Identified by Jan Gehl at 10.6 feet. (Gehl, 2006) An example of the "Geometry of Conviviality."

Lead User Innovation – When the most intensive user of a product understand its utility best, and their adaptations and modifications are often adopted into the standard product.

Learning

Cultural Learning – Subclass of Social Learning based on specific factors of human-specific culture, such as inferences about the preferences, goals, prestige, and strategies adopted or exhibited by others, and by copying the actions of others.

Individual Learning – Learning through direct observation of and interaction with the environment.

Social Learning – How an individual's learning is influenced by others. (Henrich, p 12-13)

Milgram's Theory of Overload – How people respond to situations of excessive density of people and cars. "You cope by either ignoring the people around you or doing subtle battle with them." (Montgomery P. 225)

Mind Uploading – Copying the contents of a person's brain into a computer. A theoretical possibility only, until the advent of superintelligent AI.

Moore's Law – Named for Intel Corporation co-founder Gordon Moore, describes an exponentially-improvement in the performance of computer chip technology. Moore identified this phenomenon in 1965 and published an article about it, which resulted in the name Moore's Laaw being applied to it. (See also J-curve.)

Mutual Insecurity – Interactions between two nations characterized by insecurity on both sides as a consequence of not being able to anticipate or understand the actions and intents of the other. (Kissinger, World Order, 336)

Narconomics – The economics (really finances) of illegal narcotics businesses. (See also Feakonomics)

Nature Deprivation – Lack of natural beauty in a given location or accessible to a given person. "Buildings that look out on trees and grass experience about half of the violent crime of buildings that look out on barren courtyards." (Montgomery P. 110)

NEET – Not in Employment, Education, or Training. Typically a young person. (The Economist, January 23, 2016)

Neuromorphic – Computer hardware designed to as closely as possible resemble the neural architecture of the brain. (Shanahan, 32)

Non-genetic Evolutionary Process – Evolutionary processes that are cultural rather than genetic, such as new capabilities and behaviors that emerge not based on genetic mutation. (Henrich p 35)

Non-Place – A place where people do not want to be. (Montgomery P. 168)

Non-State Actor – An entity of geopolitical significance that is not a nation-state. This is therefore typically a church or religion, a corporation, particularly a large, multi-national one, or a large-scale criminal enterprise that works across national boundaries. (See also "TCO," or Transnational Criminal Organization")

Obseogenic – Literally, fat-making. Social and cultural factors that promote obesity in humans, such as diet choices, lack of exercise, and urban designs that discourage exercise. (Montgomery P. 95)

Observer Effect – Once we begin to measure something, such as an economic variable, its behavior starts to change. "If the government starts to artificially take steps to inflate housing prices, they might well increase, but they will no longer be good measures of economic health." (Silver, 188)

ODMS, On-Demand Mobile Services – The tendency of service providers to offer a complete service experience via apps that aggregate consumer demand on mobile devices, but fulfill that demand through offline services. "ODMS deliver a "closed loop" experience by collapsing the value chain including discovery, order, payment, fulfillment (offline but within owned network) and confirmation. In the pre-mobile era we had to search yellow pages (or google), find a provider, call or email that provider, wait to connect with someone, schedule a convenient time, hope the provider arrives on time, and then pay with a credit card or cash. A new array of mobile services removes all of that friction we were used to experiencing." Source: Steve Schlafman: http://schlaf.me/post/81679927670   See also: Uberification.

Omni-connectedness – Everything is connected to everything. (See also Hyper-connectedness)

Overshoot – Excessive consumption of natural resources; refers to "overshooting" the productive capacity of Earth, i.e., using more than is produced. Technically it is possible to overshoot in a discreet given period of time due to accumulated stocks, but overshoot cannot be sustained indefinitely. For example, underground water tables that store water over a period of years or decades can provide water for agriculture, but if the water is drawn out faster than it is replenished then it will one day run out entirely.

Phase 3 – Refers to the three phases of human history. Phase 1 is the Agricultural Era; Phase 2 is the Industrial Era; and Phase 3 is the as-yet unnamed era that we are now entering. The defining point of entry is the graph of human population, which by its very shape suggests that Phase 2 is now in the process of ending as the rate of population growth that characterized Phase 2 is slowing. Demographers expect that slowing to continue based on historical rates of urbanization and reproductive rates in urban families. As more than 50 percent of the population is urbanized and urbanized families tend to have 2 or fewer children, the population explosion of 1800 – 2000 is coming to an end apparently of its own accord.

Post-Human – Along the evolutionary line a being that is no longer human but whose ancestors were human. The existence of post-humans is speculated but has not yet been demonstrated / achieved. In particular, it is expected that long-duration space flight and off-Earth habitation over multiple generations will result in the development of post-humans because they will be living and thus evolving under fundamentally different conditions than those residing on Earth. While this was once a matter of science fiction it is now a matter of legal speculation and if the Space Age continues will be a matter of law within a century or two. (See also Trans-Human)

Power Density – The amount of power (work) capable of being produced by a given resource. Similar to "energy density" but referring specifically to the work accomplished rather than the potential of work to be accomplished.

Practical Isolation – As in, "the strategy of practical isolation," that is, the strategy adopted by the Chinese government to keep its citizens isolated from news and events of the world outside of China to prevent the seeds of domestic unrest. (Skirky, 122)

Present Shock – Douglas Rushkoff coined this play on words building upon Alvin Toffler's concept of Future Shock, to describe the psychological impact that occurs when too much is happening simultaneously. (Rushkoff, Douglas. Present Shock: When Everything Happens Now. Current, 1994.)

Refugee – A person who flees their home or native country due to persecution, civil war, natural disaster, etc. (Compare: Internally-Displaced Person)

Reverse mentoring – Mentoring is a normal cultural process wherein people with more experience and expertise share advice with less. Typically this occurs when older people help or support younger ones. In reverse mentoring, however, the point is that the acceleration of change has made the knowledge of the older ones obsolete, while the younger ones have often more quickly and readily adopted new ideas and technologies, and so they coach the older ones on how to utilize all the new stuff, and what it might mean for their organizations and institutions.

Future Shock – Alvin Toffler coined this term in his book of the same title to describe hwo the acceleration of change creates and adverse psychological reaction. (Toffler, Alvin. Future Shock. Random House, 1970.)

Rolling Storage – With a glut of oil flooding the market leading supply to exceed demand, oil producers are running out of places to store it. Since there is also an abundance of railroad tanker cars that aren't needed for transporting oil, they've been turned in to storage facilities. Compare "floating storage," which is the same concept applied to oil tanker ships, again, not needed for oil transport and used instead for oil storage.

Seastead – Human-made islands in international waters outside of the jurisdiction of any nation, a project undertaken by entrepreneur Peter Thiel.

Self-domestication – As a result of the impact of human culture, evolution has favored the development of certain qualities in humans that include being inclined to social behavior, following established norms and rules, monitoring behavior of others, and sanctioning those who do not follow them. (Henrich, p. 5)

Selective Attention – The principle that people pay attention to a limited range of inputs, and select what they pay attention to according to personal and cultural biases.

Singularity – The anticipated point in time at which computers become so capable that a computer with human or human-like cognition is able to create copies of itself and/or additional computers that can learn from one another, such that the learning process proceeds exponentially, at which point the vector of human and computer evolution speeds up I a way that is incomprehensible and not able to be understood or anticipated. Or more simply, the point at which everything changes because computers become smarter than people. (Kurzweil)

Social Deficit – Lack of opportunity to socialize with other people. "We can meet almost all of our needs without gathering in public." (Montgomery P. 153)

Soft Power – The influence of culture on a society, as distinct from hard power, the influence of force. (Joseph Nye)

Stalker Economy – Massive databases compiled on individuals based on their online purchases. (Gore, P. 370)

Suicide-by-Cop – Someone who commits suicide by starting a gun battle with the police in expectation of being killed.

Swanson Effect – The declining cost of solar panels.

Systems Thinking – The process of trying to understand, or understanding, the behavior of a system, and presumably a complex one, through disciplined study.

Television Effect – Impact of the introduction of television into a community. "When TV service was introduced to otherwise healthy communities in Canada in the 1980s, it has an almost immediate corrosive effect on civic participation. Watching TV correlates with higher material aspirations, more anxiety, lower financial satisfaction, lower trust in other, and less frequent social activity." (Montgomery, P. 154)

Trained Incapacity – As trained capacity is learned skill, trained incapacity is learned non-skill, i.e., having learned how *not* to do something.

Trans-Human – The developed of evolutionarily advanced species that evolves beyond humans because of advanced capabilities, either cognitive and computational or physical. Simply, super-people. (See also Post-Human)

Transnational Criminal Organization (TCO) – A large criminal enterprise that works across national boundaries. Typically involved in drugs, money laundering, and human smuggling and prostitution.

Uberification – The tendency of service providers to offer a complete service experience. "ODMS deliver a "closed loop" experience by collapsing the value chain including discovery, order, payment, fulfillment (offline but within owned network) and confirmation. In the pre-mobile era we had to search yellow pages (or google), find a provider, call or email that provider, wait to connect with someone, schedule a convenient time, hope the provider arrives on time, and then pay with a credit card or cash. A new array of mobile services removes all of that friction we were used to

experiencing." Source: Steve Schlafman:
http://schlaf.me/post/81679927670   See also: ODMS, On-Demand
Mobile Services, Uberize.

UHNWI – Ultra-high net worth individual. A very rich person. (Abrahamian,
p 72)

Undercrowding – Insufficient urban density to create self-sustaining urban
environments. (Whyte, Project for Public Spaces)

Urban Ponzi Scheme – New real estate development in suburbs creates short
term benefits in the form of development fees, tax revenues, and
construction jobs, but create long term costs that pileup faster than cities
can pay them, in the form of infrastructure maintenance, health care costs,
and subsidies for public transit systems that are not self-sustaining. On a
wider social basis, suburban dwellers consume more natural resources and
create more pollution per person than urban residents. (Montgomery P.
260) See also, Undercrowding.

Urban Poverty Paradox – "Any attempt to fix the poverty level in a single city
may well backfire and increase the level of poverty in a city by attracting
more poor people." (Glaeser, P. 76) The same thing applies to Syrian
refugees.

Vancouverism – Designs of cities that copy the elements of Vancouver,
Canada, which is considered to be one of the world's best designed cities.
(Montgomery P. 118)

Exponents

(Forthcoming)

Selected
Bibliography

When I have money I buy books.
If any is left I buy food.

Erasmus

There are many different ways to approach the problem of the bibliography, some opting for the complete alphabetical list of every work cited or referenced, others preferring the selective list of the most interesting or useful ones. I've chosen the latter, in the hopes that it will be more helpful to the reader. It's arranged by topic in the same sequence as the chapters. A more complete and sequential listing of sources is available below in the Notes section.

Preface: The Super Predator
Introduction: The Experimenter

Bettelheim, Bruno. *The Uses of Enchantment: The Meaning and Importance of Fairy Tales.* Vintage, 1975.

Campbell, Joseph. *The Hero With a Thousand Faces.* Princeton University Press, 1949.

Doidge, Norman, M.D. *The Brain That Changes Itself: Stories of Personal Triumph from the Frontiers of Brain Science.* Penguin, 2007

Fabun, Don. *Dimensions of Change.* Glencoe Press, 1971.

Gopnik, Alison. *The Philosophical Baby: What Children's Minds Tell Us*

594

About Truth, Love, and the Meaning of Life. Farrar Strauss and Giroux, 2009

Gopnik, Alison, Andrew Meltzoff, and Patricia Kuhl. *The Scientists in the Crib: What Early Learning Tells Us About the Mind.* Harper Collins, 2001.

Henrich, Joseph. *The Secret of Our Success: How Culture is Driving Human Evolution, Domesticating Our Species, and Making Us Smarter.* Princeton University Press, 2016.

Koestler, Arthur. *The Ghost in the Machine.* Arkana, 1967.

Linden, David J. *The Compass of Pleasure: How Our Brains Make Fatty Foods, Orgasm, Exercise, Marijuana, Generosity, Vodka, Learning and Gambling Feel So Good.* Viking, 2011.

Morris, Ian. *War! What Is It Good For? Conflict and the Progress of Civilization from Primates to Robots.* Picador, 2014.

Wexler, Bruce. *Brain and Culture: Neurobiology, Ideology, and Social Change.* MIT Press, 2006.

Chapter 1: The Technologist: The Digital Revolution

Arthur, W. Brian. *The Nature of Technology: What It Is and How It Evolves.* Free Press, 2009.

Brand, Stewart. *The Media Lab: Inventing the Future at M.I.T.* Penguin, 1987.

Chandler, Alfred D. Jr. *Scale and Scope: The Dynamics of Industrial Capitalism.* Harvard/Belknap, 1990.

Diamandis, Peter H. and Steven Kotler. *Abundance: The Future Is Better Than You Think.* Free Press, 2102.

Ellul, Jacques. *The Technological Society.* Knopf, 1964.

Kodama, Fumio. *Emerging Patterns of Innovation: Sources of Japan's Technological Edge.* Harvard Business School Press, 1991.

Kurzweil, Ray. *The Singularity is Near.* Penguin Books, 2005.

Litan, Robert E. *Trillion Dollar Economists: How Economists and Their Ideas Have Transformed Business.* Wiley/Bloomberg, 2014.

Moravec, Hans. *Mind Children: The Future of Robot and Human Intelligence.* Harvard University Press, 1988.

Morris, Langdon and Ken Cox, Editors. *International Cooperation for the Development of Space.* Aerospace Technology Working Group, 2012.

Morris, Langdon and Ken Cox, Editors. *Space Commerce: The Inside Story by the People Who Are Making It Happen.* Aerospace Technology Working Group, 2010.

Piel, Gerard. *The Acceleration of History*. Knopf, 1972.

Rogers, Everett M. *Diffusion of Innovations*. Free Press, 1983.

Shanahan, Murray. *The Technological Singularity*. MIT Press, 2015.

Venter, J. Craig. *Life at the Speed of Light: From the Double Helix to the Dawn of Digital Life*. Viking, 2013.

Chapter 2: The Combustor: The Climate Revolution

Brown, Lester R. *Plan B 2.0: Rescuing a Planet Under Stress and a Civilization in Trouble*. Norton, 2006.

Martenson, Chris, PhD. *The Crash Course: The Unsustainable Future of Our Economy, Energy, and Environment*. Wiley, 2011.

Lewis, Joanna I. *Green Innovation in China: China's Wind Power Industry and the Global Transition to a Low-Carbon Economy*. Columbia University Press, 2013.

Prentiss, Mara. *Energy Revolution: The Physicis and the Promise of Efficient Technology*. Belknap Harvard, 2015.

Chapter 3: The Extractor: The Energy Revolution and the Global Economy

Engdahl, F. William. *A Century of War: Anglo-American Oil Politics and the New World Order*. Progressive Press, 2012.

Heintzman, Andrew and Evan Solomon, Editors. *Fueling the Future: How the Battle Over Energy is Changing Everything*. Anansi, 2003.

Smil, Vaclav. *Oil*. Oneworld, 2008.

Spemce, Michael. *The Next Convergence: The Future of Economic Growth in a Multispeed World*. Picador, 2011.

Yergin, Daniel and Joseph Stanislaw. *The Commanding Heights: The Battle for the World Economy*. Free Press, 2002

Yergin, Daniel. *The Prize: The Epic Quest for Oil, Money & Power*. Free Press, 2008

Chapter 4: The Builder: The Population Explosion and the Urban Revolution

Alexander, Christopher, Hajo Neis, Artemis Anninou and Ingrid King. *A New Theory of Urban Design*. Oxford University Press, 1987.

Bacon, Edmund. *Design of Cities*. Penguin, 1967.

Brugmann, Jeb. *Welcome to the Urban Revolution: How Cities Are Changing the World*. Bloomsbury Press, 2009.

Clark, David. *Urban World/Global City*. Routledge, 1996.

Glaeser, Edward. *Triumph of the City: How Our Greatest Invention*

Makes Us Richer, Smarter, Greener, Healthier, and Happier.
Penguin Books, 2011.

Kenny, Martin, Editor. *Understanding Silicon Valley: The Anatomy of an Entrepreneurial Region.* Stanford Business Books, 2000.

Kostof, Spiro. *The City Assembled: The Elements of Urban Form Through History.* Bullfinch Press, 1992.

Kostof, Spiro. *The City Shaped: Urban Patterns and Meanings Through History.* Bullfinch Press, 1991.

Hall, Peter, *Cities in Civilization.* Fromm International, 1998.

Jacobs, Jane. *Cities and the Wealth of Nations: Principles of Economic Life.* Random House, 1984.

Montgomery, Charles. *Happy City: Transforming Our Lives Through Urban Design.* Farrar, Strauss and Giroux, 2013.

Polèse, Mario. *The Wealth and Poverty of Regions: Why Cities Matter.* The University of Chicago Press, 2009.

Soleri, Paolo. *Arcology: The City in the Image of Man.* MIT Press, 1969.

Soleri, Paolo and Youngsoo Kim, Charles Anderson, Adam Nordfors, Scott Riley, and Tomiaki Tamura. *Lean Linear City: Arterial Arcology.* Cosanti Press, 2012.

Whyte, William H. *City: Rediscovering the Center.* Anchor Books, 1988.

Chapter 5: The Humanist: The Cultural Revolution

Ackroyd, Peter. *Blake.* Knopf, 1996.

Alexander, Christopher. *A Pattern Language: Towns, Buildings, Construction.* Oxford University Press, 1977.

Armstrong, Karen. *The Great Transformation: The Beginning of Our Religious Traditions.* Anchor Books, 2006.

Barzun, Jacques. *From Dawn to Decadence: 500 Years of Western Cultural Life.* Harper Collins, 2000.

Cantor, Norman F. *The Civilization of the Middle Ages.* Harper Perrennial, 1994.

Harrison, Lawrence E. and Samuel P. Huntington, Editors. Culture Matter: How Values Shape Human Progress. Basic Books, 2000.

Pope Francis. *Laudato Si': On Care for Our Common Home.* Our Sunday Visitor, 2015.

Shirky, Clay. *Here Comes Everybody: The Power of Organizing Without Organizations.* Penguin, 2008.

Watson, Peter. *Ideas: A History of Thought and Invention from Fire to Freud.* HarperCollins, 2005.

Watson, Peter. *The Modern Mind: An intellectual history of the 20th Century.* HarperCollins, 2001.

Chapter 6: The Reactionary: The Counter-Revolution

Barber, Benjamin R. *Jihad vs. McWorld: Terrorism's Challenge to Democracy.* Ballentine, 1965.

Cook, Michael. *Ancient Religions, Modern Politics: The Islamic Case in Comparative Perspective.* Princeton University Press, 2014.

Gambetta, Diego and Steffen Hertog. *Engineers of Jihad: The Curious Connection between Violent Extremism and Education.* Princeton University Press, 2016.

Hofstadter, Richard. *Anti-Intellectualism in American Life.* Vintage, 1964.

Hofstadter, Richard. *The American Political Tradition and the Men Who Made It.* Vintage, 1948, 1973.

Hofstadter, Richard. *The Paranoid Style in American Politics, and Other Essays.* Vintage, 1952.

Kuhn, Thomas S. *The Structure of Scientific Revolutions.* Second Edition, Enlarged. The University of Chicago Press, 1962, 1970.

Lakoff, Robin Tolmach. *The Language War.* University of California Press, 2000.

Martin, William. *With God on Our Side: The Rise of the Religious Right in America.* Broadway, 1996.

Mayer, Jane. *The Dark Side: The Inside Story of How the War on Terror Turned Into a War on American Ideals.* Doubleday, 2008.

Miceklthwait, John and Adrian Wooldridge. *The Right Nation: Conservative Power in America.* Penguin, 2004.

Morris, Langdon. *The War for America.* 2004.

Shorris, Earl. *The Politics of Heaven: American in Fearful Times.* Norton, 2007.

Chapter 7: The Futurist: Patterns of Change

Burke, James. *The Day the Universe Changed.* Little, Brown, 1985.

Diamond, Jared. *Guns, Germs, and Steel: The Fates of Human Societies.* Norton, 1999.

Fuller, Buckminster, *Critical Path.* St. Martin's Press, 1981.

Fuller, Buckminster, *Operating Manual for Spaceship Earth.* Clarion, 1970.

Fuller, R. Buckminster, Arthur L. Loeb (Introduction), E. J. Applewhite (Collaborator). *Synergetics: Explorations in the Geometry of*

Thinking. MacMillan, 1982

Holland, John. *Emergence: From Chaos to Order.* Persues Books, 1998.

Johnson, Steven. *Emergence: The Connected Lives of Ants, Brains, Cities, and Software.* Touchstone, 2001.

Naisbett, John. *Megatrends: Then New Directions Transforming Our Lives.* Warner Books, 1982.

Toynbee, Arnold. *Mankind and Mother Earth: A Narrative History of the World.* Oxford University Press, 1976.

Chapter 8: The Realist: Drowning in Complexity

Ackoff, Russell. *Creating the Corporate Future.* Wiley, 1981.

Bateson, Gregory. *Mind and Nature: A Necessary Unity.* Bantam Books, 1979. P. 110.

Beer, Stafford. *Brain of the Firm.* Wiley, 1972.

Beer, Stafford. *Platform for Change.* Wiley, 1975.

Beer, Stafford. *The Heart of Enterprise.* Wiley, 1979.

Calvin, William. *The Ascent of Mind: Ice Age Climates and the Evolution of Intelligence.* Bantam, 1990.

Calvin, William. *The River That Flows Uphill: A Journey from the Big Bang to the Big Brain.* MacMillan, 1986.

Deming, W. Edwards. *The New Economics for Industry, Government, Education.* MIT Press, 1993. P. 105, 109.

Drucker, Peter. *The Age of Discontinuity.* Harper Torchbooks, 1968.

Forrester, Jay. "Counter-Intuitive Behavior of Social Systems." *MIT Technology Review*, Volume 73, Number 3, January 1971.

Forrester, Jay. *Principles of Systems.* Productivity Press, 1968.

Forrester, Jay. *Urban Dynamics.* Productivity Press, 1969.

Gall, John. *Systemantics: The Underground Text of System Lore. How Systems Work and How They Fail.* The General Systemantics Press, Second Edition, 1986.

McLuhan, Marshall and Quentin Fiore. *The Medium is the Massage: An Inventory of Effects.* Penguin, 1967.

Miller, James G. *Living Systems.* McGraw Hill, 1978.

Montgomery, Charles. *Happy City: Transforming Our Lives Through Urban Design.* Farrar, Strauss and Giroux. 2013. P. 181.

Morrison, Philip and Phyllis Morrison. *Powers of Ten: About the Relative Size of Things in the Universe.* Scientific American, 1982.

Weinberg, Gerald M. and Daniela Weinberg. *General Principles of Systems Design.* Wiley, 1979.

Chapter 9: The Analyst: Evidence, and Interpretation

Ariely, Dan. *Predictably Irrational: The Hidden Forces that Shape Our Decisions*. Harper, 2008.

Kahneman, Daniel. *Thinking, Fast and Slow*. Farrar, Straus and Giroux, 2011.

Lakoff, George. *Moral Politics: What Conservatives Know that Liberals Don't*. University of Chicago Press, 1997.

Mansfield, Guy. *Developing Your Leadership Skills: From the Changing World to Changing the World*. 2013.

Mlodinow, Leonard. *Subliminal: How Your Subconscious Mind Rules Your Behavior*. Vintage, 2012.

Russo, J. Edward and Paul J.H. Schoemaker. *Winning Decisions: Getting It Right the First Time*. Crown Business, 2001.

Shermer, Michael. *The Believing Brain: From Ghosts and Gods to Politics and Conspiracies – How We Construct Beliefs and Reinforce Them as Truths*. Times Books, 2011. P. 5.

Silver, Nate. *The Signal and the Noise: Why So Many Predications Fail – But Some Don't*. Penguin, 2012.

Taleb, Nassim Nicholas. *AntiFragile: Things That Gain from Disorder*. Random House, 2012.

Taleb, Nassim Nicholas. *The Black Swan: The Impact of the Highly Improbable*. Random House, 2007.

Taleb, Nassim Nicholas. *Fooled by Randomness: The Hidden Role of Change in Life and in the Markets*. Random House, 2004.

Vaughan, Diane. *The Challenger Launch Decision: Risky Technology, Culture, and Deviance at NASA*. The University of Chicago Press, 1996.

Chapter 10: The Visionary: Understanding Foresight

Beer, Stafford. *Platform for Change*. Wiley, 1975.

Ehrlich, Paul R. *The Population Bomb*. Ballentine Books, 1968.

Franklin, Daniel, Editor. *Megachange: The World in 2050*. Wiley, 2012.

Friedman, George. *The Next 100 Years: A forecast for the 21st Century*. Anchor Books, 2010.

Gore, Al. *The Future: Six Drivers of Global Change*. Random House, 2013.

Jantsch, Eric. *The Self-Organizing Universe: Scientific and Human Implications of the Emerging Paradigm of Evolution*. Pergamon, 1980.

Meadows, Donella, Dennis L. Meadows and Jorgen Randers. *Beyond the*

Limits: Confronting Global Collapse; Envisioning a Sustainable Future. Chelsea Green, 1992.

Meadows, Donella, Jorgen Randers, Dennis L. Meadows and William W. Behrens. *The Limits to Growth: A Report for the Club of Rome's Project on the Predicament of Mankind*. Potomac, 1974.

Meadows, Donella H. and Diana Wright (Editor). *Thinking in Systems: A Primer*. Chelsea Green Publishing, 2008.

Miller, James Grier. *Living Systems*. McGraw Hill, 1978

Randers, Jorgen. *2052: A Global Forecast for the Next Forty Years*. Chelsea Green, 2012.

Rushkoff, Douglas. *Present Shock: When Everything Happens Now*. Current, 2014.

Smil, Vaclav. *Global Catastrophes and Trends: The Next Fifty Years*. The MIT Press, 2012.

Toffler, Alvin. *Future Shock*. Random House, 1970.

Chapter 11: The Map Maker: Geostrategy

Abrahamian, Atossa Araxia. *The Cosmopolites: The Coming of the Global Citizen*. Columbia Global Reports, 2015.

Acemoglu, Daron and James A. Robinson. *Why Nations Fail: The Origins of Power, Prosperity, and Poverty*. Crown Business, 2012.

Bremmer, Ian. *Superpower: Three Choices for America's Role in the World*. Penguin, 2015.

Chan, Anita, Editor. *Wal-Mart in China*. Cornell University Press, October 13, 2011.

De Blij, Harm. *The Power of Place: Geography, Destiny, and Globalization's Rough Landscape*. Oxford University Press, 2009.

Dyer, Geoff. *The Contest of the Century: The New Era of Competition with China – and How American Can Win*. Knopf, 2014.

Ferguson, Niall. *Empire: How Britain Made the Modern World*. Penguin, 2003.

Fukuyama, Francis. *The End of History and the Last Man Paperback*. Free Press, 1992.

Fulbright, J. William and Seth P. Tillman. *The Price of Empire*. Pantheon, 1989.

Kaplan, Robert D. *The Revenge of Geography: What the Map Tells Us About Coming Conflicts and the Battle Against Fate*. Random House, 2012.

Kissinger, Henry. *Diplomacy*. Simon & Schuster, 1994.

Kissinger, Henry. *On China*. The Penguin Press, 2011.

Kissinger, Henry. *World Order.* Penguin, 2014.

Lynch, Daniel C. *China's Futures: PRC Elites Debate Economics, Politics, and Foreign Policy.* Stanford University Press, 2015.

Manber, Jeffrey. *Selling Peace: Inside the Soviet Conspiracy that Transformed the U.S. Space Program.* Apogee Books, 2009.

Mahnken, Thomas G. and Dan Blumental, Editors. *Strategy in Asia: The Past, Present, and Future of Regional Security.* Stanford Security Studies, 2014.

McCants, William. *The ISIS Apocalypse: The History, Strategy, and Doomsday Vision of the Islamic State.* St. Martin's Press, 2015.

Milne, David. *Worldmaking: The Art and Science of American Diplomacy.* Farrar, Strauss and Giroux, 2015.

Morris, Ian. *Why the West Rules – For Now: The Patterns of History, and What They Reveal About the Future.* Picador, 2010.

Nye, Joseph S. Jr. *Soft Power: The Means To Success In World Politics.* Perseus Books, 2004.

Nye, Joseph S. Jr. *The Paradox of American Power: Why the World's Only Superpower Can't Go It Alone.* Oxford University Press, 2002.

Paulson, Henry M. *Dealing with China: An Insider Unmasks the New Economic Superpower.* Twelve, 2015.

Ramo, Joshua Cooper. *The Age of the Unthinkable: Why the New World Order Constantly Surprises US and What We Can Do About It.* Little, Brown, 2009.

Ridley, Matt. *The Rational Optimist.* Harper, 2010.

Shirky, Clay. *Little Rice: Smartphones, Xiaomi, and the Chinese Dream.* Columbia Global Reports, 2015.

Smith, General Rupert. *The Utility of Force: The Art of War in the Modern World.* Knopf, 2007.

Sutherland, Benjamin, Editor. *Modern Warfare, Intelligence, and Deterrence.* Wiley, 2011.

Tuchman, Barbara W. *The Guns of August.* Ballantine Books, 1962.

Tuchman, Barbara W. *The March of Folly: From Troy to Vietnam.* Ballantine Books, 1984.

Wainwright, Tom. *Narconomics: How to Run a Drug Cartel.* Public Affairs, 2016.

Zakaria, Fareed. *The Post-American World.* Norton, 2008.

Zeihan, Peter. *The Accidental Superpower: The Next Generation of American Preeminence and the Coming Global Disorder.* Grand Central Publishing, 2014.

Chapter 12: The Explorer: World Models
Chapter 13: The Planner: What if? + What if?

De Geus, Arie. *The Living Company.* Harvard Business Review Press, 1997.

Dorner, Dietrich. *The Logic of Failure: Recognizing and Avoiding Error in Complex Situations.* Perseus Books, 1986.

Kahane, Adam. *Solving Tough Problems.* Berrett-Kohler, 1999.

Kahane, Adam. *Transformative Scenario Planning.* Berrett-Kohler, 2012.

Kelly, Eamonn. *Powerful Times: Rising to the Challenge of Our Uncertain World.* Wharton School Publishing, 2006.

Mintzberg, Henry. *The Rise and Fall of Strategic Planning.* Free Press, 1994.

Ralston, Bill and Ian Wilson. *The Scenario Planning Handbook: Developing Strategies in Uncertain Times.* South-Western 206.

Schoemaker, Paul J. H. *Profiting from Uncertainty: Strategies for Succeeding No Matter What the Future Brings.* Free Press, 2002.

Schwartz, Peter. *The Art of the Long View.* Doubleday Business, 1991.

Chapter 14: The Philosopher: Feasible or Desirable

Judt, Tony. *Reappraisals: Reflections on the Forgotten Twentieth Century.* Penguin, 2008.

Judt, Tony, with Timothy Snyder. *Thinking the Twentieth Century.* Penguin, 2012.

Judt, Tony. *When the Facts Change: Essays 1995 – 2010.* Penguin, 2015.

Morris, Langdon. *Managing the Evolving Corporation.* Wiley, 1995.

Rhodes, Richard. *The Making of the Atomic Bomb.* Simon & Schuster, 1986.

Tainter, Joseph A. *The Collapse of Complex Societies.* Cambridge University Press, 1988.

Whitehead, Alfred North. *Symbolism, Its Meaning and Effect.* Fordham University Press. 1927.

Chapter 15: The Innovator: Business Model Warfare

Bhidé, Amar V. *The Origin and Evolution of New Businesses.* Oxford University Press, 2000.

Chandler, David G. *The Campaigns of Napoleon: The Mind and Method of History's Greatest Soldier.* MacMillan, 1966.

Conlon, Jerome, Moses Ma, and Langdon Morris. *Soulful Branding.* FutureLab Press, 2015.

Cronin, Vincent. *Napoleon.* HarperCollins, 1971.

Gerstner, Louis V. *Who Says Elephants Can't Dance?* HarperCollins, 2002.

Gyorffy, Laszlo and Lisa Friedman. *Creating Value with CO-STAR: An Innovation Tool for Perfecting and Pitching Your Brilliant Idea.* Enterprise Development Group, Inc, 2012.

Moore, Geoffrey. *Crossing the Chasm.* HarperBusiness, 1991.

Morris, Langdon, Moses Ma and Po Chi Wu. *Agile Innovation: The Revolutionary Approach to Accelerate Success, Inspire Engagement, and Ignite Creativity.* Wiley, 2014.

Morris, Langdon. *The Innovation Formula: The Guidebook to Innovation for Small Business Leaders and Entrepreneurs.* Innovation Academy, 2015.

Ries, Eric. *The Lean Startup: How Today's Entrepreneurs Use Continuous Innovation to Create Radically Successful Businesses.* Crown Business, 2011.

Schumpeter, Joseph. *Capitalism, Socialism, and Democracy.* Harper & Brothers, 1942.

Chapter 16: The Leader: Strategy for the 21st Century

Colvin, Geoff. *Talent Is Overrated: What Really Separates World-Class Performers from Everyone Else.* Portfolio, 2008.

De Soto, Hernando. *The Mystery of Capital: Why Capitalism Triumphs in the West and Fails Everywhere Else.* Basic Books, 2000.

Keegan, John. *Intelligence in War: Knowledge of the Enemy from Napoleon to Al-Qaeda.* Knopf, 2003.

Keegan, John. *The Mask of Command.* Penguin, 1987.

Pye, David. *The Nature and Art of Workmanship.* Cambridge University Press, 1968.

Conclusion: Super Learning and Extreme Creativity

Csikszentmihalyi, Mihaly. *Creativity: Flow and the Psychology of Discovery and Invention.* Harper, 1996.

Ray, Paul H. and Sherry Ruth Anderson. *The Cultural Creatives: How 50 Million People Are Changing the World.* Three Rivers Press, 2000.

Tharp, Twyla. *The Collaborative Habit: Life Lessons for Working Together.* Simon & Schuster, 2009.

Tharp, Twyla. *The Creative Habit: Learn It and Use It for Life.* Simon & Schuster, 2003.

About the Author

Langdon Morris is co-founder and Senior Partner of InnovationLabs, one of the world's leading innovation consultancies, and Chairman of FutureLab, a global strategy and technology firm.

His work focuses on developing and applying advanced methods in innovation and strategy to solve complex problems with very high levels of creativity. He is recognized as one the world's leading thinkers and consultants on innovation, and his original and ground-breaking work has been adopted by corporations, governments, and universities on every continent.

He is a frequent and much-appreciated public speaker at conferences and corporate events, and is author eight books including some of the most important titles in the field of innovation from the last decade, co-author of three more, and editor of the five books in the Aerospace Technology Working Group series on the future of space travel and space commerce.

He is formerly Senior Practice Scholar at the Ackoff Center of the University of Pennsylvania, and he has taught MBA courses in innovation and strategy at the Ecole Nationale des Ponts et Chaussées (France) and Universidad de Belgrano (Argentina), and has lectured at universities on 4 continents, including Chaoyang University of Technology (Taiwan), Conservatoire Nationale des Arts et Métiers (France), University of Colorado, University of North Carolina, and Rochester Institute of Technology (USA), and Shanghai Jao Tong University (China), and the University of Nairobi.

About This Book
And Acknowledgments

The journey that resulted in this book began in 1978 when I attended a seminar on systems and systems thinking at the Harvard School of Government. The guest lecturer one day was Ray Smith, who was at the time (I think), CEO of Bell of Pennsylvania. Mr. Smith made a great presentation and I spoke briefly with him afterwards. A few weeks later entirely through his kindness a copy of Stafford Beer's then most recent book *Platform for Change* arrived in my mailbox. The book made a very big impression on me, as it answered many questions that I had been wondering about concerning systems and society.

I went on to become a management consultant focusing on innovation, but I never forgot Beer and his work, and indeed I found many opportunities to apply his thinking as time went on. As I worked and wrote and studied many things have come into focus, and through it all *Platform for Change* has remained for me a critical starting point on this journey.

•••

During the long process of exploring and developing these ideas I have had the marvelous opportunity to work with and for a great many fine people and organizations who have been very generous with their thoughts and insights, and I would like to mention some of them here:

For his exemplary research support I thank Kevin Kim.

My partners and former partners at InnovationLabs and FutureLab including Bryan Coffman, Michael Kaufman, Jay Smethurst, Moses Ma, and Po Chi Wu.

My colleagues at InnovationLabs and our global network, Betty Dhamers, Jodie Engelberg, Diane Castiglioni, Paul Harvey, Doug Cheek, Christopher Fuller, Isa Olmstead, Kate Levine, Dan Newman, Michael Barry, and Sara Beckman.

Greg Gomes and Philomena Rambo of Granada High in Livermore, California, who kindly allow me to visit Greg's classroom periodically, where I spend a few hours trying to convey to the students something about what their future is likely to hold. I don't know that the students have gotten much from this, but it's been a tremendous learning experience for me.

Total Oil, which has invited me to spend time with about 1000 of its executives over the last eight years years, arranged through efforts of Antonin Fotso, Gilles Cochevelou, Guy Mansfield, Jean-Pierre Loizeau, Stephane Catel, and Alan Lambert.

The US Coast Guard's exemplary Evergreen Program that we had the privilege to support during the last few years, and its leaders Commander Eric Popeil, Lt. Commander Bill Friday, and Lt. Commander Molly Waters, along with MSI Systems' Pat Ryan and Chris Kmiecik.

Pascal Baudry of WDHB Consulting Group.

The team at Point Forward, including Gary Waymire, Tom Williams, Griff Coleman, and Bob Hall.

Capital Impact Partners former CEO Terry Simonette and COO Annie Donovan, now head of the CDFI Fund at the US Treasury Department.

Nancy Andrews of LIIF, and Kirsten Moy of the Aspen Institute.

The China Institute for Innovation, Arthur Lok, Lloyd He, and Eric Chai.

Vivian Tan of Kaiser Permanente.

Paolo Soleri.

Justin Lin.

The exceptional Ken Cox of NASA.

Airbus, Patrick Baeumle, Ian Bowcock.

Callaghan Innovation, New Zealand, Ross Pearce.

Covance, Mark Erickson.

Defense Security Service, Jim Kren, Kevin Jones, Irv Becker and Roger Dietrich.

France Télécom, Philippe Andres.

Gemalto, Christie Deydier and Philippe Vallée.

Ingersoll Rand, Dan Sondee, Dan Dykstra and Michael Wynblatt.

L'Oréal, Ghyslaine Villain, Cristina Parma, and Caroline Flandrin.

TCSAFEA, China, Director Liu and Director Michael Zheng, Emma Wang, Linda Sun

UNICEF, Sherine Guirguis, Michael Coleman, and Lorraine Shamalla.

US Navy Strategic Studies Group, Admiral James P. Wisecup, William Glenney, and Elena McCarthy.

US Naval Surface Warfare Center, Crane Division, Joe Gaines, and Brett Seidel.

US Special Operations Command, Col. Steve Nitzschke and Admiral William, McCraven.

Tata Group, Ravi Arora.

And universities where I've taught and lectured, including the French National Institute of Arts & Métiers, École Nationale des Ponts & Chaussées, Universidad del Belgrano, University of Colorado at Colorado Springs, University of North Carolina Wilmington, University of Nairobi, Shanghai Jao Tong University, Stanford University, the Ackoff Center the University of Pennsylvania, and the Rochester Institute of Technology, all of which I found immensely valuable learning opportunities.

And lastly I am most grateful for the love and support of my family, who were patient beyond reason with the countless hours that I have devoted to this project.

Notes

1   Darimont, Chris T., Caroline H. Fox, Heather M. Bryan, and Thomas E. Reimchen. "The unique ecology of human predators." *Science 21 August 2015: 858-860.*

2   Silver, Nate. *The Signal and the Noise: Why So Many Predications Fail – But Some Don't.* Penguin, 2012. P. 13.

3   Wines, Michael. "Human Activity Increases Risk of Big Quake in Oklahoma and Kansas, Experts Say." *The New York Times,* March 28, 2016. http://www.nytimes.com/2016/03/29/us/earthquake-risk-in-oklahoma-and-kansas-comparable-to-california.html?_r=0

4   http://www.anthropocene.info/

5   Subcommission on Quaternary Stratigraphy, Working Group On The 'Anthropocene:' The 'Anthropocene' is a term widely used since its coining by Paul Crutzen and Eugene Stoermer in 2000 to denote the present time interval, in which many geologically significant conditions and processes are profoundly altered by human activities. These include changes in: erosion and sediment transport associated with a variety of anthropogenic processes, including colonisation, agriculture, urbanisation and global warming. the chemical composition of the atmosphere, oceans and soils, with significant anthropogenic perturbations of the cycles of elements such as carbon, nitrogen, phosphorus and various metals. environmental conditions generated by these perturbations; these include global warming, ocean acidification and spreading oceanic 'dead zones'. the biosphere both on land and in the sea, as a result of habitat loss, predation, species invasions and the physical and chemical changes noted above. (The Subcommission on Quaternary Stratigraphy (SQS) is a constituent body of the International Commission on Stratigraphy (ICS), the largest scientific organisation within the International Union of Geological Sciences (IUGS).) http://quaternary.stratigraphy.org/workinggroups/anthropocene/

6   Fuller, Buckminster, *Operating Manual for Spaceship Earth.* Clarion, 1970.

7   Gopnik, Alison. *The Philosophical Baby.* Farrar Strauss and Girous, 2009. P 91.

8   Alison Gopnik. The Philosophical Baby. Farrar Strauss and Girous, 2009. P 87

9   Henrich, Joseph. *The Secret of Our Success: How Culture is Driving Human Evolution, Domesticating Our Species, and Making Us Smarter.* Princeton University Press, 2016. P. 3 – 7. (This is not a direct quote but a montage, and includes some paraphrasing as well.)

10 In 2012 Exxon Neftegas Ltd (ENL) completed drilling the world's deepest well in the Chayvo oil field on the Sakhalin shelf in the Russian Far East. ¬The shaft of well Z-44 is 12,376 meter deep.

11 Hall, Peter, *Cities in Civilization.* Fromm International, 1998. P. 7.

12 Toffler, Alvin. *Future Shock.* Random House, 1970.

13 Hall, Peter, *Cities in Civilization.* Fromm International, 1998. P. 932.

14 https://www.ssa.gov/planners/lifeexpectancy.html

15 Gerstner, Louis V. *Who Says Elephants Can't* Dance? Inside IBM's Historic Turnaround. HarperBusiness, 2002.

[16] Fuller, R. Buckminster, Arthur L. Loeb (Introduction), E. J. Applewhite (Collaborator). *Synergetics: Explorations in the Geometry of Thinking.* MacMillan, 1982

[17] http://www.reuters.com/article/us-gm-lyft-investment-idUSKBN0UI1A820160105

[18] http://www.npr.org/sections/alltechconsidered/2015/04/20/400988928/at-50-years-old-the-challenge-to-keep-up-with-moore-s-law

[19] Peter H. Diamandis and Steven Kotler. *Abundance: The Future Is Better Than You Think.* Free Press, 2102. P. 34.

[20] Meadows, Donella H., Diana Wright (Editor). *Thinking in Systems: A Primer.* Chelsea Green Publishing, 2008.

[21] Ehrlich, Paul R. *The Population Bomb.* Ballentine Books, 1968

[22] Sundaresan, Shankar, Rutgers University, http://crab.rutgers.edu/~sundares/MIS334Sec40.Sp08/protected/notes/hw/moores.xls, Accessed 8/6/15.

[23] Rao, Arun, A History of Silicon Valley, 11. Chipmakers: Intel's Creation and Re-Creation (1965-98), 2010

[24] Anthony, Sebastian, "Apple's A8 SoC analyzed: The iPhone 6 chip is a 2-billion-transistor 20nm monster," ExtremeTech, http://www.extremetech.com/computing/189787-apples-a8-soc-analyzed-the-iphone-6-chip-is-a-2-billion-transistor-20nm-monster

[25] Gruner & Tyrrell, George & James, "An interview with board member Om Nalamasu", IOP Science, http://m.iopscience.iop.org/2053-1613/1/1/010203/article   Accessed March 1, 2016.
$3.57 million in 1991: http://www.techpolicydaily.com/communications/much-iphone-cost-1991/

[26] January 31, 2016

[27] Bolluyt, Jess, "iPhone 6 and 6 Plus: How Much They Really Cost," CheatSheet, http://www.cheatsheet.com/technology/iphone-6-and-6-plus-how-much-they-really-cost.html/?a=viewall

[28] Kurzweil, Ray. *The Singularity is Near.* Penguin Books, 2005. P. 8.

[29] Kurzweil, Ray. *The Singularity is Near.* Penguin Books, 2005. P. 29.

[30] http://www.theroboticschallenge.org/   "Launched in response to a humanitarian need that became glaringly clear during the nuclear disaster at Fukushima, Japan, in 2011, the DARPA Robotics Challenge consisted of three increasingly demanding competitions over two years. The goal was to accelerate progress in robotics and hasten the day when robots have sufficient dexterity and robustness to enter areas too dangerous for humans and mitigate the impacts of natural or man-made disasters."

[31] http://recode.net/2015/05/11/google-no-our-self-driving-cars-arent-getting-dinged-up-that-much/

[32] US Bureau of Labor Statistics, data from 2015. http://www.bls.gov/cps/cpsaat11.pdf

[33] http://money.cnn.com/2015/08/22/pf/world-without-work/

[34] http://mashable.com/2016/01/07/uber-lyft-self-driving-cars/#MtfHzXVwREqE

[35] http://www.reuters.com/article/us-gm-lyft-investment-idUSKBN0UI1A820160105

[36] Rodrigue, Dr. Jean-Paul and Dr. Theo Notteboom "Transportation and Economic Development" Deptartment of Global Studies & Geography, Hofstra University,

New York. https://people.hofstra.edu/geotrans/eng/ch7en/conc7en/ch7c1en.html, Accessed March 28, 2016.

37 https://youtu.be/6KRjuuEVEZs; http://www.extremetech.com/extreme/183254-amazon-deploys-10000-robot-workers-a-year-after-obamas-famous-amazon-jobs-speech

38 http://finance.yahoo.com/news/truck-driving-may-be-america-s-most-popular-job--182859840.html

39 http://www.freep.com/story/news/2015/02/26/detroit-blight-removal-money/24053179/

40 This is why your grandparents call that device the "ice box;" when they were growing up it literally was a wooden or metal box that was kept cold with ice, which of course had to be delivered regularly to maintain its temperature.

41 Matier & Ross. "SF employment boom strains housing, office space." *San Francisco Chronicle*, December 28, 2014.

42 Fancher, Emily. "200,000 housing units in Bay Area pipeline. Is it enough to move the needle?" *San Francisco Business Times*, September 16, 2014.

43 US Department of Labor, Bureau of Labor Statistics, Employment Projections, December 8, 2015. http://www.bls.gov/emp/ep_table_201.htm

44 http://www.theatlantic.com/business/archive/2015/03/a-new-life-for-dead-malls/387001

45 http://www.usatoday.com/story/money/2016/01/06/macys-announces-layoffs-restructuring-after-disappointing-2015/78373358/

46 Gershgorn, Dave. "The Green Argument for Driverless Cars." *Popular Science*. July 6, 2015. http://www.popsci.com/green-argument-driverless-cars

47 Kurzweil, Ray. *The Singularity is Near*. Penguin Books, 2005. P. 309.

48 Ross, Greg. "An interview with Douglas R. Hofstadter." *American Scientist*, January 2007. http://www.americanscientist.org/bookshelf/pub/douglas-r-hofstadter

49 Gerstner, Louis V. *Who Says Elephants Can't Dance?* HarperBusiness, 2002. P. 185.

50 *The Wall Street Journal*, August 20, 2011. http://online.wsj.com/article/SB10001424053111903480904576512250915629460.html

51 Shanahan, Murray. *The Technological Singularity*. MIT Press, 2015. P. 86.

52 https://www.google.com/selfdrivingcar/

53 Moravec, Hans. *Mind Children: The Future of Robot and Human Intelligence*. Harvard University Press, 1988.

54 Baker, David R. "As state pumps oil out, Brown says world must cut back." *San Francisco Chronicle*, July 22, 2015.

55 http://ourworldindata.org/data/population-growth-vital-statistics/life-expectancy/ Accessed March 28, 2016.

56 http://www.nal.usda.gov/awic/pubs/HorseHistory/intro.shtml

57 Common, Michael, Table 8.1 Food provision energy accounts, "Sustainability and Policy: Limits to Economics," August 17, 2015, Page 199.
Max Roser, 2015. "Energy Production & Changing Energy Sources." Published online at OurWorldInData.org. Retrieved from: http://ourworldindata.org/data/resources-energy/energy-production-and-changing-energy-sources/ Accessed August 14, 2015.

58 Roser, Max (2015) – 'Energy Production & Changing Energy Sources'. Published online at OurWorldInData.org. Retrieved from:

http://ourworldindata.org/data/resources-energy/energy-production-and-changing-energy-sources/, Accessed 8/17/2015.

Madison, Angus, University of Groningen, Statistics on World Population, GDP and Per Capita GDP, 1-2008 AD, http://www.ggdc.net/MADDISON/oriindex.htm, Accessed 7/29/15.

[59] Roser, Max (2015) – 'Energy Production & Changing Energy Sources'. Published online at OurWorldInData.org. Retrieved from: http://ourworldindata.org/data/resources-energy/energy-production-and-changing-energy-sources/

[60] Roser, Max (2015) – 'Energy Production & Changing Energy Sources'. Published online at OurWorldInData.org. Retrieved from: http://ourworldindata.org/data/resources-energy/energy-production-and-changing-energy-sources/

[61] Finkenrath, Smith, & Volk; Matthias, Julian, & Dennis; "CSS Retrofit: Analysis of the Globally Installed Coal-Fired Power Plant Fleet", International Energy Agency, https://www.iea.org/publications/freepublications/publication/CCS_Retrofit.pdf, Accessed 8/18/15, Page 16.

[62] *Reuters*, "China's coal use falling faster than expected", http://www.reuters.com/article/2015/03/26/china-coal-idUSL3N0WL32720150326, Accessed 8/20/15.

[63] World Coal Association, "Frequently Asked Questions", http://www.worldcoal.org/resources/frequently-asked-questions/, Accessed 8/18/15. There are about 2300 plant locations, but many of the plants have multiple generating stations, and thus 7000 total generators.

[64] Finkenrath, Smith, & Volk; Matthias, Julian, & Dennis; "CSS Retrofit: Analysis of the Globally Installed Coal-Fired Power Plant Fleet", International Energy Agency, https://www.iea.org/publications/freepublications/publication/CCS_Retrofit.pdf, Accessed 8/18/15, Page 16.

[65] Gomes, Carlos, "Global Auto Report", ScotiaBank, August 12, 2015, http://www.gbm.scotiabank.com/English/bns_econ/bns_auto.pdf, Page 2.

[66] National Geographic. "Azerbaijan in World War II. Objective Baku - Hitler Battle for Oil." https://www.youtube.com/watch?v=7CYx1lVBldw&ebc=ANyPxKqnPnW7Csbe UQ5VeP7nQnMH3BCYO_ADwiNgyfzYxukirZPAi6mx7HP-WS_L2Zl7hk7rBlcp Accessed March 28, 2016.

[67] US Energy Information Administration, "Estimated Primary Energy Consumption in the United States, Selected Years, 1635-1945," Annual Energy Review 2009, Table E1, Appendix E, Page 385, http://www.eia.gov/todayinenergy/detail.cfm?id=10, Accessed 8/6/15. See also, Kish, J.N., "U.S. Population 1776 to Present", https://www.google.com/fusiontables/DataSource?dsrcid=225439#rows:id=1, Accessed 8/7/15. This is a public Google database with data from the US Census Bureau.

[68] US Energy Information Administration, Total Primary Energy Consumption per Capita (Million Btu per Person), International Energy Statistics, http://www.eia.gov/cfapps/ipdbproject/iedindex3.cfm?tid=44&pid=45&aid=2&cid=regions&syid=1980&eyid=2011&unit=MBTUPP, Accessed July 29, 2015.

[69] United States Environmental Protection Agency, Atmospheric Concentrations of Greenhouse Gases, Climate Change Indicators in the United States, http://www.epa.gov/climatechange/science/indicators/ghg/ghg-concentrations.html, Accessed 8/3/15.

[70] NASA Earth Observatory/Robert Simmon

[71] Intergovernmental Panel on Climate Change, "Climate Change 2014: Impacts, Adaptation, and Vulnerability", http://www.ipcc.ch/report/ar5/wg2/, Accessed 7/29/15.

http://www.jstor.org.proxy.uchicago.edu/stable/3559157?Search=yes&resultItem Click=true&searchText=climate&searchText=change&searchText=instability&se archUri=%2Faction%2FdoBasicSearch%3FQuery%3Dclimate%2Bchange%2Bins tability%26amp%3Bacc%3Don%26amp%3Bwc%3Don%26amp%3Bfc%3Doff% 26amp%3Bgroup%3Dnone&seq=6#page_scan_tab_contents

http://sauerenergy.com/index.php?option=com_content&view=article&id=150:cli mate-change-drives-instability-un-official-warns&catid=38:sector-news&Itemid=72
http://www.theguardian.com/environment/2014/mar/31/climate-change-threat-food-security-humankind

[72] Guha-Sapir, D., R. Below, Ph. Hoyois - EM-DAT: The CRED/OFDA International Disaster Database – www.emdat.be – Université Catholique de Louvain – Brussels – Belgium, Accessed August 17, 2015.

[73] http://www.emdat.be/disaster_trends/index.html Accessed March 1, 2016.
http://www.emdat.be/natural-disasters-trends
http://www.iii.org/sites/default/files/docs/pdf/MunichRe-010412.pdf
http://www.nrdc.org/health/climate/extreme-weather.asp
http://www.ncdc.noaa.gov/cag/time-series/global
http://www.c2es.org/publications/extreme-weather-and-climate-change

[74] Anderegg, William R. L., James W. Prall, Jacob Harold, and Stephen H. Schneider. "Expert credibility in climate change."
http://www.pnas.org/content/107/27/12107.full.pdf
97 percent of the 1372 published climate scientists were found to be in agreement.

[75] D. Guha-Sapir, R. Below, Ph. Hoyois - EM-DAT: The CRED/OFDA International Disaster Database – http://www.emdat.be/advanced_search/index.html, Accessed 8/20/15, Université Catholique de Louvain – Brussels – Belgium.
Other useful links:
http://www.ipcc.ch/pdf/assessment-report/ar5/wg2/WGIIAR5-Chap10_FINAL.pdf Page 680
https://www.munichre.com/site/touch-naturalhazards/get/documents_E1018449711/mr/assetpool.shared/Documents/5_T ouch/_Publications/302-08606_en.pdf

[76] Smil, Vaclav. *Global Catastrophes and Trends: The Next Fifty Years.* The MIT Press, 2012. P. 188.

[77] Bretting, Diana. " 20 Feet Sea Level Rise expected around Globe.
July 5, 2015 http://perfscience.com/content/2142261-20-feet-sea-level-rise-expected-around-globe-study#sthash.0XBOgMDR.dpuf
"The study was conducted by University of Florida researchers to predict the extent to which sea levels are likely to rise due to global warming and other climate change. The researchers analyzed the past geological history of earth,

finding that sea levels rose by around 20 feet when temperatures reached near or went above modern day global averages. The researchers chose a low-lying state area for the study as it was believed to be most affected by rising sea levels. The process for sea level rise examined by the researchers took place in climates just 1.8 to 5.4 degrees Fahrenheit warmer than our modern age. Melting ice reservoirs in Greenland and on Antarctica contributed the most to this rise in sea level."

[78]   http://www.unhcr.org/pages/49e483b76.html

[79]   Fischetti, Mark. "Climate Change Hastened Syria's Civil War: Human-induced drying in many societies can push tensions over a threshold that provokes violent conflict." *Scientific American*, March 2, 2015

[80]   https://www.mercycorps.org/articles/iraq-jordan-lebanon-syria-turkey/quick-facts-what-you-need-know-about-syria-crisis

[81]   Lyman, Rick. "Europe Lacks Strategy to Tackle Crisis, but Migrants March On." *The New York Times*, September 17, 2015.

[82]   http://www.unicef.org/drought/drought-countries.htm; http://www.usatoday.com/story/news/world/2015/07/24/historic-droughts-wreak-havoc-usa-brazil-n-korea/30513289/

[83]   Intergovernmental Panel on Climate Change. http://www.ipcc.ch/ipccreports/tar/wg2/index.php?idp=671

[84]   Overpeck, J.T. and J.L. Weiss. 2009. Projections of future sea level becoming more dire. Proceedings of the National Academy of Sciences of the United States of America 106: 21461-21462. http://www.geo.arizona.edu/dgesl/research/other/climate_change_and_sea_level/mapping_slr/

[85]   Intergovernmental Panel on Climate Change http://www.ipcc.ch/ipccreports/tar/wg2/index.php?idp=671

[86]   https://weather.com/science/environment/news/20-countries-most-risk-sea-level-rise-20140924

[87]   http://philadelphia.cbslocal.com/2015/09/30/study-sea-level-rise-increasing-major-storms-off-new-jersey/

[88]   Thompson, Don. "17 Governors Announce Clean Energy, Transportation Agreement." *Associated Press*, February 16, 2016.

[89]   Smil, Vaclav. *Oil.* Oneworld 2008. P. 161.

[90]   Smil, Vaclav. *Oil.* Oneworld, 2008.

[91]   Engdahl, F. William. *A Century of War: Anglo-American Oil Politics and the New World Order.* Progressive Press, 2012.

[92]   Senator John McCain with Mark Salter. *Hard Call: Courageous Decisions by Inspiring People.* Gibson Square, 2008. This book was written for a US presidential campaign. In its review of the book, New York Times reviewer Jacob Heilbrunn notes, "In essence, McCain depicts only the upside of history and great men. For all his emphasis on honor and nobility of character, he never confronts the fact that the Bush administration has systematically debauched those virtues in its contorted efforts to battle terrorism. The most that McCain volunteers about the Iraq war is the mild observation that "the political and military mistakes we have made in Iraq offer a variety of examples of insufficient awareness." But the Bush administration was repeatedly warned about the risks ahead of time and cavalierly chose to believe in its own version of reality. McCain, though, refuses to make that easy call. The real value of McCain's book, then, may be that it reveals why he is unlikely to win the presidency." Heilbrunn was correct; McCain lost the election decisively to Barak Obama, by 10 million votes, 70 million for Obama to

60 million for McCain. (Jacob Heilbrunn. "A Question of Character." New York Times Book Review, September 9, 2007.)

[93] Prentiss, Mara. *Energy Revolution: The Physics and the Promise of Efficient Technology*. Harvard, Belknpa, 2015. P. 3.

[94] http://www.eia.gov/dnav/pet/pet_pnp_pct_dc_nus_pct_m.htm

[95] http://www.alyeska-pipe.com/TAPS/PipelineFacts

[96] Carr, Geoffrey, "Sunny Uplands", The Economist science and technology, http://www.economist.com/news/21566414-alternative-energy-will-no-longer-be-alternative-sunny-uplands, Accessed 8/5/15.
See also: http://about.bnef.com/?cat=27&s=solar

[97] Four Peaks Technologies, Scottsdale, AZ. The table shows the Levelized Cost Of Energy (LCOE) for various sources of electricity. The LCOE is a "fair" method of comparing the cost of different complex energy technologies. It is the total life cycle cost of electricity for a given technology divided by the total life cycle electricity produced, expressed as cents per kilo-watt hour. (LCOE calculations are explained in more detail in the Utility Section below.) The table, derived from LCOE costs developed by the US Energy Information Administration (EIA) in June, 2015, estimates the raw LCOE over a 30 year period for different energy sources that are brought online in the year 2020. No subsidies are included in the calculations. http://solarcellcentral.com/cost_page.html

[98] http://www.cnbc.com/2015/06/01/bloom-energys-fuel-cell-gambit.html

[99] Note 16 of the other reference document... IHS Cambridge Energy Research Associates

[100] US Energy Information Administration, "Drilling Productivity Report", Petroleum & Other Liquids, http://www.eia.gov/petroleum/drilling/, Accessed 8/10/15.
http://blogs.wsj.com/corporate-intelligence/2015/04/01/how-much-u-s-oil-and-gas-comes-from-fracking/
http://instituteforenergyresearch.org/analysis/u-s-oil-gas-production-continues-increase-due-hydraulic-fracturing/
http://www.slate.com/articles/health_and_science/future_tense/2011/12/is_there_really_100_years_worth_of_natural_gas_beneath_the_united_states_.html

[101] International Energy Agency, "Table 1: World Oil Supply and Demand", Oil Market Report, https://www.iea.org/media/omrreports/tables/2015-07-10.pdf, Accessed 8/21/15.
Other useful links that examine how fracking is disrupting the global market:
http://www.newrepublic.com/article/121344/brookings-paper-fracking-benefits-consumers-billions-year
http://fivethirtyeight.com/datalab/the-law-of-supply-and-demand-suddenly-applies-to-oil-too/
http://instituteforenergyresearch.org/analysis/u-s-oil-gas-production-continues-increase-due-hydraulic-fracturing/

[102] California Department of Conservation, "Energy Map of California", ftp://ftp.consrv.ca.gov/pub/oil/maps/Map%20S-2.pdf, Accessed 8/18/15.

[103] http://money.cnn.com/2013/01/14/news/economy/california-oil-boom/

[104] Lochhead, Carolyn. "State Dems' plan to keep fossil fuels in ground." *San Francisco Chronicle*, February 14, 2016.

[105] "HP to power Texas data centers with wind." San Francisco Chronicle, July 22, 2105

106 APPLE: Wang, Ucilia, "Apple Inks 130MW Solar Power Contract With First Solar", http://www.forbes.com/sites/uciliawang/2015/02/10/apple-inks-130mw-solar-power-contract-with-first-solar/, Accessed 8/20/15.
GOOGLE: Parker, Leia, "Google to buy Altamont wind energy to power the Googleplex", Silicon Valley Business Journal, http://www.bizjournals.com/sanjose/news/2015/02/11/google-to-buy-altamont-wind-energy-to-power-the.html, Accessed 8/20/15.
WAL-MART: Akuo Energy, "Signing of 50MW Power Purchase Agreement with Walmart", http://www.akuoenergy.com/fileadmin/media/pdf/news-en/CP_AKE_PPA_WalMart_ENg.pdf, Accessed 8/20/15.
IKEA, HP: Ward, David, "American wind power continues to ramp up in 2015", American Wind Energy Association, http://www.awea.org/MediaCenter/pressrelease.aspx?ItemNumber=7732, Accessed 8/20/15.
MICROSOFT: Abbott, Stephen, "Microsoft's 2 Year Journey to 285 MW of Wind Energy", RMI Outlet, http://blog.rmi.org/blog_2015_08_06_microsofts_two_year_journey_to_285_mega_watts_of_wind_energy, Accessed 8/20/15.
GM: General Motors, "Wind Power to Debut on GM's Renewable Energy Roster", http://media.gm.com/media/us/en/gm/news.detail.html/content/Pages/news/us/en/2015/feb/0217-windfarm.html, Accessed 8/20/15.
IBM: IBM, "Increasing Renewable Energy", https://www.ibm.com/ibm/environment/climate/renewable_energy.shtml, Accessed 8/20/15.
CISCO: Cisco, "NRG Renew to Develop 20MW Solar Energy Facility for Cisco", http://newsroom.cisco.com/press-release-content?type=webcontent&articleId=1666280, Accessed 8/21/15.
107 https://en.wikipedia.org/wiki/United_States_Department_of_Defense#Energy_use July 22, 1015

The Department of Defense was the largest single consumer of energy in the United States in 2006. In FY 2006, the Department used almost 30,000 gigawatt hours (GWH) of electricity, at a cost of almost $2.2 billion. The Department's electricity use would supply enough electricity to power more than 2.6 million average American homes. In electricity consumption, if it were a country, the Department would rank 58th in the world, using slightly less than Denmark and slightly more than Syria (CIA World Factbook, 2006). The Department of Defense is responsible for 93% of all US government fuel consumption in 2007 (Department of the Air Force: 52%; Department of the Navy: 33%; Department of the Army: 7%; other Department components: 1%).[39] The Department of Defense uses 4,600,000,000 US gallons (1.7×1010 L) of fuel annually, an average of 12,600,000 US gallons (48,000,000 L) of fuel per day. A large Army division may use about 6,000 US gallons (23,000 L) per day. According to the 2005 CIA World Factbook, if it were a country, the Department of Defense would rank 34th in the world in average daily oil use, coming in just behind Iraq and just ahead of Sweden.[40] The Air Force is the largest user of fuel energy in the federal government. The Air Force uses 10% of the nation's aviation fuel. (JP-8 accounts for nearly 90% of its fuels.) This fuel usage breaks down as such: 82% jet fuel, 16% facility management and 2% ground vehicle/equipment.

108 Selby, Glenn. "Military's Shift Toward Renewable Energy." *Armed with Science: The Official US Defense Department Science Blog.* August 12, 2015. http://science.dodlive.mil/2015/08/12/militarys-shift-toward-renewable-energy/

109 US Energy Information Administration, "International Energy Statistics", http://www.eia.gov/cfapps/ipdbproject/IEDIndex3.cfm?tid=5&pid=57&aid=6, Accessed 8/10/15.

110 British Petroleum, Oil Total Proved Reserves, "BP Statistical Review of World Energy June 2015", http://www.bp.com/content/dam/bp/pdf/Energy-economics/statistical-review-2015/bp-statistical-review-of-world-energy-2015-full-report.pdf, Accessed 8/10/15, Page 6.

111 Arabian Business, "AB Rich List 2010", http://www.arabianbusiness.com/arabian-business-rich-list-2010-367763.html, Accessed 8/10/15.

112 Shirky, Clay. *Little Rice: Smartphones, Xiaomi, and the Chinese Dream.* Columbia Global Reports, 2015.

113 https://en.wikipedia.org/wiki/2011%E2%80%9312_Saudi_Arabian_protests

114 Hubbard, Ben. "Young Saudis See Cushy Jobs Vanish Along With Nation's Oil Wealth." *The New York Times,* February 16, 2016.

115 BP, "Oil: Production", BP Statistical Review of World Energy June 2015, http://www.bp.com/content/dam/bp/pdf/Energy-economics/statistical-review-2015/bp-statistical-review-of-world-energy-2015-full-report.pdf, Accessed 8/5/15. Other useful links:
http://oilprice.com/Energy/Crude-Oil/A-Closer-Look-At-The-Worlds-5-Biggest-Oil-Companies.html
http://www.eia.gov/finance/markets/supply-nonopec.cfm
http://www.bp.com/content/dam/bp/pdf/Energy-economics/statistical-review-2015/bp-statistical-review-of-world-energy-2015-full-report.pdf
http://www.ey.com/Publication/vwLUAssets/EY-us-oil-and-gas-reserves-study-2015/$FILE/EY-us-oil-and-gas-reserves-study-2015.pdf

116 Picker, Leslie and Julie Creswell. "Once a Coup, Pipeline Company Deal Becomes a Nightmare." *The New York Times,* February 25, 2016. http://www.nytimes.com/2016/02/26/business/dealbook/once-a-coup-energy-transfer-deal-becomes-a-nightmare.html?_r=0

117 Smil, Vaclav. Renewable Energy Sources Could Take the World by Storm." *Scientific American,* January 2014.

118 Smil, Vaclav. Renewable Energy Sources Could Take the World by Storm." *Scientific American,* January 2014.

119 Harvey, Hal. "Policies that Work." Energy Innovation Policy & Technology LLC. http://energyinnovation.org/
Energy Innovation's mission is to accelerate progress in clean energy by supporting the policies that most effectively reduce greenhouse gas emissions. Through customized research and analysis for decision makers, we uncover the strategies that will produce the largest results. We work closely with other experts, NGOs, the media, and the private sector to ensure that our work complements theirs.

120 Jones, Chuck, "Apple's US Smartphone Market Share Holding Steady Against Every Competitor," Forbes Tech, http://www.forbes.com/sites/chuckjones/2014/04/07/apples-u-s-smartphone-market-share-holding-steady-against-every-competitor/, Accessed 8/7/15.

121 Smil, Vaclav. *Global Catastrophes and Trends: The Next Fifty Years.* The MIT Press, 2012. P. 75. & P. ix

[122]   Jonah Lehrer. "A Physicist Solves the City." *New York Times Magazine*,
         December 17, 2010.
         http://www.nytimes.com/2010/12/19/magazine/19Urban_West-t.html (Diamandis
         p. 149)

[123]   Huerta, Santiago. "Technical Challenges in the Construction of Gothic Vaults:
         The Gothic Theory of Structural Design." *Construction Techniques in the Age of
         Historicism. From Theories of Gothic Structures to Building Sites in the 19th
         Century*, Hirmer Verlag, 2012.

[124]   World Bank, Urban Population (% of total), World Development Indicators,
         http://databank.worldbank.org/data//reports.aspx?source=2&country=&series=SP.
         URB.TOTL.IN.ZS&period=

[125]   US Census Bureau, Historical Estimates of World Population, International
         Programs,
         http://www.census.gov/population/international/data/worldpop/table_history.php

[126]   GOOD and ONE/Living Proof, "Teach A Wo(man) to Farm: The Agricultural
         Multiplier Effect",
         https://outrageandinspire.files.wordpress.com/2013/07/infographic-27-teach-a-
         women-to-farm.jpg, Accessed 8/17/15.
         http://www.gsma.com/mobilefordevelopment/wp-
         content/uploads/2013/10/GSMA-mAgri-Infographic_Oct2013.png

[127]   Meadows, Donella H., Jorgen Randers, Dennis L. Meadows, William W. Behrens.
         *The Limits to growth: A report for the Club of Rome's Project on the Predicament
         of Mankind.* Universe Books, 1972.

[128]   University of Pennsylvania, Population for China [POPTTLCNA173NUPN],
         retrieved from FRED, Federal Reserve Bank of St. Louis
         https://research.stlouisfed.org/fred2/series/POPTTLCNA173NUPN/, Accessed
         August 20, 2015. Note: The graph shows an extrapolated quadratic regression
         from 1960-1978 data to reflect predicted population without the One Child Policy
         in 1979.

[129]   World Bank, Population ages 15-64 male/female, Gender Statistics,
         http://databank.worldbank.org/data/reports.aspx?source=283, Accessed 8/17/15.

[130]   World Bank, "Urban population (% of total)", World Development Indicators,
         http://databank.worldbank.org/data//reports.aspx?source=2&country=&series=SP.
         URB.TOTL.IN.ZS&period, Accessed 8/10/15.

[131]   http://databank.worldbank.org/data//reports.aspx?source=2&country=&series=
         SP.URB.TOTL.IN.ZS&period#

[132]   World Bank, "Urban population (% of total)", World Development Indicators,
         http://databank.worldbank.org/data//reports.aspx?source=2&country=&series=SP.
         URB.TOTL.IN.ZS&period, Accessed 8/10/15.

[133]   http://databank.worldbank.org/data//reports.aspx?source=2&country=&series=SP.
         URB.TOTL.IN.ZS&period#

[134]   World Bank: data.worldbank.org/indicator/SP.DYN.TFRT.IN

[135]   Bloomberg Business. "World's Fastest Shrinking Countries."
         http://www.bloomberg.com/ss/10/08/0813_fastest_shrinking_countries/
         and
         World Population Data, http://www.prb.org/wpds/2015/

[136]   Zeihan, Peter. *The Accidental Superpower: The Next Generation of American
         Preeminence and the Coming Global Disorder.* Grand Central Publishing, 2014.
         P. 43- 44.

[137]   Spiegel, "Pensions Armageddon: Germans Fear Poverty Even After Life of Work", http://www.spiegel.de/international/germany/germans-fear-poverty-in-retirement-even-after-life-of-work-a-855352.html, Accessed 8/20/15.
Data from German Labor Minister Shows Pensions Sustain at Poverty Line Level Gessat, Michael, "Labor minister warns of failing pension system", Deutsche Welle, http://www.dw.com/en/labor-minister-warns-of-failing-pension-system/a-16215512, Accessed 8/20/15.

[138]   Centers for Medicare & Medicaid Services, "National Health Expenditures by type of service and source of funds, CY 1960-2013", https://www.cms.gov/Research-Statistics-Data-and-Systems/Statistics-Trends-and-Reports/NationalHealthExpendData/NationalHealthAccountsHistorical.html, Accessed 8/10/15.

[139]   Cosgrave, Jenny, "Why Greece's pensions are key to the debt deadlock", CNBC Europe: Economy, http://www.cnbc.com/2015/06/18/why-greeces-pensions-are-key-to-the-debt-deadlock.html, Accessed 8/14/15.
Greek overspending on public expenditures, pensions & understating of nation deficit: Stamouli & Bouras, Nektaria & Stelios, "Greeks Investigate Statistics Chief Over Deficit Figure", The Wall Street Journal, http://www.wsj.com/articles/deficit-drama-greek-authorities-step-up-probe-against-statistics-chief-1427060060, Accessed 8/14/15.
Greek trade deficit: Jain, Abhilash, "A Decade of Extravagance: Greece, Overspending, and the Inevitable Crisis", Quora, http://fundamentalsoffinance.quora.com/A-Decade-of-Extravagance-Greece-Overspending-and-the-Inevitable-Crisis, Accessed 8/14/15.
http://www.bbc.com/news/business-13798000

[140]   California Department of Finance, "California 2015-16 State Budget", http://www.ebudget.ca.gov/2015-16/pdf/Enacted/BudgetSummary/FullBudgetSummary.pdf, Accessed 8/17/15, Page 9.

[141]   Munford, Monty. "Silicon Plateau, Silicon Gulf and Silicon Bog: who can match the Valley?" Daily Telegraph, UK, March 10, 2013.
http://www.telegraph.co.uk/technology/news/9918665/Silicon-Plateau-Silicon-Gulf-and-Silicon-Bog-who-can-match-the-Valley.html

[142]   Eesley, Charles E. and William F. Miller. "Impact: Stanford University's Economic Impact via Innovation and Entrepreneurship." Stanford University, October 2012.
http://engineering.stanford.edu/sites/default/files/Stanford_Alumni_Innovation_Survey_Report_3-2-13.pdf

[143]   http://science.howstuffworks.com/environmental/earth/geophysics/question473.htm

[144]   http://www.aljazeera.com/indepth/features/2011/01/201111684242518839.html

[145]   https://en.wikipedia.org/wiki/Mohamed_Bouazizi#cite_note-aljazeera1-15

[146]   http://www.un.org/en/universal-declaration-human-rights/

[147]   http://www.ohchr.org/en/professionalinterest/pages/crc.aspx

[148]   Fuller, Thomas. "Thai Man May Go to Prison for Insulting King's Dog." The New York Times, December 14, 2015.

[149]   President Obama, commenting about the success of Donald Trump's presidential primary campaign in 2015. San Francisco Chronicle. "Obama: Trump Exploiting anger, fears over economy." December 22, 2015.

[150] Kuhn, Thomas S. *The Structure of Scientific Revolutions.* Second Edition, Enlarged. The University of Chicago Press, 1962, 1970. P. 7.

[151] Fukuyama, Francis. *The End of History and the Last Man Paperback.* Free Press, 1992.

[152] Nye, Joseph S. Jr. *Soft Power: The Means To Success In World Politics.* Perseus Books, 2004.

[153] McCants, William. *The ISIS Apocalypse: The History, Strategy, and Doomsday Vision of the Islamic State.* St. Martin's Press, 2015. P 144.

[154] "20,000 foreigners have joined ISIS in Iraq, Syria." February 11, 2015. https://www.rt.com/usa/231207-foreign-isis-fighters-westerners/

[155] McCants, William. *The ISIS Apocalypse: The History, Strategy, and Doomsday Vision of The Islamic State.* St. Martin's Press, 2015. P. 101.

[156] http://money.cnn.com/2015/02/10/technology/anonymous-isis-hack-twitter/

[157] Abu-Nasr, Donna, and Jeremy Hodges. "Fighting Islamic State in cyberspace." San Francisco Chronicle, January 27, 2016. Originally published by Bloomberg.

[158] McCants, William. *The ISIS Apocalypse: The History, Strategy, and Doomsday Vision of The Islamic State.* St. Martin's Press, 2015. P. 13. The phrase "hearts and minds" was apparently first used in the context of counter-insurgency warfare by British General Gerald Templer in February 1952 in Malaysia. The same phrase, amended to "winning hearts and minds," was later used by the US Army in Vietnam from 1965 - 1968 to describe how it would win the war of public opinion; the napalming of villages, however, created the opposite result, and when an American officer commented to the press after entirely destroying one such village that, "We had to destroy the village in order to save it," the war for hearts and minds was essentially lost not only in Vietnam but in the US as well. The anti-war movement in the US gained considerable strength as the absurdity of America's official government position was exposed. A book of poetry by American veterans of Vietnam was also published by McGraw Hill in 1972 with the same title, but it was filled not with optimism but bitterness.

[159] Resolution on CPC History (1949-81). "Resolution on Certain Questions in the History of Our Party Since the Founding of the People's Republic of China," adopted by the Sixth Plenary Session of the Eleventh Central Committee of the Communist Party of China on June 27, 1981. *Foreign Languages Press*, Beijing, 1981. P. 32.

[160] Toffler, Alvin. *Future Shock.* Random House, 1970.

[161] Rushkoff, Douglas. *Present Shock: When Everything Happens Now.* Current, 2014.

[162] Wingfield-Hayes, Rupert. "Why does Japan have such a high suicide rate?" BBC News, Tokyo, July 3, 2015. http://www.bbc.com/news/world-33362387

[163] http://www.who.int/mediacentre/factsheets/fs369/en/

[164] Glaeser, P. 76

[165] Hegel, Georg Wilhelm Friedrich. *The Philosophy of History.* Dover Philosophical Classics, 2004.

[166] Whitehead, Alfred North. *Symbolism, Its Meaning and Effect.* Fordham University Press, p. 88 (1927). (Also Kurzweil p 410)

[167] Rowling, J.K. *Harry Potter and the Goblet of Fire.* Scholastic, 2000.

[168] Campbell, Joseph. The Hero With a Thousand Faces. Princeton University Press, 1949. P 382.

[169] Gyorffy, Laszlo and Lisa Friedman. *Creating Value with CO-STAR: An Innovation Tool for Perfecting and Pitching Your Brilliant Idea.* Enterprise Development Group, Inc, 2012.

[170] This issue was the topic of my first book, written 20 years ago but still pertinent, as well as number of books I've authored or co-authored since then. Morris, Langdon. *Managing the Evolving Corporation.* Wiley, 1995.

[171] Sharma, Ruchir. "The Demographics of Stagnation: Whey People Matter for Economic Growth." *Foreign Affairs*, March/April 2016.

[172] Howard, Emma. "Humans have already used up 2015's supply of Earth's resources." The Guardian (UK). August 11, 2015. http://www.theguardian.com/environment/2015/aug/12/humans-have-already-used-up-2015s-supply-of-earths-resources-analysis

[173] Sharma, Ruchir. "The Demographics of Stagnation: Whey People Matter for Economic Growth." *Foreign Affairs*, March/April 2016.

[174] Taleb, Nassim Nicholas. *AntiFragile: Things That Gain from Disorder.* Random House, 2012. P. 3.

[175] Taleb, Nassim Nicholas. *AntiFragile: Things That Gain from Disorder.* Random House, 2012. P. 5. "We have been fragilizing the economy, our health, political life, education, almost everything … by suppressing randomness and volatility. … The process of discovery (or innovation, or technological progress) itself depends on antifragile tinkering, aggressive risk bearing rather than formal education."

[176] Taleb, Nassim Nicholas. *AntiFragile: Things That Gain from Disorder.* Random House, 2012. P. 76-78.

[177] Hugo, Victor. *Histoire d'un crime.* 1877. *"On resiste a l'invasion des armees; on ne resiste pas a l'invasion des idees."*

[178] Rhodes, Richard. *The Making of the Atomic Bomb.* Simon & Schuster, 1986. P. 103.

[179] Rhodes, Richard. *The Making of the Atomic Bomb.* Simon & Schuster, 1986.

[180] Miller, James Grier. *Living Systems.* McGraw Hill, 1978.

[181] Miller, James Grier. *Living Systems.* McGraw Hill, 1978. P. xiv.

[182] Bureau of Transportation Statistics: http://www.transtats.bts.gov/ A total of 631,939,829 passengers boarded domestic flights in the United States in 2010, which averages to 1.73 million passengers per day.

[183] Sierra Club. www.sierraclub.org
It takes about 8 of trees to produce between 1,000 and 2,000 pounds of paper. A typical 500-sheet packet of the paper weighs 5 pounds, that's 10,000 to 20,000 sheets per tree.

[184] *www.state.sc.us/forest/nurspa.htm*

[185] Miller, James Grier. *Living Systems.* McGraw Hill, 1978. P. 392.

[186] http://data.worldbank.org/indicator/IS.AIR.PSGR/countries?display=graph

[187] Gomes, Carlos, "Global Auto Report", ScotiaBank, August 12, 2015, http://www.gbm.scotiabank.com/English/bns_econ/bns_auto.pdf, Page 2.
Stacy C. Davis, Susan W. Diegel, and Robert G. Boundy (June 2011). "Transportation Energy Data Book: Edition 30" (PDF). Office of Energy Efficiency and Renewable Energy, U.S. Department of Energy. Retrieved 2012-09-24. See Tables 3.1 and 3.2 for figures from 1960 to 2005
Stacy C. Davis, Susan W. Diegel, and Robert G. Boundy (July 2012). "Transportation Energy Data Book: Edition 31" (PDF). Office of Energy Efficiency and Renewable Energy, U.S. Department of Energy. Retrieved 2012-09-25. See Tables 3.2 and 3.3 for 2009 figures

Stacy C. Davis, Susan W. Diegel, and Robert G. Boundy (July 2014). "Transportation Energy Data Book: Edition 33" (PDF). Office of Energy Efficiency and Renewable Energy, U.S. Department of Energy. Retrieved 2015-03-14. See Tables 3.2 and 3.3 for 2010 and 2012 figures

[188] http://www.statista.com/statistics/273018/number-of-internet-users-worldwide/

[189] https://en.wikipedia.org/wiki/Arab_Spring

[190] Dainotti, Alberto. "Analysis of Country-wide Internet Outages Caused by Censorship." University of Napoli Federico II. http://www.caida.org/publications/papers/2011/outages_censorship/outages_censorship.pdf

[191] O'Donnell, Catherine. "New study quantifies use of social media in Arab Spring." University of Washington, *UW Today,* September 12, 2011. http://www.washington.edu/news/2011/09/12/new-study-quantifies-use-of-social-media-in-arab-spring/

[192] http://www.statista.com/statistics/264810/number-of-monthly-active-facebook-users-worldwide/

[193] *Fast Company.* "How Top Brands Like Gatorade And The Super Bowl Use Social-Media Command Centers." http://www.fastcompany.com/1841131/how-top-brands-gatorade-and-super-bowl-use-social-media-command-centers

[194] https://en.wikipedia.org/wiki/Metcalfe's_law: Metcalfe's law states that the value of a telecommunications network is proportional to the square of the number of connected users of the system (n2). Metcalfe's law was originally presented, c. 1980, not in terms of users, but rather of "compatible communicating devices" (for example, fax machines, telephones, etc.). Only more recently with the launch of the Internet did this law carry over to users and networks as its original intent was to describe Ethernet purchases and connections.

[195] http://linuxworlddominationillustrated.blogspot.com/2010/06/first-inkscape-graph-metcalfes-law.html

[196] http://spectrum.ieee.org/computing/networks/metcalfes-law-is-wrong

[197] McLuhan, Marshall and Quentin Fiore. *The Medium is the Massage: An Inventory of Effects.* Penguin, 1967. P. 63.

[198] https://www.youtube.com/yt/press/statistics.html

[199] http://www.reelseo.com/hours-minute-uploaded-youtube/

[200] http://www.statista.com/statistics/263055/cotton-production-worldwide-by-top-countries/

[201] http://cottonaustralia.com.au/cotton-library/fact-sheets/cotton-fact-file-the-australian-cotton-industry

[202] http://www.ers.usda.gov/topics/crops/cotton-wool/background.aspx
Trade is particularly important for cotton. About 30 percent of the world's consumption of cotton fiber crosses international borders before processing, a larger share than for wheat, corn, soybeans, or rice. Through trade in yarn, fabric, and clothing, much of the world's cotton again crosses international borders at least once more before reaching the final consumer.

[203] Elmer-DeWitt, Philip. "By the numbers: How Foxconn churns out Apple's iPhone 5S." *Fortune Magazine*, November 27, 2013 http://fortune.com/2013/11/27/by-the-numbers-how-foxconn-churns-out-apples-iphone-5s/

[204] Chan, Anita, Editor. *Wal-Mart in China.* Cornell University Press, October 13, 2011.

205 Cardinal, David. "Amazon deploys 10,000 robot workers, a year after Obama's famous Amazon jobs speech." Extreme Tech, May 30, 2014. http://www.extremetech.com/extreme/183254-amazon-deploys-10000-robot-workers-a-year-after-obamas-famous-amazon-jobs-speech

206 Temperton, James. "Samsung developing robots to replace cheap Chinese labour." Wired UK. 19 October 2015. http://www.wired.co.uk/news/archive/2015-10/19/samsung-south-korea-robots-cheap-labour

207 Canal, Emily. "ISIS Halves Fighters' Salaries Following Losses Of Territory, Oil And Cash." Forbes. January 20, 2016. http://www.forbes.com/sites/emilycanal/2016/01/20/isis-halves-fighters-salaries-following-losses-of-territory-oil-and-cash/#638f47273d7f

208 Shah, Anup. "Loss of Biodiversity and Extinctions" http://www.globalissues.org/article/171/loss-of-biodiversity-and-extinctions Data from the Brazilian National Space Research Agency (INPE), graph compiled by Secretariat of the Convention on Biological Diversity (2010) Global Biodiversity Outlook 3, May 2010. https://www.cbd.int/

209 http://www.ipsnews.net/2012/10/palau-proves-sharks-worth-more-alive-than-dead/
Sharks play a crucial role in the health of marine ecosystems, including coral reefs, said Anisha Grover, the policy officer on oceans and coasts for the Hamburg, Germany-based World Future Council. Sharks are considered a keystone species in maintaining the marine food web. They eat the sick and weak, and scavenge on the dead. With too few sharks, coral reefs, lagoons and other parts of the ocean degrade, scientists have learned.
The people of Palau recognise the importance of sharks to the health of their ocean territory. And they now know they make far money from shark tourism than shark fishing, Grover told IPS from Hyderabad. Catching 100 reef sharks would bring the Palau government a one-time benefit amounting to 10,800 dollars, a recent Australian report has shown. Those same 100 reef sharks now visited by tourists nets 18 million dollars on an annual basis, according to the report, "Wanted Dead or Alive? The relative value of reef sharks as a fishery and an ecotourism asset in Palau". Reef sharks live 10 to 25 years.
"Wanted Dead or Alive? The relative value of reef sharks as a fishery and an ecotourism asset in Palau."

210 United States Department of Agriculture, Economic Research Service, November 2015. http://www.ers.usda.gov/topics/crops/corn/background.aspx

211 Smil, Vaclav. *Oil*. Oneworld, 2008. P. 16.

212 United States Department of Agriculture, Economic Research Service, World Agricultural Outlook Board, World Agricultural Supply and Demand Estimates, Updated November 2015. http://www.ers.usda.gov/topics/crops/corn/background.aspx

213 Bullis, Kevin. "Ethanol Blamed for Record Food Prices: A more flexible policy could ease the impact of ethanol mandates on worldwide markets. *Technology Review*, March 23, 2011. https://www.technologyreview.com/s/423385/ethanol-blamed-for-record-food-prices/

214 Gall, John. *Systemantics: The Underground Text of System Lore. How Systems Work and How They Fail.* The General Systemantics Press, Second Edition, 1986.

215 Kleiner, Art. *The Age of Heretics: A History of Radical Thinkers Who Reinvented Corporate Management.* Jossey-Bass, 2008.

216   Forrester, Jay. "Counter-Intuitive Behavior of Social Systems." *MIT Technology Review*, Volume 73, Number 3, January 1971.

217   Montgomery, Charles. *Happy City: Transforming Our Lives Through Urban Design.* Farrar, Strauss and Giroux. 2013. P. 181.

218   Kuhn, Thomas S. *The Structure of Scientific Revolutions.* Second Edition, Enlarged. The University of Chicago Press, 1962, 1970. P. 93.

219   Calvin, William. *The River That Flows Uphill: A Journey from the Big Bang to the Big Brain.* MacMillan, 1986.

220   http://www.cnn.com/2016/01/06/politics/house-obamacare-repeal-planned-parenthood/

221   Keynes, John Maynard. *The Economic Consequences of the Peace.* 1919.

222   "The Mother of All Demos" is a name given retrospectively to Douglas Engelbart's December 9, 1968, computer demonstration at the Fall Joint Computer Conference in San Francisco. The live demonstration featured the introduction of a complete computer hardware and software system called the oN-Line System or more commonly, NLS. The 90-minute presentation essentially demonstrated almost all the fundamental elements of modern personal computing: windows, hypertext, graphics, efficient navigation and command input, video conferencing, the computer mouse, word processing, dynamic file linking, revision control, and a collaborative real-time editor (collaborative work). Engelbart's presentation was the first to publicly demonstrate all these elements in a single system. The demonstration was highly influential and spawned similar projects at Xerox PARC in the early 1970s. The underlying technologies influenced both the Apple Macintosh and Microsoft Windows graphical user interface operating systems in the 1980s and 1990s. https://en.wikipedia.org/wiki/The_Mother_of_All_Demos

223   Beer, Stafford. *Platform for Change.* Wiley, 1975.

224   Soleri, Paolo. *Arcology: The City in the Image of Man.* MIT Press, 1969.

225   Randers, Jorgen. *2052: A Global Forecast for the Next Forty Years.* Chelsea Green, 2012.

226   http://www.2052.info/

227   May 7, 2012

228   Randers, Jorgen. *2052: A Global Forecast for the Next Forty Years.* Chelsea Green, 2012. P. 235.

229   Jevremovic, Tatjana. *Nuclear Principles in Engineering.* Springer, 2005. P. 397.

230   Kahney, Leander. *Inside Steve's Brain.* Portfolio, 2008.

231   Deming, W. Edwards. *The New Economics for Industry, Government, Education.* MIT Press, 1993.

232   Another visionary, the prodigal genius physicist Freeman Dyson, was once asked by Kenneth Brower about his unique thinking ability. "I asked Dyson whether as a boy he had speculated much about his gift. Had he asked himself why he had this special power? Why he was so bright? Dyson is almost infallibly a modest and self-effacing man, but tonight his eyes were blank with fatigue, and his answer was uncharacteristic. 'That's not how the question phrases itself,' he said. 'The question is: why is everyone else so stupid?' Brower, Kenneth. *The Starship and the Canoe.* HarperPerennial, 1983.

233   Andrews, Edmund L. "Greenspan Concedes Error on Regulation." The New York Times, October 23, 2008.
http://www.nytimes.com/2008/10/24/business/economy/24panel.html

234   Judt, Tony. *When the Facts Change.* Essays 1995 – 2010. Penguin Press, 2015.

235 Lakoff, George. *Moral Politics: What Conservatives Know that Liberals Don't*. University of Chicago Press, 1997.

236 Henrich, Joseph. *The Secret of Our Success: How Culture is Driving Human Evolution, Domesticating Our Species, and Making Us Smarter*. Princeton University Press, 2016. P. 186.

237 Janis, Irving L. *Groupthink*. Houghton Mifflin Company, 1982. Second Edition. P. 3.

238 Tuchman, Barbara W. *The Guns of August*. Ballantine Books, 1962. P 224

239 Gershwin, George and Ira. *Porgy and Bess*. 1934.

240 Shermer, Michael. *The Believing Brain: From Ghosts and Gods to Politics and Conspiracies – How We Construct Beliefs and Reinforce Them as Truths*. Times Books, 2011. P. 5.

241 Kahneman, Daniel. *Thinking, Fast and Slow*. Farrar, Straus and Giroux, 2011.

242 Russo, J. Edward and Paul J.H. Schoemaker. *Winning Decisions: Getting It Right the First Time*. Crown Business, 2001.

243 Mansfield, Guy. *Developing Your Leadership Skills: From the Changing World to Changing the World*. 2013.

244 Taleb, Nassim Nicholas. *Fooled by Randomness: The Hidden Role of Change in Life and in the Markets*. Random House, 2004.

245 https://en.wikipedia.org/wiki/List_of_ongoing_armed_conflicts. Accessed April 1, 2016.

246 Roig-Franzia, Manuel. "Brooksley Born, the Cassandra of the Derivatives Crisis." *The Washington Post*, May 26, 2009. http://www.washingtonpost.com/wp-dyn/content/article/2009/05/25/AR2009052502108.html

247 Taleb, Nassim Nicholas. *The Black Swan: The Impact of the Highly Improbable*. Random House, 2007. P. 225.

248 Taleb, Nassim Nicholas. *The Black Swan: The Impact of the Highly Improbable*. Random House, 2007. P. xvii.

249 Janis, Irving L. *Groupthink*. Houghton Mifflin Company, 1982. Second Edition. P. 136.

250 Shermer, Micahel. *The Believing Brain: From Ghosts and Gods to Politics and Conspiracies – How We Construct Beliefs and Reinforce Them as Truths*. Times Books, 2011. P. 4.

251 Henry Kissinger. *On China*. The Penguin Press, 2011. P 264.

252 Smil, Vaclav. *Global Catastrophes and Trends: The Next Fifty Years*. MIT Press, 2008. P. 120.

253 Kissinger, Henry. *World Order*. Penguin Books, 2014. P. 93.

254 Zeihan, Peter. *The Accidental Superpower: The Next Generation of American Preeminence and the Coming Global Disorder*. Grand Central Publishing, 2014. P. 73.

255 Keller, Bill. "Soviet Cartographer Says Nation's Maps Inaccurate." *The New York Times*, September 10, 1988.

256 https://polastre.com/2013/02/what-the-map/

257 Gopnik, Alison. The Philosophical Baby. Farrar Strauss and Girous, 2009. P 39

258 Shirky, Clay. *Little Rice: Smartphones, Xiaomi, and the Chinese Dream*. Columbia Global Reports, 2015. P. 21.

259 Abrahamian, Atossa Araxia. *The Cosmopolites: The Coming of the Global Citizen*. Columbia Global Reports, 2015. P. 17.

260 Kissinger, Henry. *On China*. The Penguin Press, 2011. P. 11.

261   Swanson, Ana. How China used more cement in 3 years that the U.S. did in the entire 20th century. *Washington Post*, March 24, 2015.

262   Data: World Bank

263   Kissinger, Henry. *On China*. The Penguin Press, 2011. P 264.

264   Cheng Li. "The Political Mapping of China's Tobacco Industry and Anti-Smoking Campaign." John L. Thornton China Center Monograph Series, Brookings Institution, October 2012.

265   Martin, Andrew. "The Chinese Government Is Getting Rich Selling Cigarettes." *Bloomberg*, December 11, 2014.

266   Fisher, Max. "How China Stays Stable Despite 500 Protests Every Day." The Atlantic, January 5, 2012. http://www.theatlantic.com/international/archive/2012/01/how-china-stays-stable-despite-500-protests-every-day/250940/

267   Outdoor air pollution ranked fourth both in mortality and in the overall burden on health rates in China, where it contributed to 1.2 million deaths and 25 million healthy years of life lost in 2010, according to the 2010 Global Burden of Disease (GBD) report: http://www.china.org.cn/china/2013-04/11/content_28513523.htm

268   Orlik, Tom. "Unrest Grows as Economy Booms." The Wall Street Journal, September 26, 2011. http://www.wsj.com/articles/SB10001424053111903703604576587070600504108

269   Keliher, Macabe and Hsinchao Wu. "How to Discipline 90 Million People." *The Atlantic*. April 7, 2015. http://www.theatlantic.com/international/archive/2015/04/xi-jinping-china-corruption-political-culture/389787/

270   You can retrieve the most current numbers from the US Bureau of Labor Statistics: http://www.bls.gov/webapps/legacy/cesbtab1.htm

271   *The Economist*. "China's army: Lifting the veil. Xi Jinping is bringing a corrupt army to heel. Now he must make it behave responsibly." February 14, 2015. http://www.economist.com/news/leaders/21643140-xi-jinping-bringing-corrupt-army-heel-now-he-must-make-it-behave-responsibly-lifting

272   https://www.stratfor.com/geopolitical-diary/china-abandons-one-child-policy

273   Lakdawalla, Emily. "Updates on China's lunar missions." *The Planetary Society*. January 14, 2016. http://www.planetary.org/blogs/emily-lakdawalla/2016/01141307-updates-on-change-program.html

274   Kan, Michael. "Foxconn expects robots to take over more factory work." *IDG News Service, PCWorld News*, February 27, 2015. http://www.pcworld.com/article/2890032/foxconn-expects-robots-to-take-over-more-factory-work.html

275   Barnett, Jon, Sarah Rogers, Michael Webber, Brian Finlayson, and Mark Wang. "Sustainability: Transfer project cannot meet China's water needs." *Nature*, November 18, 2015. http://www.nature.com/news/sustainability-transfer-project-cannot-meet-china-s-water-needs-1.18792

276   Ana Swanson. How China used more cement in 3 years that the U.S. did in the entire 20th century. Washington Post, March 24, 2015.

277   Shirky, Clay. *Little Rice: Smartphones, Xiaomi, and the Chinese Dream*. Columbia Global Reports, 2015. P. 50.

278   Shirky, Clay. *Little Rice: Smartphones, Xiaomi, and the Chinese Dream*. Columbia Global Reports, 2015. P. 21

279 Rose, Scott. "Putin's Approval Rating Rises to 88% in October, Levada Says." Bloomberg, October 28, 2015. Levada Center is an independent, Moscow-based polling company. http://www.bloomberg.com/news/articles/2015-10-28/putin-s-approval-rating-rises-to-88-in-october-levada-says

280 Smil, Vaclav. *Global Catastrophes and Trends: The Next Fifty Years.* MIT Press, 2008. P. 120.

281 Zeihan, Peter. *The Accidental Superpower: The Next Generation of American Preeminence and the Coming Global Disorder.* Twelve Books, 2014. P. 184.

282 Kastrenakes, Jacob. "Obama jokes about creating 'Iron Man,' but military is already doing it." The Verge, February 27, 2014. http://www.theverge.com/2014/2/27/5454602/obama-iron-man-joke-military-actually-building-talos-armor

283 Kissinger, Henry. *World Order.* Penguin, 2014. P 87

284 Pyper, Julia. "Debt-plagued Greece sees economic gains in adapting to climate change." *ClimateWire*, Tuesday, September 24, 2013. "In the country's latest comprehensive climate risk assessment, the Bank of Greece determined that if no action is taken to reduce man-made greenhouse gas emissions, the cumulative loss to the Greek economy in terms of gross domestic product by 2100 will be the equivalent of $945 billion." http://www.eenews.net/stories/1059987706

285 http://blog.euromonitor.com/2016/01/top-100-city-destinations-ranking-2016.html

286 Plumer, Brad. "Wonkblog: America's staggering defense budget, in charts." *Washington Post*, January 7, 2013. https://www.washingtonpost.com/news/wonk/wp/2013/01/07/everything-chuck-hagel-needs-to-know-about-the-defense-budget-in-charts/

287 Randers, Jorgen. *2052: A Global Forecast For The Next Forty Years.* Chelsea Green, 2012. P. 235.

288 Zeihan, Peter. *The Accidental Superpower: The Next Generation of American Preeminence and the Coming Global Disorder*. Grand Central Publishing, 2014. P. 81.

289 Morris, Langdon. *The War for America.* 2004.

290 Hofstadter, Richard. *The Paranoid Style in American Politics, and Other Essays.* Vintage, 1952.

291 Tomasky, Michael. "The Dangerous Election." *The New York Review of Books, March 24, 2016.*

292 Sanchez, Ray. "Death and guns in the USA: The story in six graphs." *CNN*, October 3, 2015. http://www.cnn.com/2015/10/03/us/gun-deaths-united-states/ See also: http://www.shootingtracker.com/Main_Page

293 Wainwright, Tom. *Narconomics: How to Run a Drug Cartel.* Public Affairs, 2016.

294 Abrahamian quoting Samuel Huntington from "Dead Souls: The Denationalism of the American Elite"

295 Henry Kissinger. World Order. Penguin, 2014. P 2, 331, 375.

296 Naisbett, John. *Megatrends: Then New Directions Transforming Our Lives.* Warner Books, 1982.

297 Gore, Al. *The Future: Six Drivers of Global Change.* Random House, 2013. The mind map, which is also the book's table of contents, was accessed from: http://whyy.org/cms/radiotimes/2013/02/05/al-gores-six-drivers-of-global-change/

298 Silver, Nate. *The Signal and the Noise: Why So Many Predications Fail – But Some Don't.* Penguin, 2012. P. 390.

299 Kahane, Adam. *Solving Tough Problems.* Berrett-Kohler, 1999. Kahane has also written a more recent and also quite fine book, *Transformative Scenario Planning.*

300 Kahane, Adam. *Solving Tough Problems: An Open Way of Talking, Listening, and Creating New Realities.* Berrett-Kohler, 2004. P. 20.

301 Kahane, Adam. *Solving Tough Problems: An Open Way of Talking, Listening, and Creating New Realities.* Berrett-Kohler, 2004. P. 23.

302 The Mt. Fleur Scenarios document can be found online at http://www.generonconsulting.com/publications/papers/pdfs/Mont%20Fleur.pdf This version was republished by the consulting firm Global Business Network, or GBN, a firm created by many former members of the Shell scenario planning team. GBN subsequently became part of Monitor Group that was later acquired by Deloitte.

303 Kahane, Adam. *Solving Tough Problems: An Open Way of Talking, Listening, and Creating New Realities.* Berrett-Kohler, 2004. P. 26.

304 The term "co-opetition" evokes the same sentiment, whereby two companies both co-operate in some markets and compete in others. Sometimes they even compete in the same market.

305 Kissiinger, Henry. *World Order.* Penguin, 2014. P 226.

306 During the last ten years our firm has led more than a dozen scenario planning workshops for Total, the large French-based oil firm.

307 Schwartz, Peter. *The Art of the Long View.* Doubleday Business, 1991.

308 De Geus, Arie. *The Living Company.* Harvard Business Review Press, 1997.

309 Kleiner, Art. "The Man Who Saw the Future." *Strategy & Business*, Spring 2003.

310 http://www.shell.com/energy-and-innovation/the-energy-future/shell-scenarios.html

311 http://www.uscg.mil/strategy/evergreen.asp. Our firm, InnovationLabs, conducted many of the scenario planning workshops for the Coast Guard during the 2014-2015 cycle.

312 Kahane, Adam. *Solving Tough Problems.* Berrett-Kohler, 2004. P. 311.

313 Nixon, Richard. *Six Crises.* Pocket Books, 1962.

314 Rhodes, Richard. *The Making of the Atomic Bomb.* Simon and Schuster, 1986. P. 751.

315 Tuchman, Barbara W. *The Guns of August.* Random House, 1962. P. 439.

316 Nixon, Richard. *Six Crises.* Pocket Books, 1962.

317 Marvin Minsky. (Kurzweil p 289)

318 Forrester, Jay. "Counter-Intuitive Behavior of Social Systems." *MIT Technology Review*, Volume 73, Number 3, January 1971

319 USSTRATCOM Space Control and Space Surveillance. https://www.stratcom.mil/factsheets/11/Space_Control_and_Space_Surveillance/

320 Smil, Vaclav. *Global Catastrophes and Trends: The Next Fifty Years.* MIT Press, 2008. P. 170

321 Robert A. Lewis was the co-pilot on the Enola Gay, the US aircraft that dropped the atomic bomb on Hiroshima on August 6, 1945. The plane released the bomb over Hiroshima and then banked away as steeply as possible to avoid getting hit with the blast wave that would result. Within a minute of releasing the bomb, it exploded 10,000 feet in the air above Hiroshima, and the sky was filled with an impossibly bright light. Lewis saw it all, and he realized the implications of a weapon that massive. In his logbook that day he wrote, "My God, what have we done?"

322 Kissinger, Henry. *World Order.* Penguin, 2014. P. 159.

323 Tainter, Joseph A. *The Collapse of Complex Societies.* Cambridge University Press, 1988.

324   Ehrenfreund, Max. "Obama's skin looks a little different in these GOP campaign ads." *Washington Post*, December 29, 2015

325   Bishop, Rachel. "Republicans have been making Barack Obama look darker in campaign literature." *Metro.co.uk*, December 31, 2015. http://metro.co.uk/2015/12/31/republicans-have-been-blacking-up-barack-obama-in-campaign-literature-5592833/

326   Fisher, Max. "How China Stays Stable Despite 500 Protests Every Day." *The Atlantic*. January 5, 2012.

327   This section is adapted from a previous book of mine. Morris, Langdon. *Managing the Evolving Corporation*. Wiley, 1995. Chapter 5.

328   Beer, Stafford. *The Heart of Enterprise*. Wiley, 1979. P. 283.

329   Bateson, Gregory. *Mind and Nature: A Necessary Unity*. Bantam Books, 1979. P. 110.

330   Deming, W. Edwards. *The New Economics for Industry, Government, Education*. MIT Press, 1993. P. 105, 109.

331   Drucker, Peter. *The Age of Discontinuity*. Harper Torchbooks, 1968. P. 269.

332   Ackoff, Russell. This graphic is adapted from his presentation to the 10ᵗʰ annual conference of GOAL/QPC, November 8, 1993. In his presentation Ackoff noted that the distinction between "doing things right" and "doing the right thing" was originally Peter Drucker's.

333   Beer, Stafford. *Brain of the Firm*. Wiley, 1972.

334   Einstein, Albert. *The World As I See It*. Citadel Press, 1979.

335   Schumpeter, Joseph. *Capitalism, Socialism, and Democracy*. Harper & Brothers, 1942.

336   Cronin, Vincent. *Napoleon*. HarperCollins, 1971. P. 128.

337   Eesley, Charles E. and William F. Miller. "Impact: Stanford University's Economic Impact via Innovation and Entrepreneurship." Stanford University, October 2012. http://engineering.stanford.edu/sites/default/files/Stanford_Alumni_Innovation_Survey_Report_3-2-13.pdf

338   Morris, Langdon, Moses Ma and Po Chi Wu. *Agile Innovation: The Revolutionary Approach to Accelerate Success, Inspire Engagement, and Ignite Creativity*. Wiley, 2014.
Ries, Eric. *The Lean Startup: How Today's Entrepreneurs Use Continuous Innovation to Create Radically Successful Businesses*. Crown Business, 2011.
Moore, Geoffrey. *Crossing the Chasm*. HarperBusiness, 1991.

339   Portions of this chapter are adapted from a series of innovation books and papers that I've authored and co-authored during the last few years, including *Agile Innovation, The Innovation Master Plan*, and *Permanent Innovation*.

340   Google Finance, "Eastman Kodak Company," https://www.google.com/finance/historical?cid=10501&startdate=Jan+1%2C+1998&enddate=Jul+28%2C+2015&num=30&ei=4wa4VYH0A-fvigKajIzoDg, Accessed July 28, 2015.

341   It is precisely for this reason that Stafford Beer, whom we met in Chapter 10, named his life's work the viable system model for he clearly foresaw that the rate of change was accelerating and that this acceleration was a threat to the viability of all organizations. He was entirely correct, of course, and a study of his work yields numerous insights about systems, organizations, fragility, and viability. See Beer, Stafford. *Brain of the Firm*. Wiley, 1972.

342 Blanc-Jouvan, Xavier. "Worldwide Influence of the French Civil Code of 1804, On the Occasion of Its Bicentennial Celebration." *Cornell Law School*, September 27, 2004.
http://scholarship.law.cornell.edu/cgi/viewcontent.cgi?article=1003&context=biss _papers

343 Chandler, David G. *The Campaigns of Napoleon: The Mind and Method of History's Greatest Soldier.* MacMillan, 1966.

344 Gerstner, Louis V. *Who Says Elephants Can't* Dance? Inside IBM's Historic Turnaround. HarperBusiness, 2002.

345 *Booz & Company.* "Ninth Annual Global Innovation 1000 Study: Navigating the Digital Future." October 22, 2013. http://www.marketwired.com/press-release/ninth-annual-global-innovation-1000-study-navigating-the-digital-future-1843425.htm

346 Conlon, Jerome, Moses Ma, and Langdon Morris. *Soulful Branding.* FutureLab Press, 2015.

347 Kissinger, Henry. *On China.* The Penguin Press, 2011. P 215.

348 Morris, Langdon, Moses Ma and Po Chi Wu. *Agile Innovation: The Revolutionary Approach to Accelerate Success, Inspire Engagement, and Ignite Creativity.* Wiley, 2014.

349 Fell, Mark. "As Mark Zuckerberg Turns 30, His 10 Best Quotes as CEO." *Entrepreneur Magazine*, May 14, 2014.
http://www.entrepreneur.com/article/233890

350 Baron Funds Quarterly Report, March 31, 2014.
http://www.baronfunds.com/BaronFunds/media/Quarterly-Reports/Quarterly-Report-33114.pdf

351 Henrich, Joseph. The Secret of Our Success: *How Culture Is Driving Human Evolution, Domesticating Our Species, and Making Us Smarter.* Princton University Press, 2016. P. 5.

352 Lakhani, Karim R. and Jill Panetta, "The Principles of Distributed Innovation. Innovations: Technology, Governance, Globalization." Summer, Vol. 2, No. 3, 2007; *The Berkman Center for Internet and Society* Research Paper No. 2007-7. Available at SSRN: http://ssrn.com/abstract=1021034

353 Campbell, Joseph. *The Hero With a Thousand Faces.* Princeton University Press, 1949. P 19 & 29.

354 Janis, Irving L. *Groupthink.* Houghton Mifflin Company, 1982. Second Edition. P. 136.

355 Morris, Langdon. *The Innovation Formula: The Guidebook to Innovation for Small Business Leaders and Entrepreneurs.* Innovation Academy, 2015.

356 Campbell, Joseph. *The Hero With a Thousand Faces.* Princeton University Press, 1949. P 389, 391.

357 Henrich, Joseph. *The Secret of Our Success: How Culture Is Driving Human Evolution, Domesticating Our Species, and Making Us Smarter.* Princton University Press, 2016. P. 210.

INDEX

(Forthcoming)

31273408R10397

Made in the USA
Middletown, DE
24 April 2016